MW01640309

PosterAnnual2004 Graphis Mission Statement: *Graphis* is committed to presenting exceptional work in international design, advertising, illustration and photography. Since 1944, we have presented individuals and companies in the visual communications industry who have consistently demonstrated excellence and determination in overcoming economic, cultural and creative hurdles to produce true brilliance.

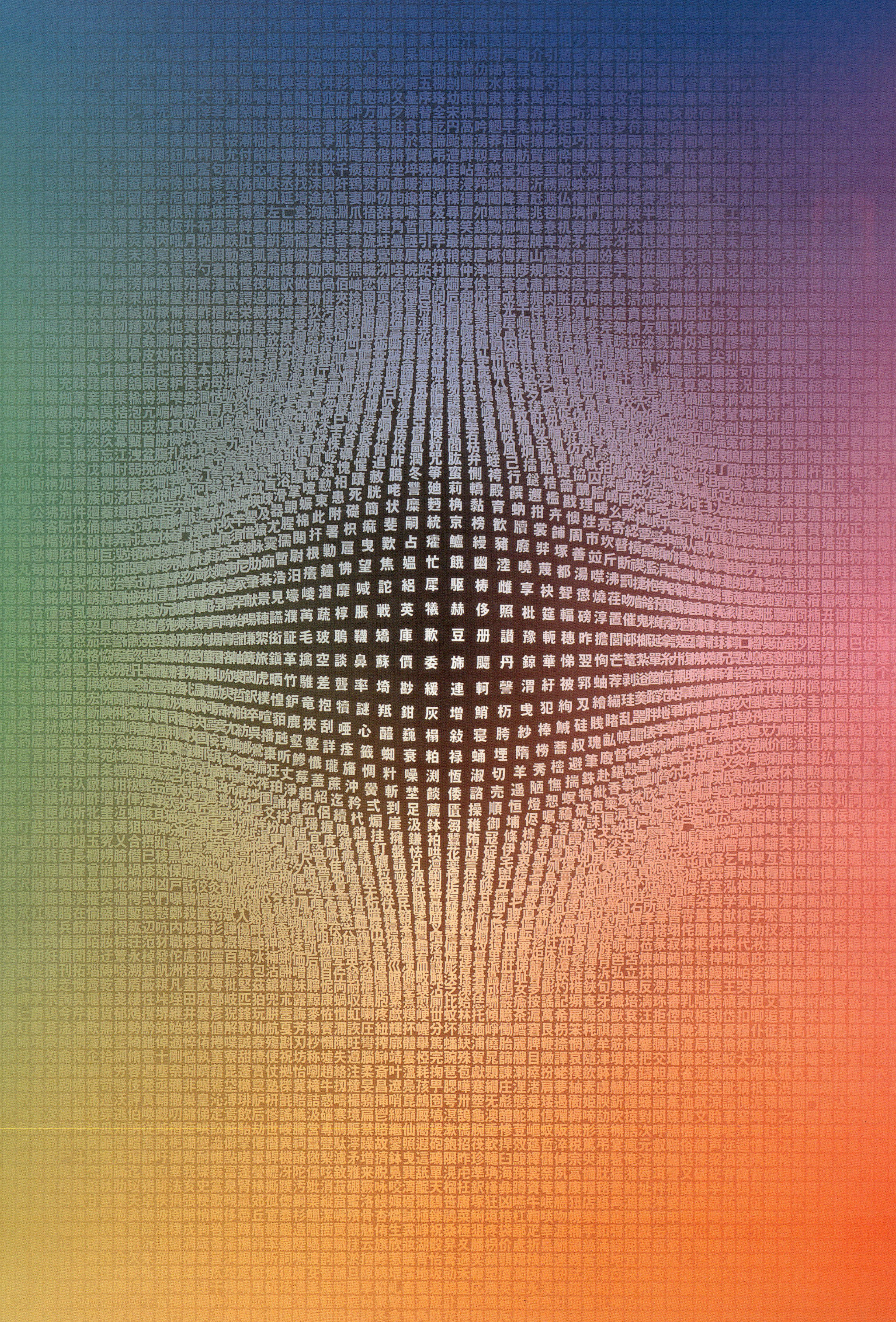

PosterAnnual2004

CEO & Creative Director: B. Martin Pedersen

Editors: Laetitia Wolff & Betsey McLain
Art Directors: Andrea Vélez & Jennifer Kinon
Design & Production: Luis Diaz

Photographer: Alfredo Parraga

Published by Graphis Inc.

This book is dedicated to
Ikko Tanaka
(1930-2002)

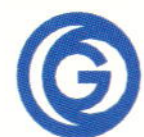

(opposite) Morisawa Font for Morisawa & Company Ltd. by Shinnoske, Inc., page 236 and (following page) AIGA Landor Associates Poster for AIGA San Francisco by Morla Design, Inc. page 51

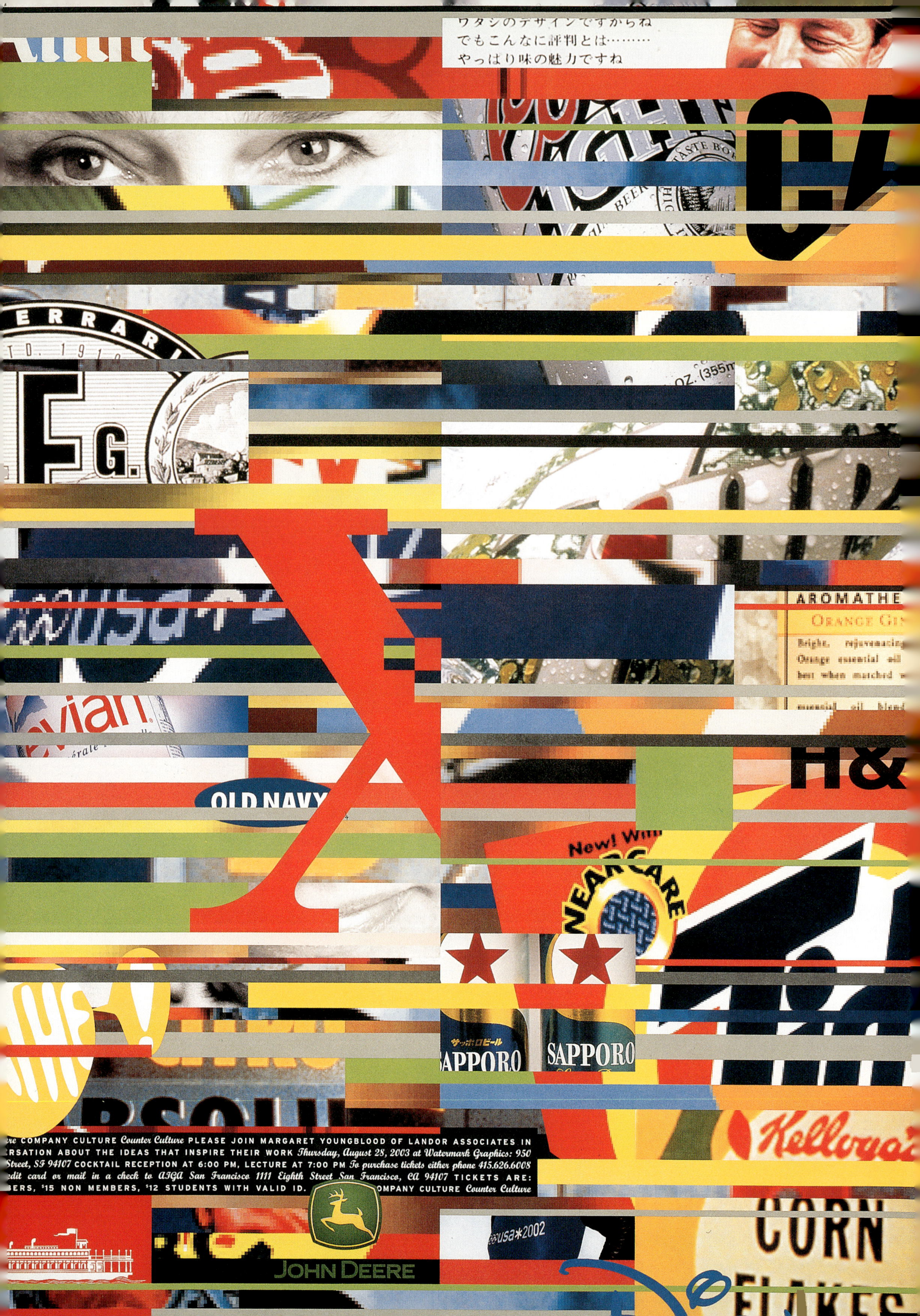
ワタシのデザインですからね
でもこんなに評判とは………
やっぱり味の魅力ですね
AROMATHE
OLD NAVY
evian
New! With
SAPPORO
SAPPORO
Kellogg's
CORN
H&
re COMPANY CULTURE Counter Culture PLEASE JOIN MARGARET YOUNGBLOOD OF LANDOR ASSOCIATES IN
RSATION ABOUT THE IDEAS THAT INSPIRE THEIR WORK Thursday, August 28, 2003 at Watermark Graphics: 950
Street, SF 94107 COCKTAIL RECEPTION AT 6:00 PM, LECTURE AT 7:00 PM To purchase tickets either phone 415.626.6008
edit card or mail in a check to AIGA San Francisco 1111 Eighth Street San Francisco, CA 94107 TICKETS ARE:
BERS, $15 NON MEMBERS, $12 STUDENTS WITH VALID ID. OMPANY CULTURE Counter Culture
JOHN DEERE
usa*2002

Contents Inhalt Sommaire

Remarks: We extend our heartfelt thanks to contributors throughout the world who have made it possible to publish a wide and international spectrum of the best work in this field. Entry instructions for all Graphis Books may be requested from: **Graphis Inc.**, 307 Fifth Avenue, Tenth Floor, New York, New York 10016, or visit our Web site at www.graphis.com.

Anmerkungen: Unser Dank gilt den Einsendern aus aller Welt, die es uns ermöglicht haben, ein breites, internationales Spektrum der besten Arbeiten zu veröffentlichen. Teilnahmebedingungen für die Graphis-Bücher sind erhältlich bei: **Graphis Inc.**, 307 Fifth Avenue, Tenth Floor, New York, New York 10016. Besuchen Sie uns im World Wide Web, www.graphis.com.

Remerciements: Nous remercions les participants du monde entier qui ont rendu possible la publication de cet ouvrage offrant un panorama complet des meilleurs travaux. Les modalités d'inscription peuvent être obtenues auprès de: **Graphis Inc.**, 307 Fifth Avenue, Tenth Floor, New York, New York 10016. Rendez-nous visite sur notre site web: www.graphis.com.

 ISBN: 1-931241-36-8 Printed in Korea.

If your
only tool is
a hammer,
all
problems
look like
nails.

MARK TWAIN

STOP
GENDER
VIOLENCE

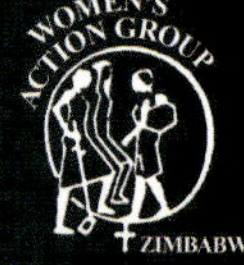

P.O. Box 135
Harare
Tel: 339161 / 308738 / 339292
E Mail: wag@wag.co.zw

Special Consultative Status with the UN ECOSOC

Q&A with Chaz Maviyane-Davies, Zimbabwe

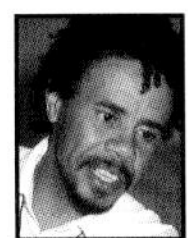

Chaz Maviyane-Davies work has been described by UKs Design *magazine as "the guerrilla of graphic design." For more than two decades the award-winning, controversial Zimbabwean designer's powerful work has taken on issues of consumerism, health, nutrition, social responsibility, the environment, and human rights. His credentials include a M.A. in Graphic Design from the Central School of Art and Design in London, and an Advanced Diploma in Post-graduate film-making from the Central St. Martins College of Art and Design in London. He spent a year in Japan studying three-dimensional design and ten months in Malaysia working on various world-reaching design projects for the International Organization of Consumers Unions and Just World Trust (JUST). His design work experience includes time with Fulcrum (Design Consultants), Newell and Sorrell Design Ltd., as well as a stint in the graphic design department of BBC Television. From 1983 until recently he ran a design studio in Harare called The Maviyane-Project. As a result of the social, humane, and confrontational nature of his work, he felt compelled to temporarily leave his homeland because of adverse political climate. He is presently an Associate Professor of design at the Massachusetts College of Art in Boston. Chaz Maviyane-Davies has been recognized for his films, which have been screened and awarded in many international film festivals. His design work has been represented in most of the largest international graphic, invitational, and poster exhibitions from 1980 to the present time.*

What is your proudest achievement in design so far?
The poster series that is based on 12 of the articles from the United Nations Universal Declaration of Human Rights. I needed to express my design philosophy on a larger scale and share it with a wider audience. For many, "Africa" conjures up images of a continent torn apart by hatred and brutality, corpses and corruption. Ignore these images and the continent has no other identity. As an African, I experience life on a continent where in many parts, fundamental human rights are obliterated. This is my warning: continue to ignore it and we will all be destroyed by our own lack of humanity. Envisaging this project meant many things to me:
a) In this project I could utilize my creative ideas to serve the fight for human rights in Africa. Without the respect of these rights, real development cannot be sustained.
b) I used these posters as a form of education. They propose ways of seeing that are alternative to common aesthetics and attempt to rekindle some of the images we lost when we adopted the prepackaged, off-the-shelf, foreign images that now envelope us.
c) It also meant that we look at our predicament through our own eyes and not limit human rights only to abuse (I can let the media do that). Instead, we look at it as an integral part of the celebration of the human spirit and intelligence, thereby emphasizing the cultural diversity that abounds us. I hope the viewer sees himself in the images, and sees the essence of civilization, inherent in all cultures and traditions.
Who are the 3-5 designers you most admire?
Dave McKean–prolific with a dark vivid imagination and all the skills to pull it off. The late Paul Peter Piech—woodcut/linocut poster visionary of the social message, and Wieslaw Walkuski—Polish genius of the sublime surreal. Also, Pierre Bernard—founder of *Grapus* in France who put his skill and intelligence in the service of humanity.
How much does technology influence your work?
It doesn't. Technology in the form of Photoshop is my tool of choice for the moment, but I see this as only a means to an end and not as a factor that defines my creativity.
How do you keep up with current trends in design?
While I look around to see what is happening in the world of design, I don't believe that current styles and trends are meant to alter my vision and imagination. The underlying fact today is that too many design trends are software driven and not conceptual or skill driven, with a look-alike mediocrity labelled 'in' by those who benefit from it. It is a designers duty to offer a new vitality, energy, and greater appreciation of diversity through creativity.
What part of your work do you find most demanding?
The organization, planning, and number crunching.
What interests do you have outside work?
Politics, justice, and dancing. Dancing is in my blood, and Salsa, Samba and Rhumba, because of their origins, are the types of dance I enjoy most. There is a Zimbabwean proverb that says: 'If you can walk you can dance, if you can talk you can sing.'
Have you ever turned down a client?
Yes, several times, mainly because they regarded me merely as executor of their own vision.
What questions do your clients most often ask?
Can you tone it down a bit? How much will the job cost me? Can you have it ready in two days?
What creative philosophy do you communicate to a student audience? a professional audience? a client?
To my students I say: Believe in yourself, really believe in yourself. Research, work as hard as you can at the process and not the ends, strive to realize your vision, listen with your eyes, see with your ears, and let your soul dictate.
To my professional audience I say: In our quest for "progress," we have relegated huge chunks of our culture into the recesses of our subconscious as opposed to using it to define our role in the world. This means that any icons or visual manifestations of our traditions and past are considered inferior as we readily adopt the global (American) lifestyles and attitudes. By using a symbolic and visual language that is meaningful not only to us, but enriching to a world that has run out of ideas other than market forces, we must adapt and develop traditions and values, defining our truly independent future.
To my clients I say: I am a professional, let me do what I do best.
How involved are you with the design community?
I participate in several design juries and conferences.
Do you teach a course on design?
I am presently an associate professor at the Massachusetts College of Art, teaching Graphic Design and Digital Photography.
How important is it to win awards?
It isn't always the "best" work that is rewarded. There are too many cultural, political, and stylistic issues inherent in the way that competitions are judged. I enter many exhibitions as a way of sharing and the spirit of participating to promote what we do. If I am awarded something for my work then fine. If not, then it's not important.
Which of your skills would you most like to perfect?
Illustration.
Where would you like to be five or ten years from now?
In a more humane world.
What do you consider good design?
Good design is when a project's intent is felt and appreciated by the user or observer. If something is intended to instruct, then it should instruct. If it is meant to inform then there should be a learning experience. If it is meant to move us then we should feel the emotion. Too often design does not meet this mandate neither conceptually nor aesthetically; that is why mediocrity rules. Never forget, it is artistic license coupled with intelligence that creates a good design.

Opening page: "Stop Gender Violence," 1999, Client: Women's Action Group, Zimbabwe. Photography: Bob Davey. Designed by Chaz Maviyane-Davies. Opposite left Page: "Rights," 1996, Client: Chaz Maviyane-Davies. Designed by Chaz Maviyane-Davies. Photography: Ian Murphy. Opposite right page: "Rights," 1996, Client: Chaz Maviyane-Davies. Designed by Chaz Maviyane-Davies. Photography: Ian Murphy

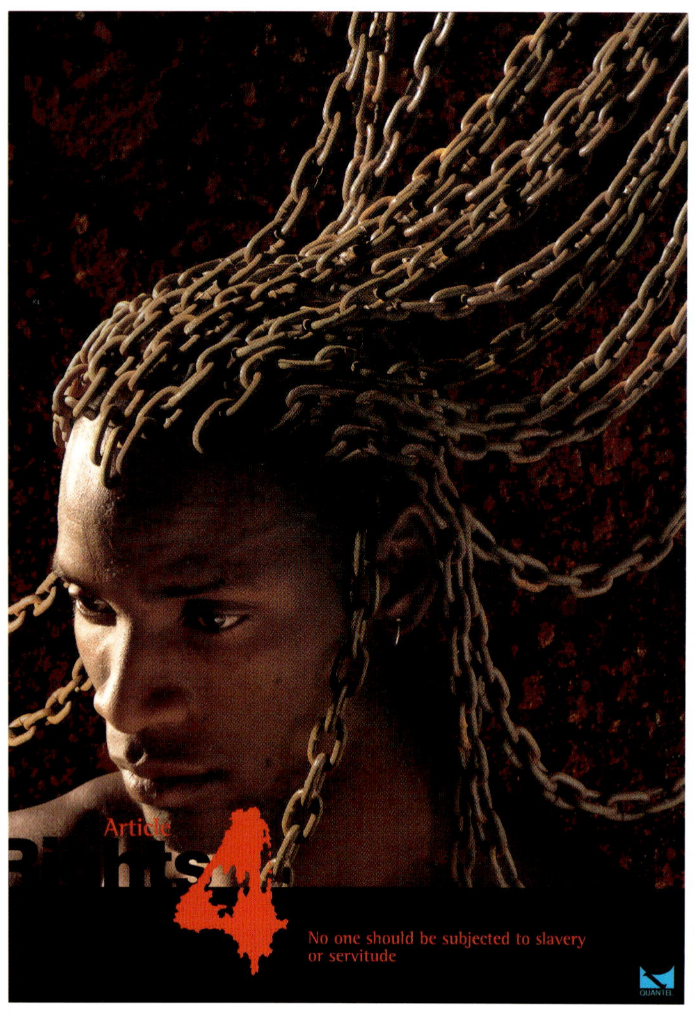
Article
4
No one should be subjected to slavery
or servitude
QUANTEL

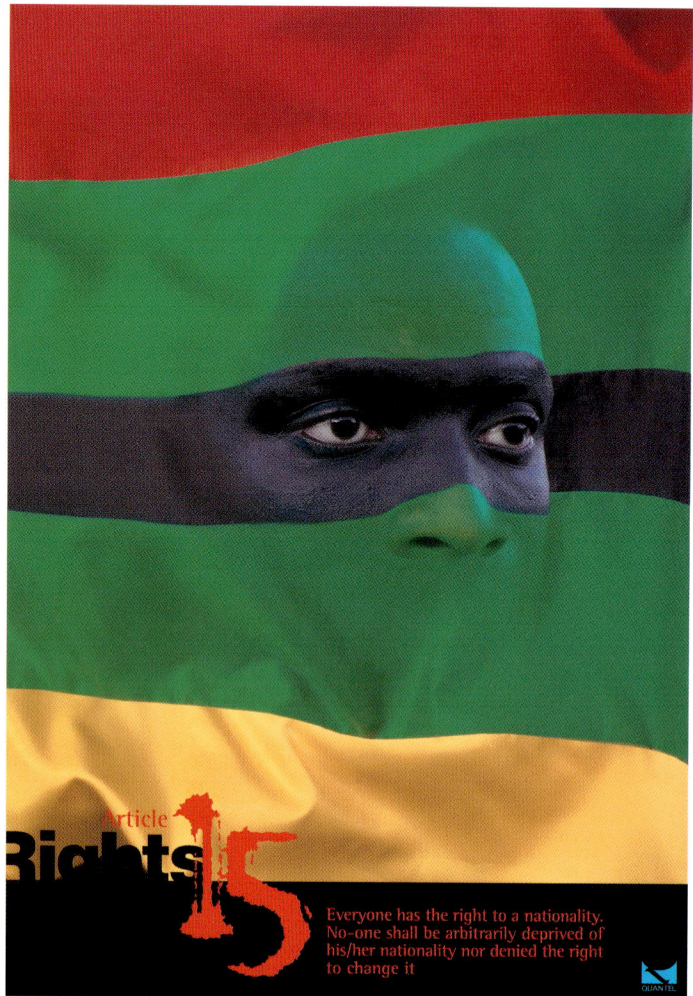
Article
15
Everyone has the right to a nationality.
No-one shall be arbitrarily deprived of
his/her nationality nor denied the right
to change it
QUANTEL

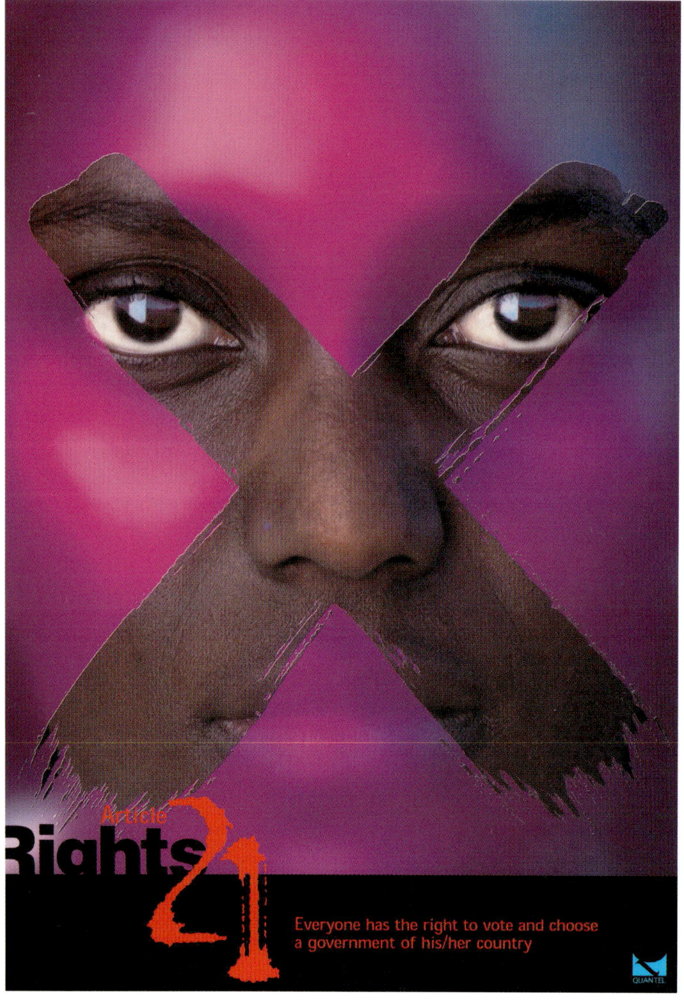
Article
21
Everyone has the right to vote and choose
a government of his/her country
QUANTEL

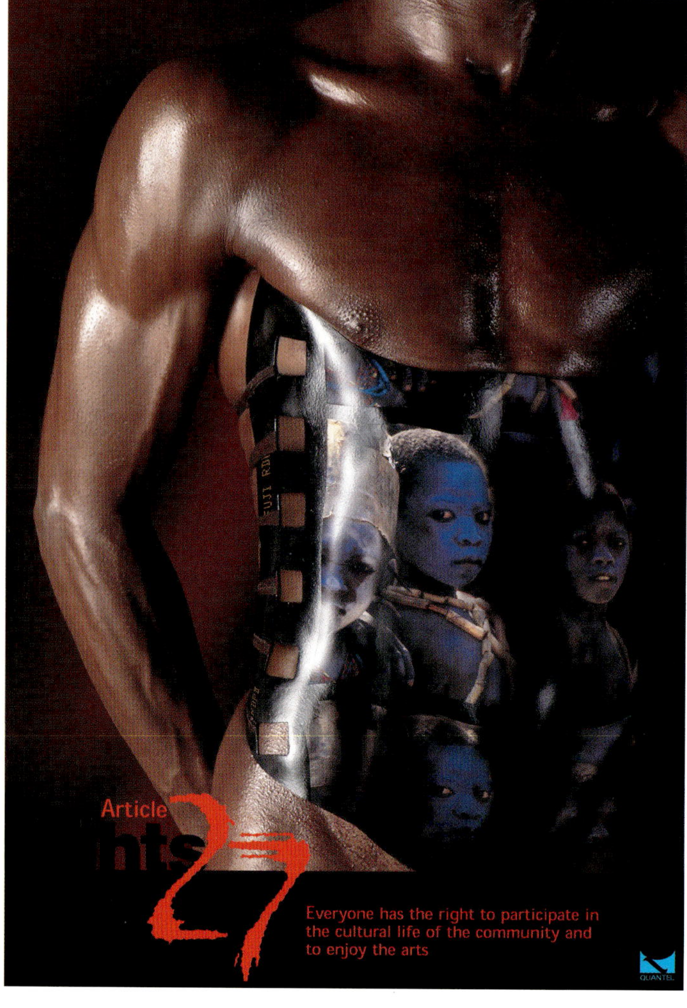
Article
27
Everyone has the right to participate in
the cultural life of the community and
to enjoy the arts
QUANTEL

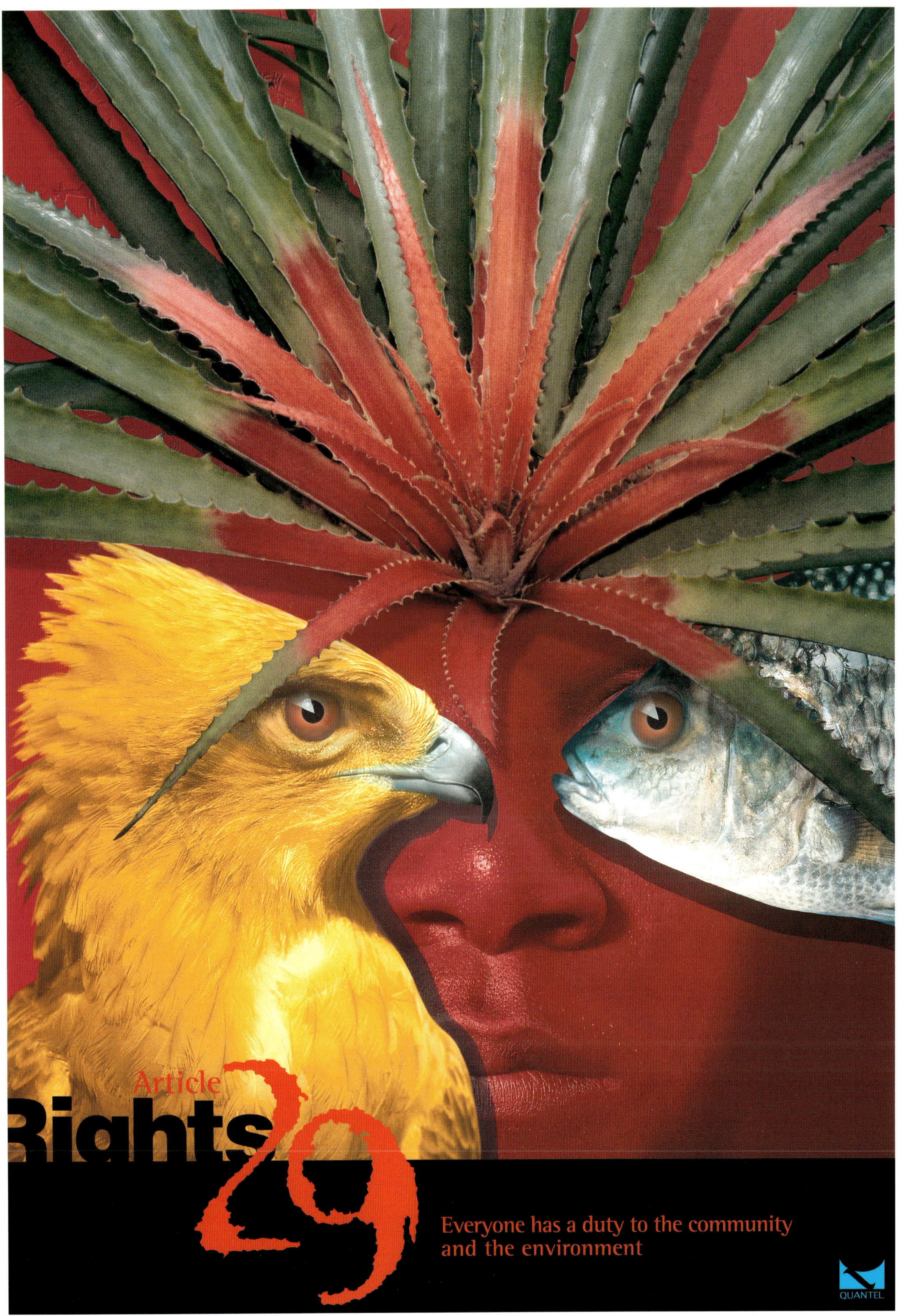
Article
Rights 29
Everyone has a duty to the community
and the environment
QUANTEL

Crossmedia: die Kompetenz der Druck- und Medienindustri

Q&A with Uwe Loesch, Germany

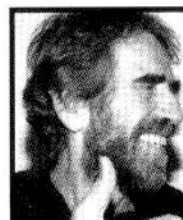

Uwe Loesch, born in 1943 in Germany, is one of the world's leading poster designers. His work is represented in all important museums and collections such as the Museum of Modern Art New York and the Bibliothèque Nationale in Paris. More than 30 one-man-exhibitions have shown his poster design worldwide, lately in the Galerie Anatome in Paris and the GGG Ginza graphic gallery Tokyo. His work has been honored with numerous awards including two Grand Prix of the International Poster Biennial in Lahti, the ICOGRADA Excellence Award, the Gold Medal of the International Biennial of Graphic Design Brno, the Gold Medal of the Art Directors Club of Europe, the Silver Medal of the Art Directors Club New York and the Festival d'Affiches de Chaumont and many awards by the Type Directors Club New York. Since 1990 he has held a professorship for Communication Design at the University of Wuppertal, Germany.

What direction and advice do you give to students about portfolios?
Good portfolios are never seen again, unless, that is, the artist got the job. I tell them that a portfolio is the best business card they possess in the present and in the years following their graduation. Students begin to work on their portfolio after their first semester so by the end of their studies they have a worthy book!
A portfolio is essential and informative; short text and concepts to accompany the assignments are just as efficient as the names of the dear teachers. The dates in which each assignment was being developed must always be stated. The first non-school related assignments that students get, when hired by agencies and design studios, needs to specify clearly their part in the production process. Who was the art director? Who wrote the text? Students need to know if the work is worth showing, or if simply stating the name is more impressive. A good portfolio shows a process. Design is process! Often times, a step in the middle of the process is better than the end result. A portfolio needs to impress within three minutes. The CD-ROM is only looked at when the portfolio has created enough curiosity.

What is your proudest achievement in teaching so far?
There are students that are potentially very creative but they face great difficulties using their creativity in a practical way. To motivate them and to encourage their crazy ideas—as long as it takes—until an intelligent solution is reached, this is what my job as an educator is. Eight of my former students are now active professors on their own. Many of them work in San Francisco, New York, London, Amsterdam, Seoul, Hong Kong, Jakarta, Vienna, Barcelona, Paris, and Berlin.

What is your fondest experience as a teacher?
I love to see work that at first seems to be totally missing the point evolve in such ways that it eventually turns out to surpass other works. These surprises always make me happy. On the other hand, there are students whose intelligence paradoxically stands in their way; they have become lazy and distracted.

What part of academia do you find most demanding?
The biggest challenge in studying is to remain true to oneself. It is even harder to establish criteria by which one looks at their own work from a distance. To ask oneself, what is it that I truly see here? What did I make noticeable in this work? Why is it red and not green? Does the color have a meaning? If so, what is it? Or is it simply decorative? Who am I trying to reach? Is it legible and comprehensive, or does it require explanations? Does my message trigger sympathy? What spontaneous associations are provoked? Trust yourself!

Name 3-5 colleagues you most admire.
There are many colleagues whose work I greatly value, but here are five names: Werner Jeker, Gérard Paris Clavel, Philippe Apeloig, Makoto Saito, and Bruno Monguzzi.

What do you tell your students about the professional world?
I tell them about the way things work in reality. I tell them the truth. In the professional world, most jobs are like a dream job that sometimes turns into a nightmare. (But it depends on who your client is.)

What are some of your frustrations with students today?
Many students have too little interest in literature, music, architecture, art, and history. Mainly, there is a lack of knowledge of other graphic designers and artists of the 20th century and as a result, they tend to overestimate their own accomplishments. The postmodern human being celebrated himself and decorated himself with feathers that are not his own.

How do you inspire your students?
We go together to the museum.

Do you think design can be taught or is it something innate?
Creativity is innate. Therefore, it can neither be taught nor learned. From this point of view, I, as a teacher, am only the mediator of critical consciousness. Everything is behind me—and everything is still ahead of you! You are better than I am. Just Think!

What is your philosophy on grades/grading?
The successful designer is the one who one day doesn't need the applause from the wrong side anymore. Autodidacts are the actual heroes. The presentable work is what truly counts. The students just have to do it and those who work well also graduate. The actual learning process, not graduating, is what really counts. One day they might be able to use their diploma or MA to decorate their office or perhaps to be a civil servant—what a horrible thought!

What is your advice to students entering the job market?
The job market is a challenge. The experience of having worked in an advertising agency is worth gold. As a result, one will become self employed and responsible and eventually will work for non-profit and will create his own customers.

Where do you tell students to find inspiration?
In love!

What is the most important element of good design?
To arouse sympathy and interest.

How do you encourage your students' growth?
You are much better than I am. But I am 35 years ahead of you. Catch up with me.

Is a master's degree in your field relevant, or even necessary?
A master's degree is helpful. Now or never: you have to do it.
Doubi doubi doo!

What's your biggest fear about sending your students out into the professional world?
The art of failing. It does not matter whose great idea it is, it does not necessarily have to be your own if you work in a team. Don't immediately give up because of this, there are going to be many defeats along the way, but from all, you can learn.

What philosophy on design do you communicate to a student audience?
Blueberries are red when they are green. Our world is just as irritating as we are. It is an art to learn to express yourself with minimal means. Avoid every unnecessary decoration and arbitrariness unless your employer is a wallpaper factory.

Left Page: "X-medil: Crossmedia. the competence in print and media industries," 2001, Client: German Printing and Media Industries Federation
Opposite Left Page: "a dios, 2000," 2001, Client: Museum fur angewandtk Kunst, Frankfurt am Main (Trans. Museum for Applied Arts, Frankfurt am Main) Designed by Uwe Loesch
Opposite Right Page: "Posters by Uwe Loesch," 2002. Client: ggg Gallery Tokyo. Designed by Uwe Loesch and Ikko Tanaka

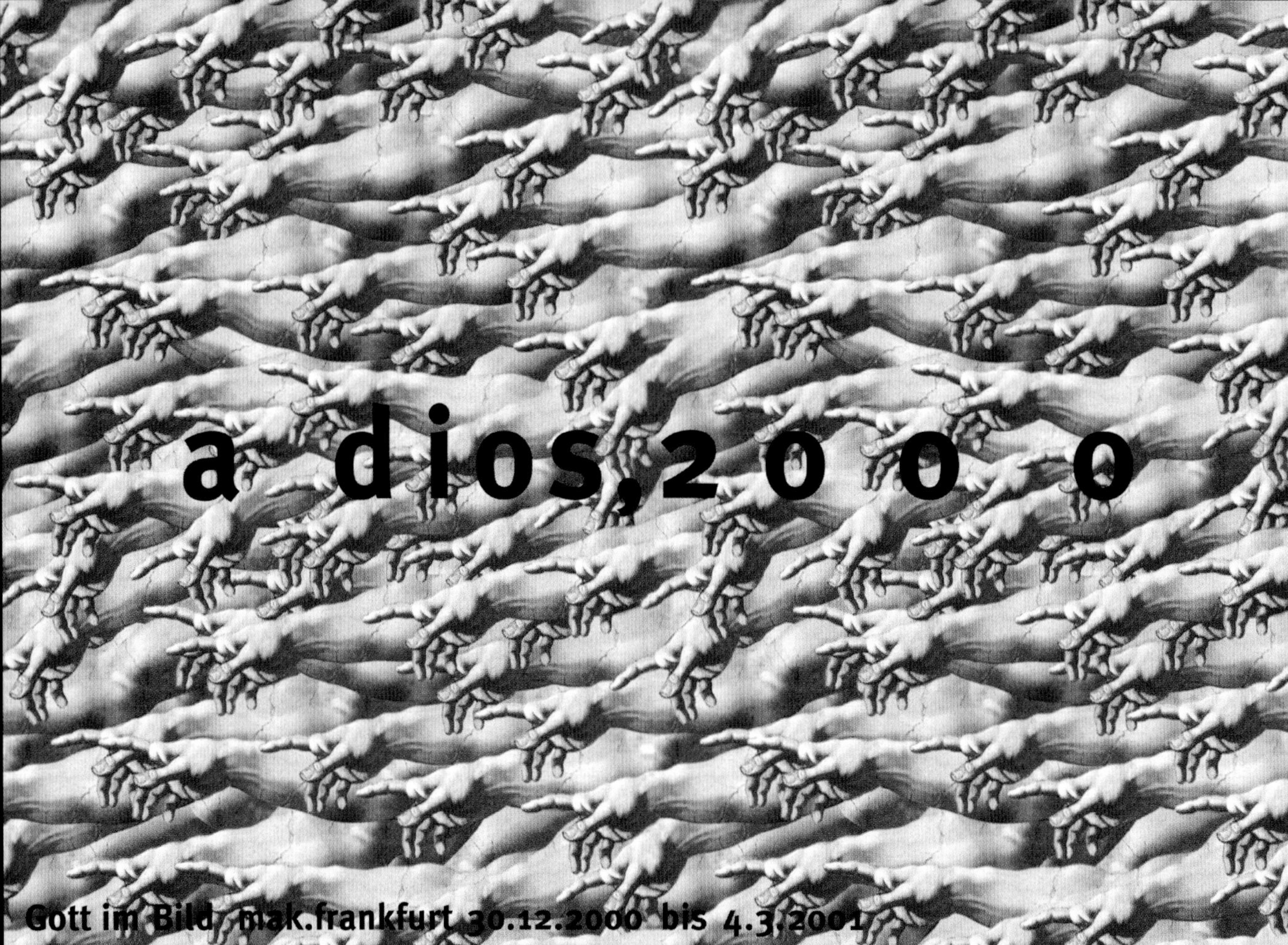
a dios,2 0 0 0
Gott im Bild mak.frankfurt 30.12.2000 bis 4.3.2001

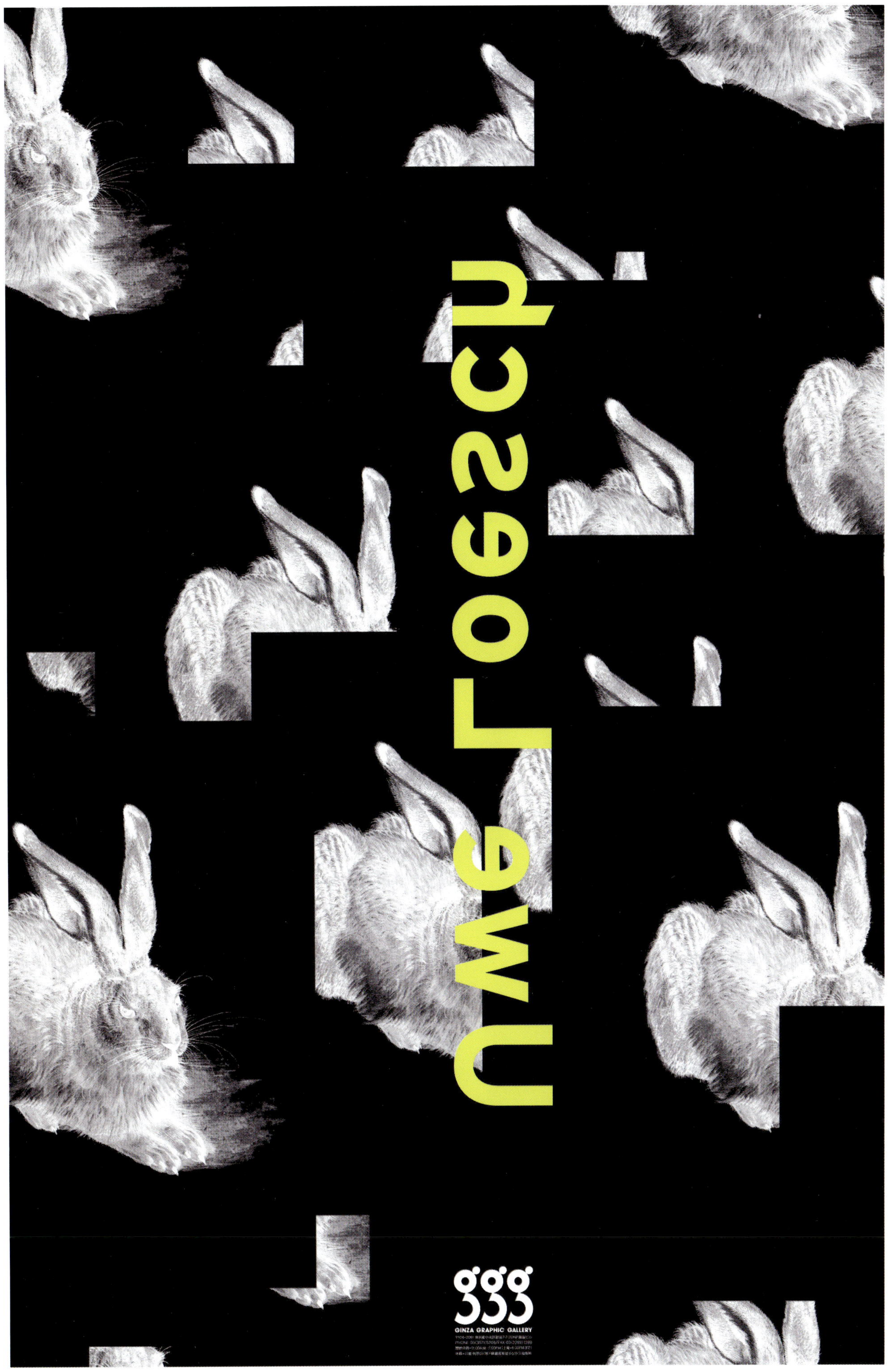
Uwe Loesch
ggg
GINZA GRAPHIC GALLERY

AZZ IN WILLISAU FR. 31. OKT. 200
20.30 UHR CLUB FORUM
ETHNIC HERITAGE ENSEMBLE

Q&A with Niklaus Troxler, Switzerland

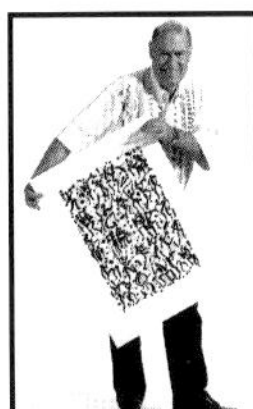

***Niklaus Troxler** was born in Willisau, Switzerland in 1947. After earning a degree in graphic design from the Art School of Lucerne, Switzerland, he become the Art Director at Hellenstein Création in Paris. In 1973 he created his own design firm in Willisau, and has held the title of Professor at the State Academy of Fine Arts in Stuttgart, Germany since 1998. Troxler has been highly involved in the Willisau Jazz scene since 1966 as the organizer of the Willisau jazz concerts and festivals. Troxler's work has achieved resounding praise and his numerous awards include the Vestag Cultural Prize, Lucerne, Switzerland (1977), the Cultural Prize of Central Switzerland (1982), the Touristique Prize of Central Switzerland (1989), Honorary citizen of Willisau (1994), the Swiss scholarship for Applied Art (2000) and the ADC Special Award for the Jazz Festival in Willisau (2000). Receiving high acclaim in his native Switzerland, Troxler has won 22 Swiss Posters of the Year Awards (1977-99) and 2 Gold, 18 Silver and 26 Bronze/Distinctive Merit prizes from the Art Directors Club of Switzerland (1979-2000). He has also won prizes from the Art Directors Club New York, the Art Directors Club of Europe, the Type Directors Club New York and the Tokyo Type Directors Club. He has also participated in and received prizes in competitions such as the Warsaw Poster Biennial, the Brno Design Biennial, the Toyama Poster Triennial, the Mexico Poster Biennial, the Lahti Poster Biennial, the Helsinki Poster Biennial, the Moscow Poster Biennial and the China International Poster Biennial Hangzhou a.m.o. His posters have been featured in various collections such as the MOMA New York, the Poster Museum Essen, the Zurich Poster Collection, and the Basel Poster Collection. Troxler is also the author of* Niklaus Troxler: Jazz Posters *(Edition Oreos/Germany o.o.p, 1991),* Jazz Boulevard: Niklaus Troxler Posters *(Lars Müller Publishers, 1999) and* Niklaus Troxler: A Designers Design Life *(Wang Xu Publishers, Guangzhou, China, 1999).*

What is your proudest achievement in design so far?
Designing the posters for all the jazz concerts and festivals I've organized myself. Designing posters for my favorite musicians has always been a great challenge, because when I started my design education, I also started organizing jazz concerts in Willisau. So for me, design and jazz have always held the same importantance and passion.

How much of your work day is spent on actual design?
If I manage to get half a day of actual design work, I am happy.

Do you think that having a distinctive style is important?
Yes. I think it's important to make statements with your design. The importance of a distinct style lies in the fact that it is part of the strength of the message.

How do you keep up with current trends in design?
The trends influence me, of course, like everything else around me.

How much does technology influence your work?
Technology doesn't initially influence my work, but essentially every new tool influences my work. The photocopier or Letraset did the same in earlier times.

What part of your work do you find most demanding?
Poster design, of course. Posters, especially in Switzerland, are placed in the streets, lending to a direct contact with the public. But since people don't go to streets to see posters, the poster has to reach the passer-by and therein lies the challenge.

Has globalization changed the way you work?
I think so. Globalization has enabled me to be in contact with people from all over the world—and that is great. It builds a greater sense of community as well as communication between the designers. First, design is a communication to the direct receiver and second, a communication between the designers worldwide, which fosters an exchange of ideas.

Have you ever turned down a client—and why?
Yes, because they didn't care for the environment.

What questions do your clients most often ask?
How much does it cost?

Where would you like to be ten years from now?
I hope to still design with the same great pleasure I design now, and I hope to still find new solutions for upcoming problems.

Which of your skills would you most like to perfect?
Illustration.

How do you see your work evolving in the next five years?
I feel freer now than in the past, so I think that in the future I will achieve new design results more easily.

How important is it to win awards?
It's always a nice gesture to be recognized, but it is not so important. It's a good feeling to be receiving awards together with a younger generation of designers.

How involved are you with the design community?
I usually meet other designers at jury sessions and design conferences, and these are always good moments to meet designers from all over the world.

Do you enjoy speaking at design conferences?
I like it very much! I also love talking to and having discussions with students and aspiring designers after my lectures!

Name the three artists you most admire.
Charlie Parker, Cecil Taylor, and Saul Steinberg

Do you teach a course on design?
Yes, at the State Academy of Stuttgart, Germany.

What philosophy on design do you communicate to a student audience? a professional audience? a client?
I tell them to work hard! They need to work until they reach the perfect idea for a specific subject. The message has priority over form, so does creativity over aesthetics, and expression over perfect design. This is the philosophy I tell all my students, professionals, and clients.

What interests do you have outside work?
Jazz, jazz, jazz. Art, traveling, and love.

Left Page: "Ethnic Heritage Ensemble," 2003, Client: Jazz in Willisau. Designed by Niklaus Troxler Opposite Left Page: "Christy Doran's New Bag," 2002, Client: Jazz in Willisau. Designed by Niklaus Troxler.

JAZ IN WILL SAU

SAMSTAG, 12. OKTOBER 02

20.00 UHR IM NEUEN

CLUB FOROOM / WELLIS AG

CHRISTY DORAN'S

NEW BAG

CHRISTY DORAN G

BRUNO AMSTAD VOICE

HANS PETER PFAMATTER P

FABIAN KURATLI DR, PERC

WOLFGANG ZWIAUER E-B

CD-TAUFE UND

IR OPEN NG

PosterAnnual2004

LYCEUM

A Traveling Fellowship in Architecture

COMPETITION

2003

2003 JURY:

Chairperson: **Carol Burns, AIA**
Taylor & Burns Architects
Boston, MA

Allison Arieff
Editor in Chief
Dwell Magazine

Jennifer Siegal
Architect
Office of Mobile Design
Los Angeles, CA

Elliot Fabri
CEO, New Era Building Systems
Manufacturer of modular housing
Strattanville, PA

Peter Vincent, AIA
Architect
Peter Vincent & Associates, LLC
Honolulu, HI

PRIZES:

First Prize • $10,000 for 6 months travel

Second Prize • $6,000 for 3 months travel abroad

Third Prize • $1,000 grant

Alternate • citation

INVITED SCHOOLS:

The Boston Architectural Center
McGill University
Rhode Island School of Design
Southern California Institute of Architecture
University of Arizona
University of Cincinnati
University of Illinois at Chicago
University of Hawaii at Manoa

The House on Wheels

Program Author: Carol Burns

The "mobile home" and its "park" are still-common sites across North America, even though the present-day house on wheels is not so mobile anymore, usually making only one move from the factory to the site. Today's houses on wheels–manufactured housing–provide a realistic option for dwelling. However, neither this house nor its site has been informed by architectural design thinking. The challenge of the competition is to reconceive the house on a permanent chassis along with its setting.

Lyceum Fellowship Committee

Peter Vincent, AIA

www.lyceum-fellowship.org

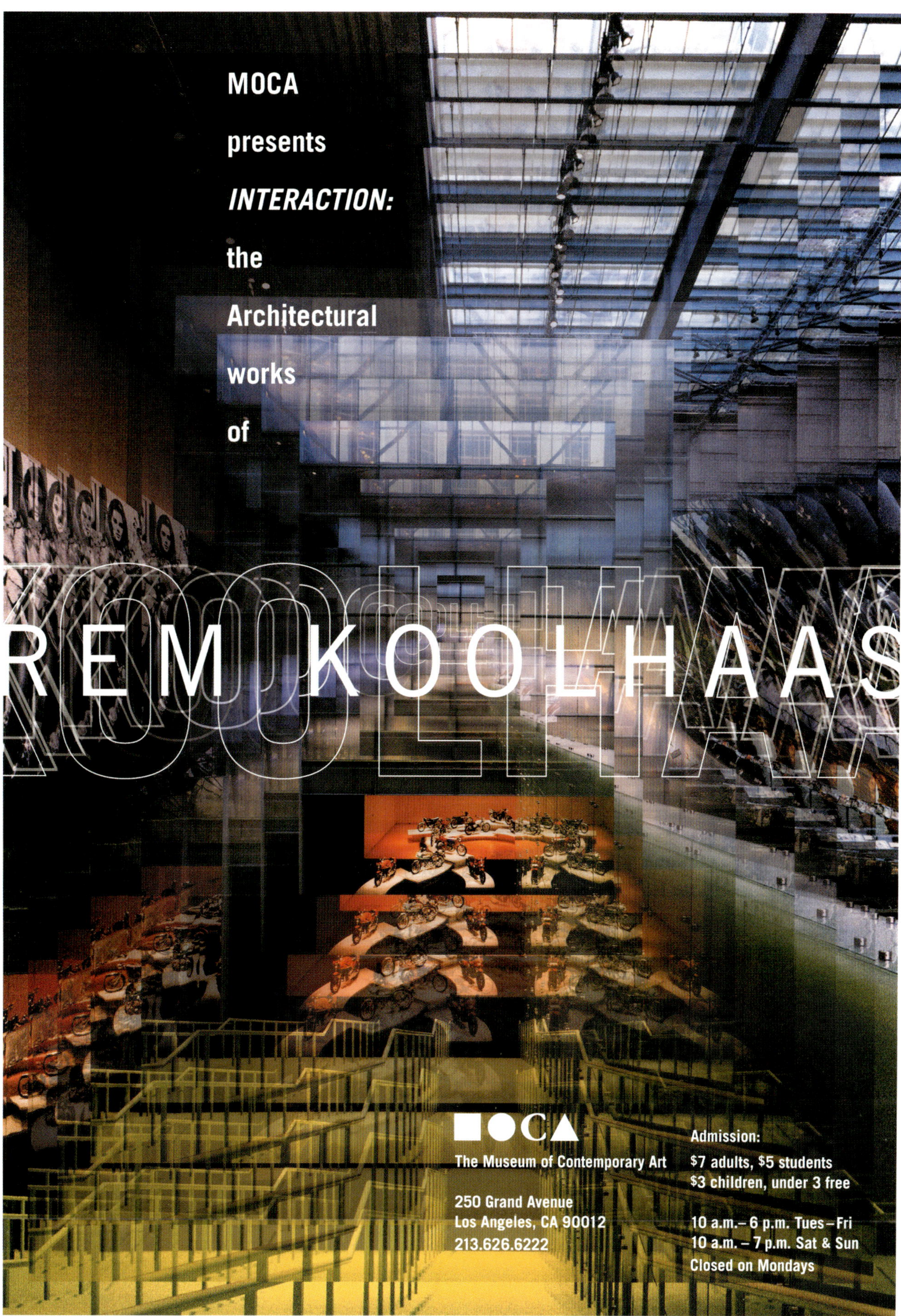

Irene Yuan/Art Center College of Design/MOCA

LEONARD P. ZAKIM
BUNKER HILL BRIDGE

BOSTON, MASSACHUSETTS

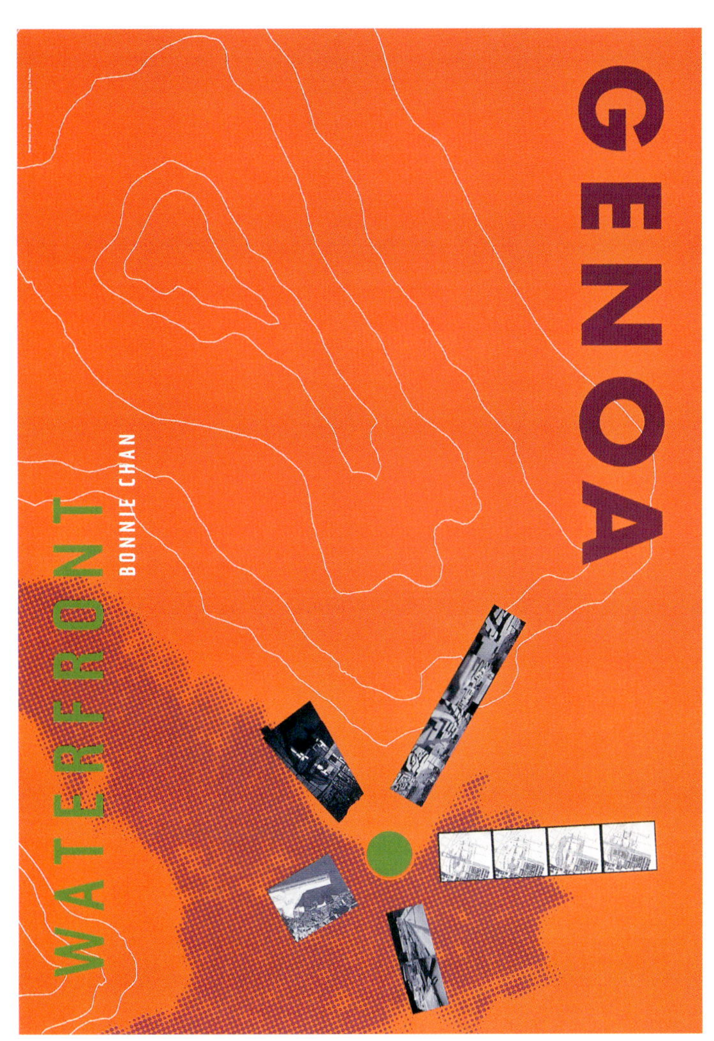

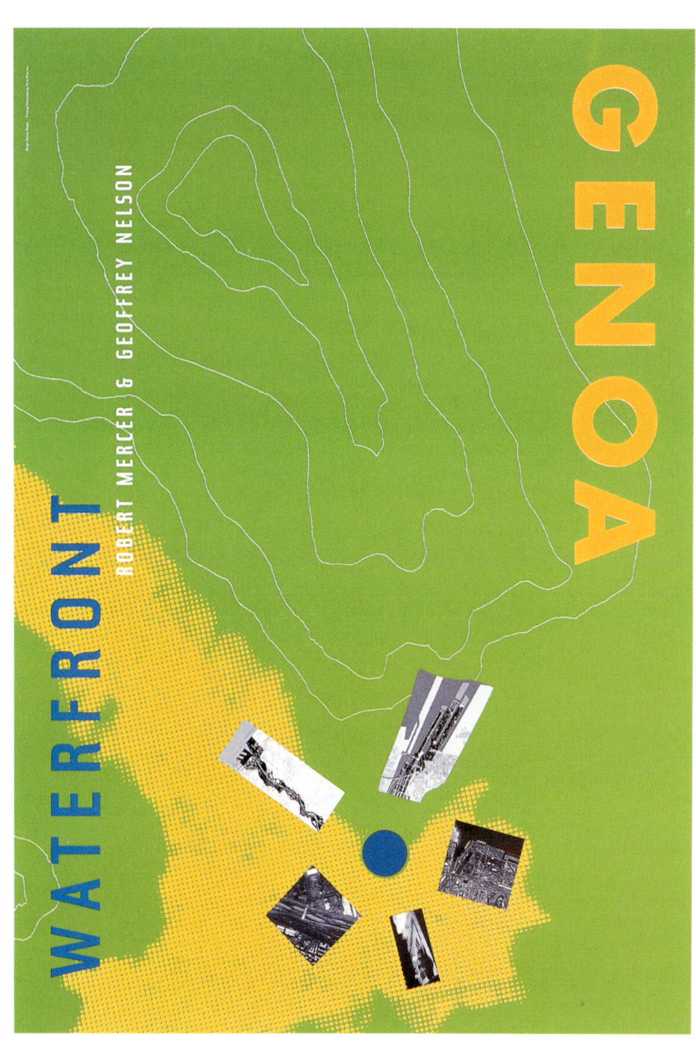

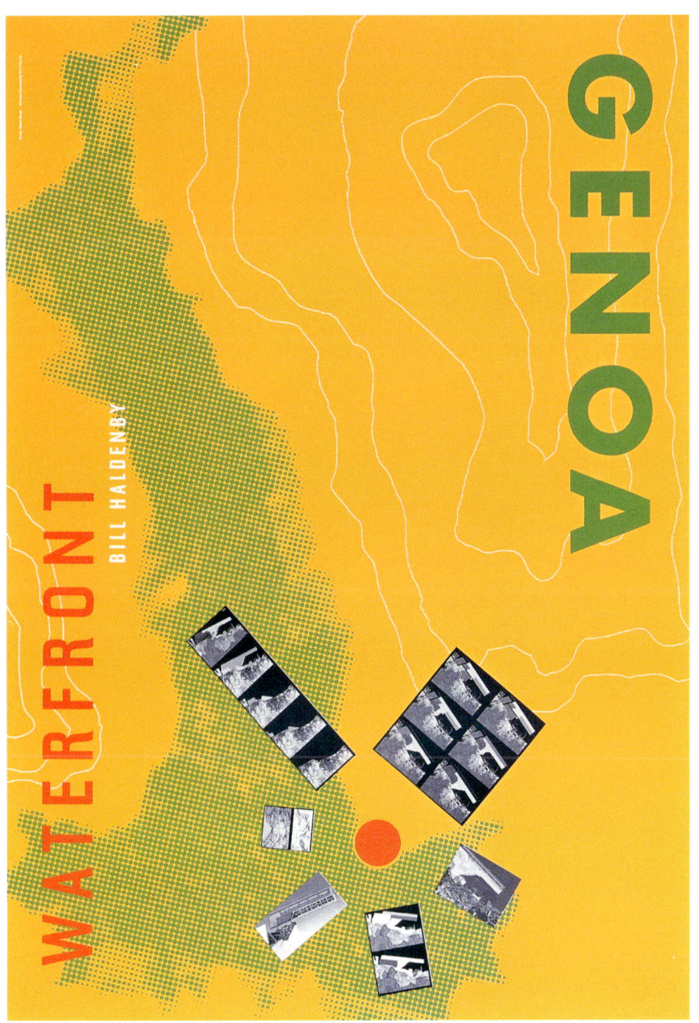

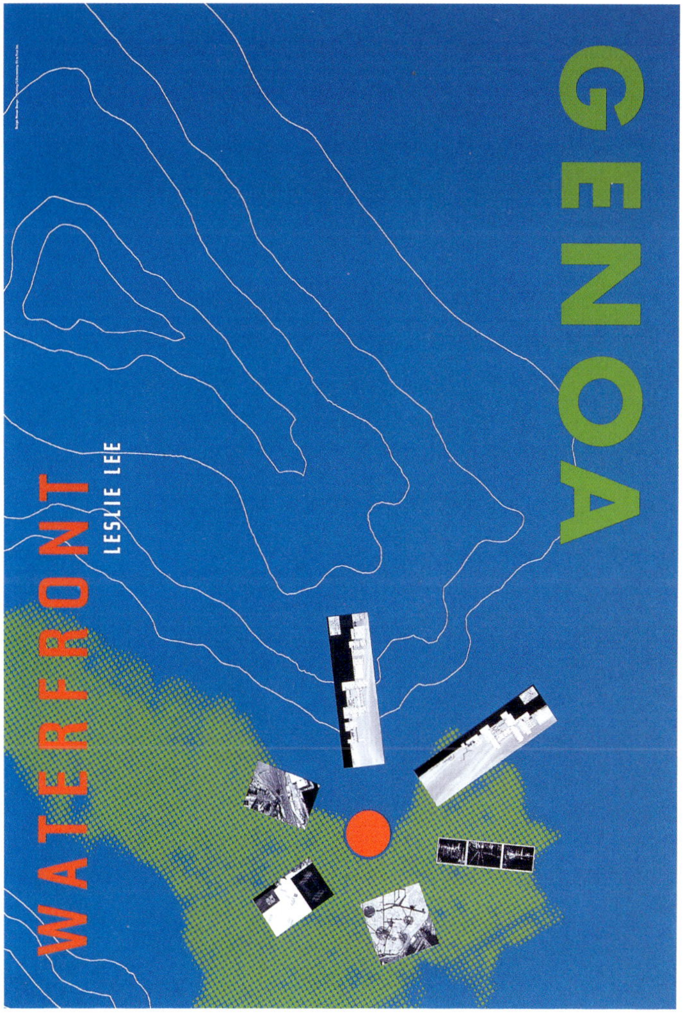

Nassar Design/Harvard Design School

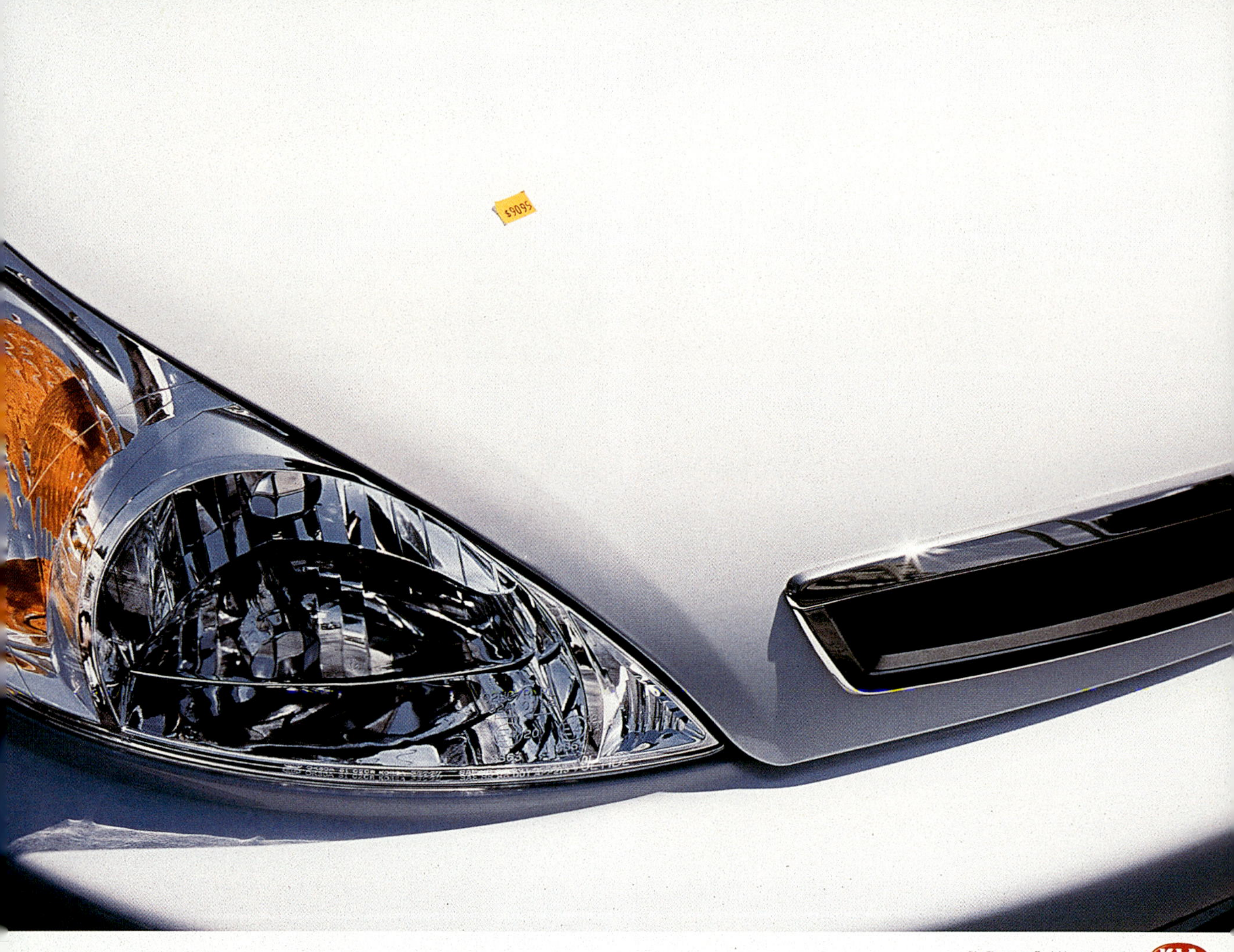
$9095

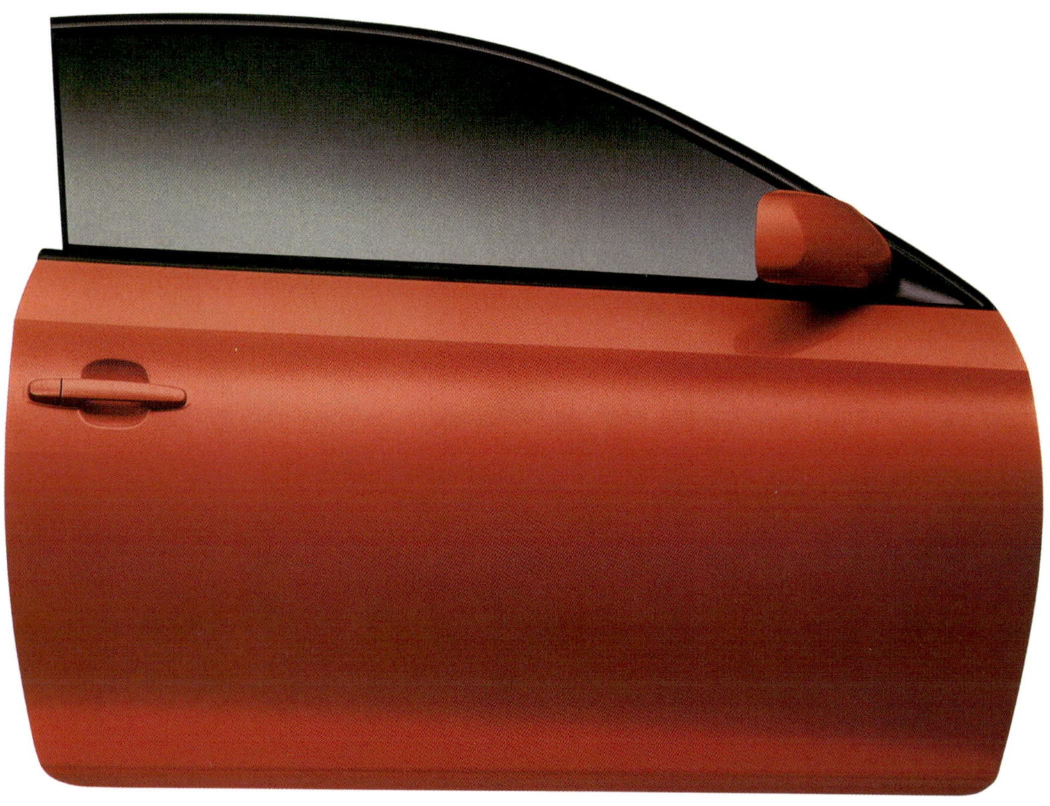

"Door." 2004. Enamel on steel panel with glass, 44" x 56 1/2."
Part of the complete exhibit called "Solara" on loan to the New York Auto Show.
From the Toyota Collection. Exhibit closes April 27.

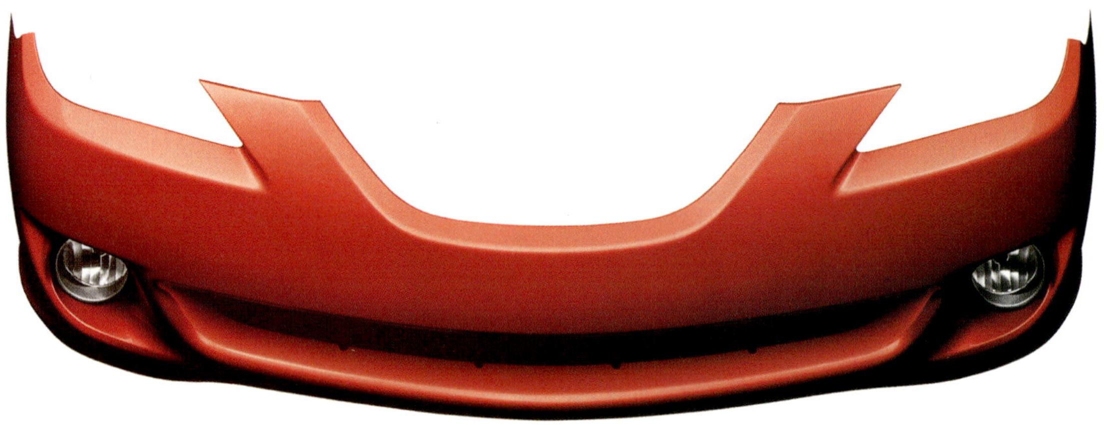

"Fascia." 2004. Enamel on Super Olefin Polymer, 16" x 97 3/4."
Part of the complete exhibit called "Solara" on loan to the New York Auto Show.
From the Toyota Collection. Exhibit closes April 27.

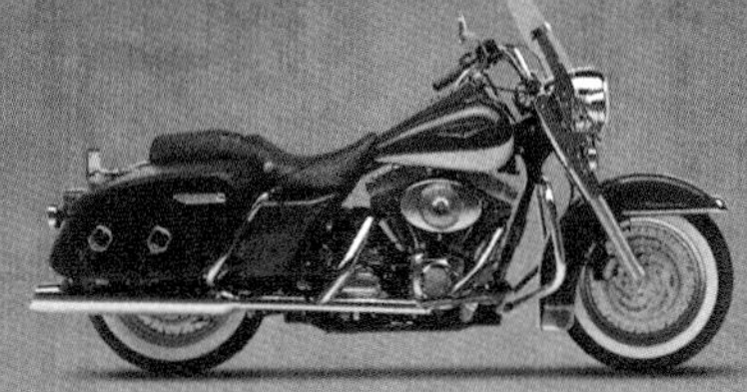

ELVIS RODE

SO DID DWIGHT EISENHOWER, STEVE McQUEEN AND CHARLES LINDBERGH. PETER FONDA AND DENNIS HOPPER STILL RIDE. SO DO BRUCE SPRINGSTEEN, SHERYL CROW, JOHN TRAVOLTA, MICKEY ROURKE AND SOME GUY NAMED MITCH WITH A JUICED-UP, CHROMED-OUT, CUSTOM-PAINTED 1972 V-TWIN SHOVELHEAD. AND SO DO YOU. HERE'S TO THOSE WHO RODE, THOSE WHO RIDE AND THOSE WHO WILL RIDE.

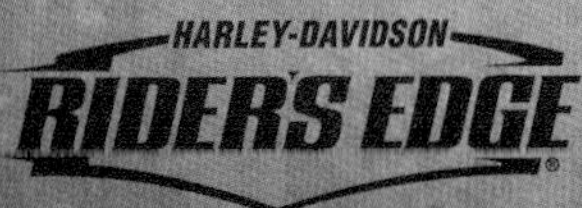

Shine Advertising/Harley-Davidson Motor Company

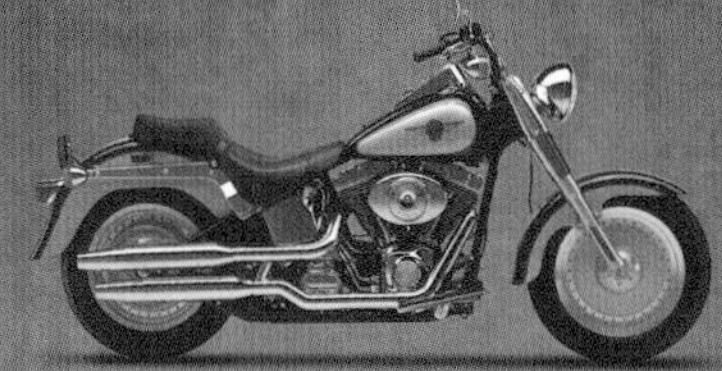

NO CAGES

A DREAM. NO COUPES. NO SEDANS. NO WAGONS. NO SPORT UTILITIES. AND FOR THE LOVE OF GOD, NO MINIVANS. NO MORE CAGES. AND WHILE THE MASSES SEE THEIR CAGE AS A REFUGE FROM THE ELEMENTS, WE KNOW IT'S REALLY JUST A PRISON FOR THEIR SOUL. SEPARATING IT FROM THE WIND AND THE SUN AND THE RAIN AND LIFE. HERE'S TO THOSE WHO RODE, THOSE WHO RIDE AND THOSE WHO WILL RIDE.

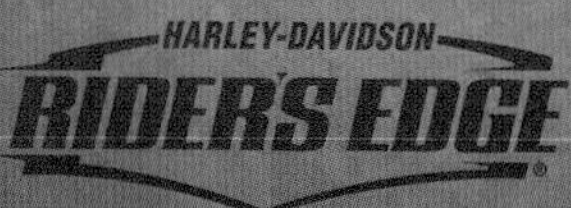

Shine Advertising/Harley-Davidson Motor Company

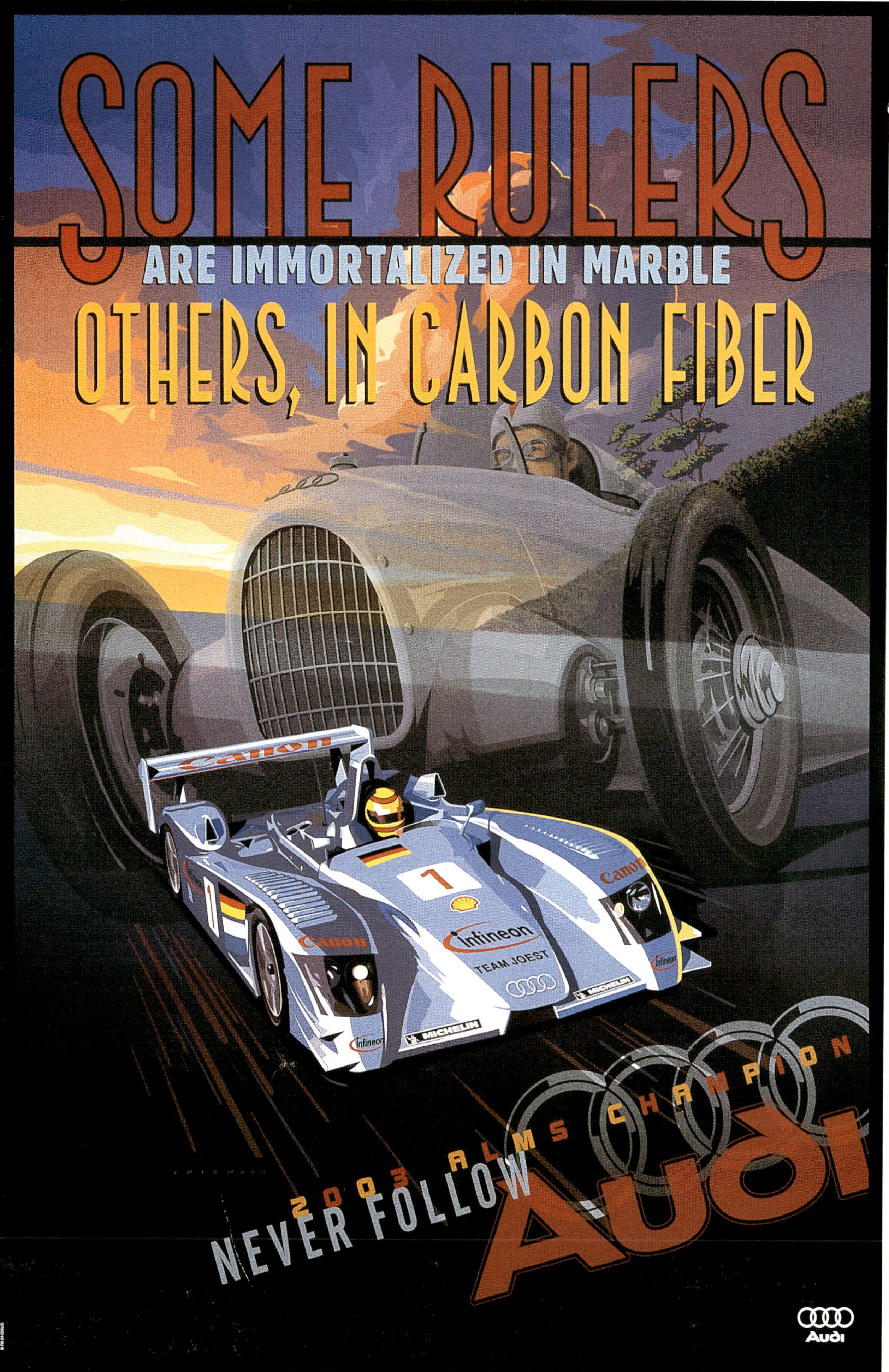

McKinney + Silver/Audi of America

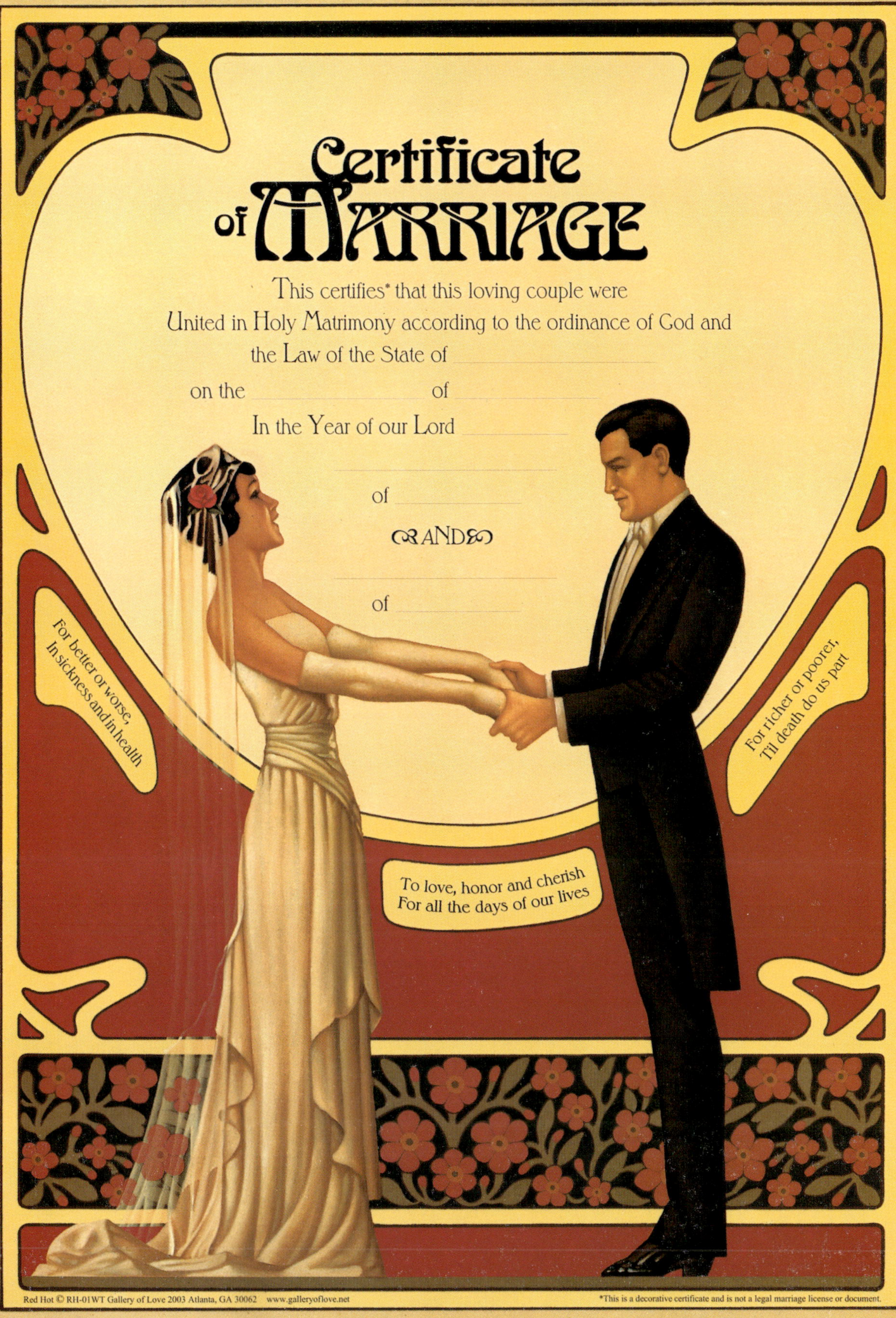
Certificate of Marriage
This certifies* that this loving couple were
United in Holy Matrimony according to the ordinance of God and
the Law of the State of
on the of
In the Year of our Lord
of
AND
of
For better or worse,
In sickness and in health
For richer or poorer,
Til death do us part
To love, honor and cherish
For all the days of our lives
Red Hot © RH-01WT Gallery of Love 2003 Atlanta, GA 30062 www.galleryoflove.net
*This is a decorative certificate and is not a legal marriage license or document.

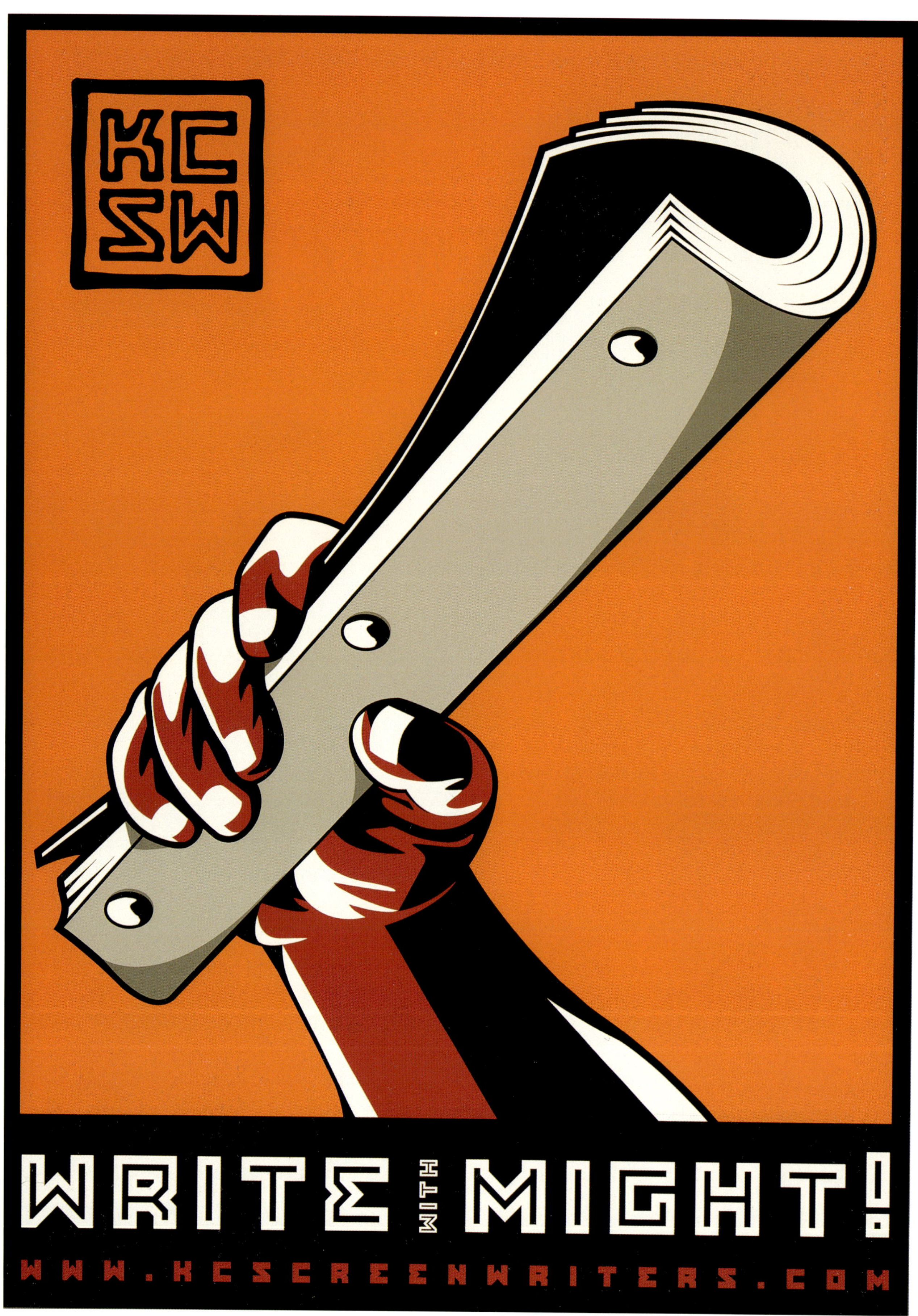

Muller+Company/The Kansas City Screenwriters

LET ME OUT OF HERE!

technology trap *technologiefalle*

designbüro behr/Plakation Detlef Behr & Germar Wambach

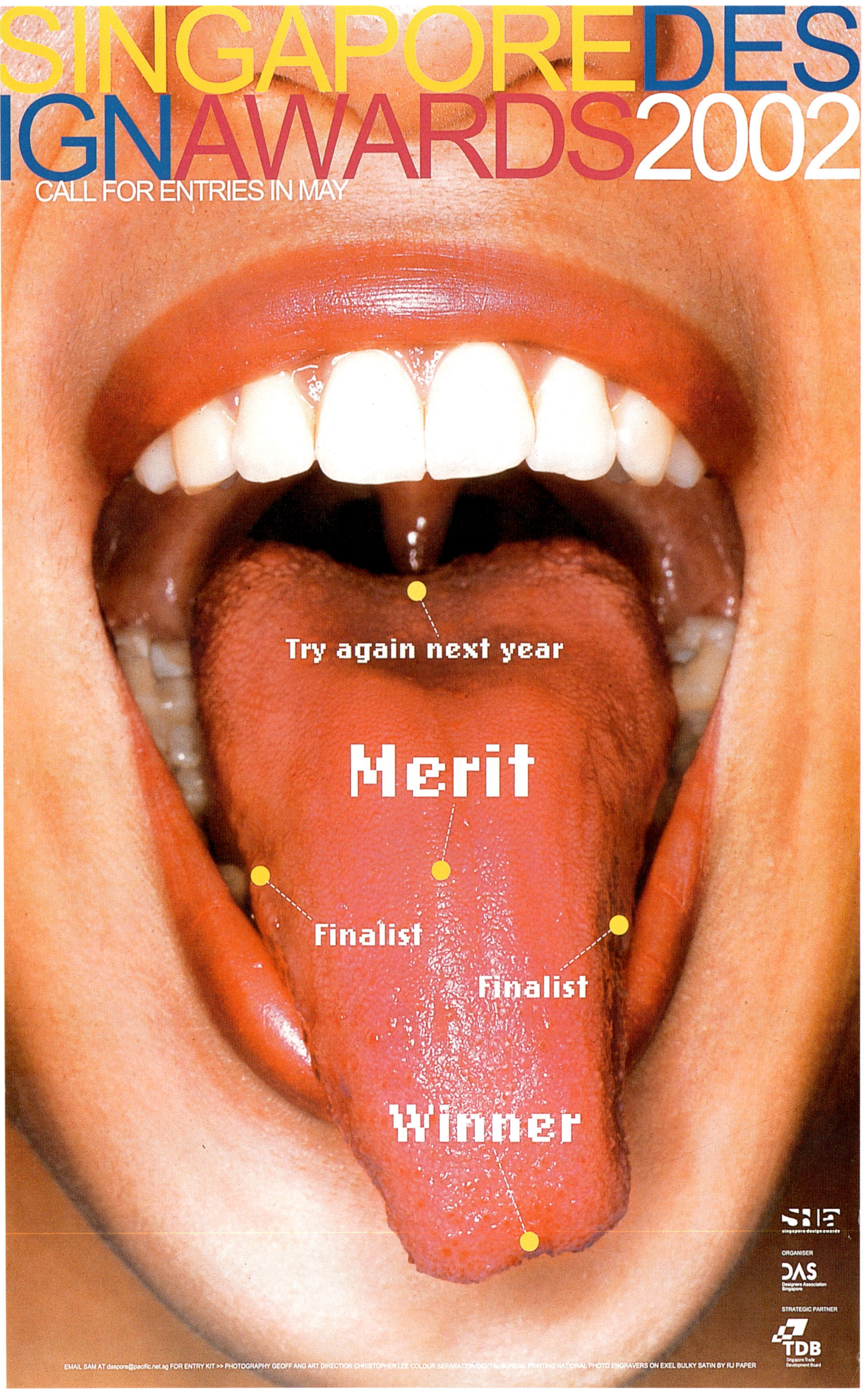

Duffy Singapore Pte Ltd/Designers Association of Singapore

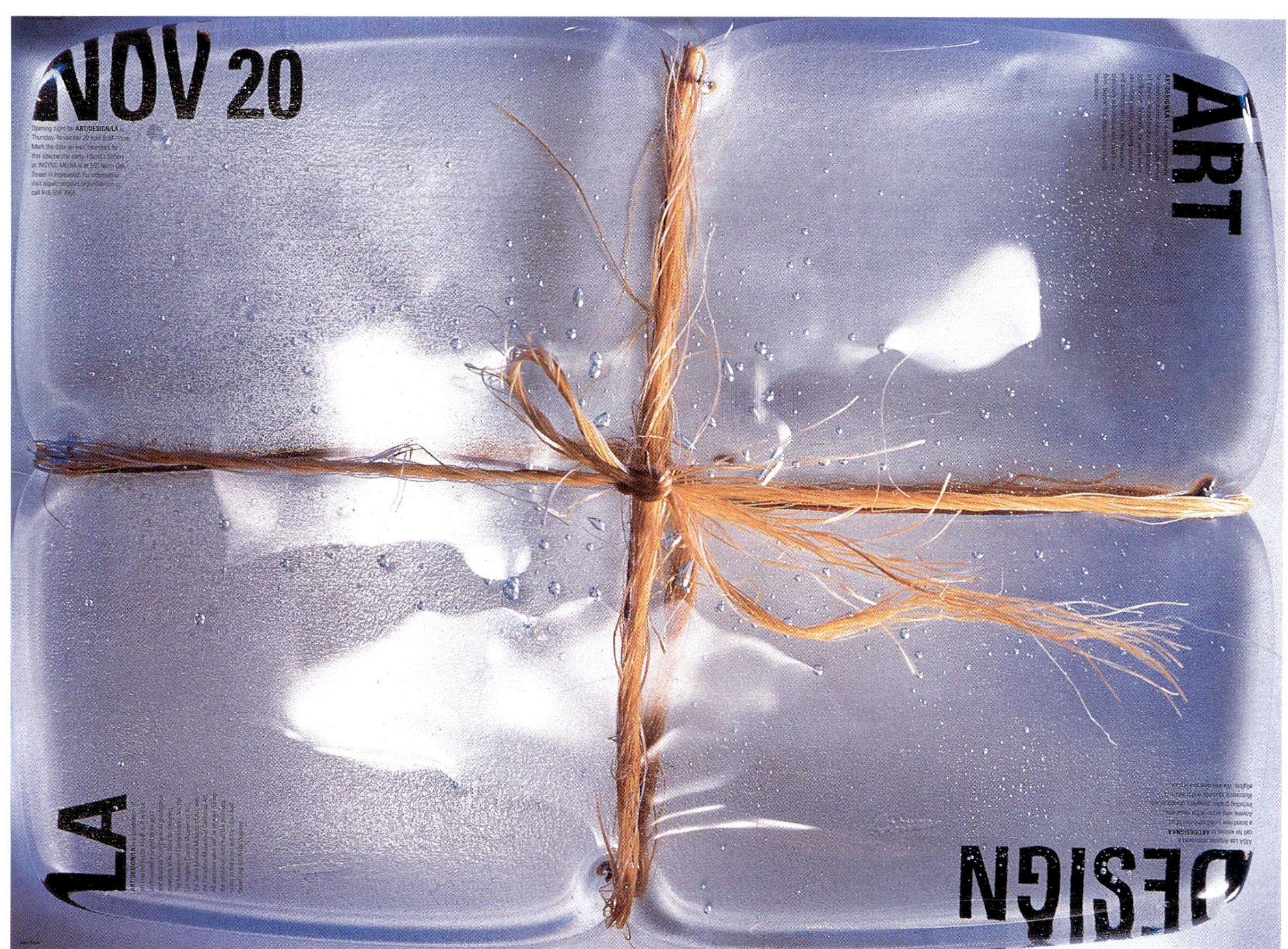

Looking/AIGA Los Angeles, Harold's Gallery at Insync Media

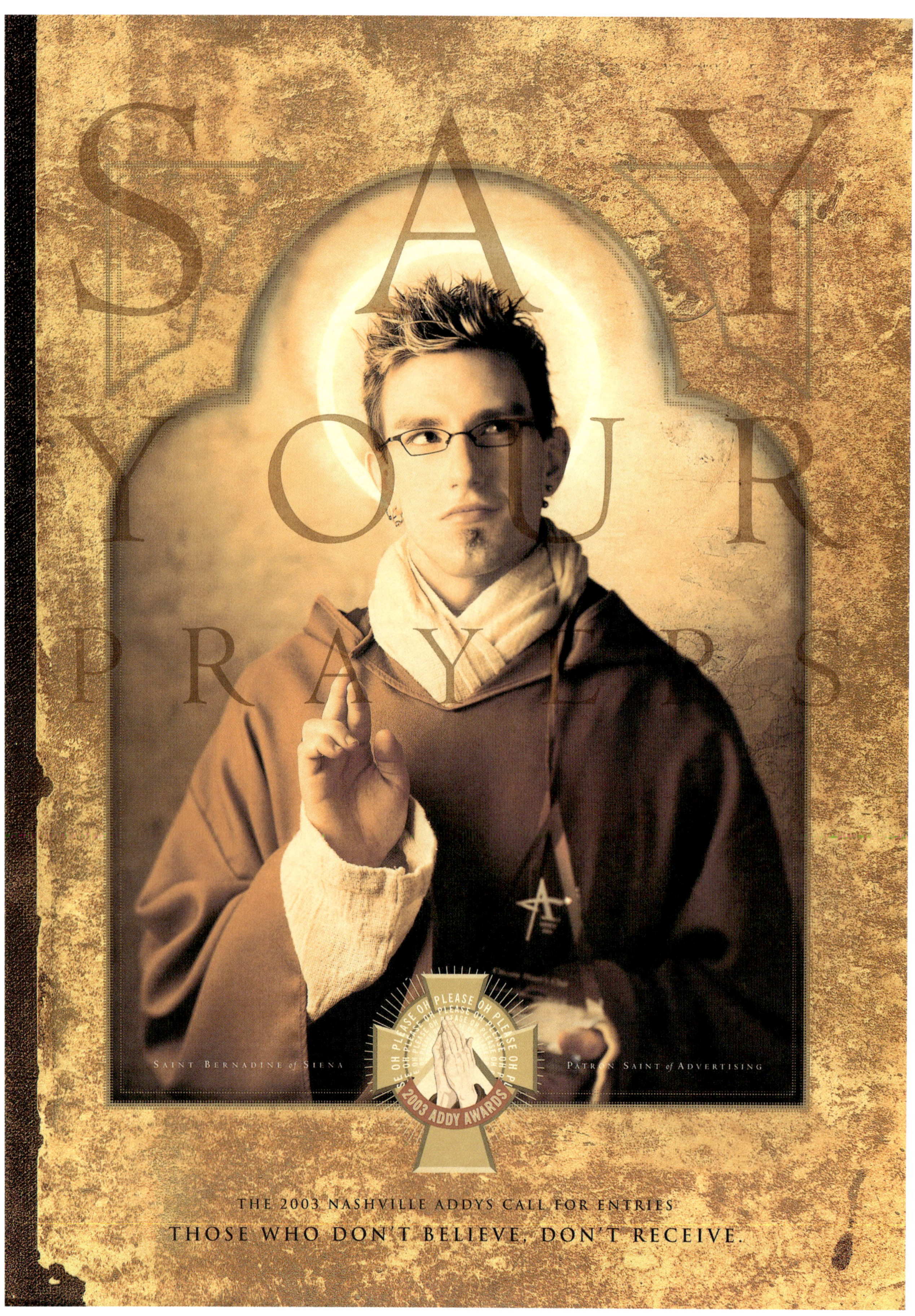

Bohan Advertising/Marketing/Nashville Advertising Federation

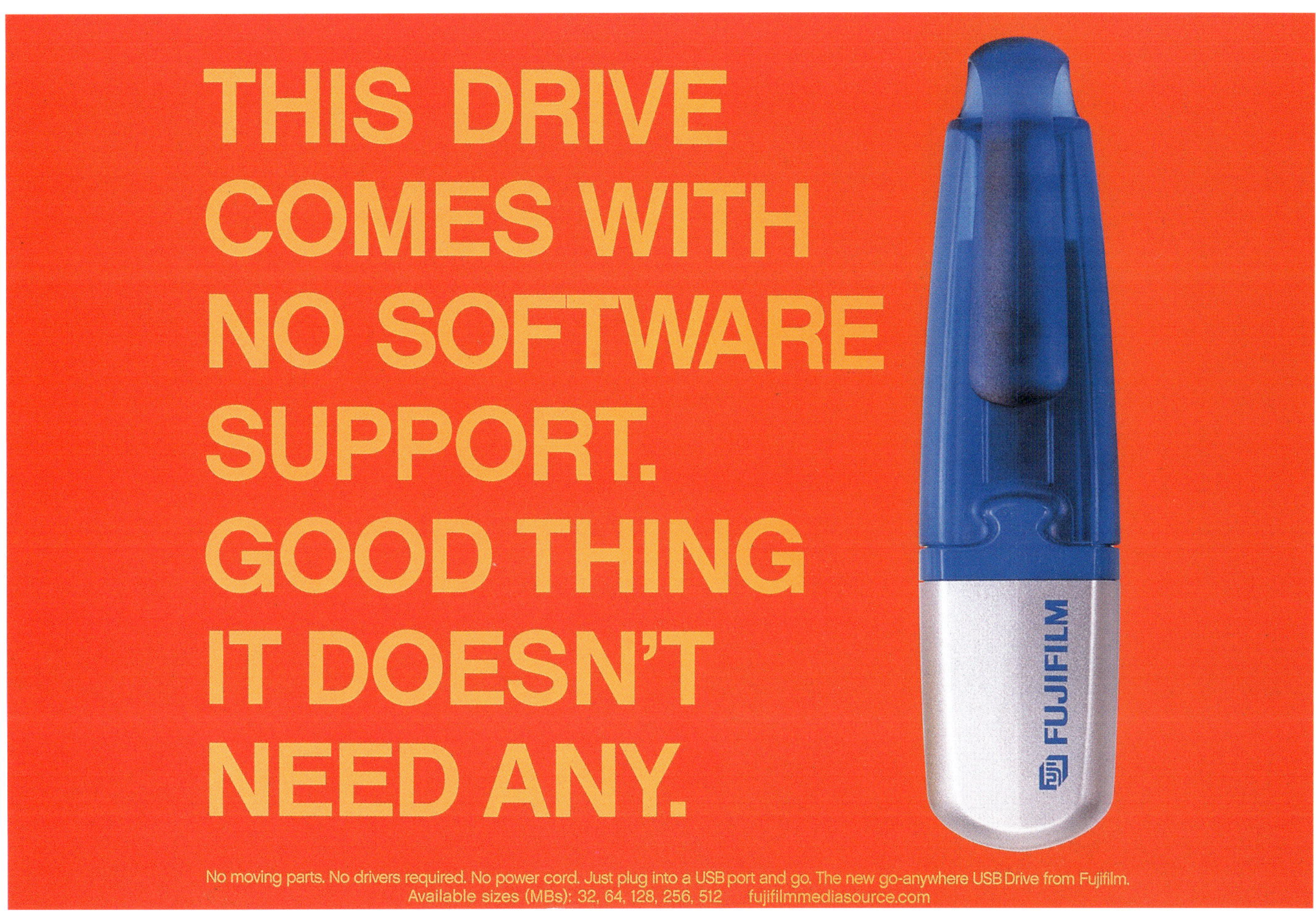

ADK America/Fujifilm

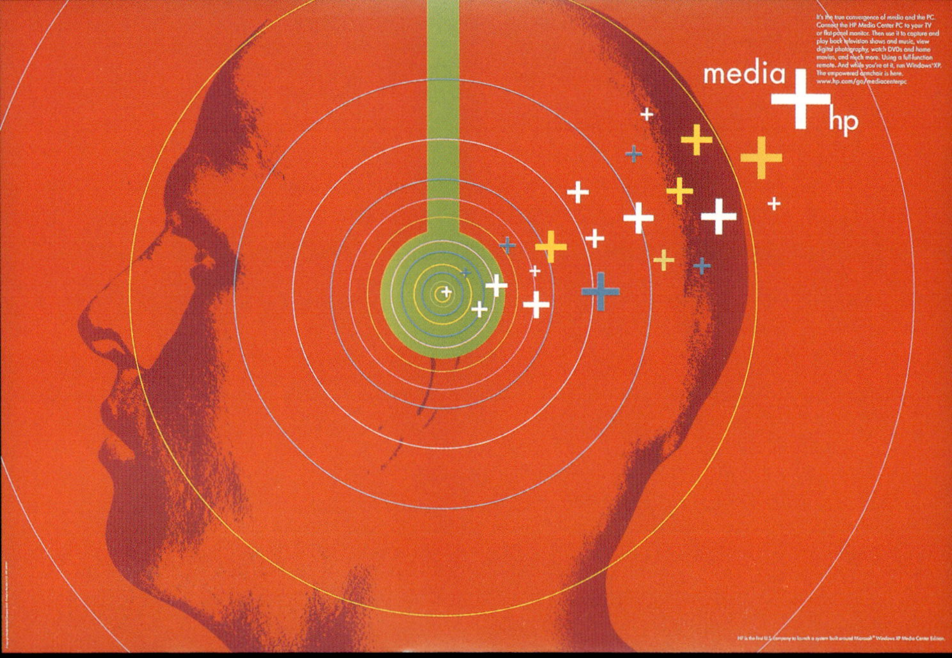

It's the true convergence of media and the PC. Connect the HP Media Center PC to your TV or flat-panel monitor. Then use it to capture and play back television shows and music, view digital photography, watch DVDs and home movies, and much more. Using a full-function remote. And while you're at it, run Windows® XP. The empowered armchair is here. www.hp.com/go/mediacenterpc

media + hp

HP is the first U.S. company to launch a system built around Microsoft® Windows XP Media Center Edition.

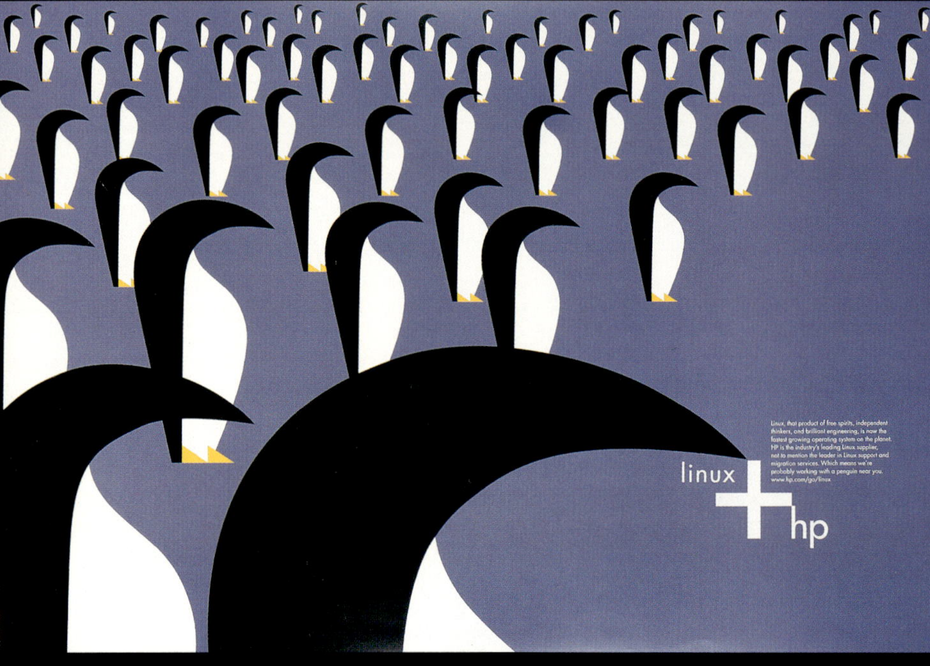

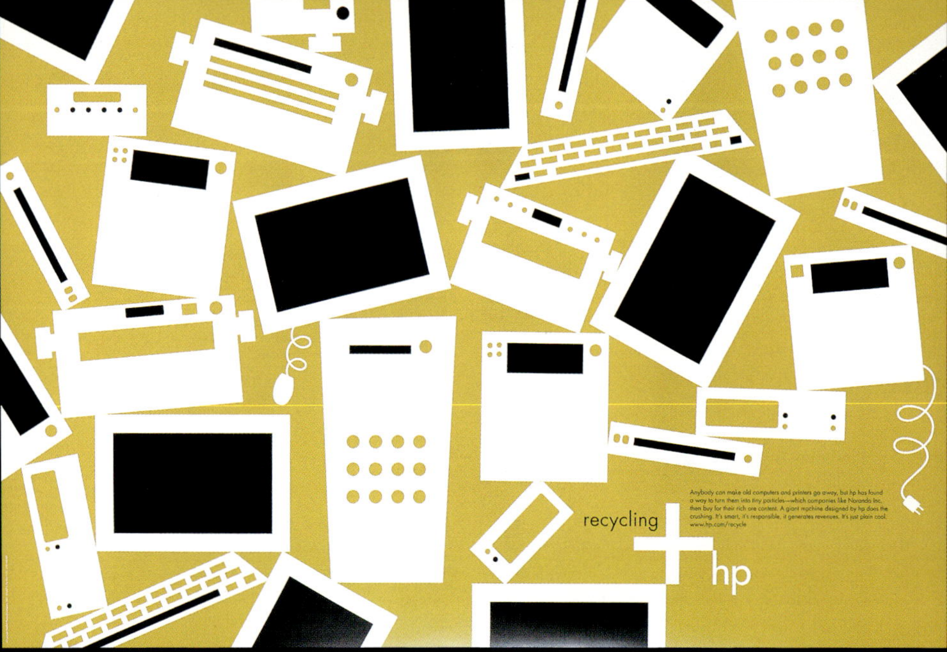

Seed Communications/Hewlett-Packard Company

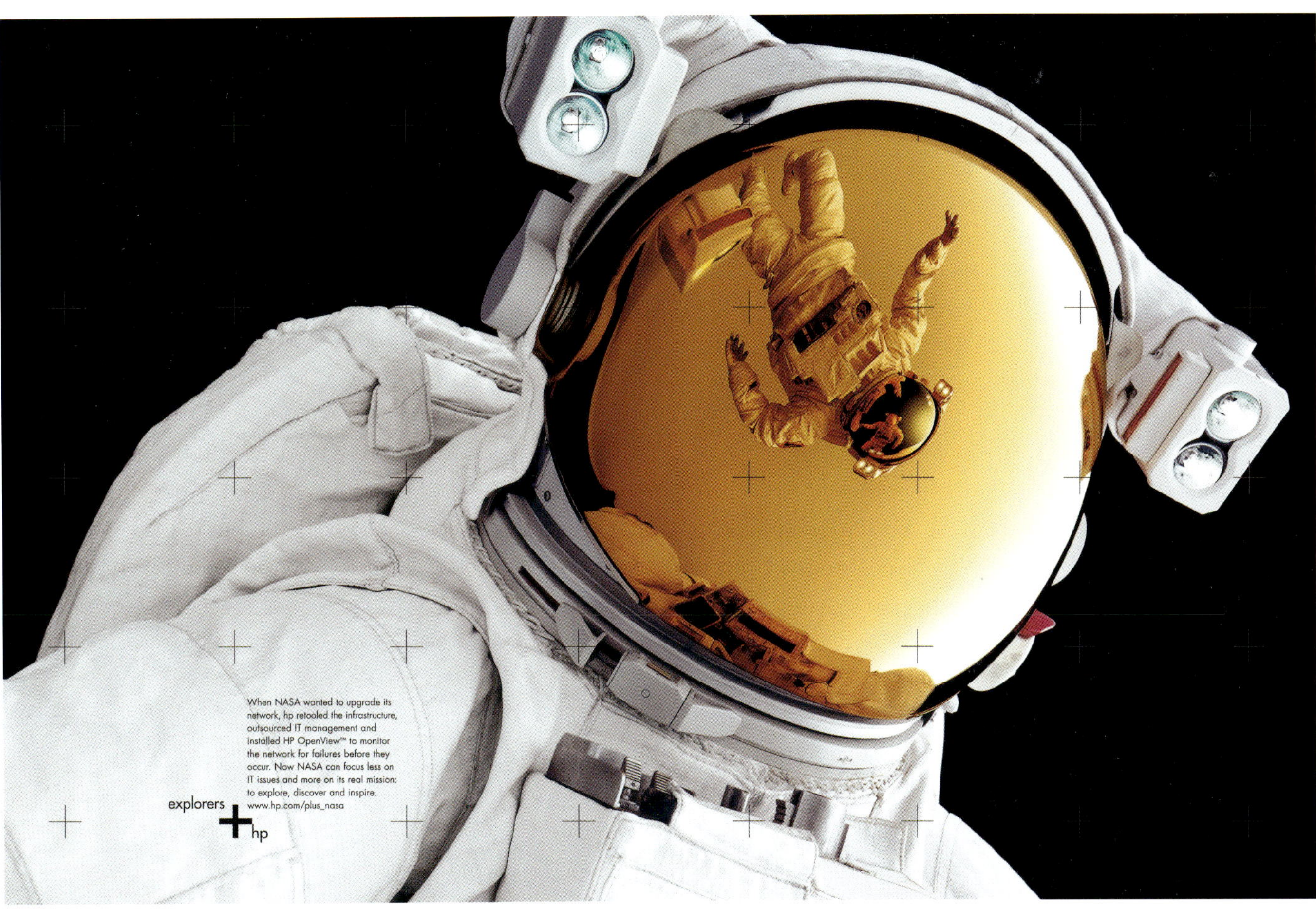

Goodby Silverstein & Partners/Hewlett-Packard Company

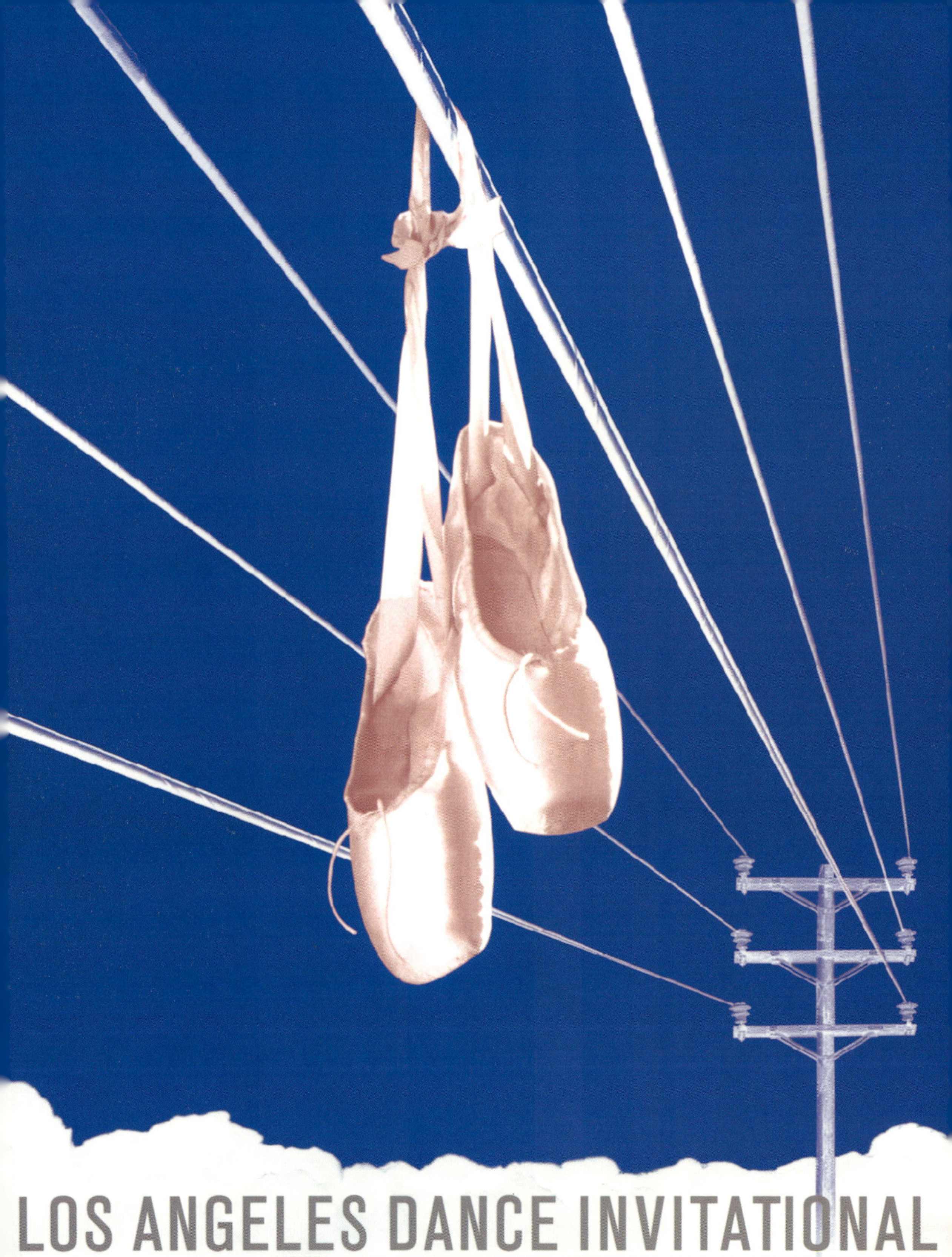
LOS ANGELES DANCE INVITATIONAL
FRI. & SAT. JUNE 6-7 • EL PORTAL THEATRE • HONOREE: MITZI GAYNOR • TICKETS 323-655-TKTS • SPONSOR: WELLS FARGO
CHOREOGRAPHERS: TERRY BEEMAN, PATRICK DAVID BRADLEY (SAN PEDRO CITY BALLET), MAGGIE DANIELSEN, MARIE DE LA PALME, MARIA GILLESPIE, LIZ IMPERIO (INSTINCTS DANCE CO), KELLY KEMP, JENNIFER BACKHAUS MCIVOR (BACKHAUS DANCE), REGAN PATNO & JULIA SNYDER (THE TWEAKSTERS), ERICA REBOLLAR & KENNETH WALKER

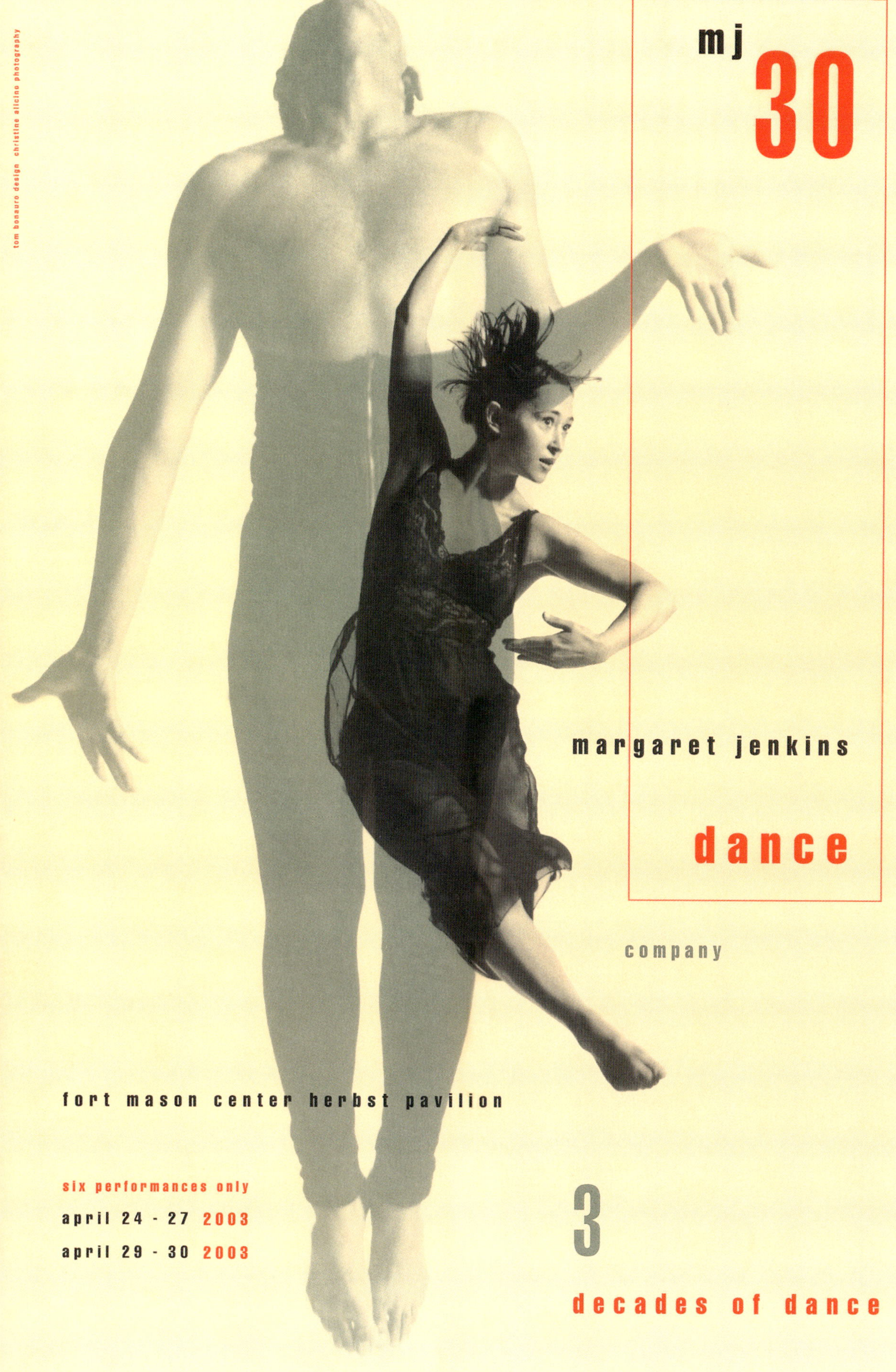
tom bonauro design christine alcino photography
mj 30
margaret jenkins
dance
company
fort mason center herbst pavilion
six performances only
april 24 - 27 2003
april 29 - 30 2003
3
decades of dance
$20 $25 tickets now on sale (415) 392-4400 www.mjdc.org

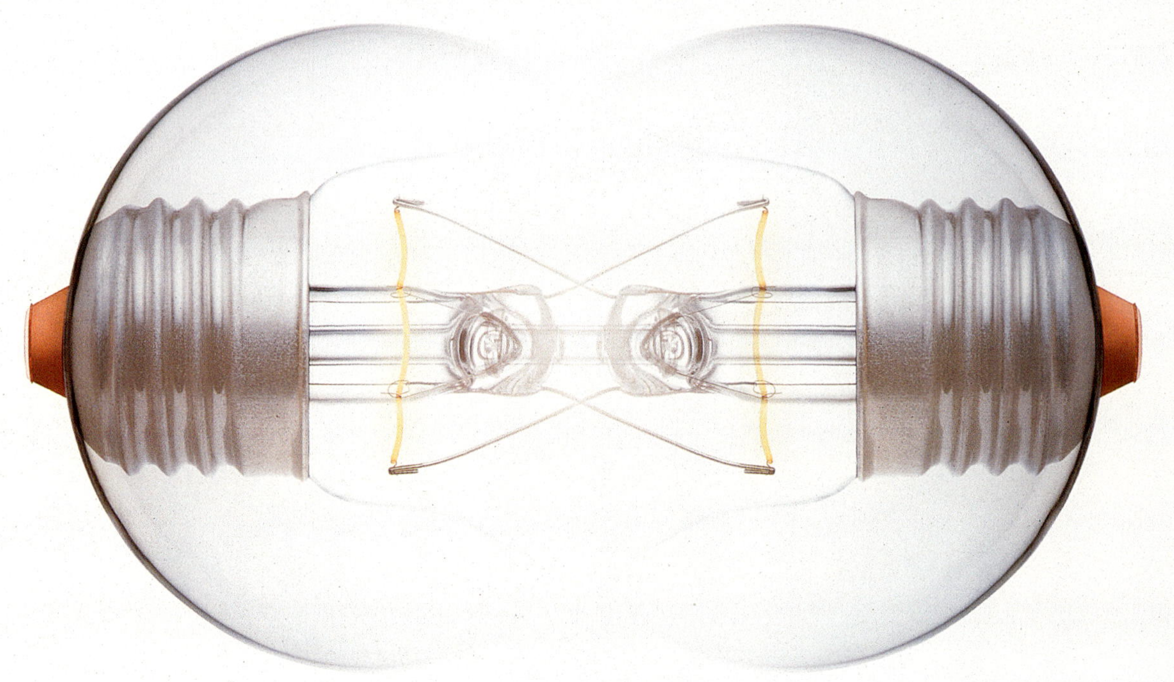

THE MOTHER OF ALL ENERGY AND CREATIVITY

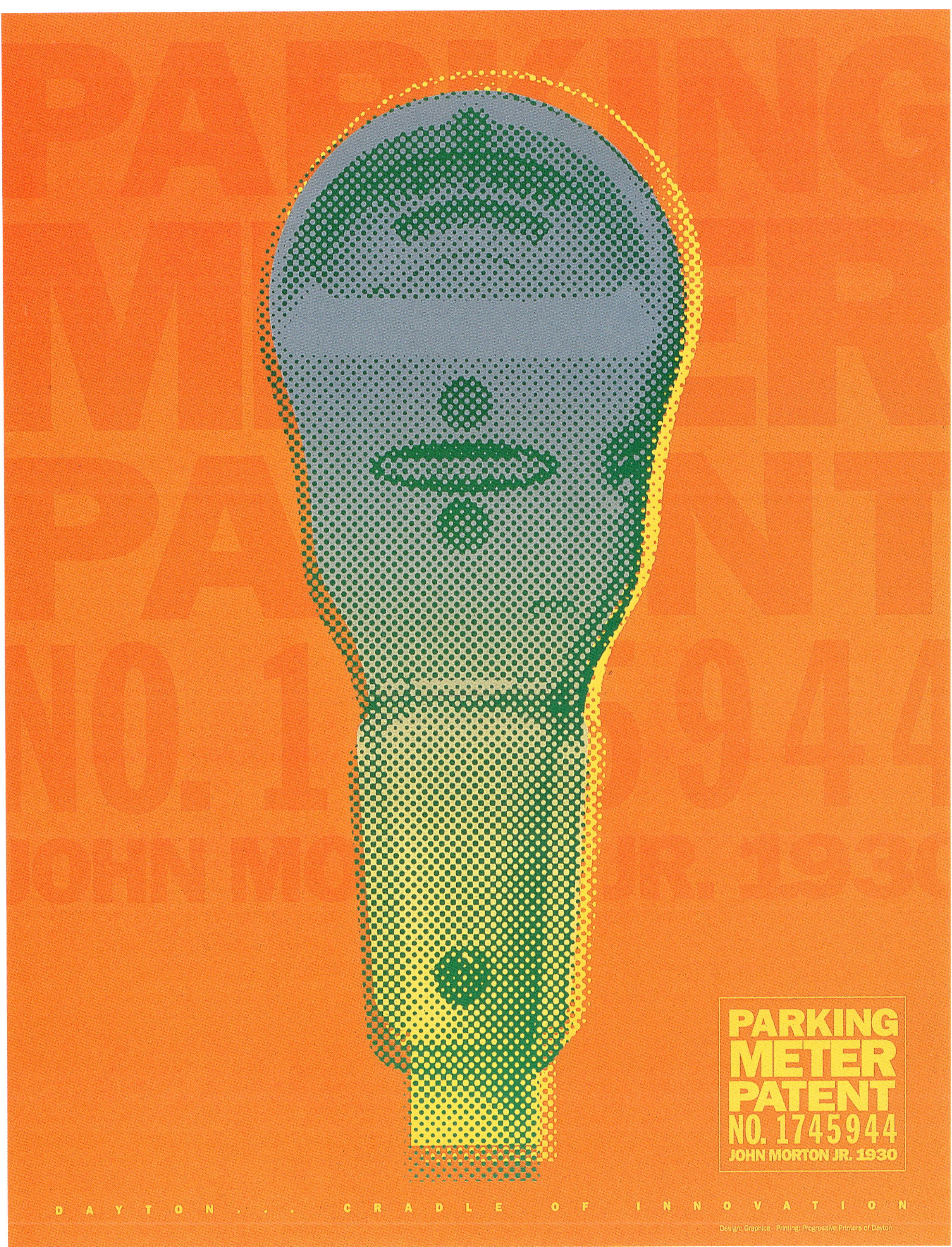

Graphica, Inc./Graphica, Inc. and Progressive Printers

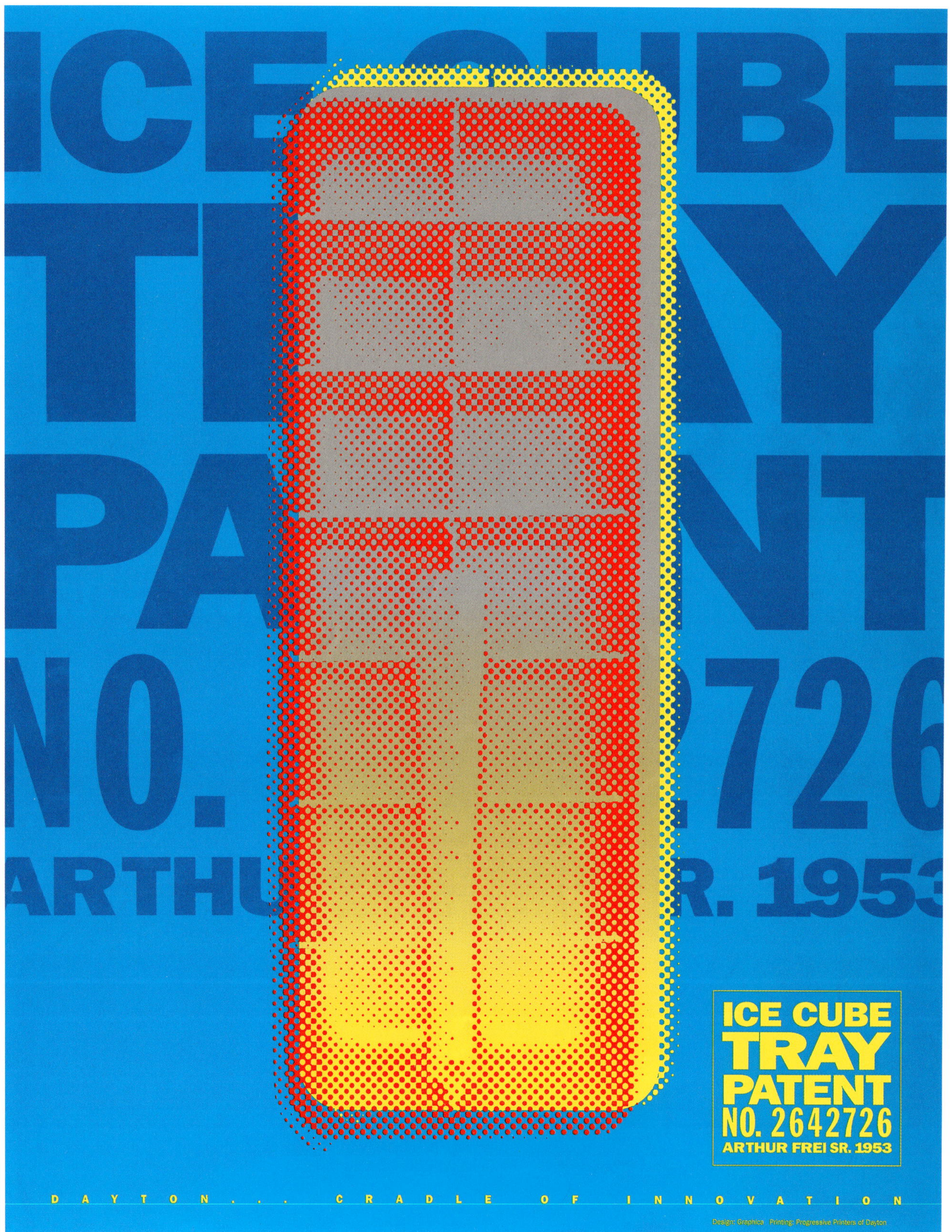

Graphica, Inc./Graphica, Inc. and Progressive Printers

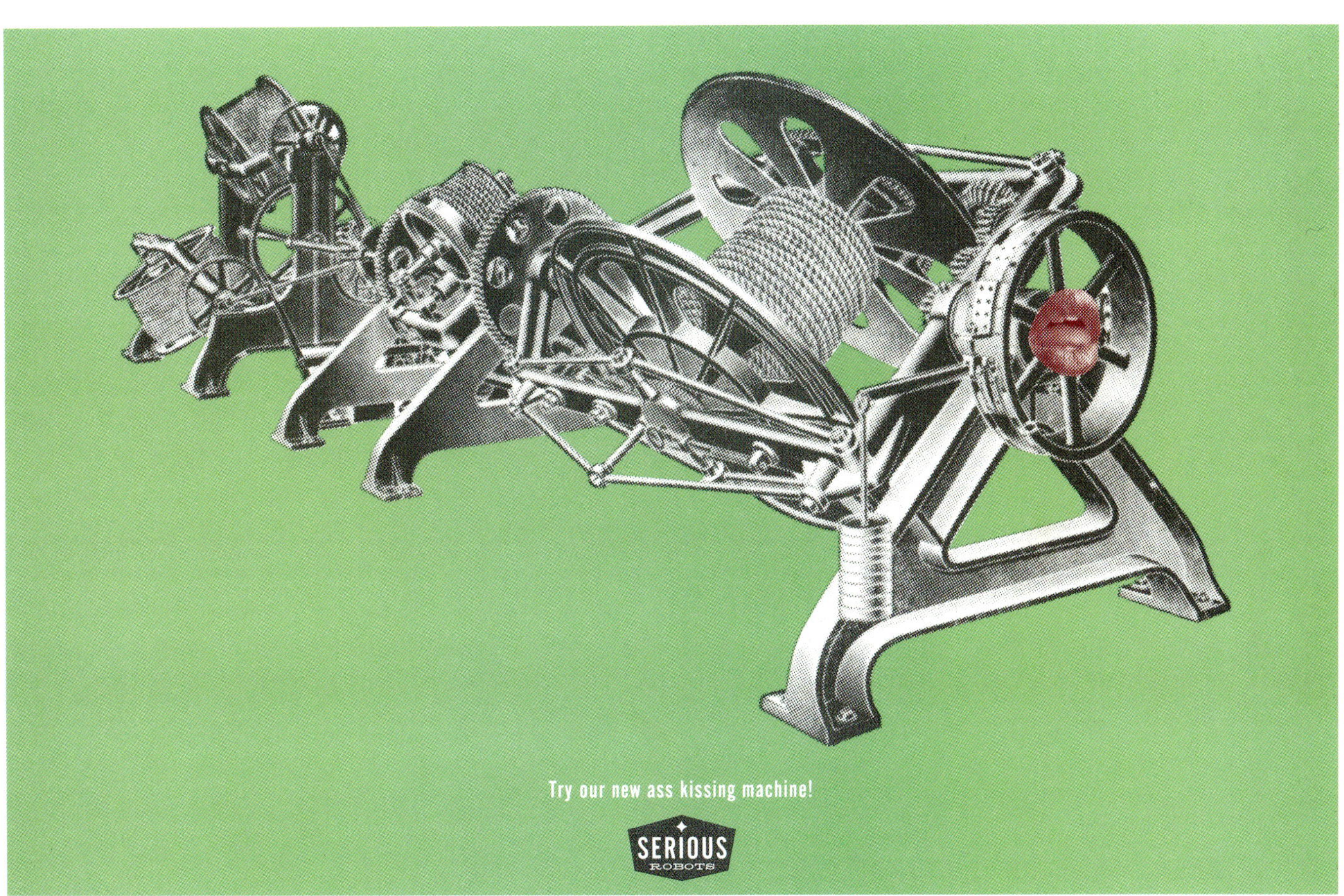

The Republik/Serious Robots

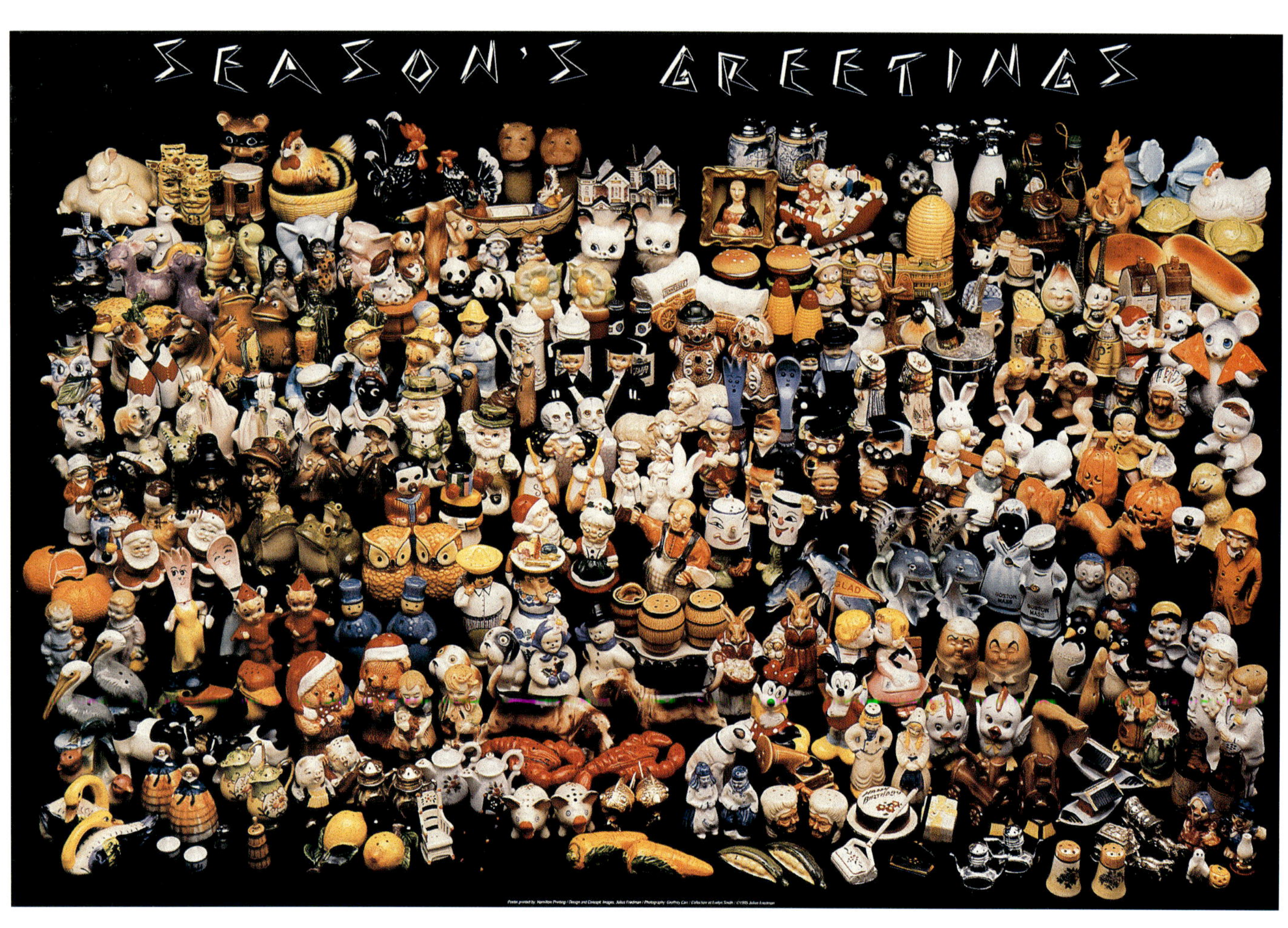

Images/Images and Hamilton Printing

The Bozell & Jacobs Summer Internship Program.
Positions available in Account Service, Art Direction, Copywriting, Interactive, Media, and Public Relations. For more information or to download an application, log on to www.bozelljacobs.com/Summerintern.

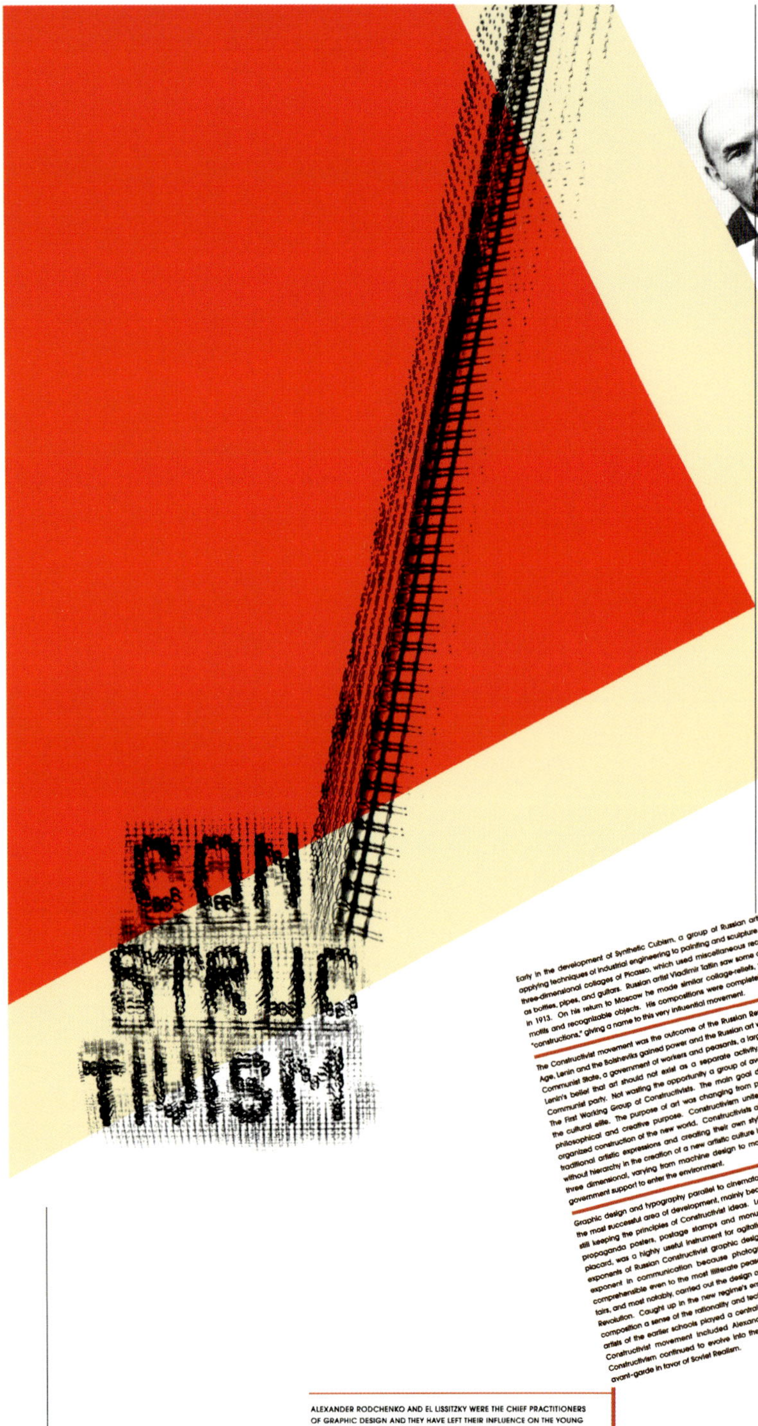

CON STRUC TIVISM

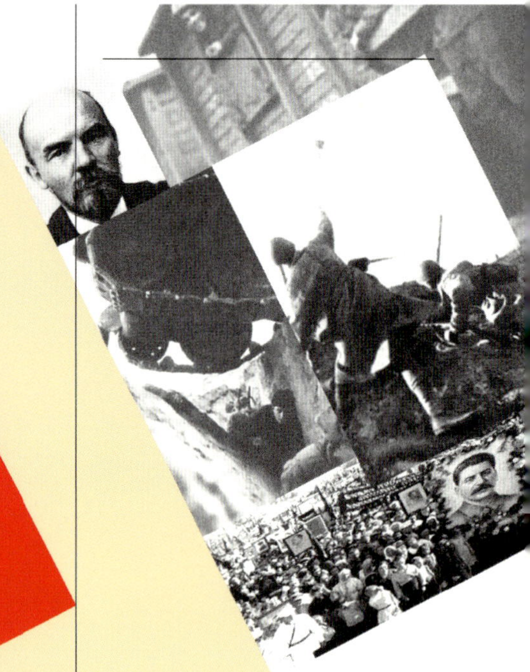

Early in the development of Synthetic Cubism, a group of Russian artists working in Moscow became interested in applying techniques of industrial engineering to painting and sculpture. Their point of departure was some of the more three-dimensional collages of Picasso, which used miscellaneous recognizable objects out of the environment, such as bottles, pipes, and guitars. Russian artist Vladimir Tatlin saw some of these collages, when he visited Picasso in Paris in 1913. On his return to Moscow he made similar collage-reliefs, which significantly excluded all representational motifs and recognizable objects. His compositions were completely abstract, the first of their kind. These he called "constructions," giving a name to this very influential movement.

The Constructivist movement was the outcome of the Russian Revolution of 1917. Russia progressed to the Industrial Age, Lenin and the Bolsheviks gained power and the Russian art world turned upside down. Revolution created the first Communist State, a government of workers and peasants, a largely illiterate population in need of education. It was Lenin's belief that art should not exist as a separate activity, but should come under the central authority of the Communist party. Not wasting the opportunity a group of avant-guard artists including Tatlin formed the club called The First Working Group of Constructivists. The main goal during this period was to create art for the people, not the cultural elite. The purpose of art was changing from purely aesthetic to having a social, political, ideological, philosophical and creative purpose. Constructivism united art, science, technology, politics and society into an organized construction of the new world. Constructivists aimed to totally transform the environment, by rejecting the traditional artistic expressions and creating their own style that would bring together all the arts as artistic activity without hierarchy in the creation of a new artistic culture in a communist society. Although, most of their designs were three dimensional, varying from machine design to model monuments or buildings, very few of them actually got government support to enter the environment.

Graphic design and typography parallel to cinematography, architecture, costume design and product design had the most successful area of development, mainly because it was the easiest way of winning government support and still keeping the principles of Constructivist ideas. Lenin wanted to sell his vision to the illiterate population, through propaganda posters, postage stamps and monuments. Graphic design, particularly as applied in the political placard, was a highly useful instrument for agitation, as it was both direct and economical. One of the important exponents of Russian Constructivist graphic design was the photomontage. Photomontage became an important exponent in communication because photography brought direct contact with the real world and this was comprehensible even to the most illiterate peasant. They produced political posters, organized street pageants and fairs, and most notably, carried out the design of the country's great public spaces for anniversary celebrations of the Revolution. Caught up in the new regime's emphasis on the importance of industrial power, they began to bring to composition a sense of the rationality and technological focus of industrial work and design. Many of the prominent artists of the earlier schools played a central role in Constructivism, especially Tatlin. Other well-known artists of the Constructivist movement included Alexander Rodchenko, El Lissitzky, Varvara Stepanova, and Liubov Popova. Constructivism continued to evolve into the late 1920s, when the conservatism of the Stalinist State renounced the avant-garde in favor of Soviet Realism.

ALEXANDER RODCHENKO AND EL LISSITZKY WERE THE CHIEF PRACTITIONERS OF GRAPHIC DESIGN AND THEY HAVE LEFT THEIR INFLUENCE ON THE YOUNG GENERATIONS OF GRAPHIC DESIGNERS EVEN TODAY.

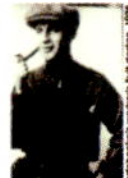
Rodchenko's worker's suit design, 1925.

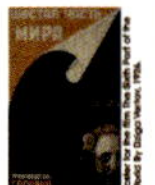
Poster for the film The Sixth Part of the World By Dziga Vertov, 1926.

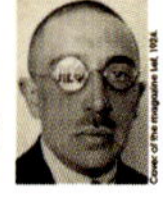
Cover of the magazine Lef, 1924.

Alexander Rodchenko (1891-1956) Alexander Rodchenko was a Russian graphic designer, photographer, painter, constructor, costume designer and director who was influenced by Futurism, Cubism and Art Nouveau, and most of all his mentor, Vladimir Tatlin. In 1921-1922 he did illustrative work in theater, films, typography and advertising, and continued throughout the 1920's to provide cover designs for a remarkably wide range of publications - from the poet Mayakovsky's books (1925-1929) to scientific and technical literature for Moscow publishers. Rodchenko experimented with the ideas of integrating photograph and type into new areas that were questioning form and spatial understanding. He re-educated the public to look in a new way through his photographs of ordinary objects from totally unexpected angles. Rodchenko began photo-reporting during 1926, working for the magazines Ogonok, Radioslushatel, Prozhektor, Krasnoye Studenchestvo, Dayosh, Za rubezhom, Smena, Borba klassov and the daily Vechernaya Moskva, among others. In 1932 the photographer, whose work was - and still is - widely exhibited, began working in photomontage. Also involved in the film world, Rodchenko shot a newsreel series directed by Dziga Vertov, originally called *Kino-Pravda* and later called *One-sixth of the World*, which was begun in 1922. Between the years 1927 and 1930 he was "constructor-artist" of the films *The Woman Journalist*, *Moscow in October*, *Albidum*, *The Puppet Millionaire* and *What Shall I Be?*. He also directed the documentary *The Chemicalization* of the Forest. Seemingly unlimited in his versatility, Rodchenko was one of Russia's foremost painter, collagist and poster artist, also involved in theater, designing the costumes and props for Glebov's Pendulum and The Bed Bug in 1929.

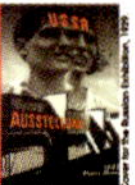
Cover for the Russian Exhibition, 1929.

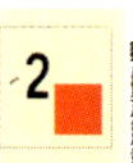

Children's book by Lissitzky, 1922.

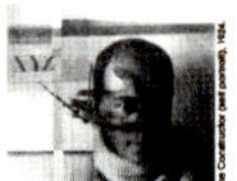
The Constructor (self portrait), 1924.

Lazar El Lissitzky (1890-1941) Russian-Jewish middle class painter, typographer, and designer, was a pioneer of nonrepresentational art in the early 20th century. His innovations in typography, advertising, and exhibition design were particularly influential. Lissitzky was influenced by Malevich, the painter and founder of the Suprematist movement, which advocated the supremacy of pure geometric form over representation. Lissitzky was also developing his own synthesis of painting and architecture, known as Proun. Thereby displaying the Constructivist desire to apply art to social and industrial needs, such as integrating art with architecture, and experimenting with design. His experiments in spatial construction led him to devise new techniques in exhibitions, printing, photomontage, and architecture, which have had much influence in Western Europe. El Lissitzky often made frequent use of expressive possibilities of photographic techniques in his graphic work, exhibition designs and architectural projects. High point of El Lissitzky's work in book design is the volume of poems by Mayakovksy called Dlia Golosa (for the voice) published in Berlin 1923.

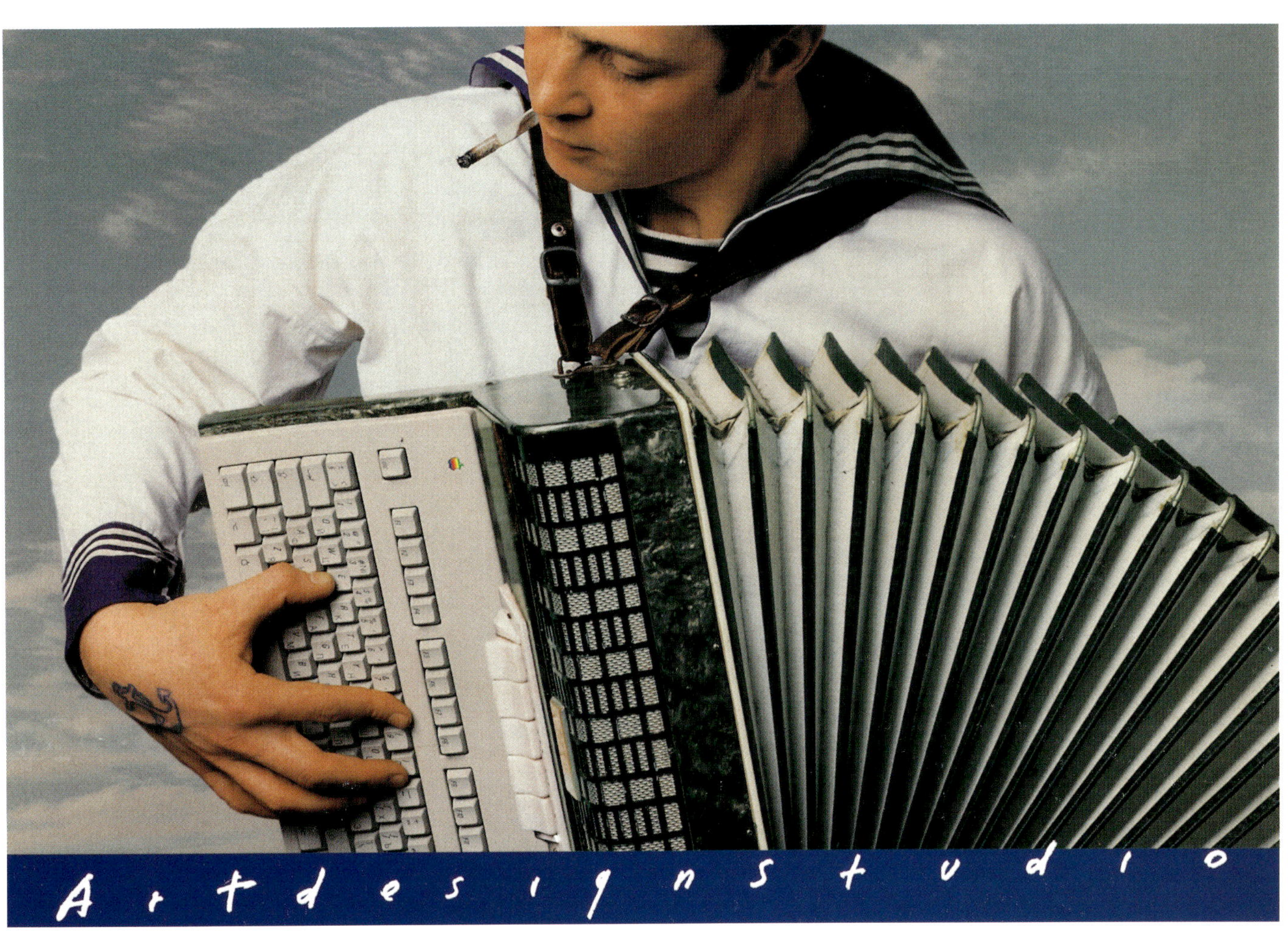

ArtDesignStudio/Linea Grafic

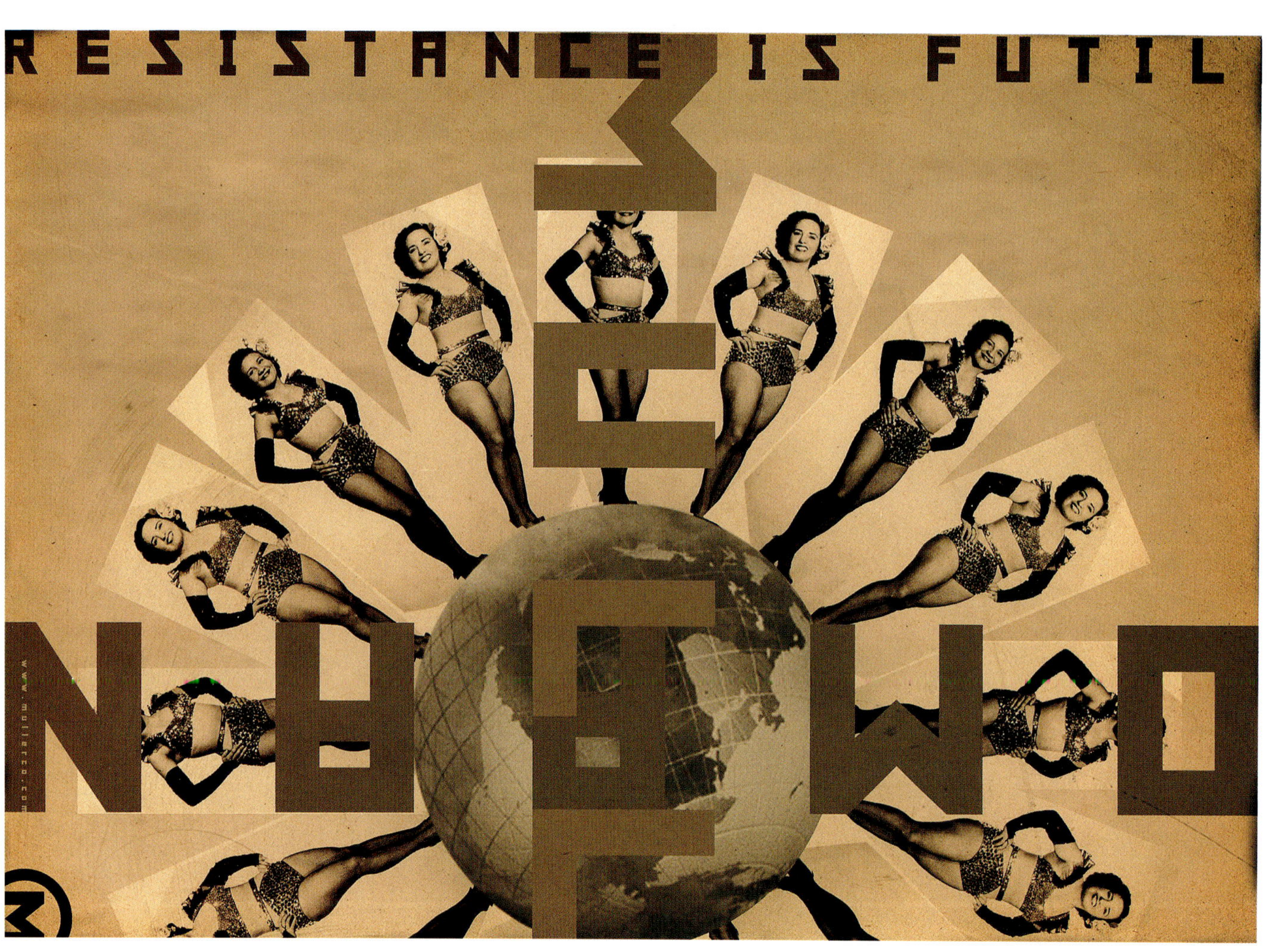

Muller + Company/Muller + Company

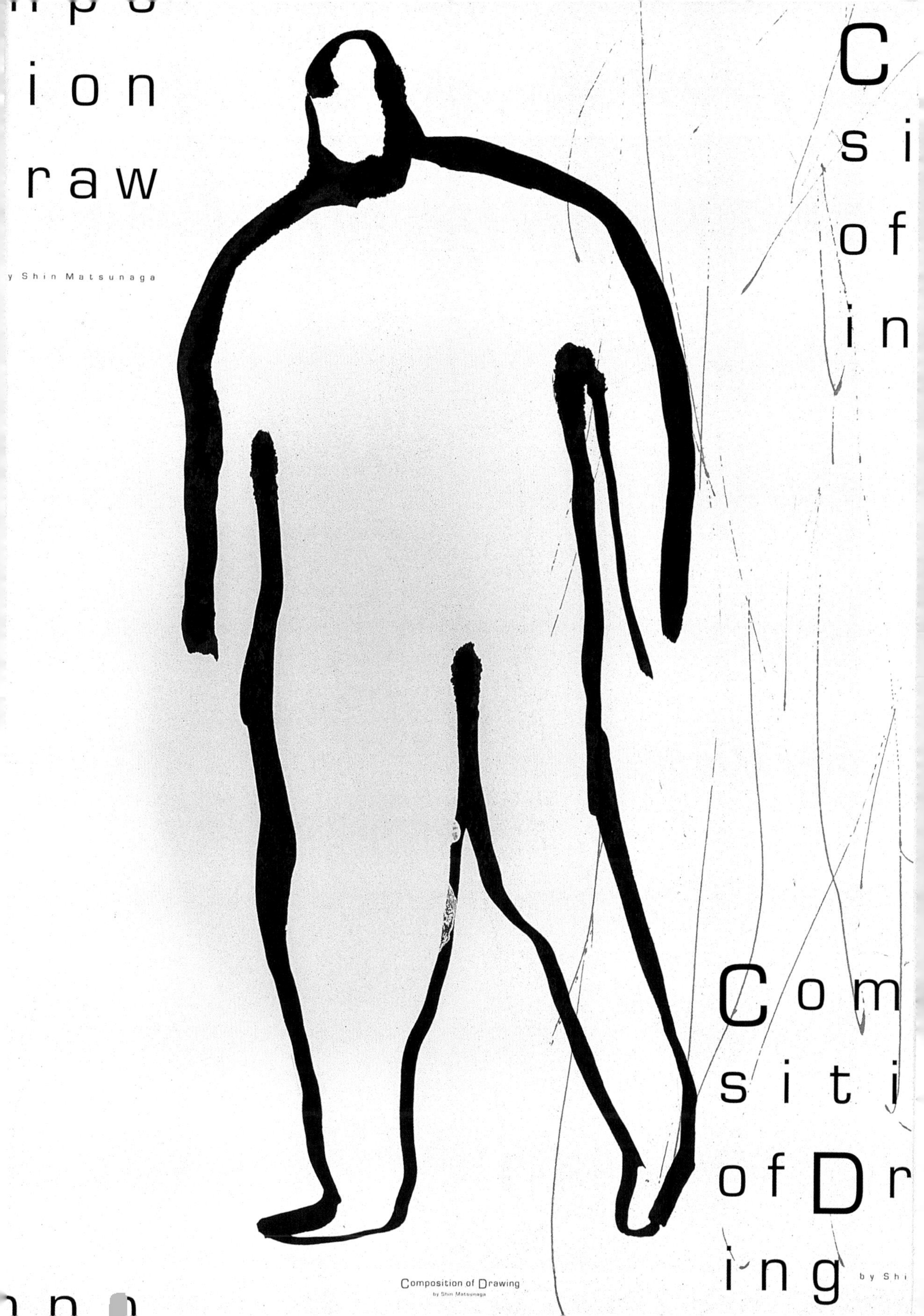
ion
raw
y Shin Matsunaga
C
si
of
in
Com
siti
of D r
ing
by Shi
Composition of Drawing
by Shin Matsunaga

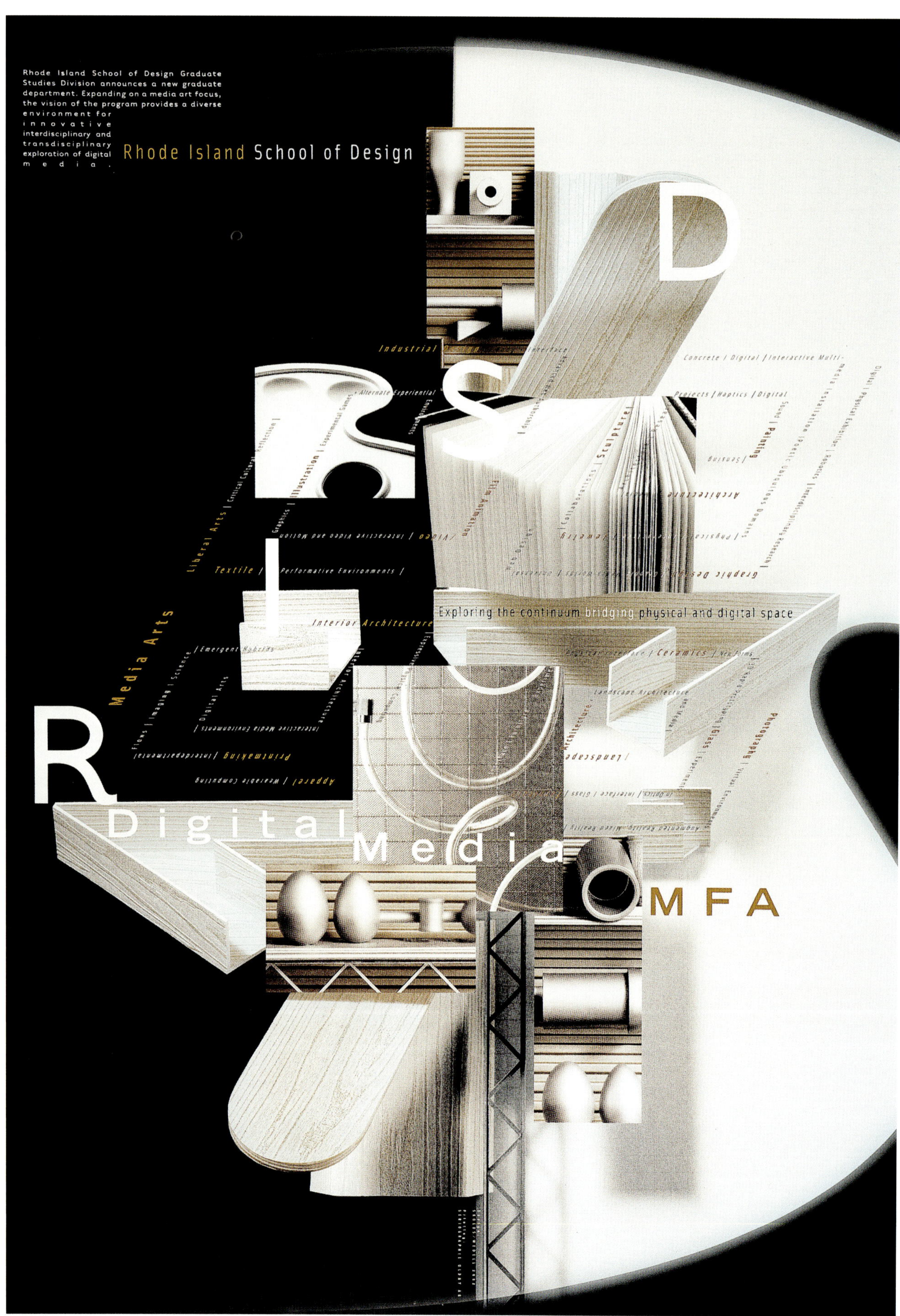

Skolos/Wedell/Rhode Island School of Design, Department of Digital Media

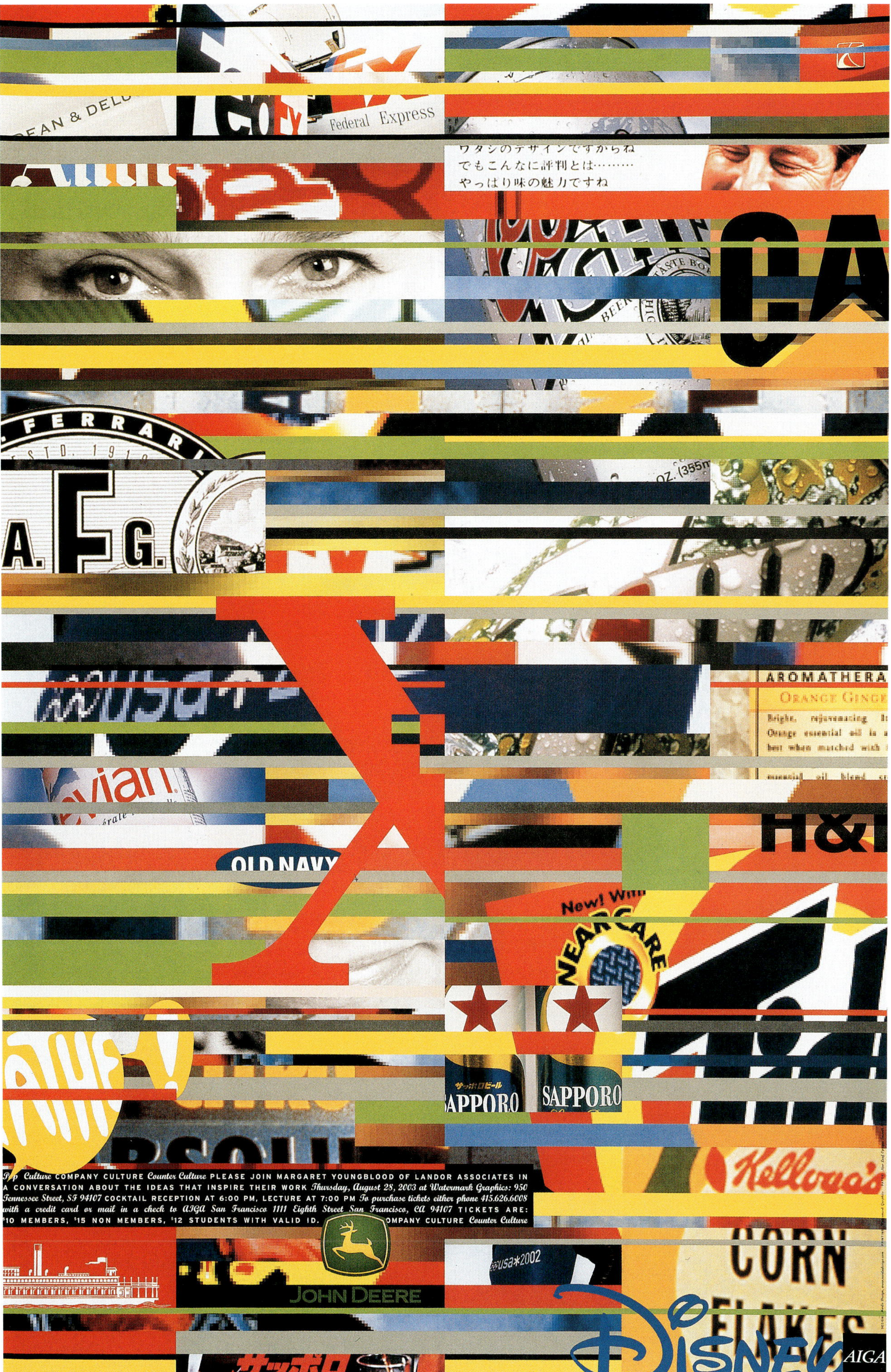

Morla Design, Inc./AIGA San Francisco Chapter

Rhode Island School of Design
Museum of Art
September 28
October 28
2001

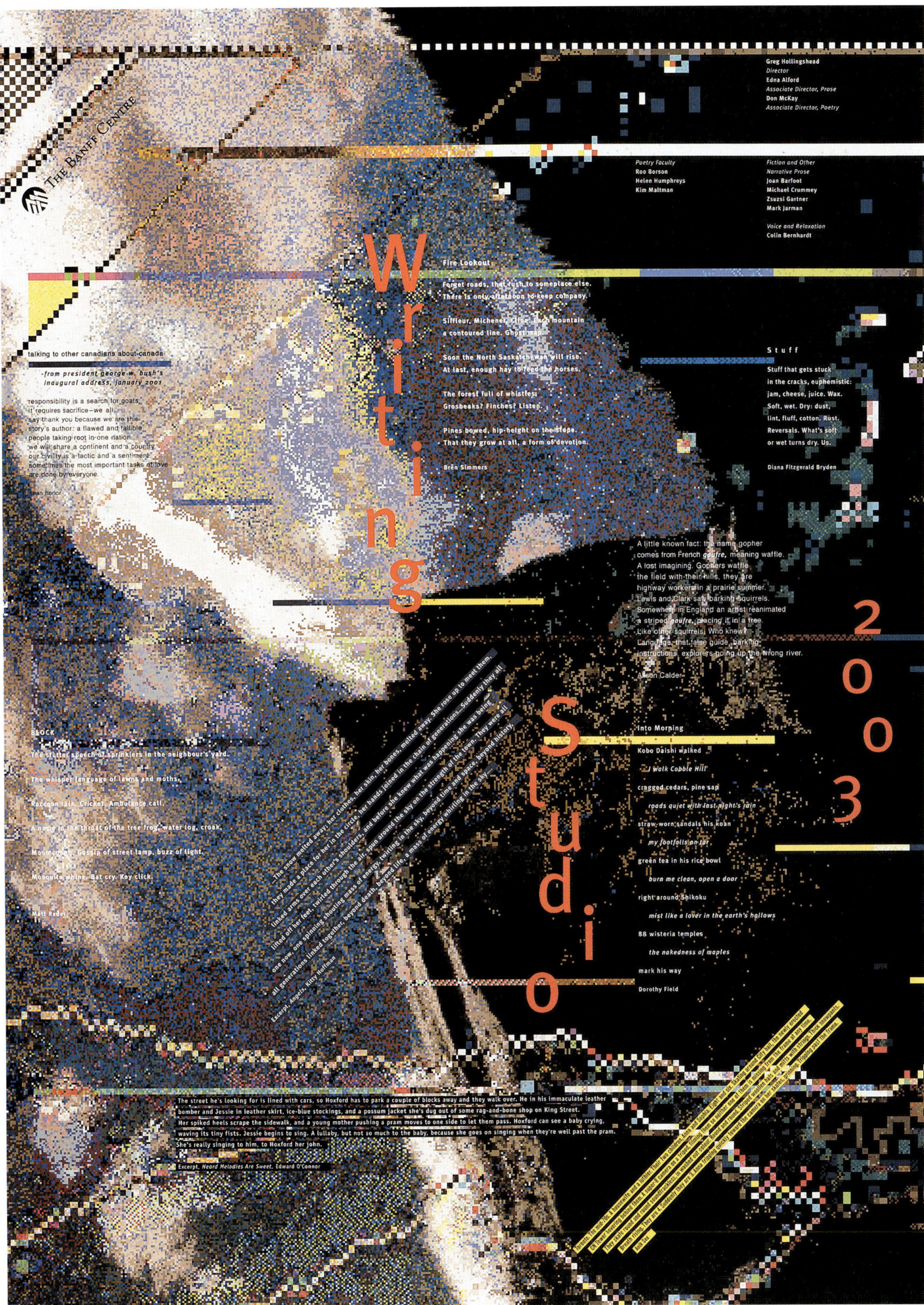

Malcolm Wadell Associates/The Banff Centre

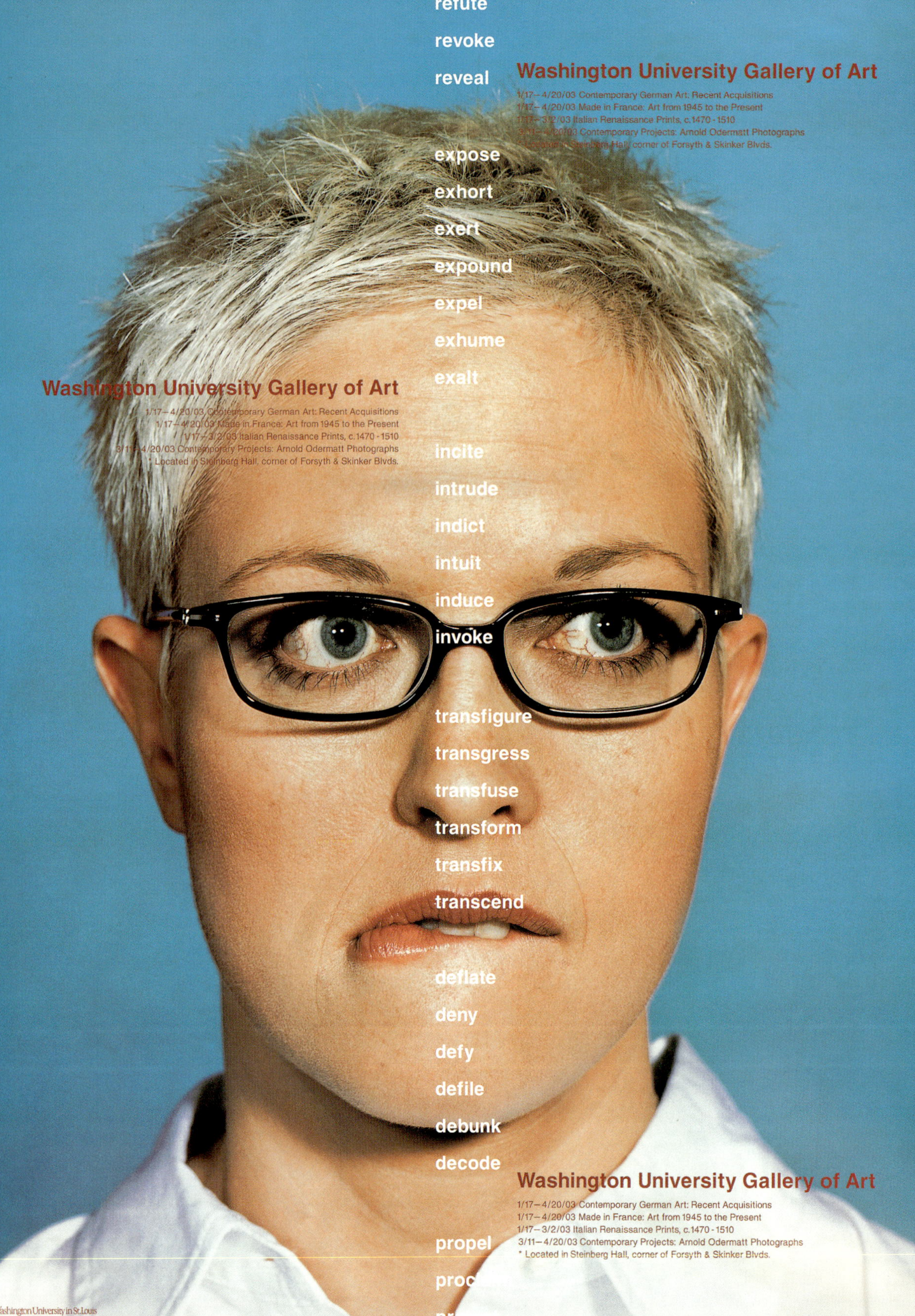

refute
revoke
reveal
Washington University Gallery of Art
1/17–4/20/03 Contemporary German Art: Recent Acquisitions
1/17–4/20/03 Made in France: Art from 1945 to the Present
1/17–3/2/03 Italian Renaissance Prints, c.1470 - 1510
3/11–4/20/03 Contemporary Projects: Arnold Odermatt Photographs
* Located in Steinberg Hall, corner of Forsyth & Skinker Blvds.
expose
exhort
exert
expound
expel
exhume
exalt
incite
intrude
indict
intuit
induce
invoke
transfigure
transgress
transfuse
transform
transfix
transcend
deflate
deny
defy
defile
debunk
decode
propel
Washington University in St.Louis

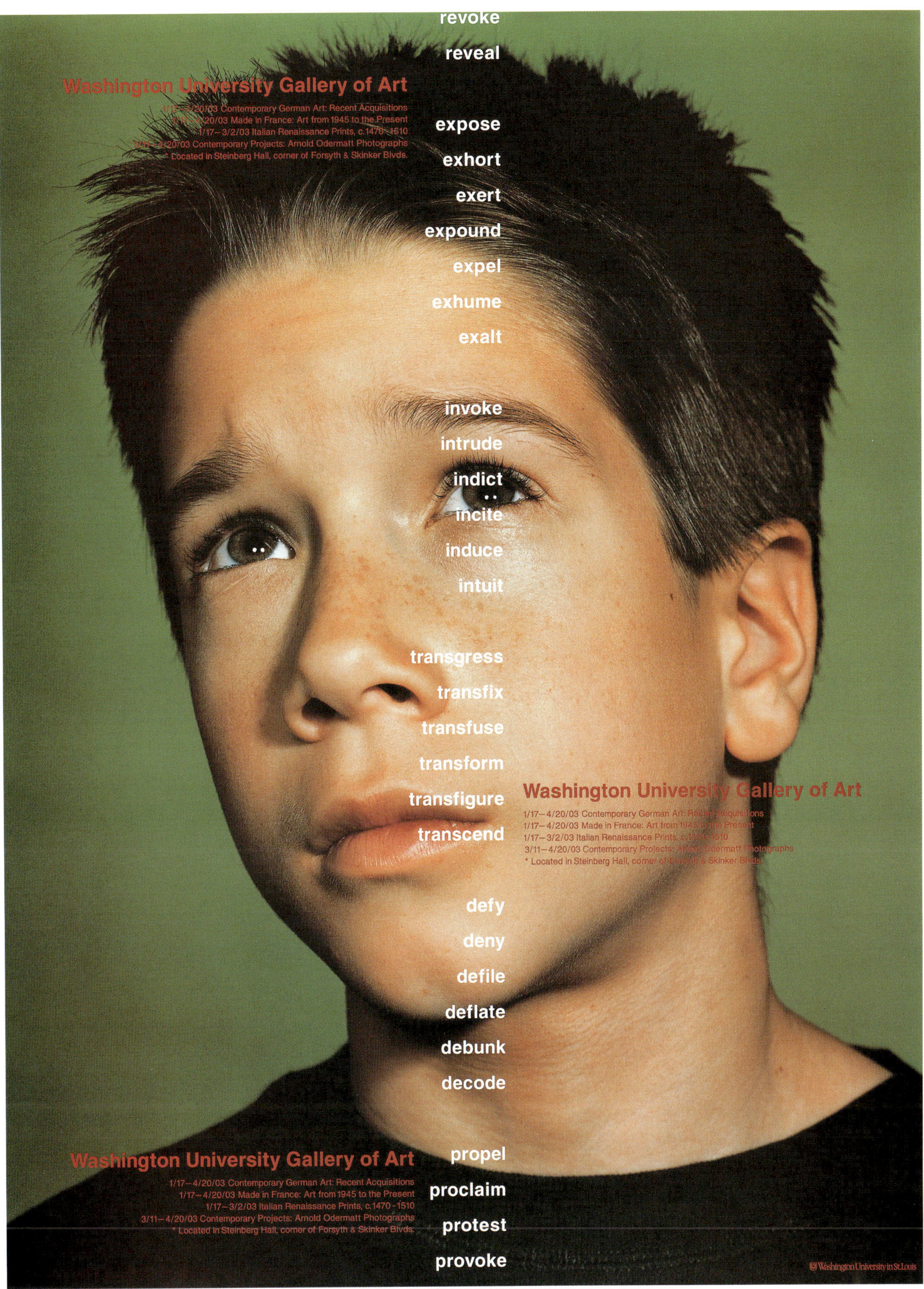

Arnold Worldwide - St. Louis/Washington University Gallery of Art

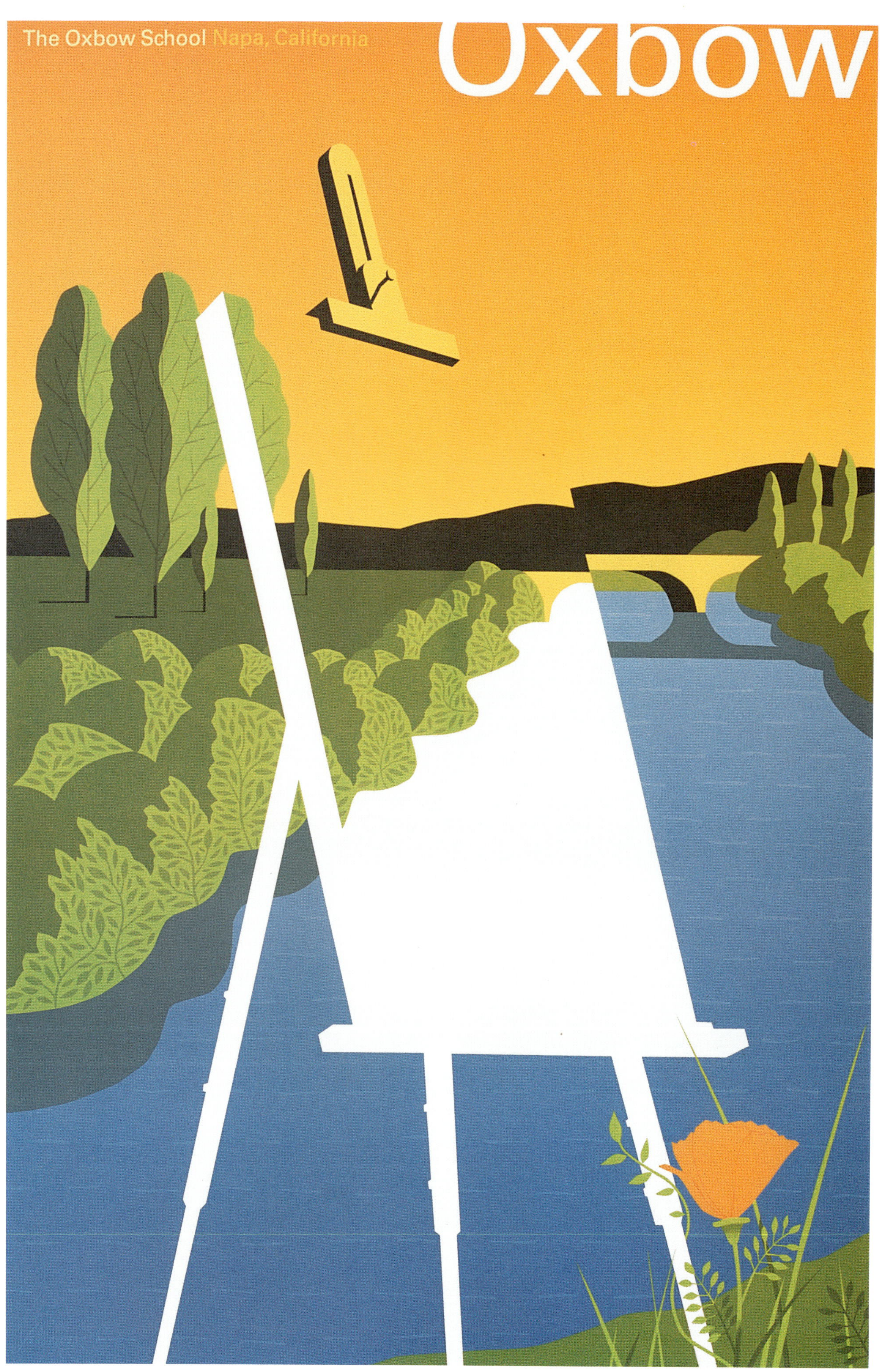

Craig Frazier Studio/The Oxbow School, Napa, CA

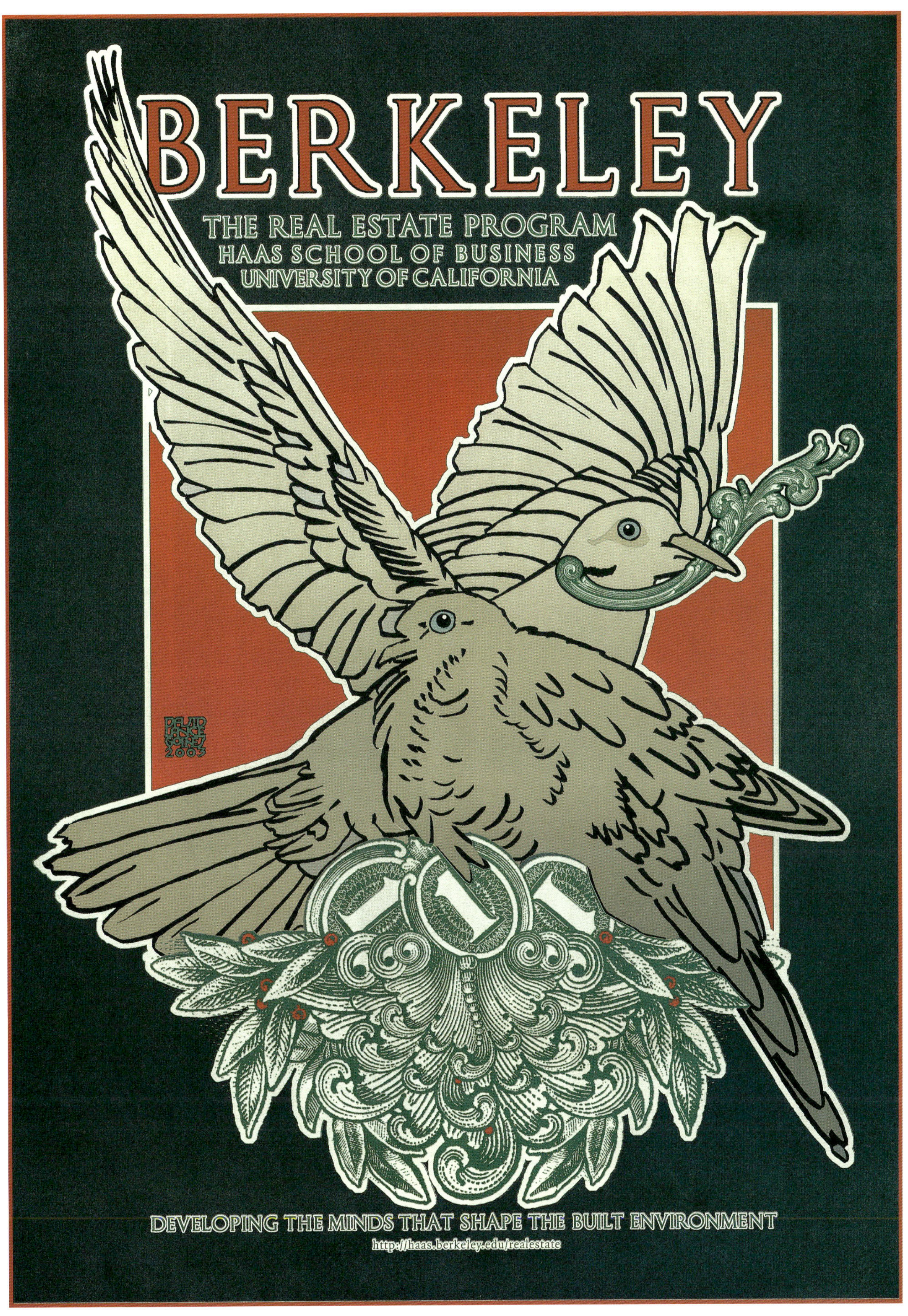

Saint Hieronymus Press/Berkeley Real Estate Program, Haas School of Business, University of California, Berkeley

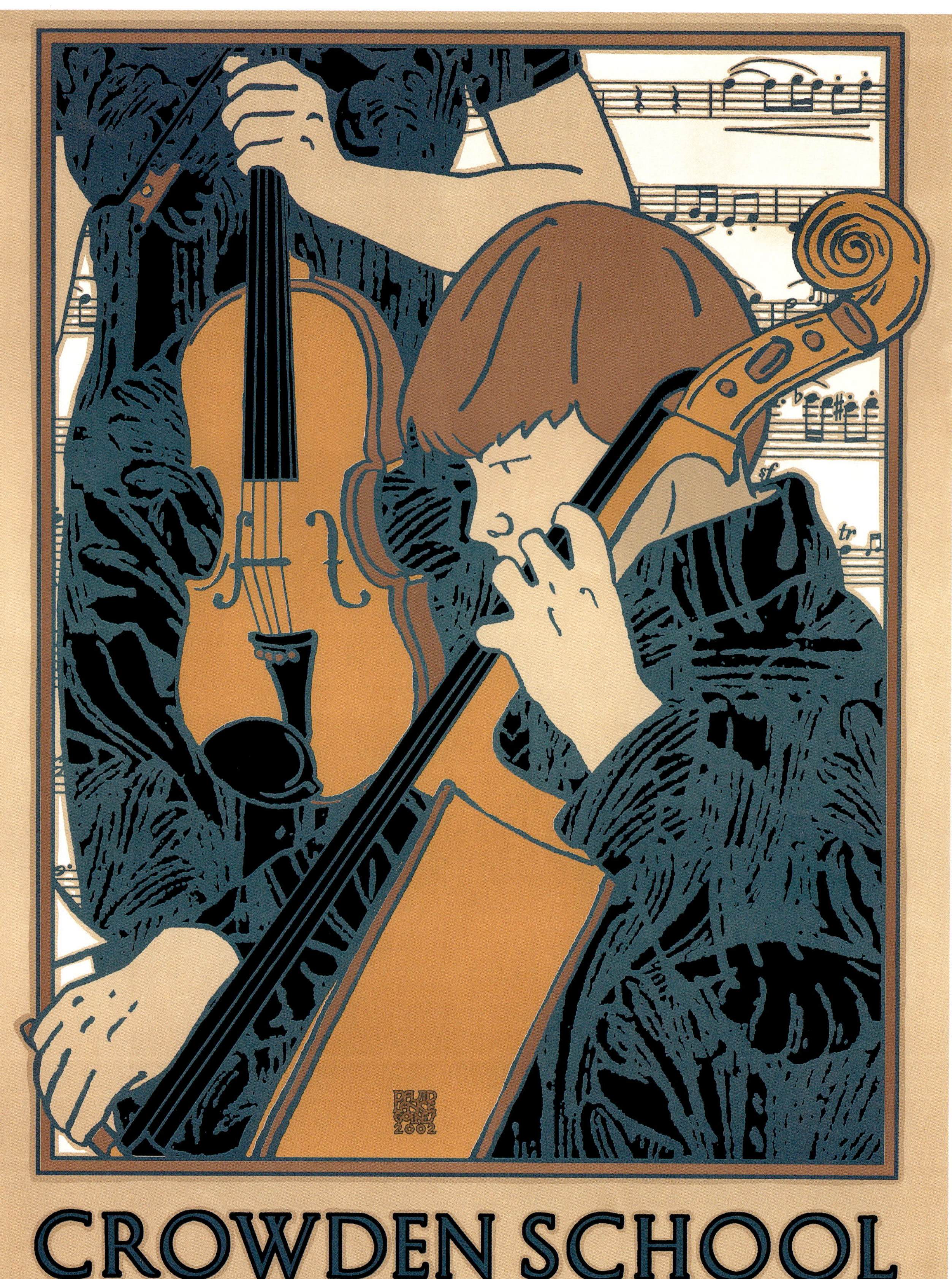

Saint Hieronymus Press/The Crowden School

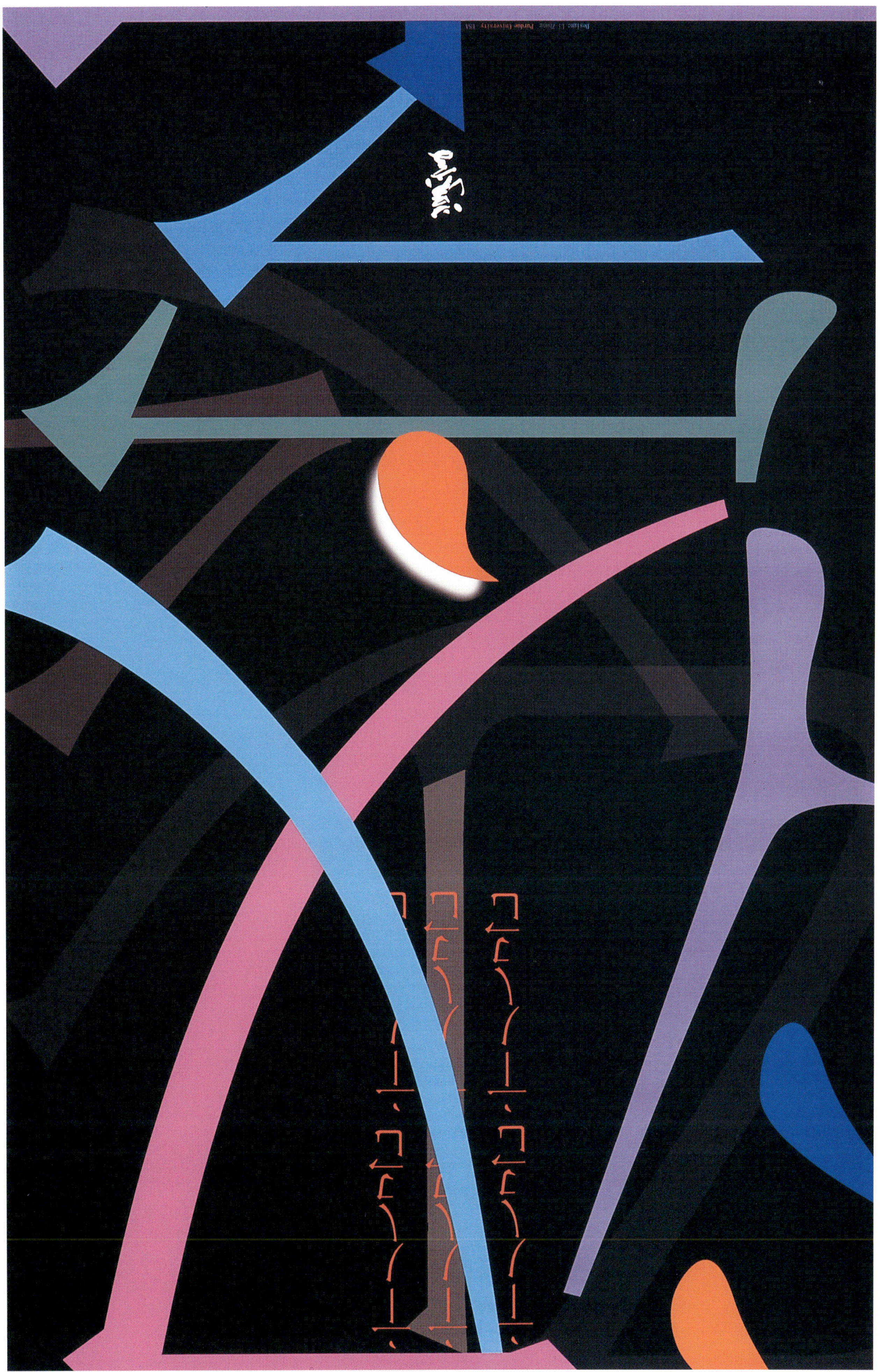

Purdue University, Visual and Performing Arts/Taiwan Poster Design Association, Tung Fang Institute of Technology

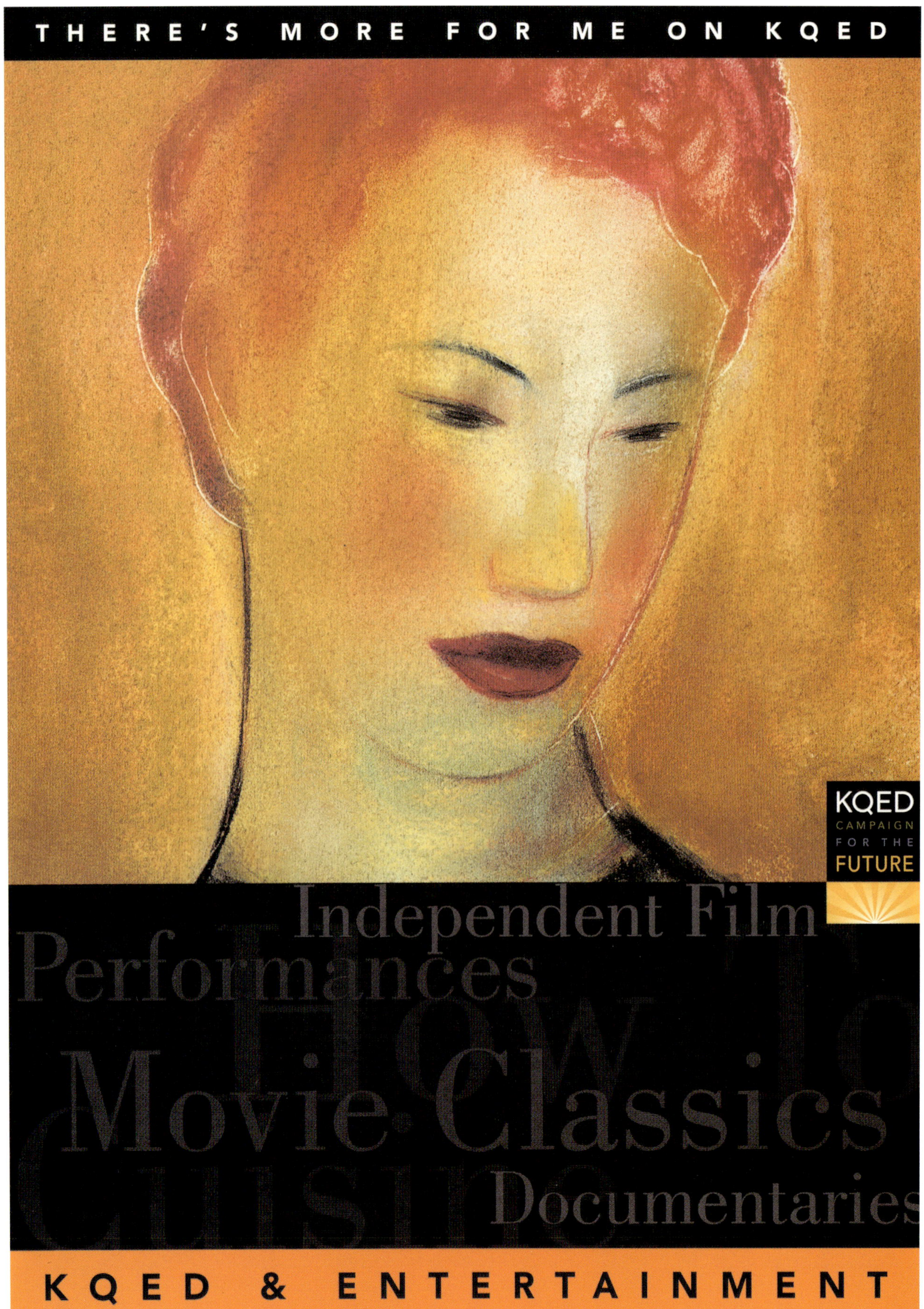

Pentagram/KQED

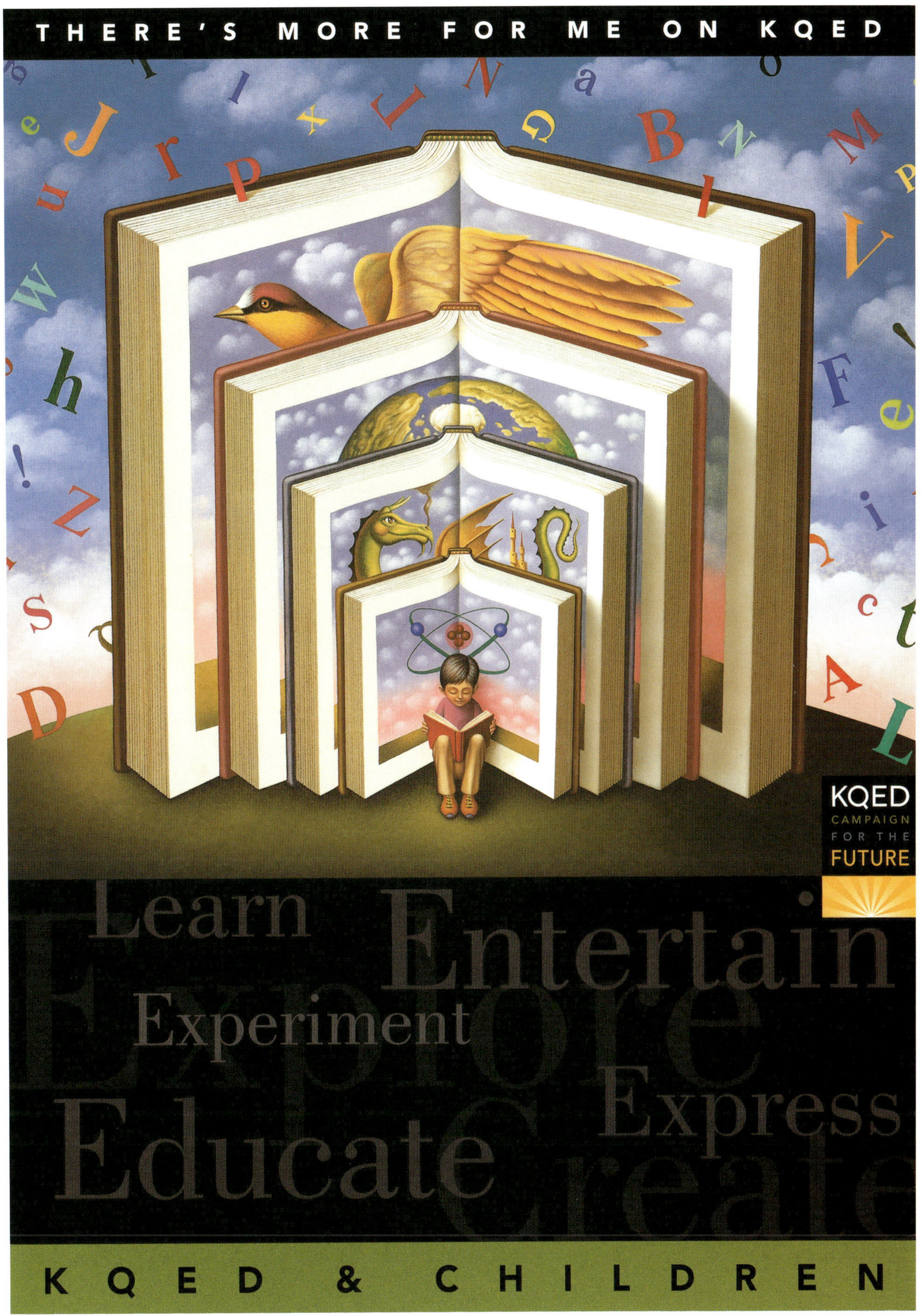

Pentagram/KQED

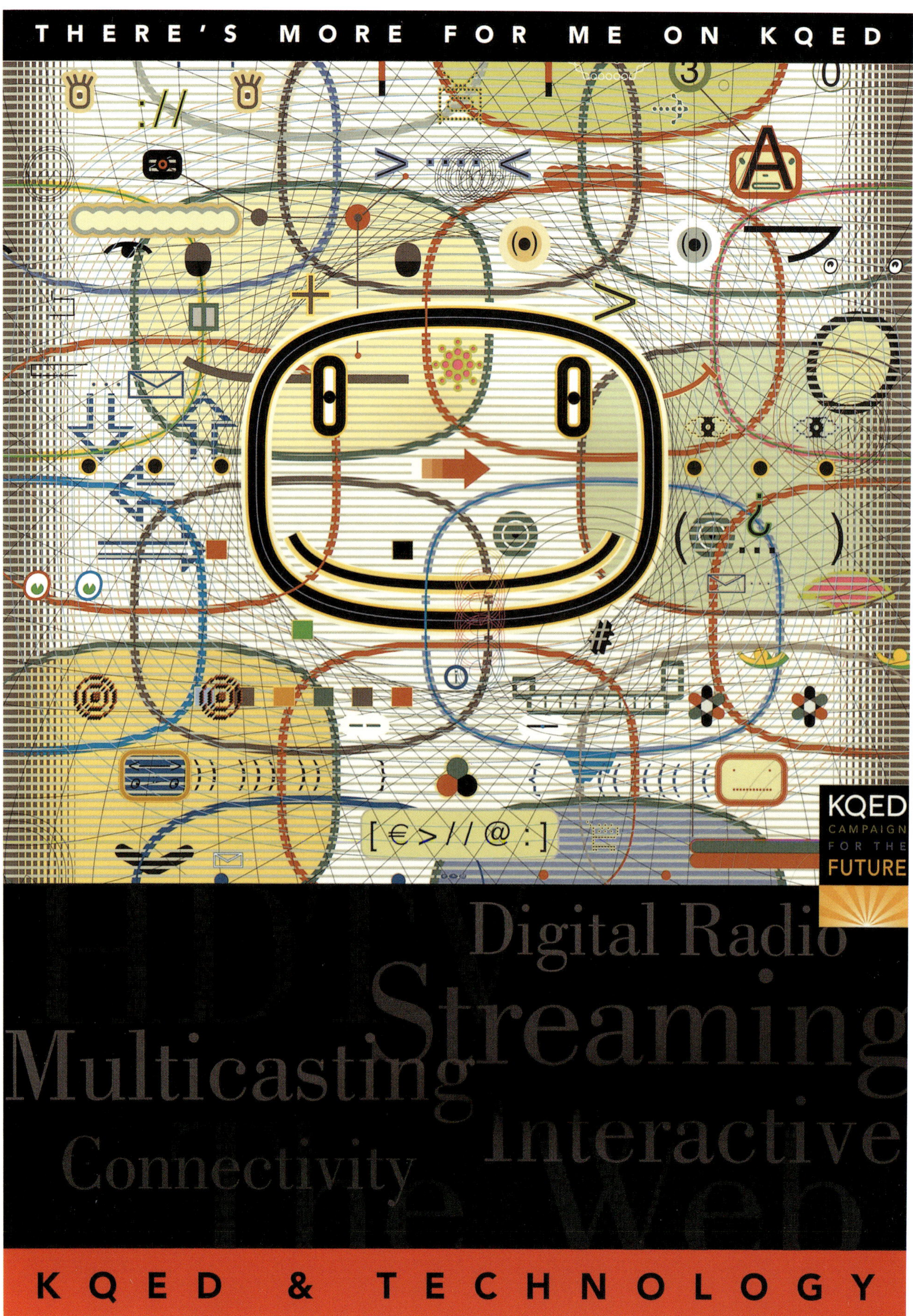

Pentagram/KQED

A TIME OF REFLECTION 4/23/2003

Question/Deliberate/Explore
What special obligation do institutions of higher learning have to use their resources toward understanding conflict?

Design: John Rousseau / Visual Communication Design

The War in Iraq

University Classes
8:30am–2:30pm
An optional opportunity to explore the meaning and consequences of war in regularly scheduled classes

Workshops/Lectures/Discussions
2:30pm–6:00pm
Special topics presented by UW students, faculty and staff

+ Evening Events

For program details, visit:
http://washington.edu/oue/wariniraq

University of Washington
If you would like to request accommodations due to a disability, please contact Disabled Student Services, 448 Schmitz Hall, (206) 543-8924 (V/TTY)

John Rousseau Design/University of Washington School of Art one of a series

A PRECEPT E FOR EDUCATION 200

TO 160

KNOW 120

WHAT I 80

THINK, I 60

MUST SEE 50

WHAT I SAY. 40

ANN DRENNAN - ON 30

WRITING TO MATERIALIZE 25

THOUGHT, AND REVISION OF THE 20

WORDS TO FOCUS TRULY GREAT IDEAS. 15

Literary exegesis by Ann Drennan on an original quotation by E.M. Forester; profiles in art and education series

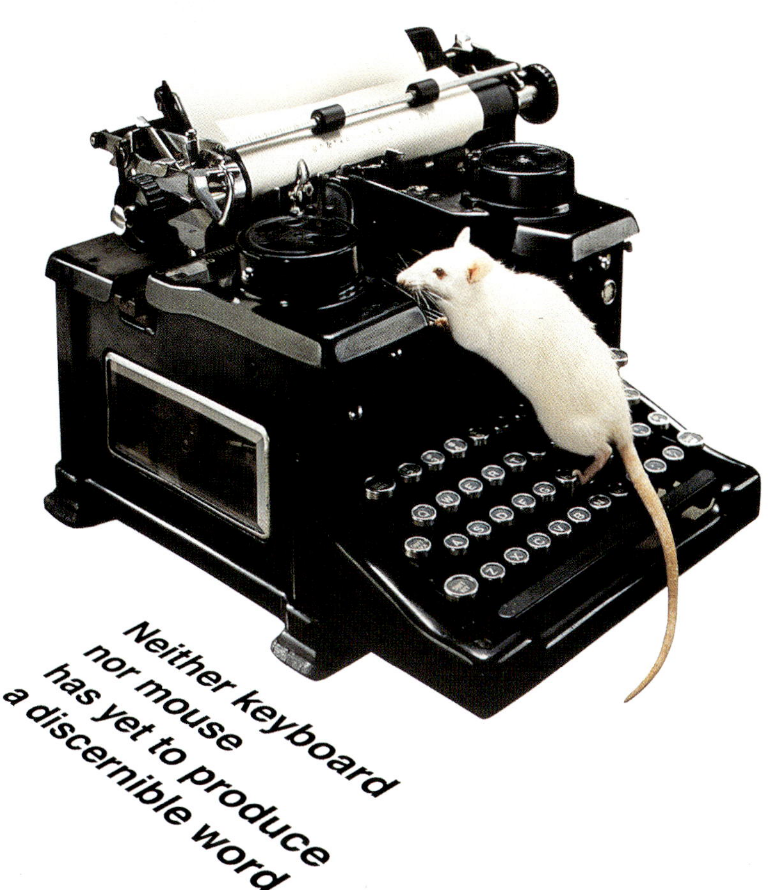

As for creativity, the product can be no better than the humanity.

fred drennan
on design and technology

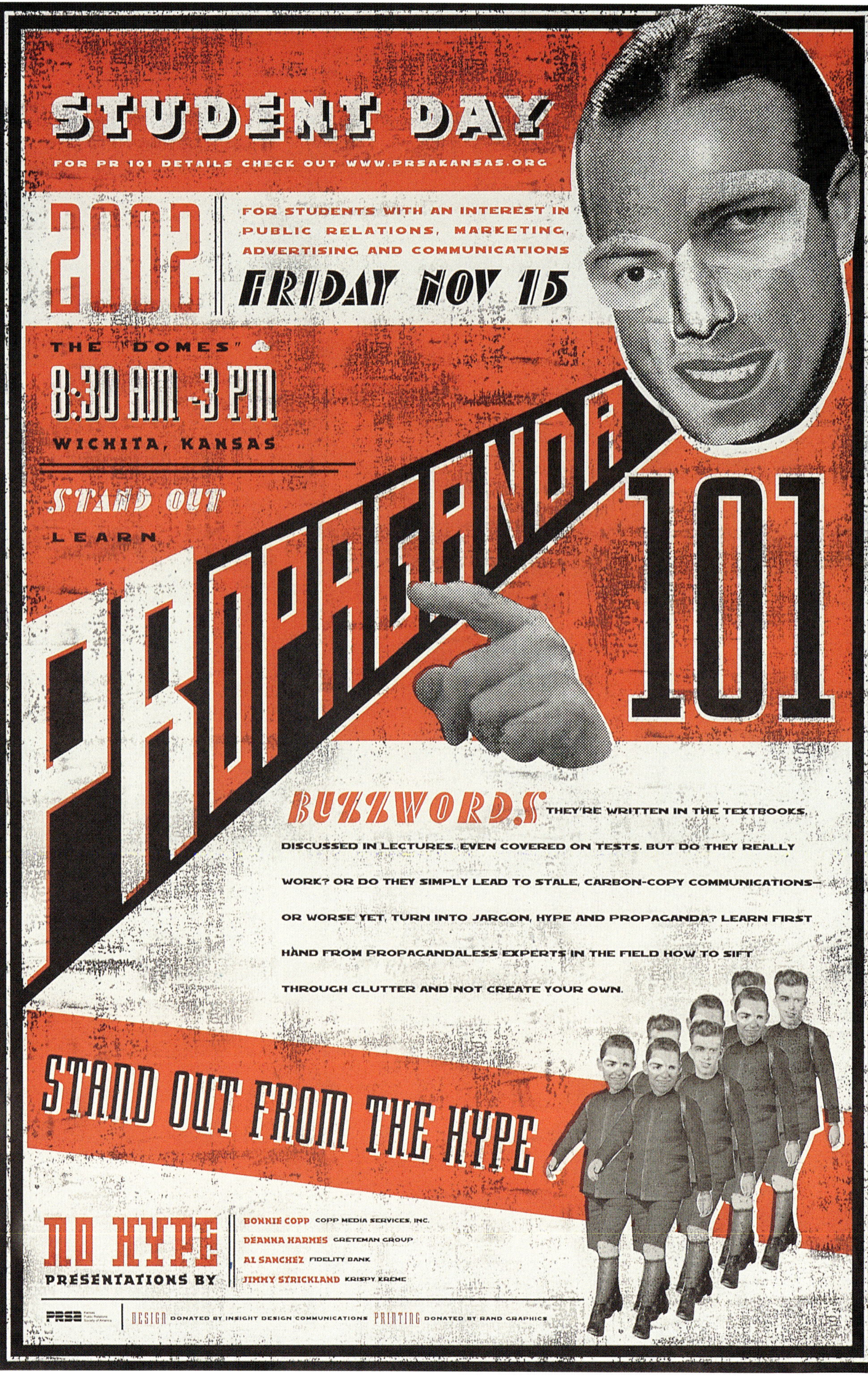

Insight Design Communications/Public Relations Society of America

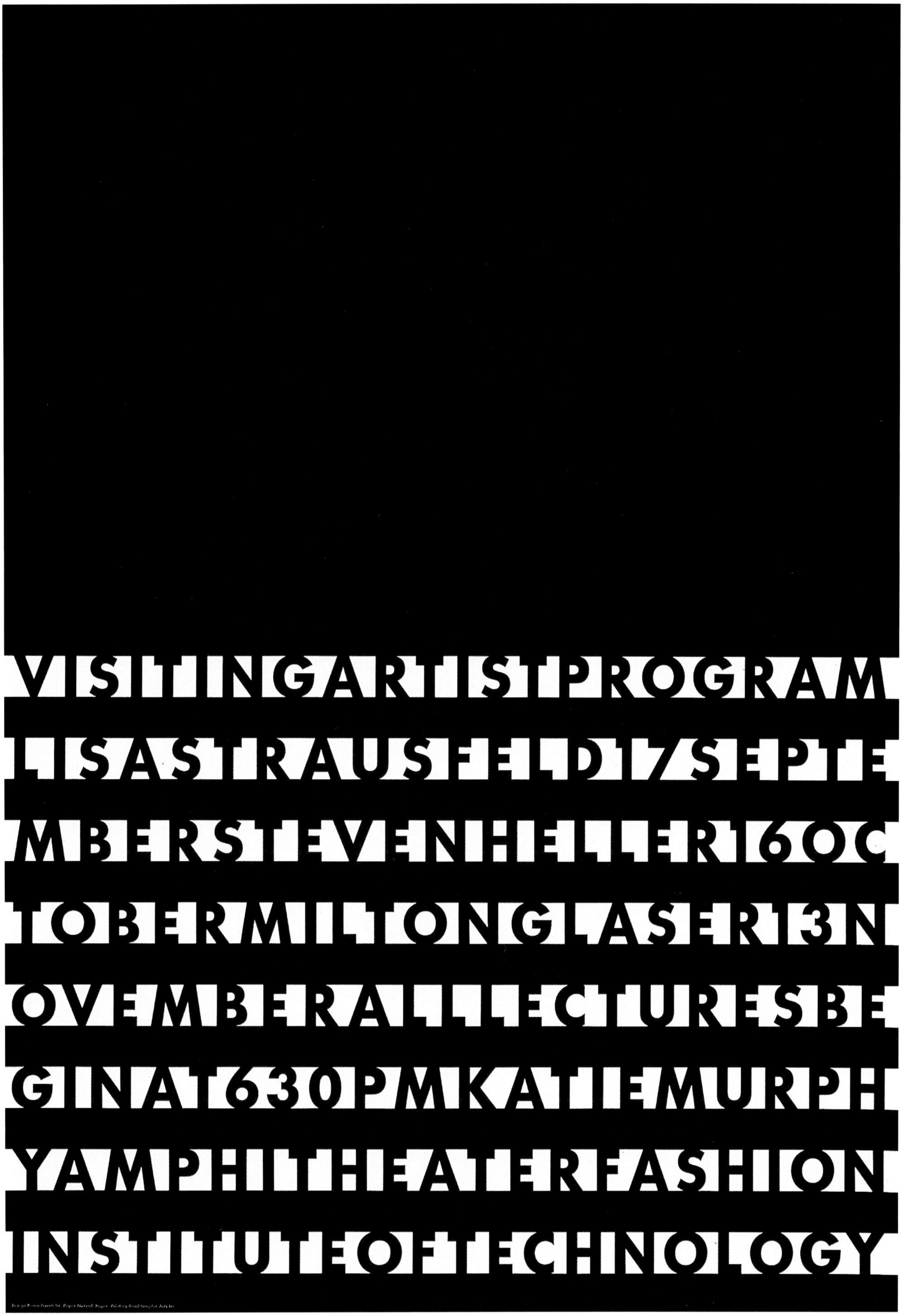

VISITINGARTISTPROGRAM
LISASTRAUSFELD17SEPTE
MBERSTEVENHELLER16OC
TOBERMILTONGLASER13N
OVEMBERALLECTURESBE
GINAT630PMKATIEMURPH
YAMPHITHEATERFASHION
INSTITUTEOFTECHNOLOGY

Piscatello Design Centre/Fashion Institute of Technology

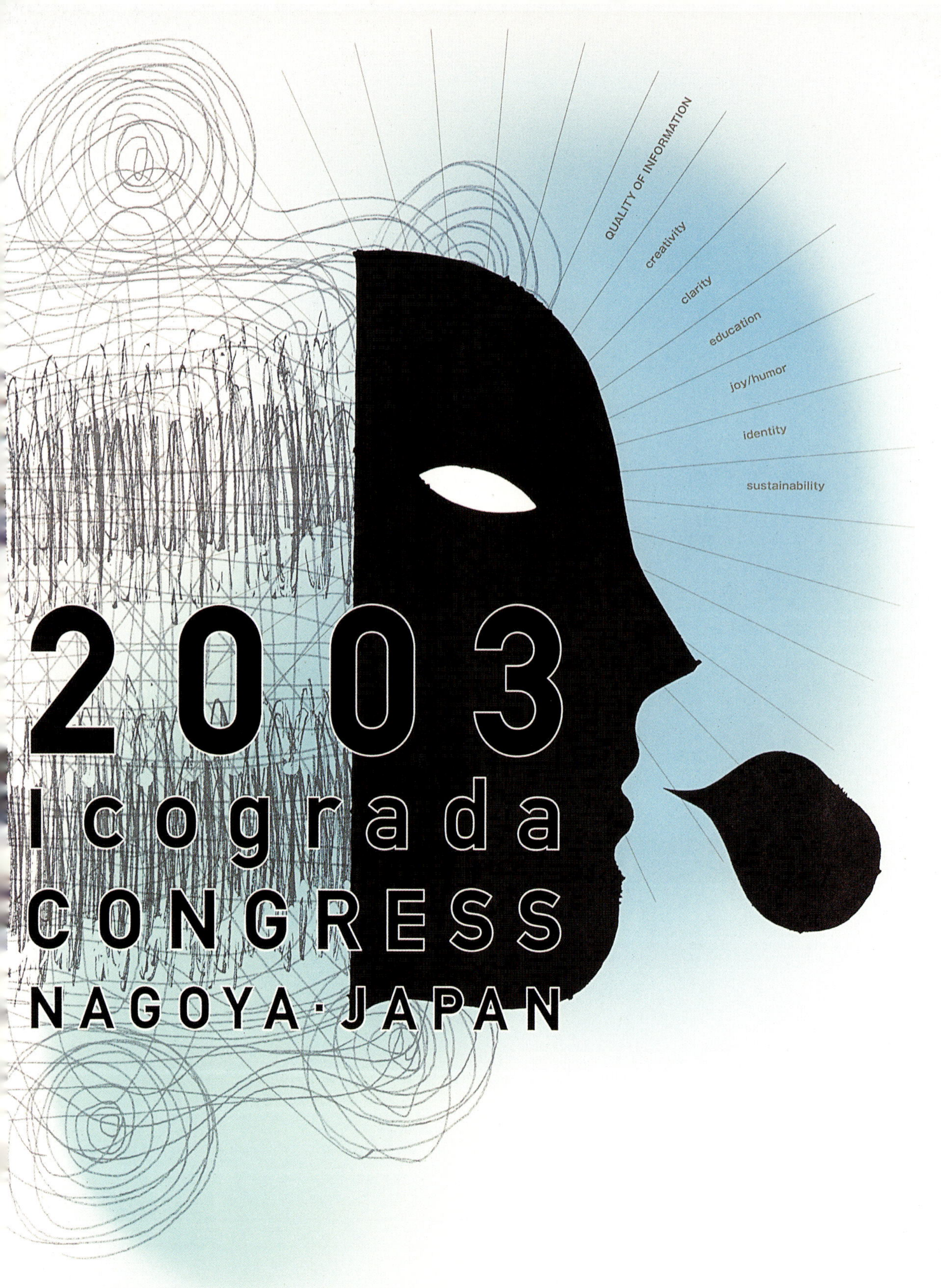

世界グラフィックデザイン会議・名古屋

VISUALOGUE

2003年10月8日 水 13日 月・祝

名古屋国際会議場

www.visualogue.com

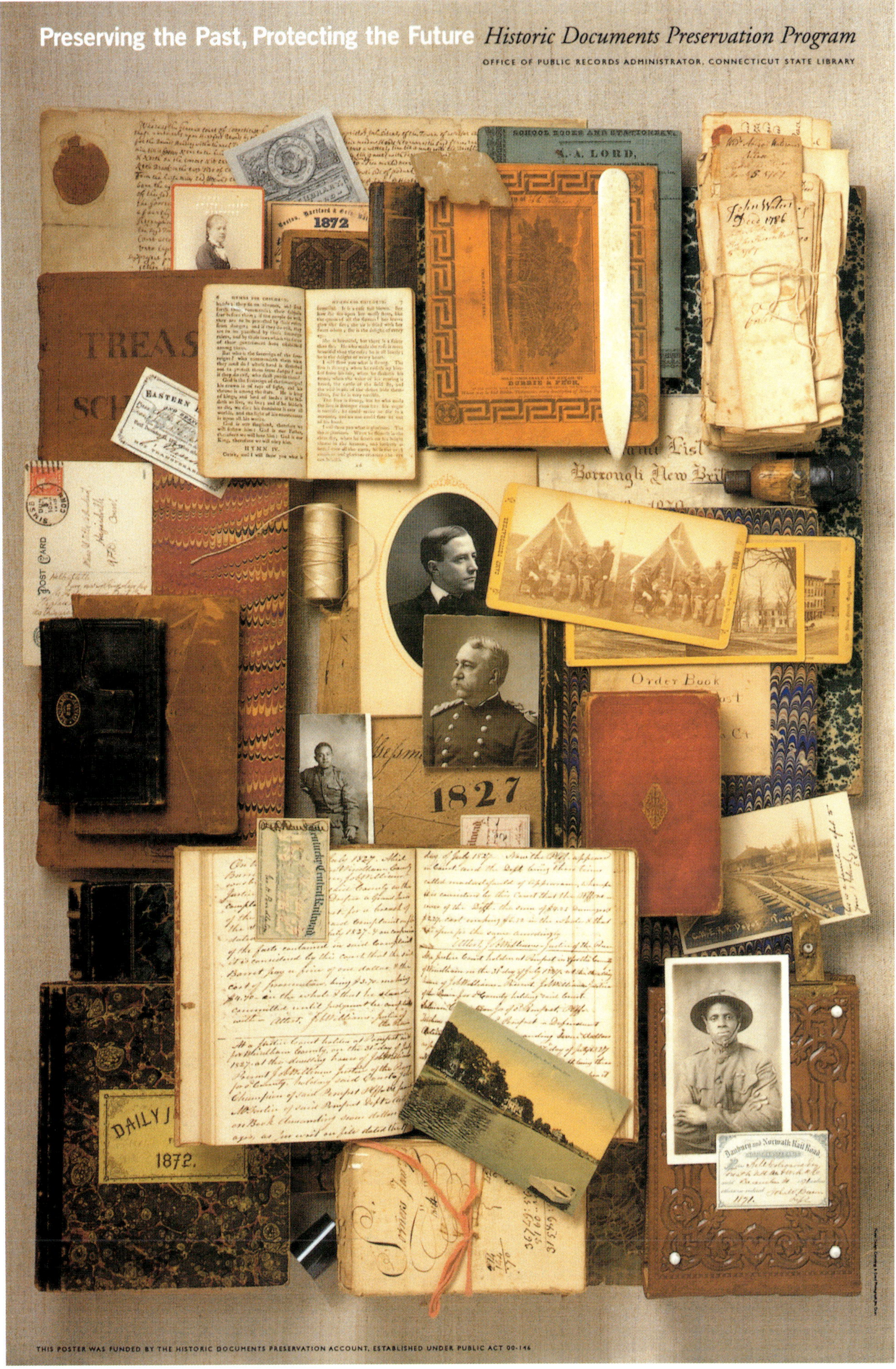

Cummings & Good/Connecticut State Library

3 ECOLOGICAL SINS

SEVEN DEADLY

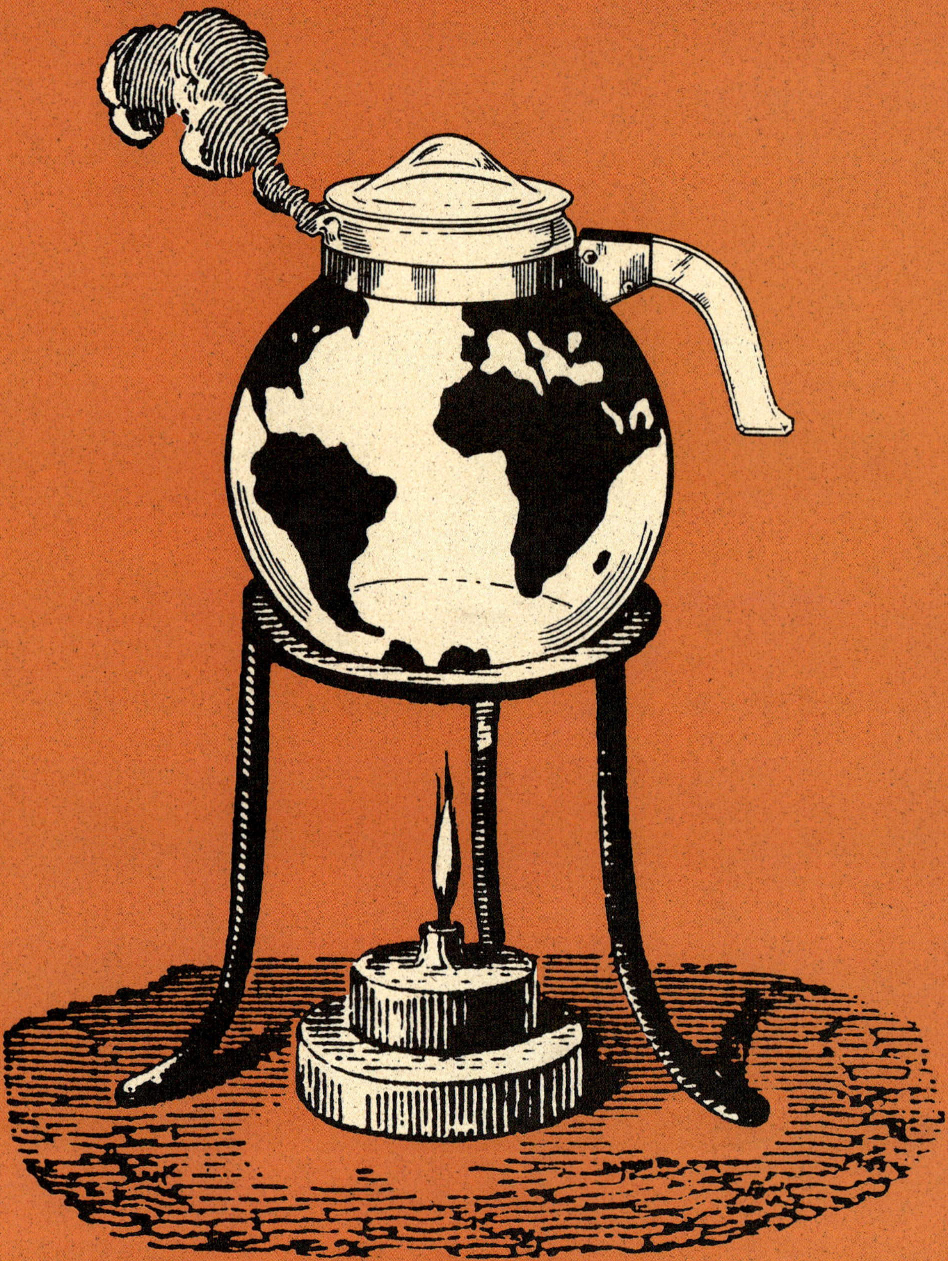

WARMING

GLOBAL 3

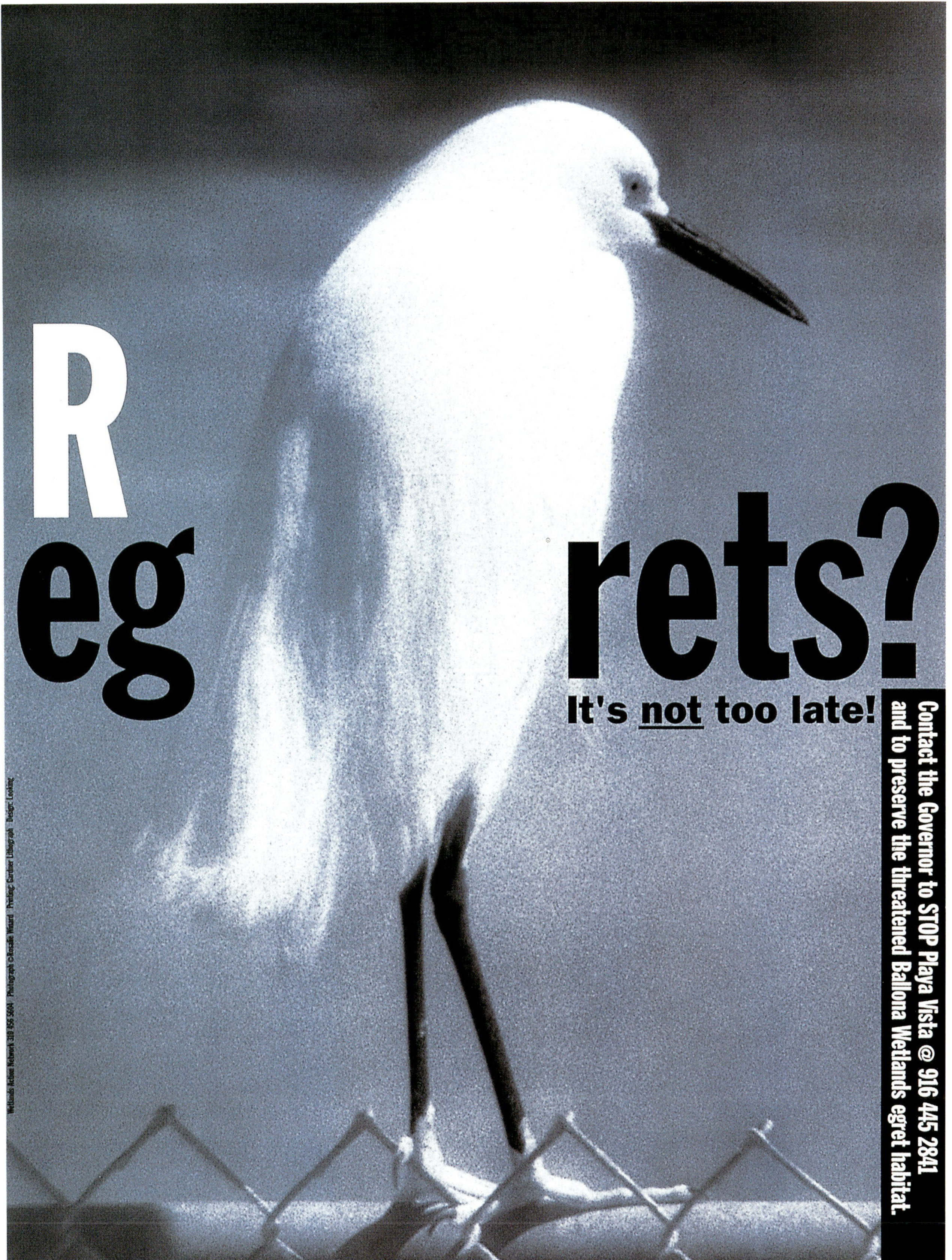

Looking/Wetland Action Committee

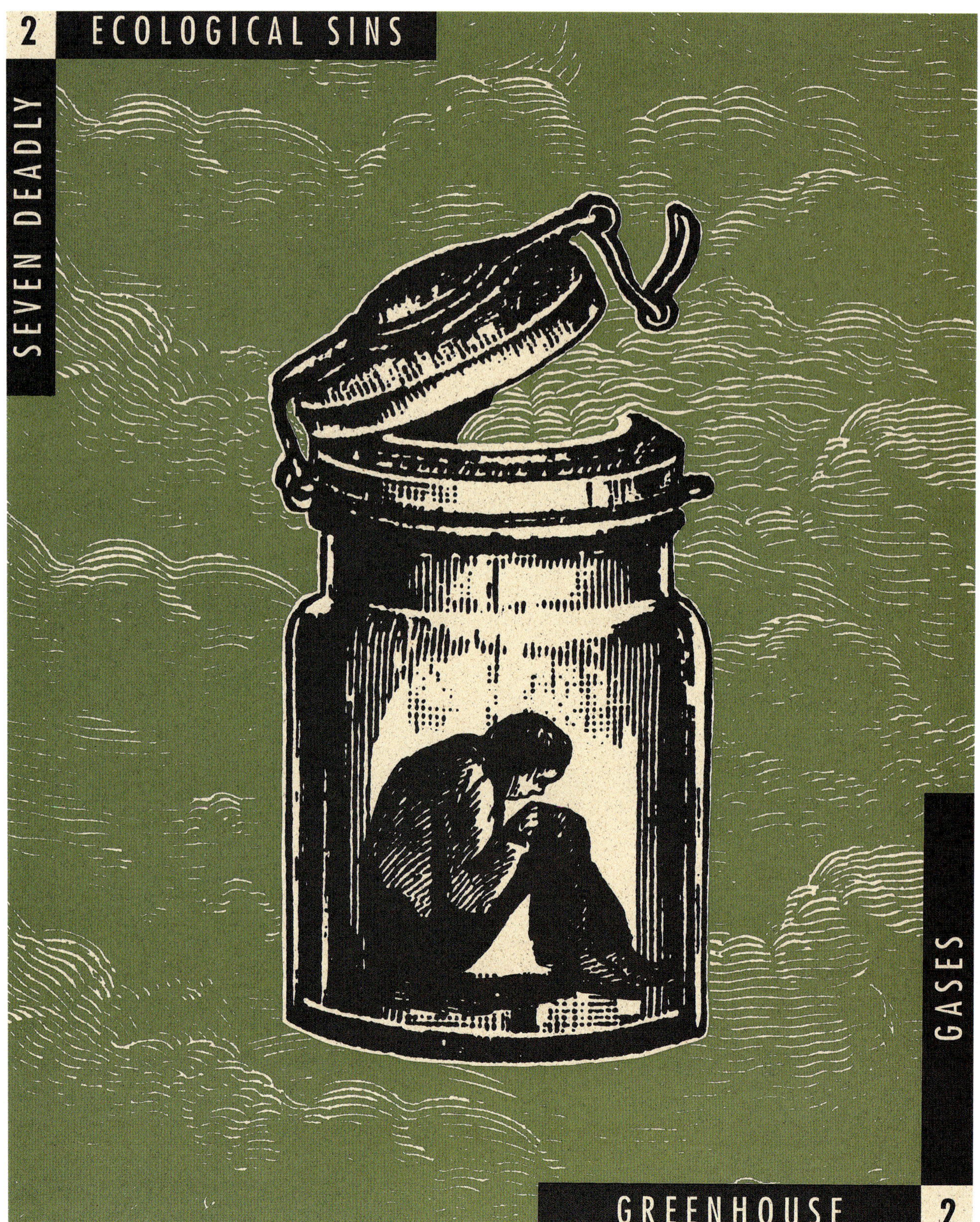

Stephanie Knopp Designs/Stephanie Knopp

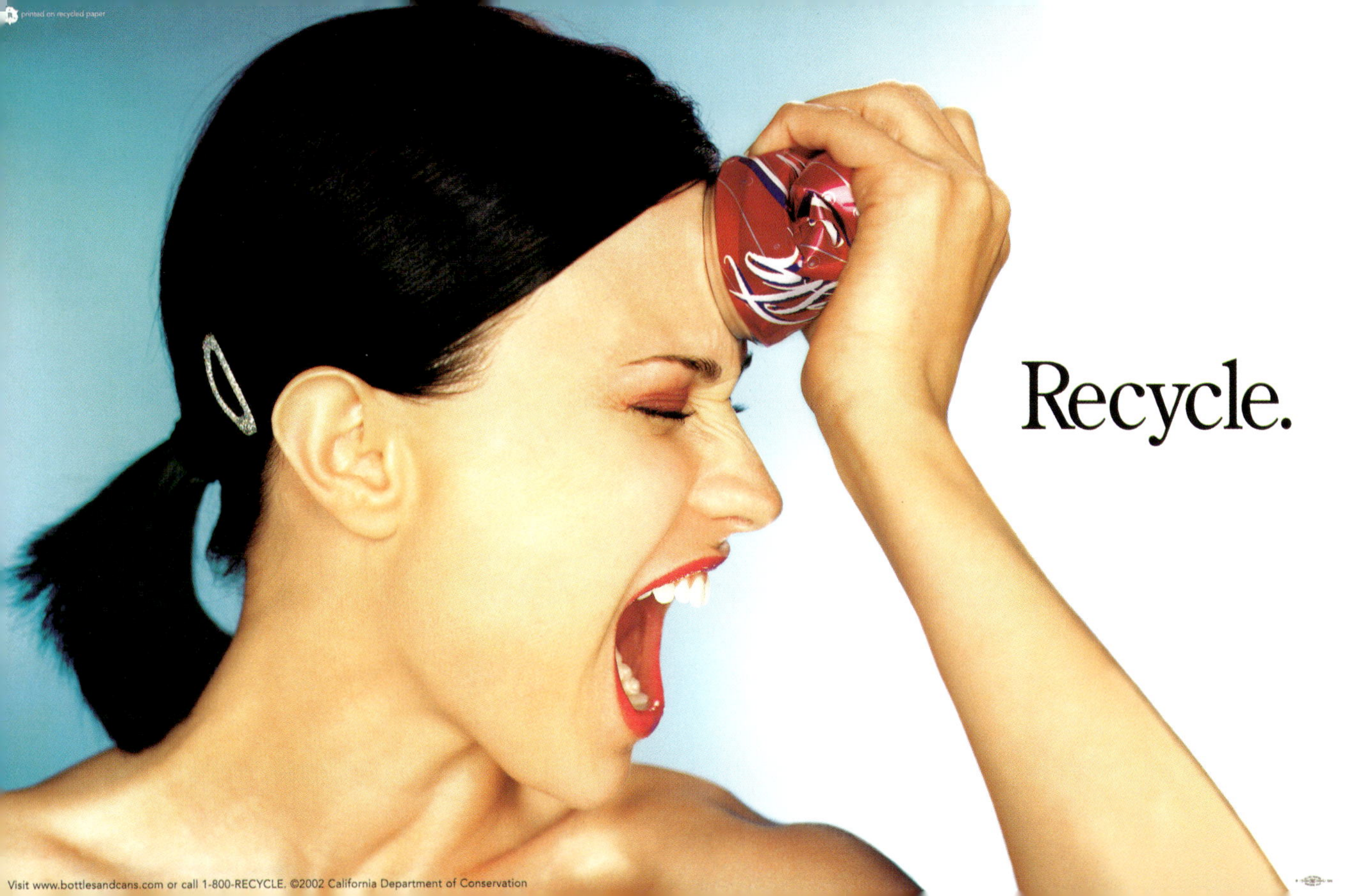
printed on recycled paper
Recycle.
Visit www.bottlesandcans.com or call 1-800-RECYCLE. ©2002 California Department of Conservation

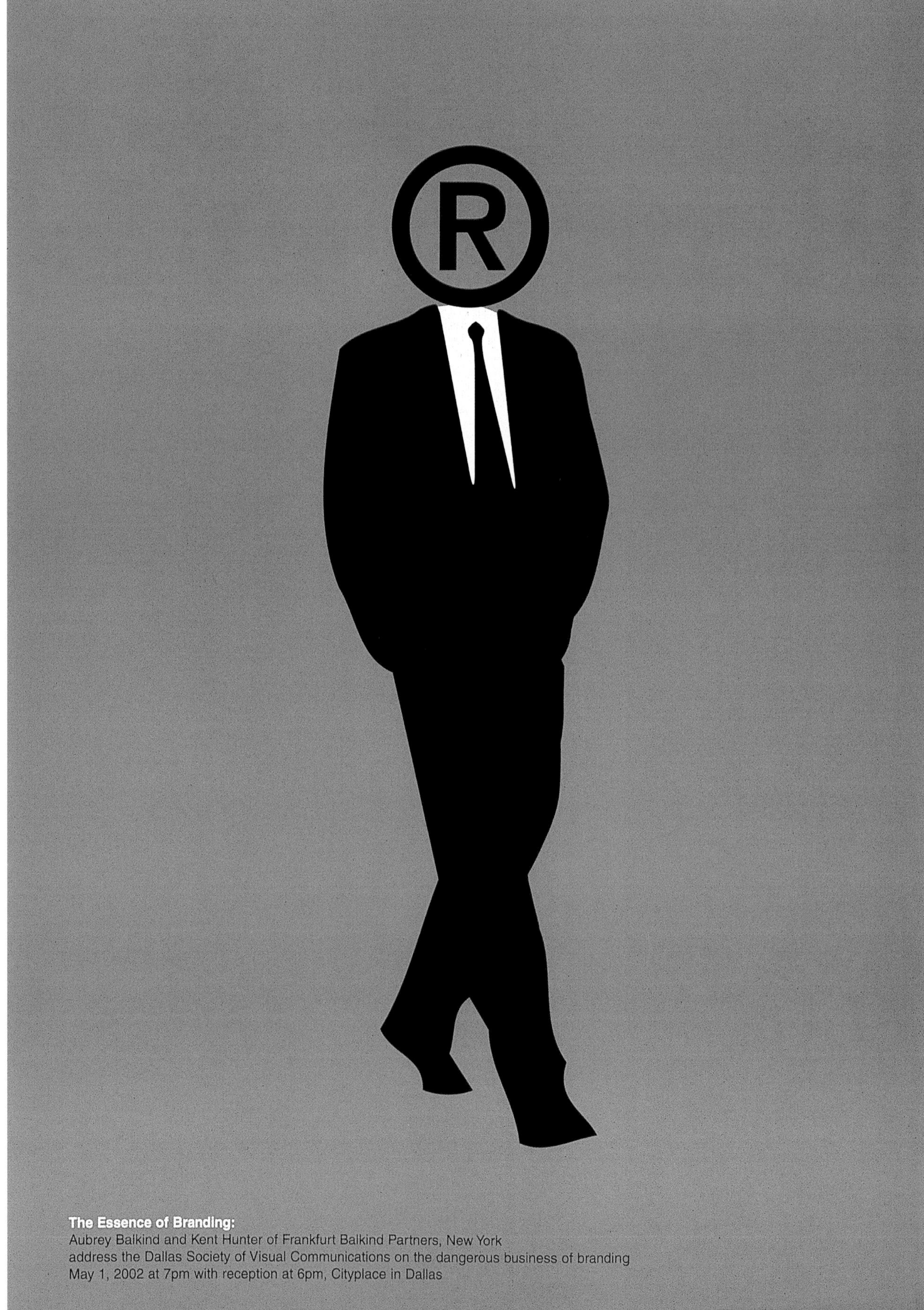

Eisenberg and Associates/The Dallas Society of Visual Communications (DSVC)

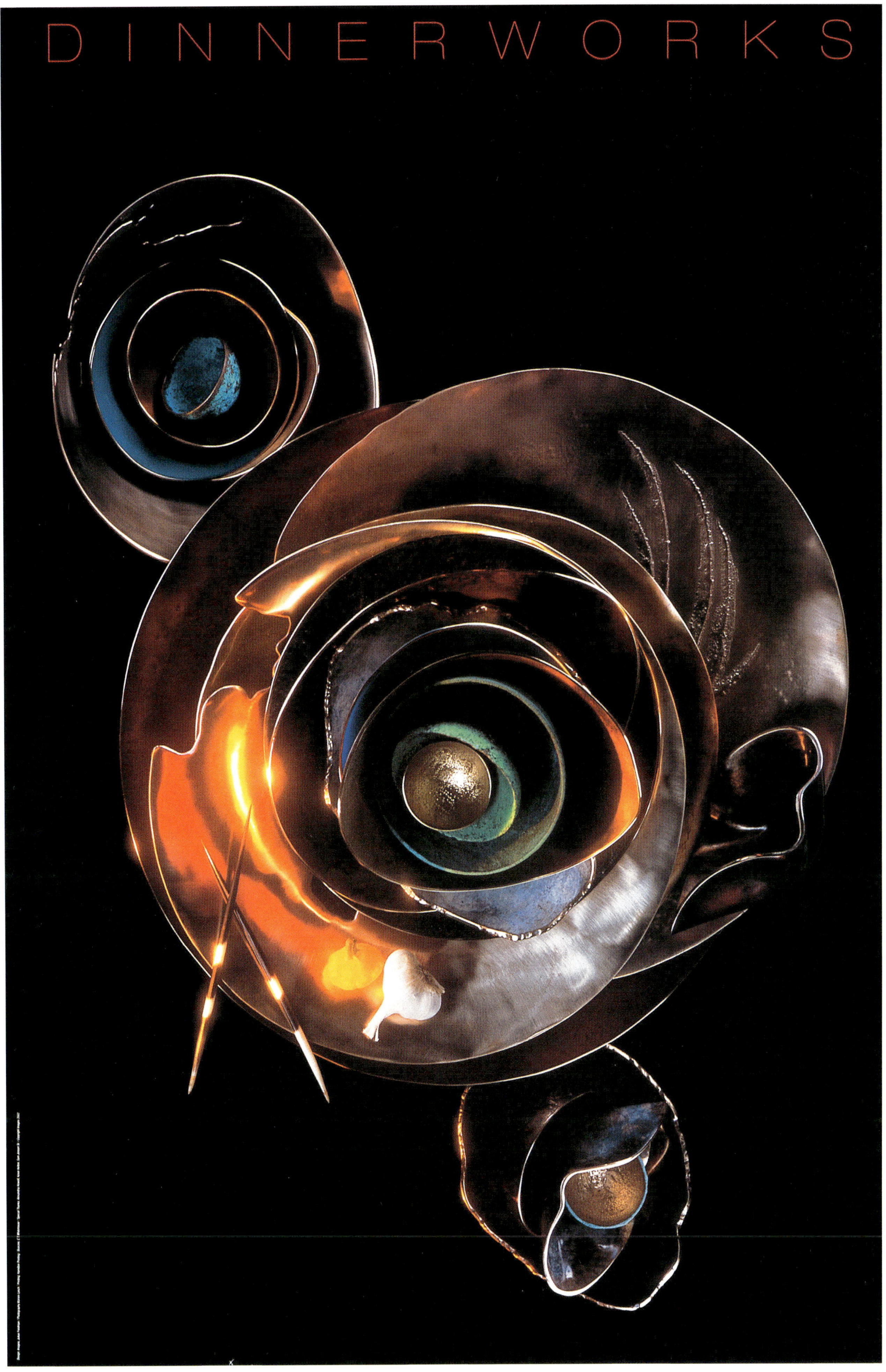

Images/Louisville Visual Art Association

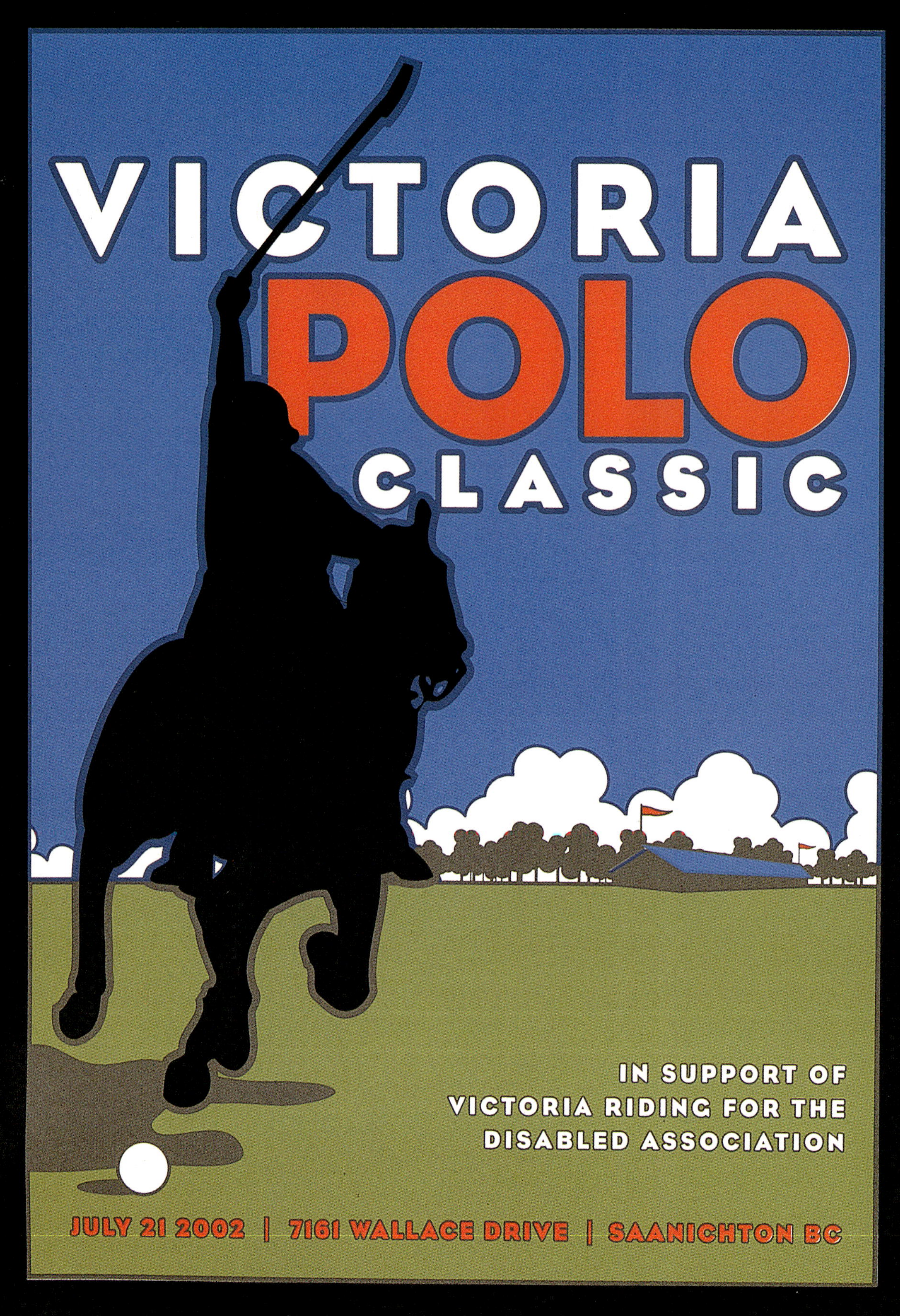

Hangar 18 Creative Group/Victoria Riding for the Disabled Association

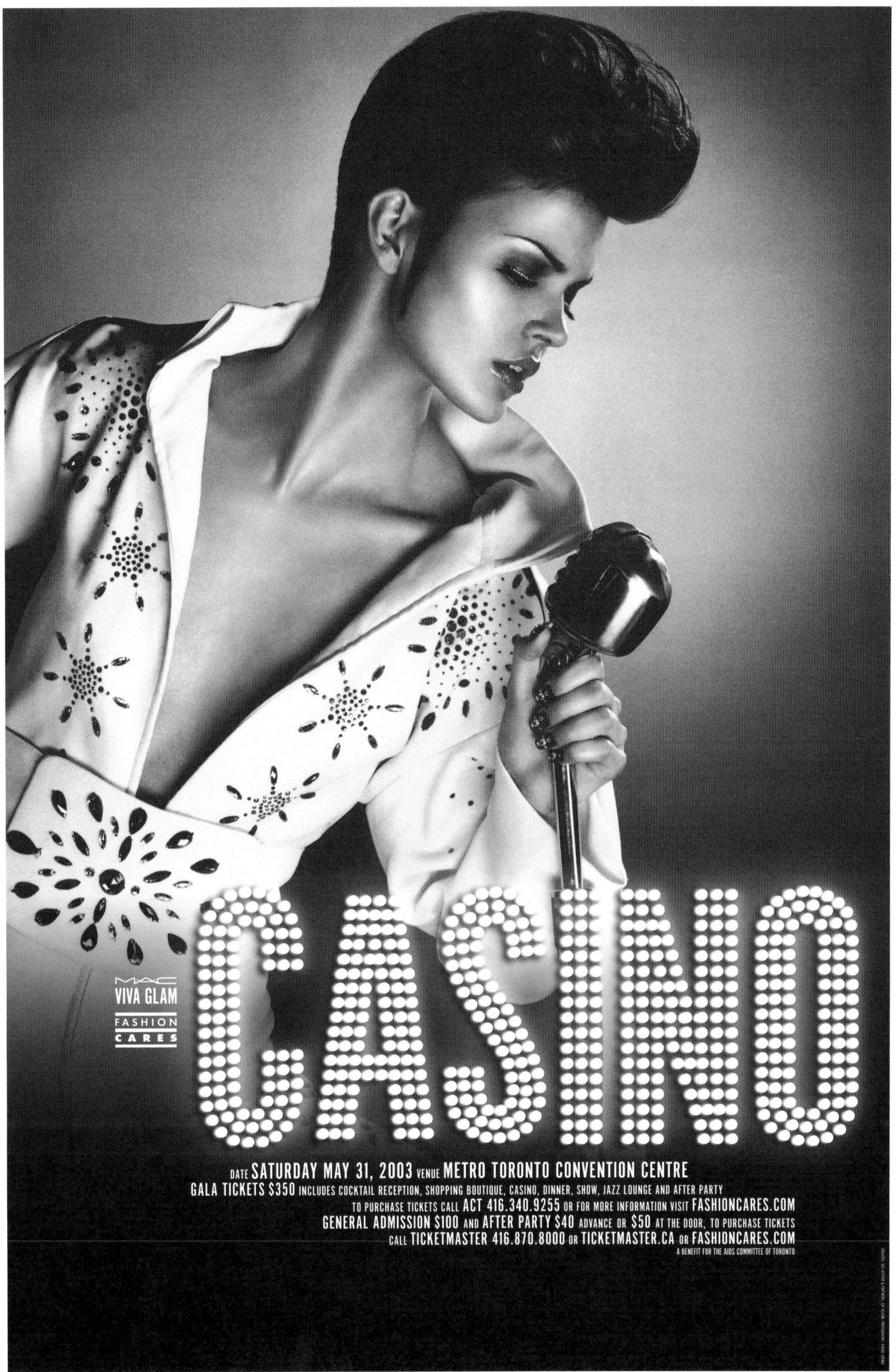

GJP Design/Fashion Cares/AIDS Committee of Toronto

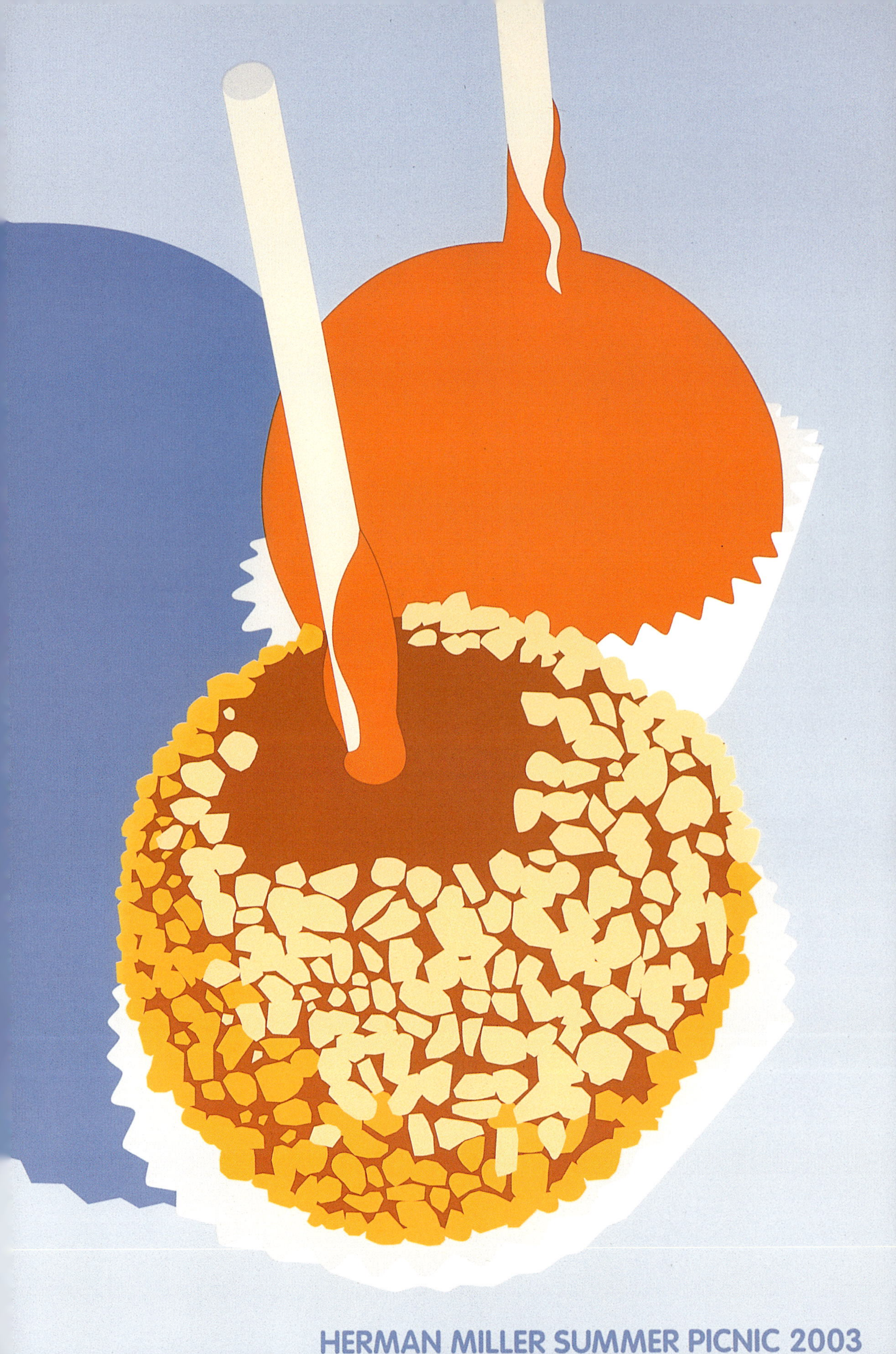
HERMAN MILLER SUMMER PICNIC 2003

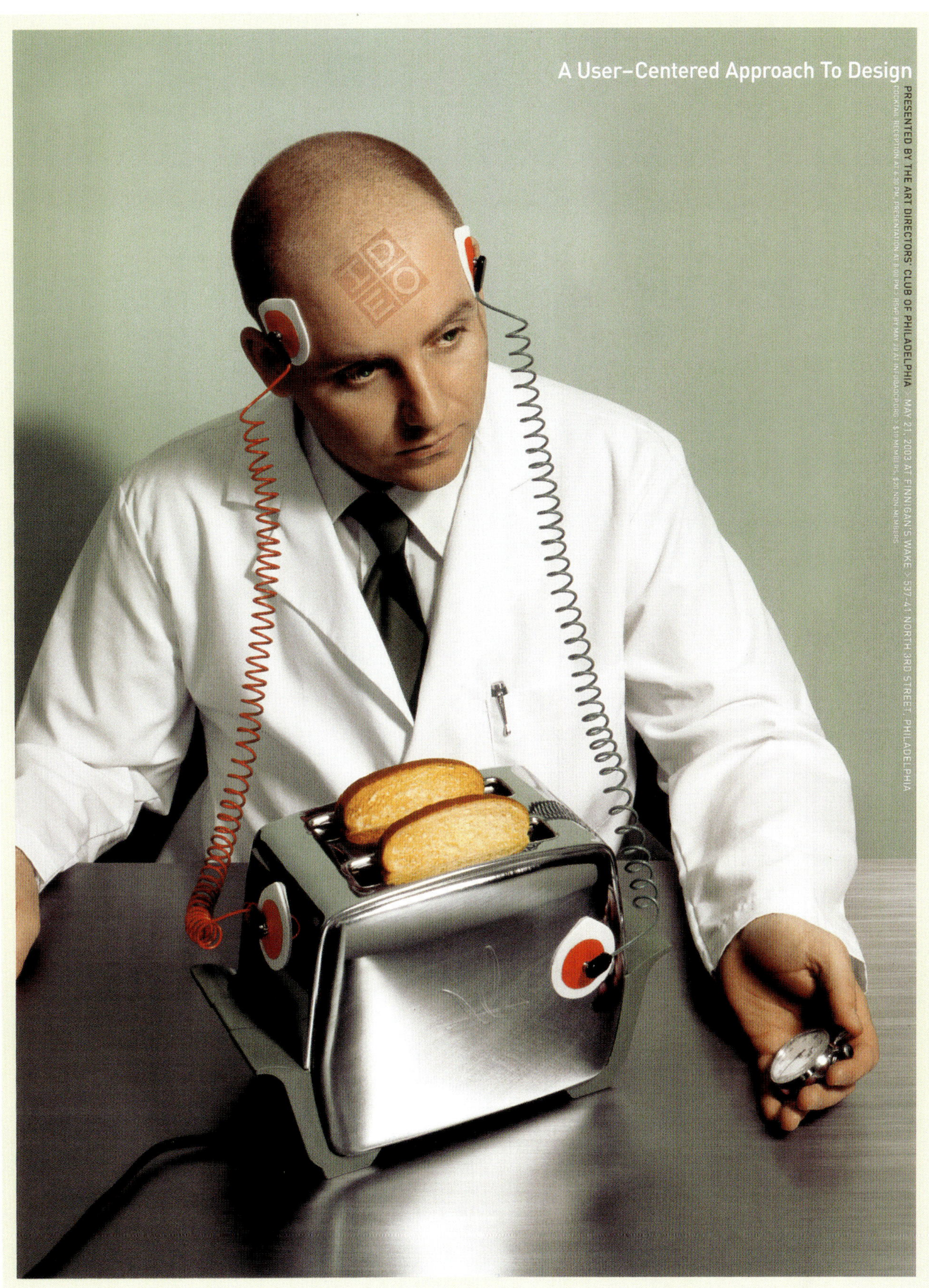

NDW Communications/Art Directors Club of Philadelphia

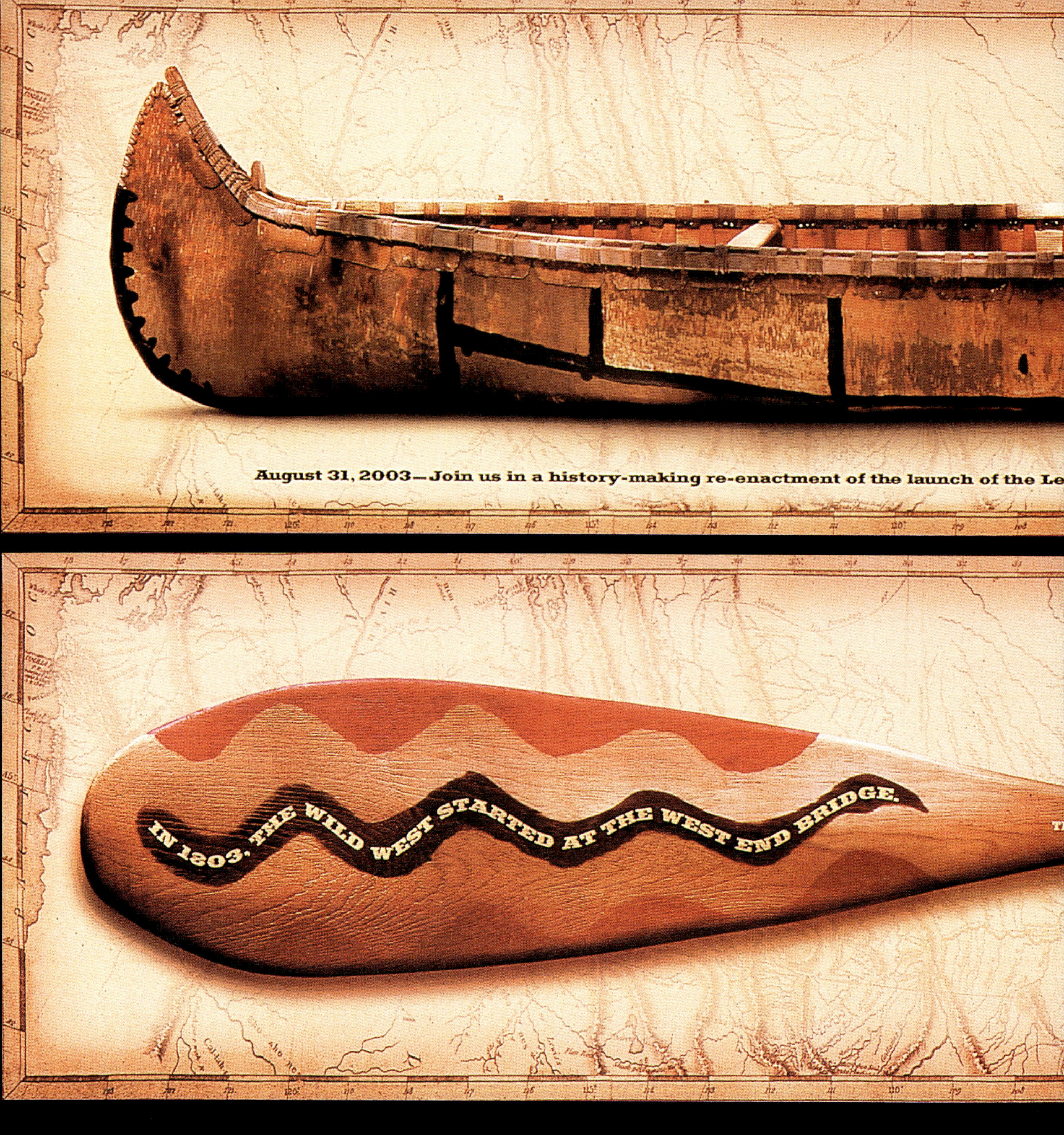
August 31, 2003—Join us in a history-making re-enactment of the launch of the Le
IN 1803, THE WILD WEST STARTED AT THE WEST END BRIDGE.

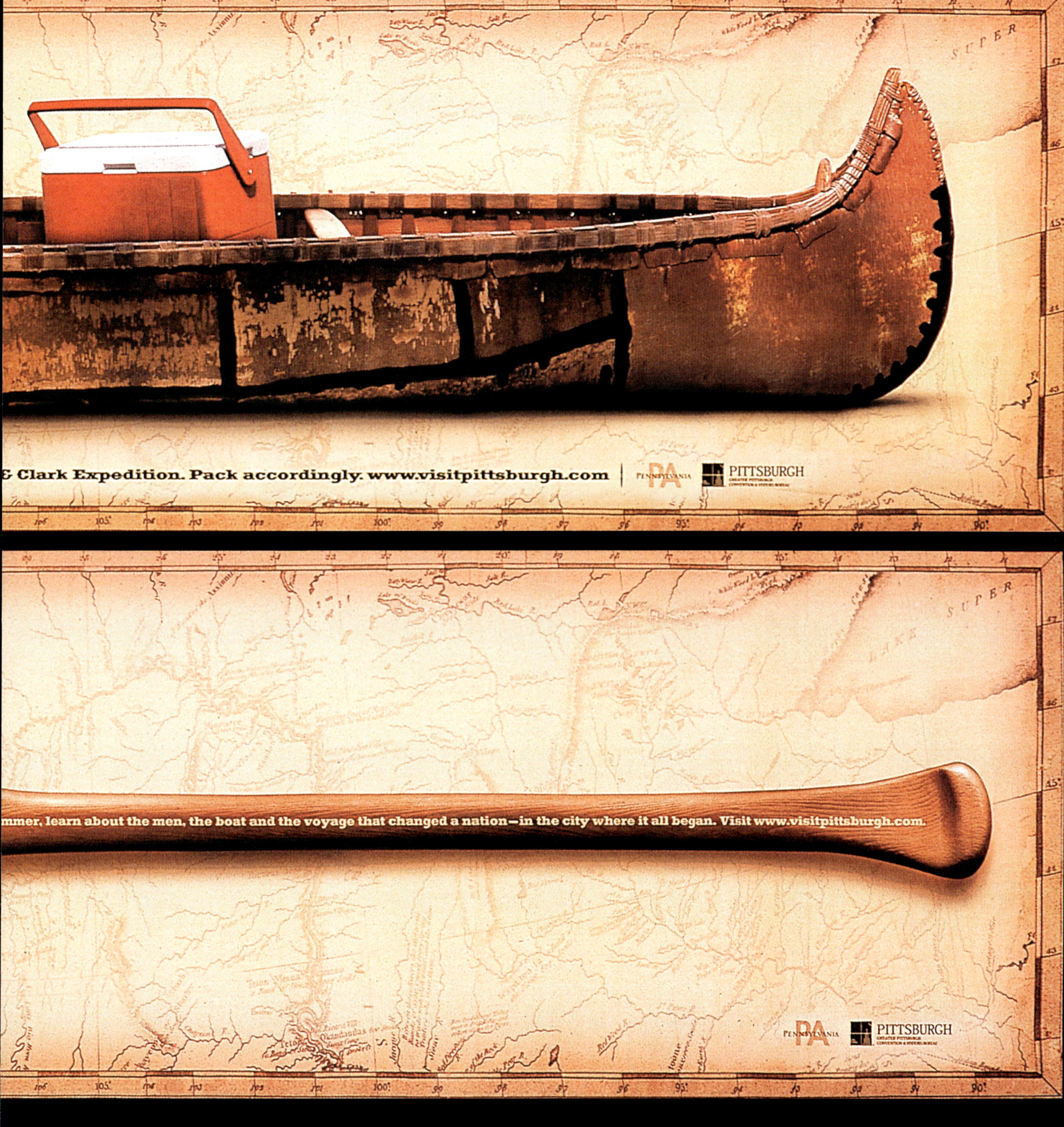
& Clark Expedition. Pack accordingly. www.visitpittsburgh.com
PENNSYLVANIA PA
PITTSBURGH
mmer, learn about the men, the boat and the voyage that changed a nation—in the city where it all began. Visit www.visitpittsburgh.com.
PENNSYLVANIA PA
PITTSBURGH

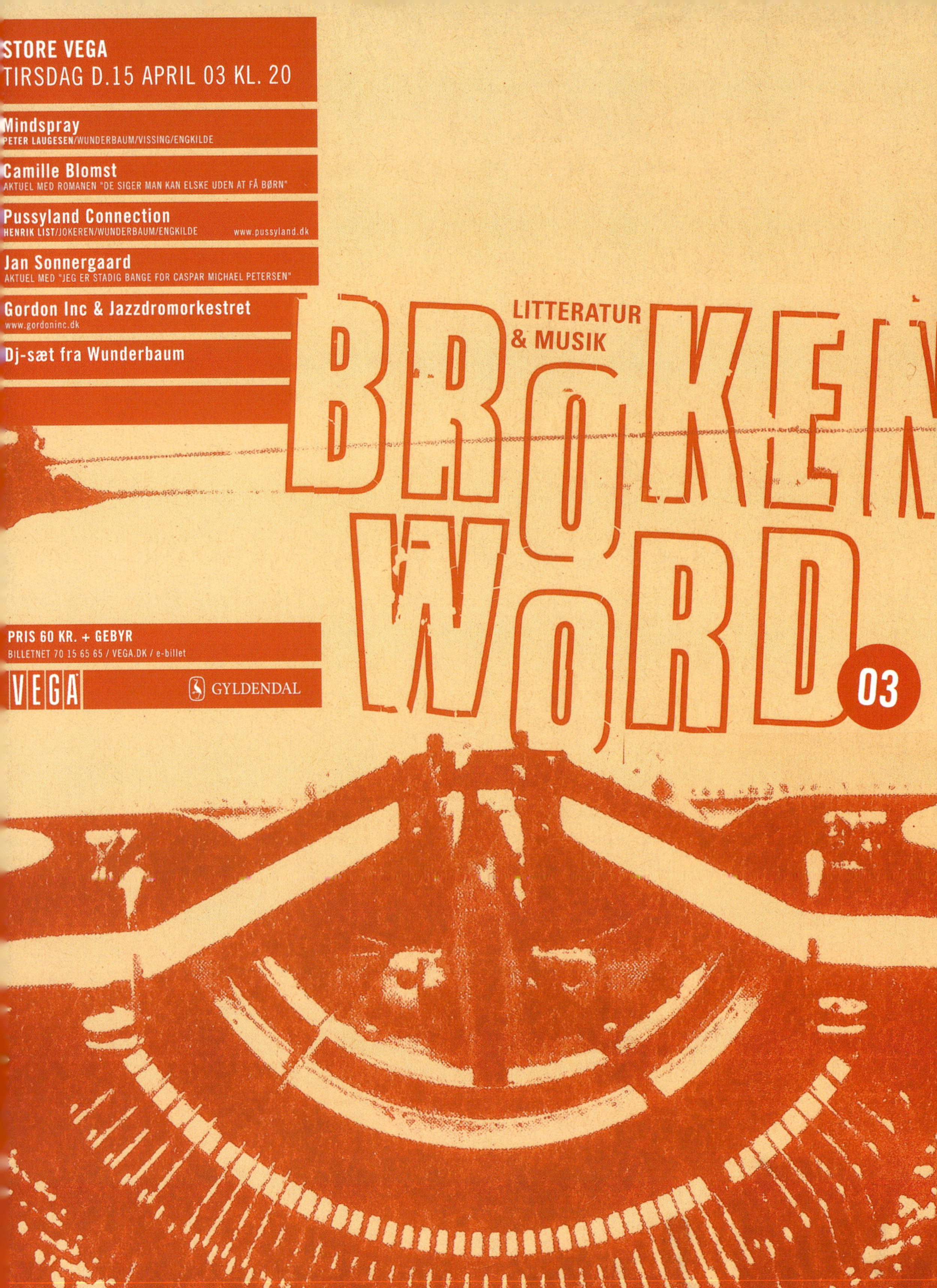

re:public

ORD & BEATS, LYRIK & LYD, HISTORIER & STEMNINGER, RAP & RYTME

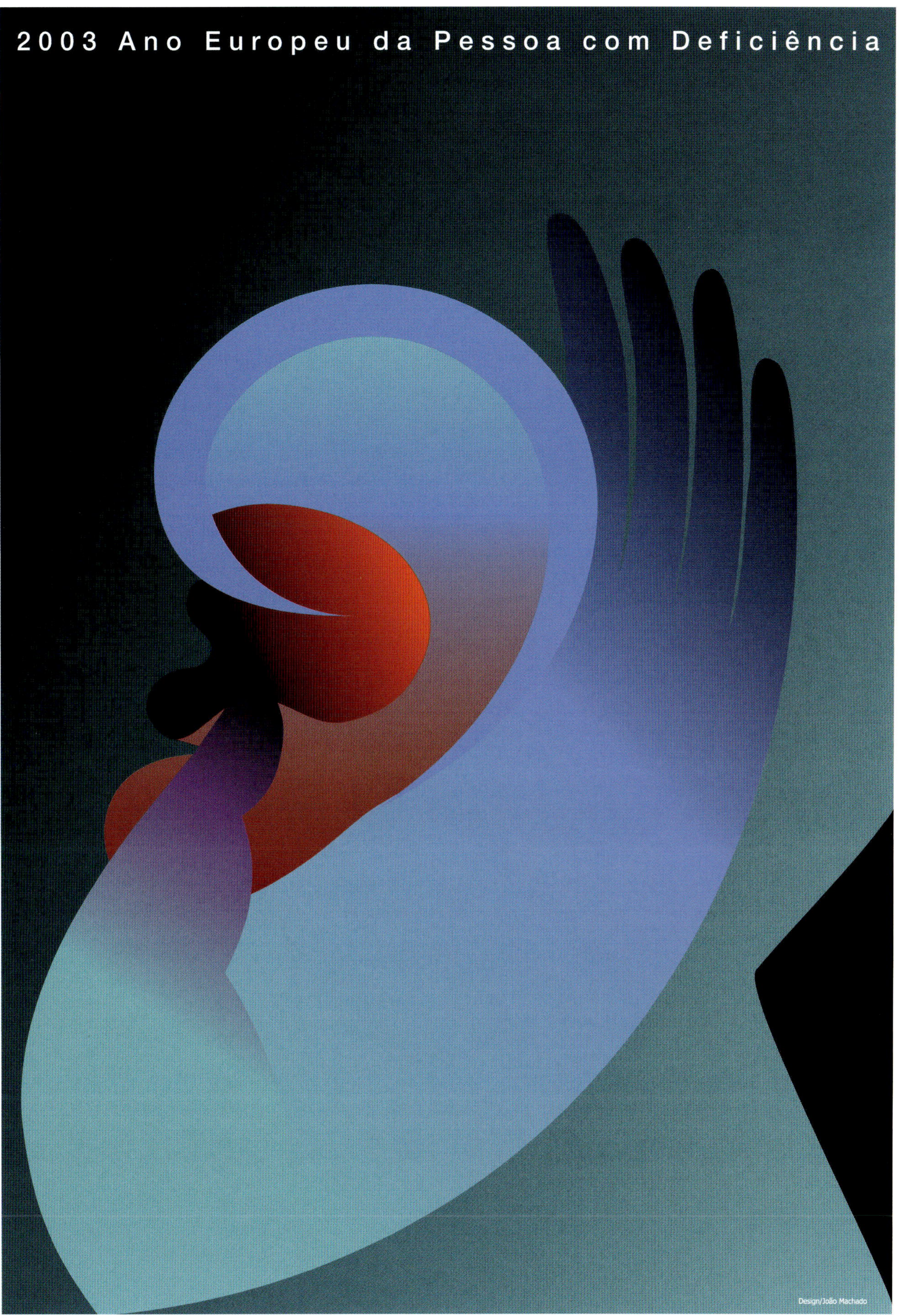

João Machado Design Lda/CTT

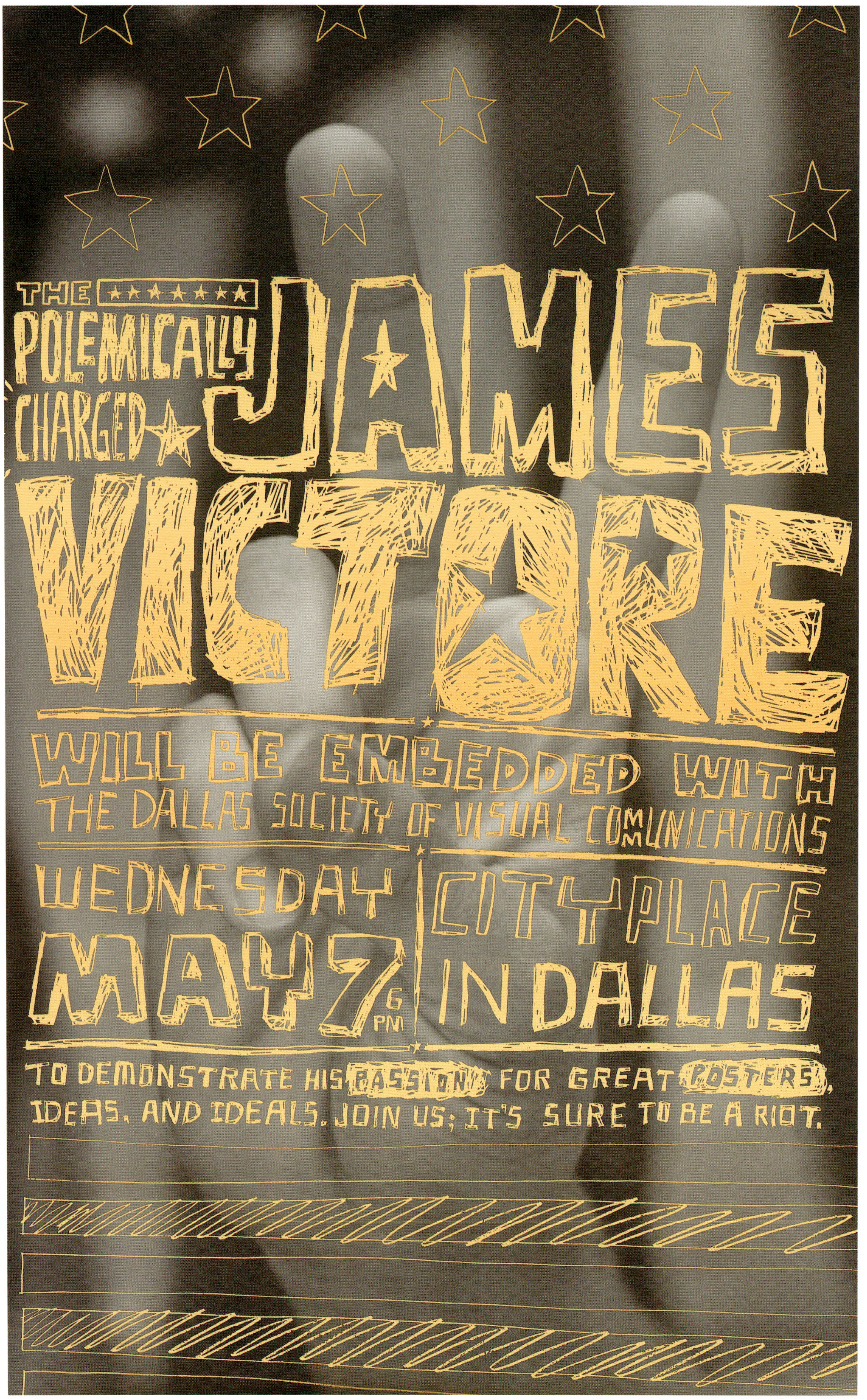

Eisenberg and Associates/The Dallas Society of Visual Communications (DSVC)

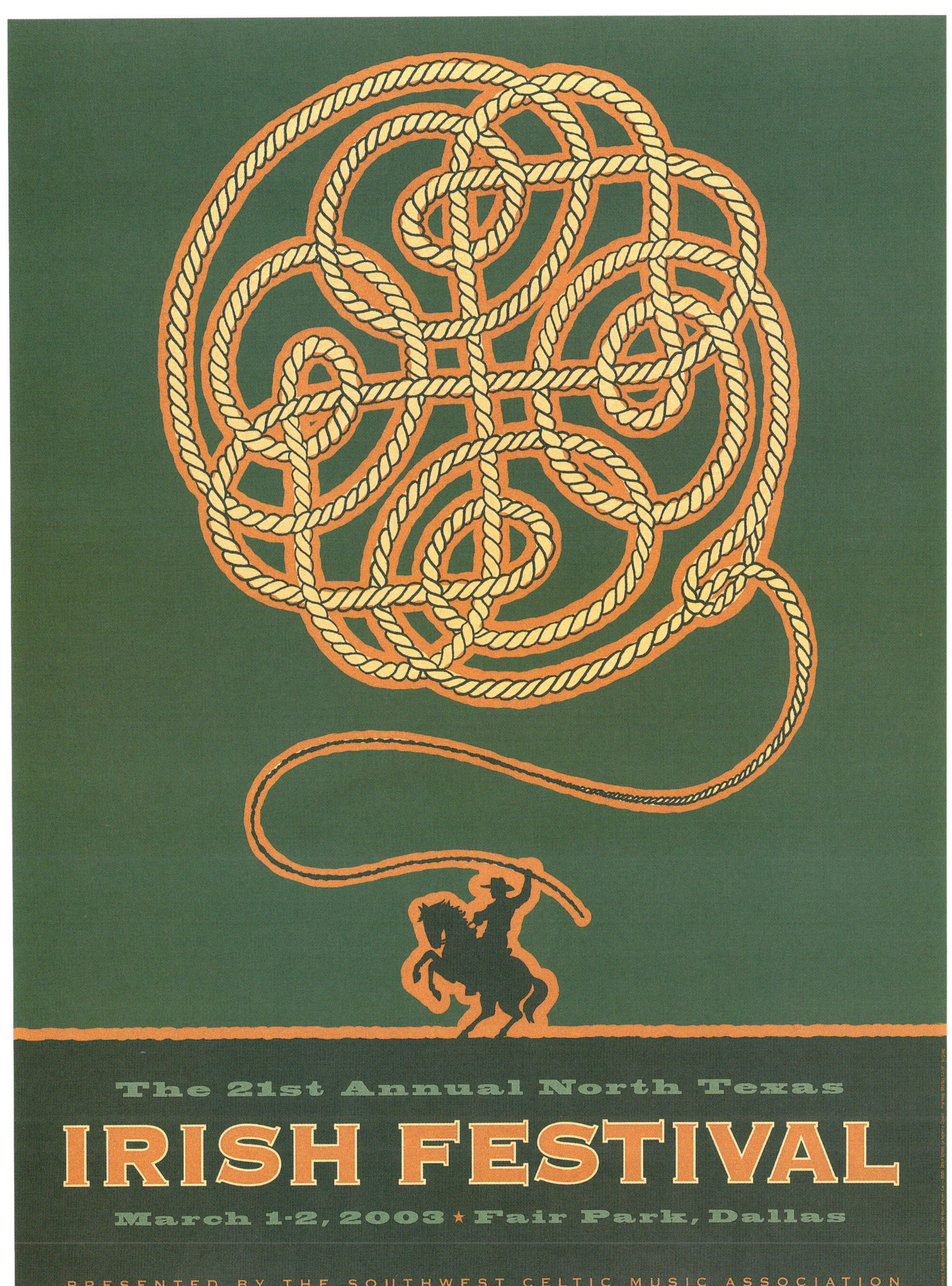

SullivanPerkins, Inc./Southwest Celtic Music Association

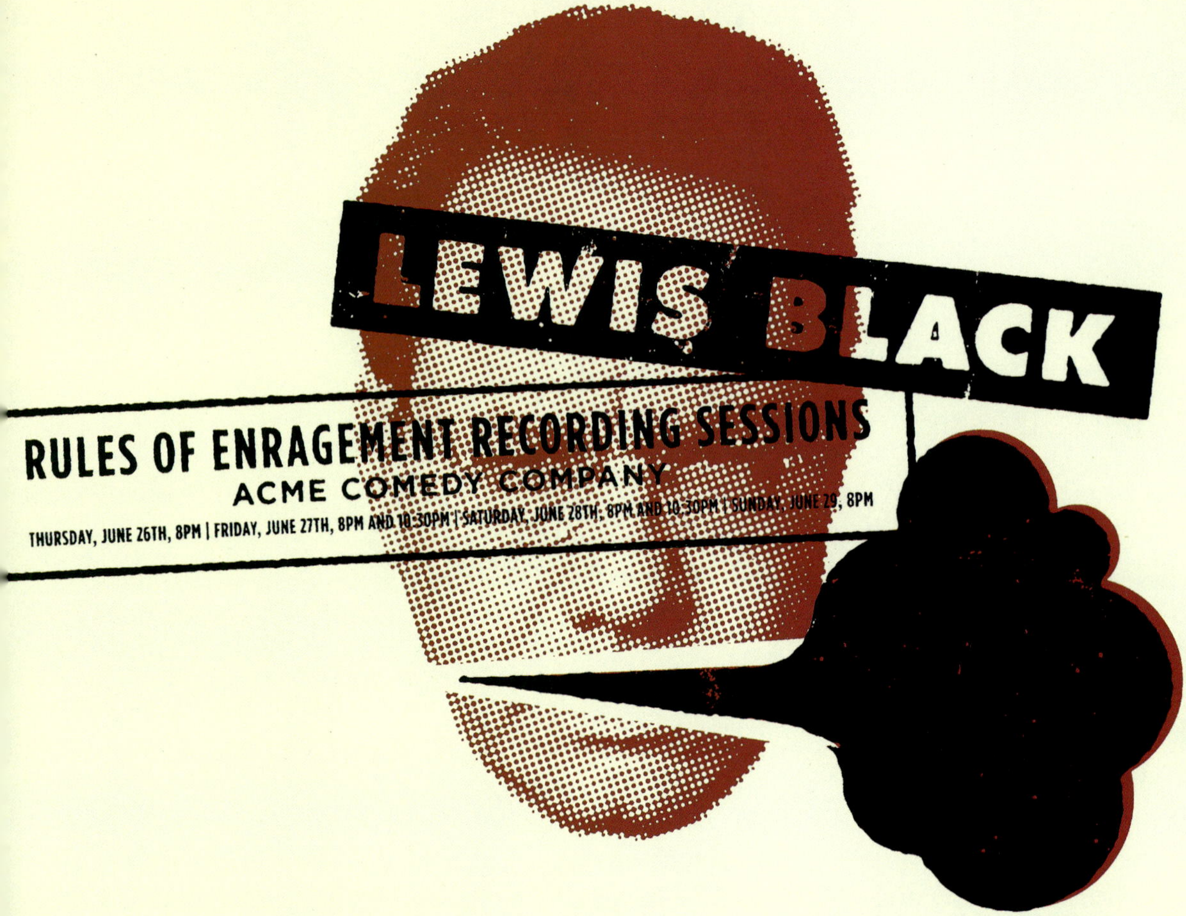

LEWIS BLACK

RULES OF ENRAGEMENT RECORDING SESSIONS

ACME COMEDY COMPANY

THURSDAY, JUNE 26TH, 8PM | FRIDAY, JUNE 27TH, 8PM AND 10:30PM | SATURDAY, JUNE 28TH, 8PM AND 10:30PM | SUNDAY, JUNE 29, 8PM

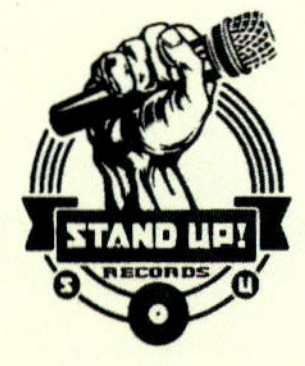

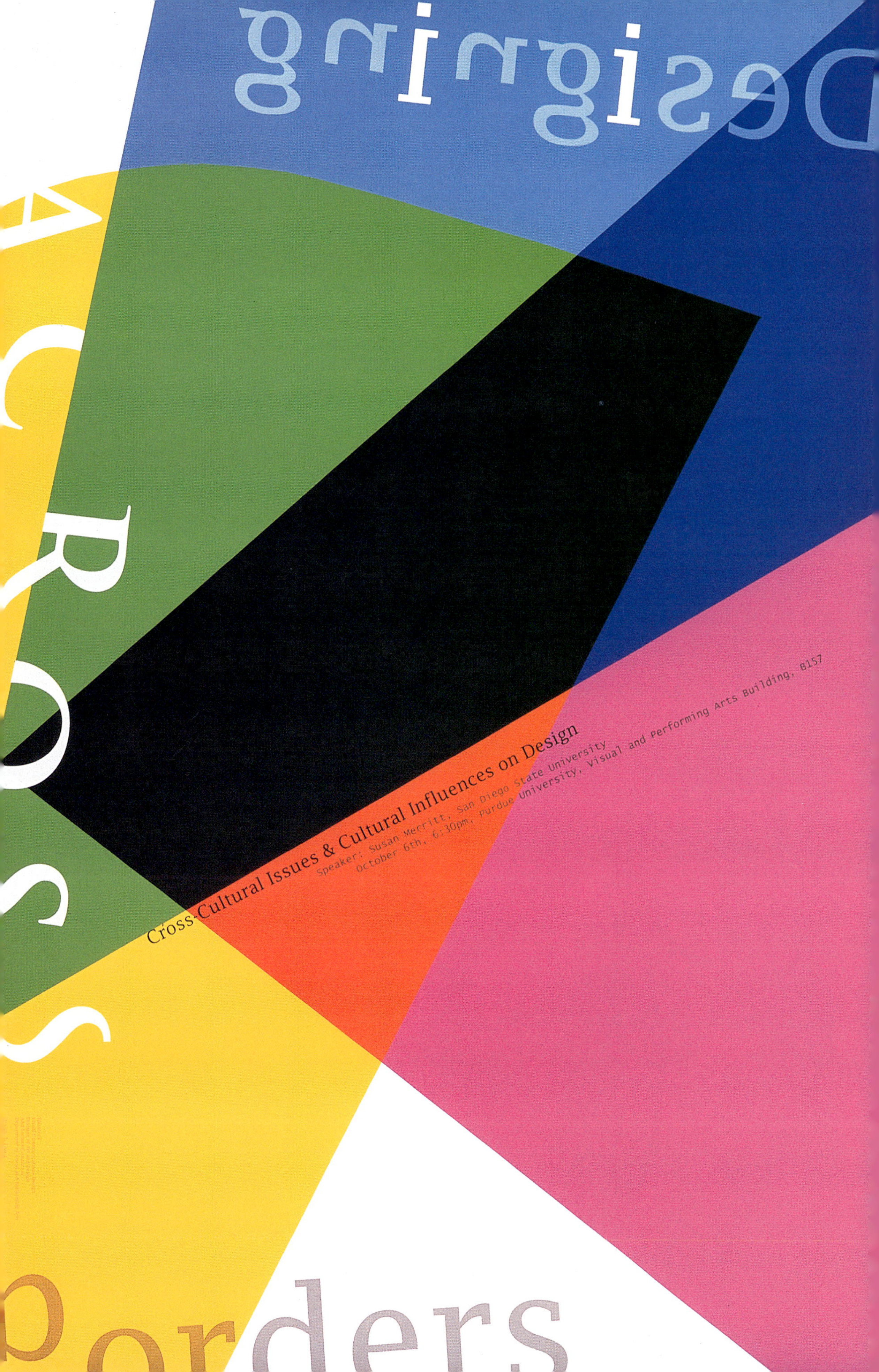
Designing
Across
Borders
Cross-Cultural Issues & Cultural Influences on Design
Speaker: Susan Merritt, San Diego State University
October 6th, 6:30pm, Purdue University, Visual and Performing Arts Building, B157

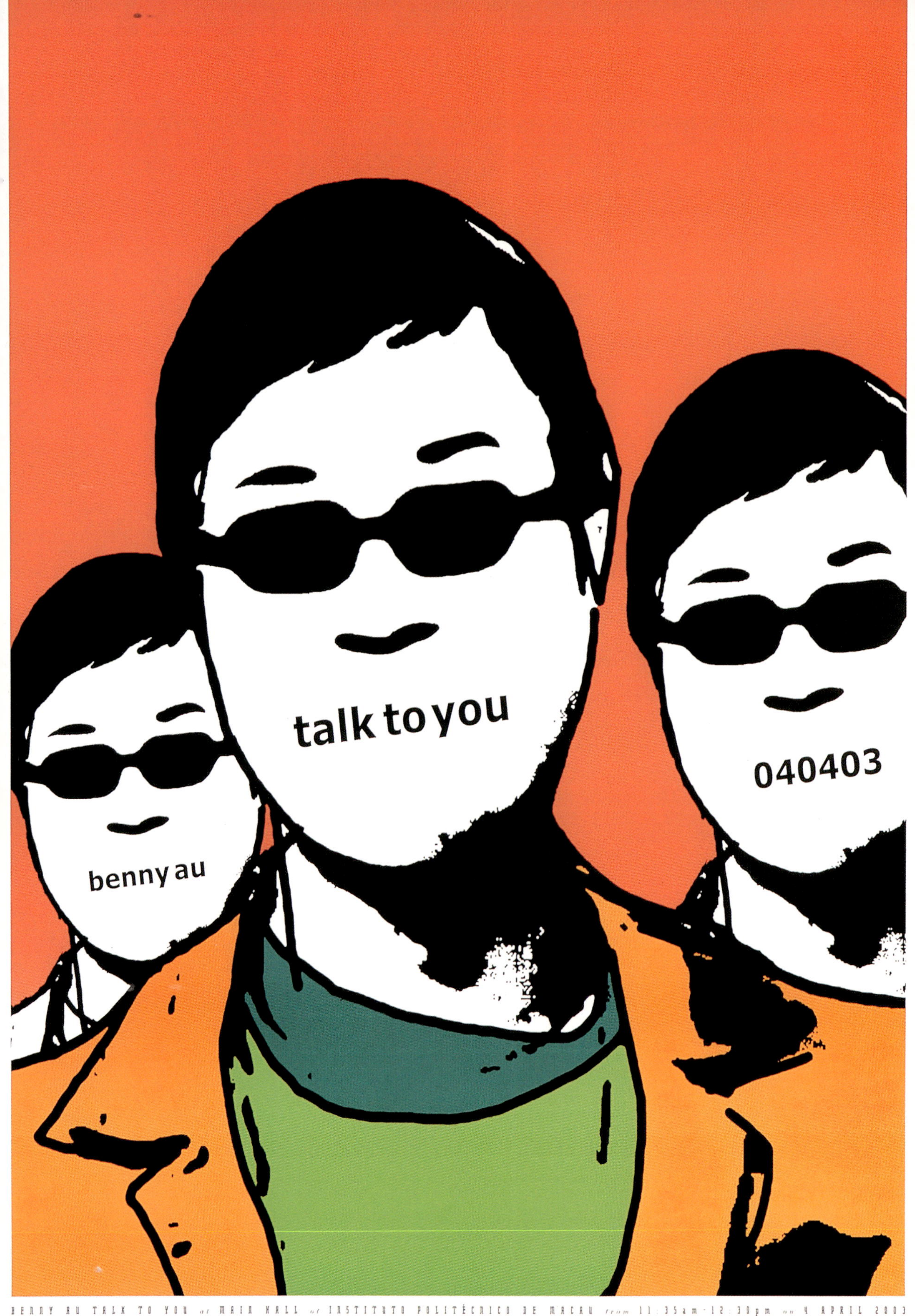
talk to you
benny au
040403
BENNY AU TALK TO YOU at MAIN HALL of INSTITUTO POLITÉCNICO DE MACAU from 11:35am-12:30pm on 4 APRIL 2003

FINISH

the physical
distance
is 26.2 miles
CROSS THE LINE
and the
personal journey
is immeasurable
City Hall
26
Chestnut St
Union Station
STL
RKET ST
Compton
24
spirit of st louis marathon & family fitness weekend
marathon : half marathon : relay : Mayor's 5K run/walk : kid's fun runs : read, right & run marathon : 2003 USA women's marathon championship
april 5 & 6
stlouismarathon.com 314 727 0800

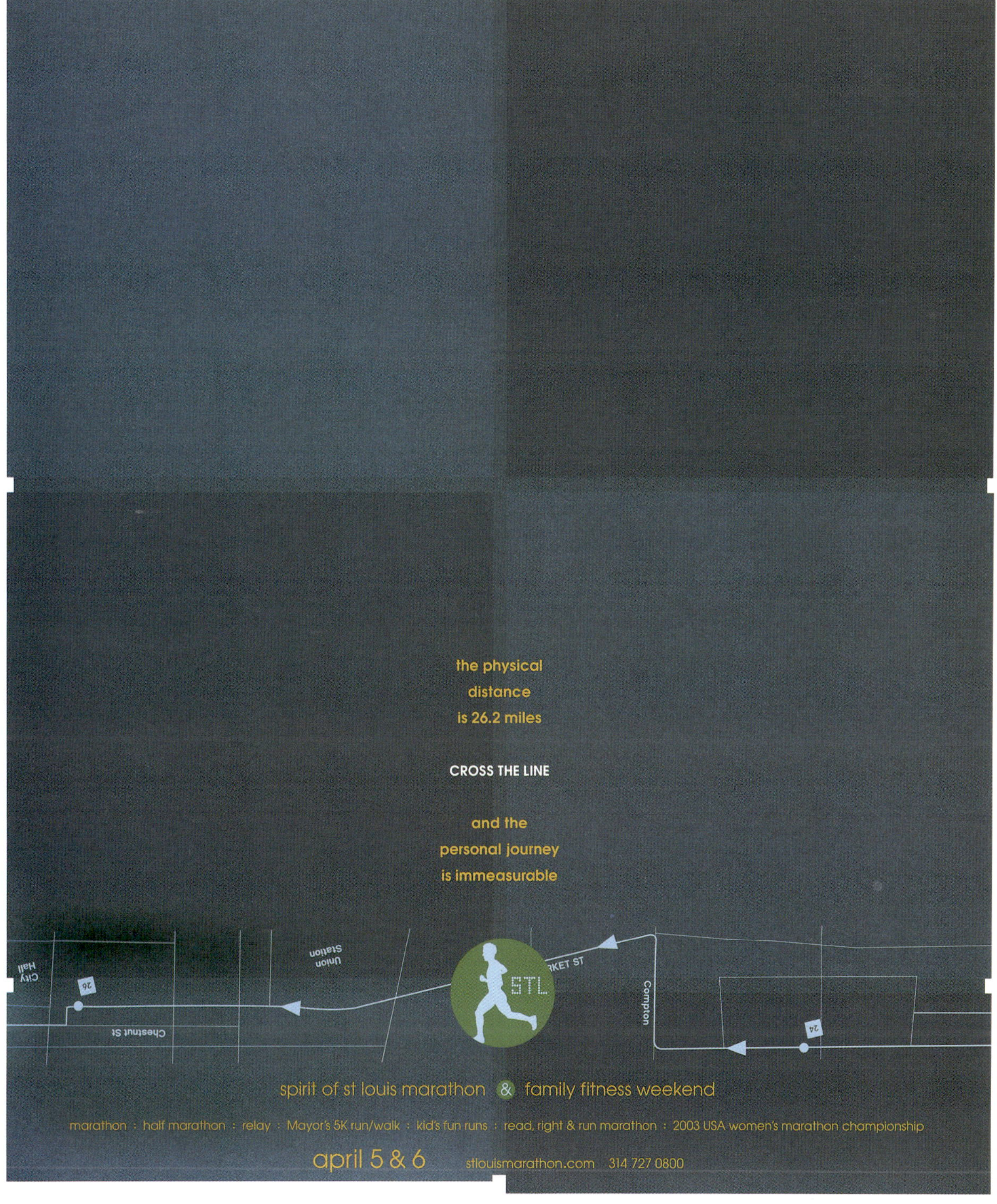

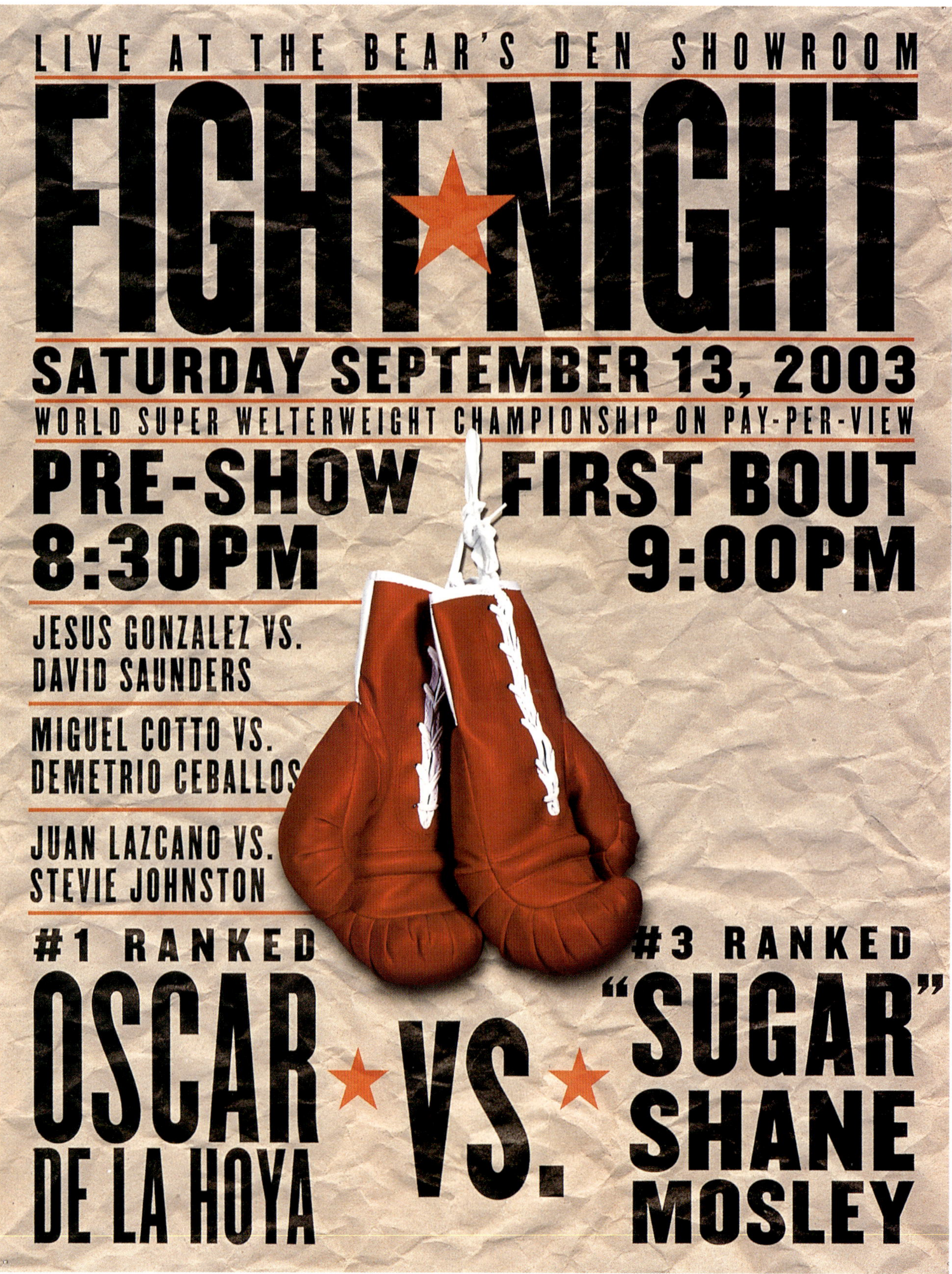

Partners in Marketing, LLC/Seneca Niagara Casino

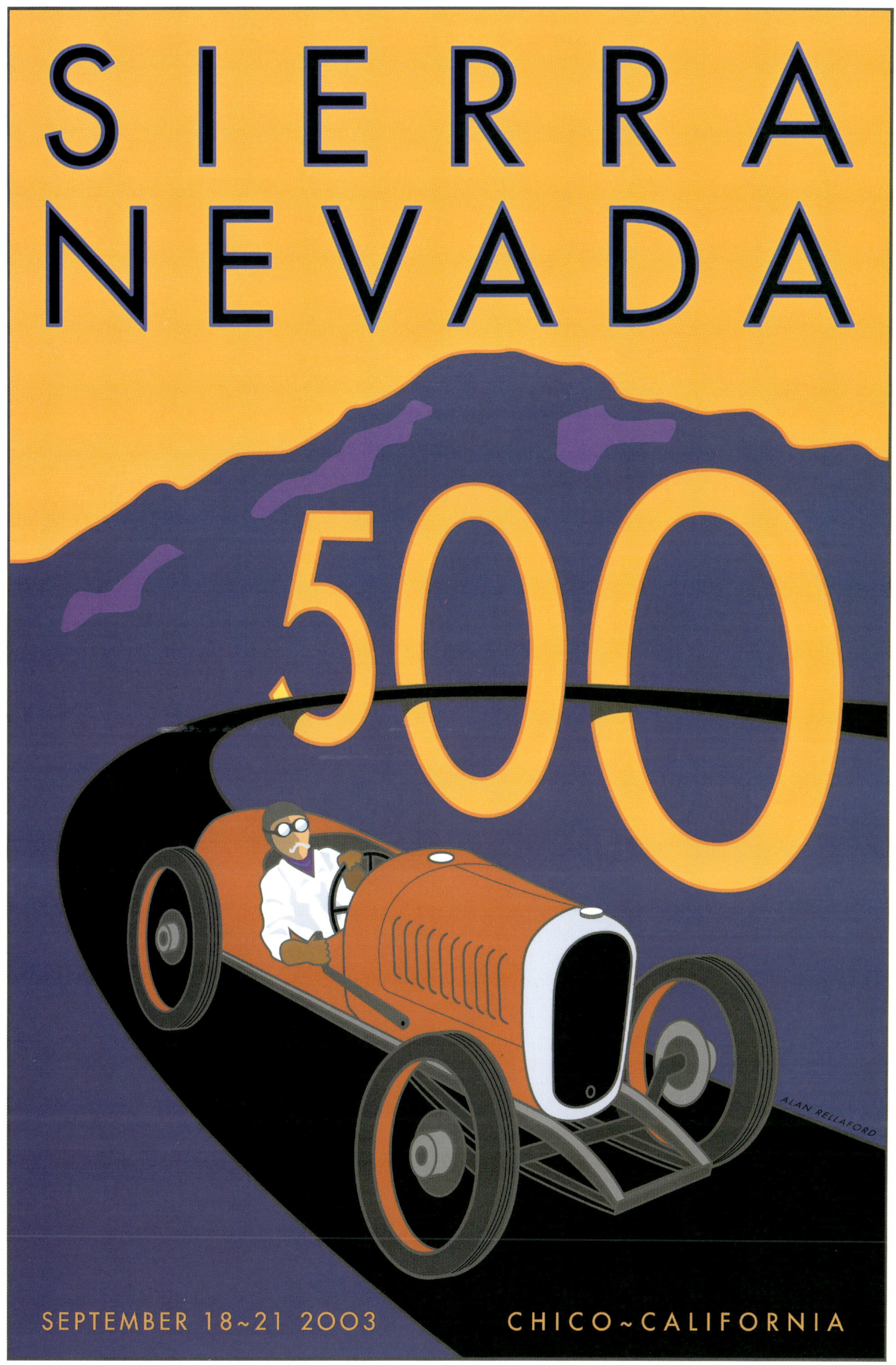

Alan Rellaford Graphic Design/Sierra Nevada 500

DOING GOOD

SEPTEMBER 12–14, 2003

ASILOMAR CONFERENCE CENTER
PACIFIC GROVE, CALIFORNIA

FOR MORE INFORMATION. GO TO WWW.AIACC.ORG OR CALL (916) 448-9082

JOIN HUNDREDS OF DESIGN PROFESSIONALS FOR A WEEKEND OF PEERING INSIDE THE HEADS OF A CROSS SECTION OF OUR PEERS TO GET A GLIMPSE OF WHAT THEY ARE DOING, AND WHERE THEIR IDEAS ORIGINATE. DON'T MISS THE OPPORTUNITY TO EXPERIENCE THE EXPRESSION OF IDEAS AND EXPLORE THE PERIPHERAL ISSUES AND COLLABORATIVE OPPORTUNITIES AFFECTING THE FUTURE OF ARCHITECTURE.

"You're making something that belongs to all of us, otherwise you are really producing very little or almost nothing—if not really nothing. Of course that tells you that almost everybody fails, and it's quite true...

THIS GOOD UP

GIVE

GROW

THIS GOOD UP

...But I don't think Mozart was a failure, do you? And don't you think Mozart makes a society? Did society make Mozart? No. It's the man, the man only, not a committee, not a mob—nothing makes anything but a man, a single, single, man." –Louis Kahn, 1965

AIA California Council

FOR SEASONED AS WELL AS UP-AND-COMING ARCHITECTS, ASSOCIATES, STUDENTS, ALLIED PROFESSIONALS, GUESTS AND CHILDREN

WHETHER GROWING OR GIVING, WHAT IS DOING GOOD FOR YOU? TELL US AT WWW.AIACC.ORG/CONFERENCES/MDC

THE 16TH AIACC MONTEREY DESIGN CONFERENCE

DOING GOOD

Volume Design, Inc./American Institute of Architects California Council

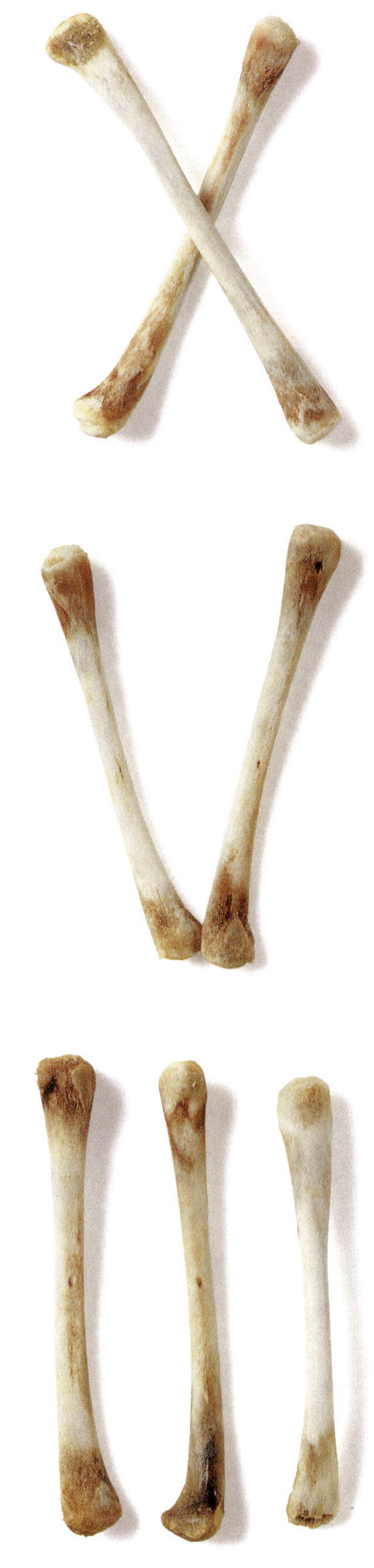

Bare Bones - Creative Survival Creative Summit 18 www.creativesummit.com

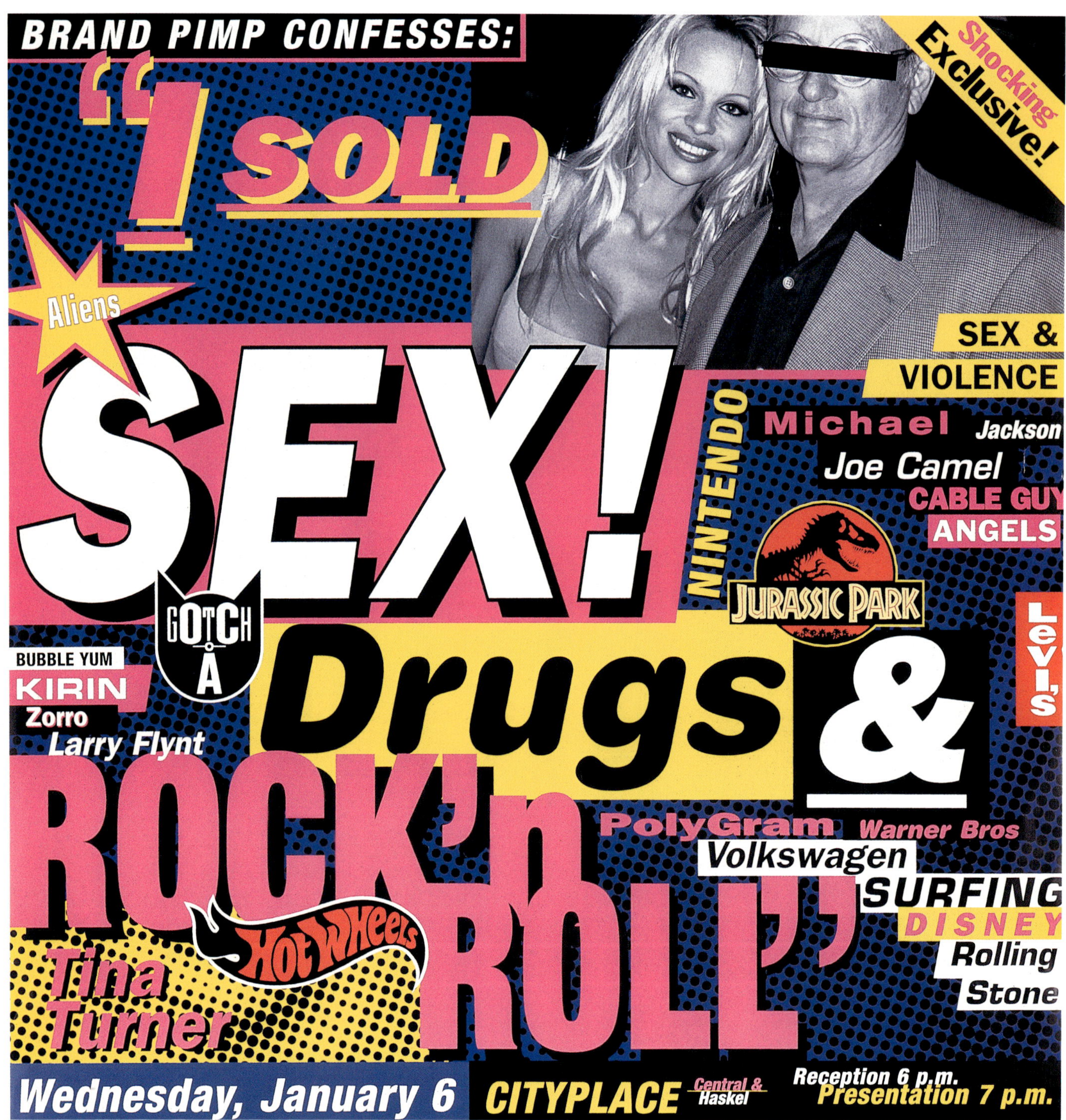

Mike Salisbury LLC/Dallas Society of Communication Arts

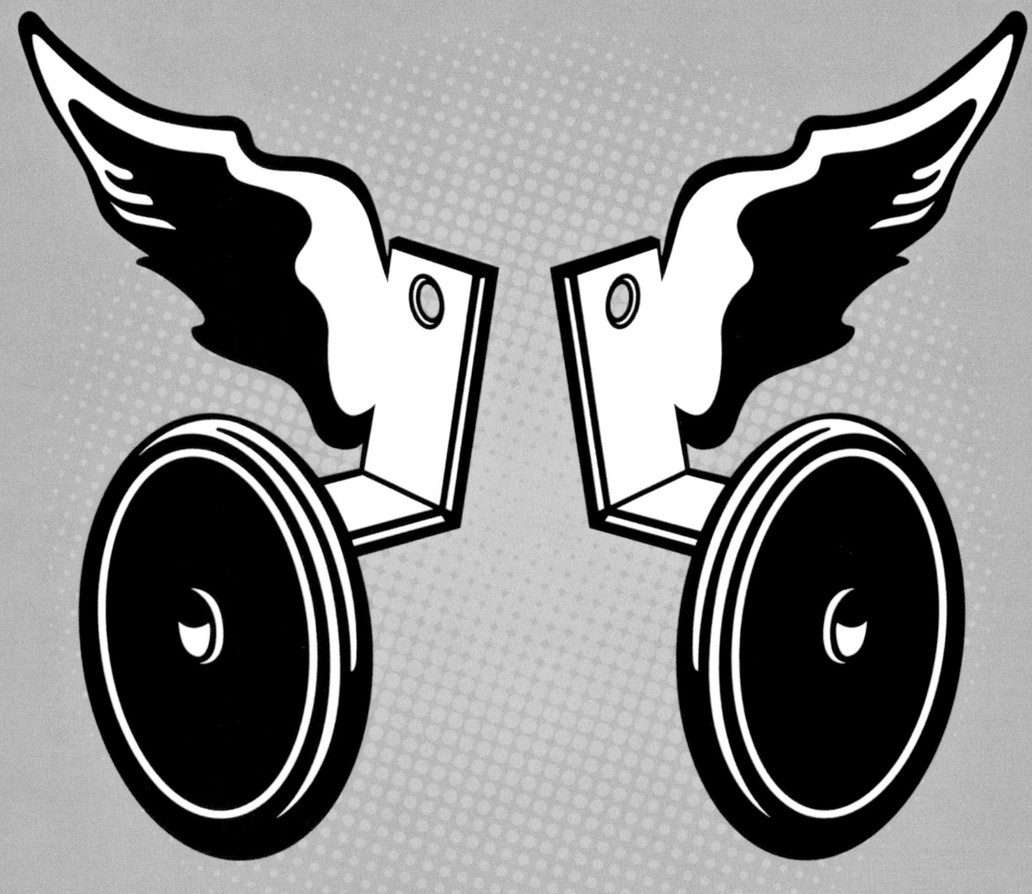

DONATE YOUR LEGS

TREK FOR KIDS

A BIKE RIDE TO BENEFIT BOYS & GIRLS CLUB OF DANE COUNTY

SATURDAY, JULY 26, 2003

EDGEWOOD HIGH SCHOOL, MADISON

REGISTER AT WWW.TREKFORKIDS.ORG OR 608-257-2606

The Hiebing Group/Boys and Girls Club of Dane County

567

The average number of calories burned during a 10K run.

Join the 2003 Omaha Corporate Cup 10K Team. Sign up with Ben Matiyow in the Union Pacific Fitness Center by August 15 or call 402.271.2184.

UNION PACIFIC

BUILDING AMERICA™

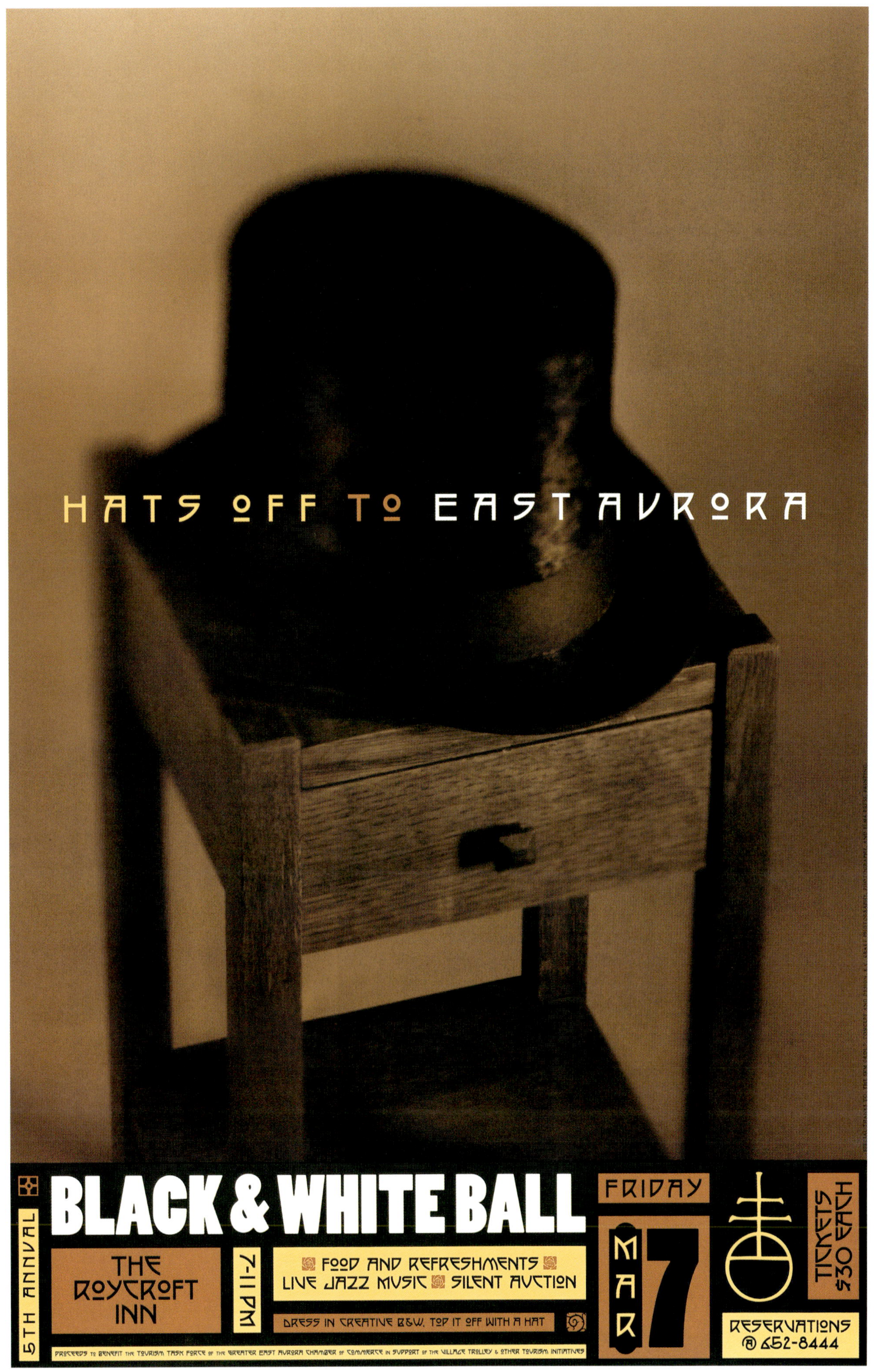

SKM Group/Greater East Aurora Chamber of Commerce

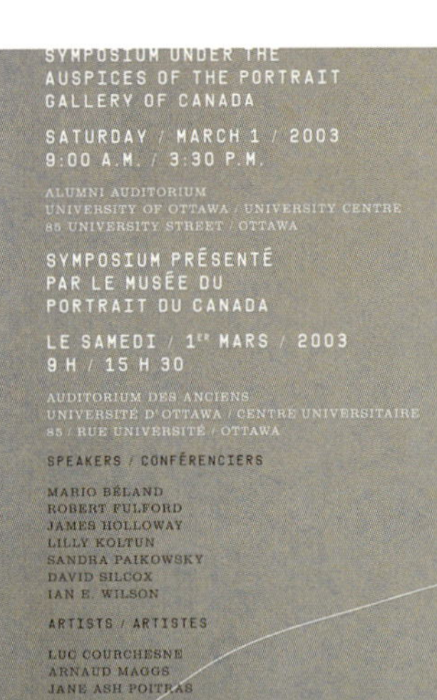
SYMPOSIUM UNDER THE
AUSPICES OF THE PORTRAIT
GALLERY OF CANADA
SATURDAY / MARCH 1 / 2003
9:00 A.M. / 3:30 P.M.
ALUMNI AUDITORIUM
UNIVERSITY OF OTTAWA / UNIVERSITY CENTRE
85 UNIVERSITY STREET / OTTAWA
SYMPOSIUM PRÉSENTÉ
PAR LE MUSÉE DU
PORTRAIT DU CANADA
LE SAMEDI / 1ER MARS / 2003
9 H / 15 H 30
AUDITORIUM DES ANCIENS
UNIVERSITÉ D'OTTAWA / CENTRE UNIVERSITAIRE
85 / RUE UNIVERSITÉ / OTTAWA
SPEAKERS / CONFÉRENCIERS
MARIO BÉLAND
ROBERT FULFORD
JAMES HOLLOWAY
LILLY KOLTUN
SANDRA PAIKOWSKY
DAVID SILCOX
IAN E. WILSON
ARTISTS / ARTISTES
LUC COURCHESNE
ARNAUD MAGGS
JANE ASH POITRAS
JOANNE TOD
WWW.PORTRAITS.GC.CA
613 / 985 / 5575
PORTRAITURE
between /
NARRATIVE
and /
l'art du /
PORTRAIT
entre la /
NARRATION
et l' /
ABSTRACTION
DESIGN / KOLEGRAM PHOTO / JF PLANTE
National Archives of Canada and
National Library of Canada
Archives nationales du Canada et
Bibliothèque nationale du Canada
Canada

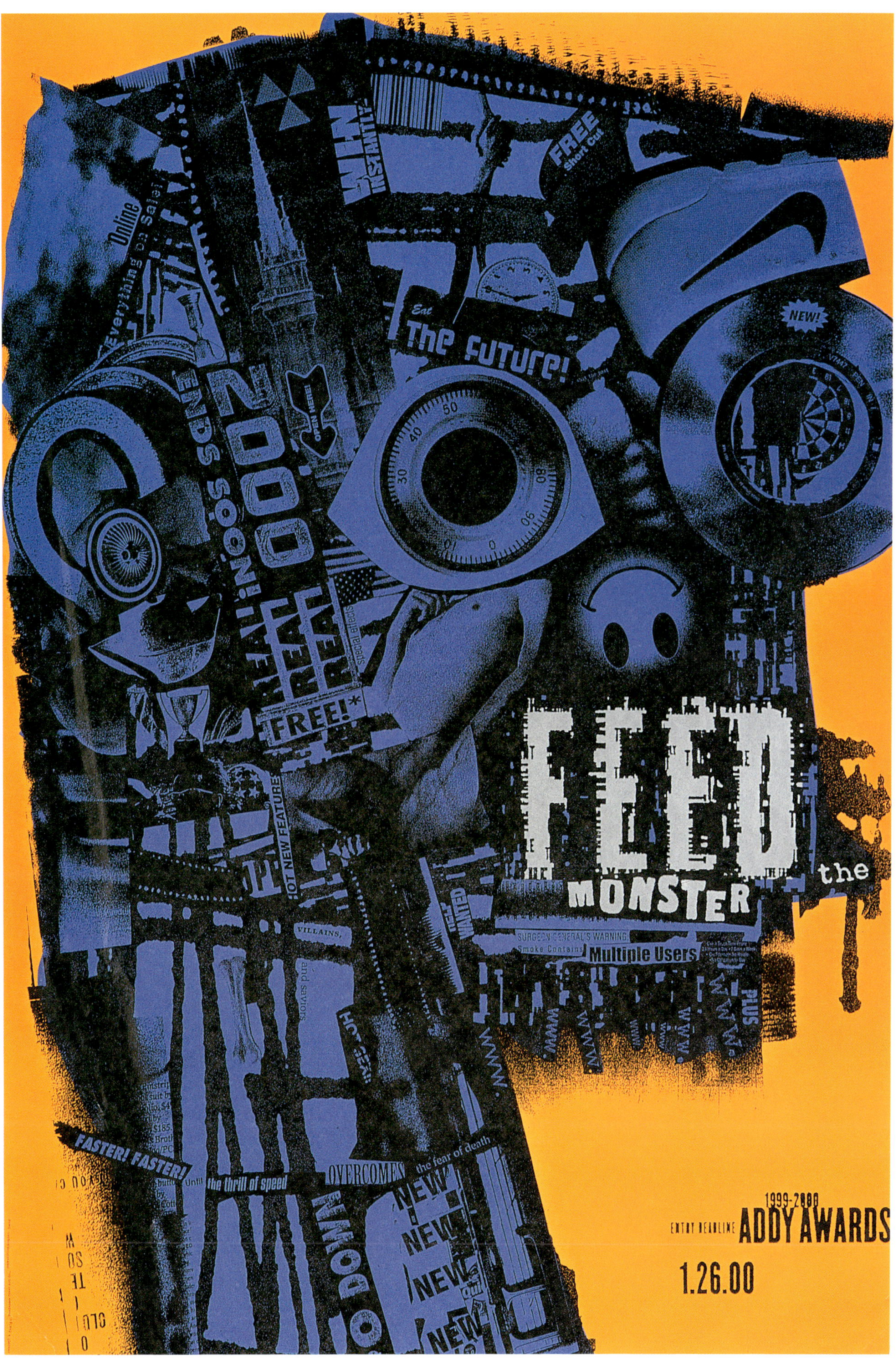

HendersonBromsteadArt Co./American Advertising Federation

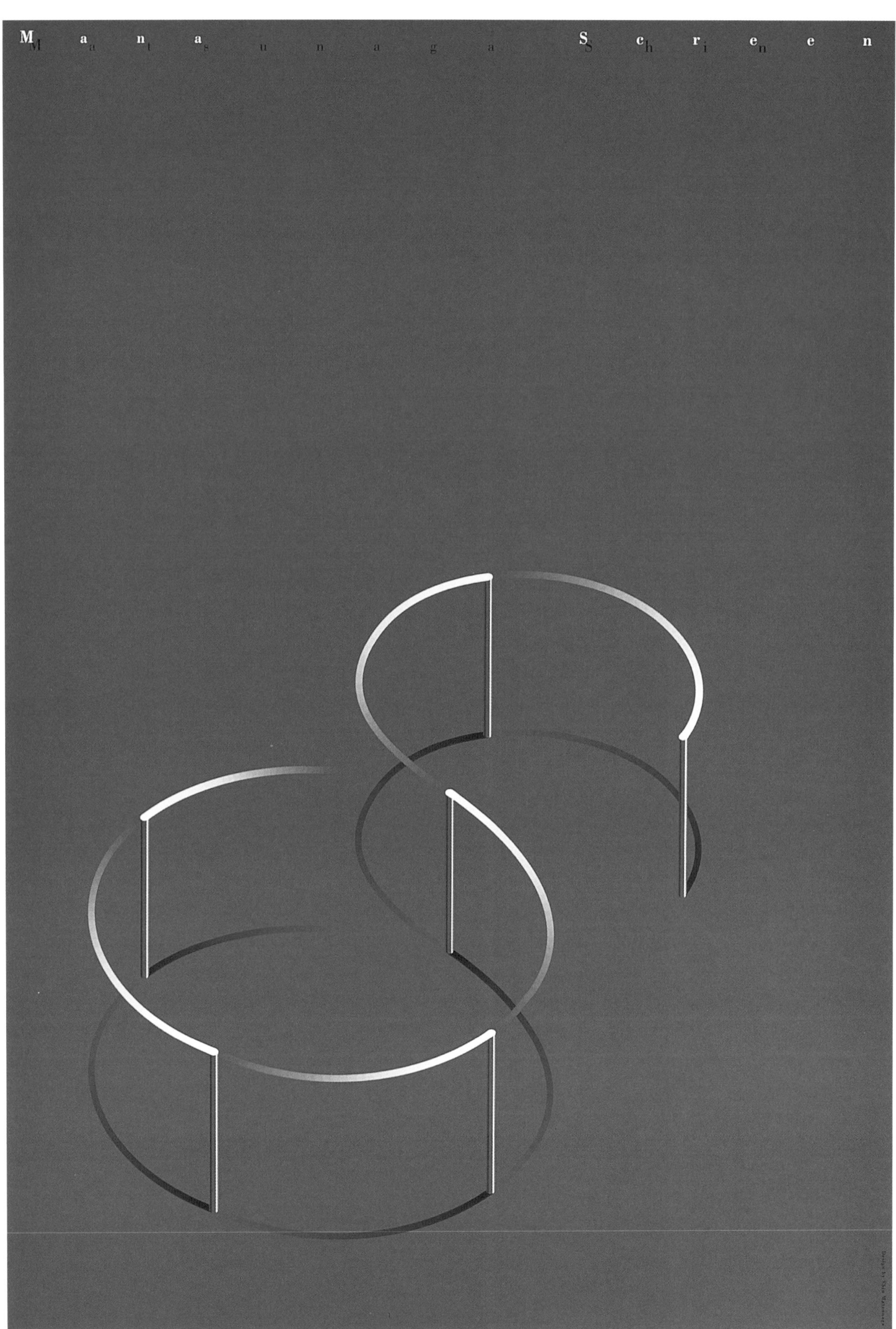

Shin Matsunaga Design Inc./Mana Screen Co., Ltd.

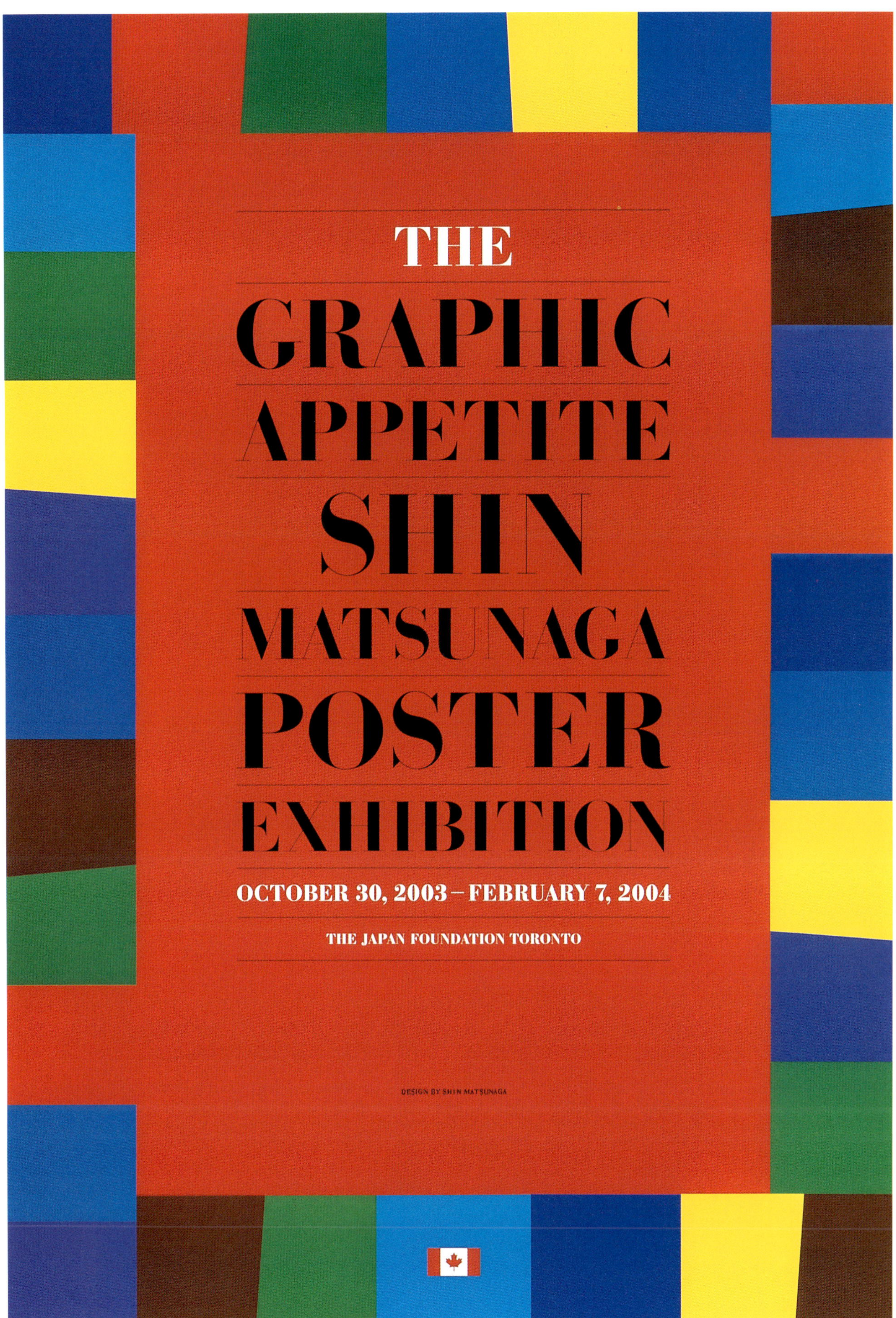

Shin Matsunaga Design Inc./The Japan Foundation

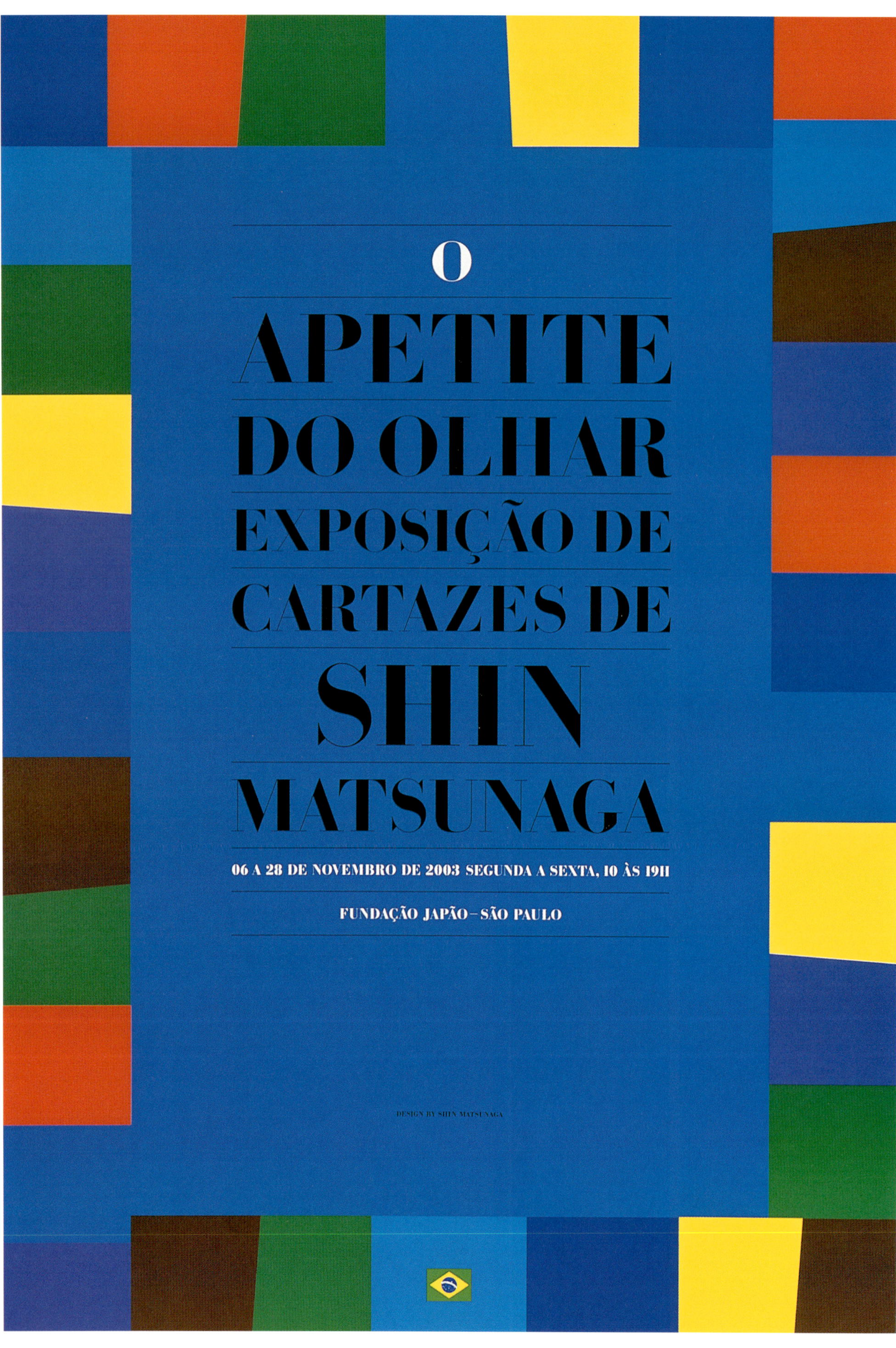

Shin Matsunaga Design Inc./The Japan Foundation

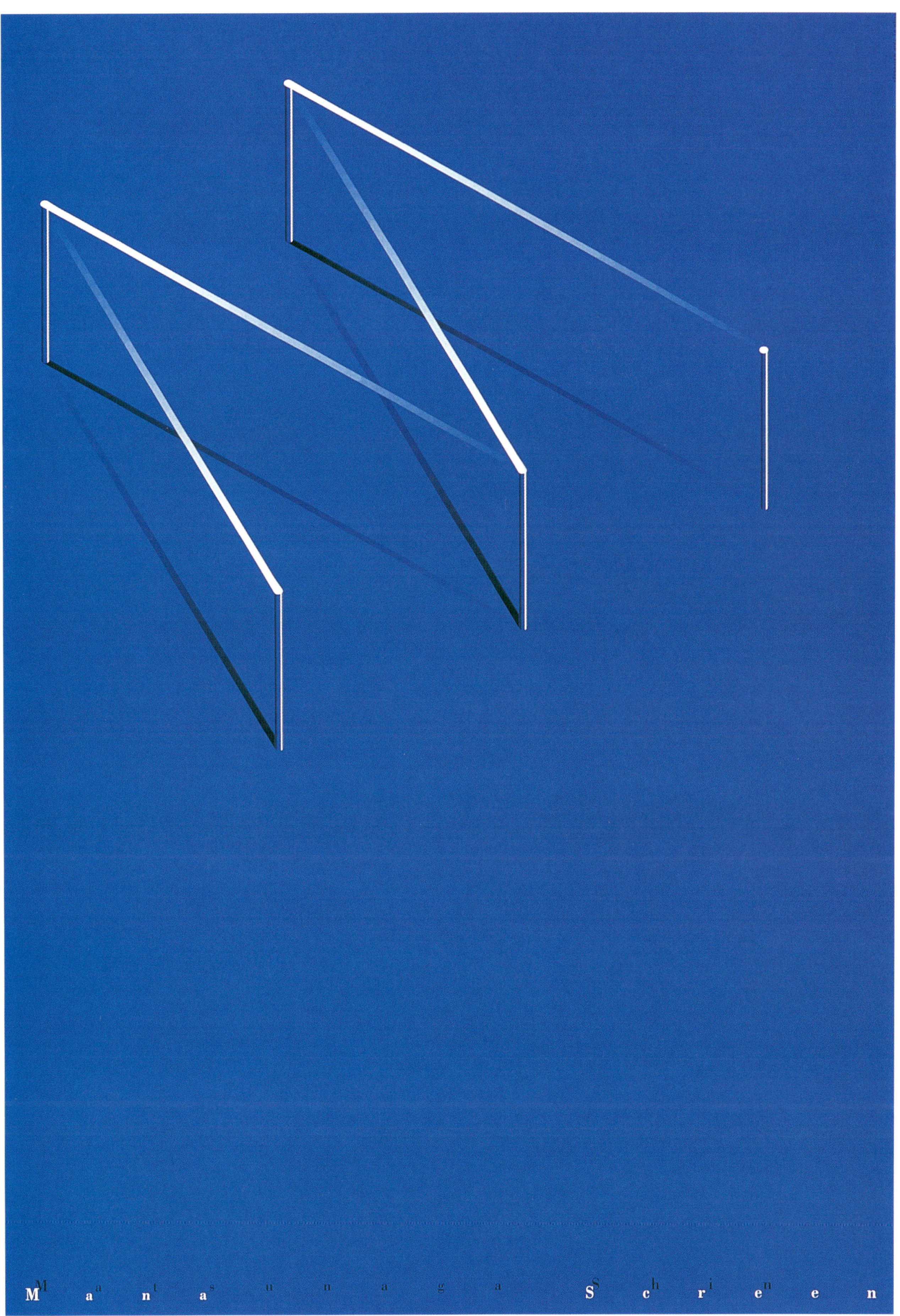

Shin Matsunaga Design Inc./Mana Screen Co., Ltd.

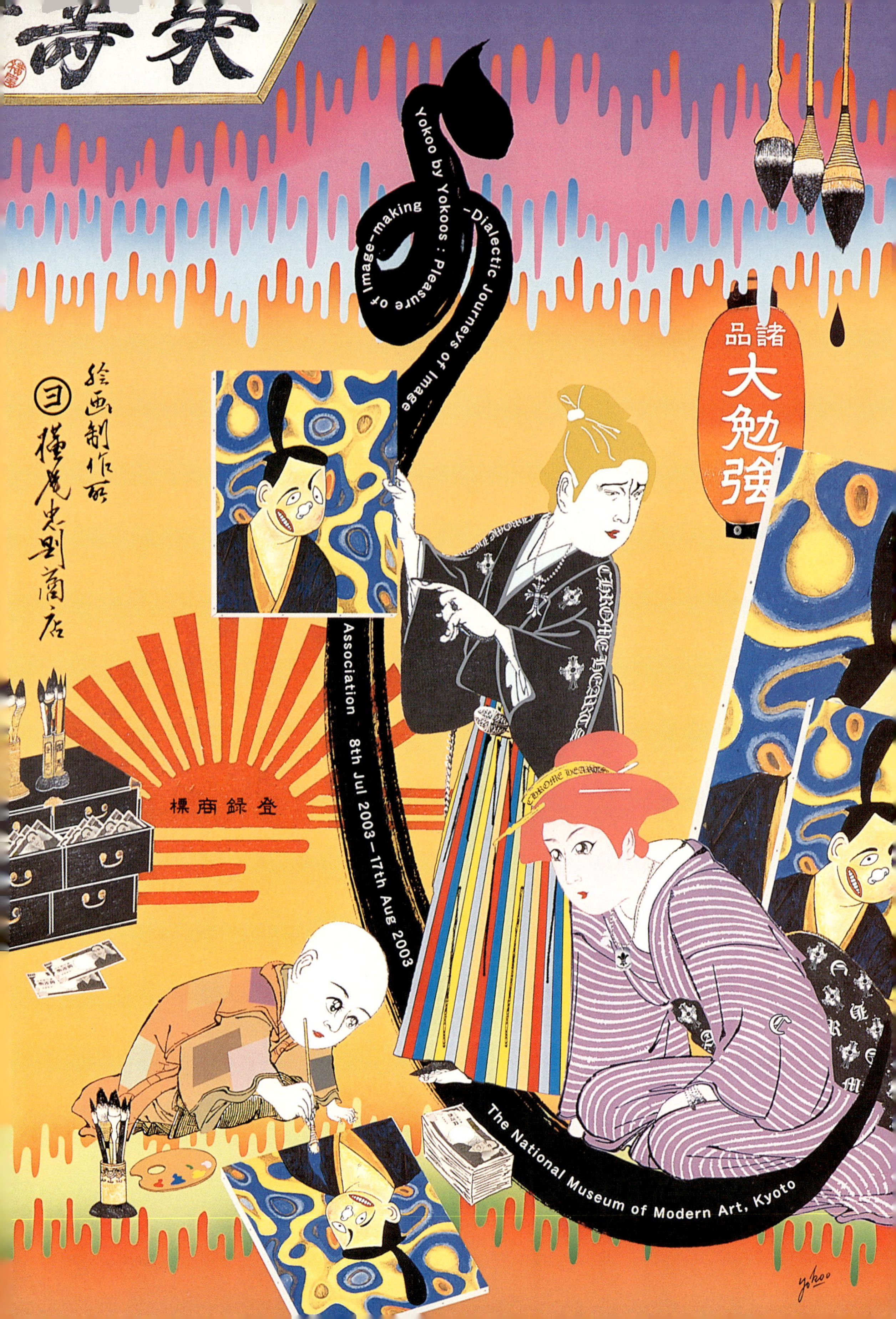

Yokoo by Yokoos : Pleasure of Image-making
-Dialectic Journeys of Image
Association
8th Jul 2003–17th Aug 2003
The National Museum of Modern Art, Kyoto
諸品
大勉強
絵画制作所
横尾忠則商店
登録商標
CHROME HEARTS
yokoo

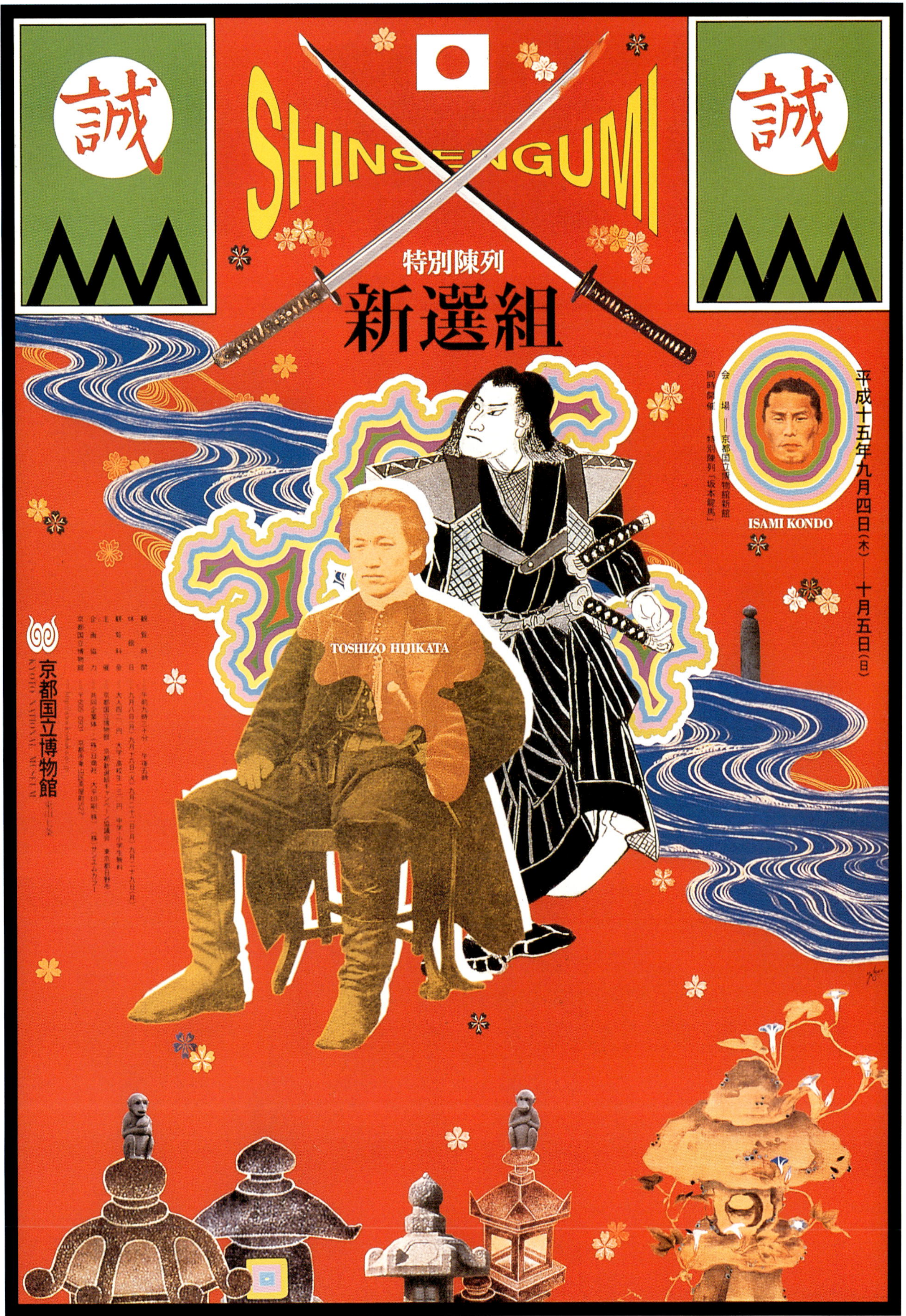

Yokoo's Circus Co., Ltd./Kyoto National Museum

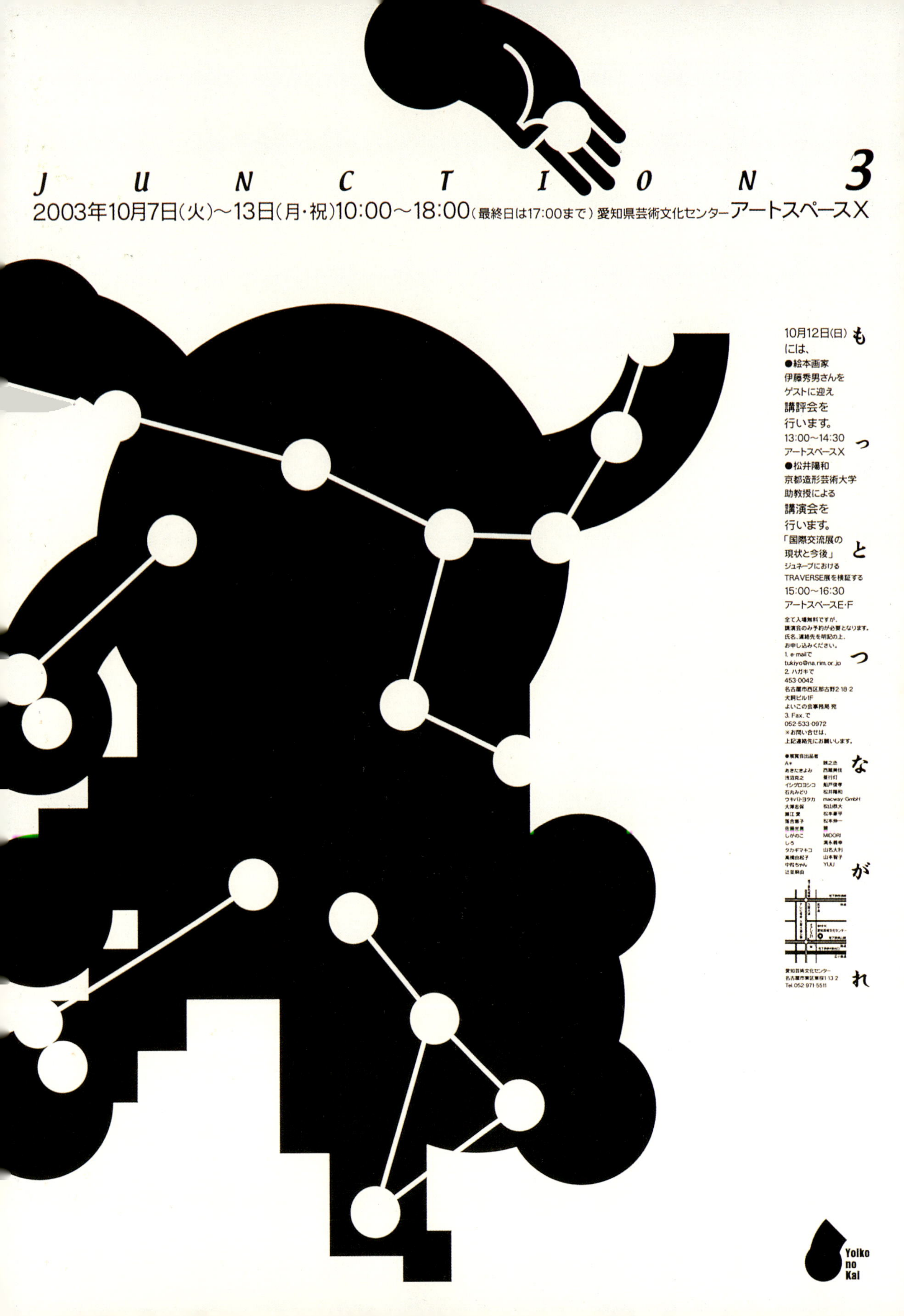

J U N C T I O N 3

2003年10月7日(火)〜13日(月・祝)10:00〜18:00(最終日は17:00まで) 愛知県芸術文化センター アートスペースX

もっとつながれ

10月12日(日)には、

●絵本画家
伊藤秀男さんを
ゲストに迎え
講評会を
行います。
13:00〜14:30
アートスペースX

●松井陽和
京都造形芸術大学
助教授による
講演会を
行います。
「国際交流展の
現状と今後」
ジュネーブにおける
TRAVERSE展を検証する
15:00〜16:30
アートスペースE・F

全て入場無料ですが、
講演会のみ予約が必要となります。
氏名、連絡先を明記の上、
お申し込みください。
1. e-mailで
tukiyo@na.rim.or.jp
2. ハガキで
453-0042
名古屋市西区那古野2-18-2
大野ビル1F
よいこの会事務局 宛
3. Fax.で
052-533-0972
※お問い合せは、
上記連絡先にお願いします。

●展覧会出品者

A+	誠之助
あきたきよみ	西願美佳
浅沼克之	[illegible]
イシグロヨシコ	船戸俊孝
石丸みどり	松井陽和
ウキバトヨタカ	macway GmbH
大澤志保	松山恭大
[illegible]	松本慶平
落合恵子	松本伸一
佐藤世貴	[illegible]
しがのこ	MIDORI
しろ	清水義幸
タカギマキコ	山名大判
髙橋由起子	山本智子
中野ちゃん	YUU
辻並麻由	

愛知芸術文化センター
名古屋市東区東桜1-13-2
Tel.052-971-5511

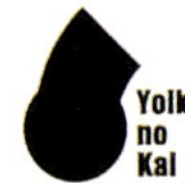

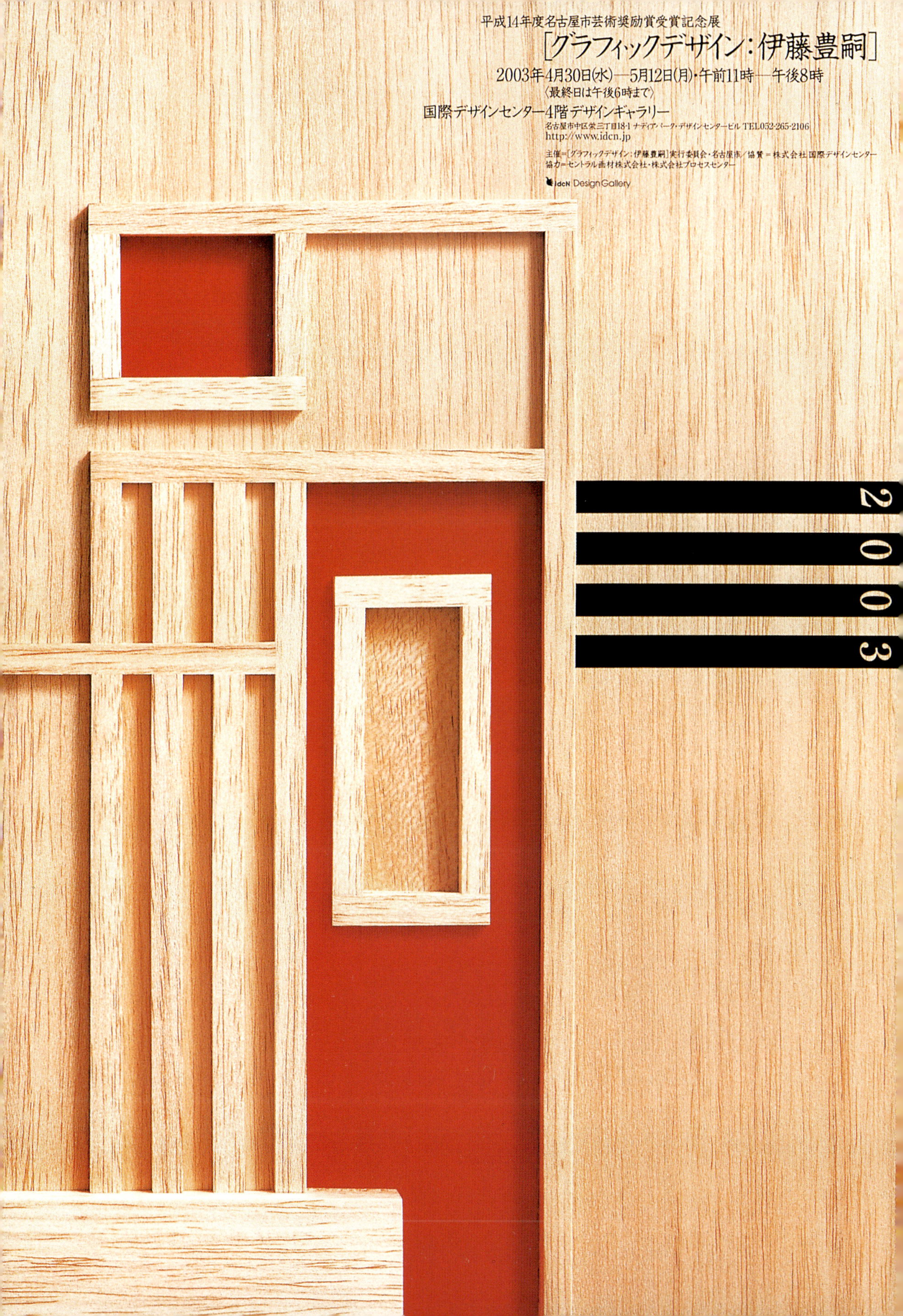
平成14年度名古屋市芸術奨励賞受賞記念展
[グラフィックデザイン：伊藤豊嗣]
2003年4月30日(水)—5月12日(月)・午前11時—午後8時
〈最終日は午後6時まで〉
国際デザインセンター4階デザインギャラリー
名古屋市中区栄三丁目18-1 ナディアパーク・デザインセンタービル TEL052-265-2106
http://www.idcn.jp
主催=[グラフィックデザイン：伊藤豊嗣]実行委員会・名古屋市／協賛=株式会社国際デザインセンター
協力=セントラル画材株式会社・株式会社プロセスセンター
idcN DesignGallery
2003

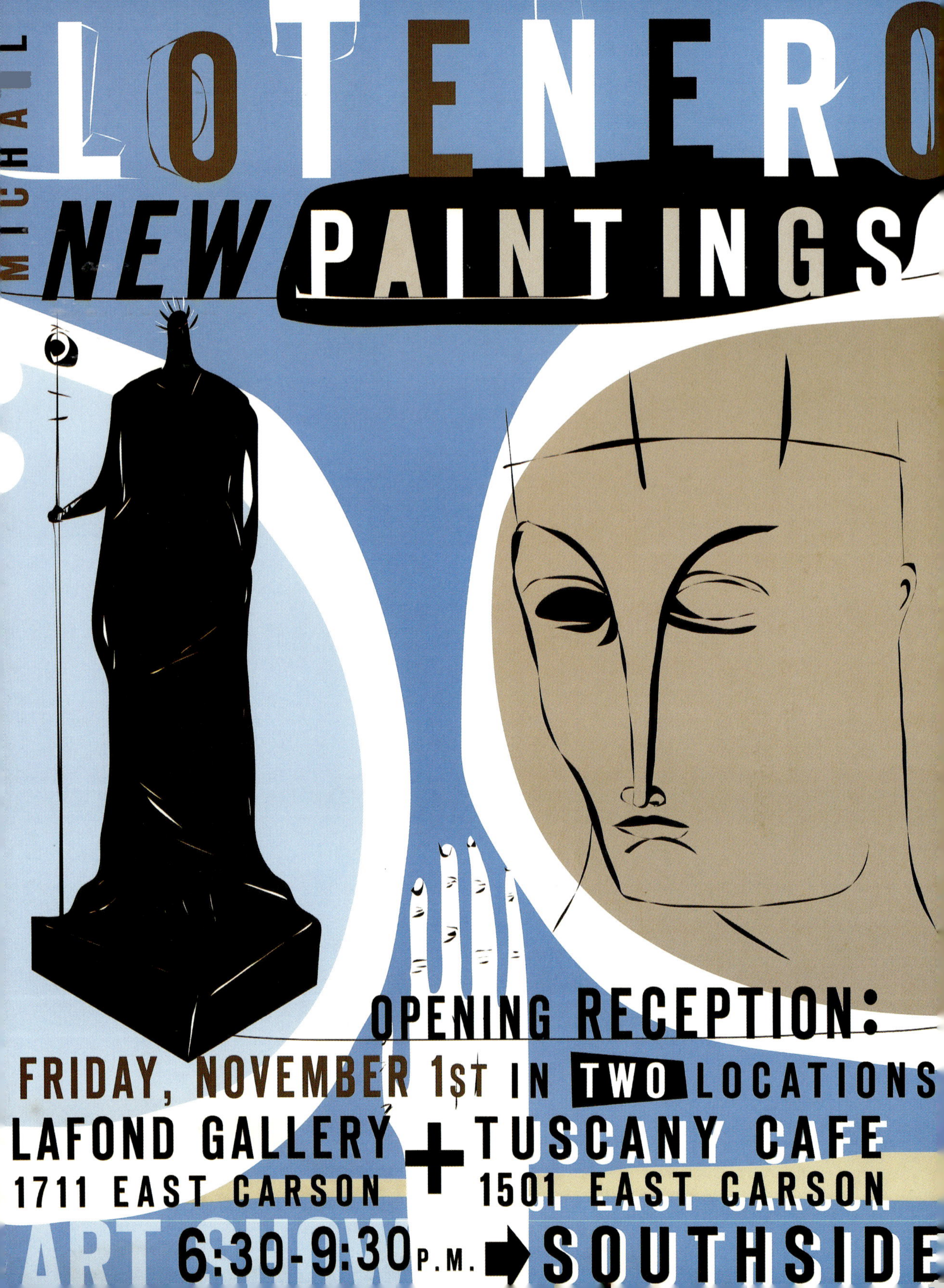
MICHAIL
LOTENERO
NEW PAINTINGS
OPENING RECEPTION:
FRIDAY, NOVEMBER 1ST IN TWO LOCATIONS
LAFOND GALLERY + TUSCANY CAFE
1711 EAST CARSON
1501 EAST CARSON
ART SHOW
6:30-9:30 P.M.
SOUTHSIDE

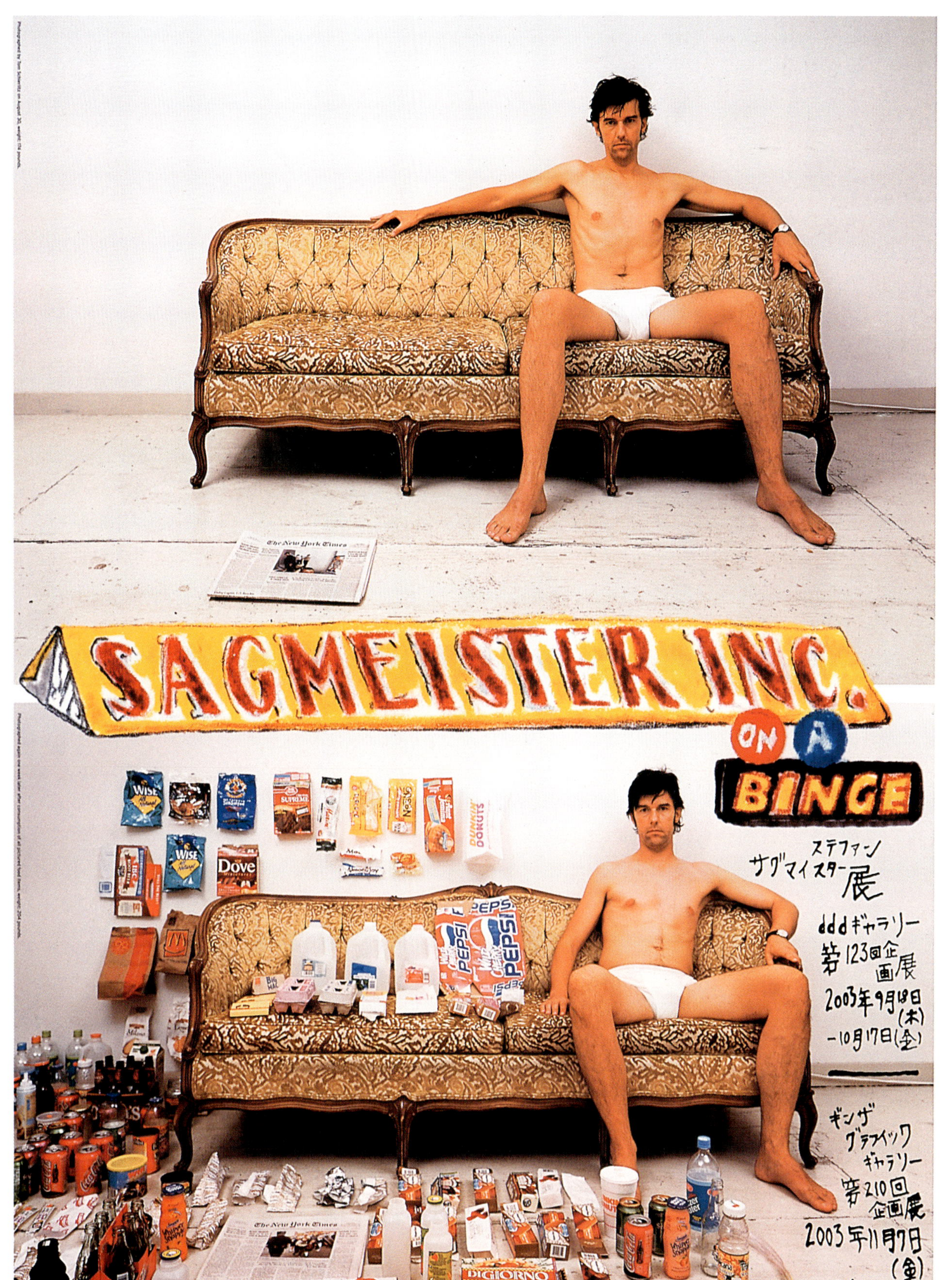

SAGMEISTER INC.
ON A
BINGE
ステファン
サグマイスター展
dddギャラリー
第123回企画展
2003年9月18日(木)
-10月17日(金)
ギンザ
グラフィック
ギャラリー
第210回
企画展
2003年11月7日
(金)
-26日(水)
後援:オーストリア大使館

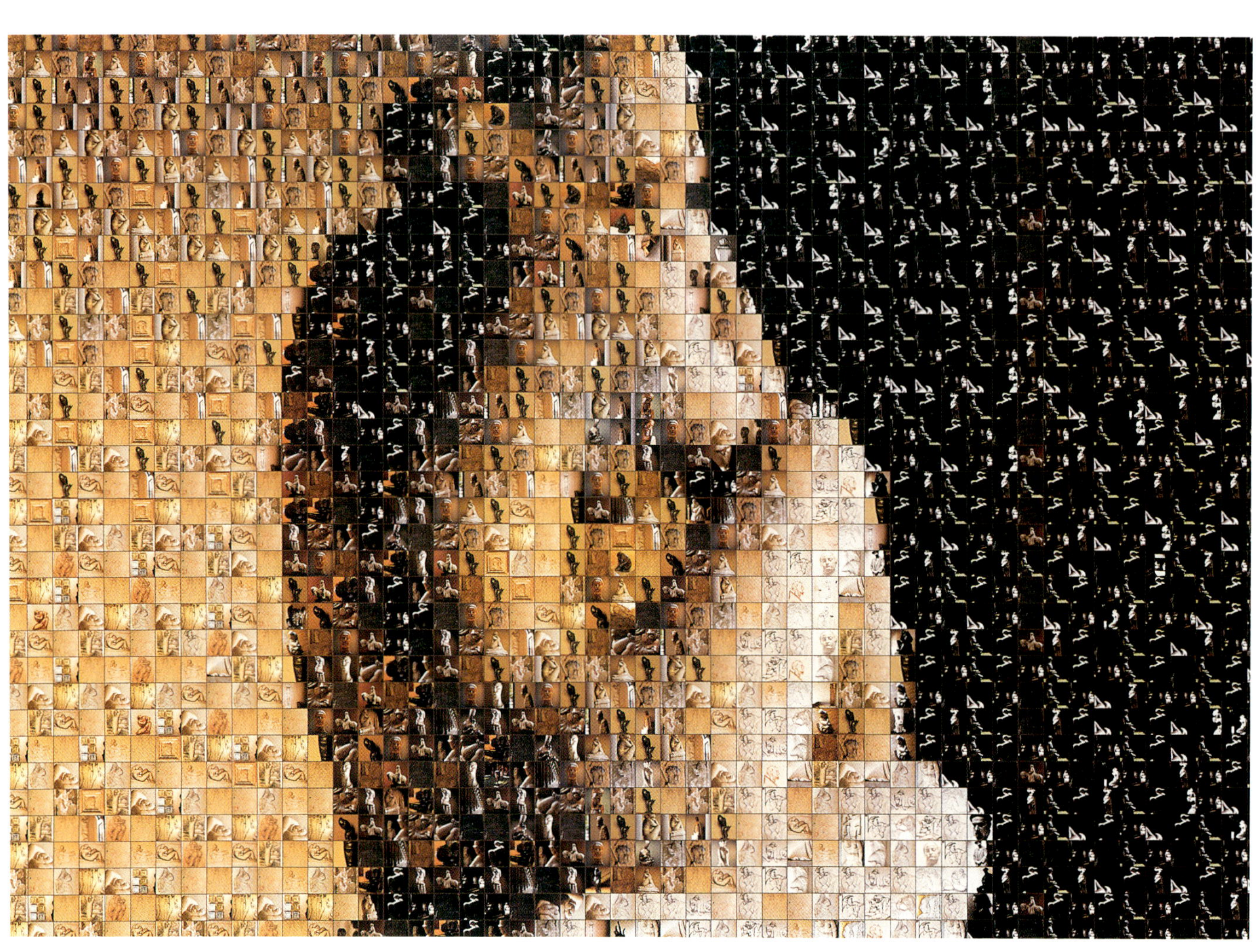

Studio International/Fundacija Ivana Mestrovica (Ivan Mestrovic Foundation)

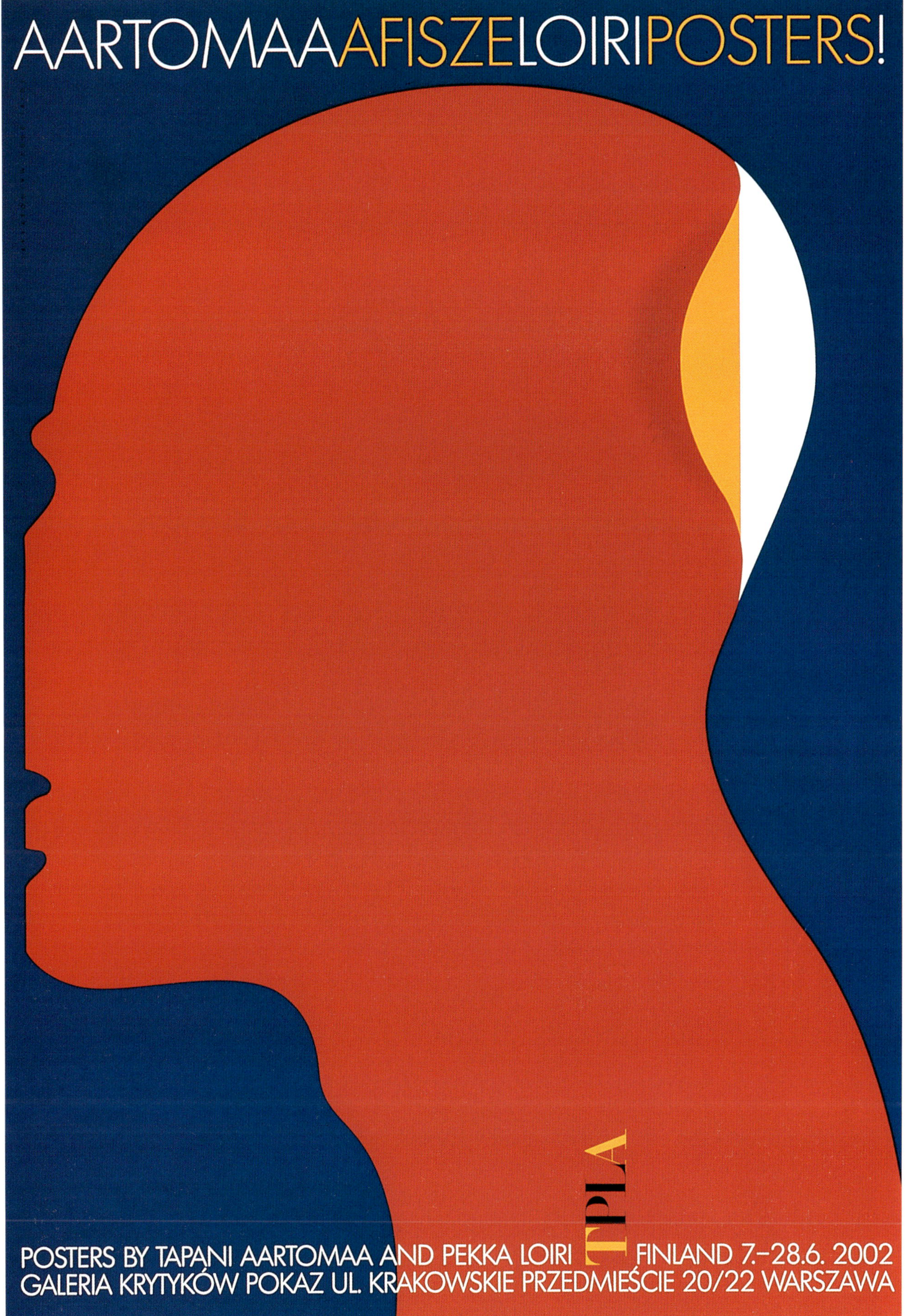

Original Loiri Inc./Galeria Krytykow Pokaz

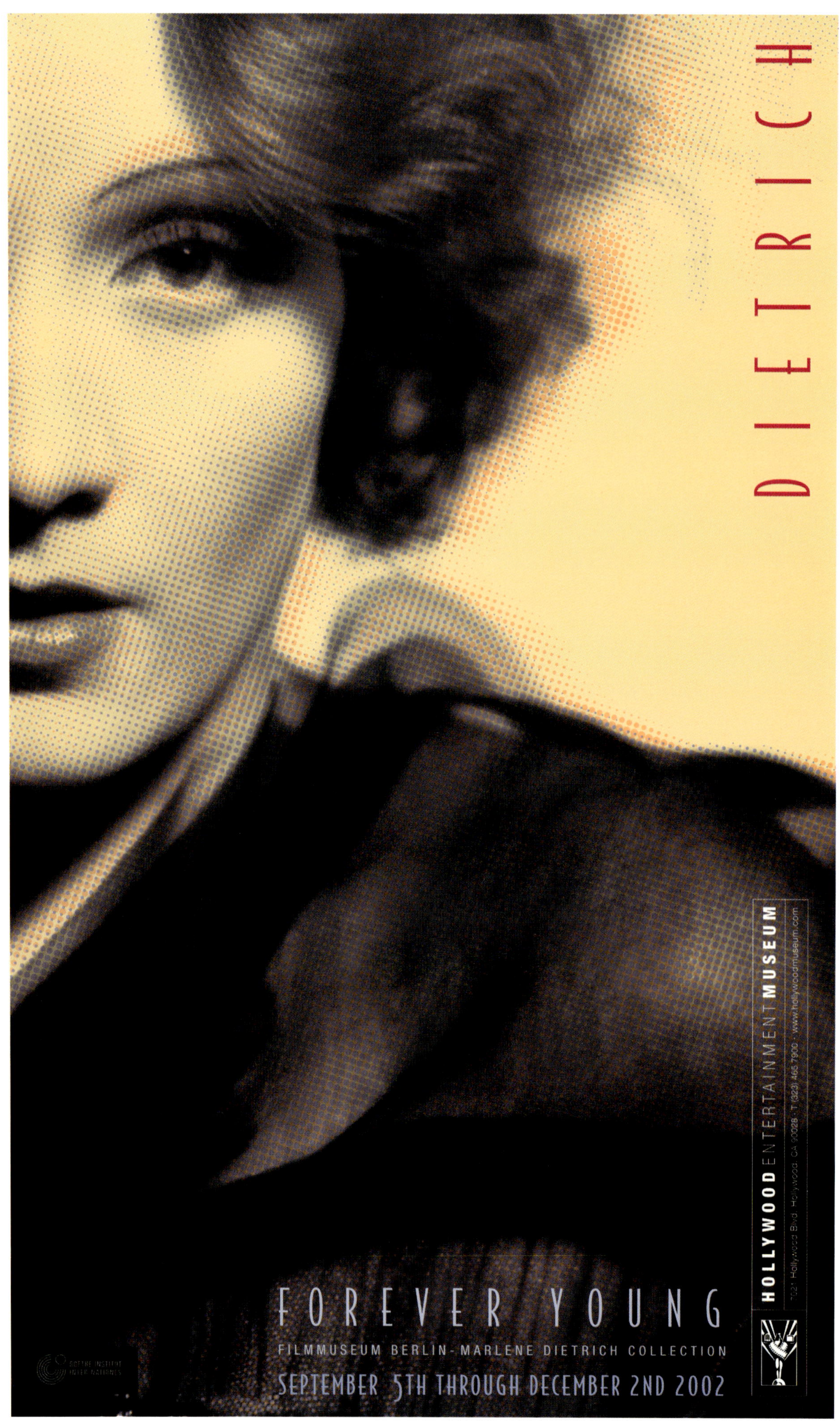

Garza Group Communications/Hollywood Entertainment Museum

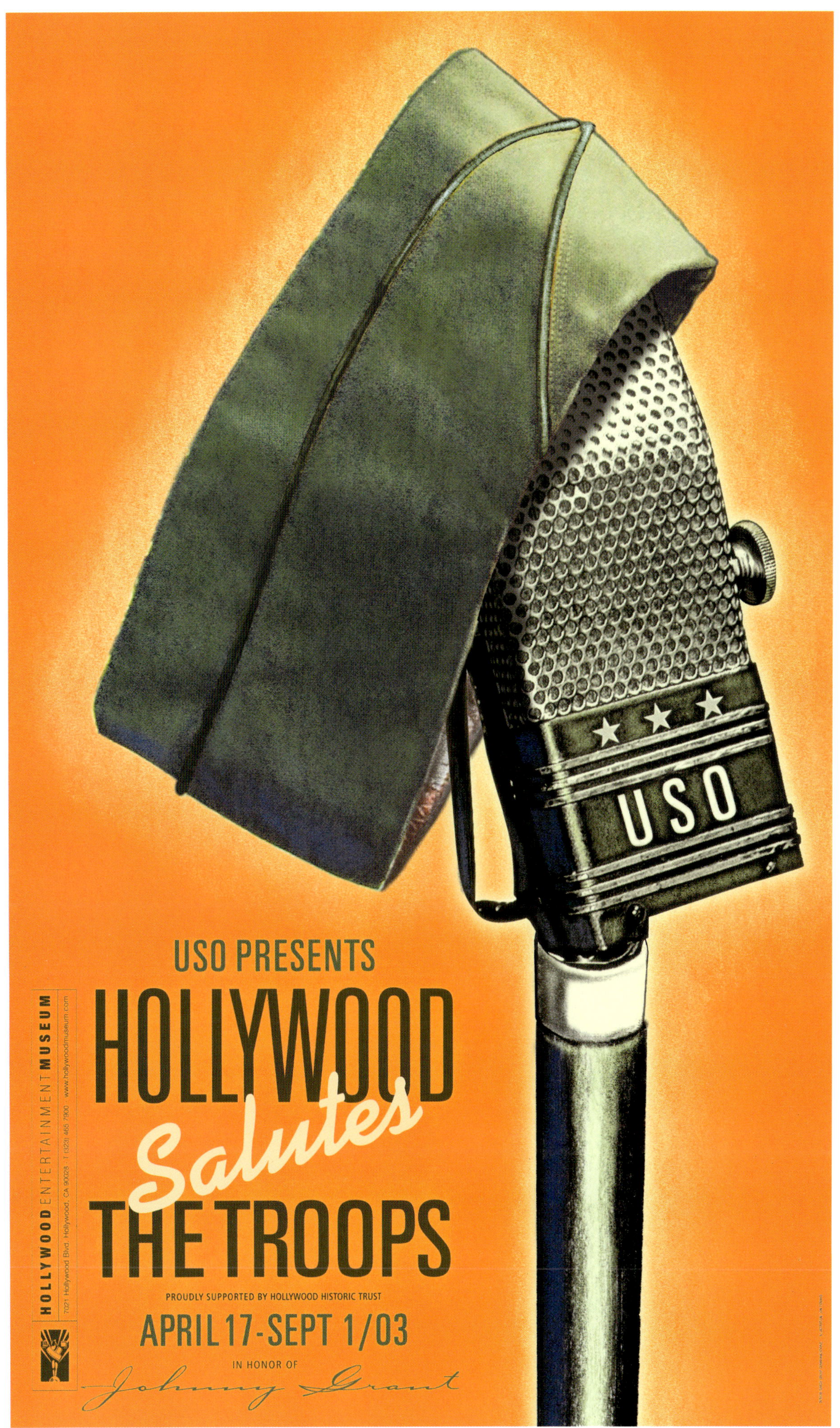

Garza Group Communications/Hollywood Entertainment Museum

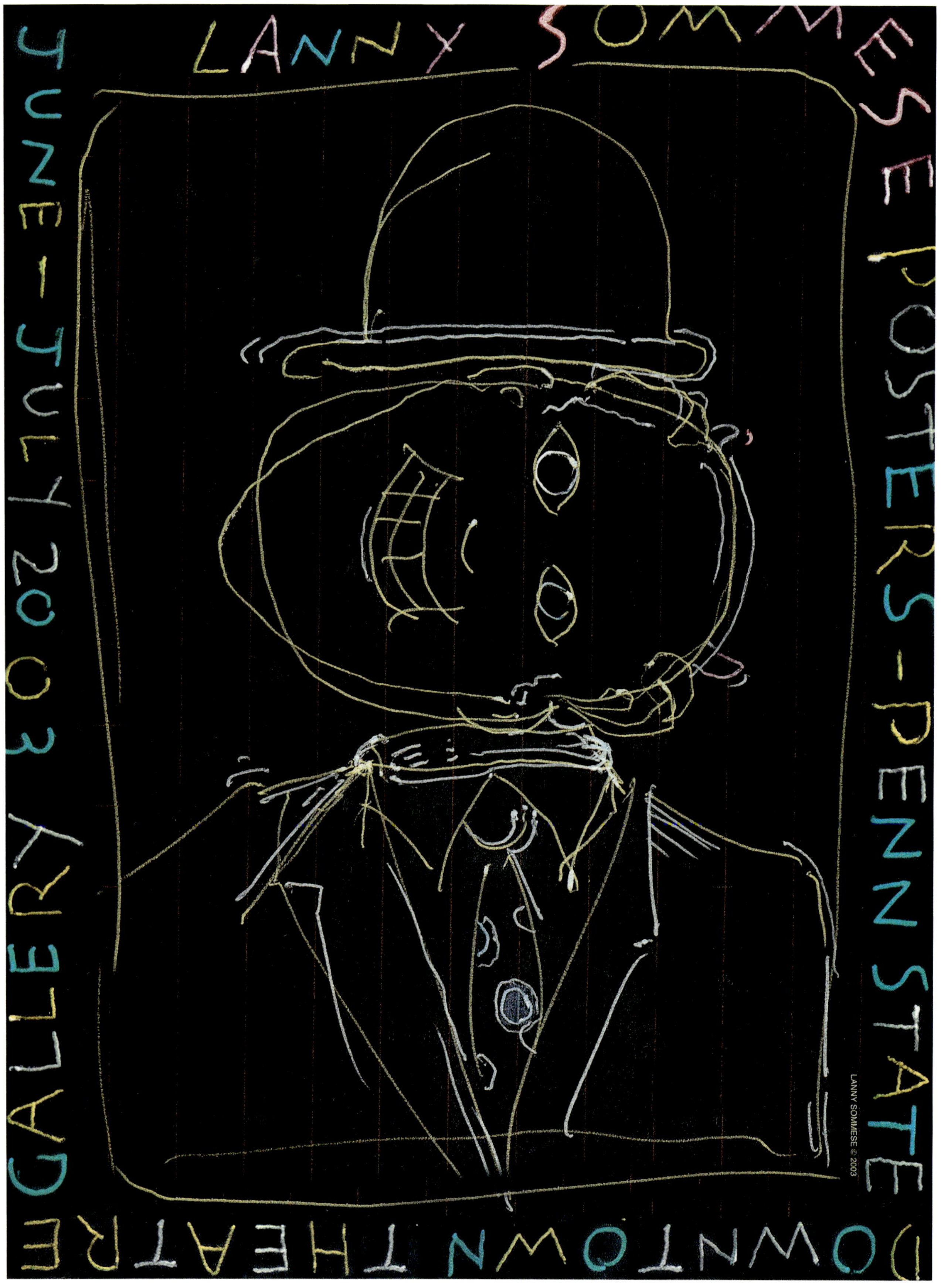

Sommese Design/Penn State College of the Arts and Architecture

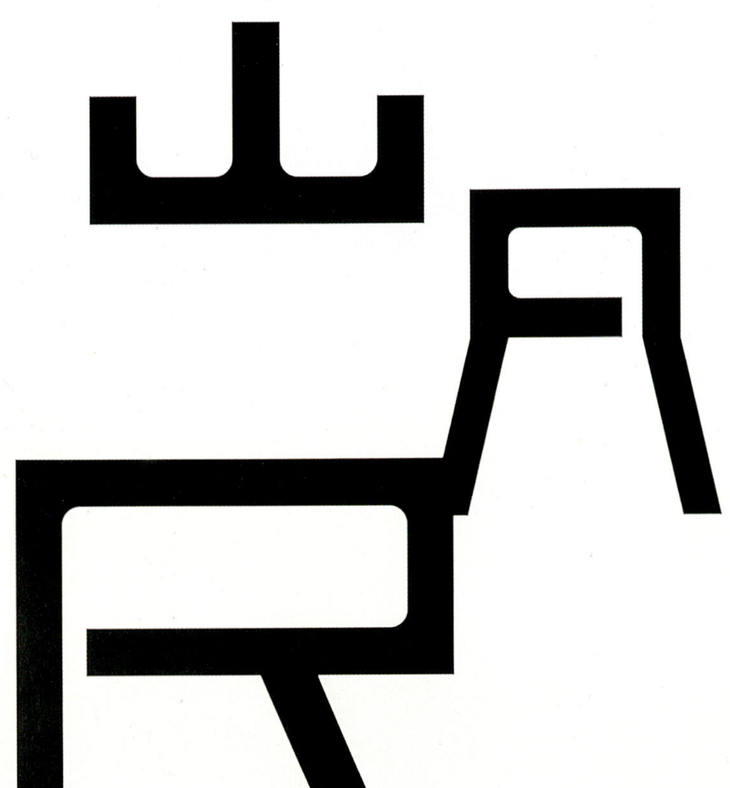

纸。生活

将战意化为暖意

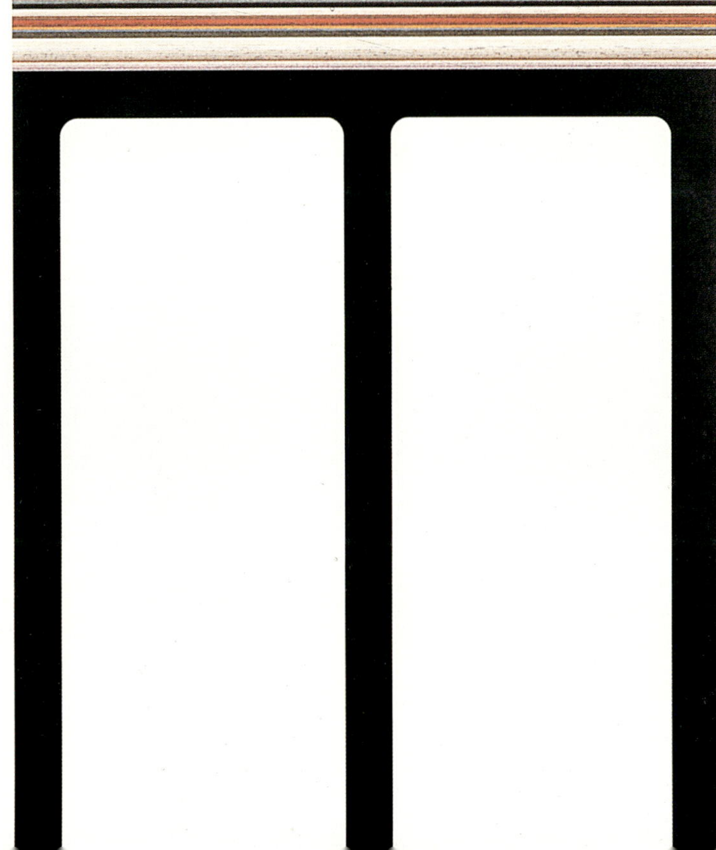

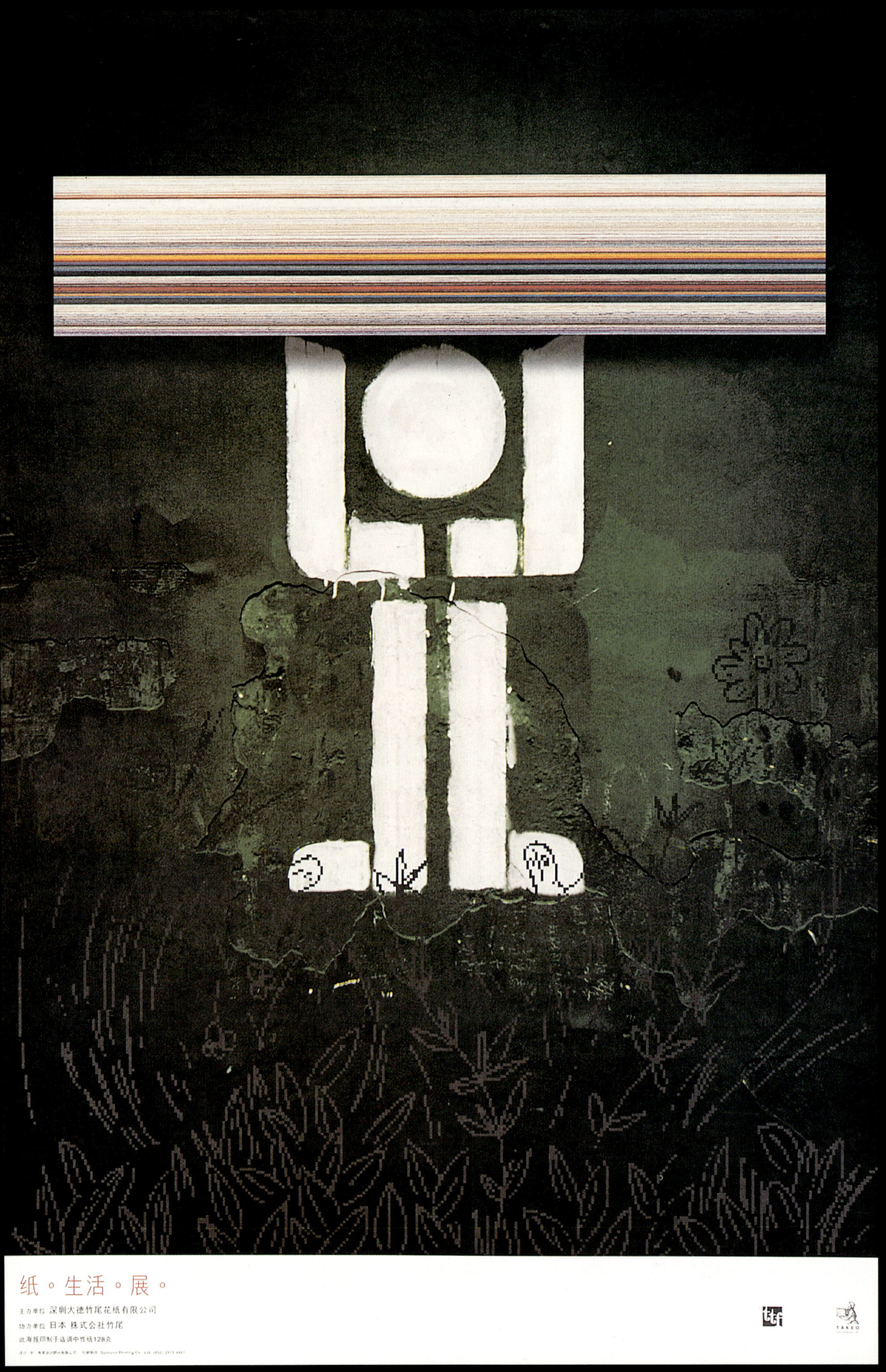

纸 ◦ 生活 ◦ 展 ◦

主办单位 深圳大德竹尾花纸有限公司

协办单位 日本 株式会社竹尾

此海报印制于适调中性纸128克

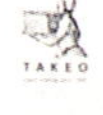

Amazing Angle Design Consultants Ltd./Shenzhen Tai Tak Takeo Fine Paper Co., Ltd.

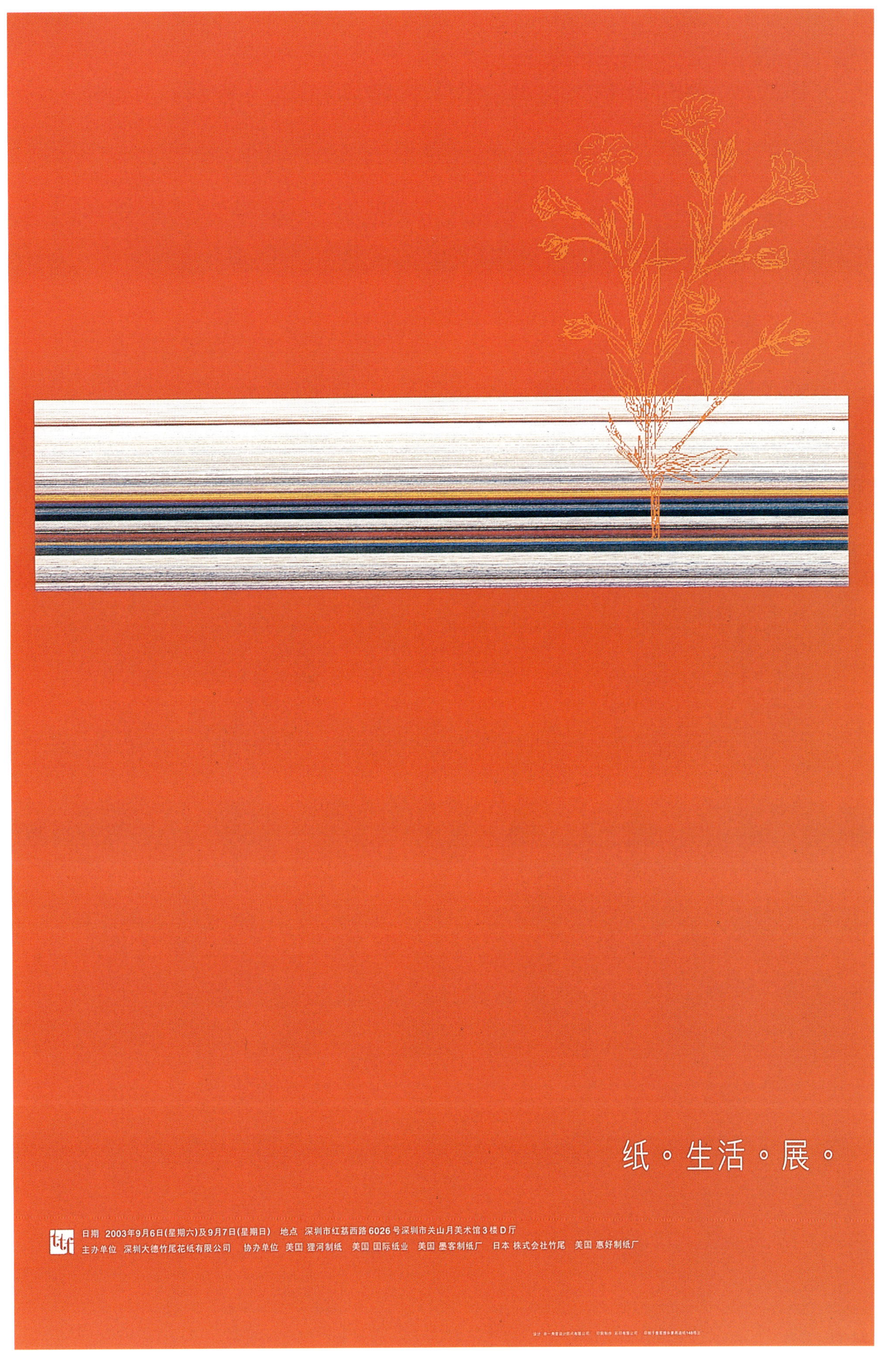

Amazing Angle Design Consultants Ltd./Shenzhen Tai Tak Takeo Fine Paper Co., Ltd.

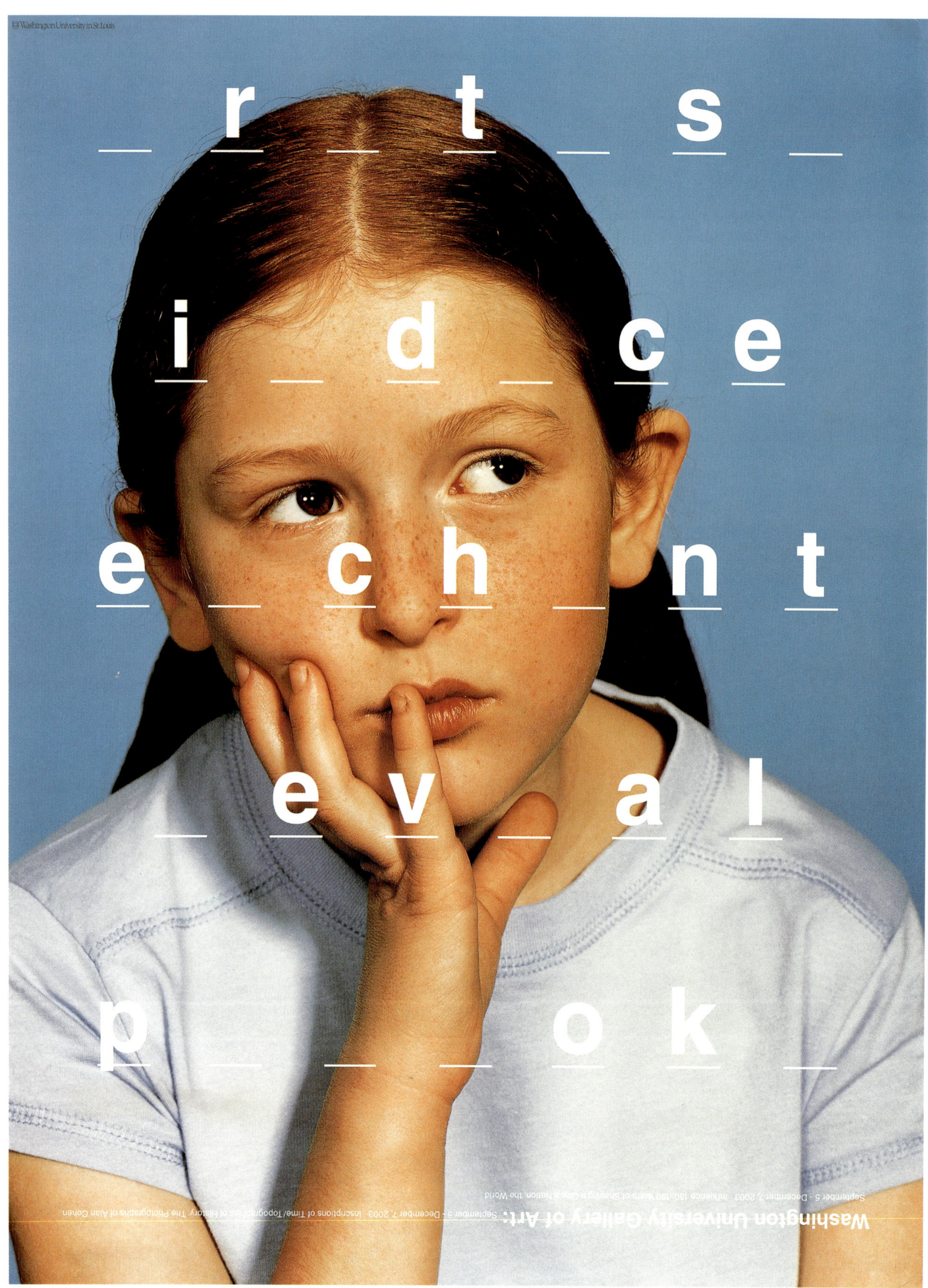

Arnold Worldwide - St. Louis/Washington University Gallery of Art

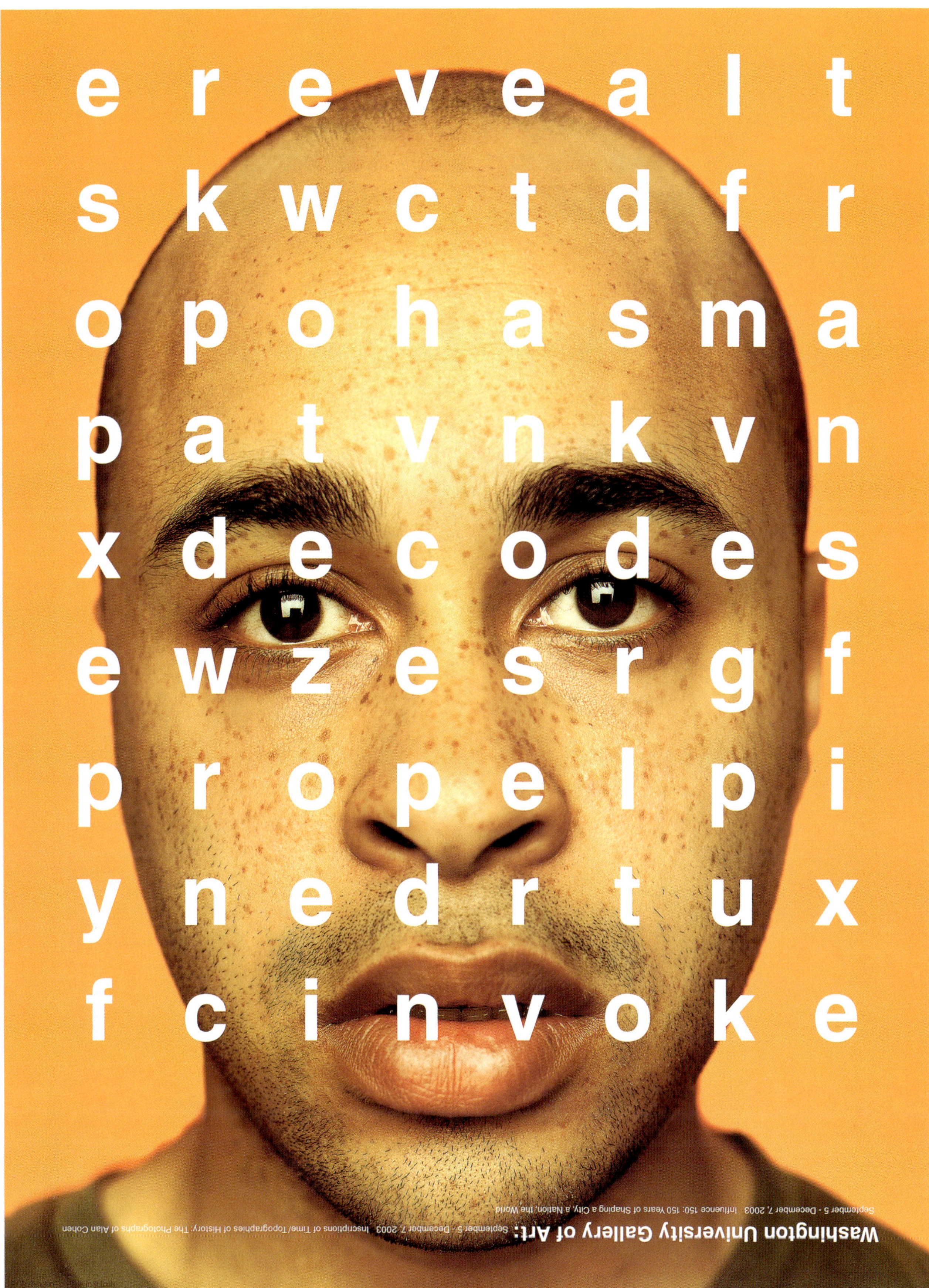

Arnold Worldwide - St. Louis/Washington University Gallery of Art

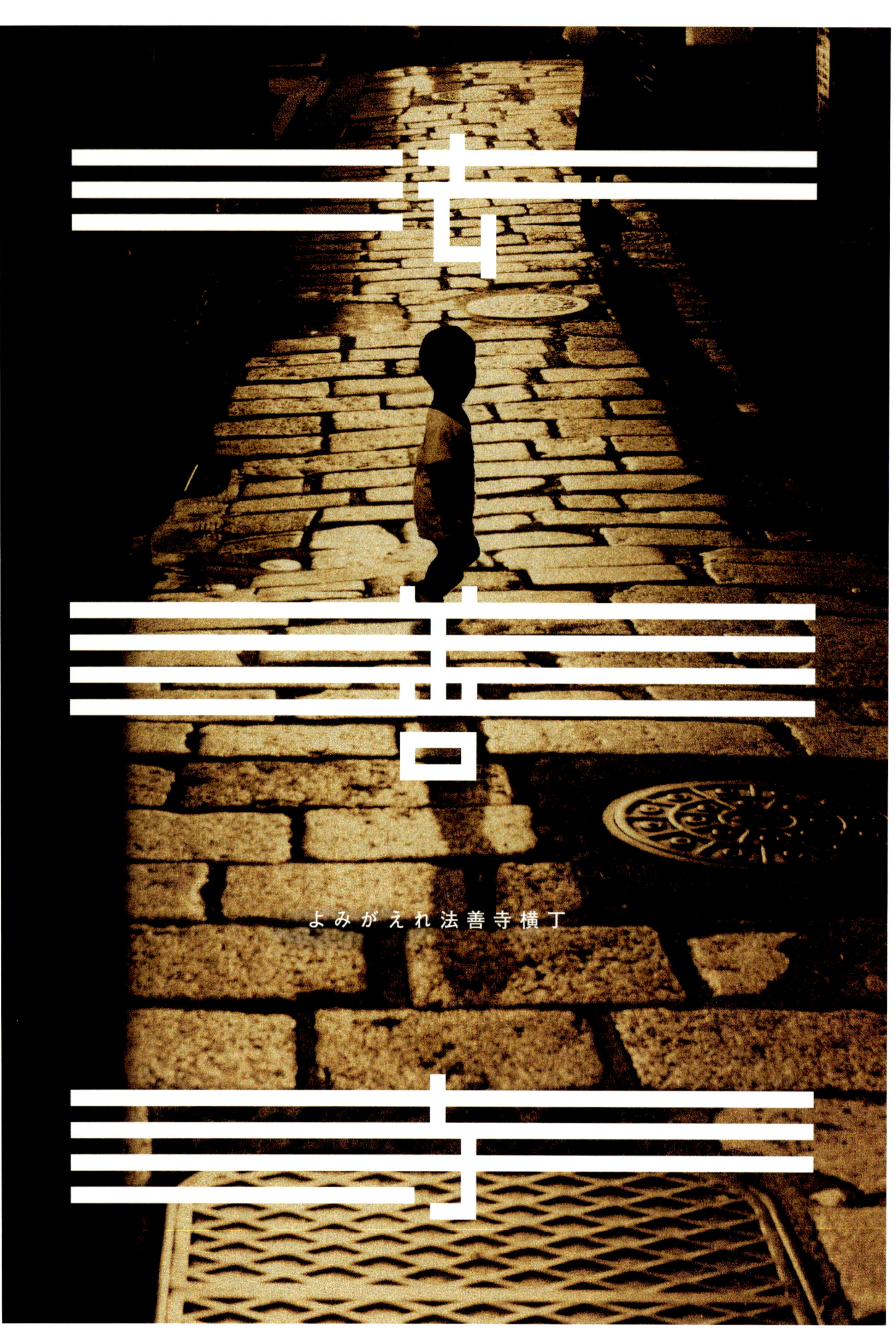

Kokokumaru Inc./Japan Graphic Designers Association

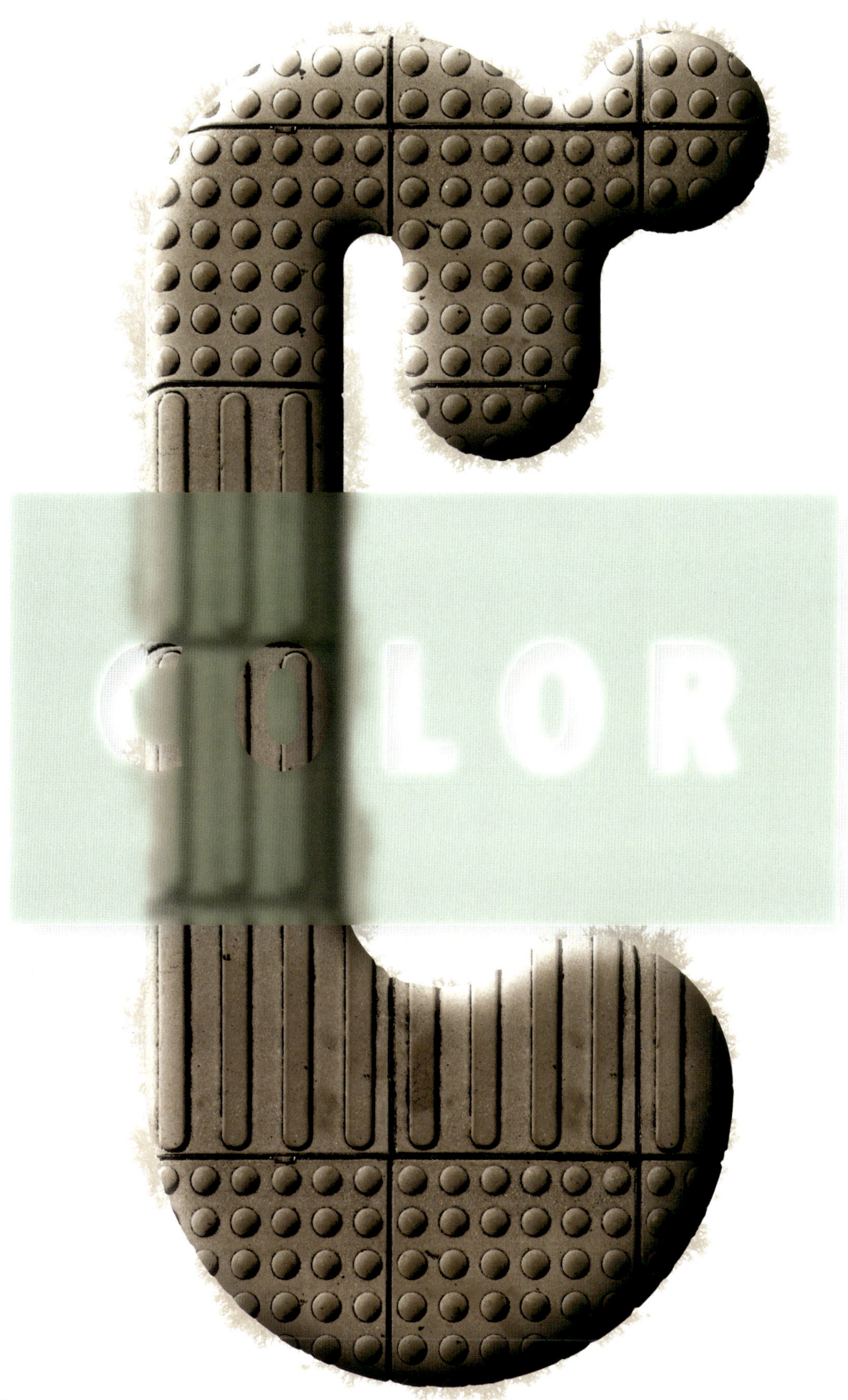
COLOR
WcLock

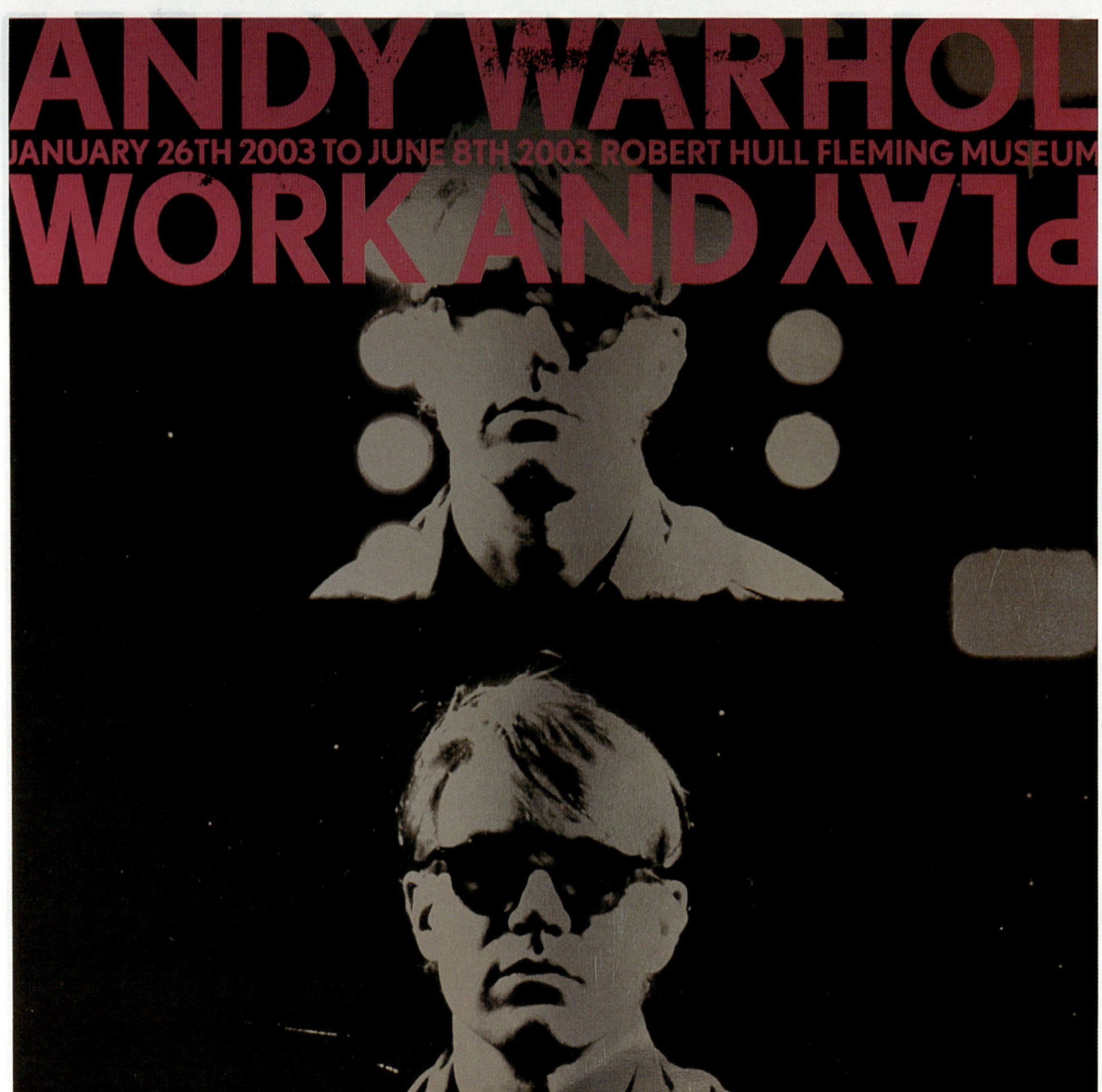
ANDY WARHOL
JANUARY 26TH 2003 TO JUNE 8TH 2003 ROBERT HULL FLEMING MUSEUM
WORK AND PLAY

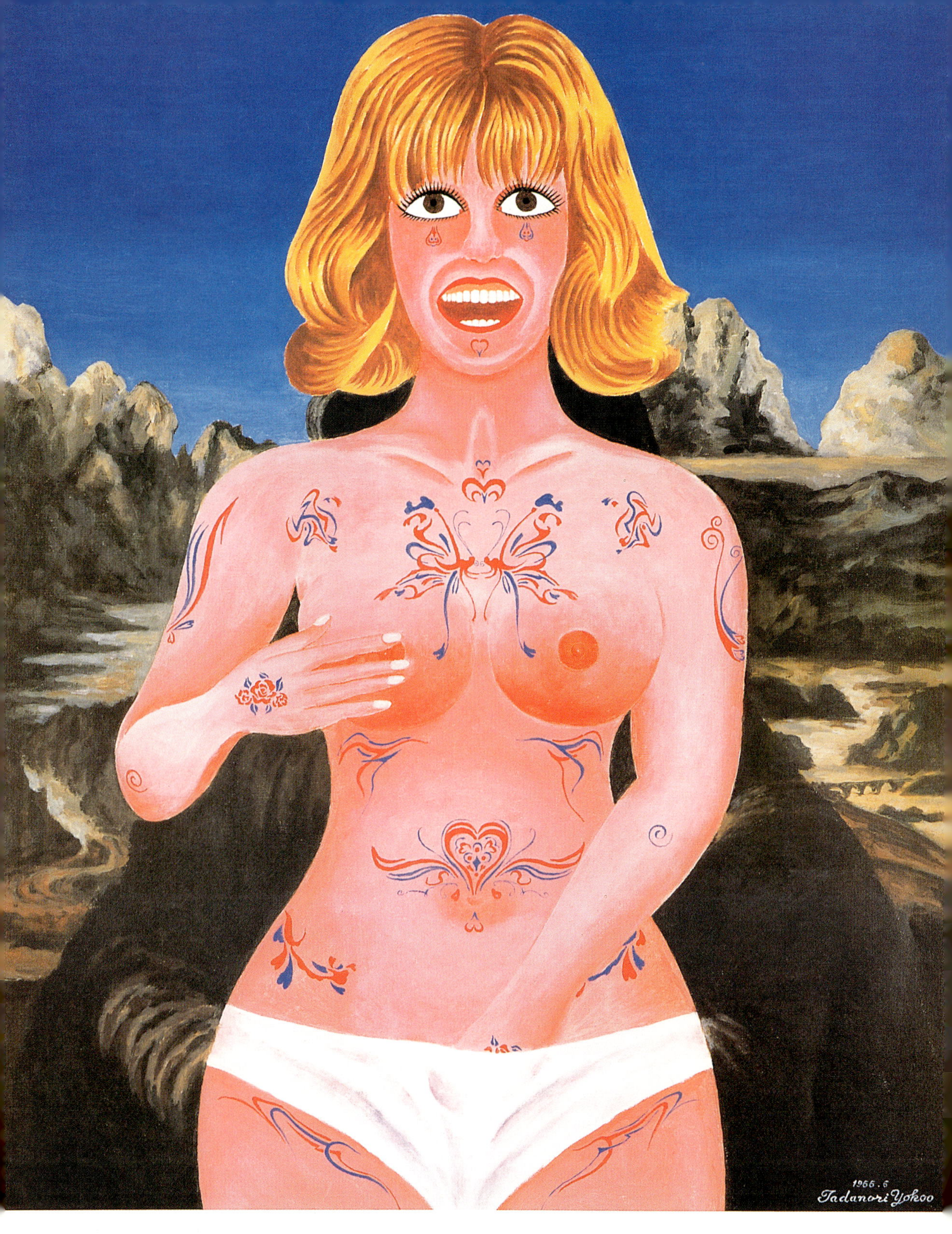

ISSEY MIYAKE

BY NAOKI TAKIZAWA

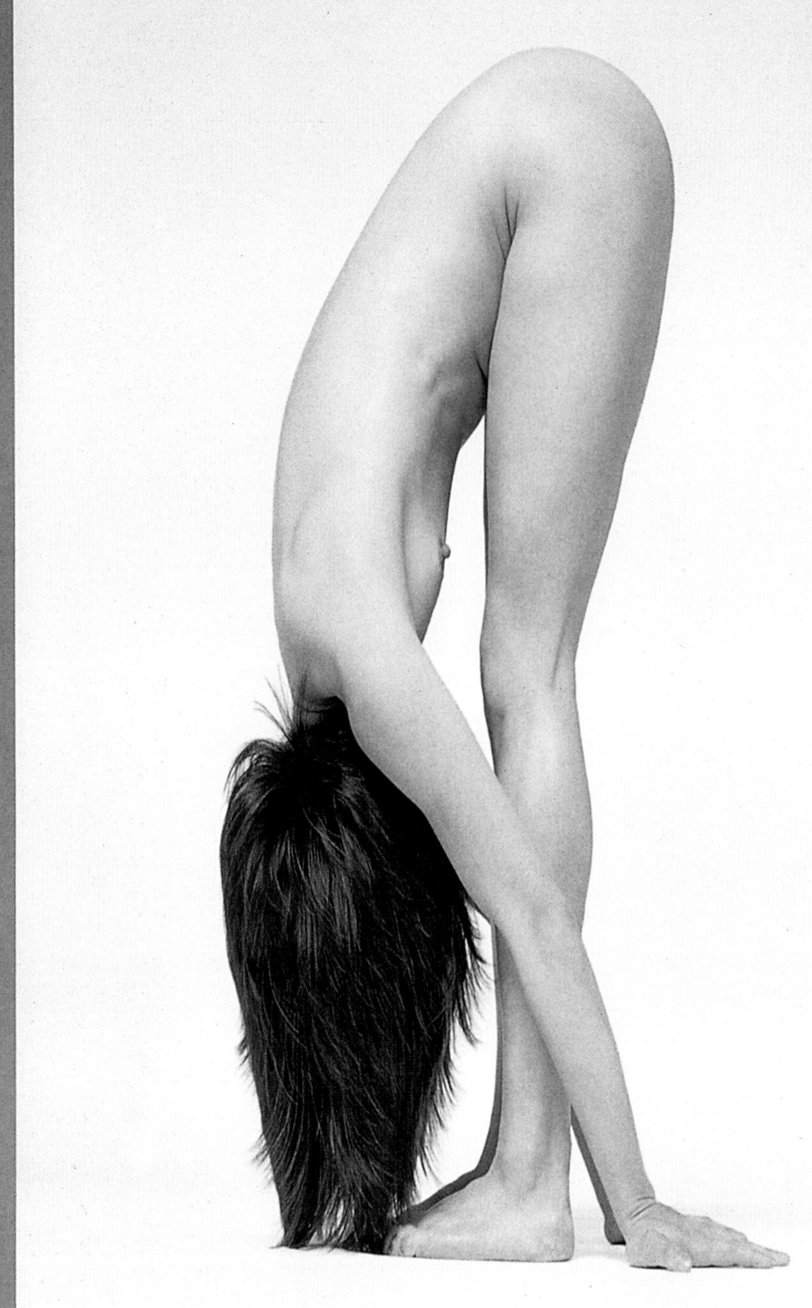
with thanks to Getty Images
exhibition [21st century platinum]
photography by peter dazeley
The Coningsby Gallery, 30 Tottenham Street, London W1 T4RJ
OPEN Monday - Saturday 9am - 6pm, Sunday 11am - 5pm
Nearest Tube station Goodge Street
21st July - 2nd August 2003

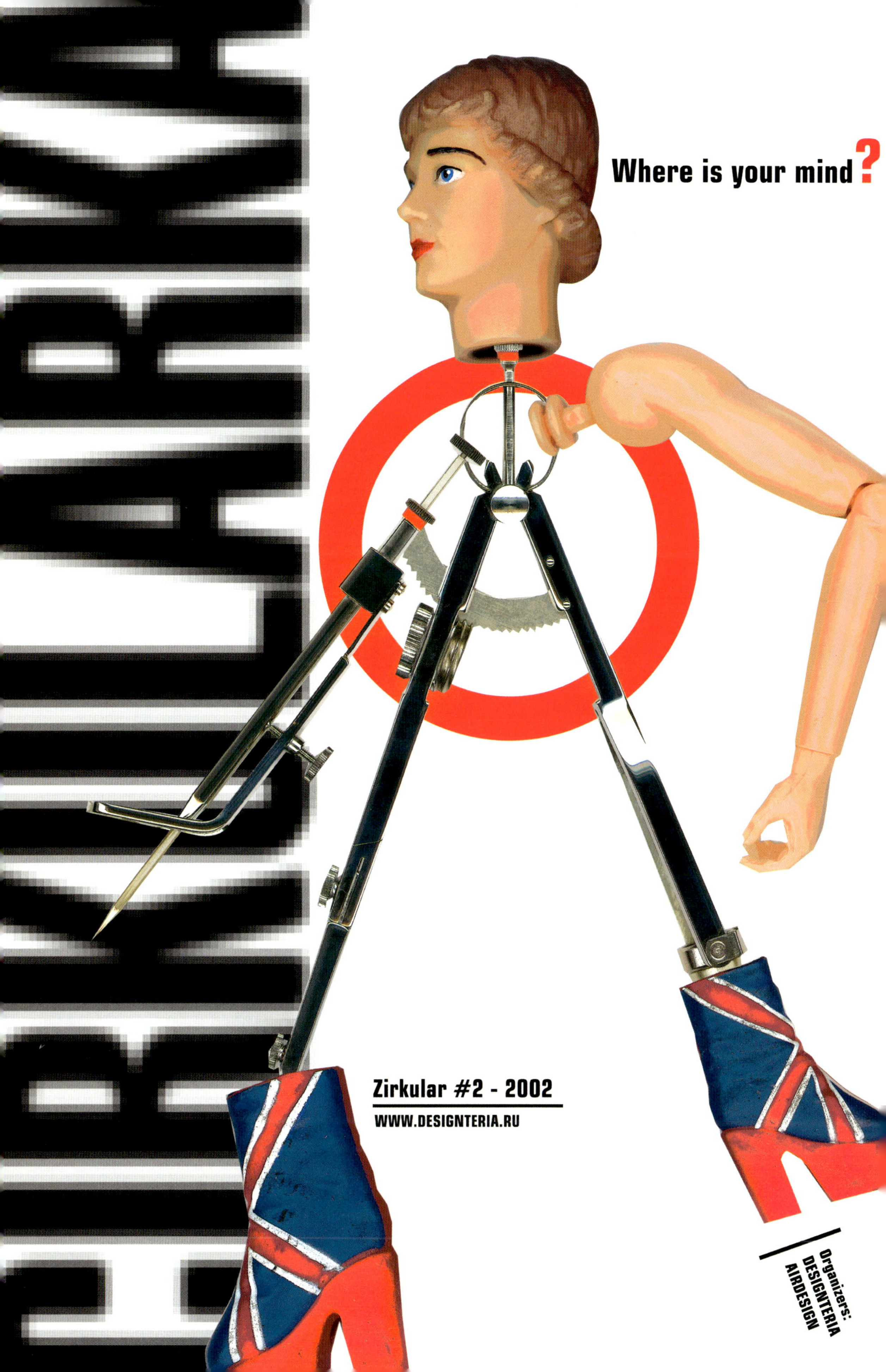
Where is your mind?
Zirkular #2 - 2002
WWW.DESIGNTERIA.RU
Organizers:
DESIGNTERIA
AIRDESIGN

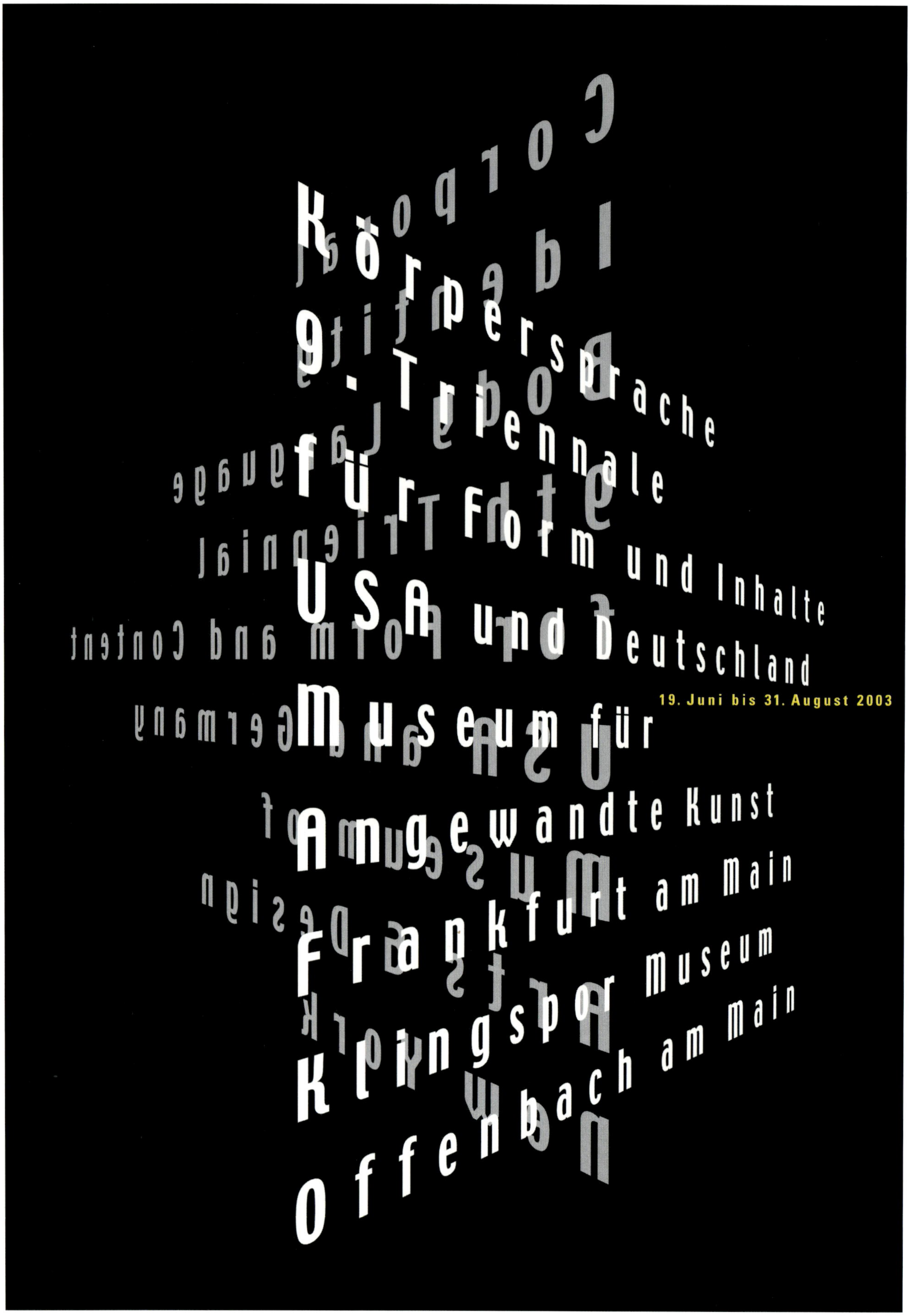

Körpersprache
9. Triennale
für Form und Inhalte
USA und Deutschland
19. Juni bis 31. August 2003
Museum für
Angewandte Kunst
Frankfurt am Main
Klingspor Museum
Offenbach am Main

Uwe Loesch/Museum of Arts & Crafts New York, Museum fur angewandte Kunst, Frankfurt am Main, Klingspor Museum, Offenbach

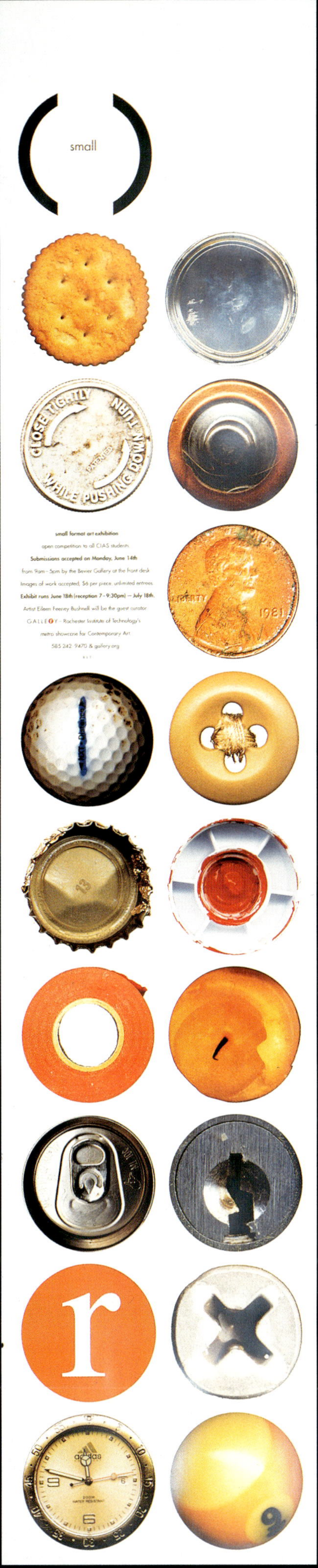

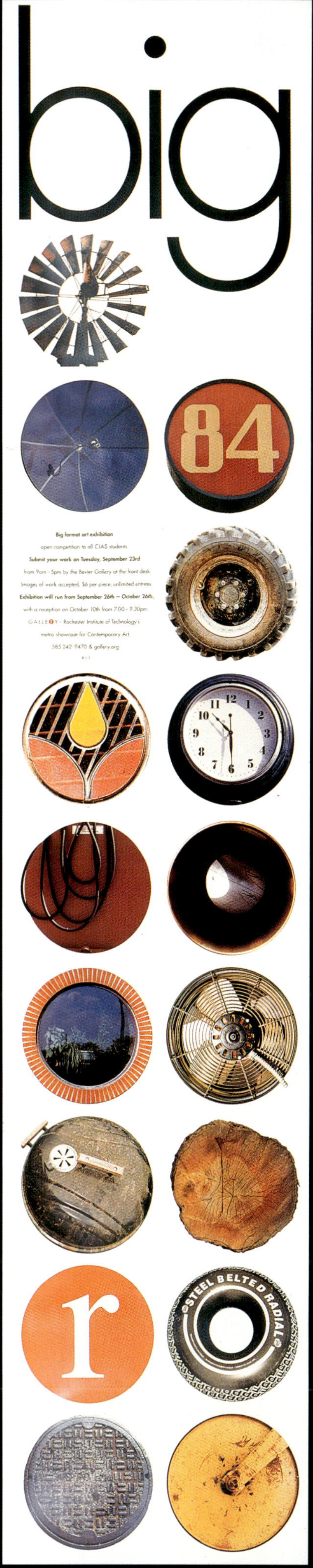

(small)

small format art exhibition

open competition to all CIAS students.

Submissions accepted on Monday, June 14th

from 9am – 5pm by the Bevier Gallery at the front desk.

Images of work accepted, $6 per piece, unlimited entrees.

Exhibit runs June 18th (reception 7 – 9:30pm) — July 18th.

Artist Eileen Feeney Bushnell will be the guest curator.

GALLERY – Rochester Institute of Technology's

metro showcase for Contemporary Art.

585 242 9470 & gallery.org

RIT

big

Big format art exhibition

open competition to all CIAS students.

Submit your work on Tuesday, September 23rd

from 9am – 5pm by the Bevier Gallery at the front desk.

Images of work accepted, $6 per piece, unlimited entrees.

Exhibition will run from September 26th — October 26th,

with a reception on October 10th from 7:00 – 9:30pm

GALLERY – Rochester Institute of Technology's

metro showcase for Contemporary Art.

585 242 9470 & gallery.org

RIT

3dub Design/Gallery R

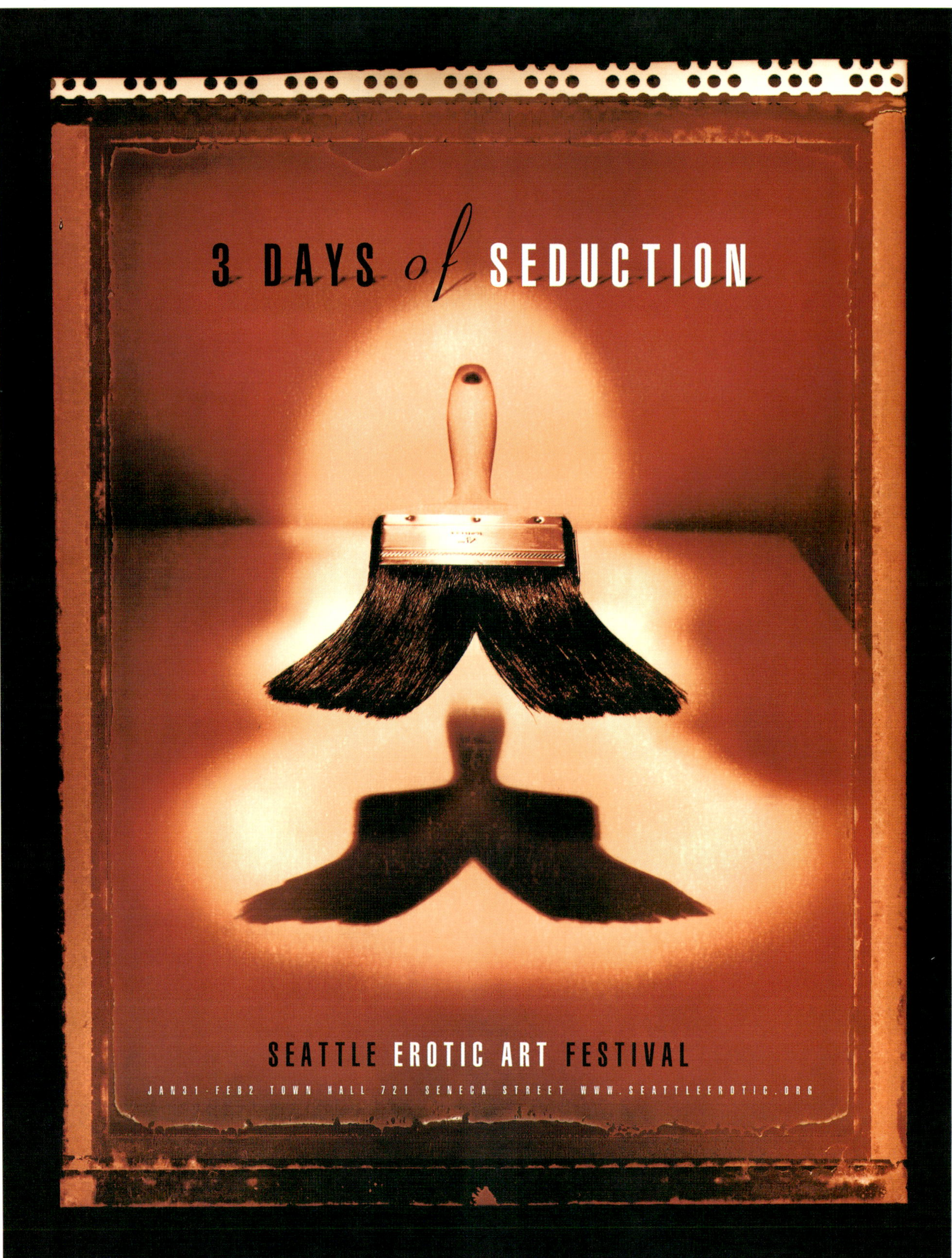

Cole & Weber/Red Cell/Seattle Erotic Art Festival

JAGDA MEMBERS' POSTER EXHIBITION 2003

ベストワン・ポスター展

日本グラフィックデザイナー協会会員によるベストワンポスター展（JAGDA年鑑1981年～2003年に掲載された作品から自選）

MY BEST POSTER EXHIBITION

2003年10月8日(水)－11日(土)

会場＝国際会議場2号館1階「展示室」／入場無料

主催＝世界グラフィックデザイン会議開催運営会
構成団体（愛知県、名古屋市、(社)日本グラフィックデザイナー協会、(財)国際デザイン交流協会、(株)国際デザインセンター、(財)日本産業デザイン振興会、名古屋商工会議所、(社)中部経済連合会）
後援＝経済産業省、文化庁、外務省、国土交通省、愛知県教育委員会、名古屋市教育委員会
協力＝国際観光振興会

世界グラフィックデザイン会議・名古屋

VISUALOGUE

2003年10月8日(水)–13日(月·祝)
名古屋国際会議場
www.visualogue.com

Design by Shin Matsunaga

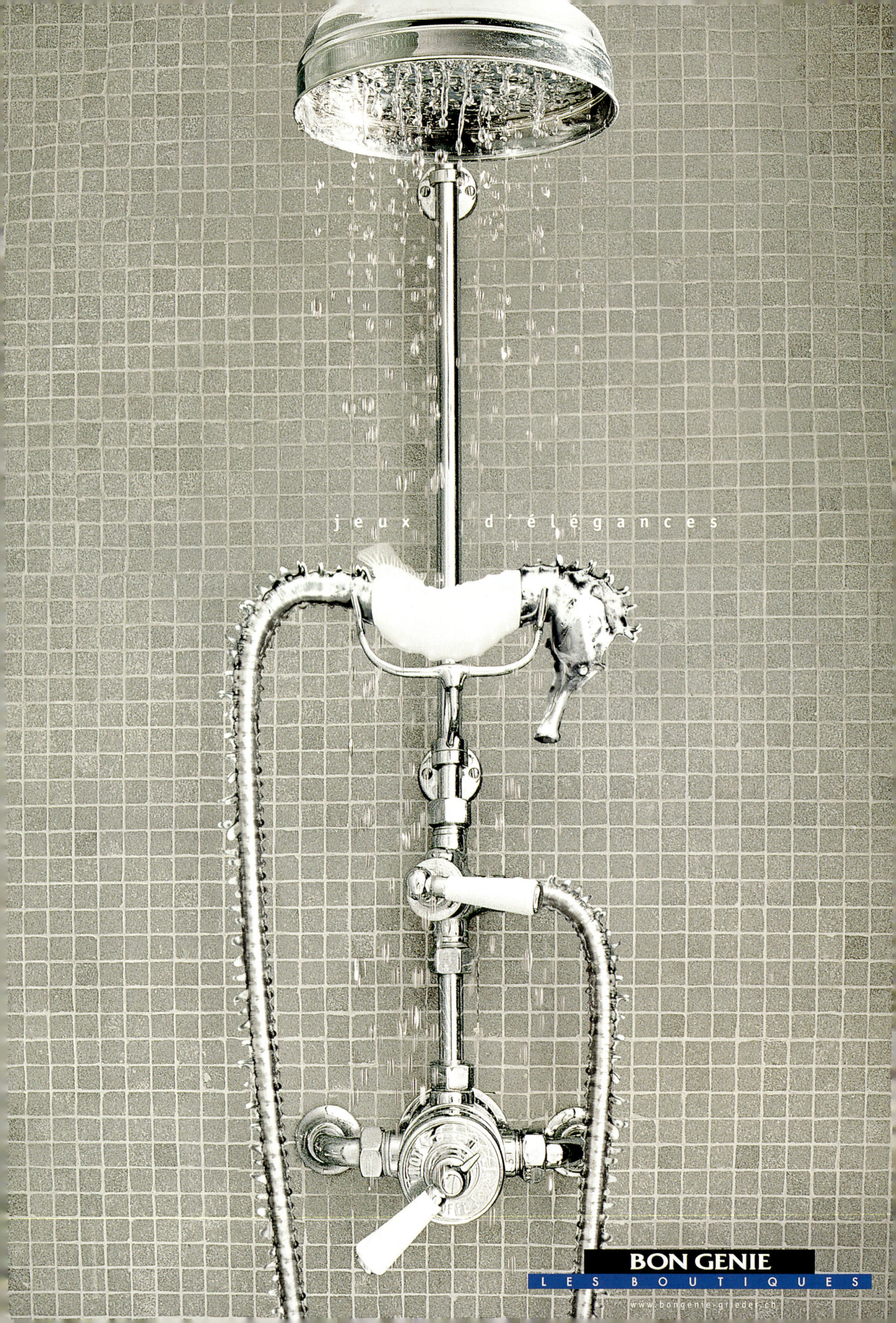
jeux d'élégances
BON GENIE
LES BOUTIQUES
www.bongenie-grieder.ch

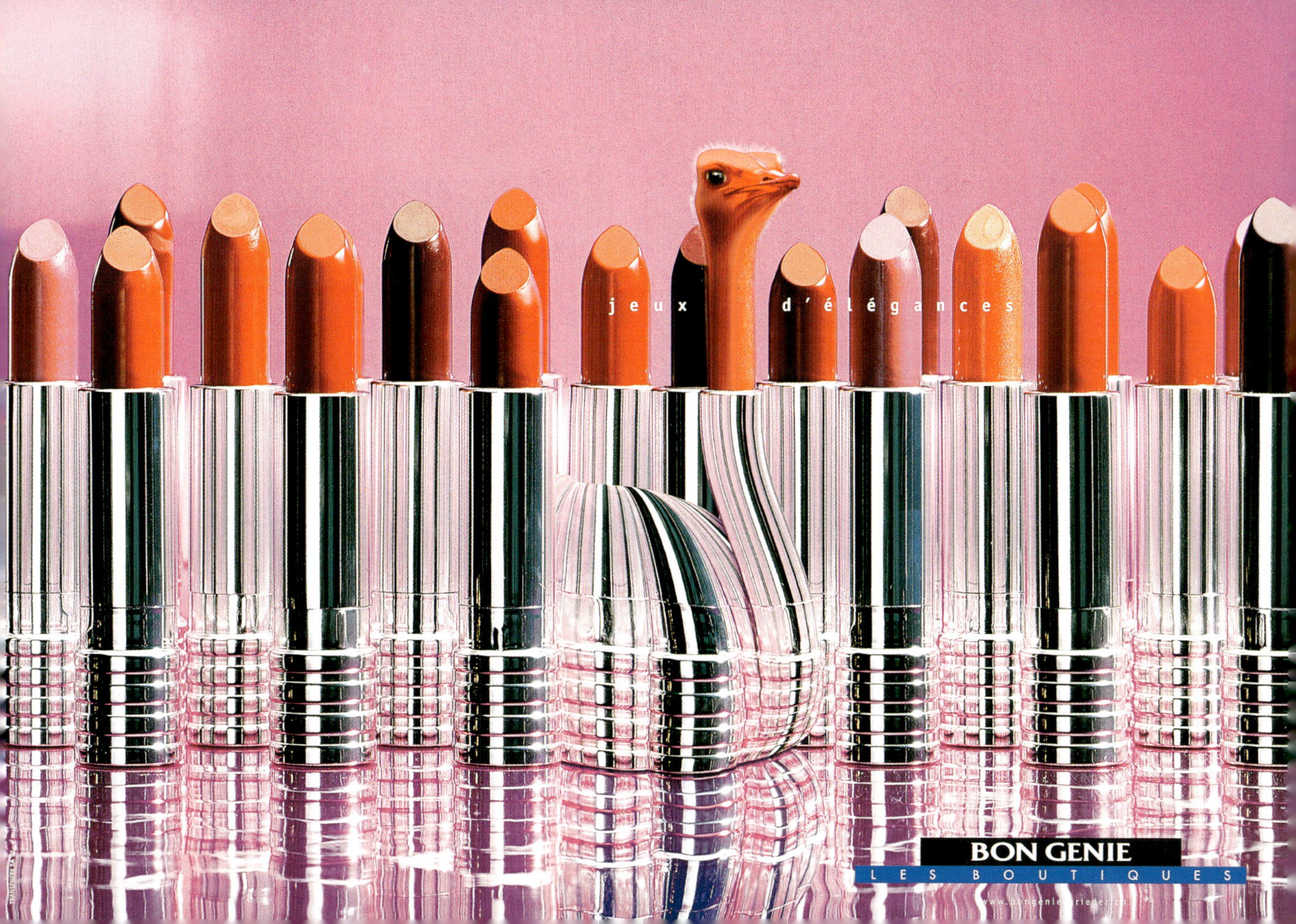

jeux d'élégances
BON GENIE
LES BOUTIQUES

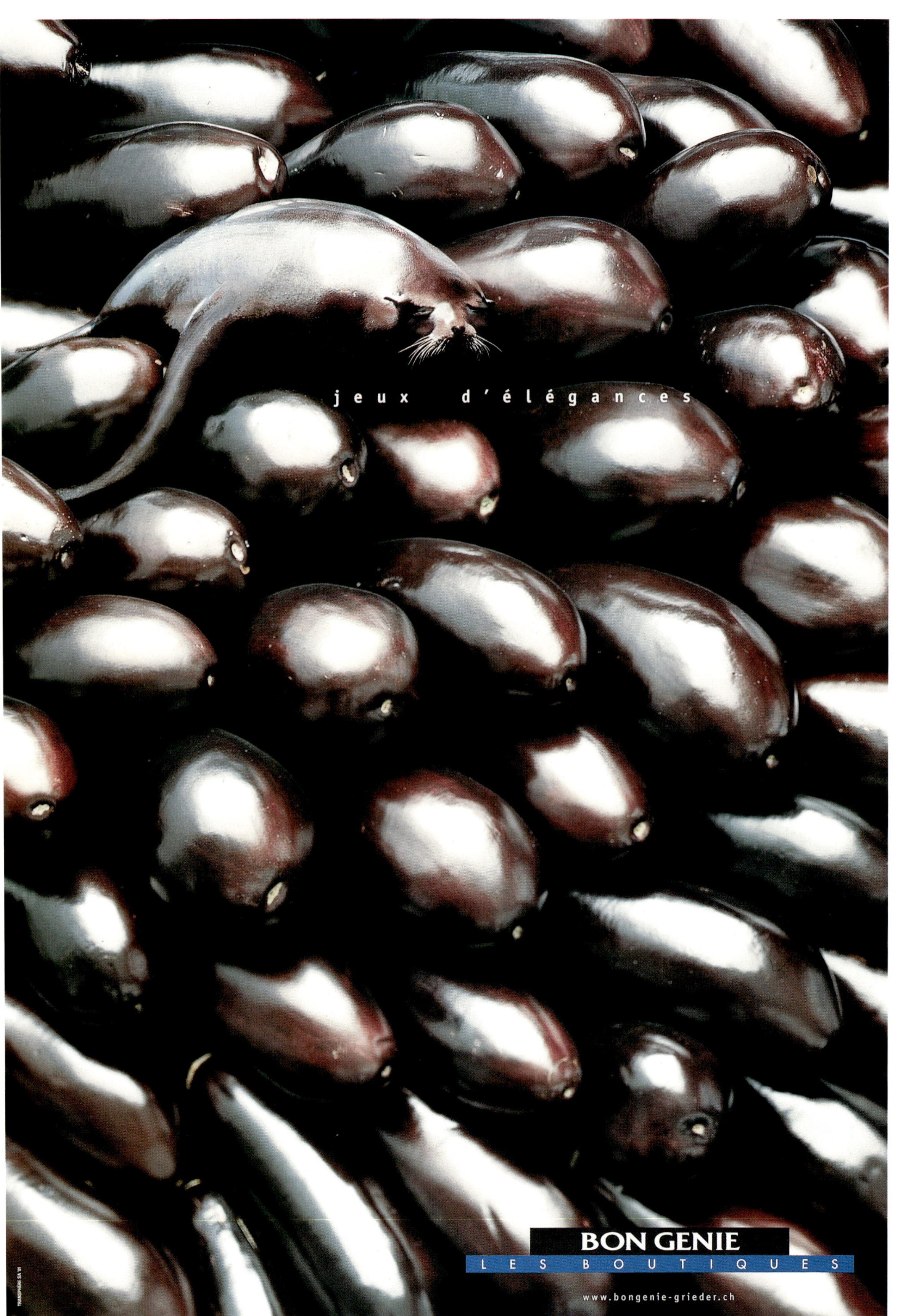

Transphère SA/Bon Génie/Grieder

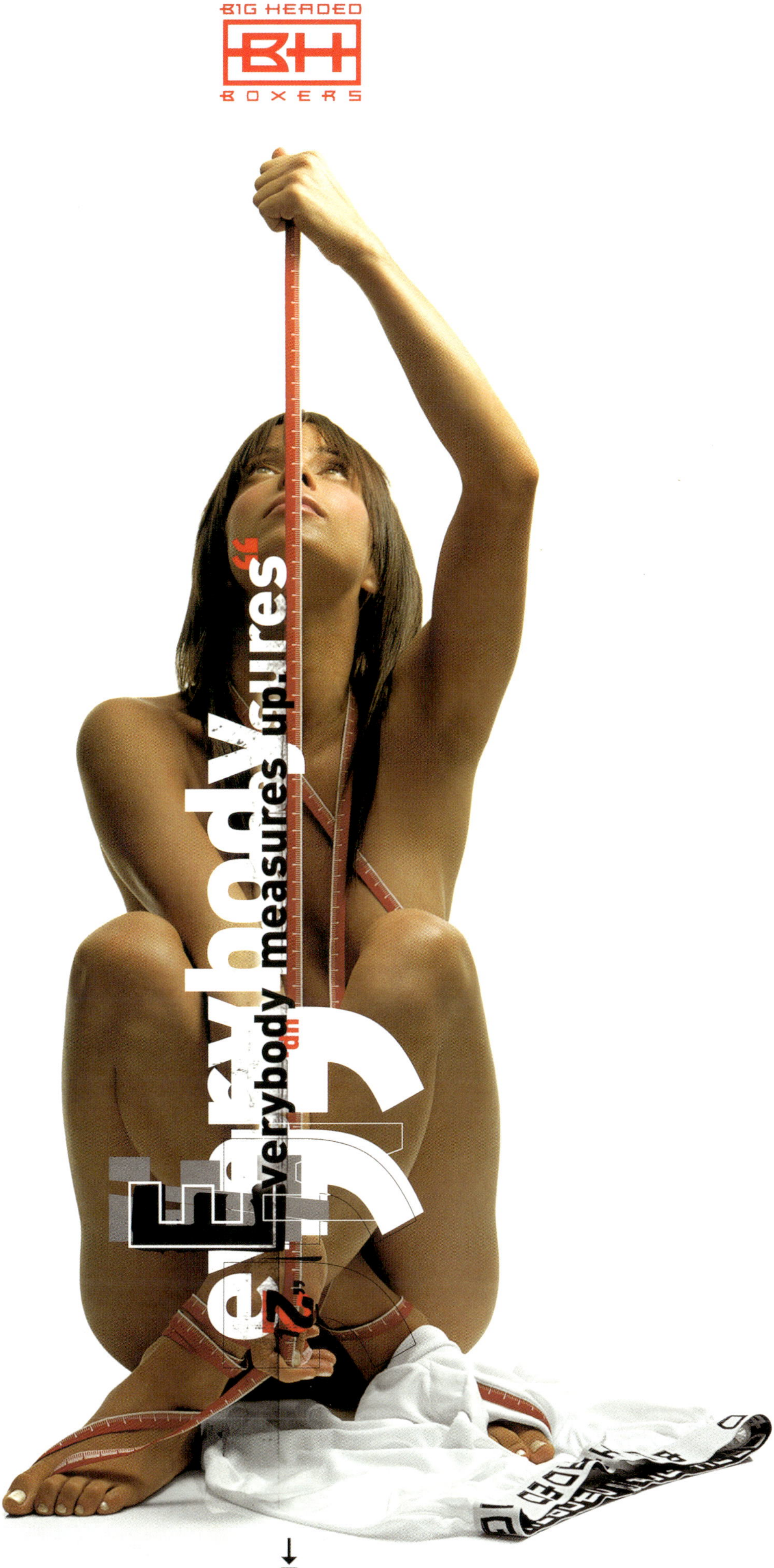

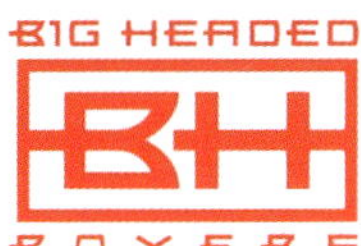

everybody measures up

12"

RON TAFT PHOTOGRAPHY

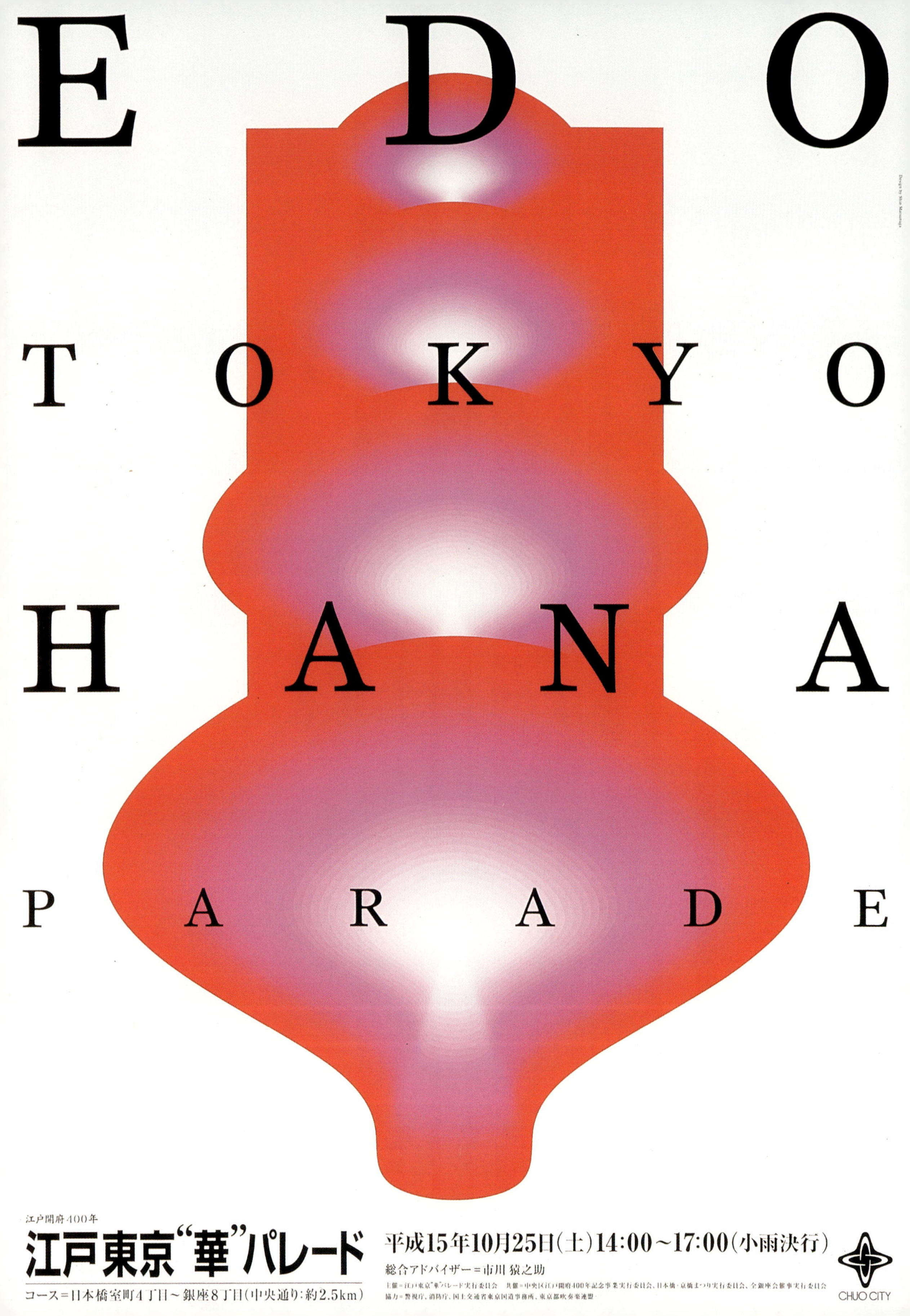

E D O

T O K Y O

H A N A

P A R A D E

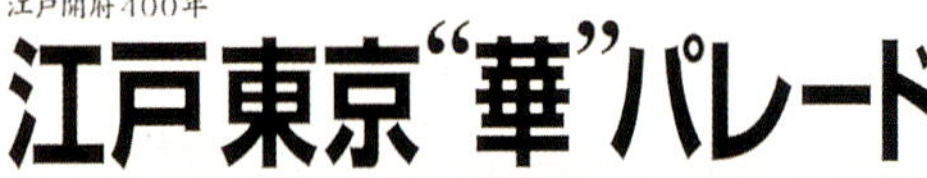

平成15年10月25日(土)14:00～17:00(小雨決行)

総合アドバイザー＝市川 猿之助

主催＝江戸東京"華"パレード実行委員会　共催＝中央区江戸開府400年記念事業実行委員会、日本橋・京橋まつり実行委員会、全銀座会催事実行委員会

協力＝警視庁、消防庁、国土交通省東京国道事務所、東京都吹奏楽連盟

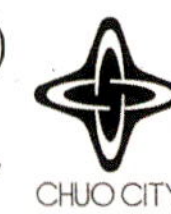

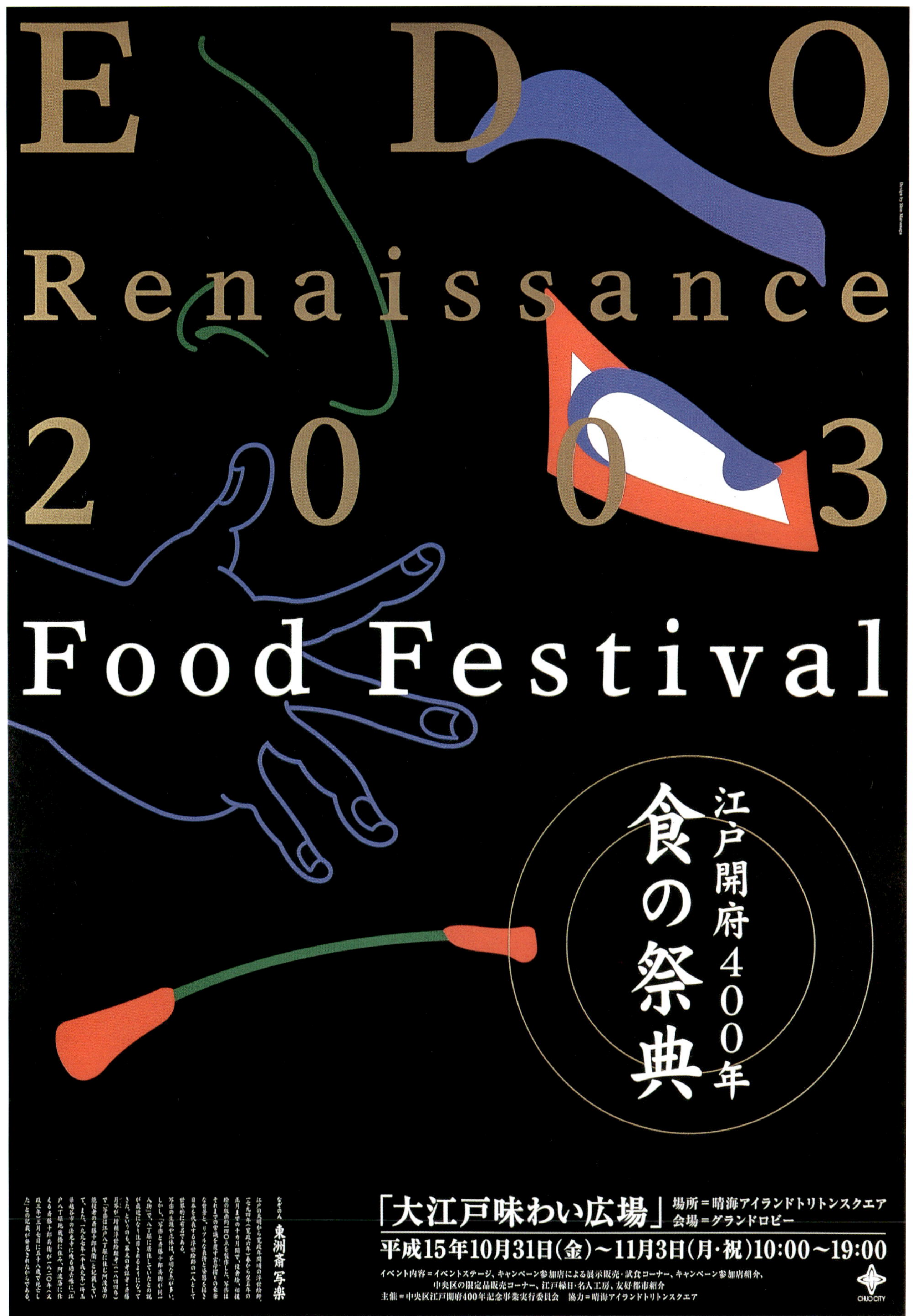

Shin Matsunaga Design Inc./Chuo City

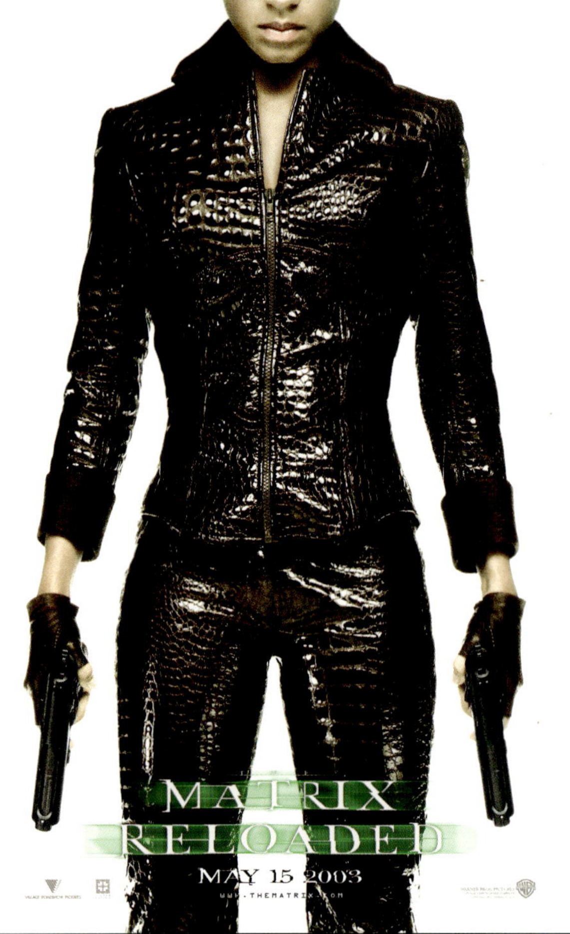
MATRIX
RELOADED
MAY 15 2003
WWW.THEMATRIX.COM

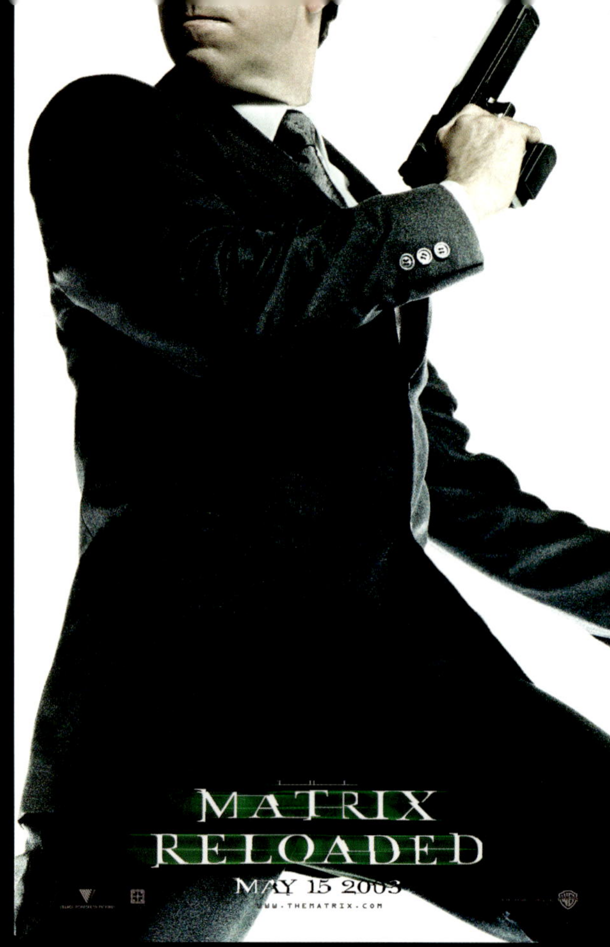
MATRIX
RELOADED
MAY 15 2003
WWW.THEMATRIX.COM

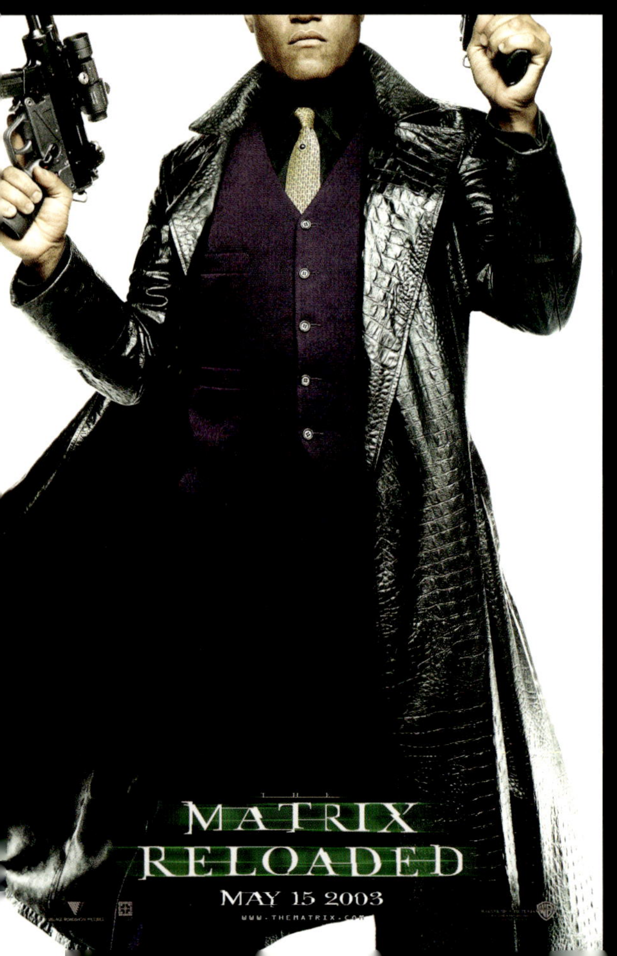
MATRIX
RELOADED
MAY 15 2003
WWW.THEMATRIX.COM

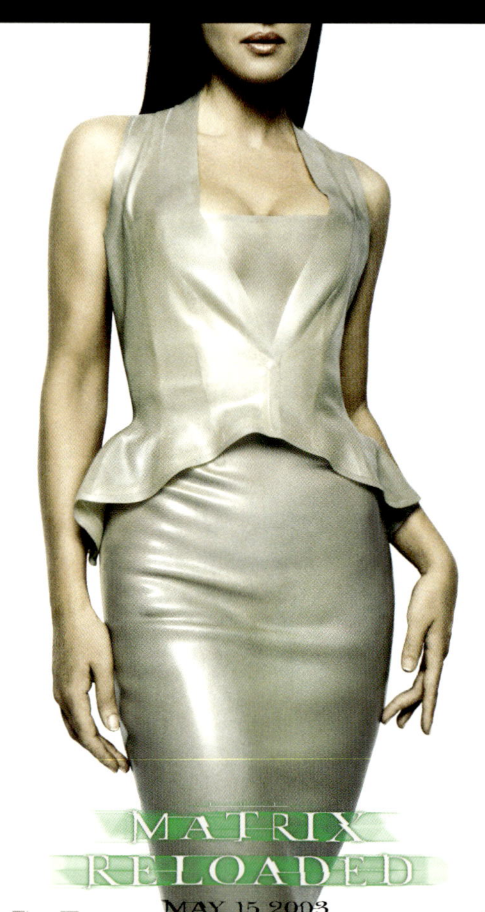
MATRIX
RELOADED
MAY 15 2003
WWW.THEMATRIX.COM

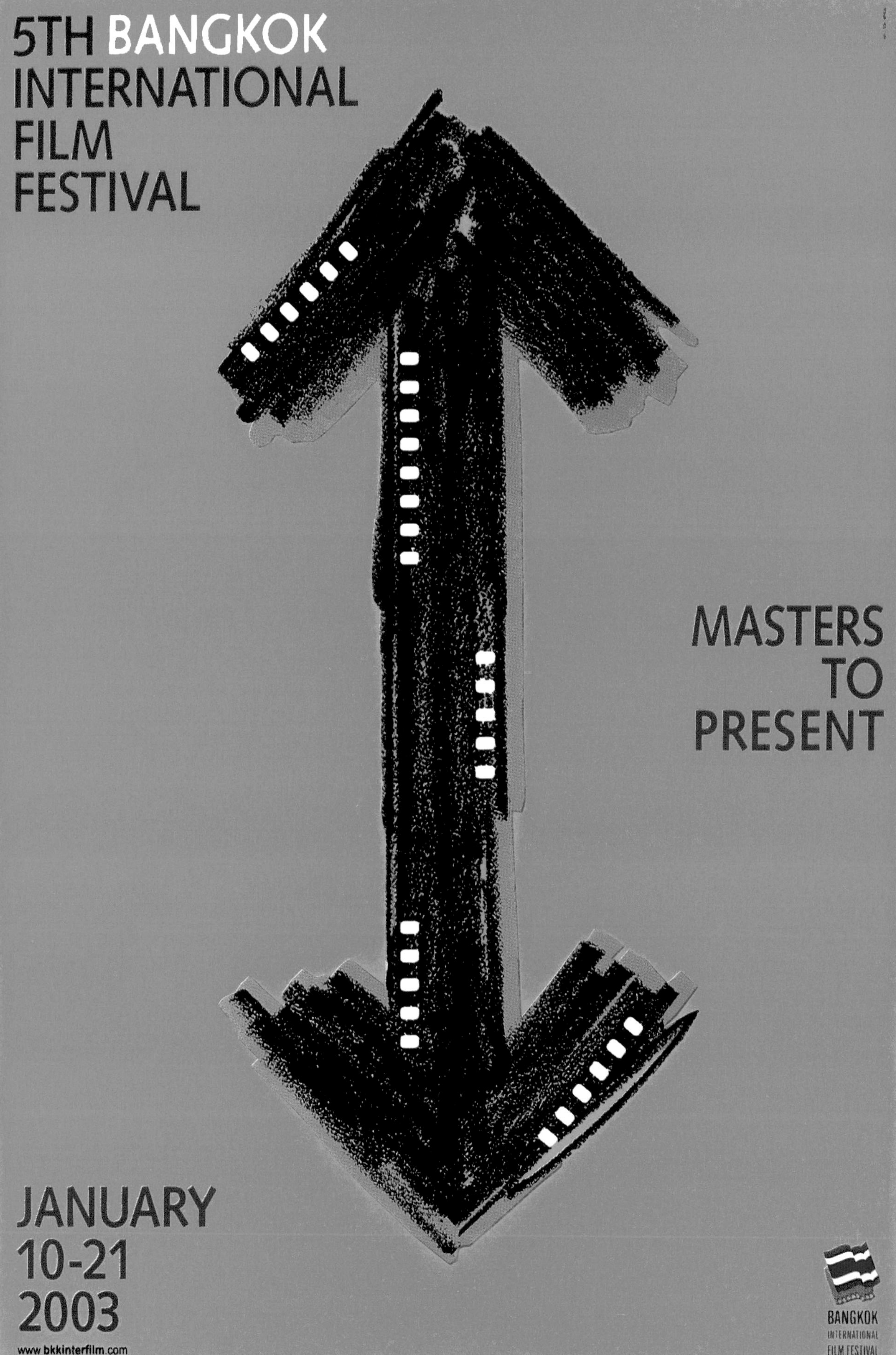
5TH BANGKOK
INTERNATIONAL
FILM
FESTIVAL
MASTERS
TO
PRESENT
JANUARY
10-21
2003
www.bkkinterfilm.com
BANGKOK
INTERNATIONAL
FILM FESTIVAL

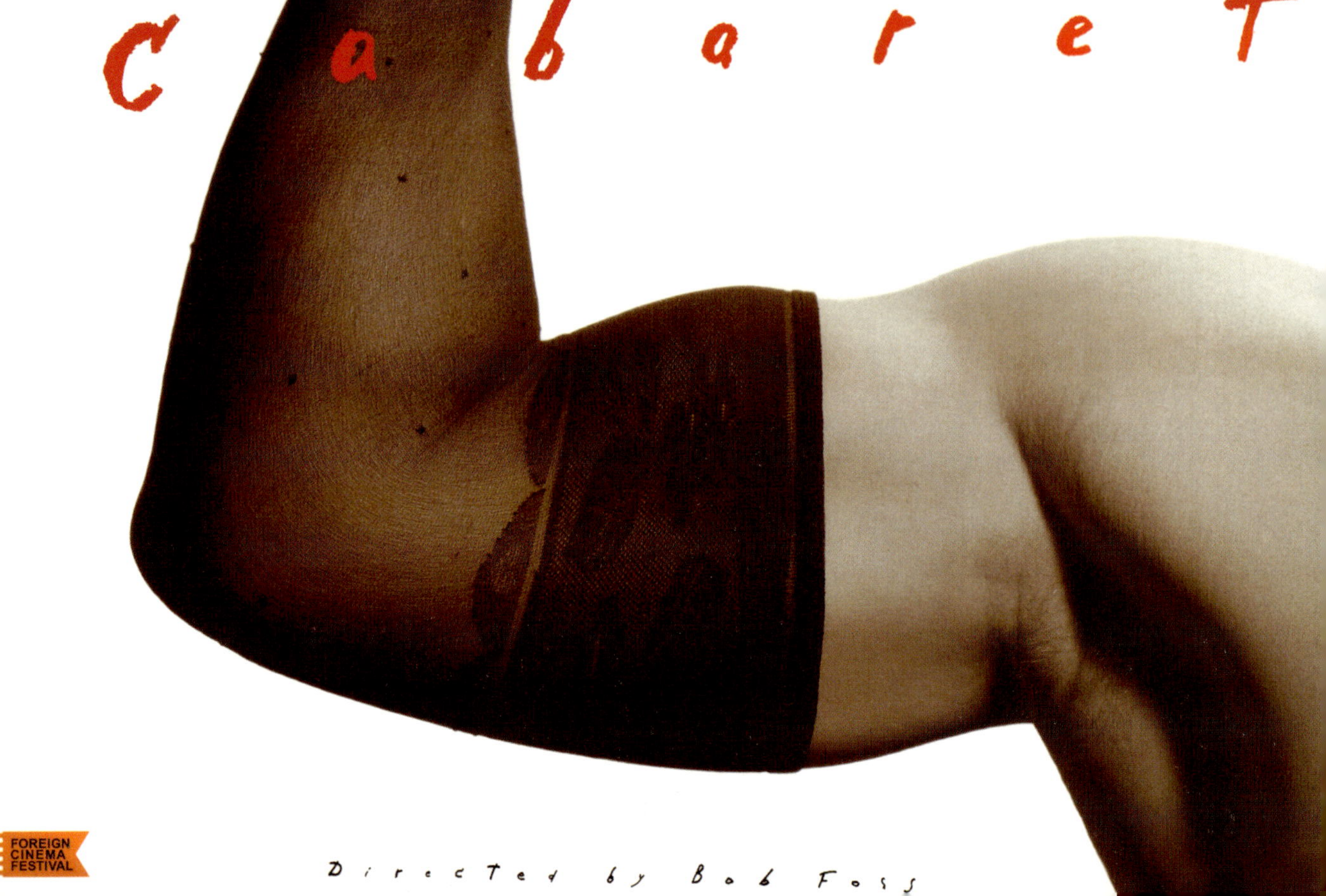
Cabaret
FOREIGN
CINEMA
FESTIVAL
Directed by Bob Foss

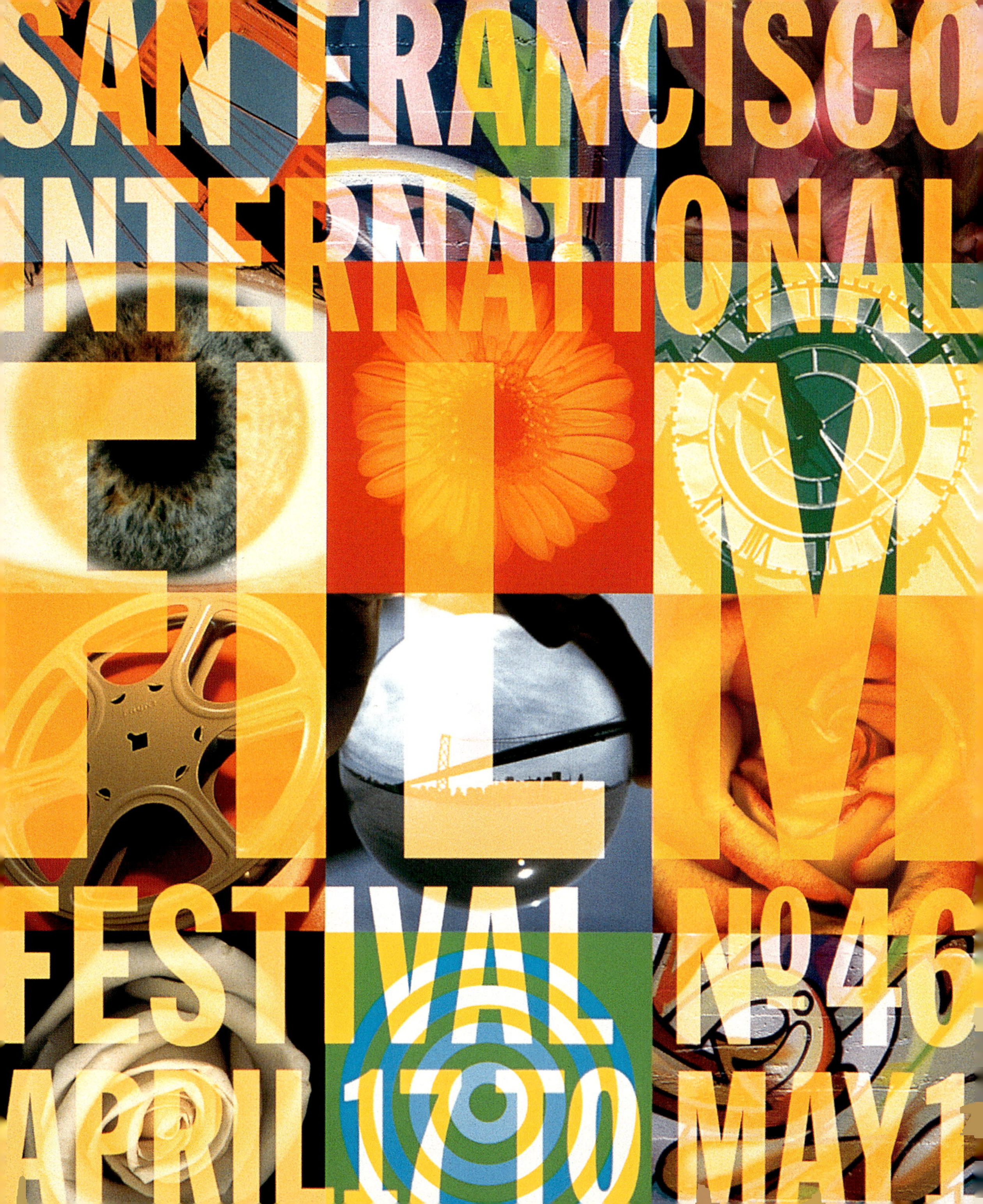
SAN FRANCISCO
INTERNATIONAL
FILM
FESTIVAL Nº46
APRIL 17 TO MAY 1

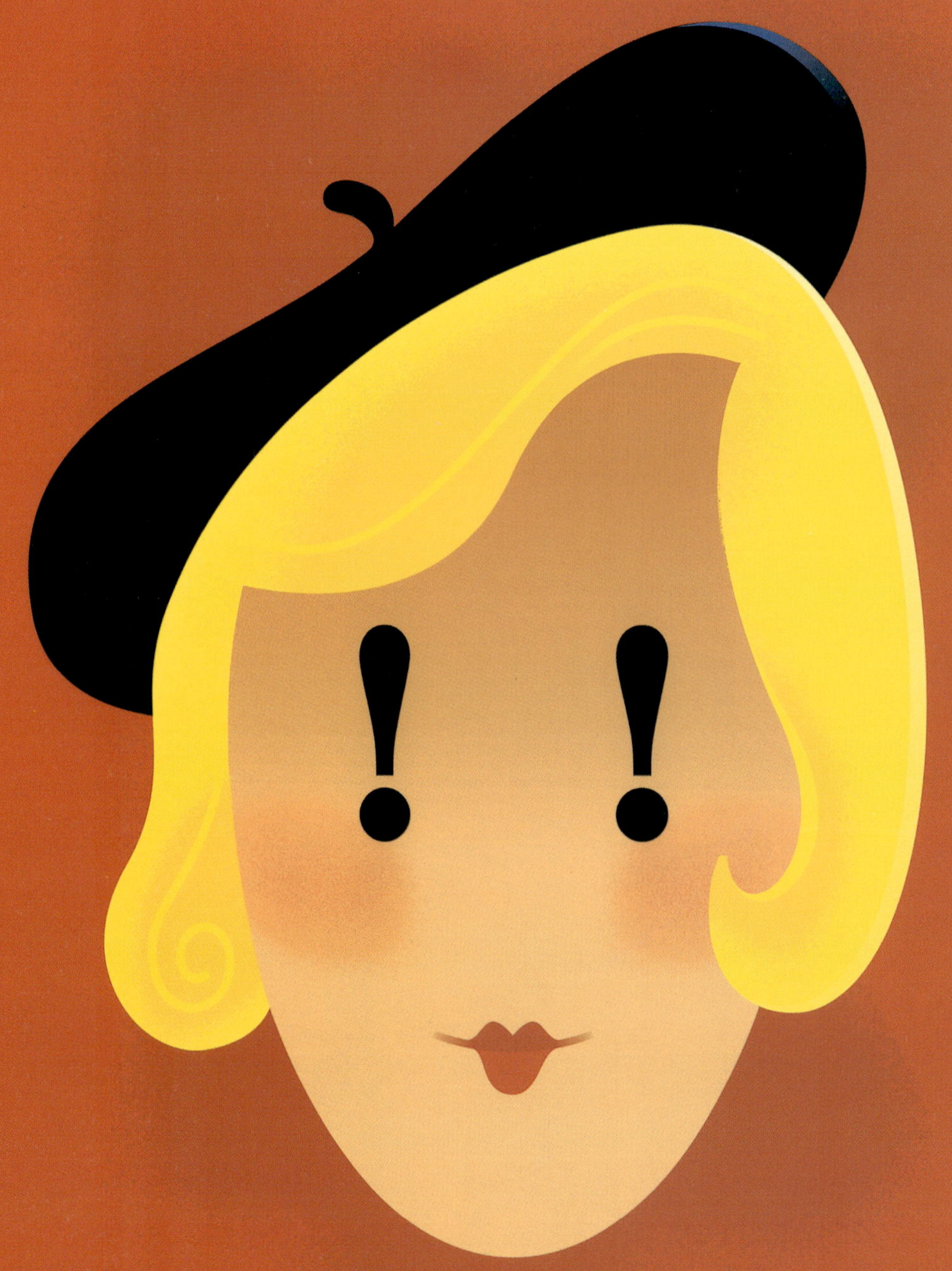

NO DÉJÀ VU

SEATTLE INTERNATIONAL FILM FESTIVAL 2003

MAY 22ND - JUNE 15TH

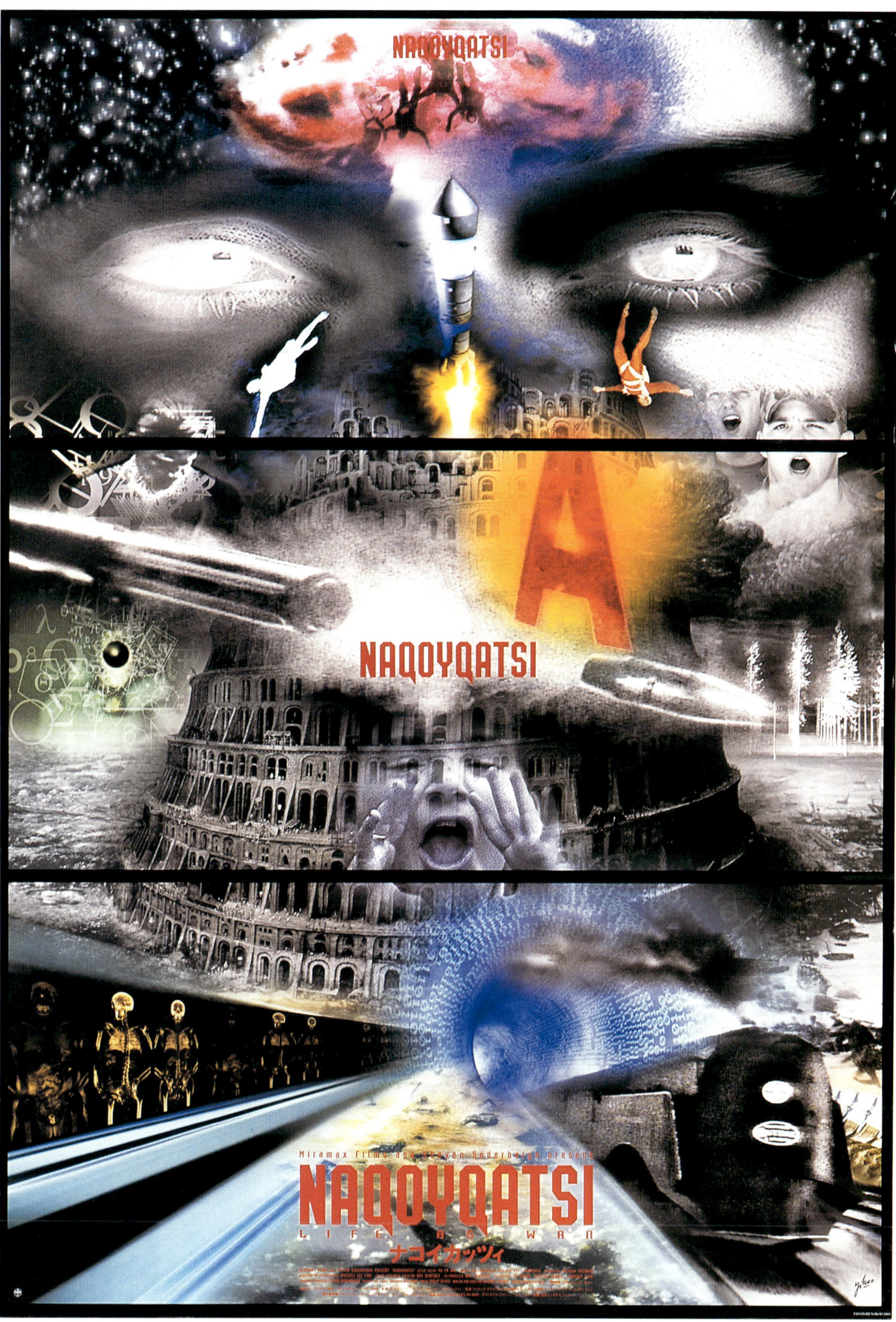

Yokoo's Circus Company, Ltd./Toshiba Entertainment Inc.

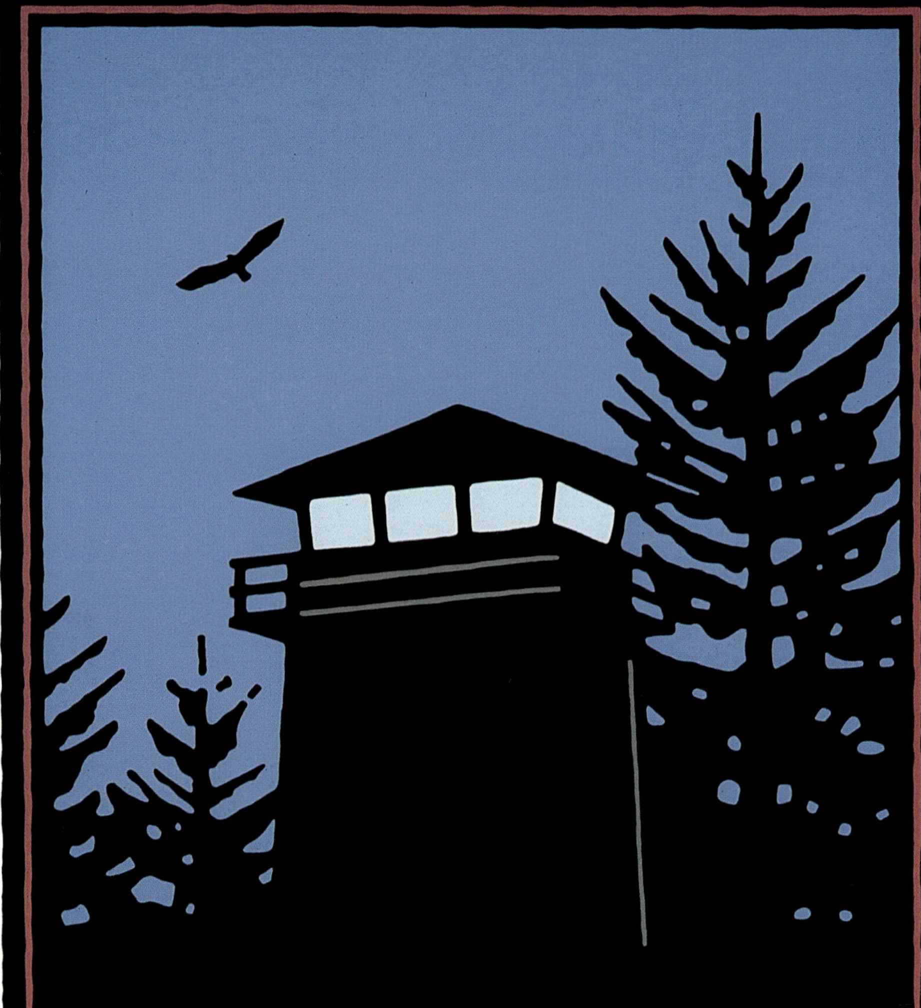

SIGNAL
RIDGE
VINEYARD

SCHWAB

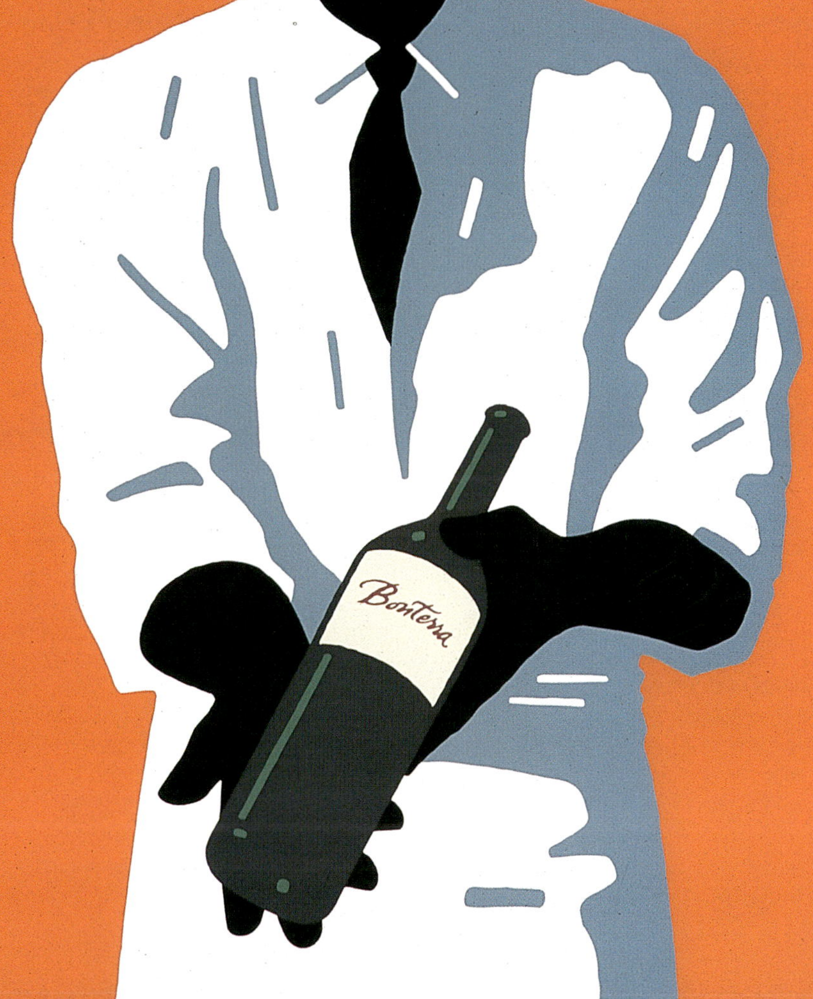
BONTERRA
VINEYARDS
Bonterra
SCHWAB
ORGANICALLY GROWN GRAPES
OFFICIAL WINE OF THE SUNDANCE FILM FESTIVAL
WWW.BONTERRA.COM

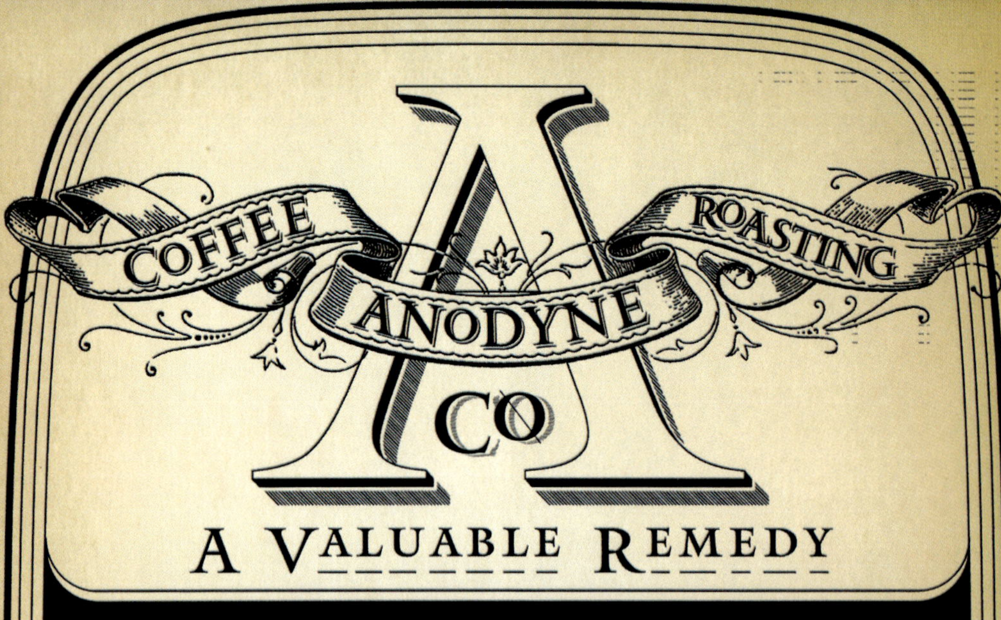

MIND TONIC

HELPS GET THINGS DONE

ENHANCES REASONING POWER

FIGHTS CONFUSION

STIMULATES BRAIN CELLS

AN AID TO CONVERSATION

RELIEVES SLUGGISHNESS

COFFEE THAT CURES

To the muddleheaded: coffee is a natural tonic for the mind. It increases the ability to think clearly, improves alertness and concentration, enhances memory and reasoning power, stimulates energy and boosts motivation. It also has positive effects on motor skills, endurance, and reaction time. It brightens conversation. Anodyne is an independent, local coffee company devoted to lifting the spirits and improving the brain power of our community. We donate 2500 pounds of coffee every year to Milwaukee charities. We were the first coffee company in Milwaukee to purchase certified Fair Trade beans. Our beans are of the highest quality and several organic varieties are available. Anodyne truly is the soon-to-be-recognized cure-all for tired minds.

ANODYNE COFFEE ROASTING COMPANY · MILWAUKEE · WISCONSIN · A

ROASTED IN SMALL BATCHES WITH ACCURACY & PURITY

ANODYNE COFFEE ROASTING CO

A VALUABLE REMEDY

1208 East Brady Street Milwaukee, WI 53202 414.276.8081

www.anodynecoffee.com

CYD Design Ltd./Anodyne Coffee Roasting Company

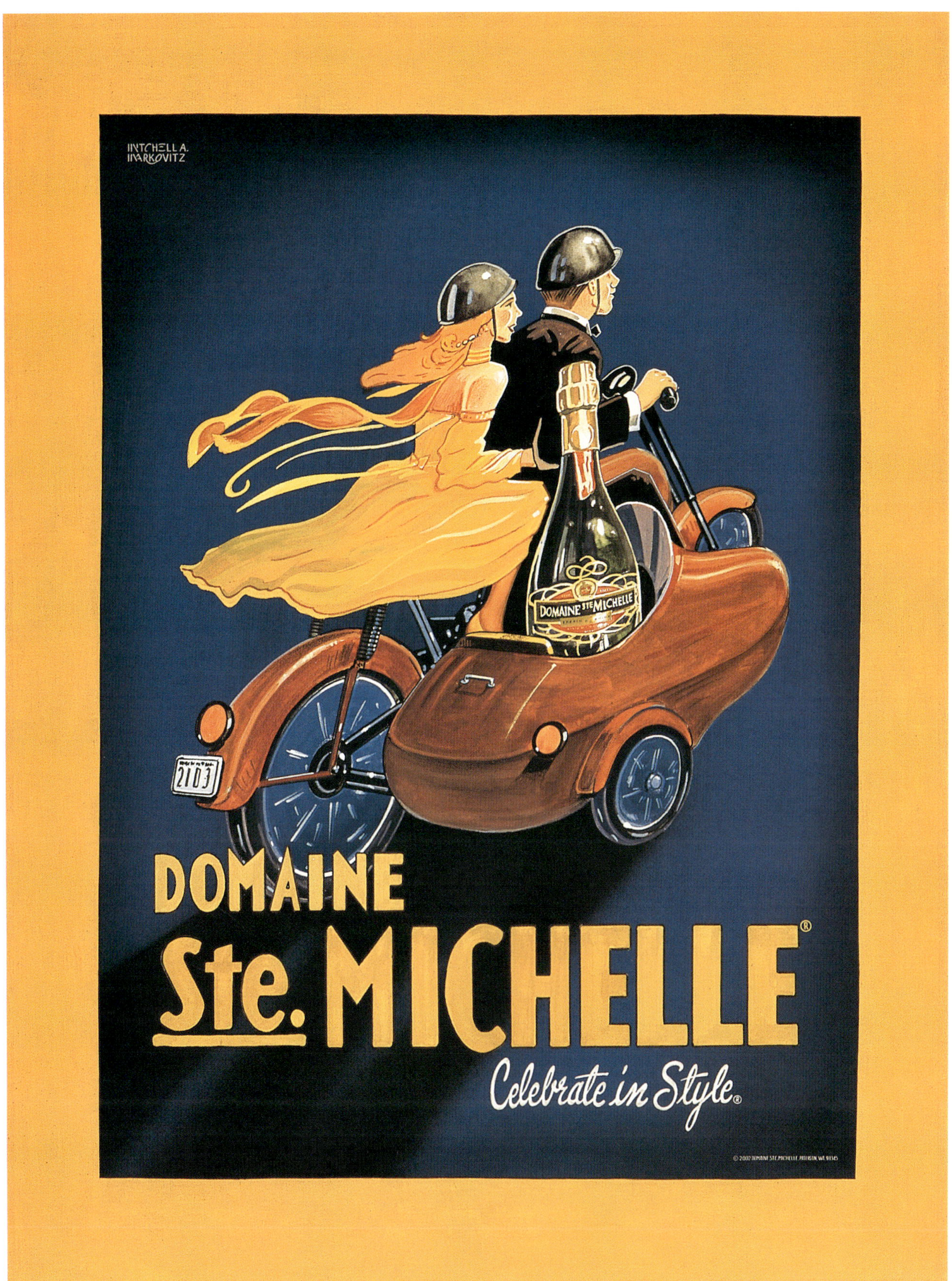

DDB Seattle/Domaine Ste.Michelle

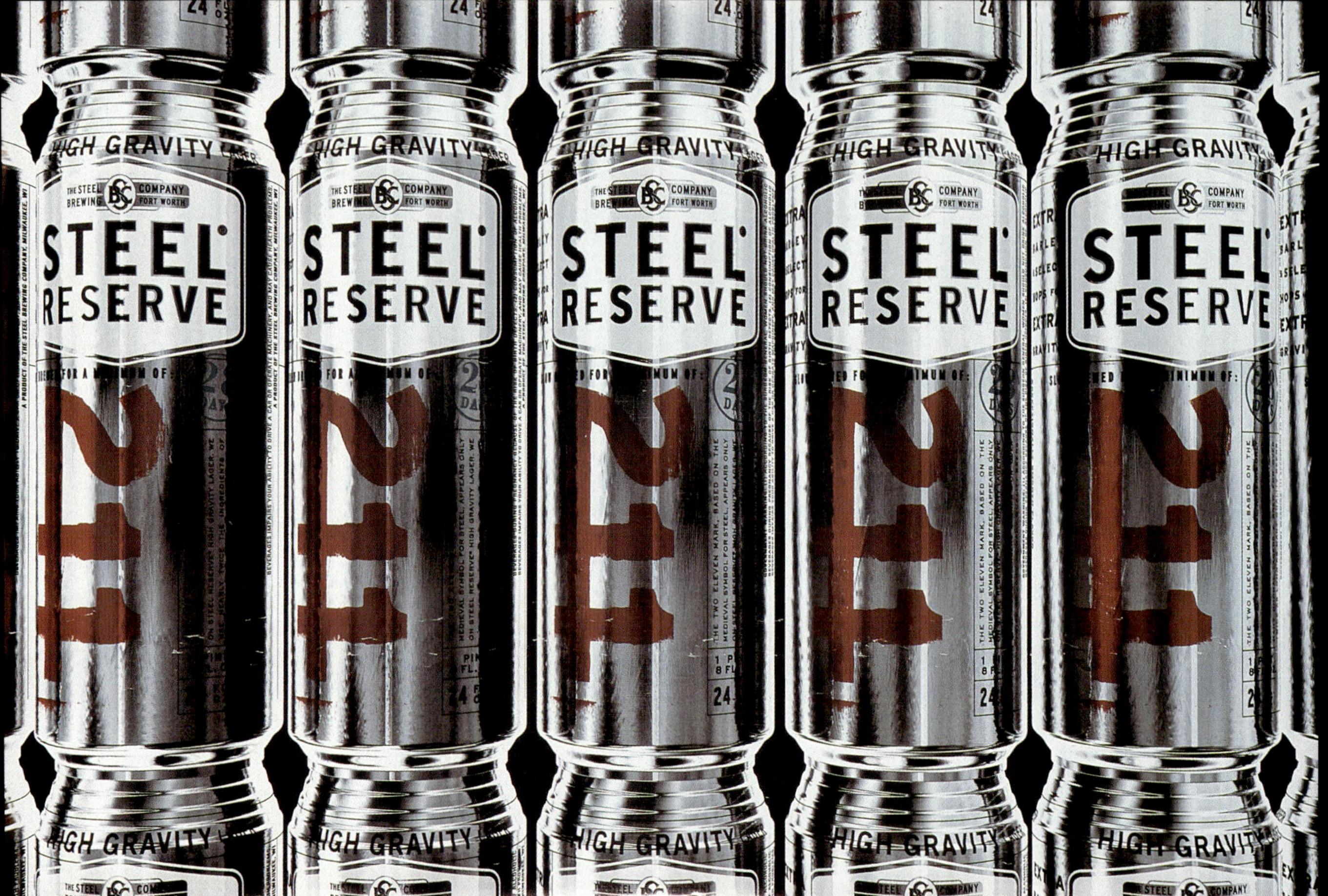
HIGH GRAVITY LAGER
THE STEEL BREWING COMPANY FORT WORTH
STEEL RESERVE
HIGH GRAVITY
THE STEEL BREWING COMPANY FORT WORTH
STEEL RESERVE
HIGH GRAVITY
THE STEEL BREWING COMPANY FORT WORTH
STEEL RESERVE
HIGH GRAVITY
THE STEEL BREWING COMPANY FORT WORTH
STEEL RESERVE
HIGH GRAVITY
COMPANY FORT WORTH
STEEL RESERVE
HIGH GRAVITY
HIGH GRAVITY
HIGH GRAVITY
HIGH GRAVITY
HIGH GRAVITY

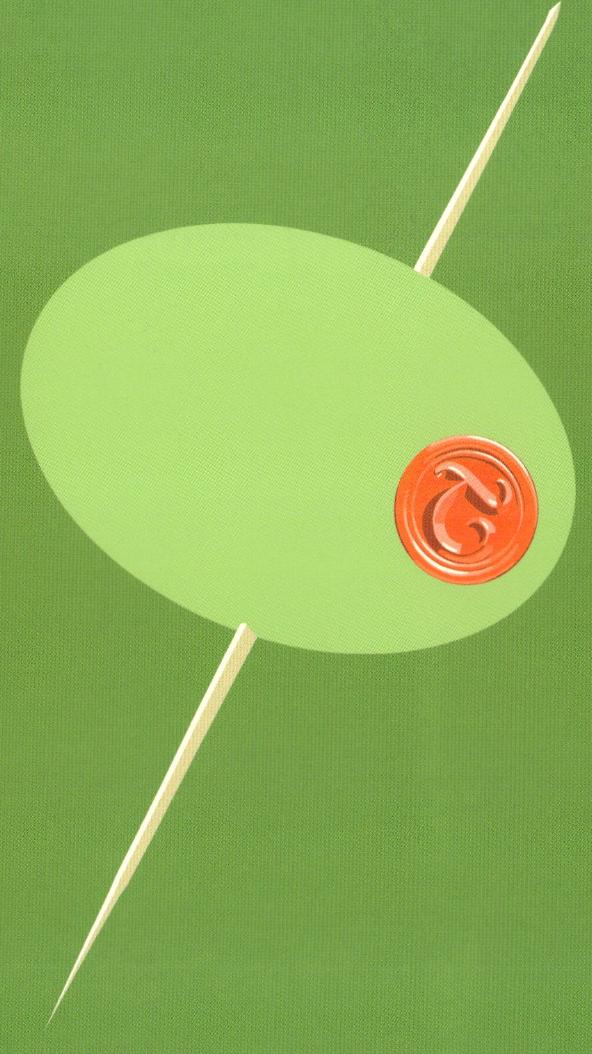
Tanqueray®

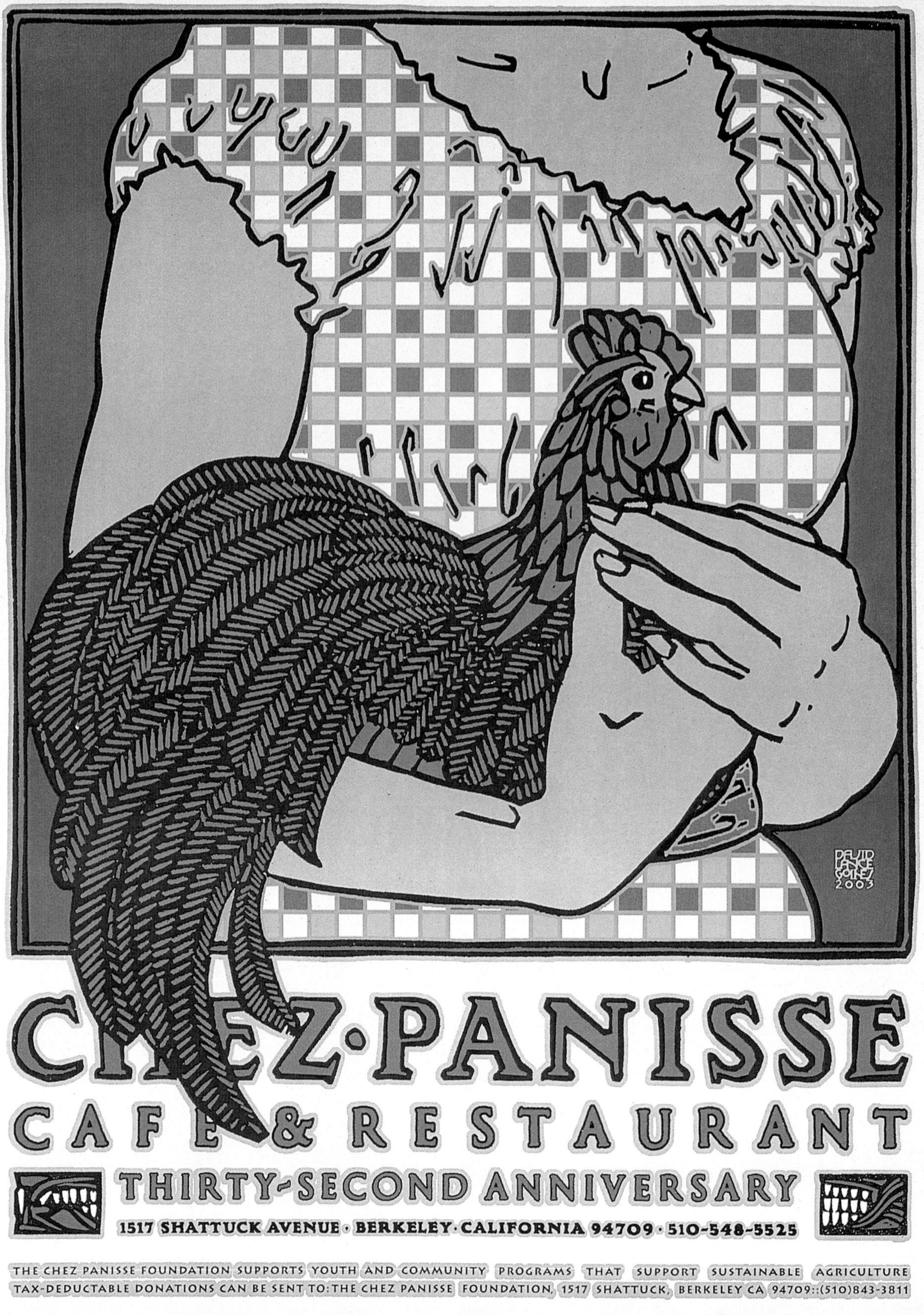

DAVID LANCE GOINES 2003

CHEZ·PANISSE

CAFE & RESTAURANT

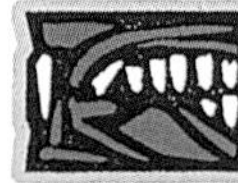

THIRTY-SECOND ANNIVERSARY

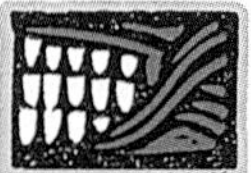

1517 SHATTUCK AVENUE · BERKELEY · CALIFORNIA 94709 · 510-548-5525

THE CHEZ PANISSE FOUNDATION SUPPORTS YOUTH AND COMMUNITY PROGRAMS THAT SUPPORT SUSTAINABLE AGRICULTURE
TAX-DEDUCTABLE DONATIONS CAN BE SENT TO: THE CHEZ PANISSE FOUNDATION, 1517 SHATTUCK, BERKELEY CA 94709::(510)843-3811

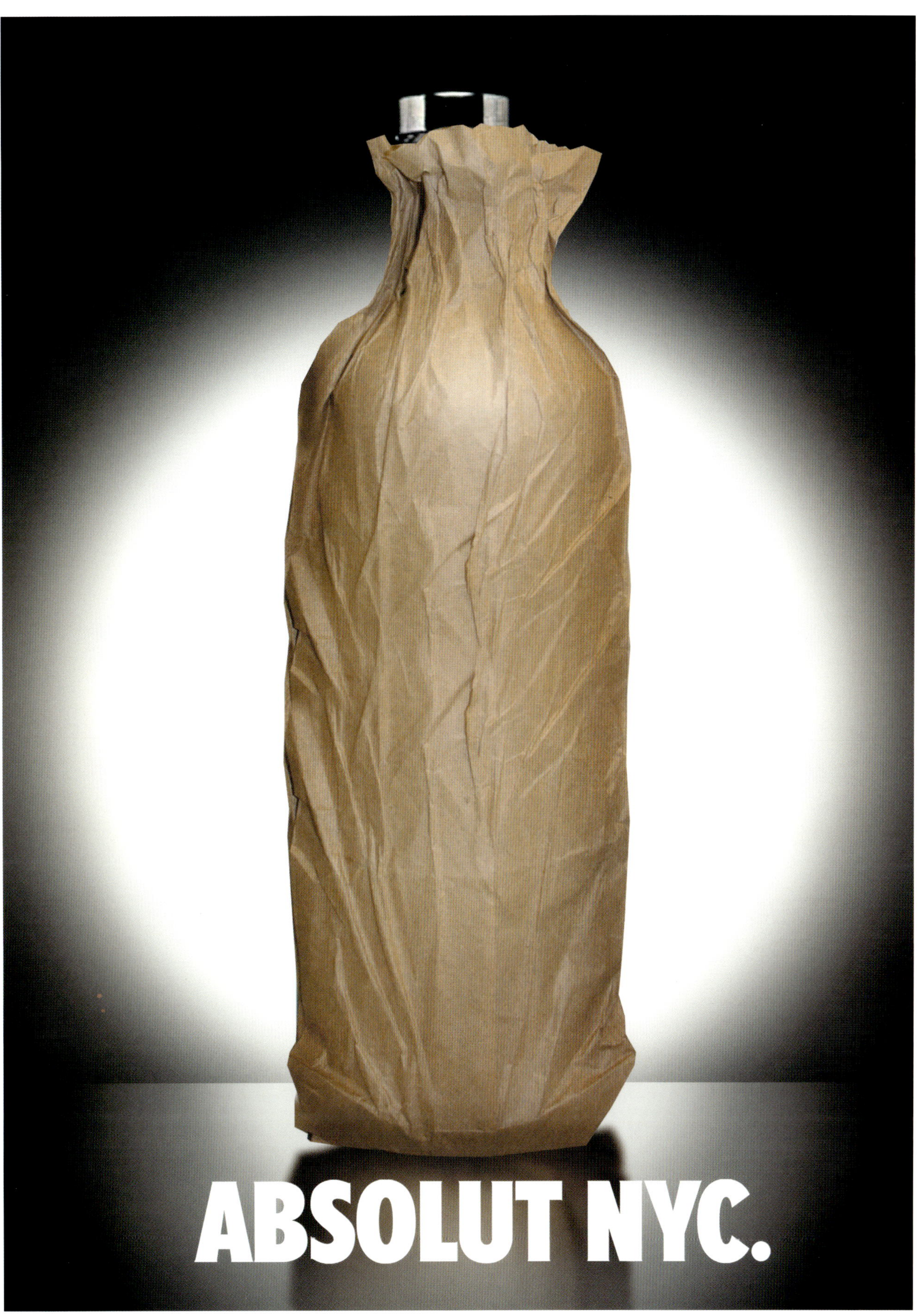

The Right Hand/Absolut Company (volunteer project)

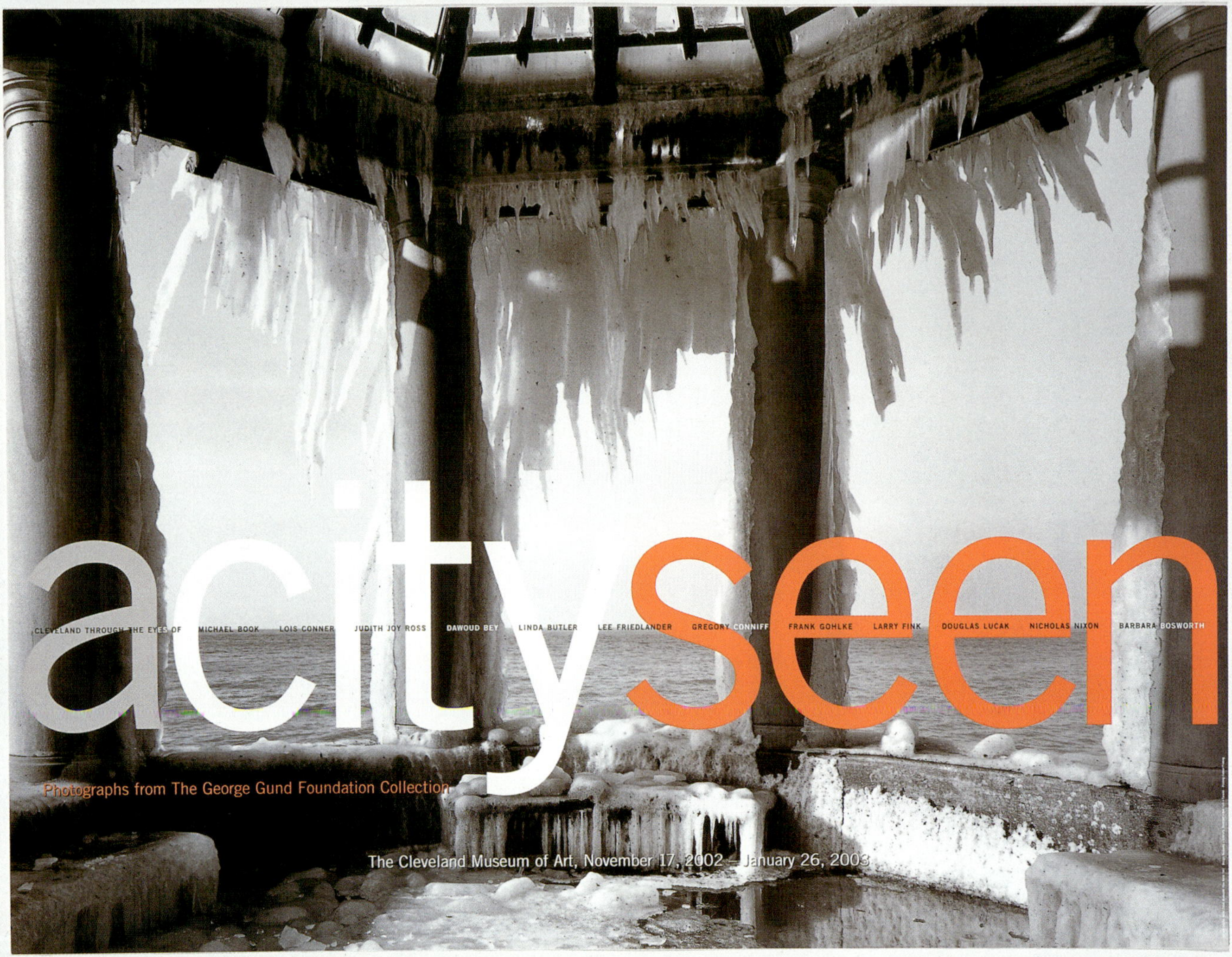

a city seen

CLEVELAND THROUGH THE EYES OF MICHAEL BOOK LOIS CONNER JUDITH JOY ROSS DAWOUD BEY LINDA BUTLER LEE FRIEDLANDER GREGORY CONNIFF FRANK GOHLKE LARRY FINK DOUGLAS LUCAK NICHOLAS NIXON BARBARA BOSWORTH

Photographs from The George Gund Foundation Collection

The Cleveland Museum of Art, November 17, 2002 – January 26, 2003

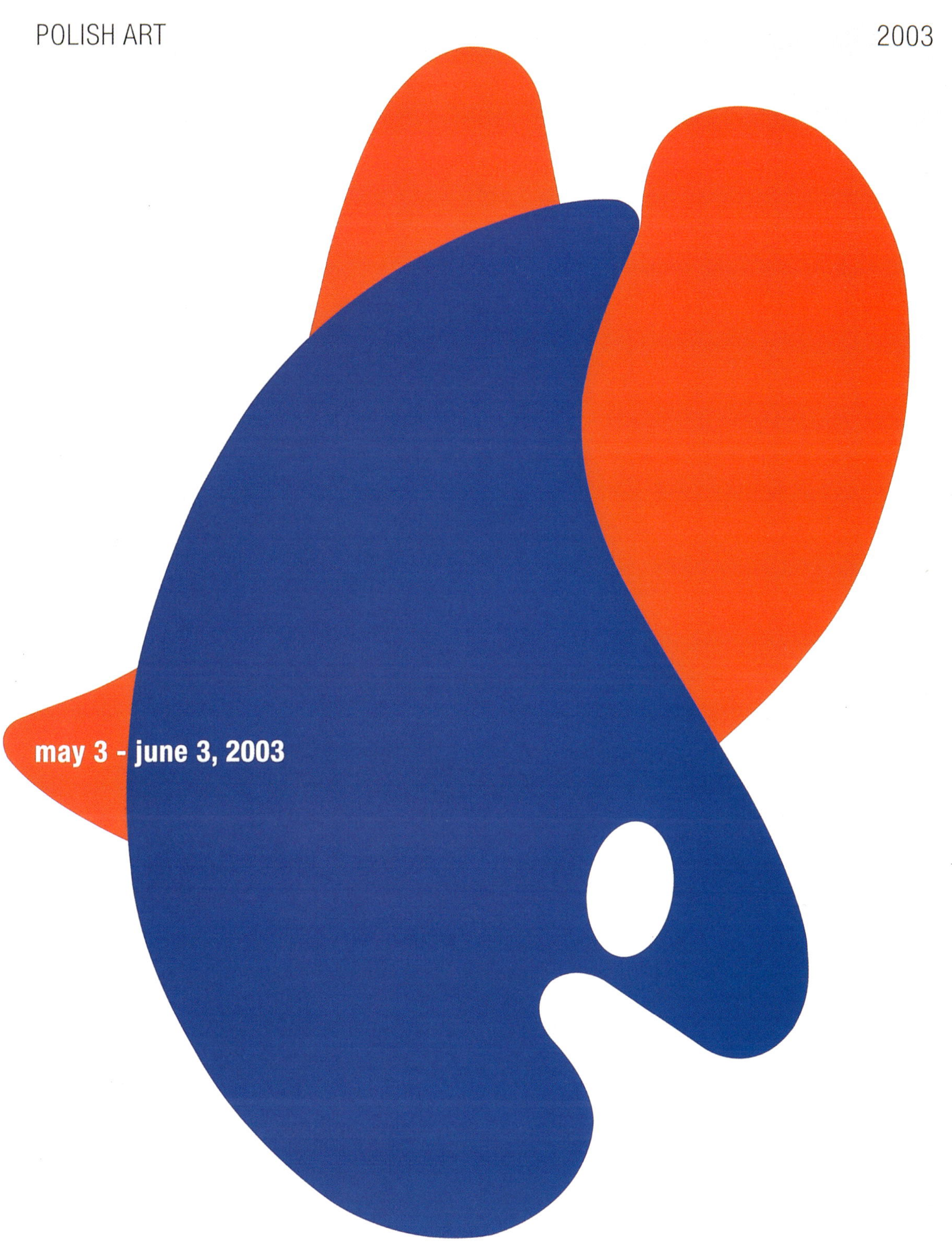
CONFRONTATIONS
POLISH ART
2003
may 3 - june 3, 2003
Modern Art Gallery in Los Angeles

NEW YORK CENTRAL

RAILROAD MUSEUM

ELKHART • INDIANA

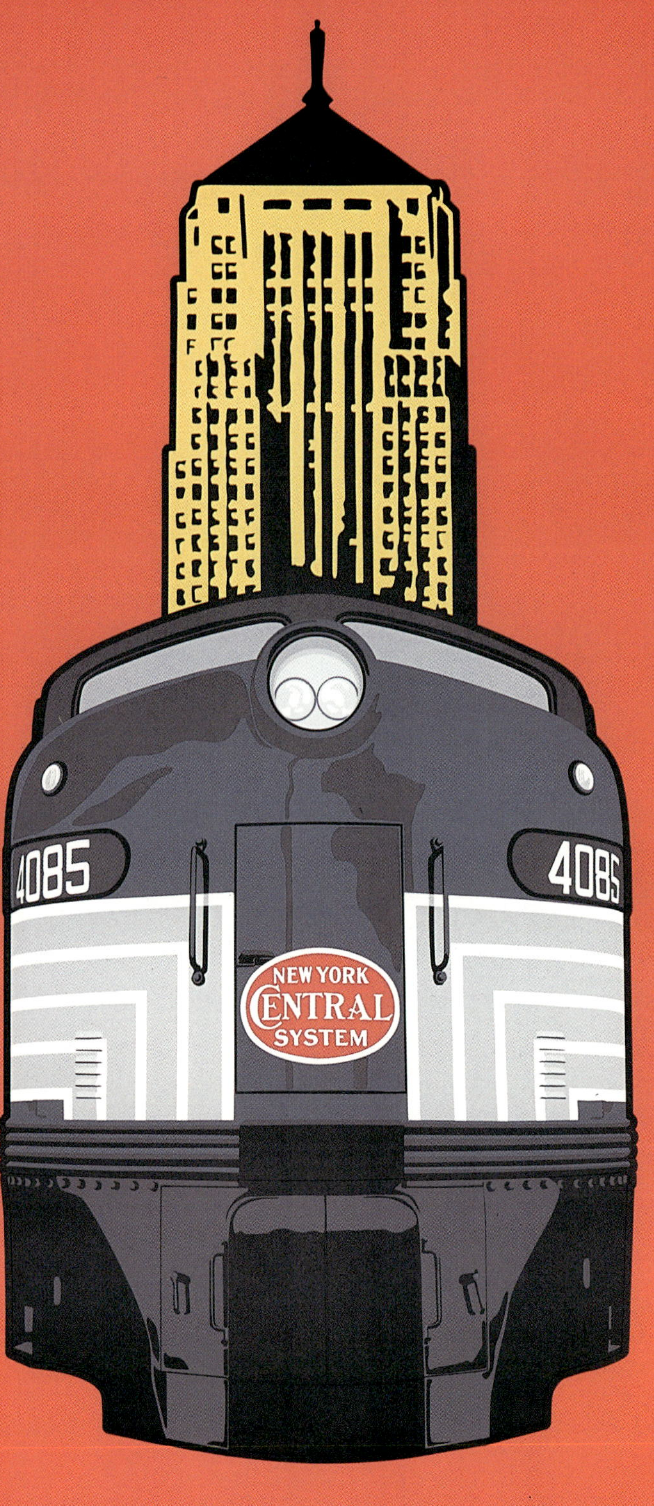

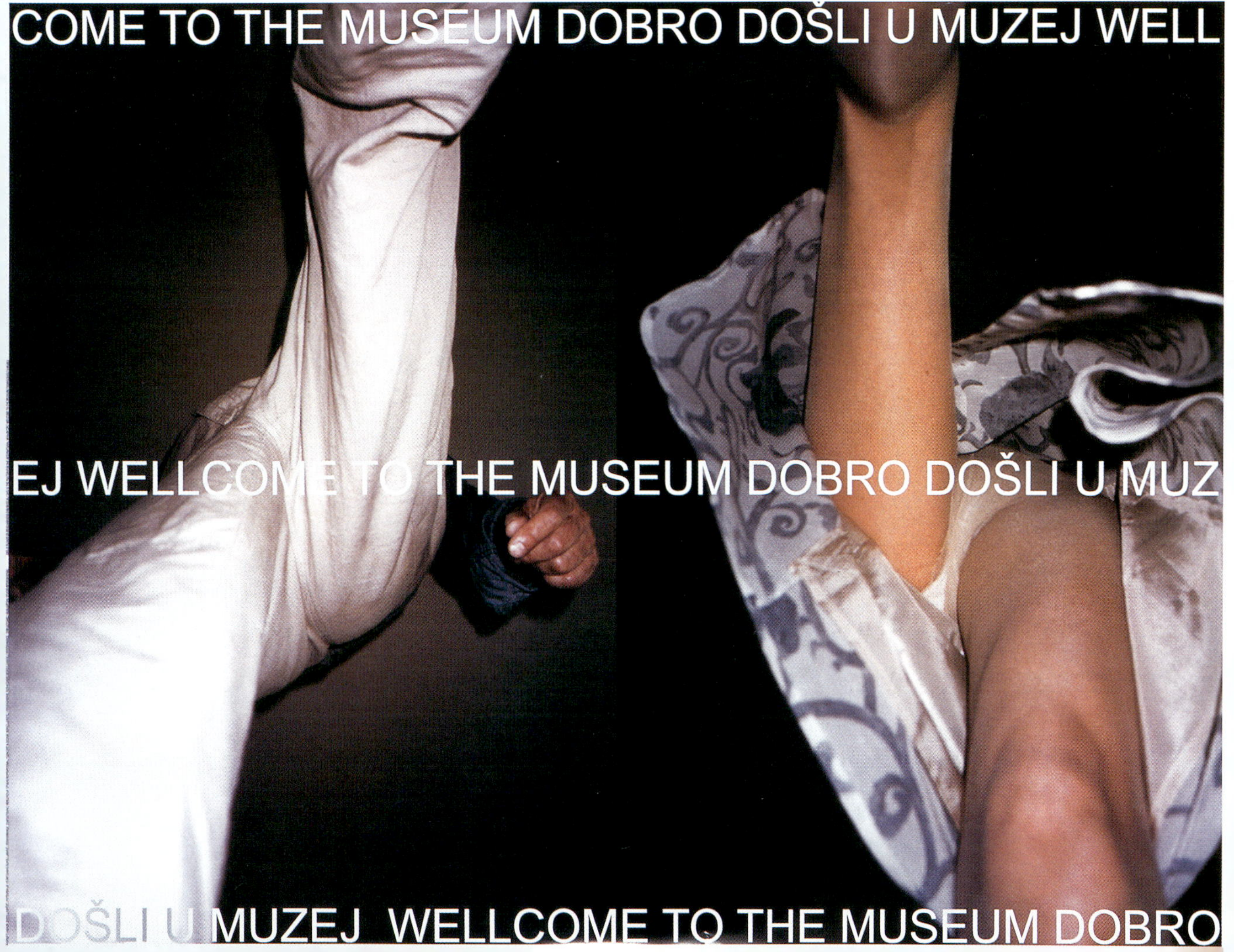
COME TO THE MUSEUM DOBRO DOŠLI U MUZEJ WELL
EJ WELLCOME TO THE MUSEUM DOBRO DOŠLI U MUZ
DOŠLI U MUZEJ WELLCOME TO THE MUSEUM DOBRO

The Manchester String Quartet *Dawn of the String Quartet*

Hyun-Woo Kim, violin
Marissa Regni, violin
Daniel Foster, viola
Glenn Garlick, cello

A series of eight concerts celebrating the legacy of classical Vienna

7
April 28, 2003
BRAHMS
Quartet in C Minor, opus 51 #1

8
May 19, 2003
DVORAK
Quartet in D Minor, opus 34

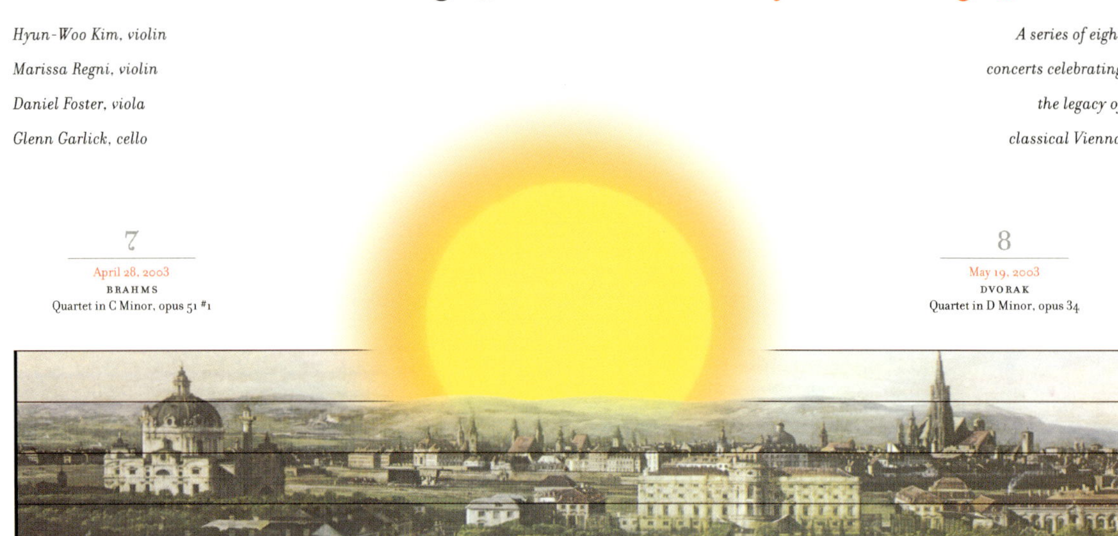

5
February 3, 2003
BEETHOVEN
Quartet in C sharp Minor, opus 131

6
March 31, 2003
SCHUMANN
Quartet in A Minor, opus 41 #1

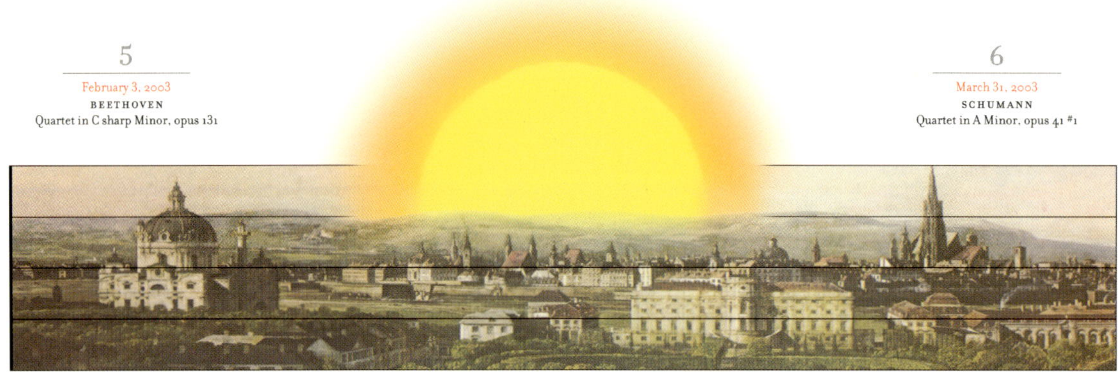

3
December 9, 2002
SCHUBERT
Quartet in A Minor, opus 29 #1 D. 804

4
January 13, 2003
MENDELSSOHN
Quartet in E flat Major, opus 12

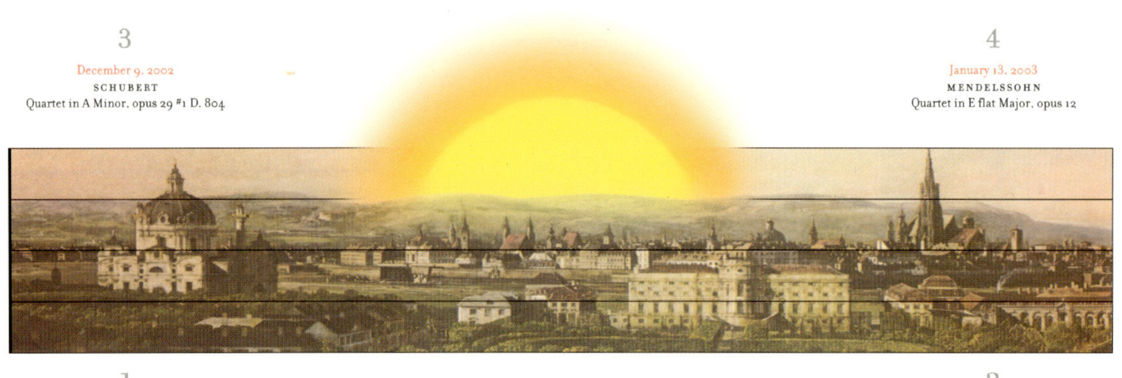

1
October 21, 2002
HAYDN
Quartet in B flat Major, opus 76 #4 "Sunrise"
BEETHOVEN
Quartet in C Minor, opus 18 #4

2
November 25, 2002
MOZART
Quartet in A Major, K. 464
BEETHOVEN
Quartet in A Major, opus 18 #5

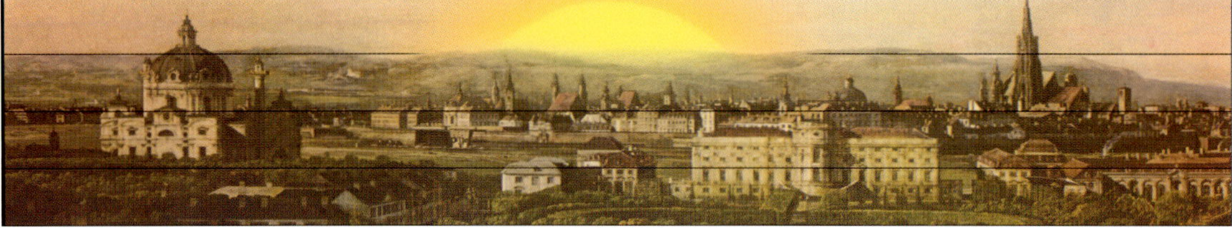

This series is made possible by a grant from the Merck Company Foundation.
All concerts are free and begin at 12:30 p.m. in Masur Auditorium, Building 10, NIH Medical Center.

For further information, contact the NIH Visitor Information Center, (VIC) 301-496-4713.

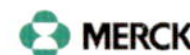

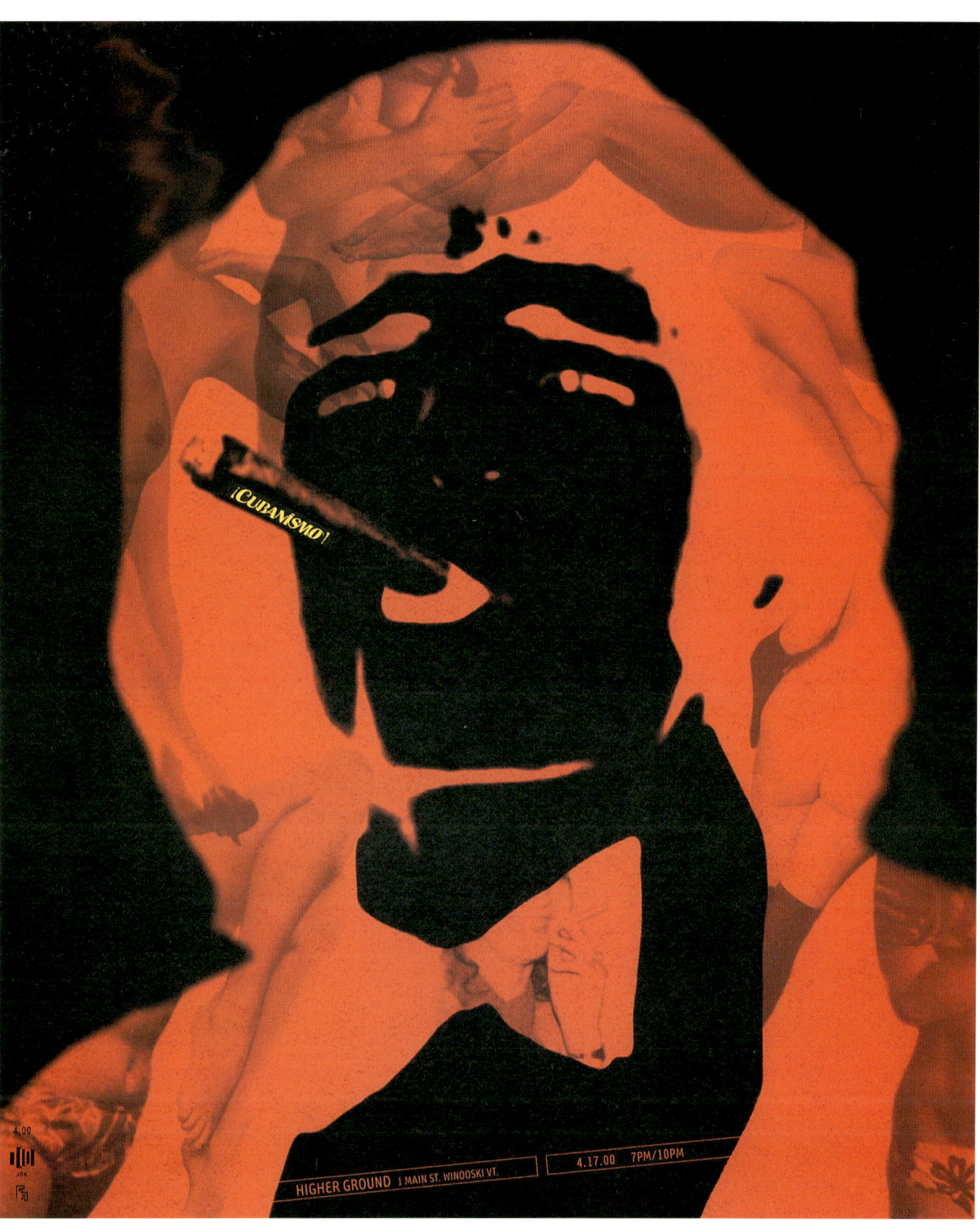

Jager Di Paola Kemp Design/Higher Ground

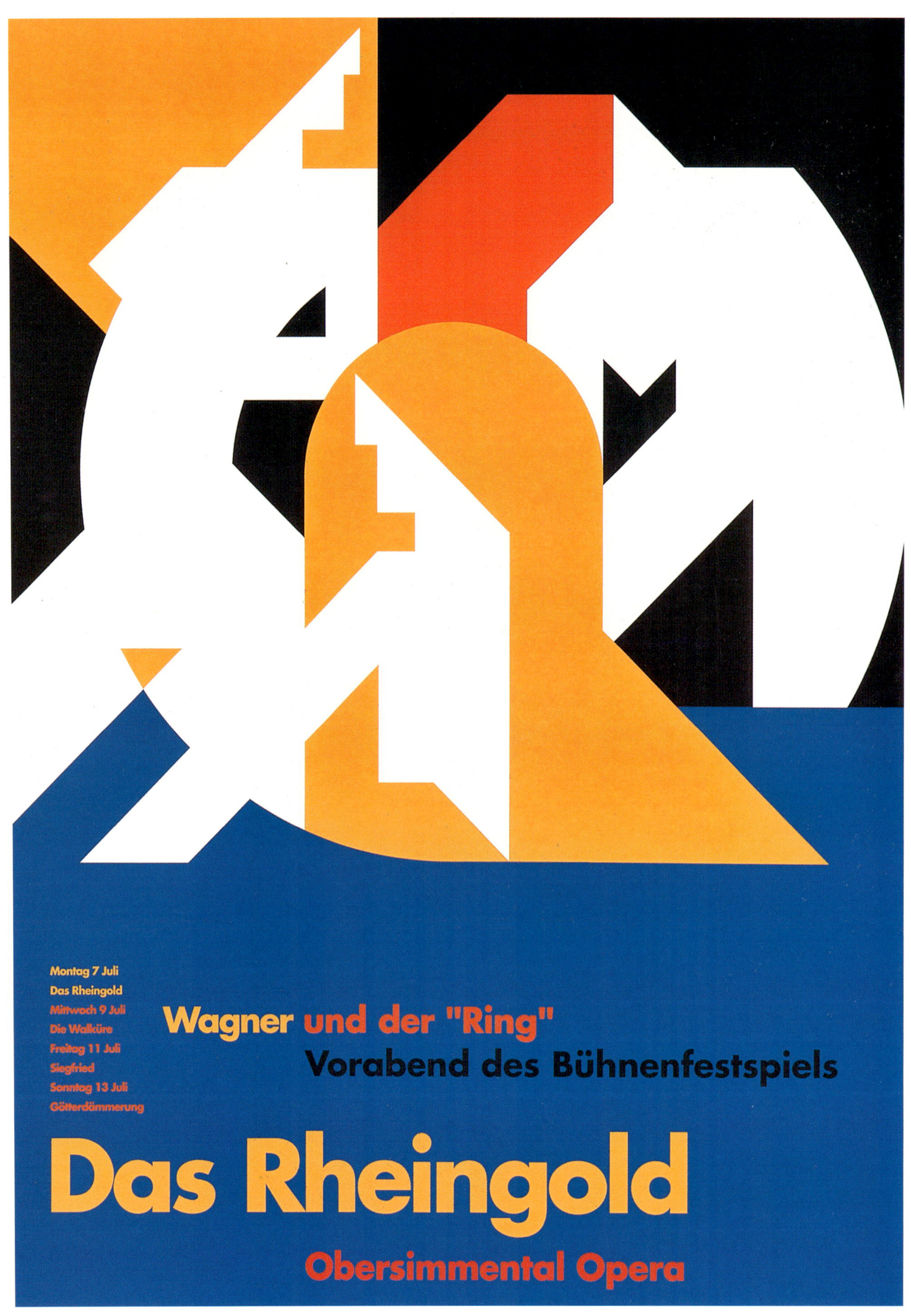

John Rieben Design/Obersimmental Opera

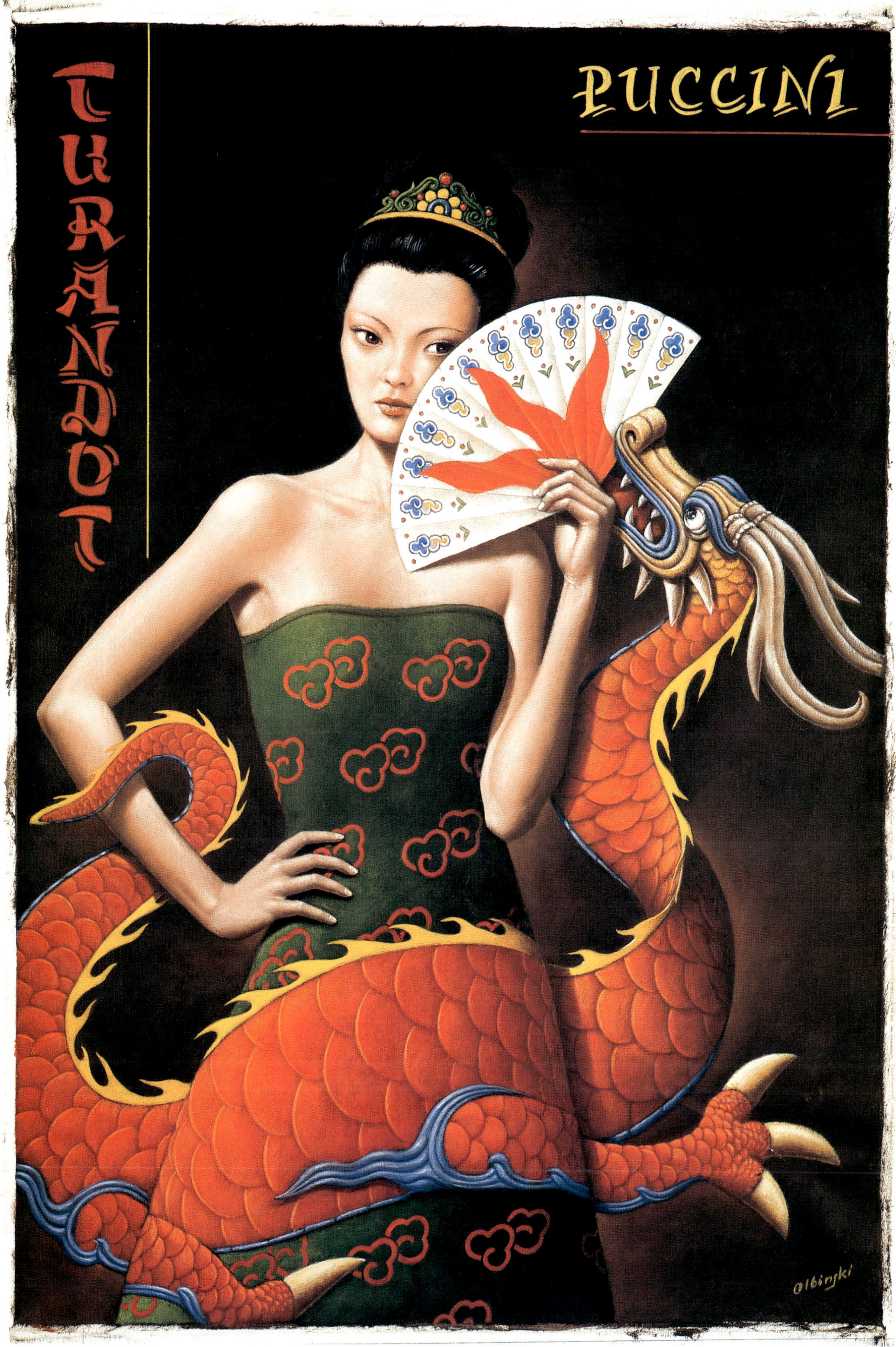

Olbinski Studio/Allegro Corporation

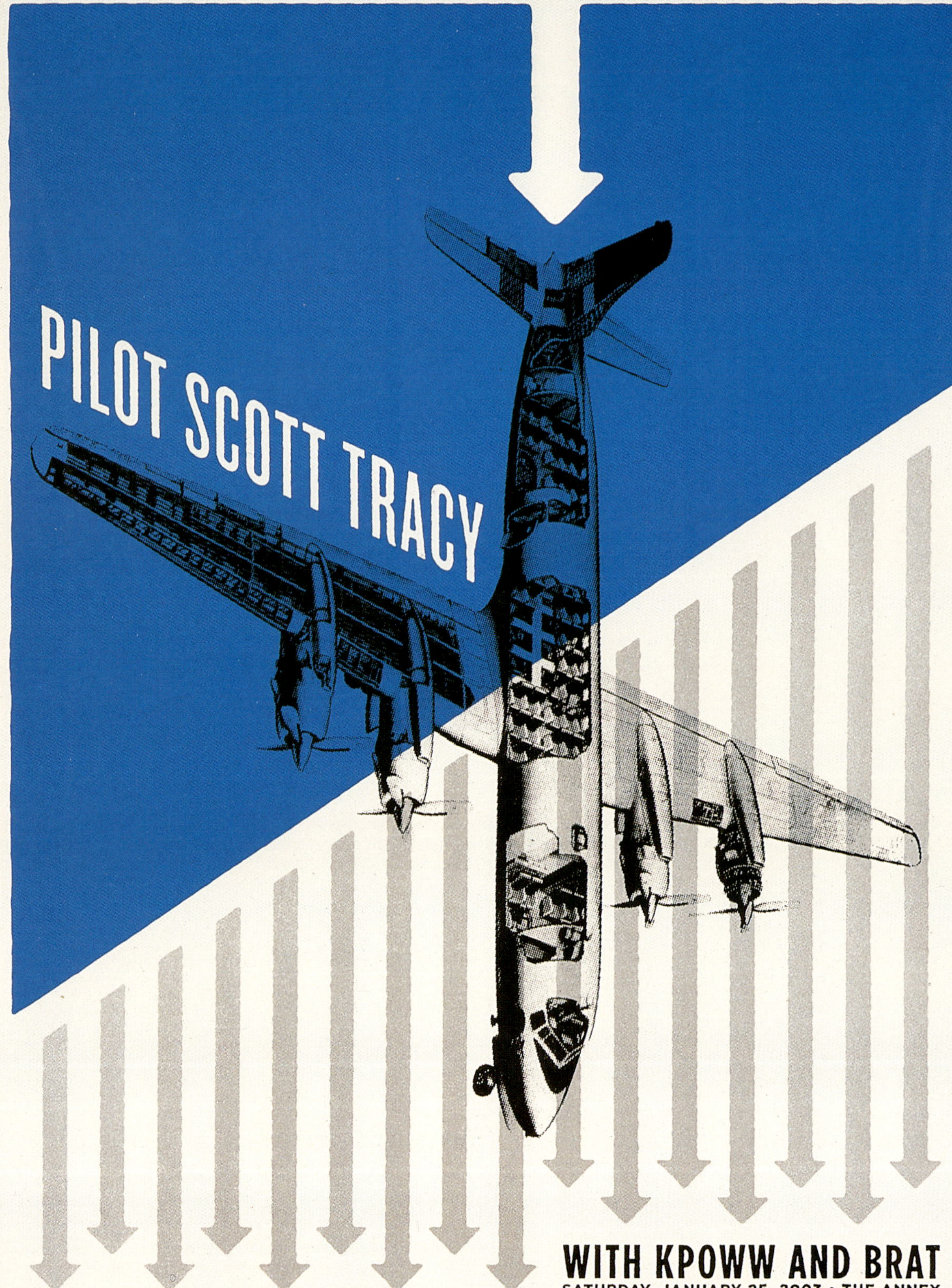
PILOT SCOTT TRACY
WITH KPOWW AND BRAT
SATURDAY, JANUARY 25, 2003 • THE ANNEX

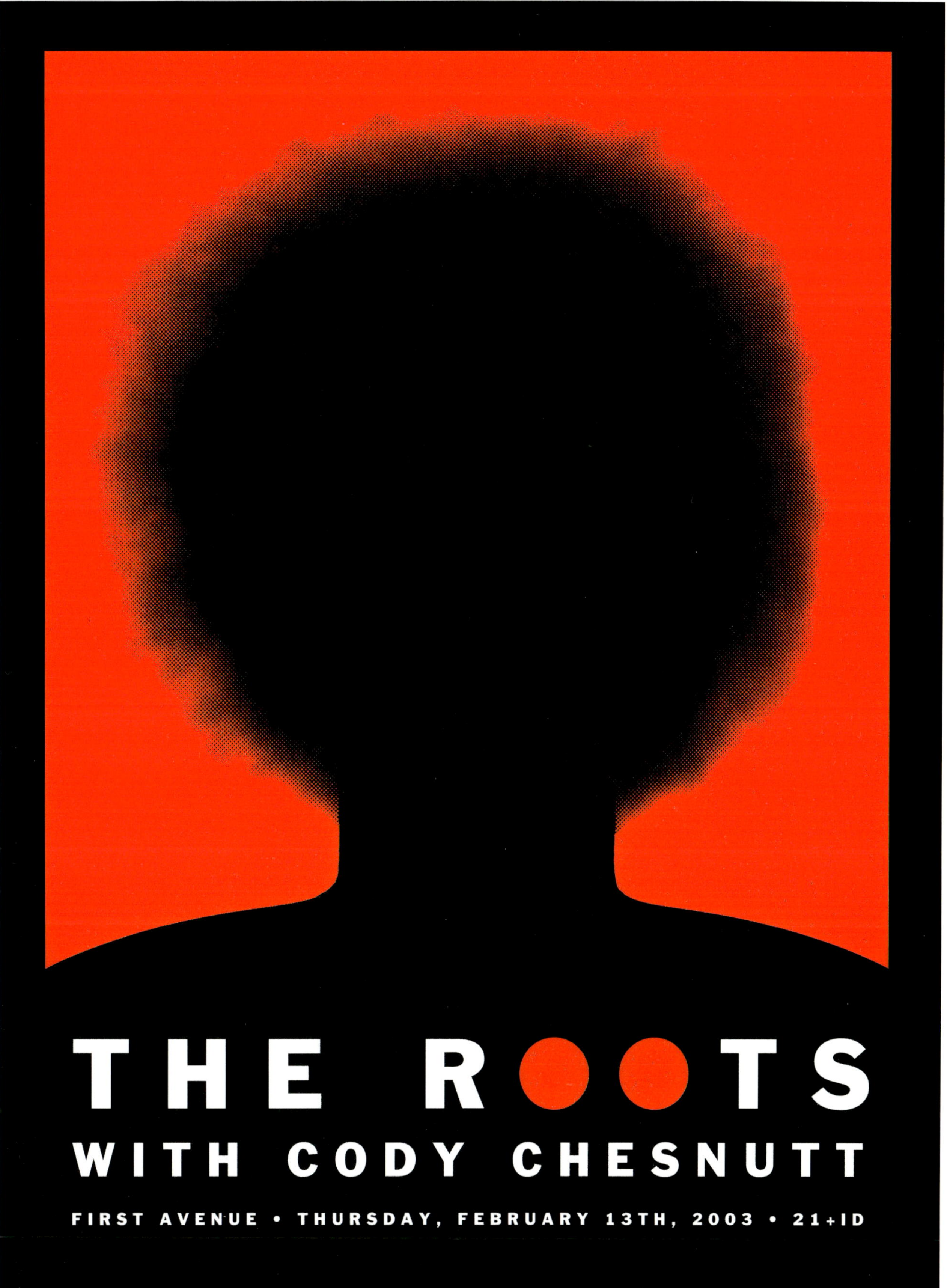

Aesthetic Apparatus/First Avenue

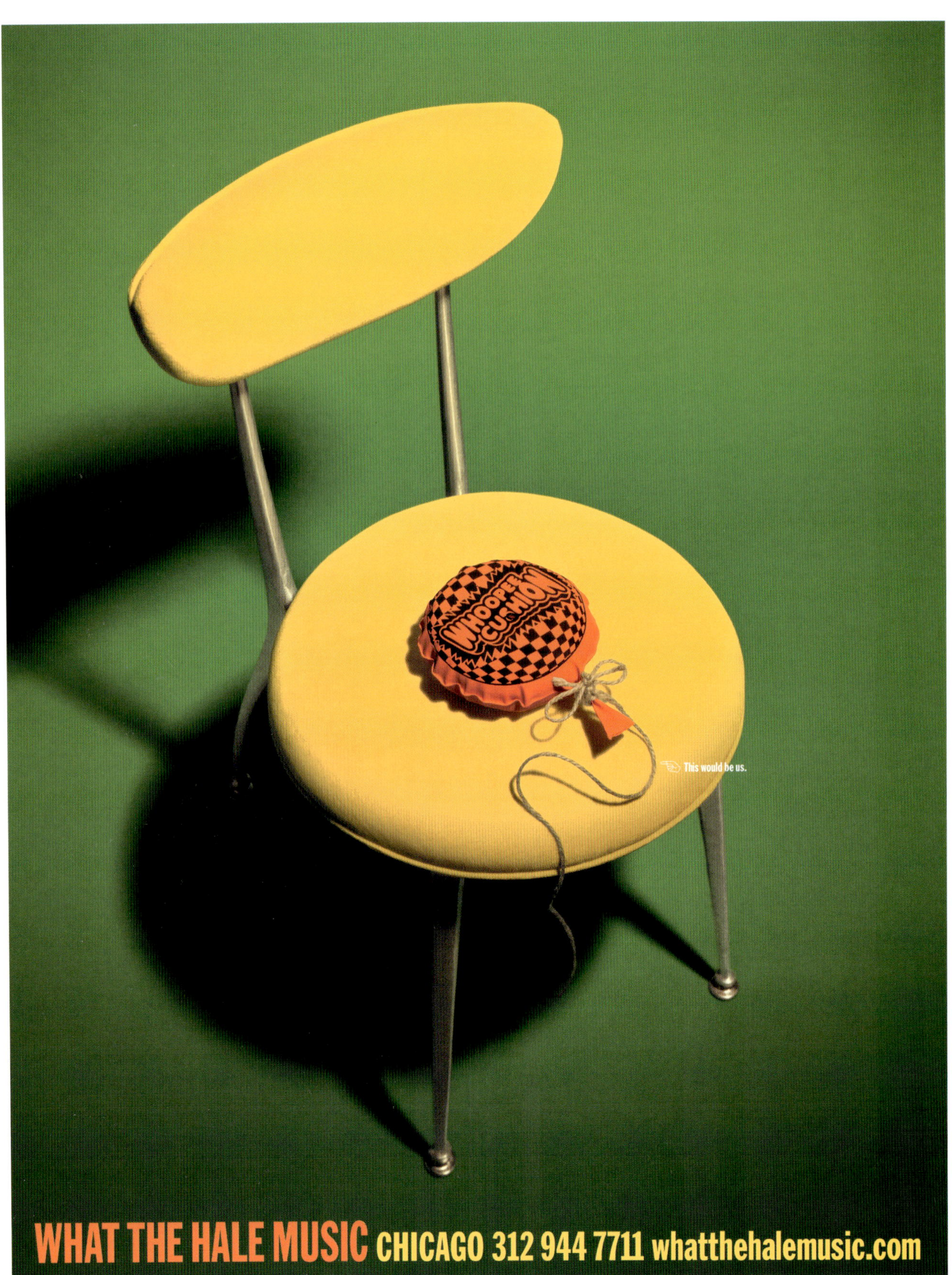

Hoffman York Inc./What the Hale Music

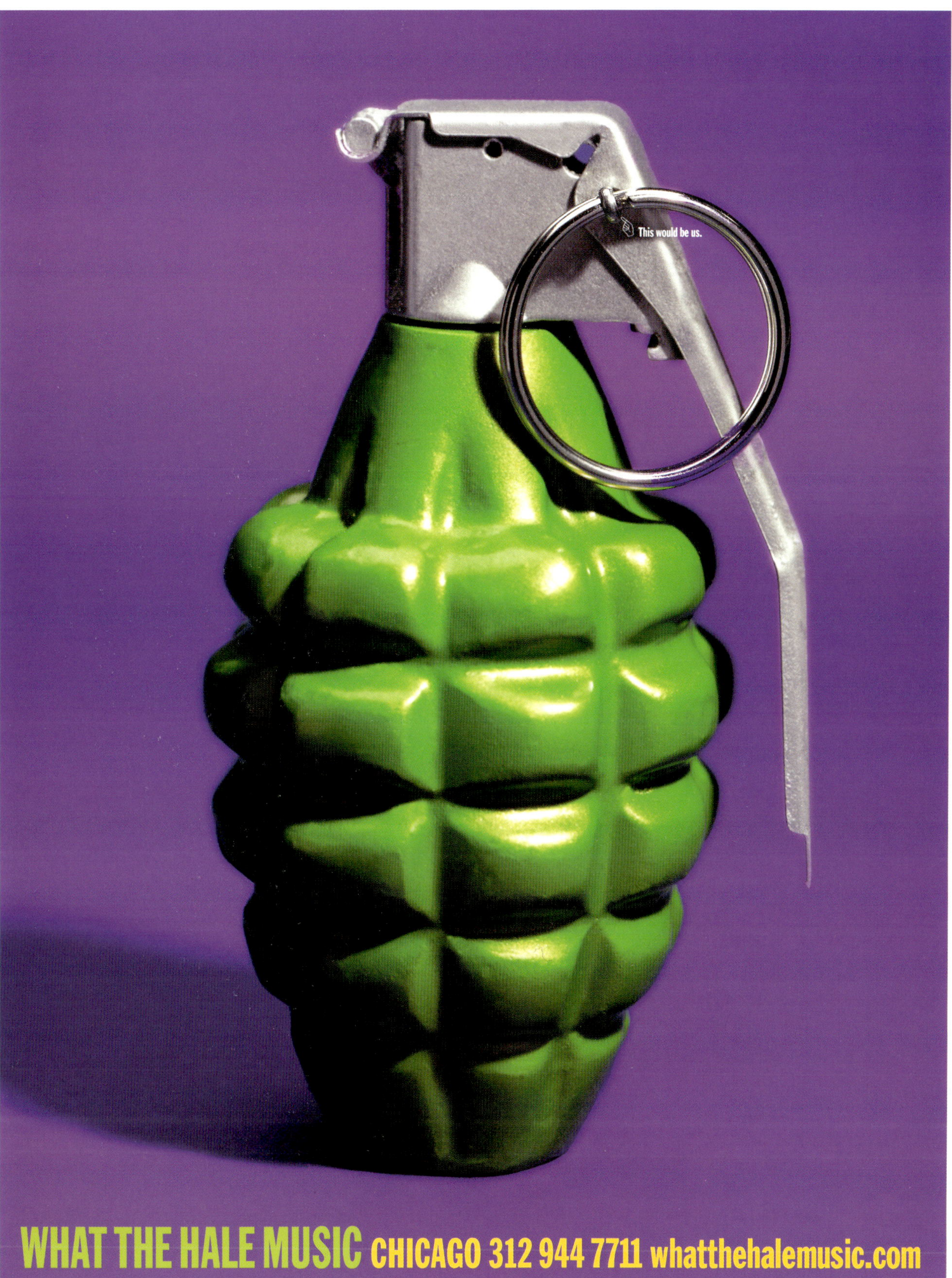

Hoffman York Inc./What the Hale Music

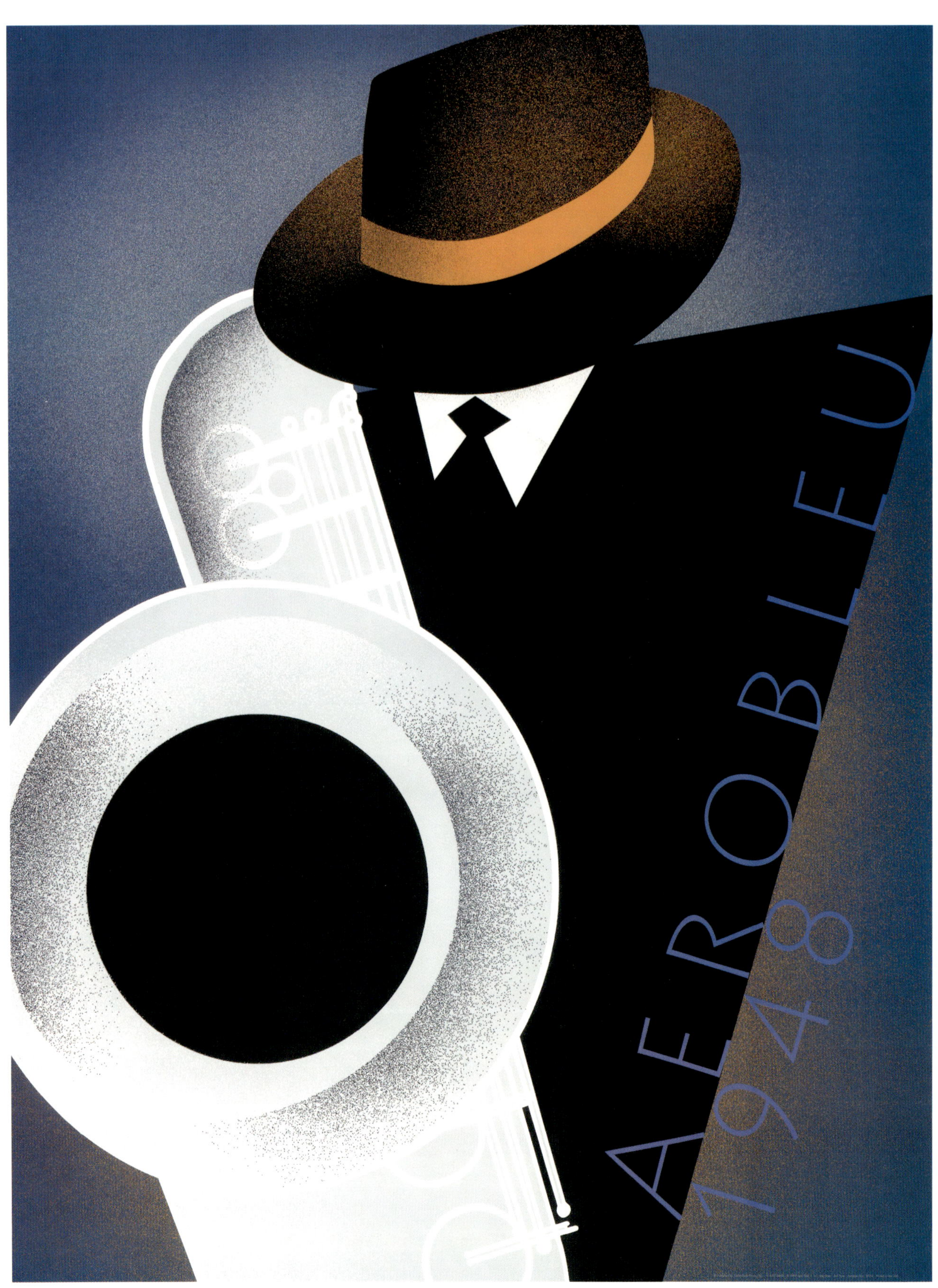

Rod Dyer International/Brooks Branch

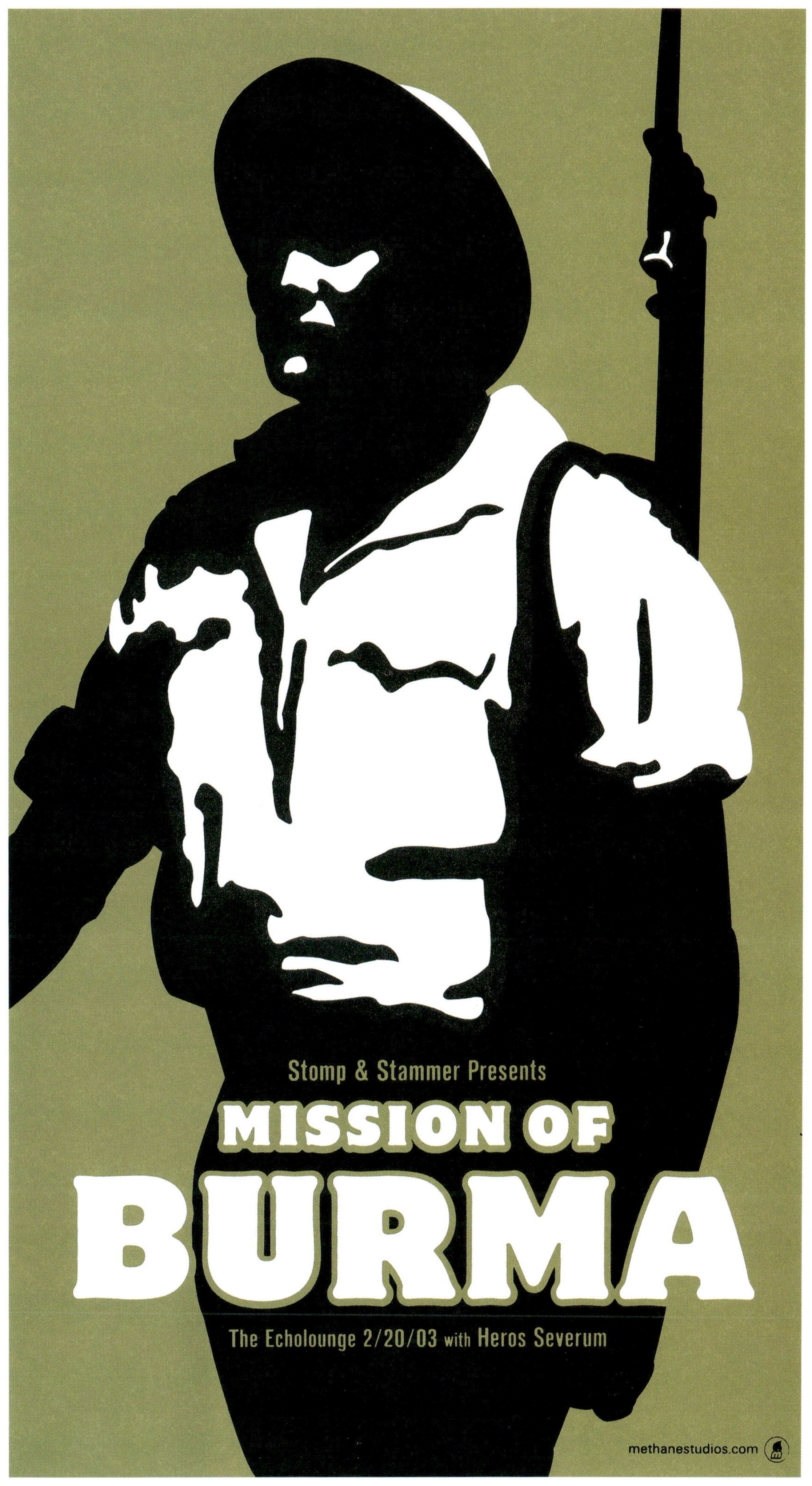

Methane Studios, Inc./The Echo Lounge

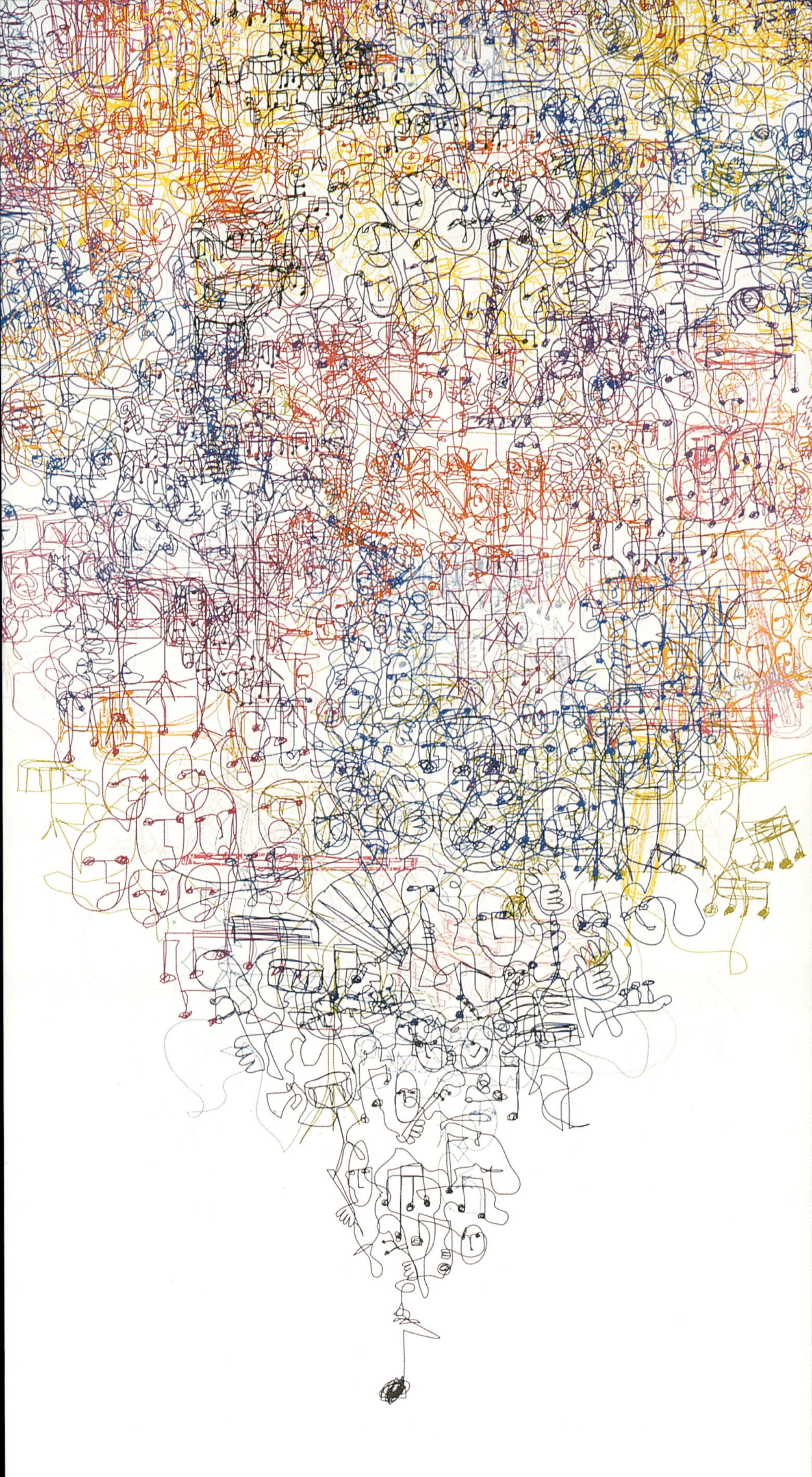

winston-salem symphony 2000/2001 season

HendersonBromsteadArt Co./Winston-Salem Symphony

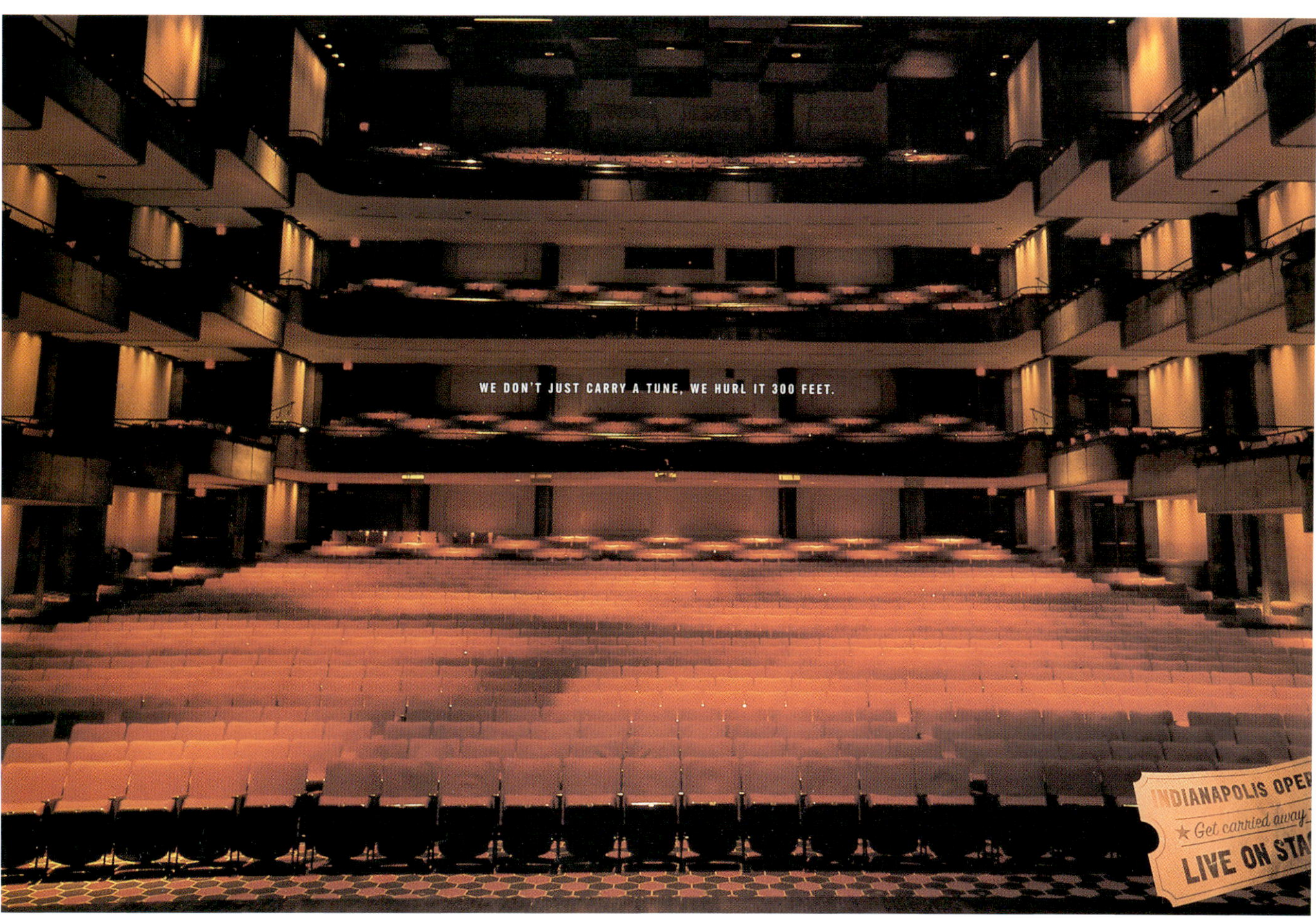

Roman Brand Group/Indianapolis Opera

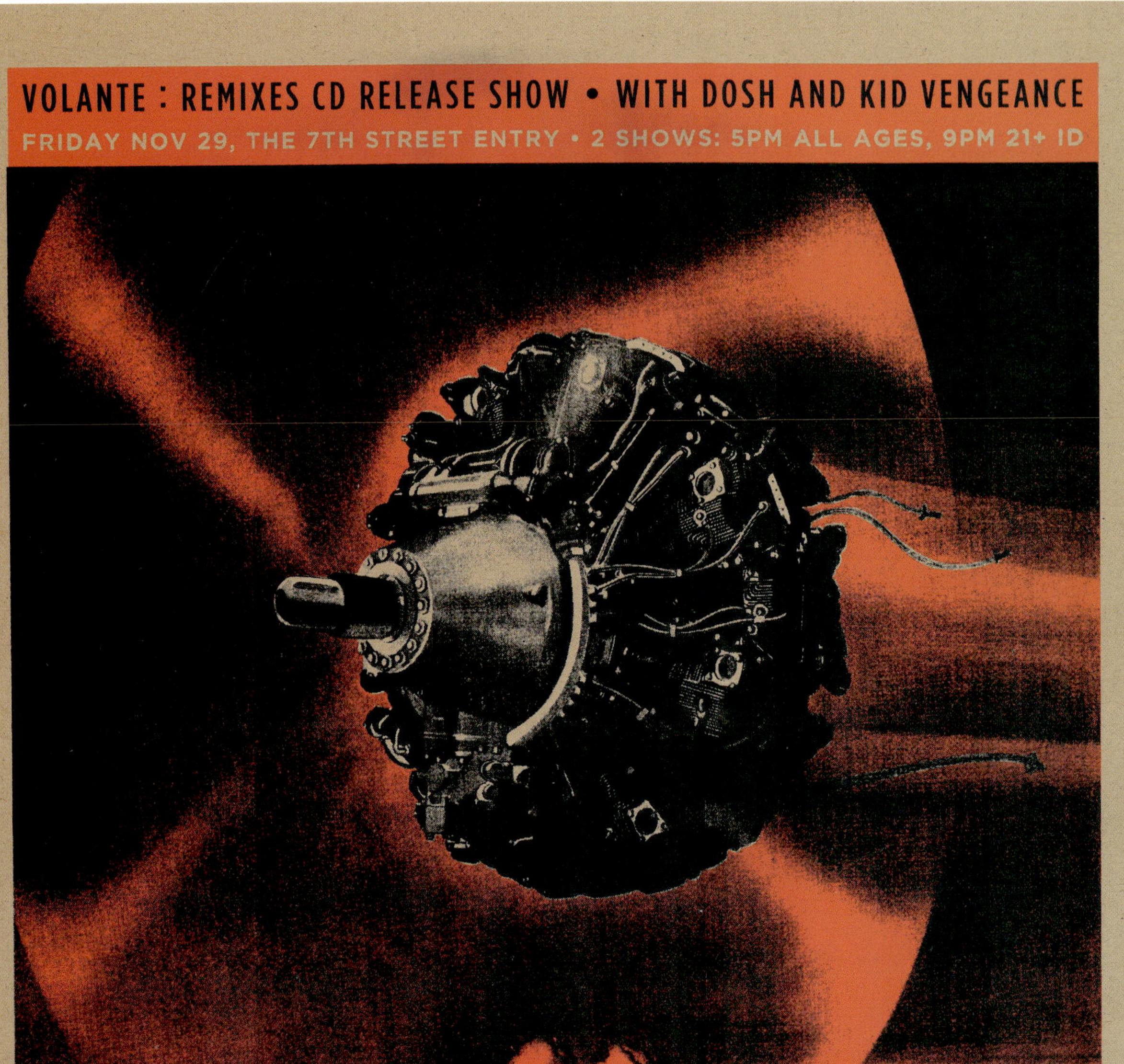

Aesthetic Apparatus/Volante

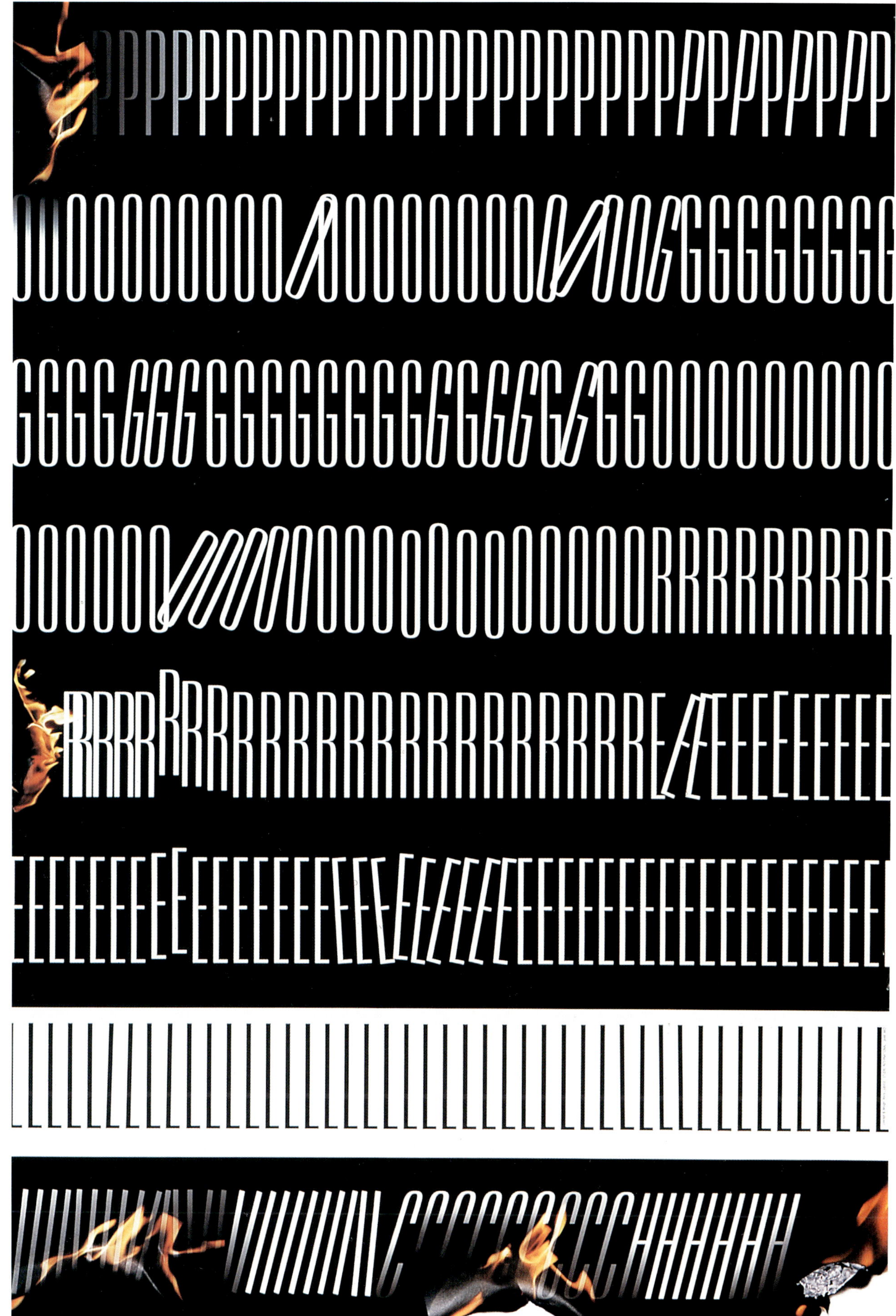

Studio International/Rotary Club Zagreb

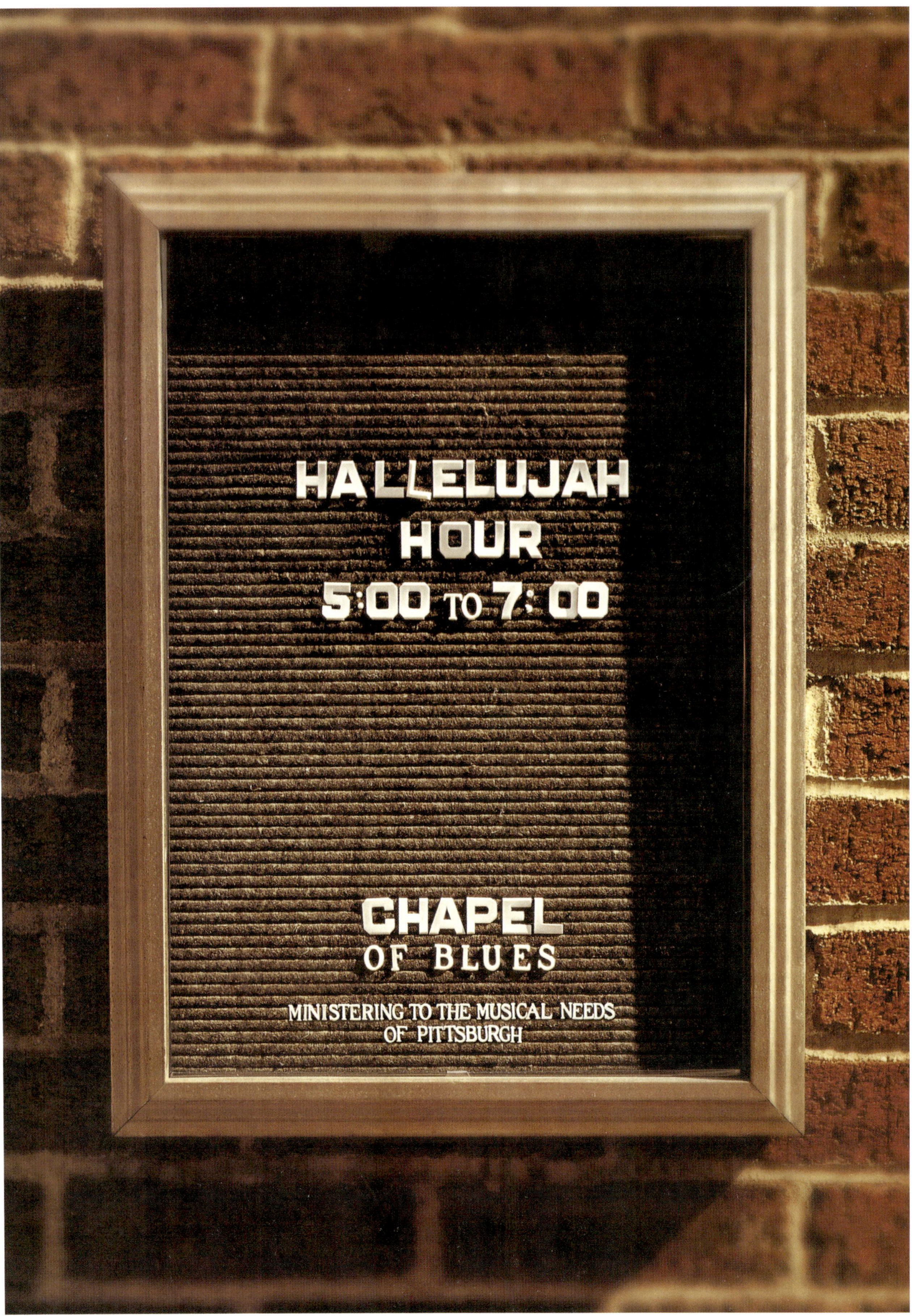

Blattner Brunner/Chapel of Blues

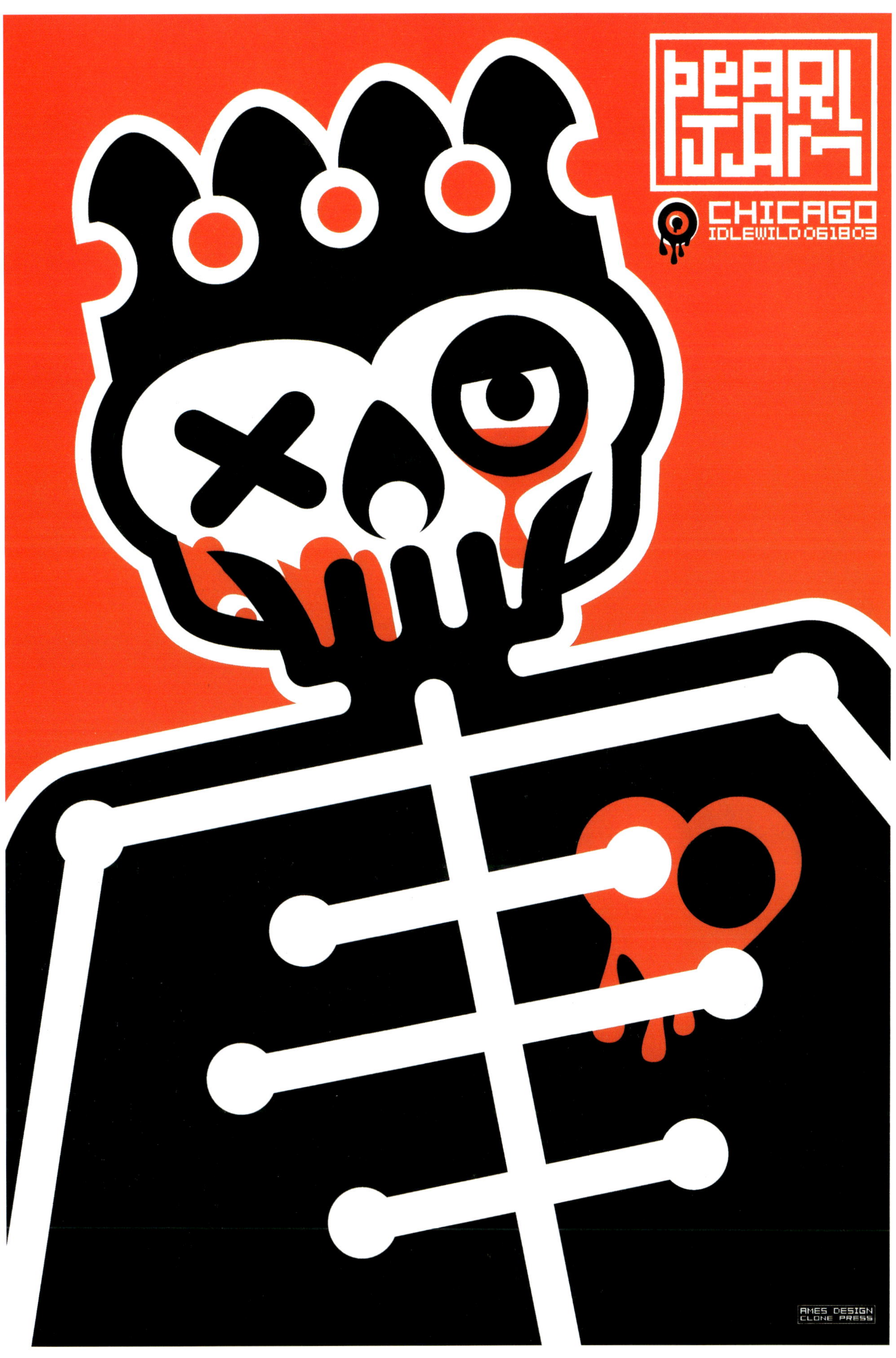

(this page) Ames Design/Pearl Jam (following spread) Taxi/Mini - BMW Group Canada

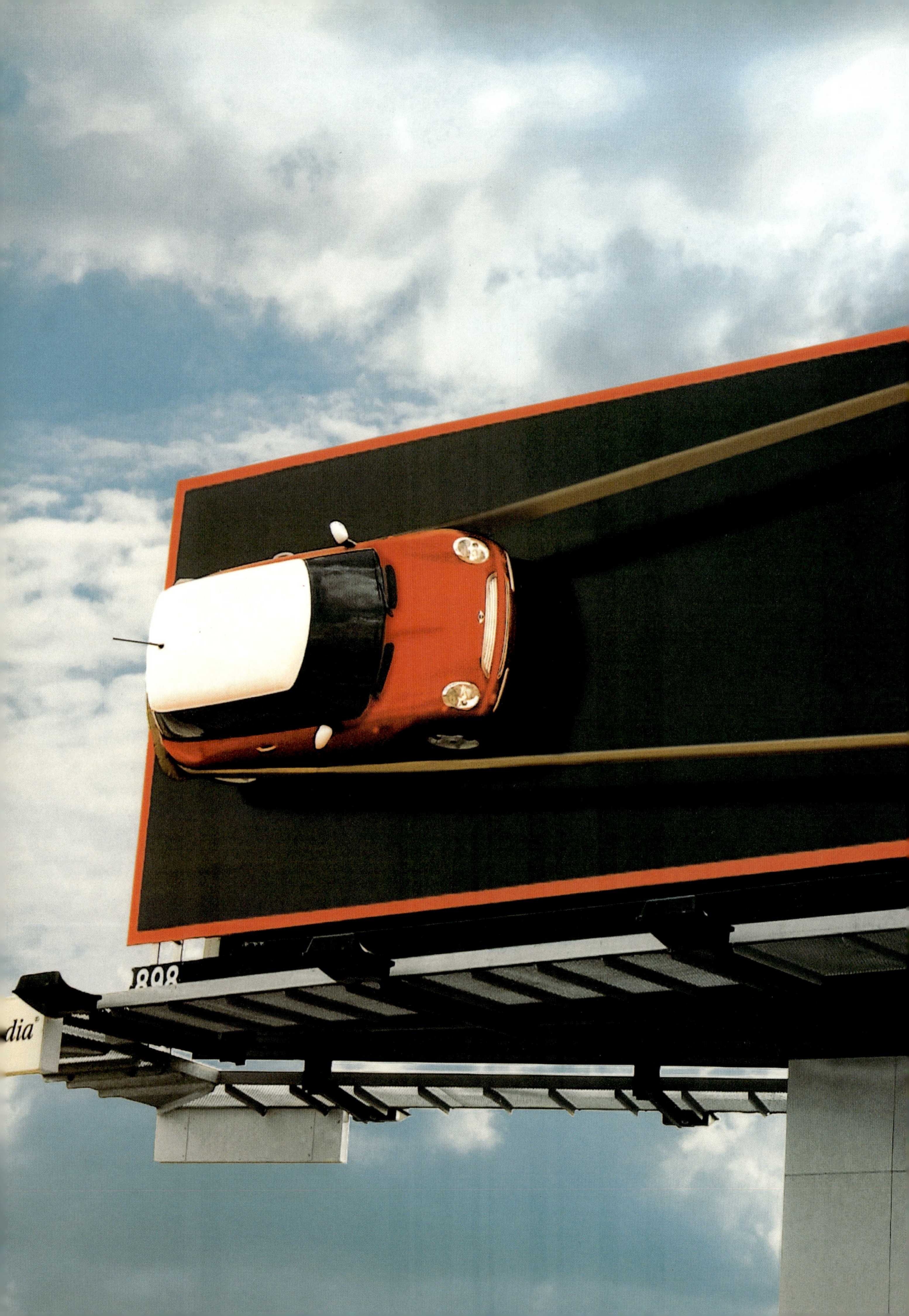
898
dia®

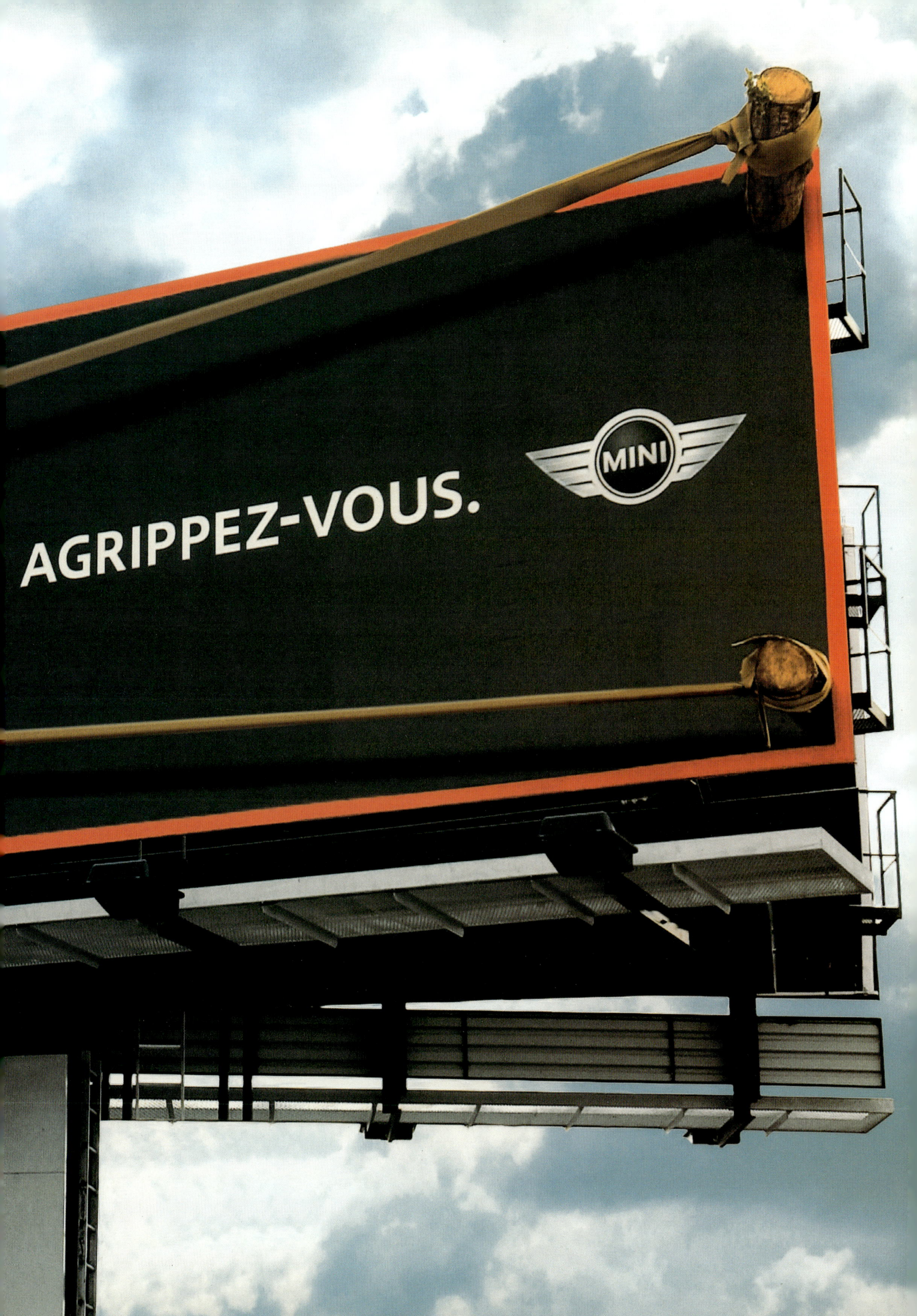
MINI
AGRIPPEZ-VOUS.

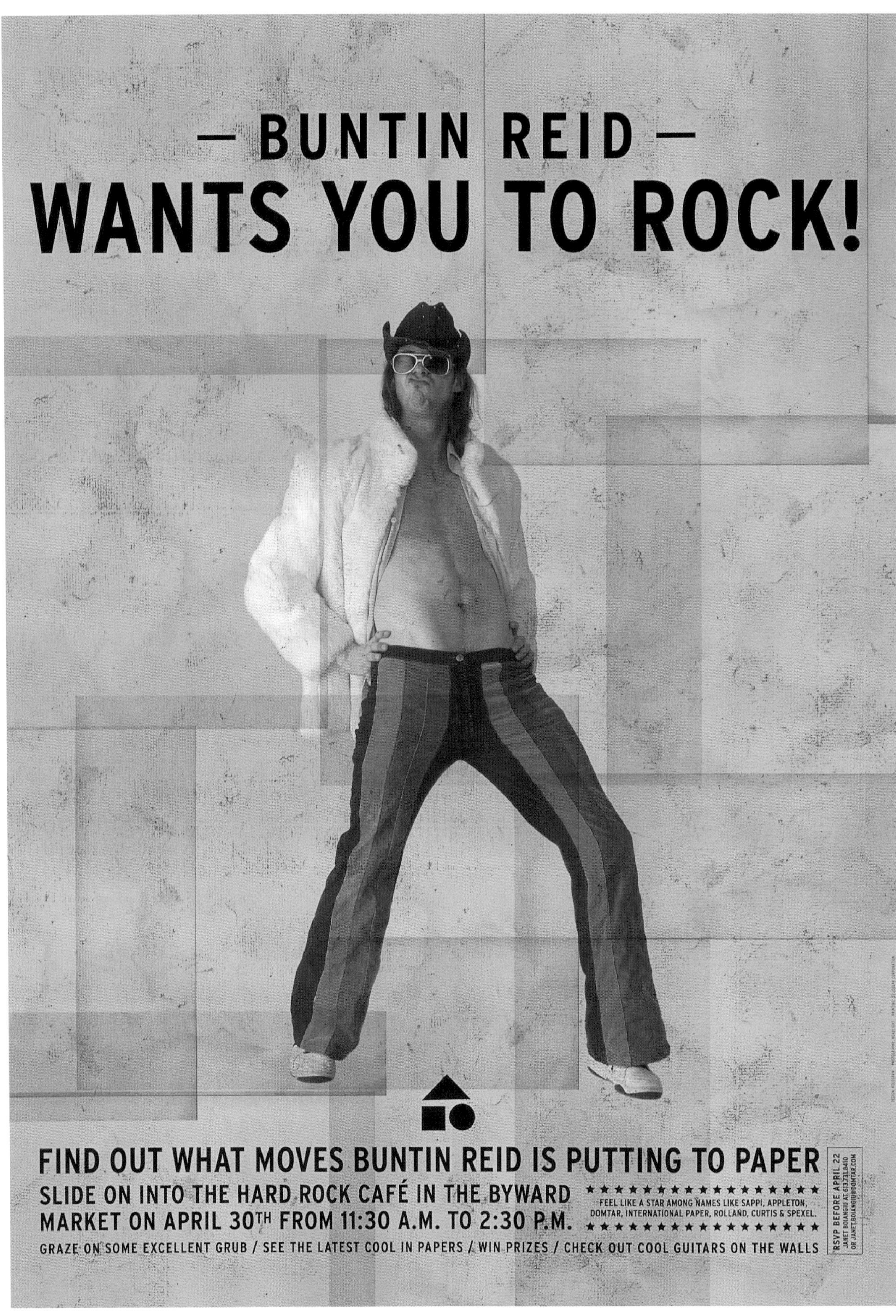

Kolegram Design/Buntin Reid

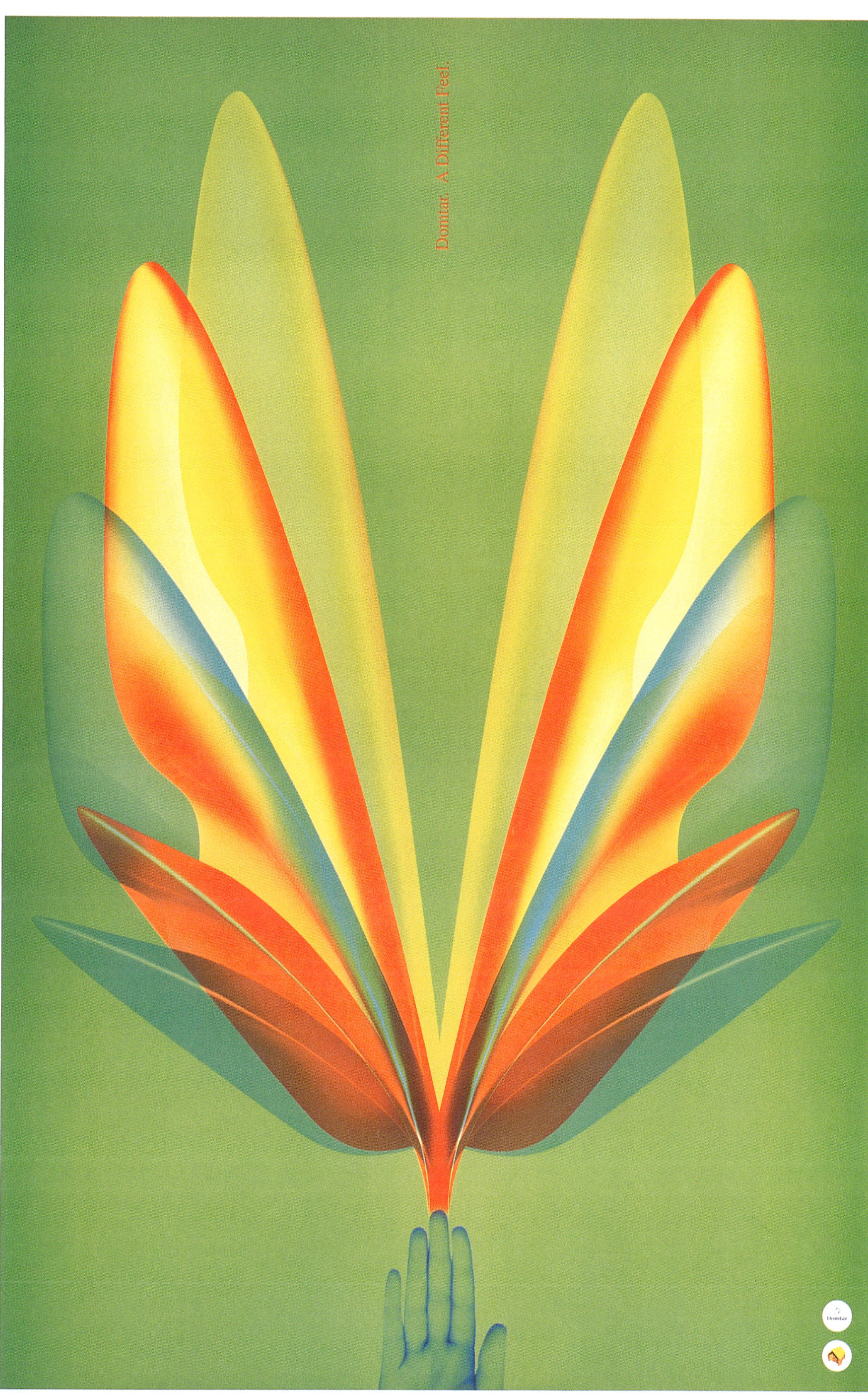
Domtar. A Different Feel.
Domtar

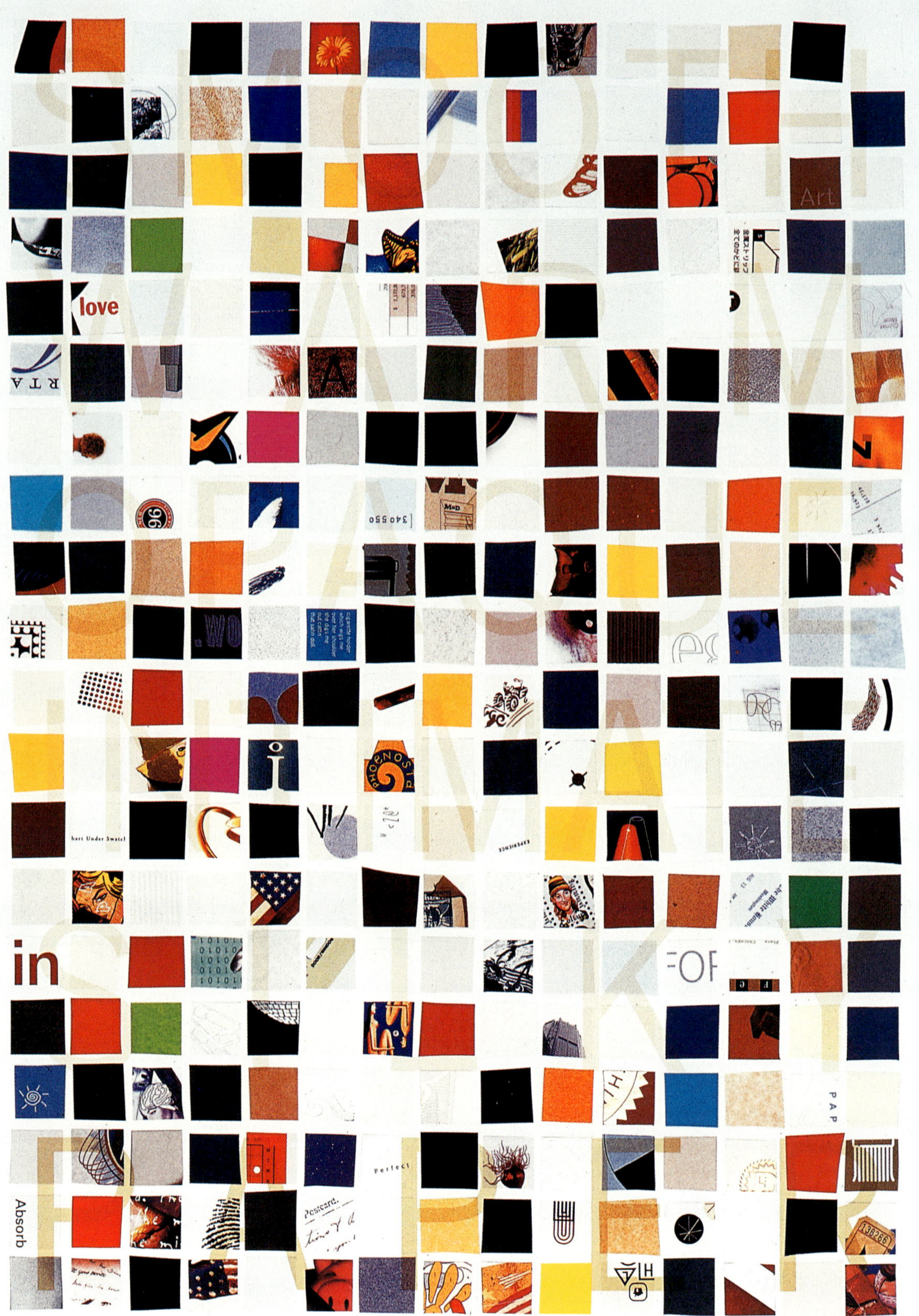

CLAMPITT PAPER SHOW

OCT 17.02

WARWICK HOTEL

LAFONTAINE BALLROOM

5:30 to 8:00 [PM]

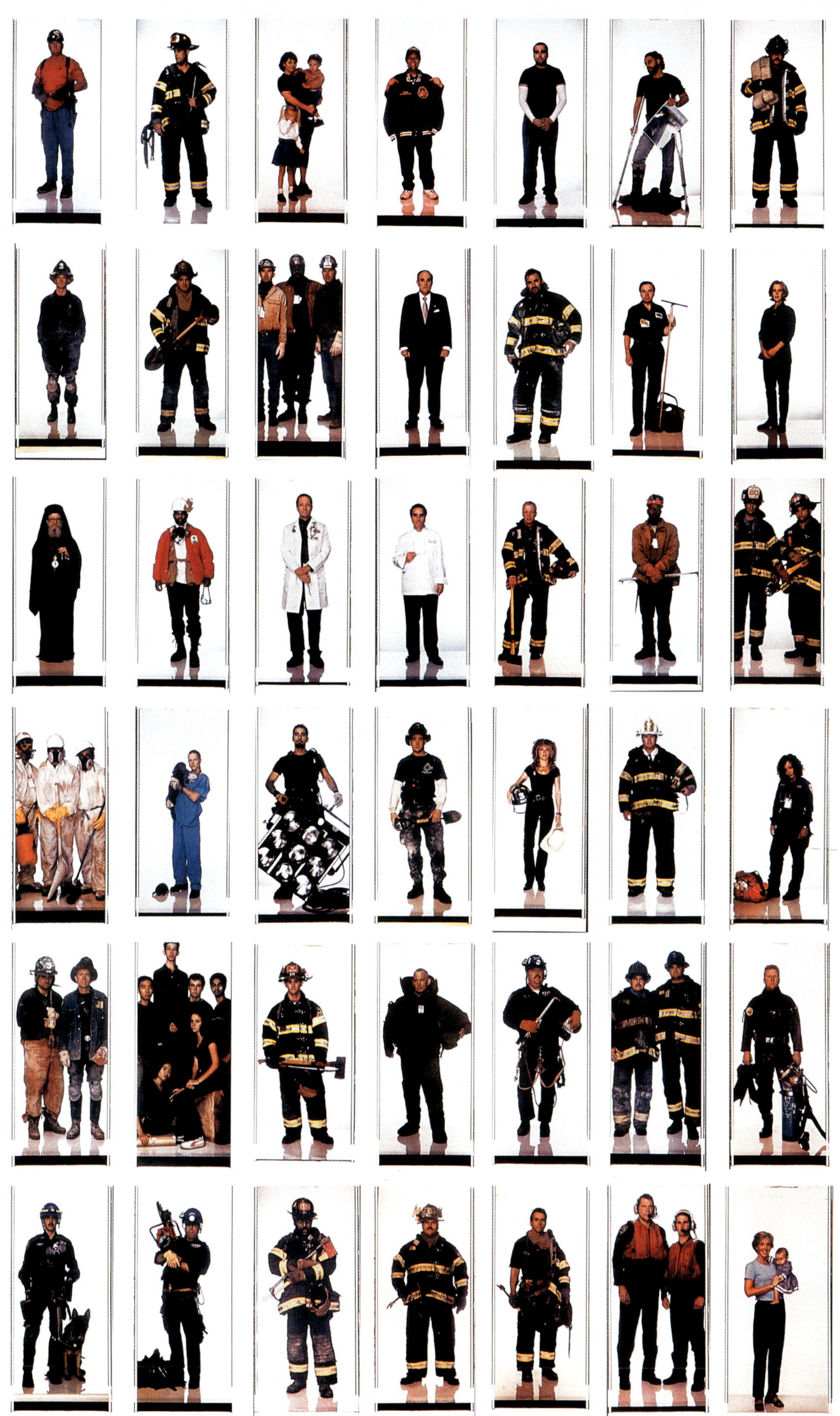

Joe McNally Photography

Faces of Ground Zero >> Giant Polaroid Collection

www.joemcnally.com >> 914.478.7728

Joe McNally Photography, Inc./Joe McNally

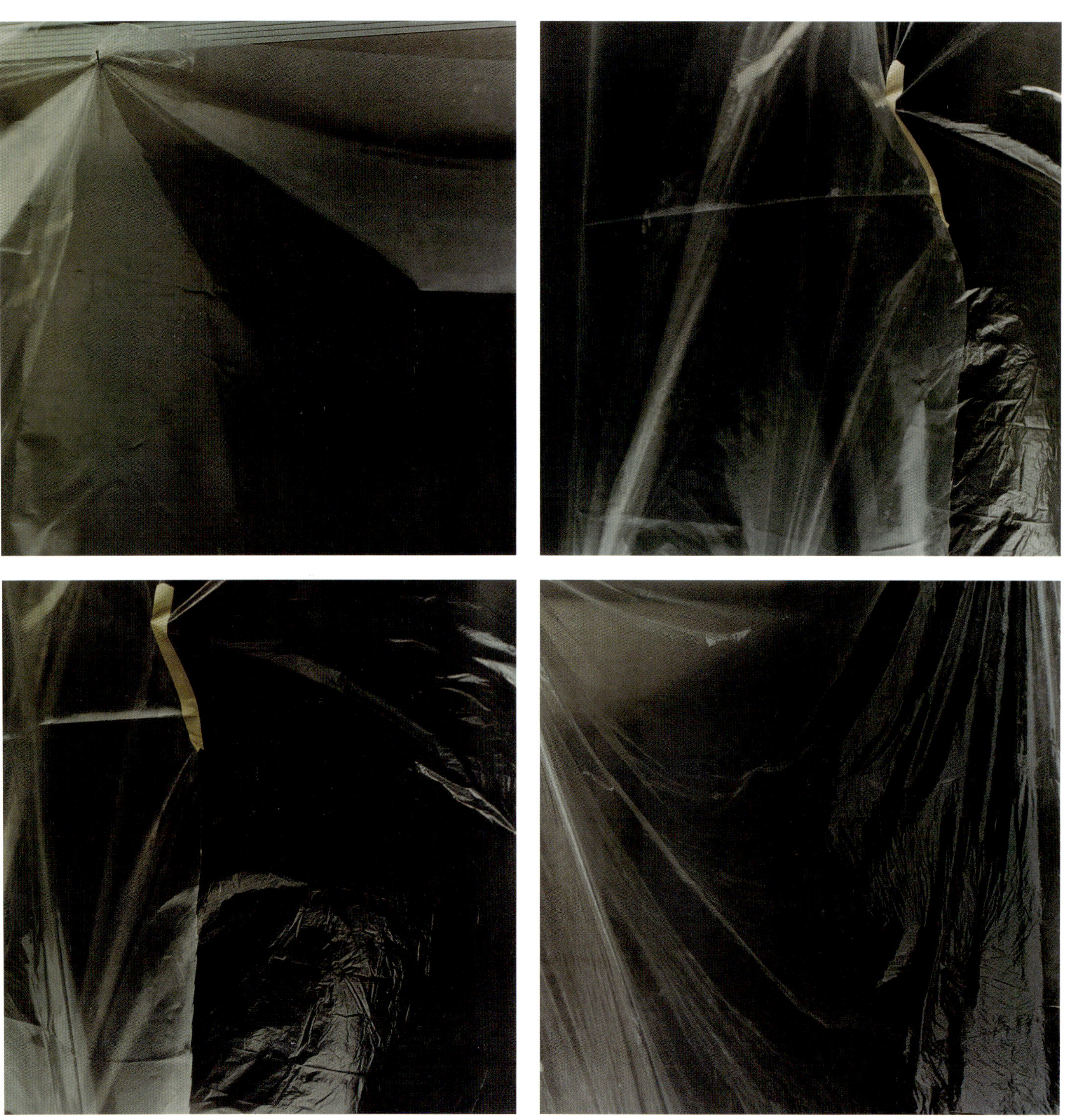

GJP Design/Michael Myersfeld

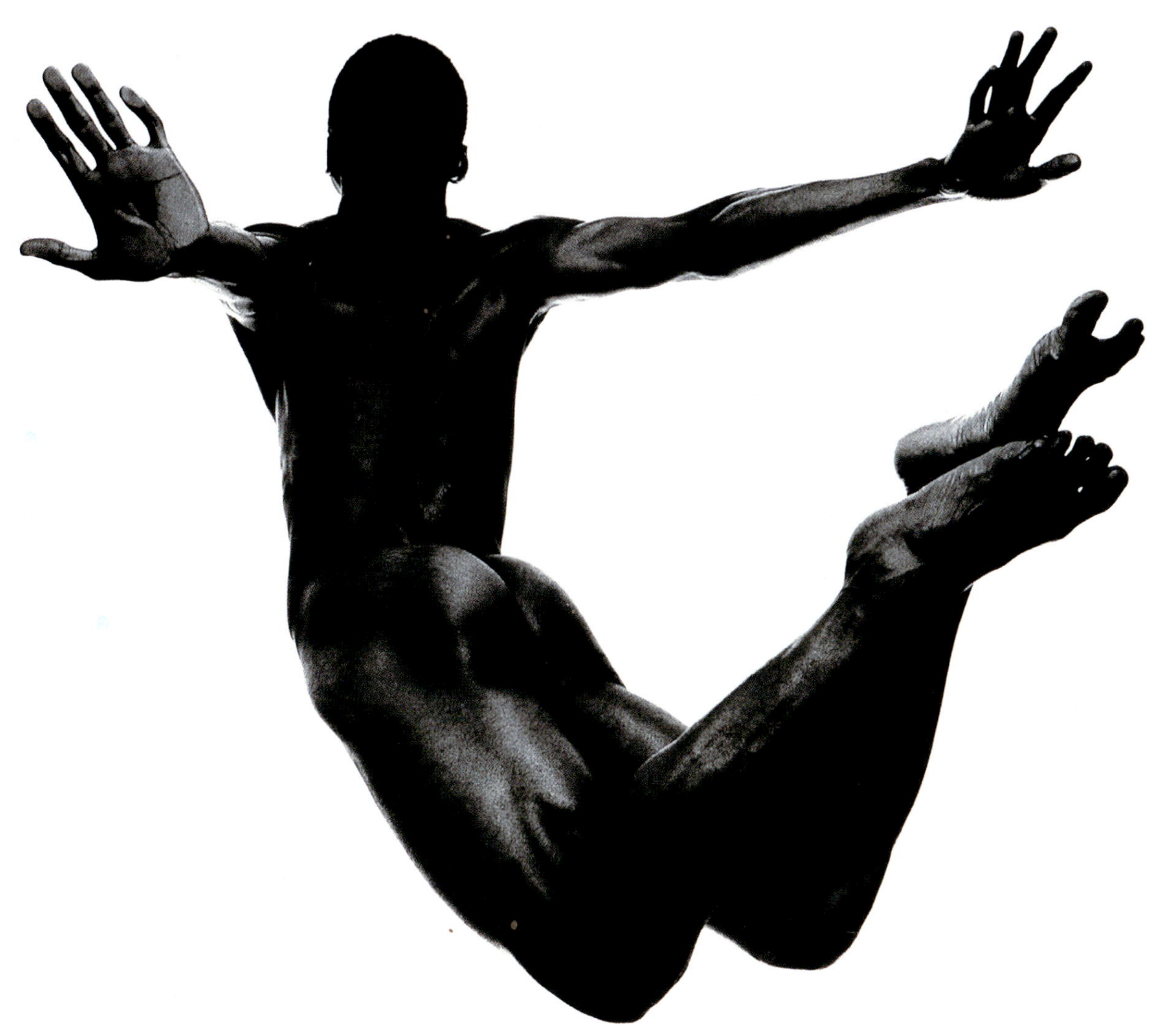

SANDRO
FIGURE E
RITRATTI

Nude Dancer on Plexiglass   Centro Internazionale di Fotografia Scavi Scaligeri   Verona, Italy   25 Oct, 2002   05 Jan, 2003

MAKE LİFE

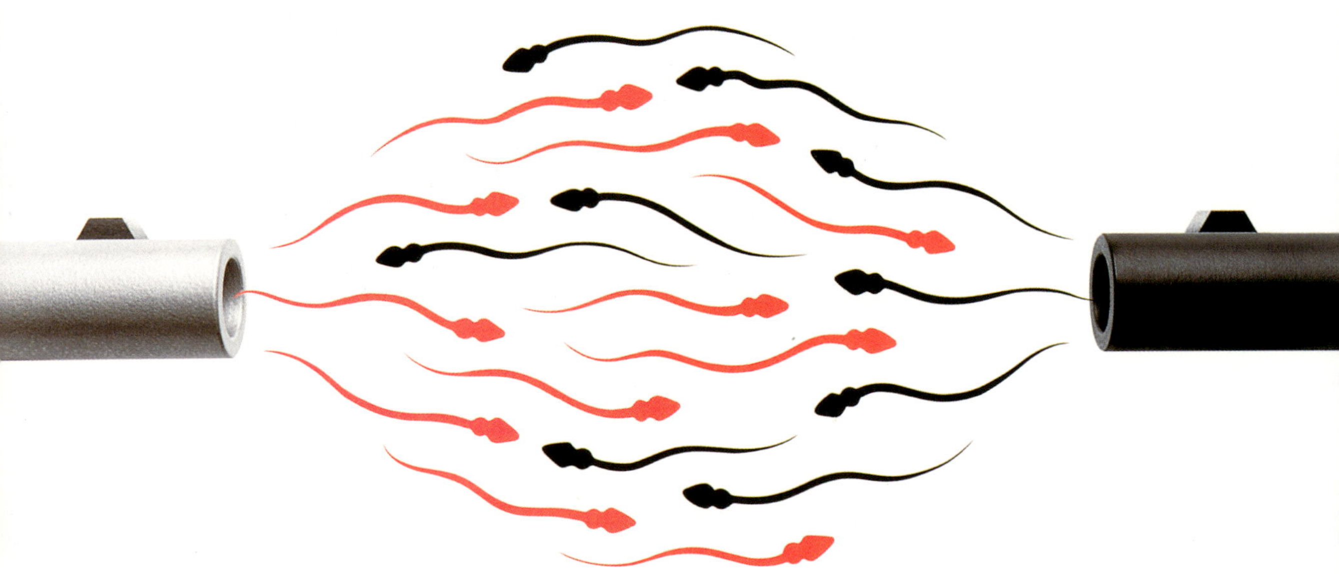

NO WaR

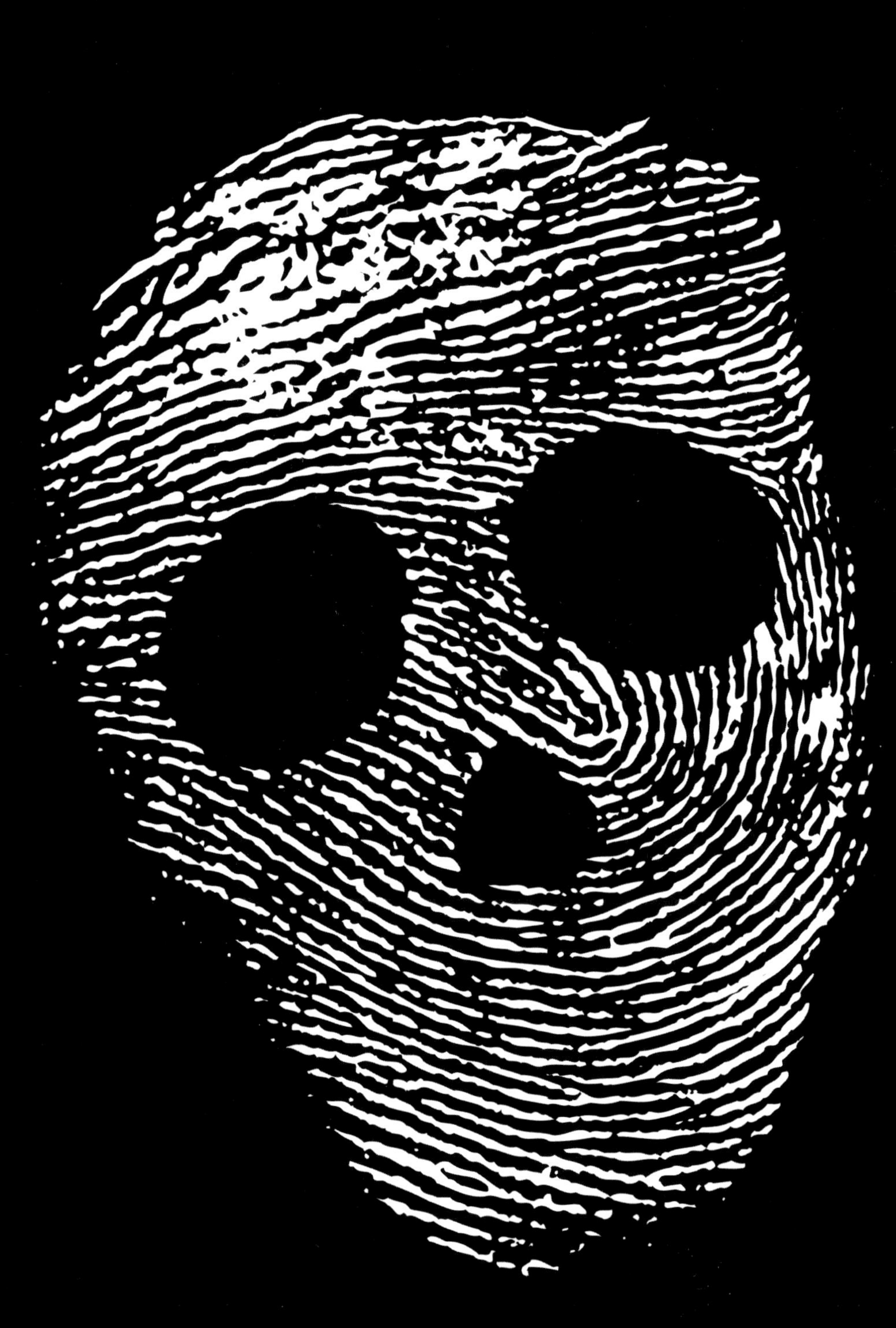

COLOMBIA

MAS DE LA MITAD DE TODOS LOS ATENTADOS TERRORISTAS EN EL MUNDO OCURREN AQUI

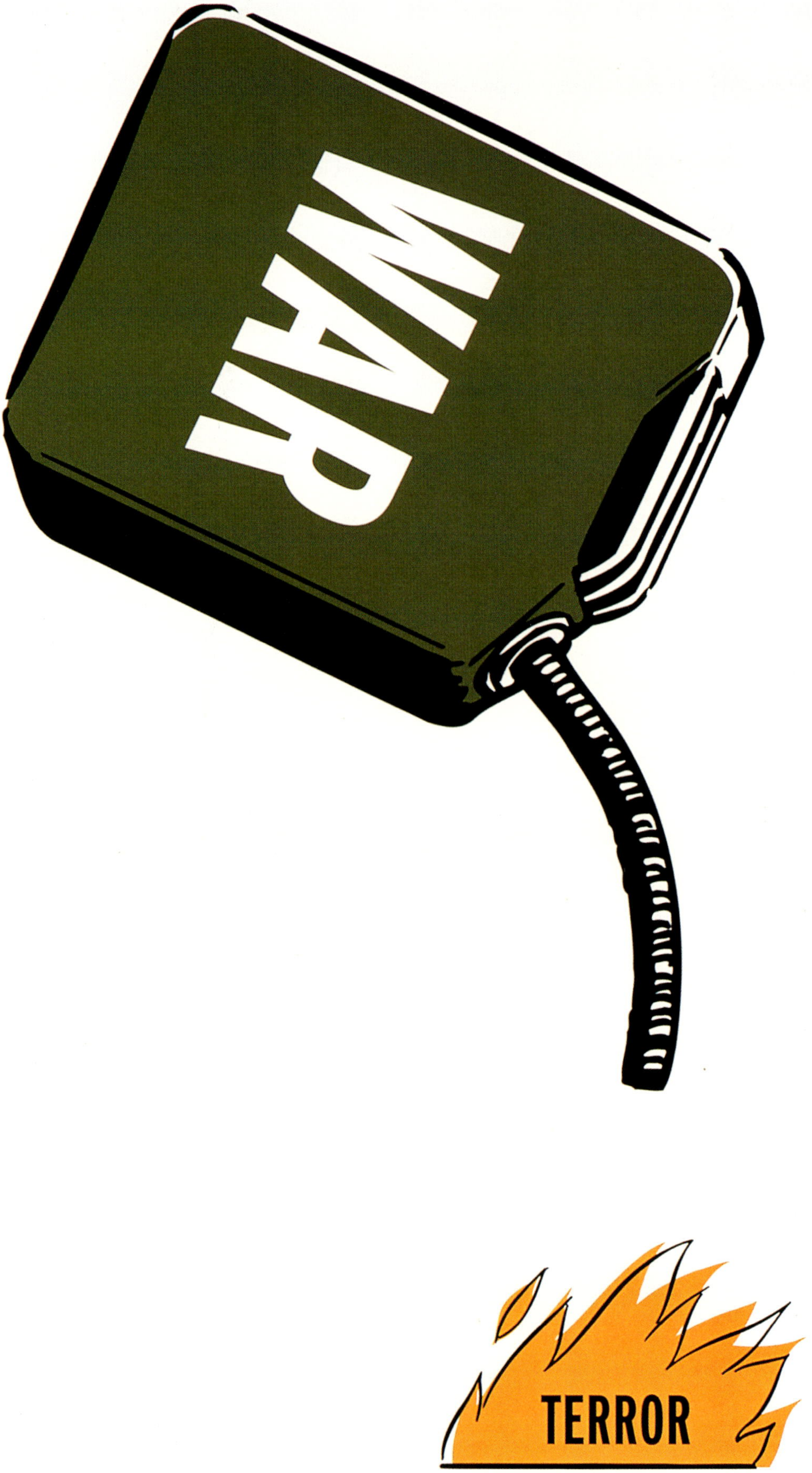

WAR

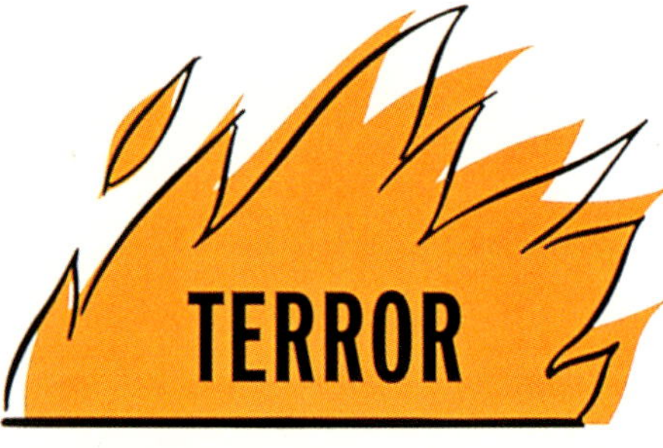

DOWNLOAD THIS POSTER FREE AT WWW.ANOTHERPOSTERFORPEACE.COM DESIGN: MARTY NEUMEIER

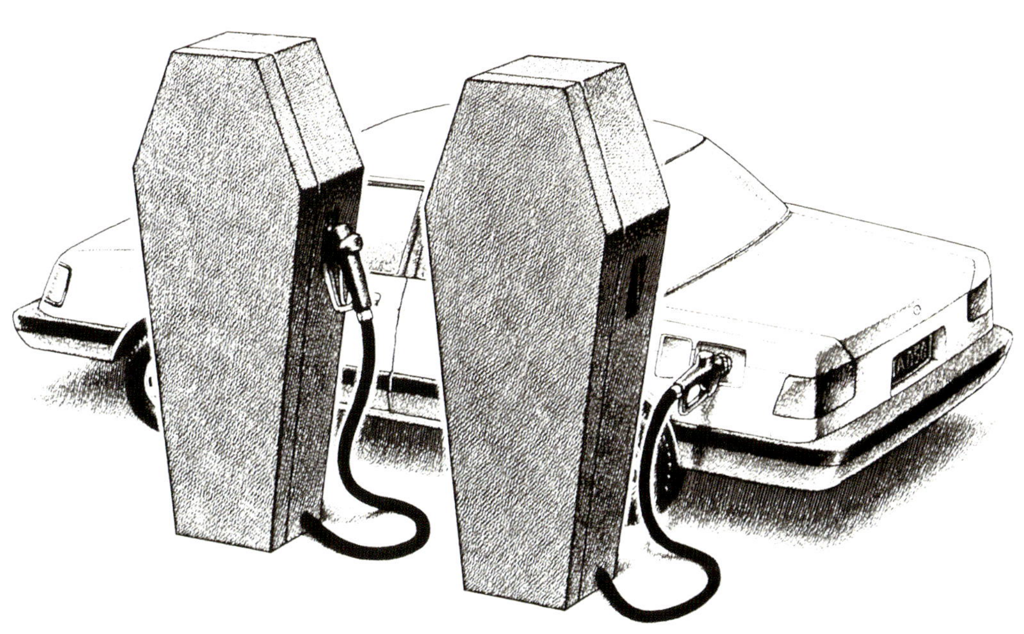

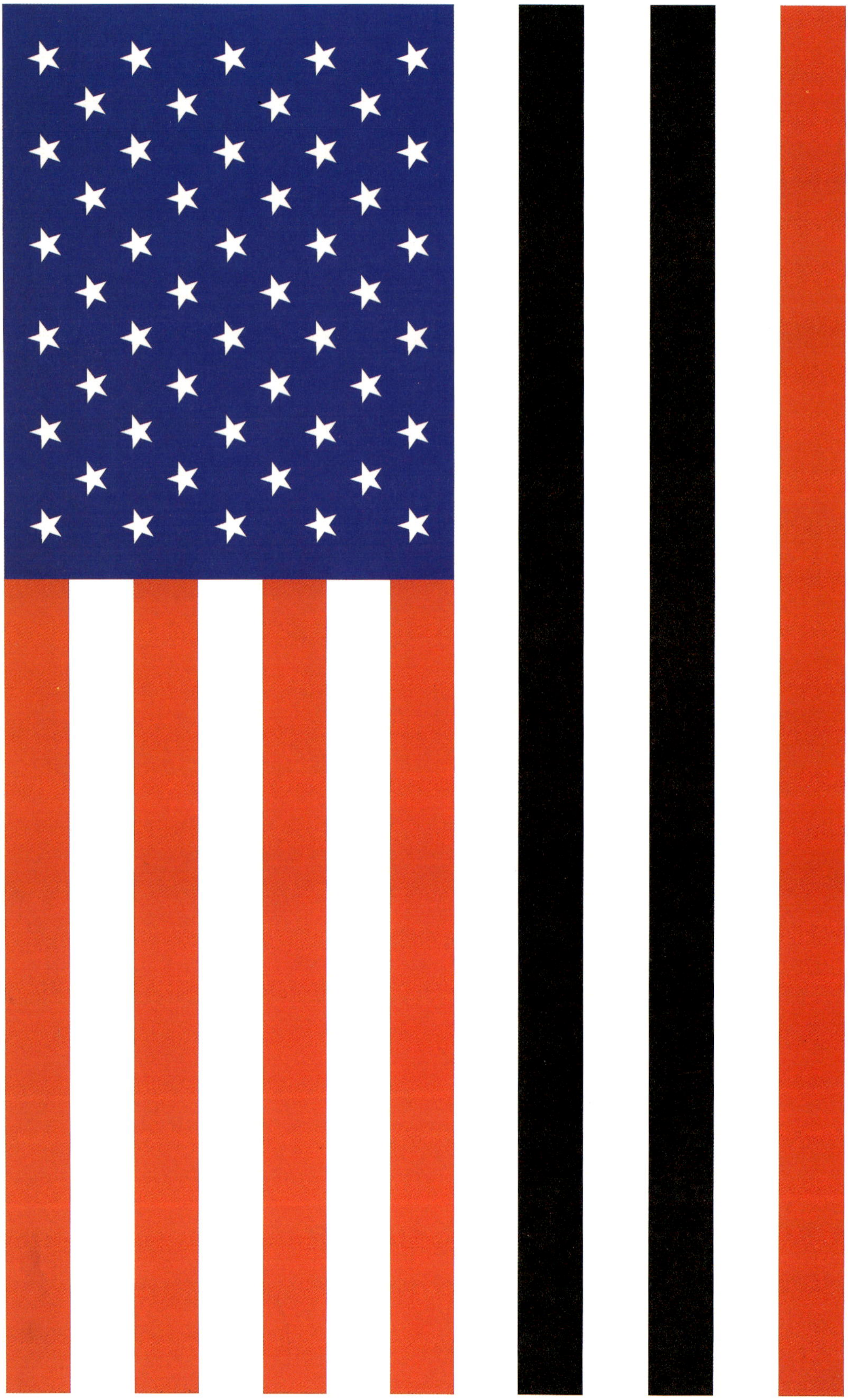

In memoriam

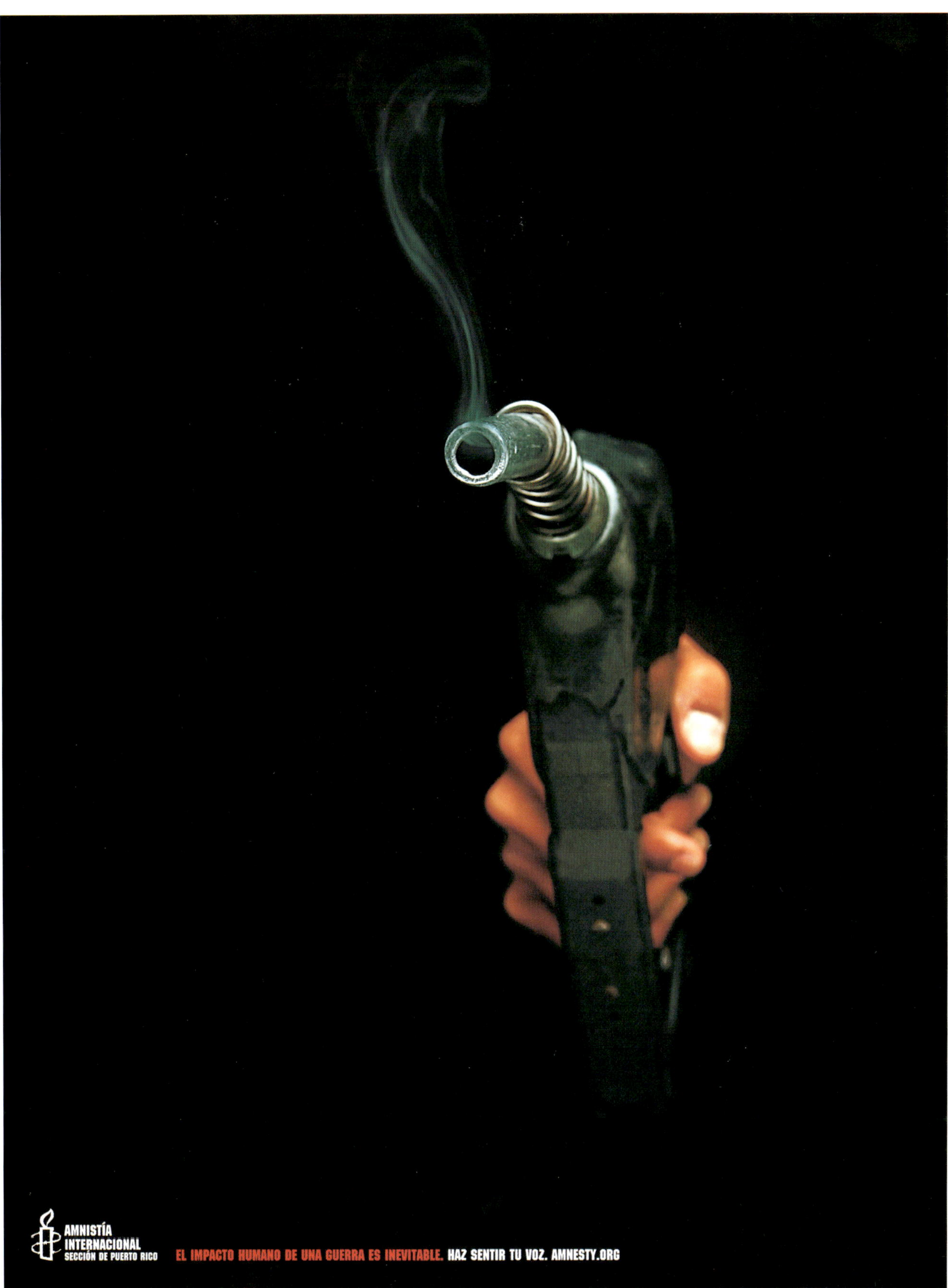

Cima Communications/Amnesty International Puerto Rico

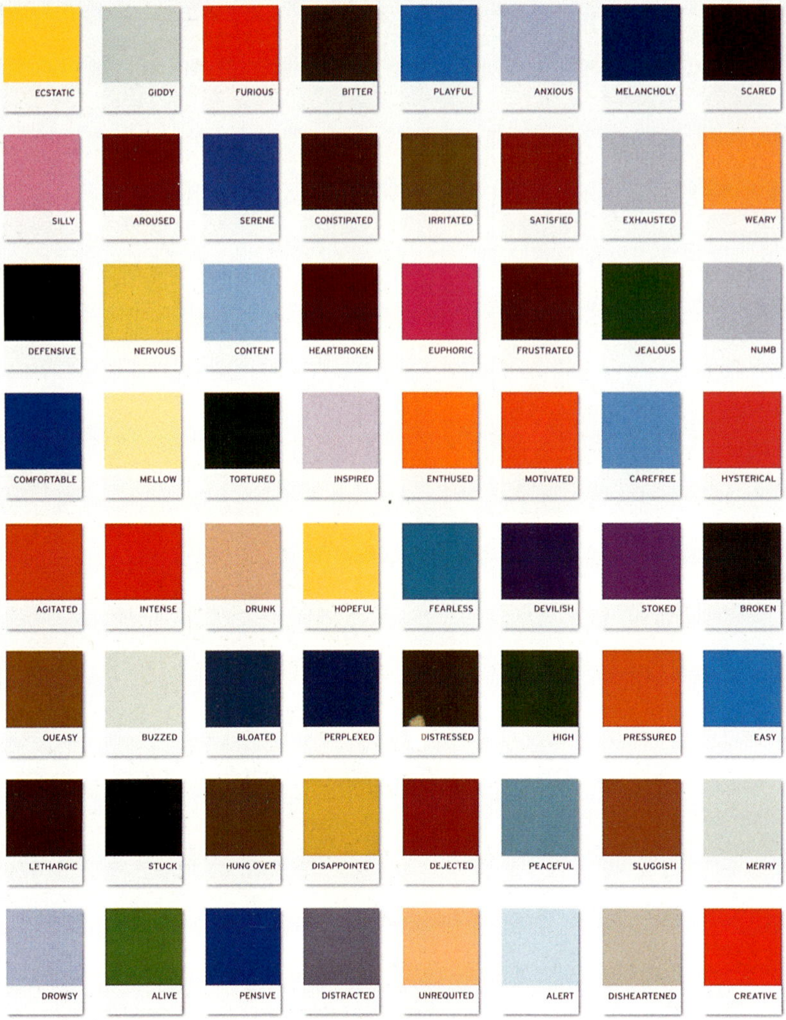

ECSTATIC	GIDDY	FURIOUS	BITTER	PLAYFUL	ANXIOUS	MELANCHOLY	SCARED
SILLY	AROUSED	SERENE	CONSTIPATED	IRRITATED	SATISFIED	EXHAUSTED	WEARY
DEFENSIVE	NERVOUS	CONTENT	HEARTBROKEN	EUPHORIC	FRUSTRATED	JEALOUS	NUMB
COMFORTABLE	MELLOW	TORTURED	INSPIRED	ENTHUSED	MOTIVATED	CAREFREE	HYSTERICAL
AGITATED	INTENSE	DRUNK	HOPEFUL	FEARLESS	DEVILISH	STOKED	BROKEN
QUEASY	BUZZED	BLOATED	PERPLEXED	DISTRESSED	HIGH	PRESSURED	EASY
LETHARGIC	STUCK	HUNG OVER	DISAPPOINTED	DEJECTED	PEACEFUL	SLUGGISH	MERRY
DROWSY	ALIVE	PENSIVE	DISTRACTED	UNREQUITED	ALERT	DISHEARTENED	CREATIVE

THE PERSONALITY OF COLOR

Have you ever come down with a case of the Monday blues? Has a client ever made you see red? We all know color does so much more than cover paper. It sets the mood and reveals feelings without using words. At Williamson Printing Corporation, we know that you appreciate color more than anyone else. Every color palette has as much personality as the designer or art director who creates it, and every combination tells a different story. So whether you're feeling process or Pantone®, we'll make sure your ideas hit the right spot.

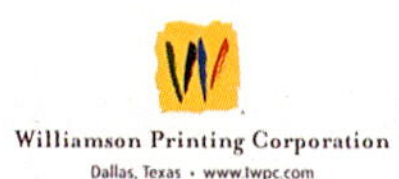

5750.

A COMPLETE AND TOTAL ENTITY. A HIGHLY EVOLVED EIGHT-COLOR HEIDELBERG PRESS CREATED TO MAKE EACH PRINT PROJECT MORE PROFOUND AND POWERFUL THAN EVER. **PR1MARYCOLOR** SCALES UP WITH THE MAXIMUM OF EASE AND CONVENIENCE.

HANNUM AVENUE CULVER CITY CALIFORNIA 90230 T 310.841.0250

EIGHT!

McGAW AVENUE **IRVINE** CA 92614 T 949.660.7080

2361

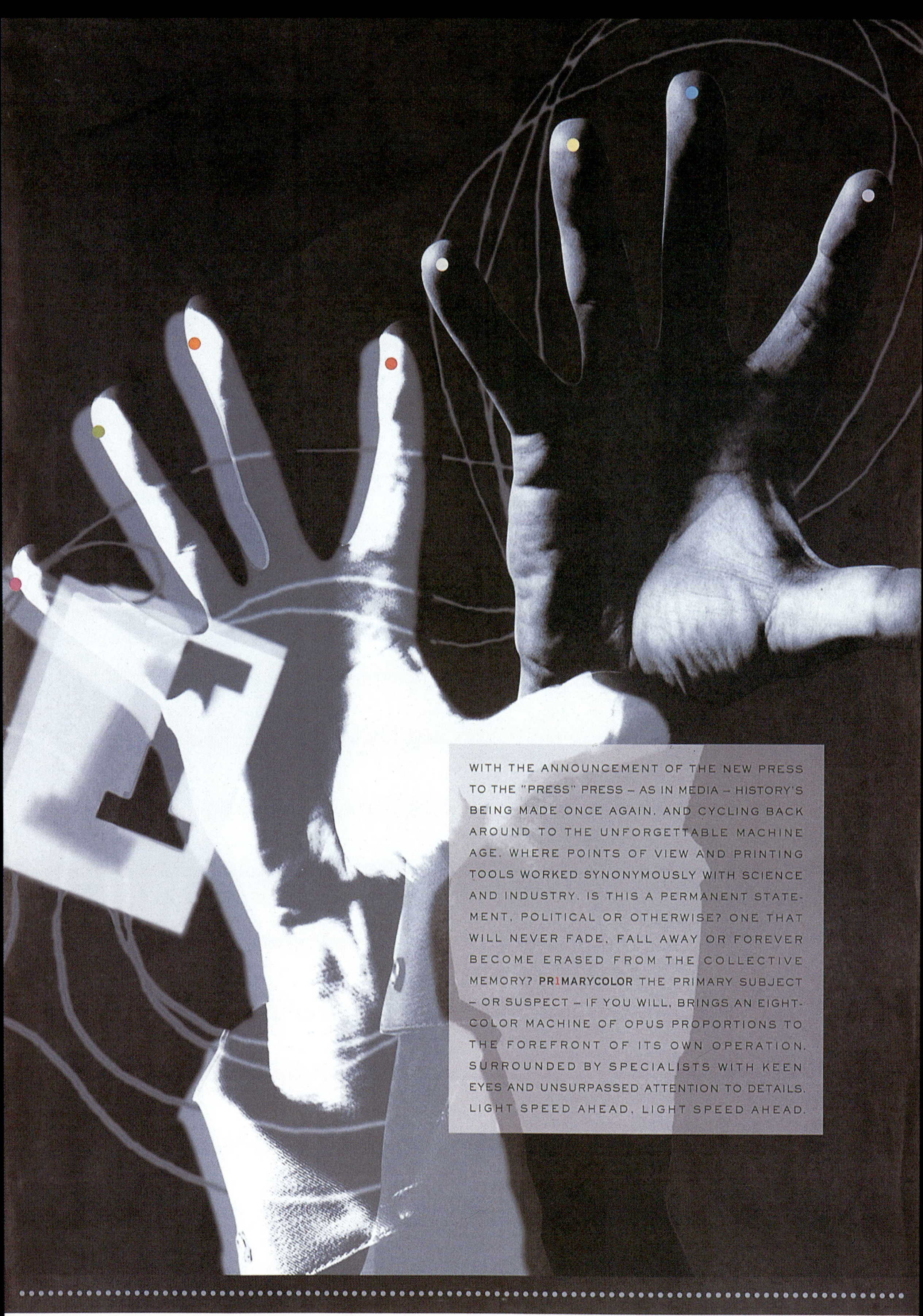

Ph.D/Primary Color

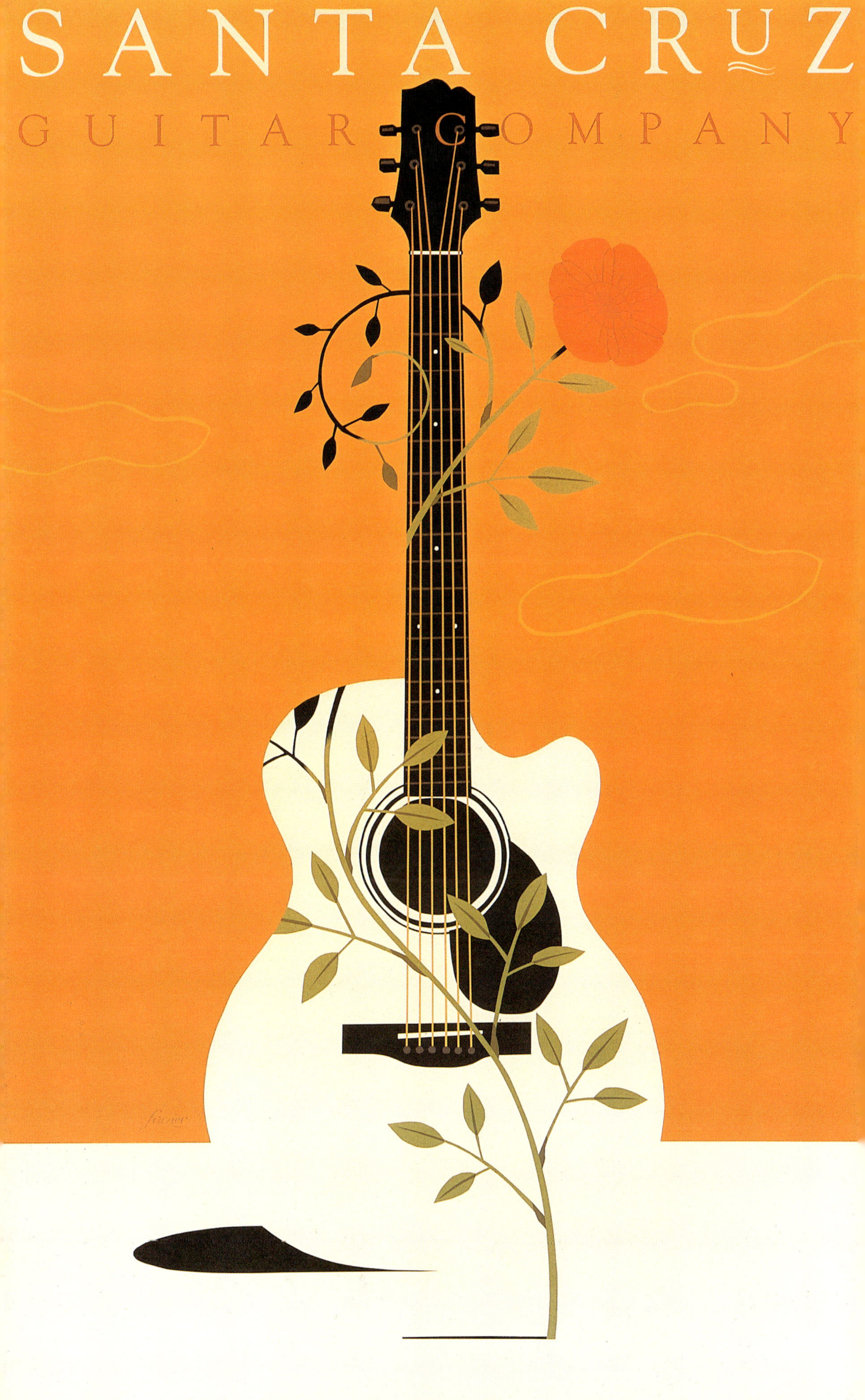
SANTA CRUZ
GUITAR COMPANY

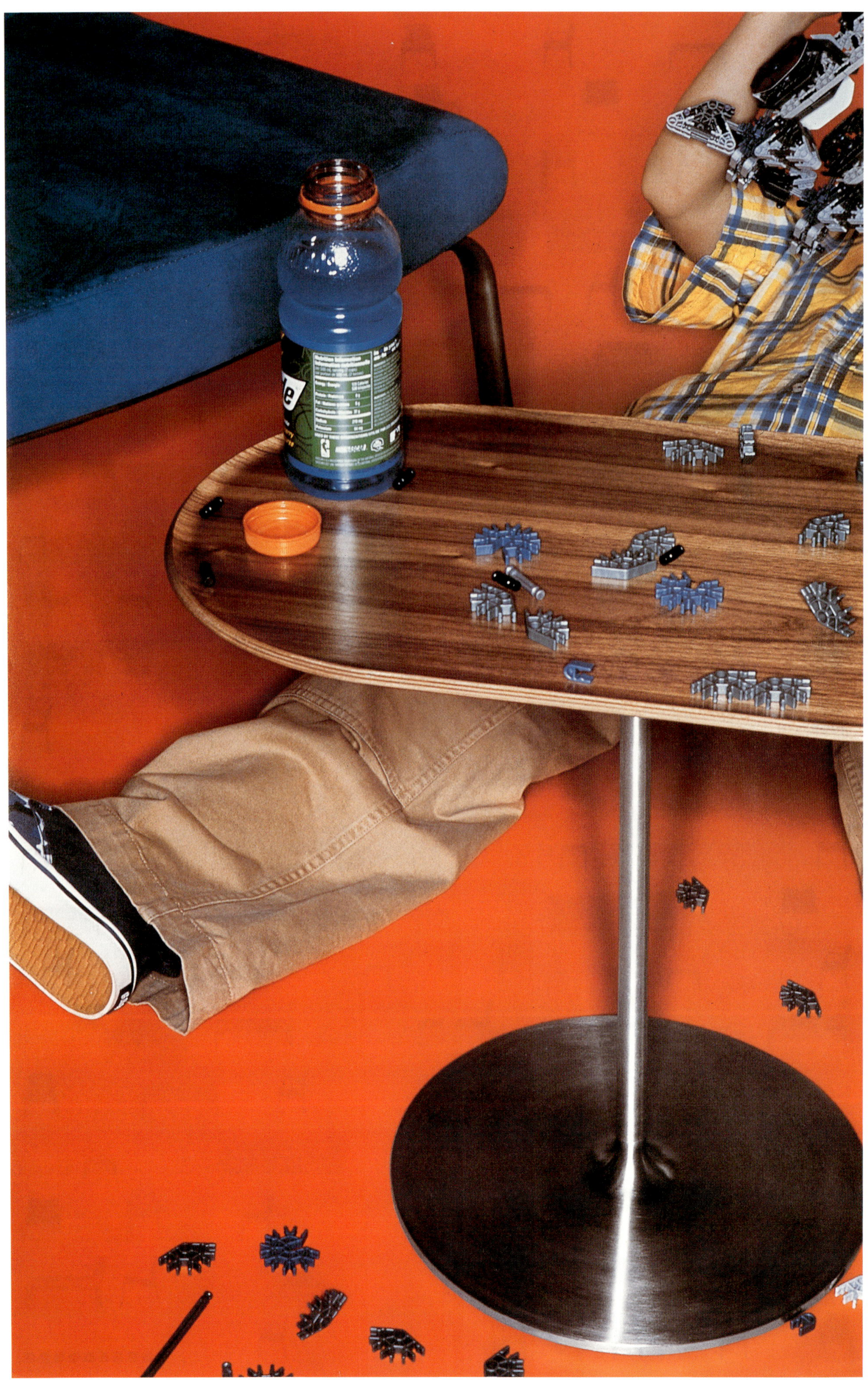

Concrete Design Communications/Keilbauer

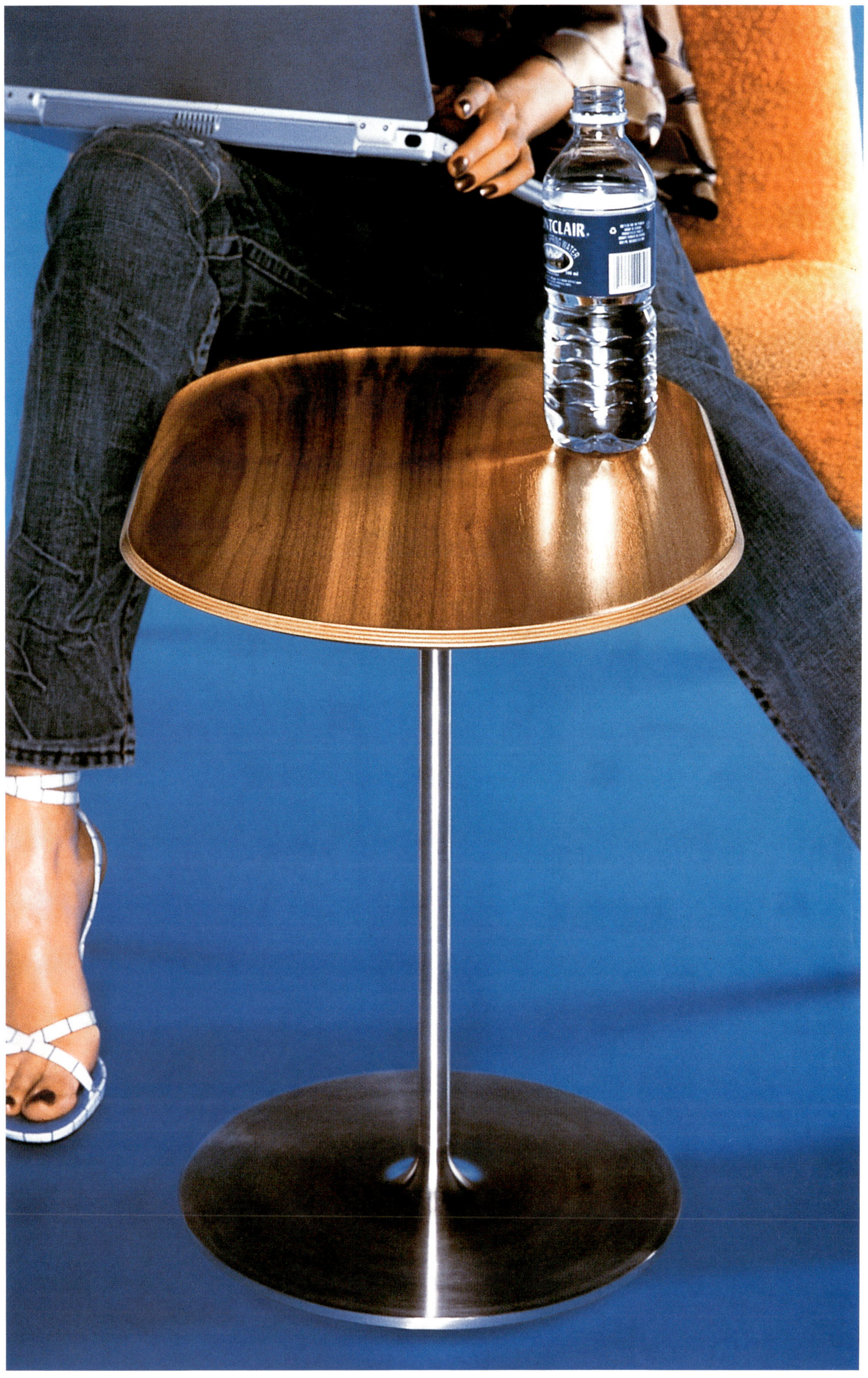

Concrete Design Communications/Keilhauer

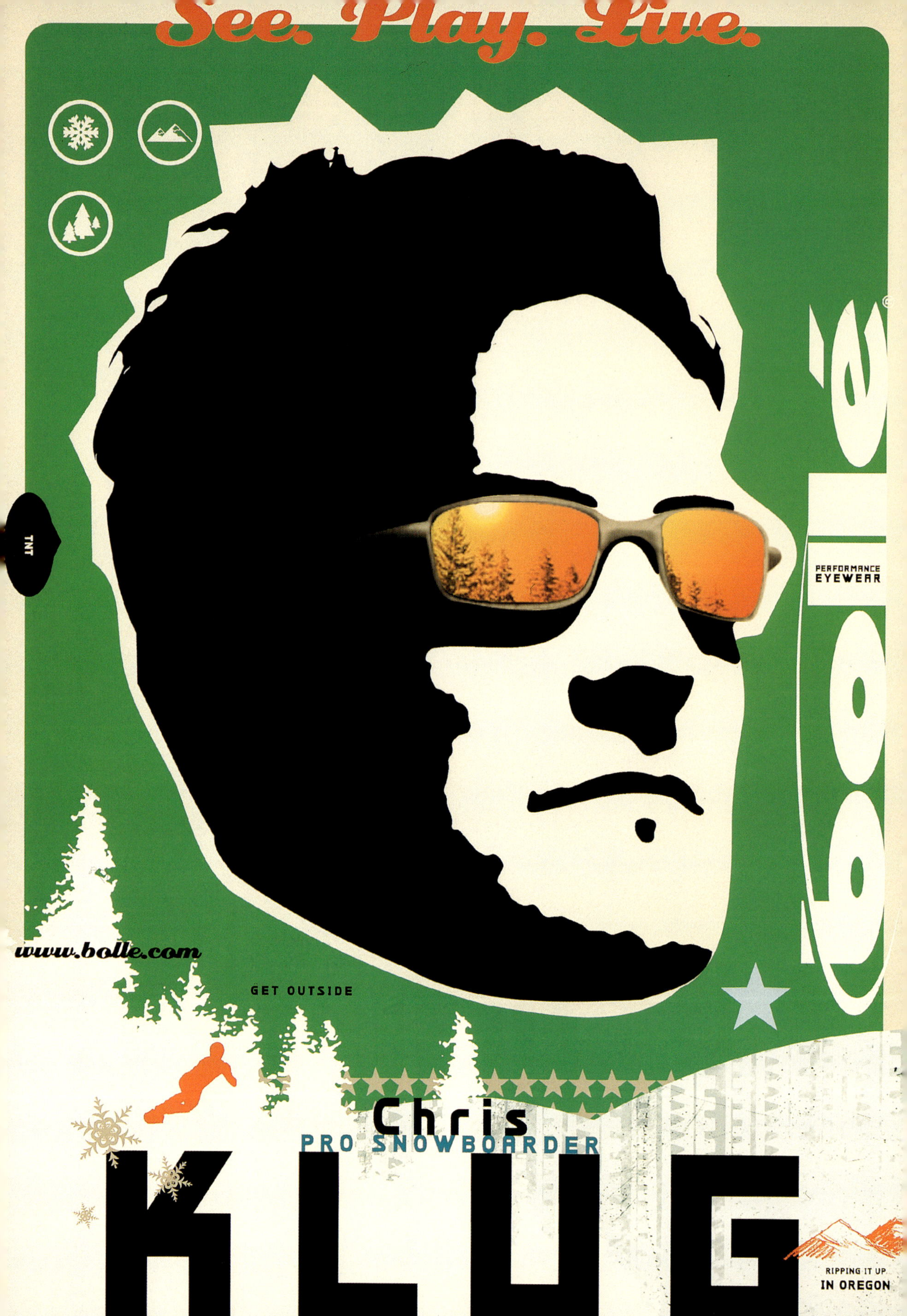

See. Play. Live.
TNT
bollé
PERFORMANCE EYEWEAR
www.bolle.com
GET OUTSIDE
Chris
PRO SNOWBOARDER
KLUG
RIPPING IT UP
IN OREGON

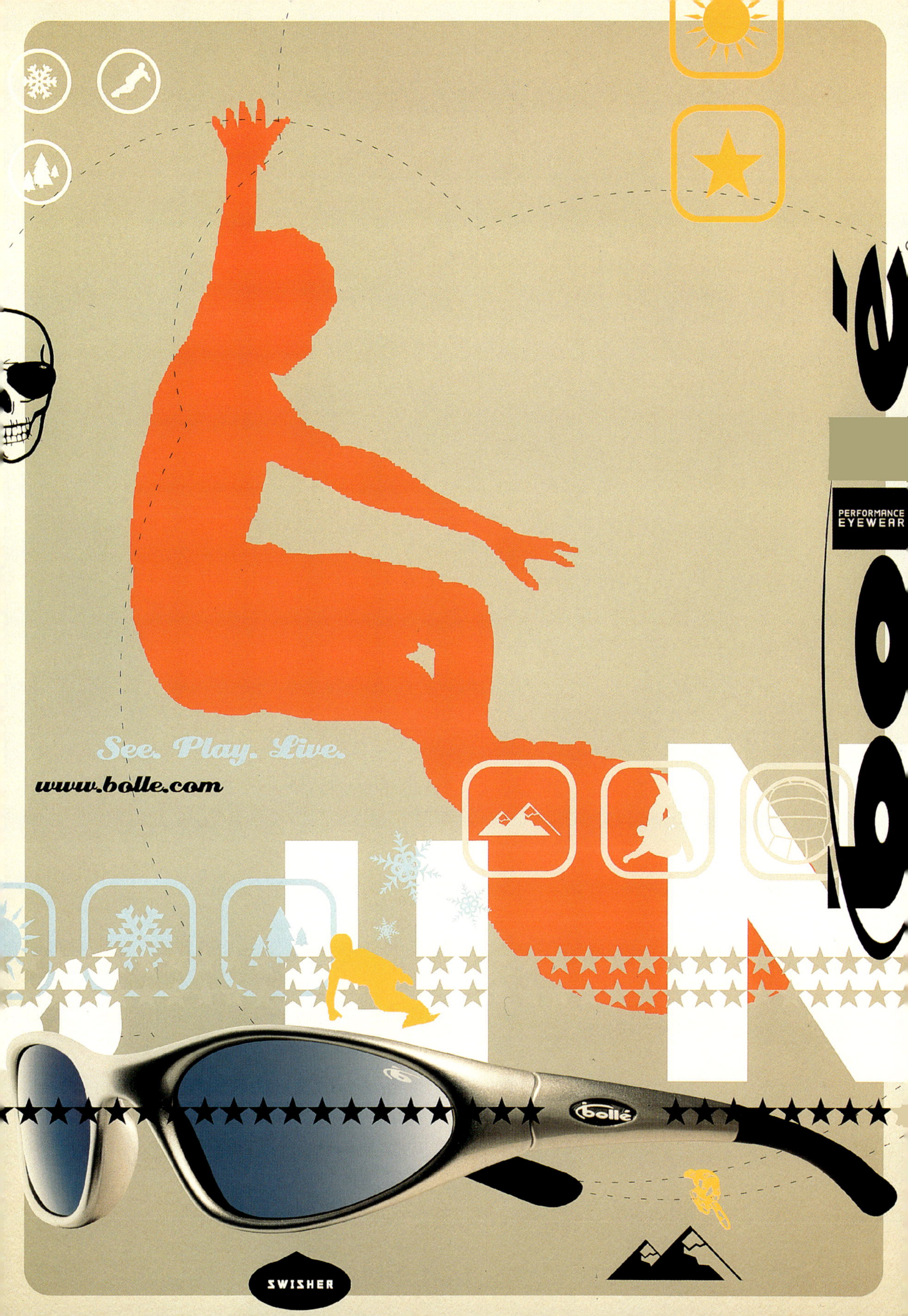

See. Play. Live.
www.bolle.com
bollé
PERFORMANCE EYEWEAR
SWISHER

bulthaup

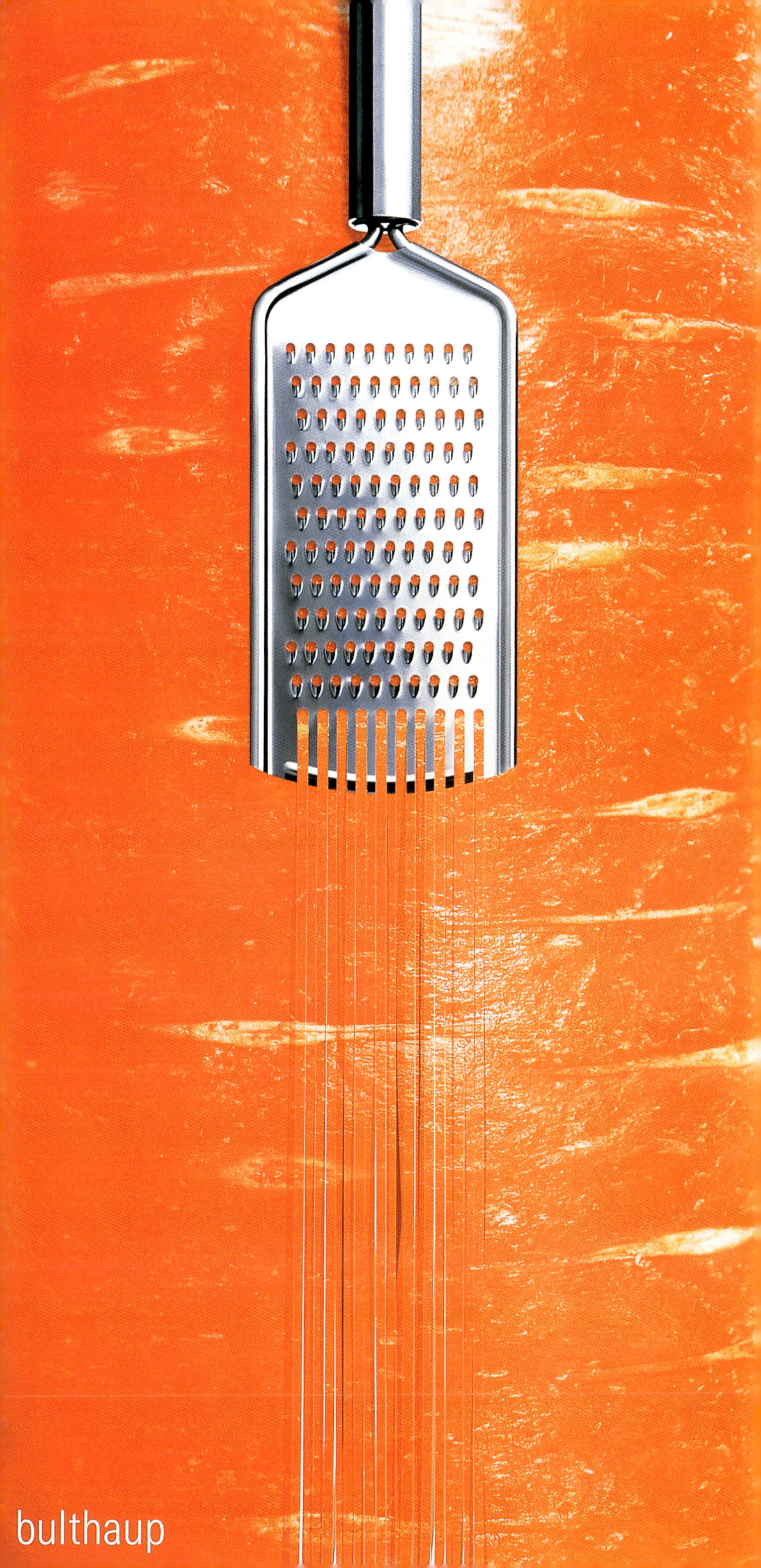
bulthaup

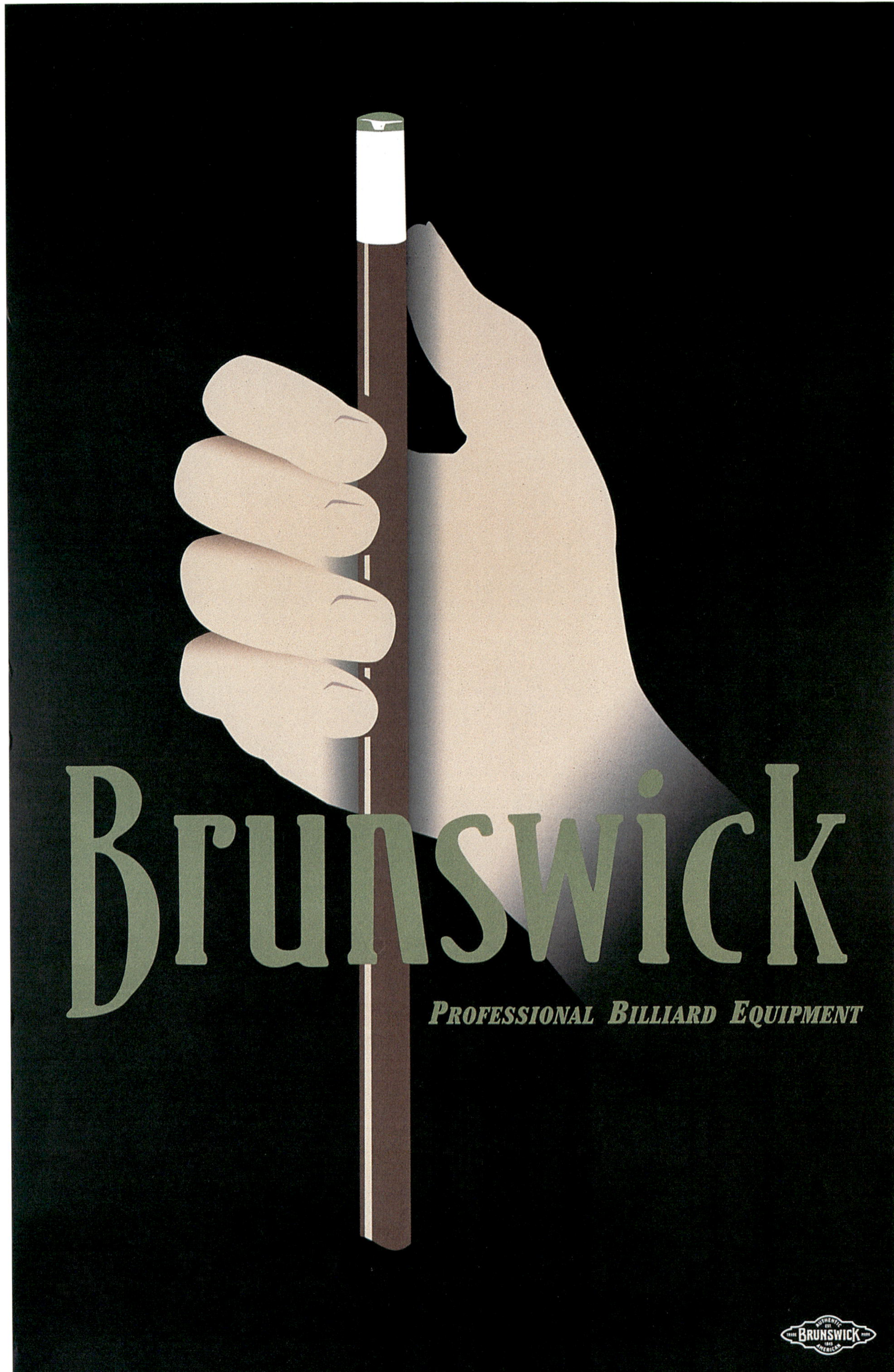

IA Collaborative/Brunswick Billiards

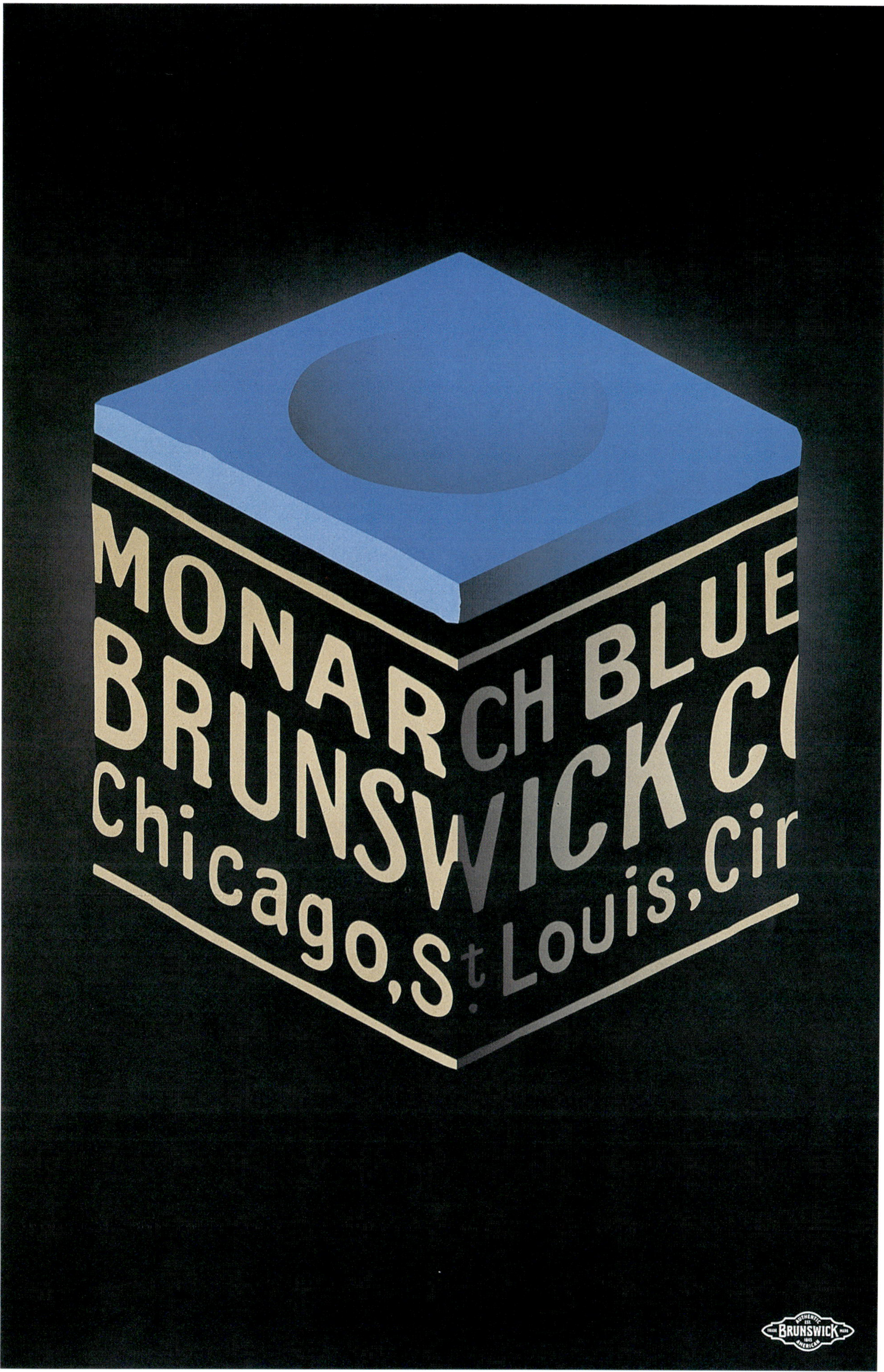

IA Collaborative/Brunswick Billiards

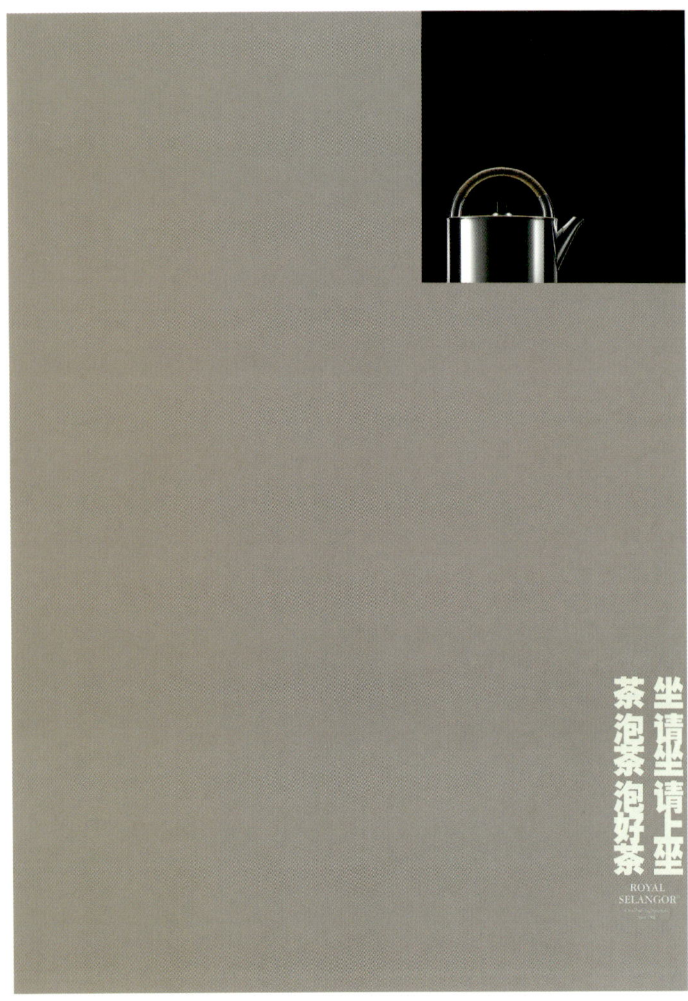

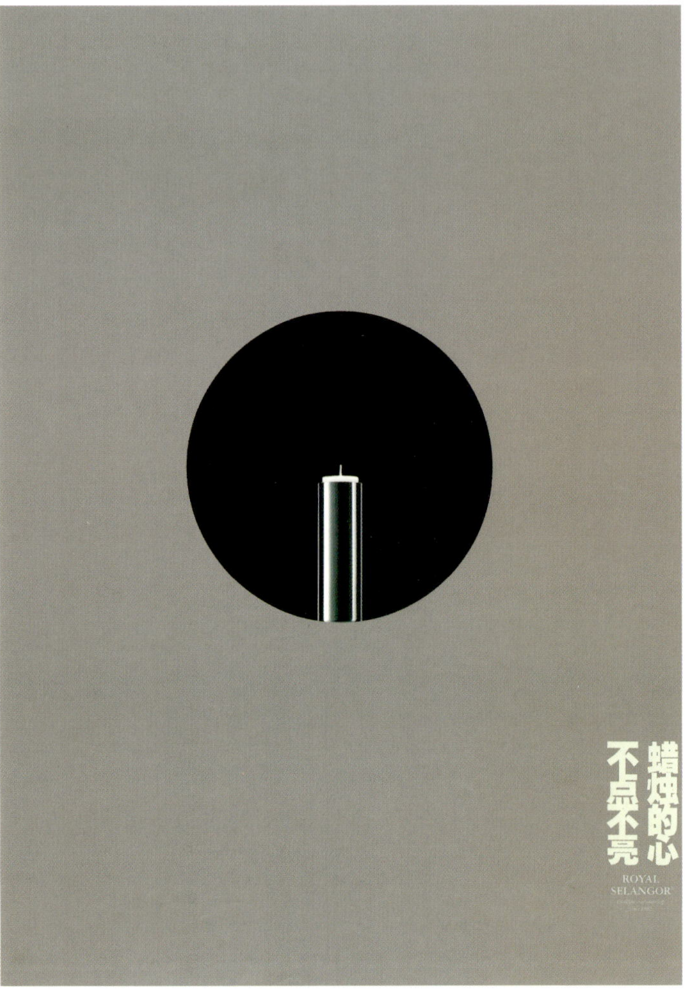

FCB Singapore/Royal Selangor

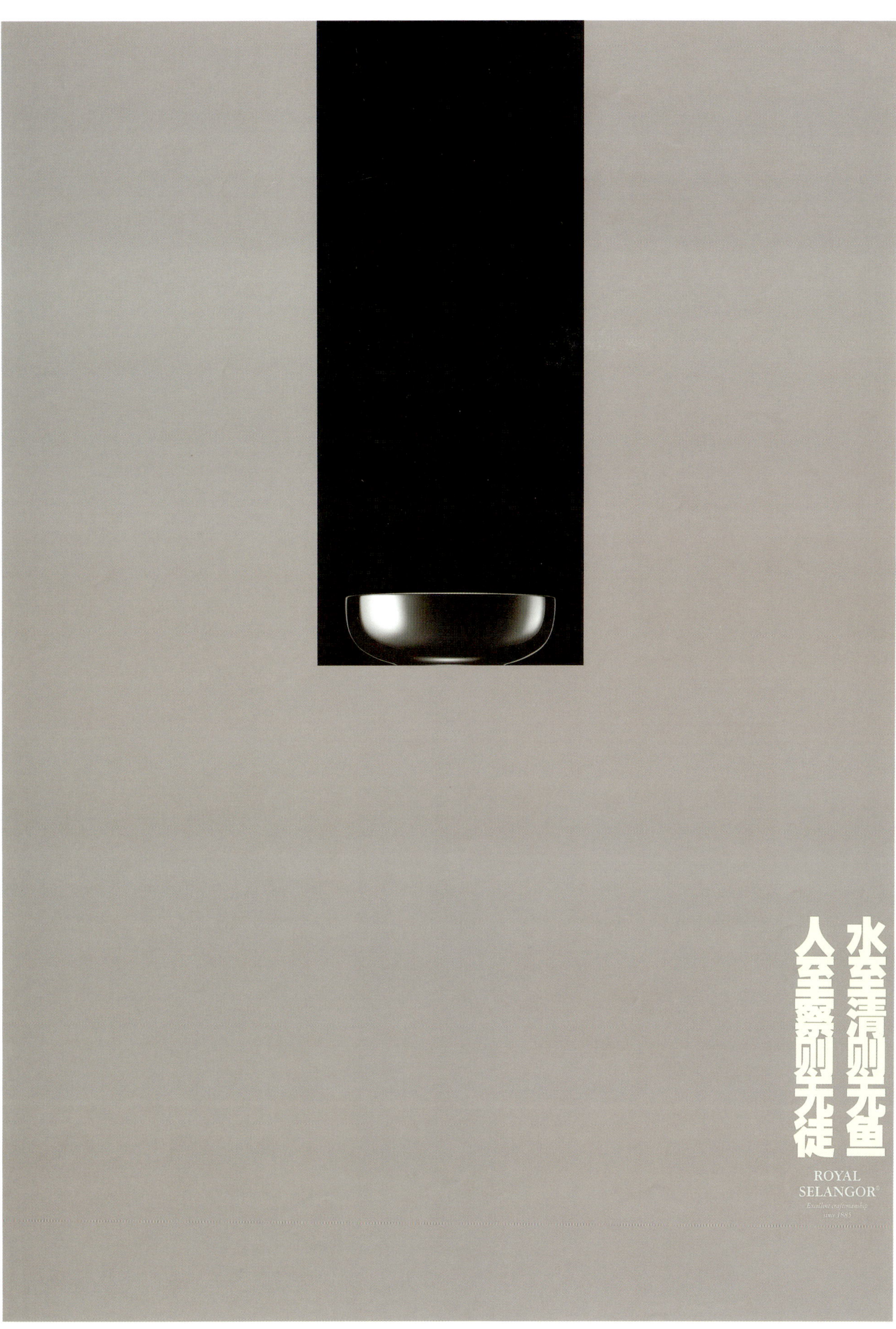

FCB Singapore/Royal Selangor

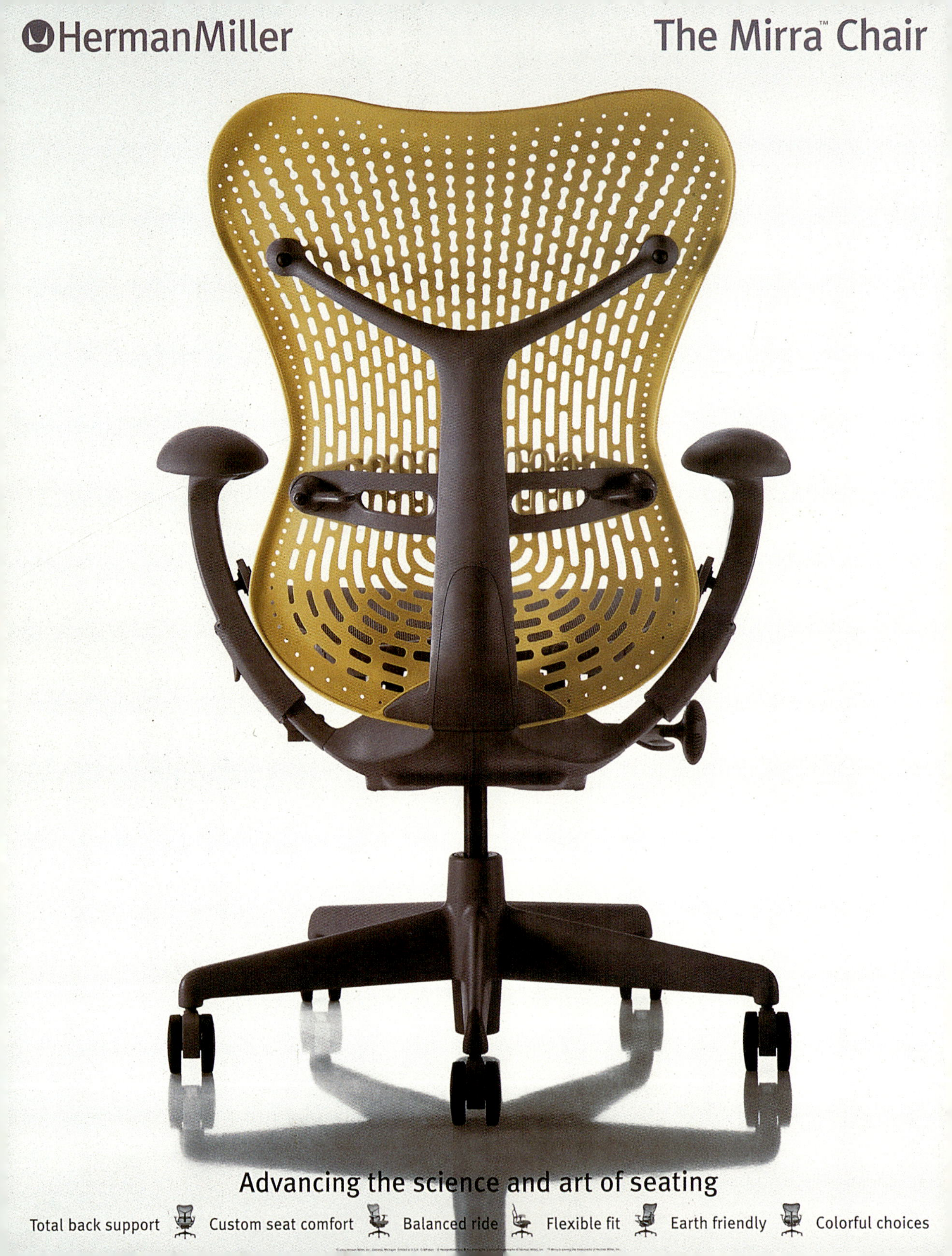

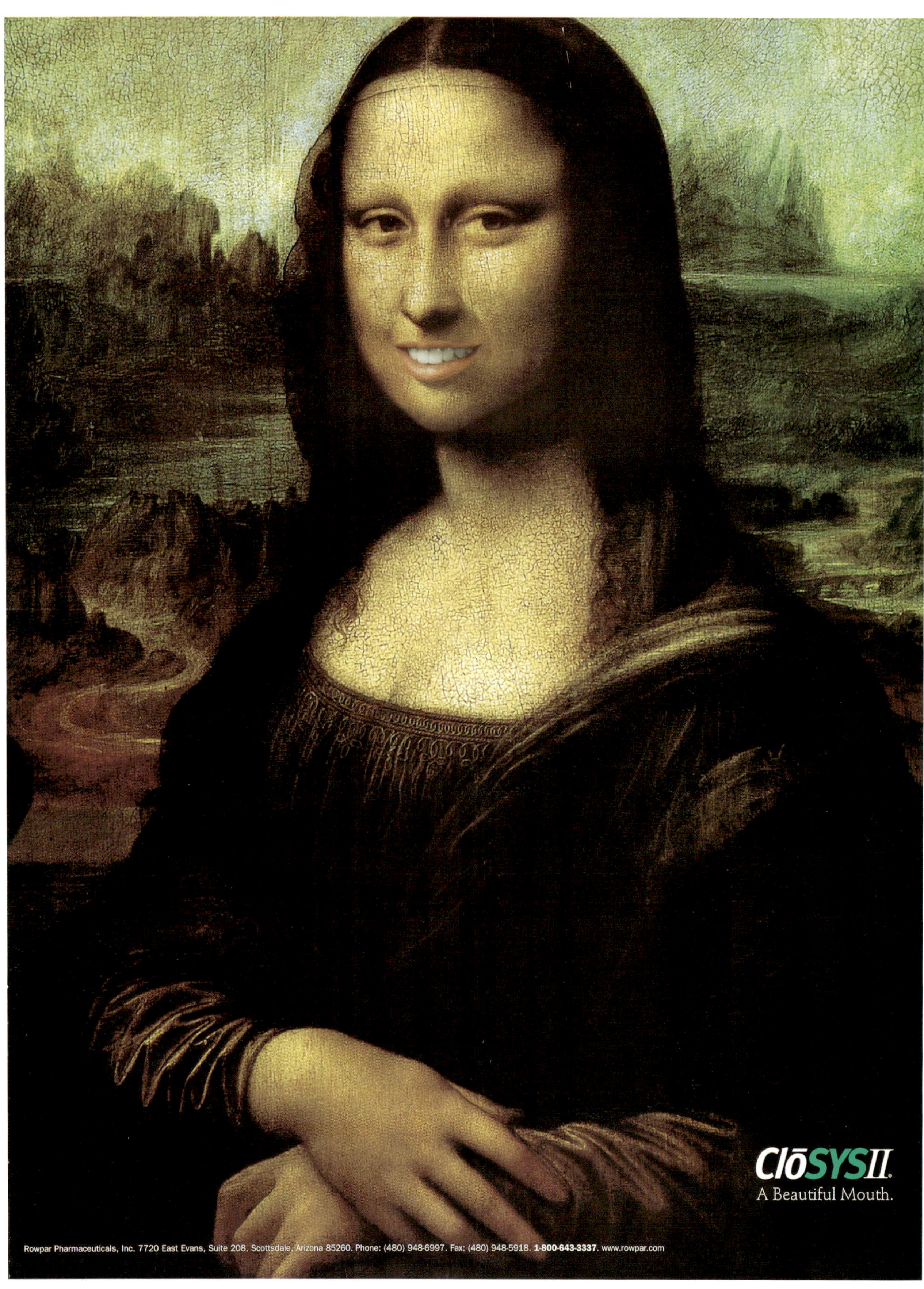

Kellam Montgomery Phillips Advertising/Rowpar Pharmaceuticals

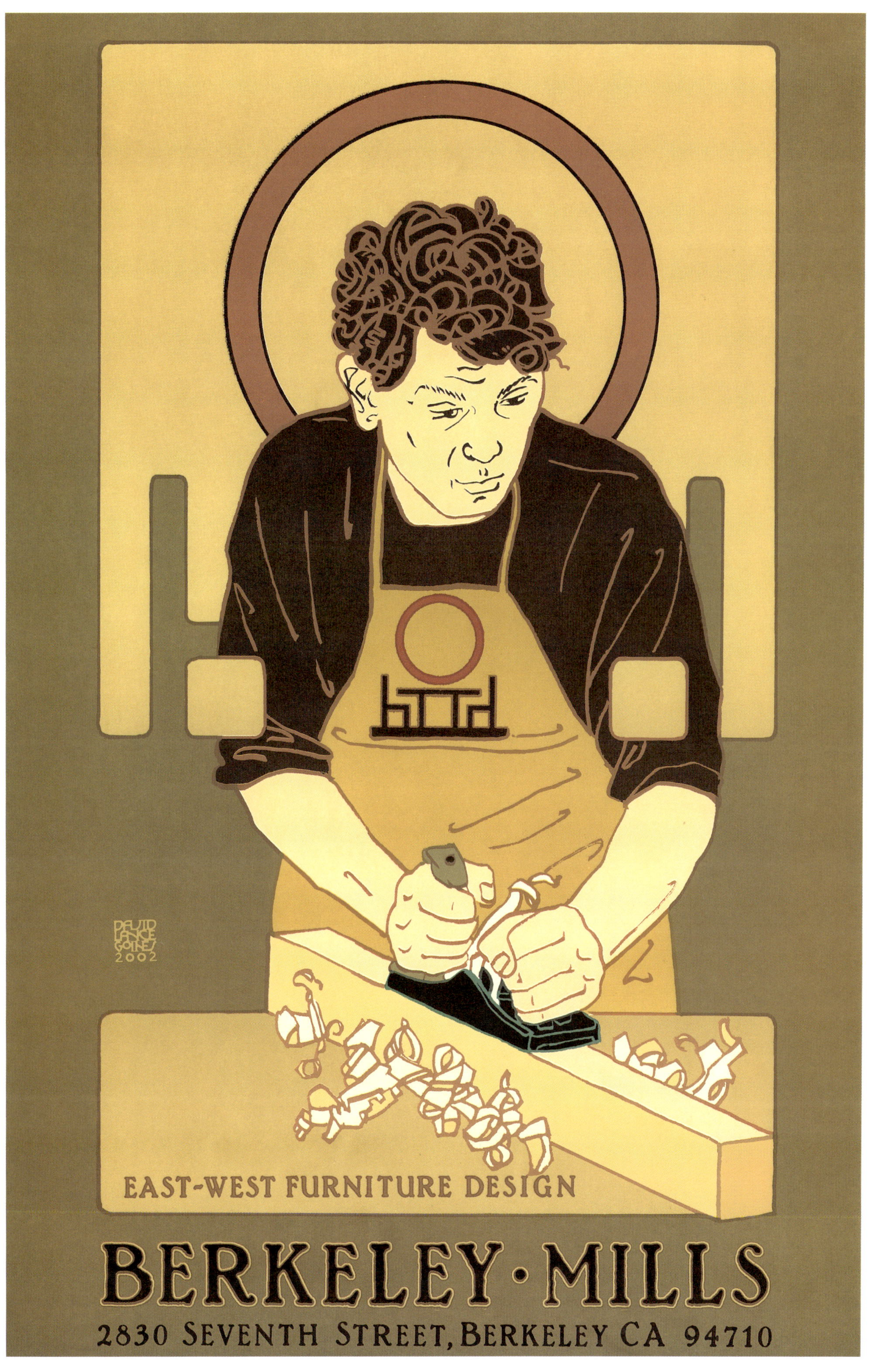

Saint Hieronymus Press/Berkeley Mills

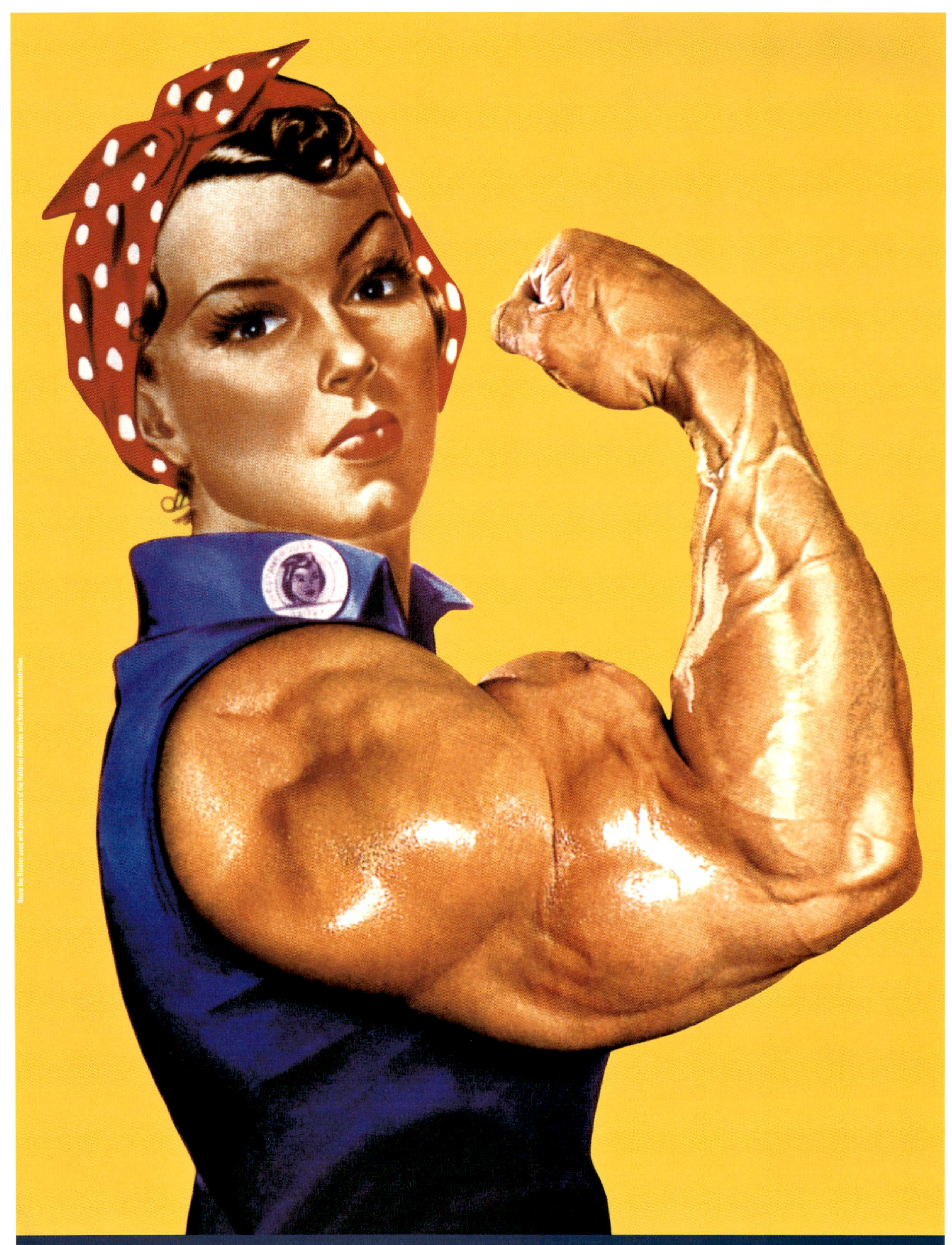

BBDO New York/The Ad Council

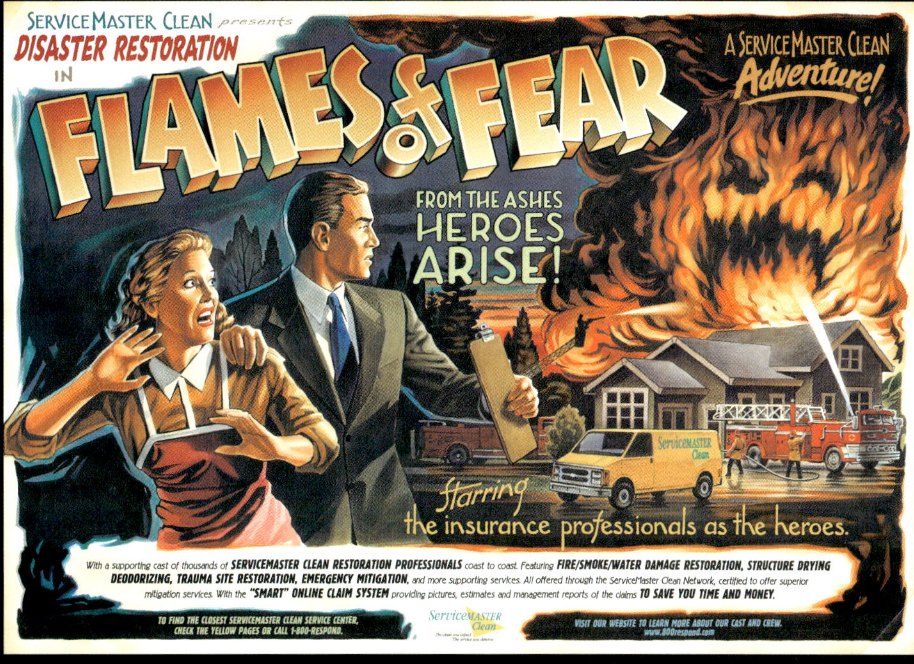

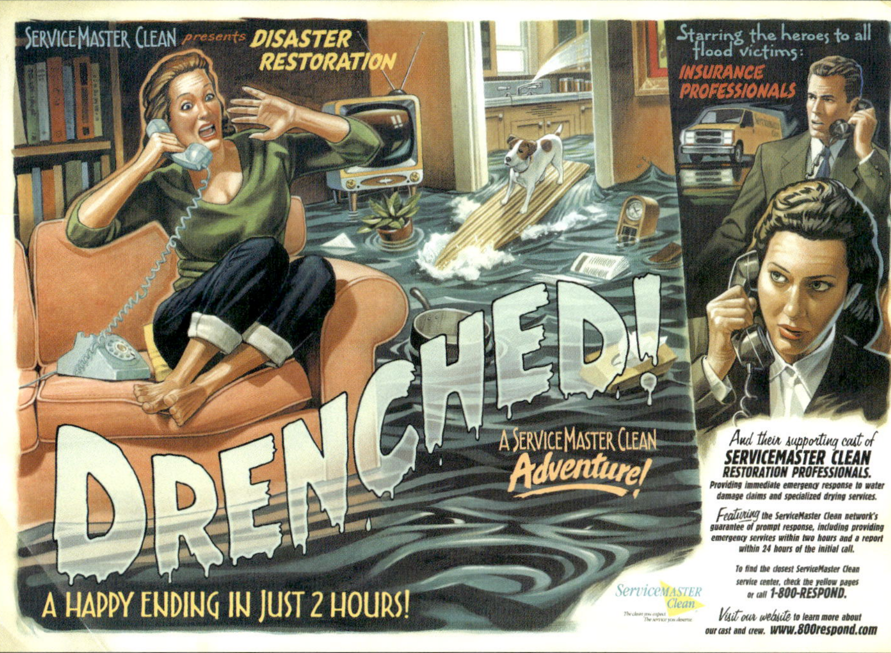

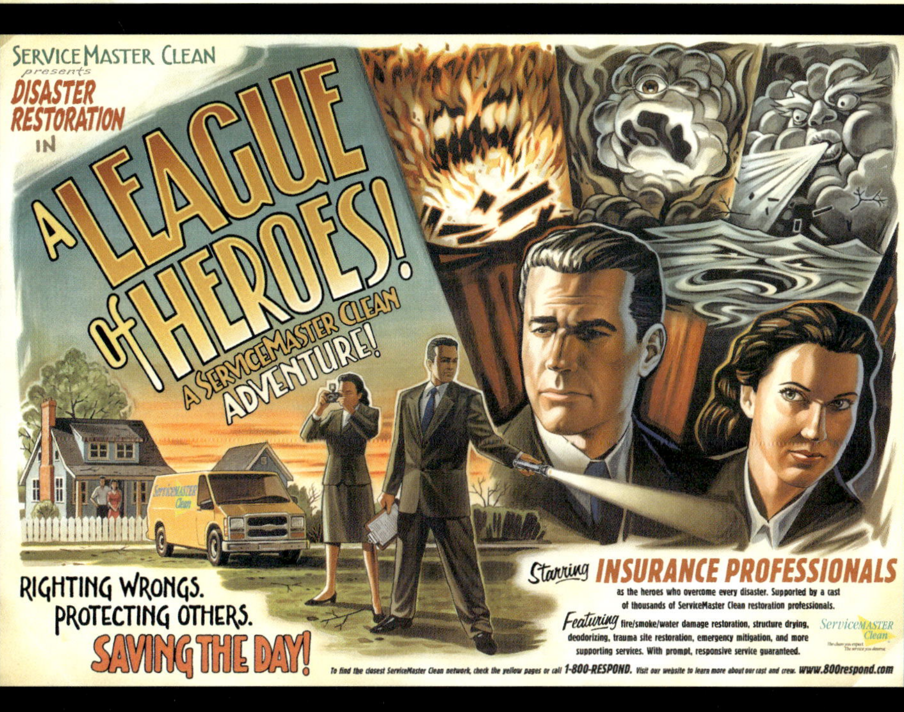

Jeff Foster Illustration and Design Take Out/Archer Malmo Adv. and Service Master

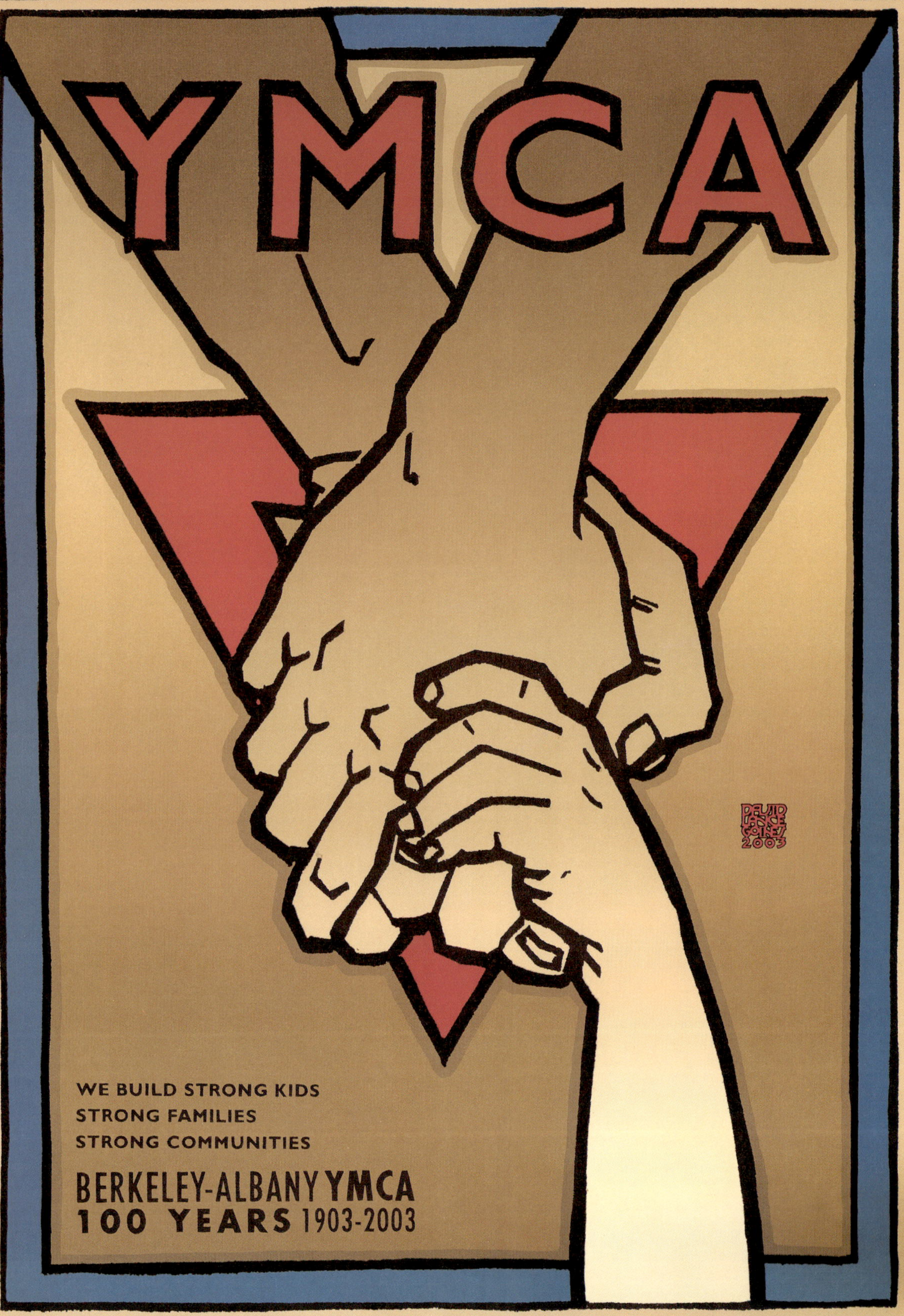
YMCA
DAVID LANCE GOINES 2003
WE BUILD STRONG KIDS
STRONG FAMILIES
STRONG COMMUNITIES
BERKELEY-ALBANY YMCA
100 YEARS 1903-2003

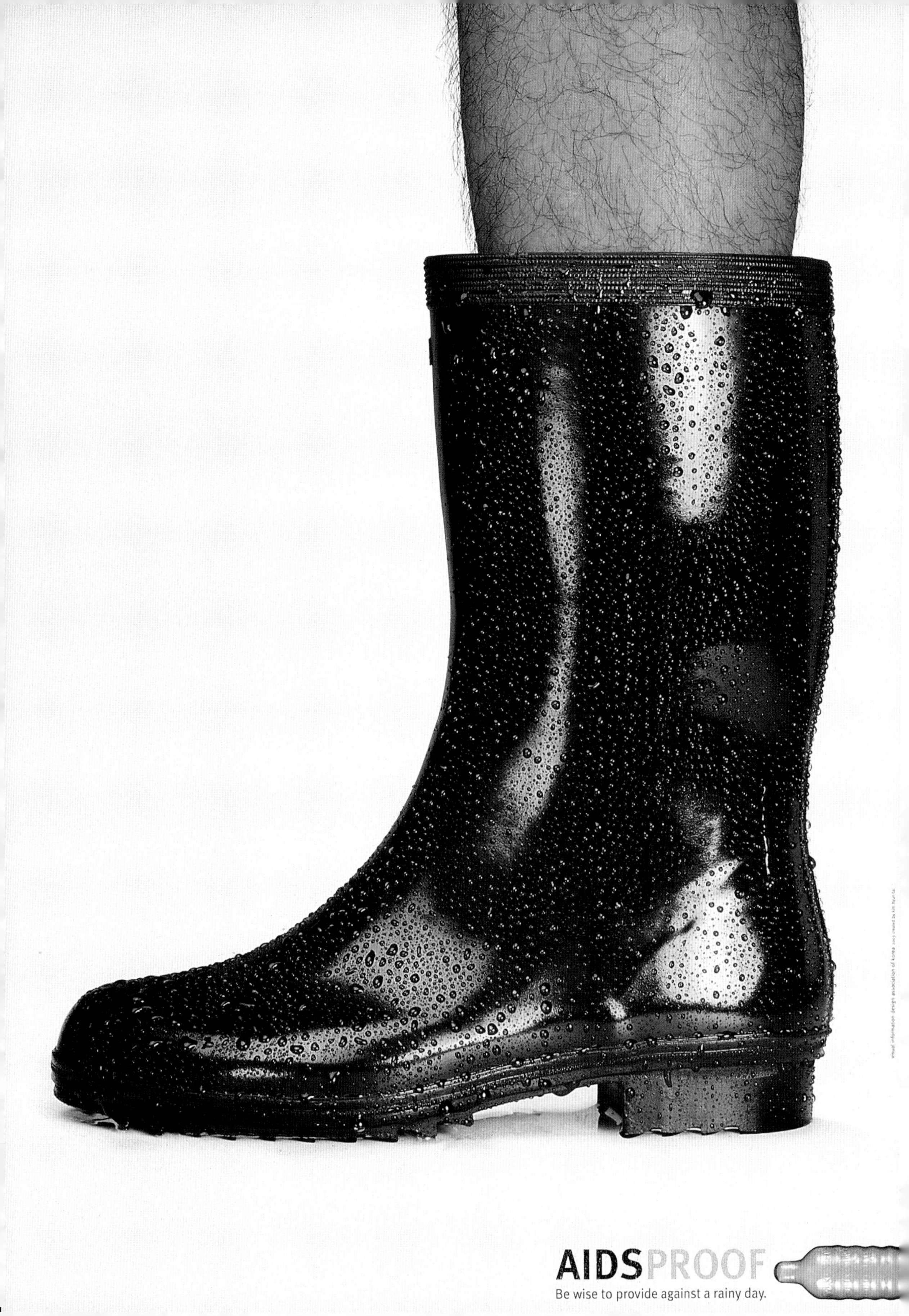

visual information design association of korea

AIDSPROOF

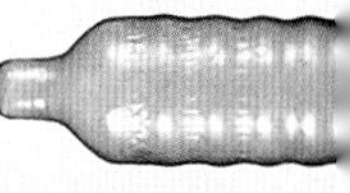

Be wise to provide against a rainy day.

CAMP KITAKI NEEDS YOUR HELP. GIVE BY CALLING 434-9205.

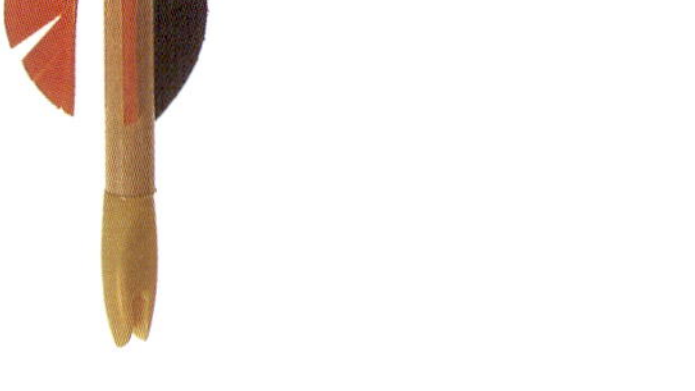

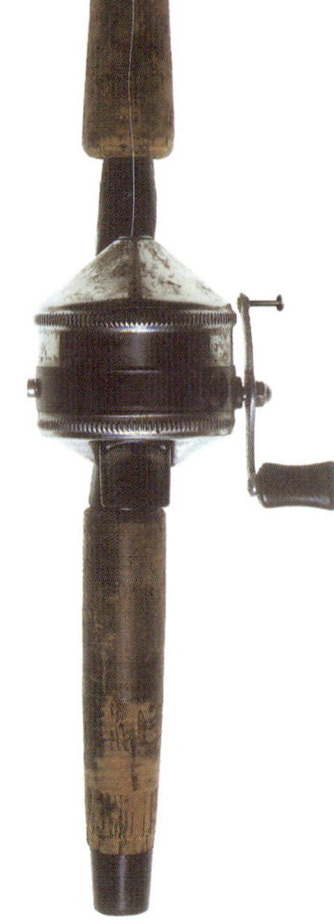

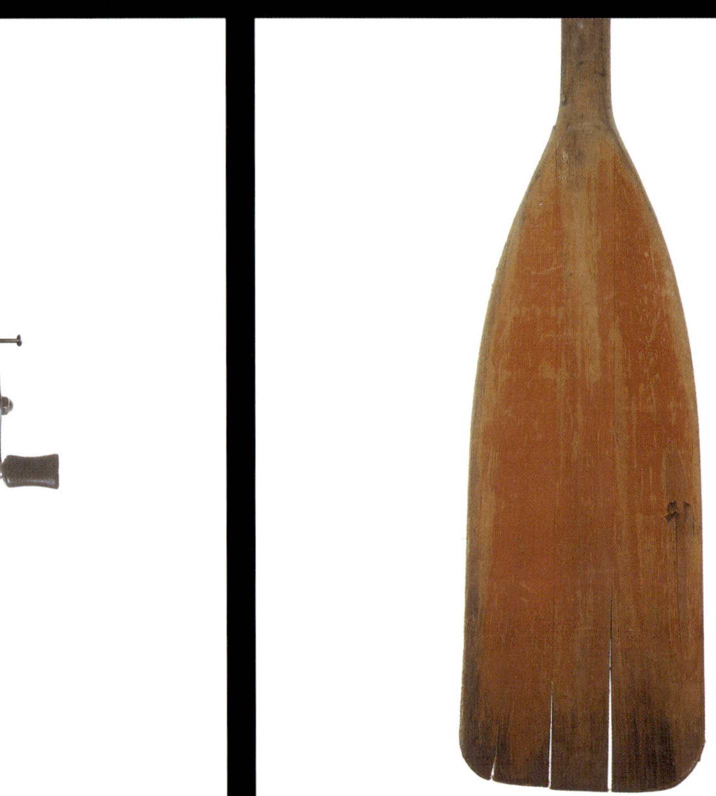

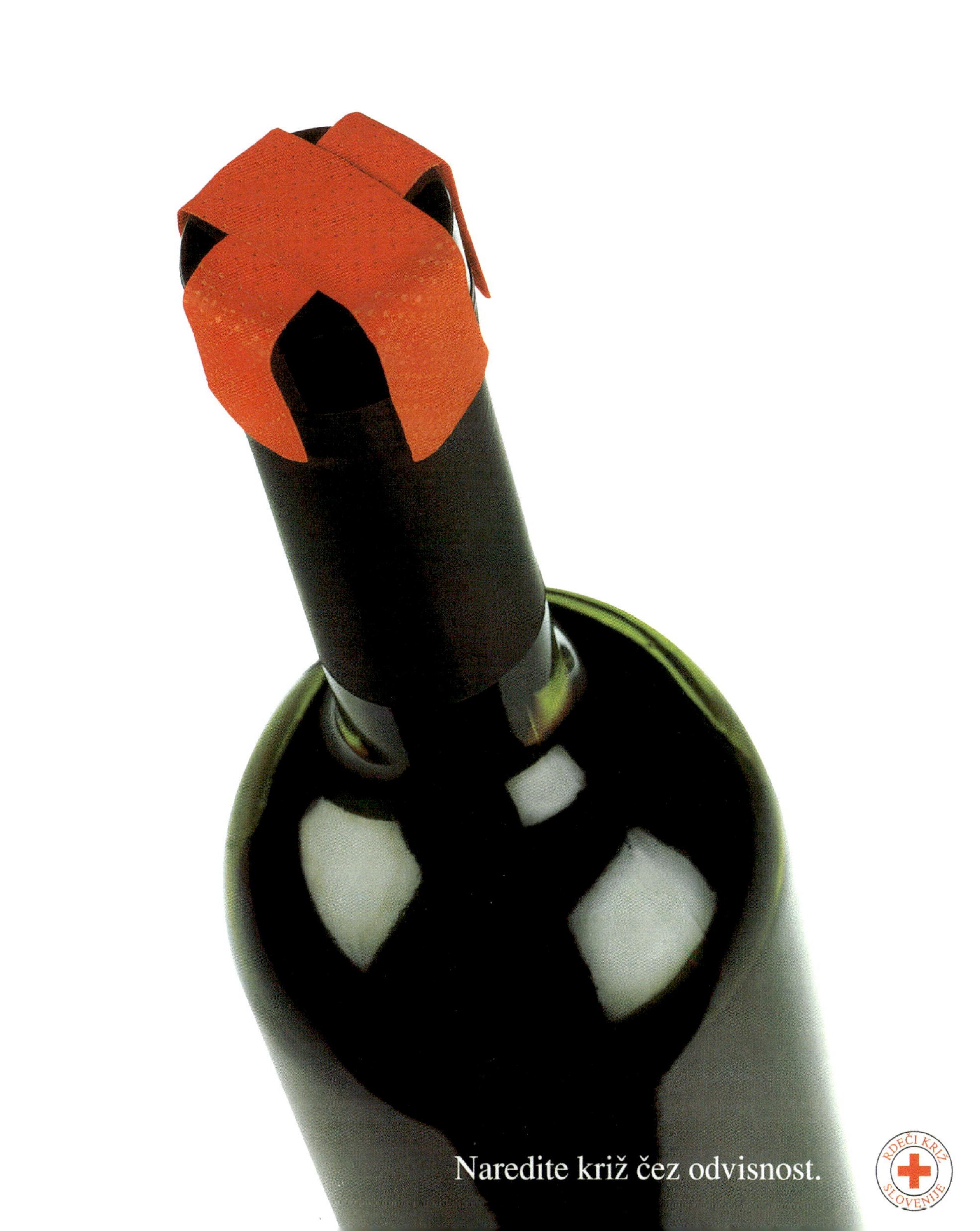

Naredite križ čez odvisnost.

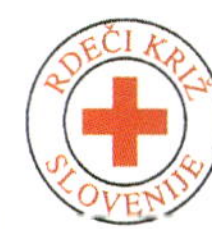

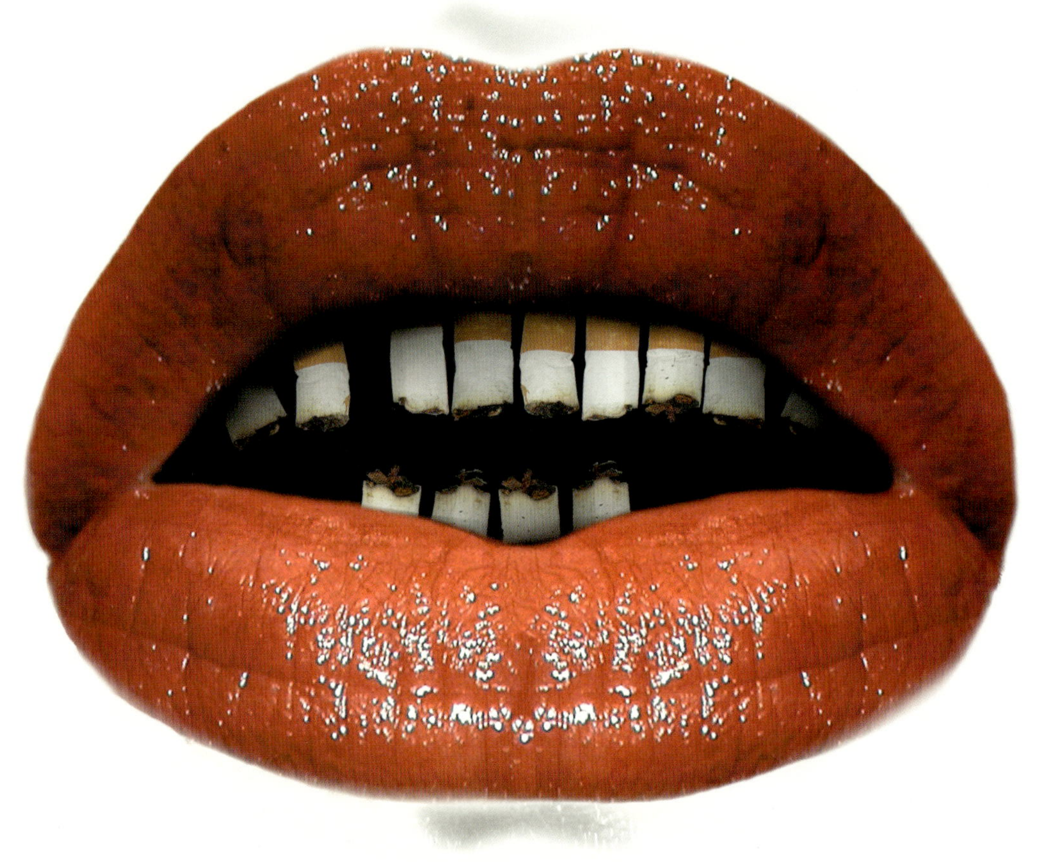

QUIT NOW

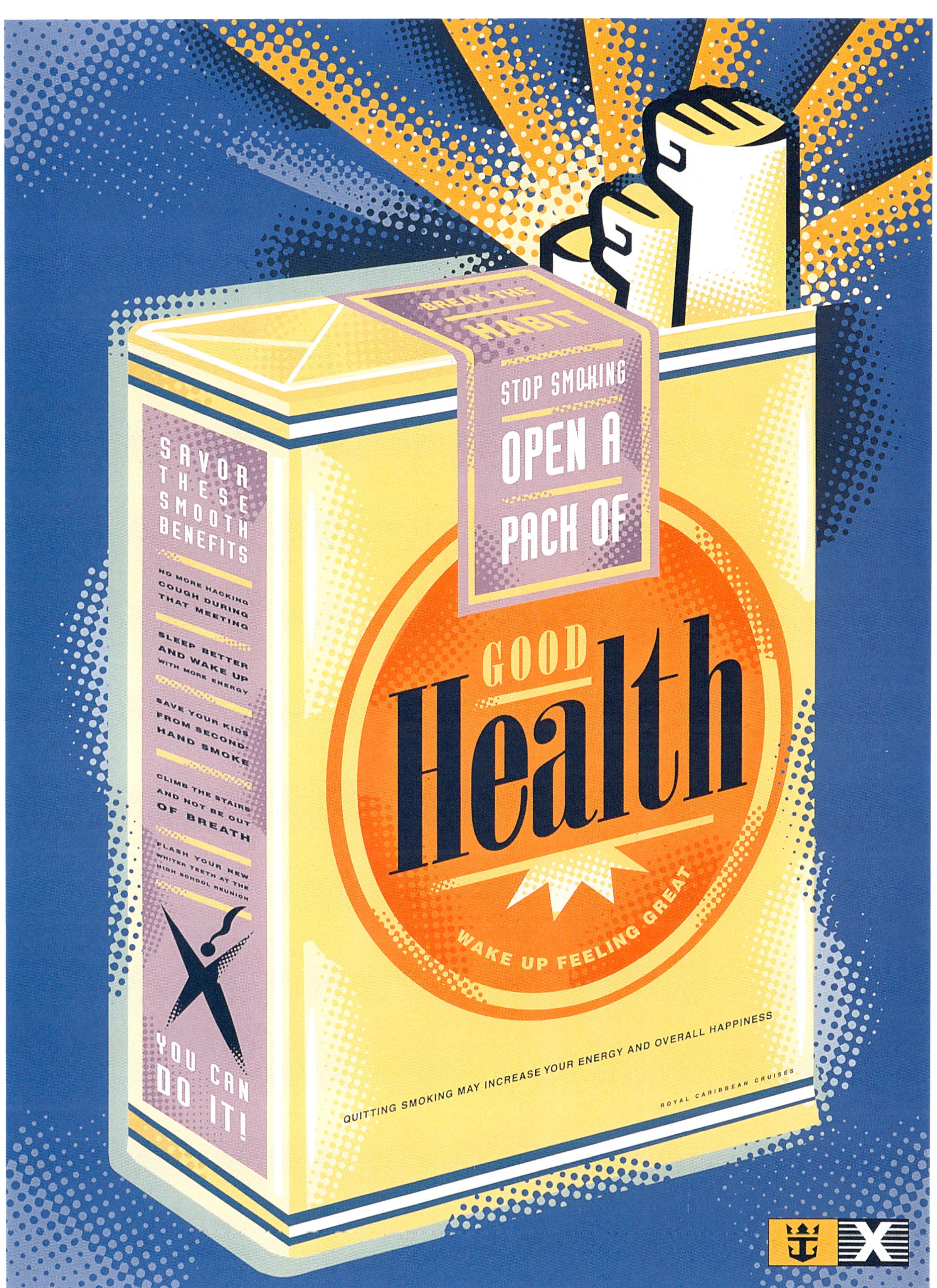

Greteman Group/Royal Carribean Cruise Lines

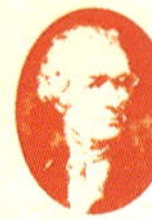

NEW YORK POST

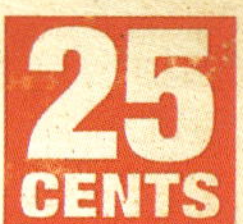

LATE CITY FINAL

SATURDAY, DECEMBER 18, 1903 / Breezy, cold. High 40 / Weather: Page 28 25¢

FIRST MANNED FLIGHT

WILBUR WETS HIS PANTS

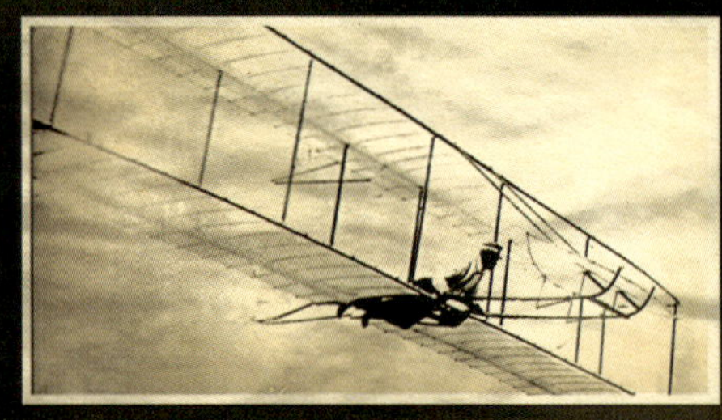

Two brothers made history yesterday with the first successful manned, powered flight in Kitty Hawk, North Carolina. Oliver Wright coasted along in their handmade flying machine for 120 feet. Then Wilbur Wright made the longest and, by all accounts, scariest flight when the craft suddenly dove toward the ground after flying 800 feet or so.

EXCLUSIVE: PAGE 5

New York's most colorful paper for over two hundred years.

GSD&M/New York Post

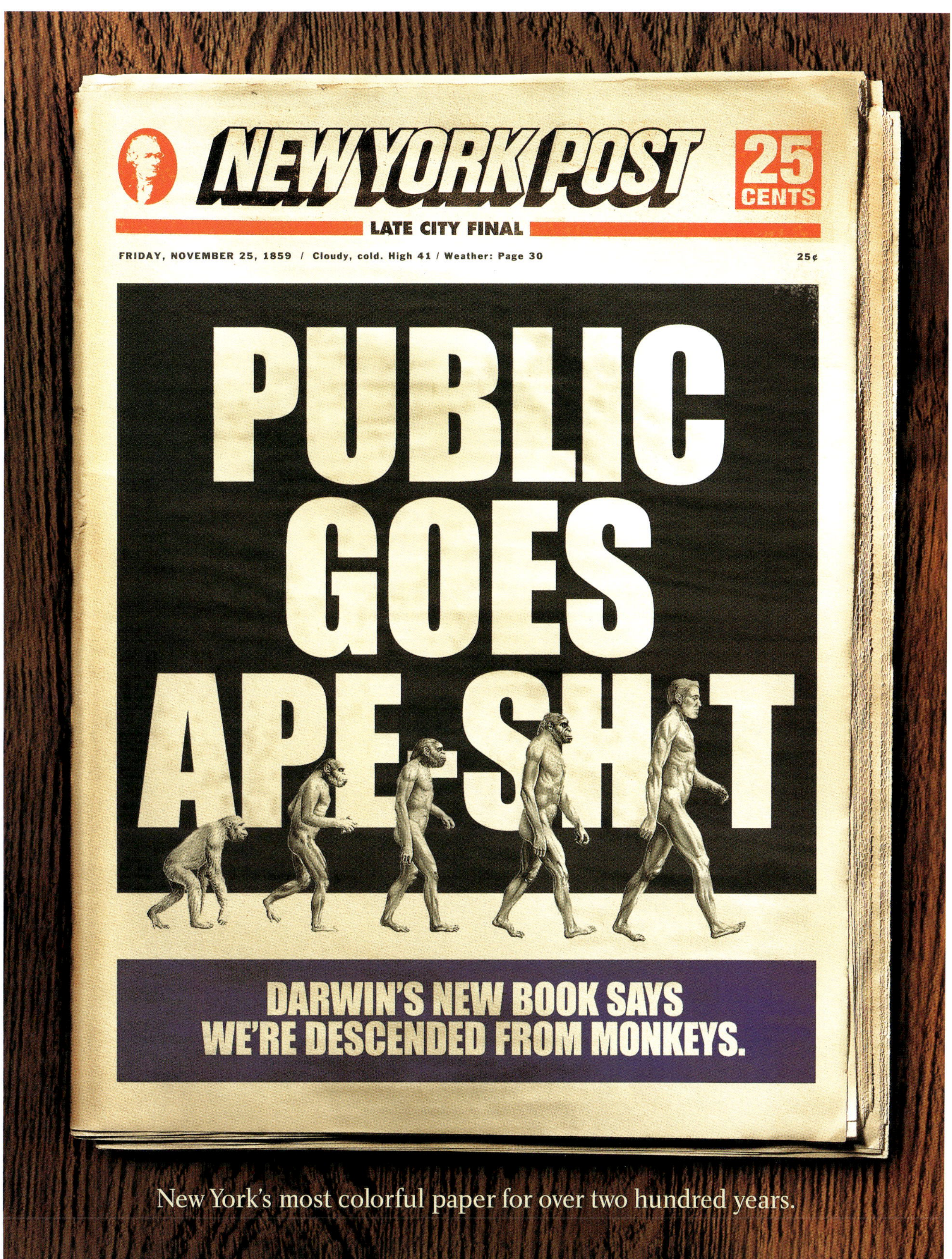

GSD&M/New York Post

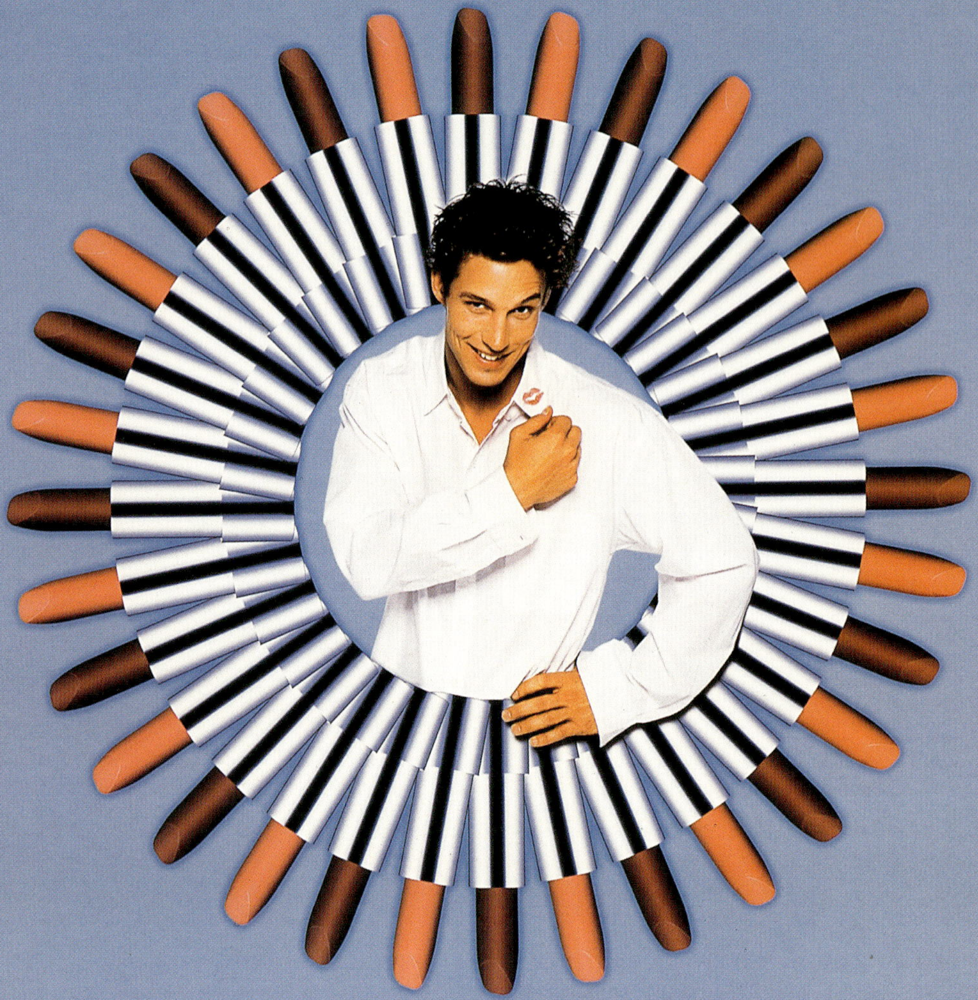

more shirts. more ways to leave your mark. more Targets. 1000 stores now open.

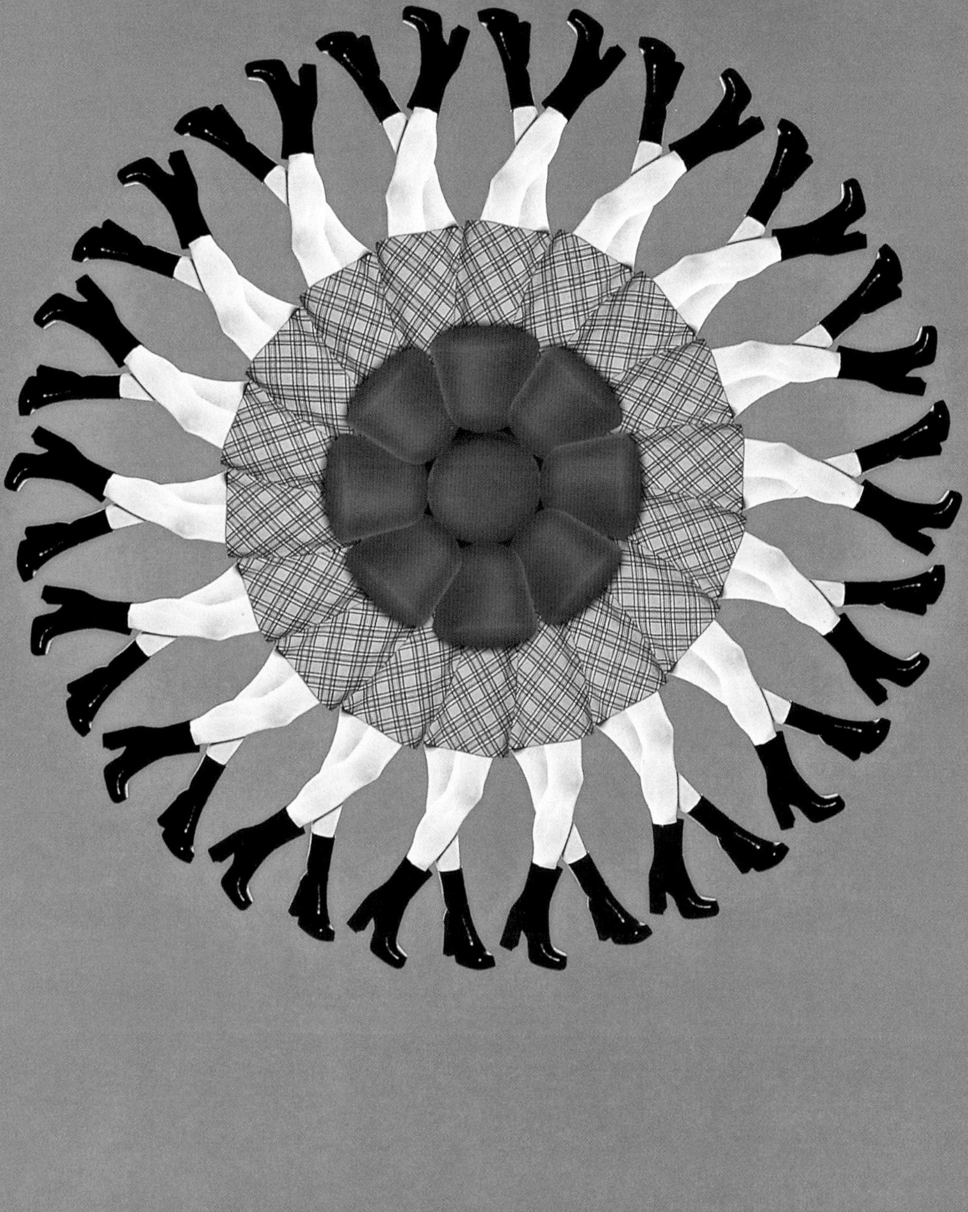

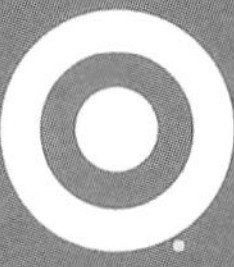

more gumdrops. more eye candy. more Targets. 1000 stores now open.

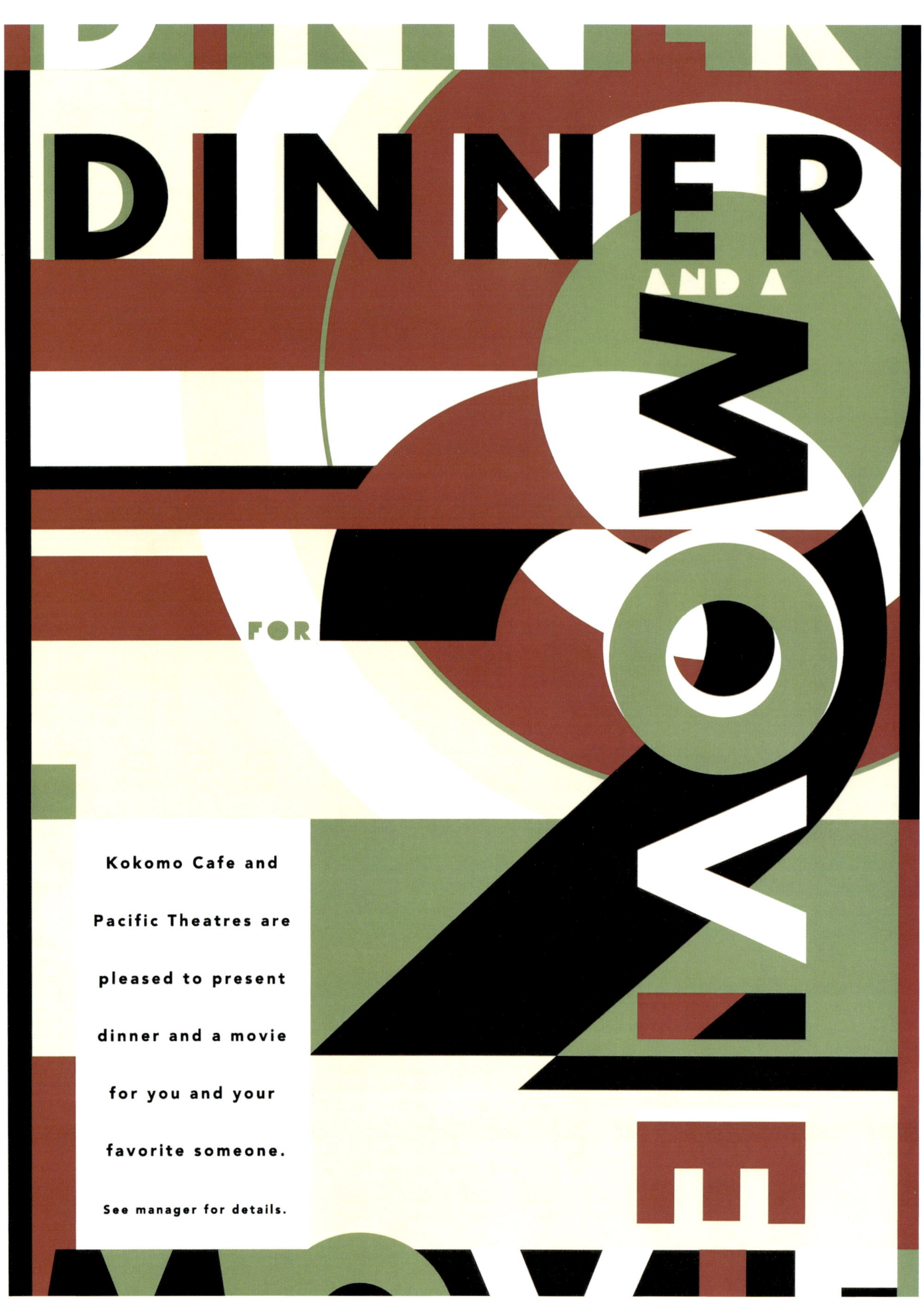

David Croy/Kokomo Cafe

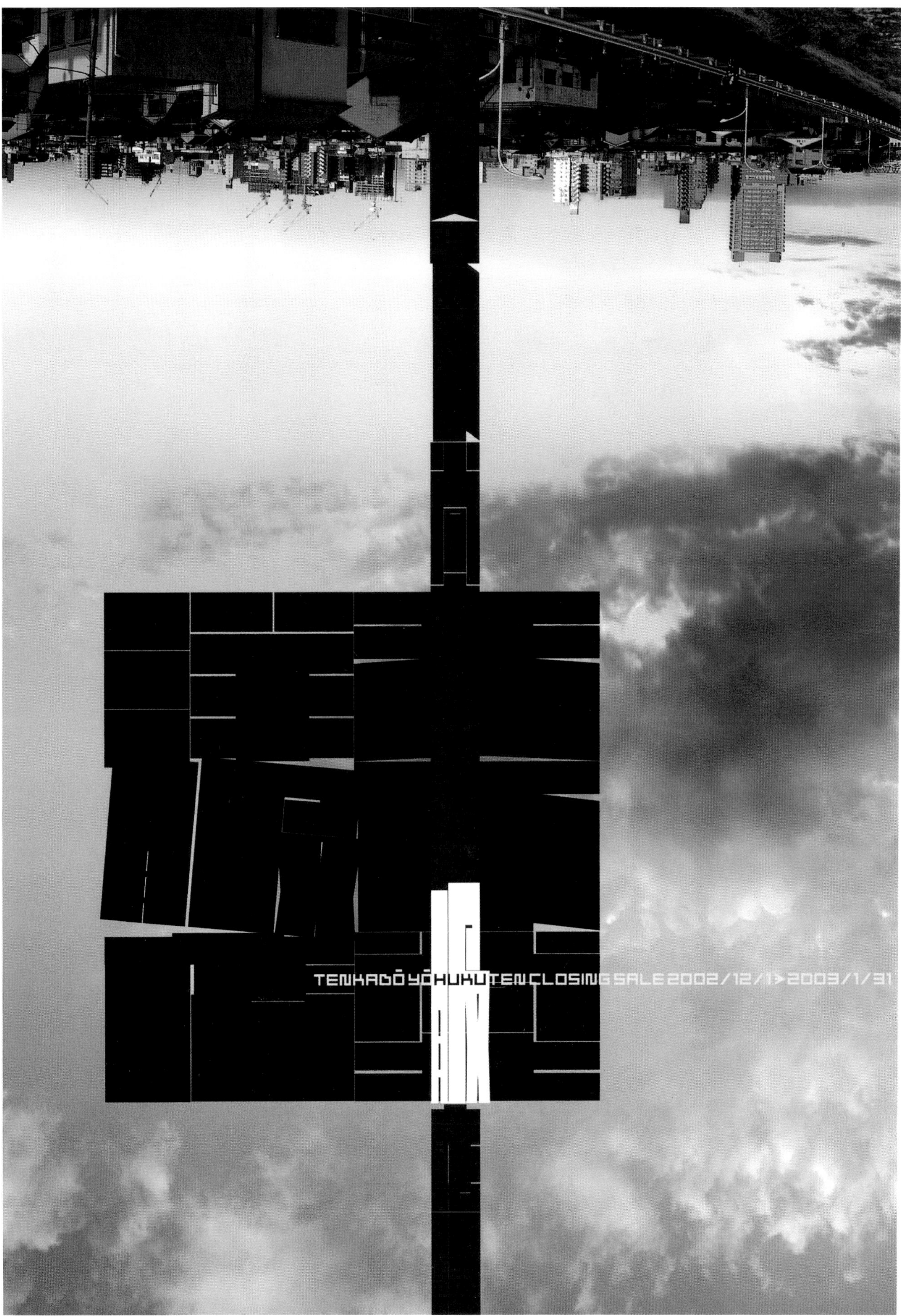

Nippon Design Center/Tenkado Yohukuten

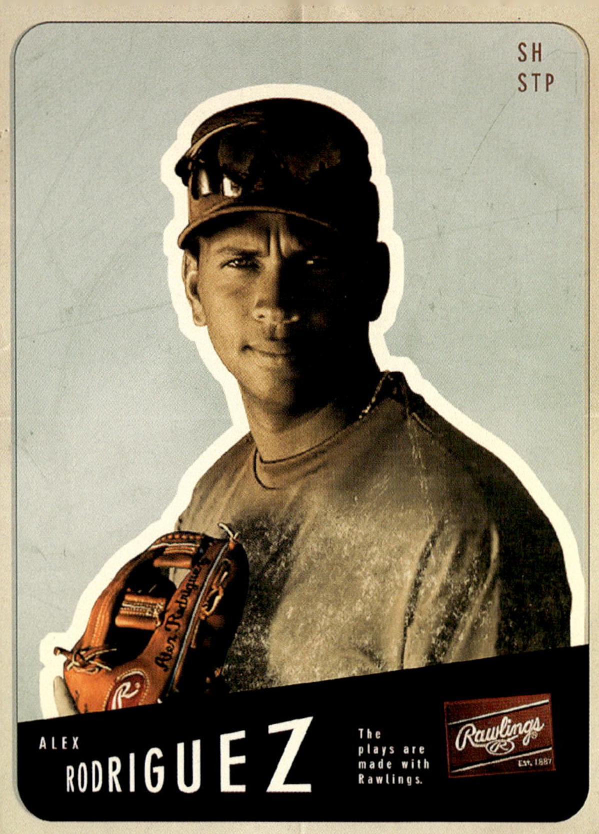
SH
STP
ALEX
RODRIGUEZ
The plays are made with Rawlings.
Rawlings
EST. 1887

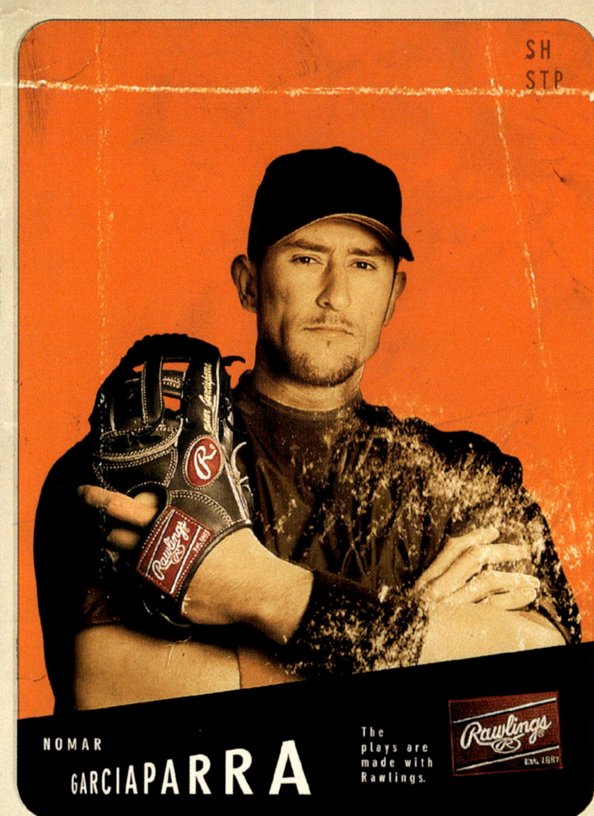
SH
STP
NOMAR
GARCIAPARRA
The plays are made with Rawlings.
Rawlings
EST. 1887

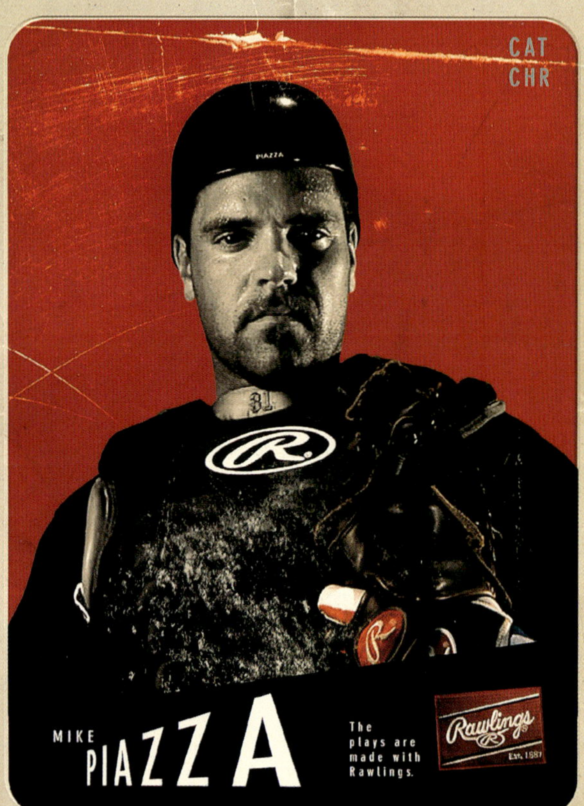
CAT
CHR
MIKE
PIAZZA
The plays are made with Rawlings.
Rawlings
EST. 1887

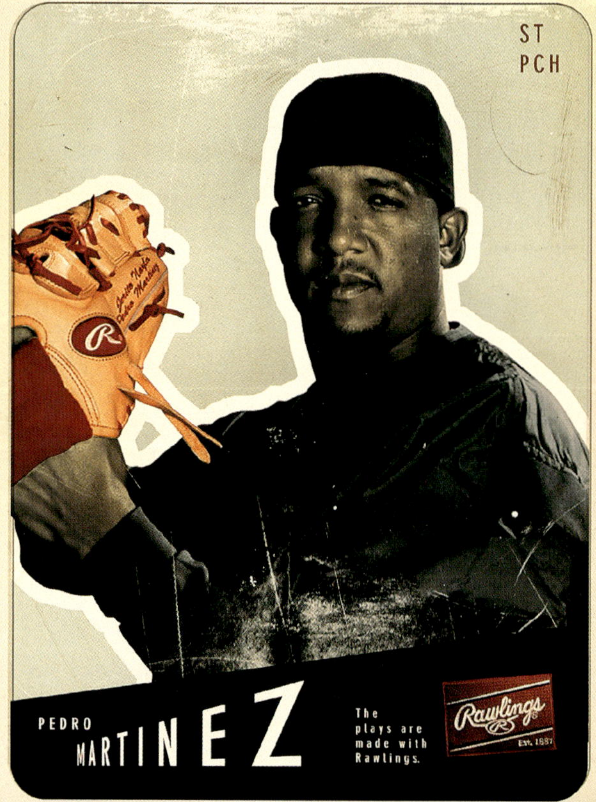
ST
PCH
PEDRO
MARTINEZ
The plays are made with Rawlings.
Rawlings
EST. 1887

BACK TO THE GAME. BACK TO PRIDE. BACK TO A BACKBOARD, A RIM AND A BALL. BACK TO THE EDGE OF YOUR SEAT. BACK TO HEAVEN AND HELL ON A HARDWOOD FLOOR. BACK TO SQUEAK, SQUEAK, ROAR. BACK TO CORN DOGS DIPPED IN ADRENALINE. BACK TO A LITTLE KNOWN POINT GUARD BECOMING A GOD. BACK TO BIRD MEN FLYING THROUGH THE CHARLOTTE AIR. BACK TO ARGUMENTS IN BARBER SHOPS. BACK TO LESSONS LEARNED OUT OF SCHOOL. BACK TO HUGGING THE GUY NEXT TO YOU. BACK TO TAKING ON THE WORLD. BACK TO THE GAME.

GOOD LUCK TO THE NEW CHARLOTTE BOBCATS FROM PRICE McNABB.

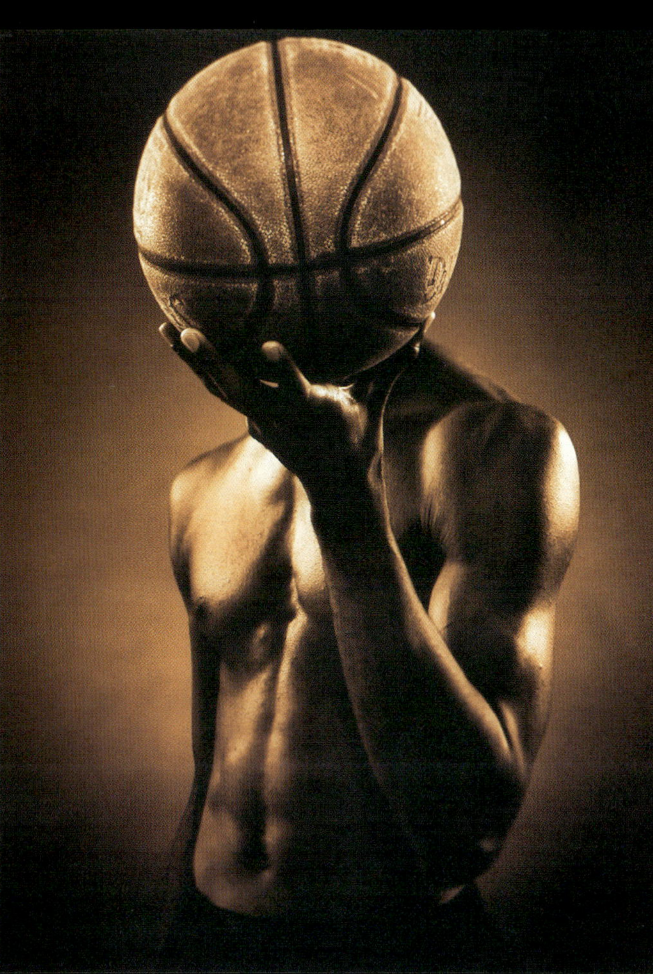

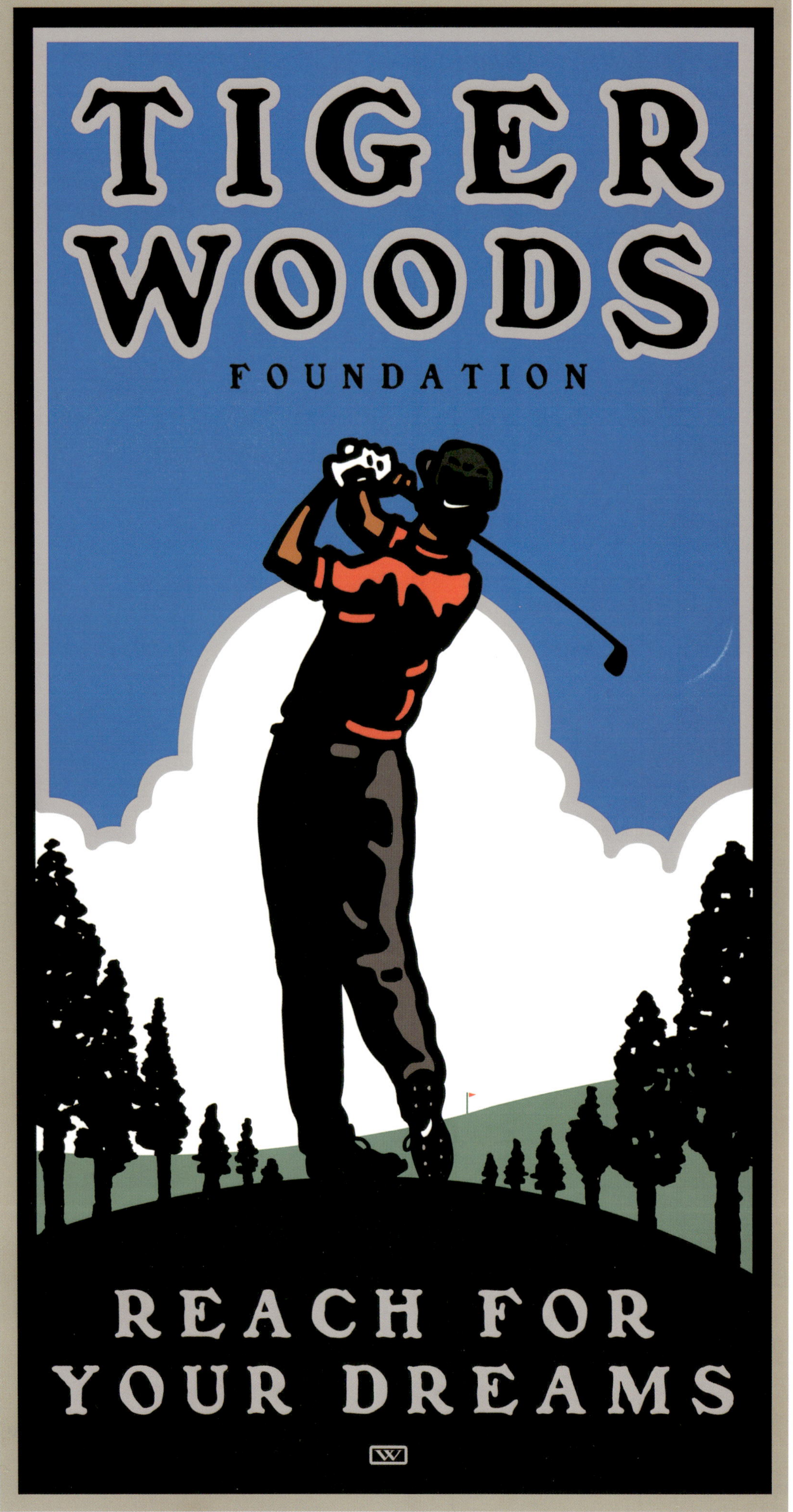

Subzero Design/Tiger Woods/Coca Cola

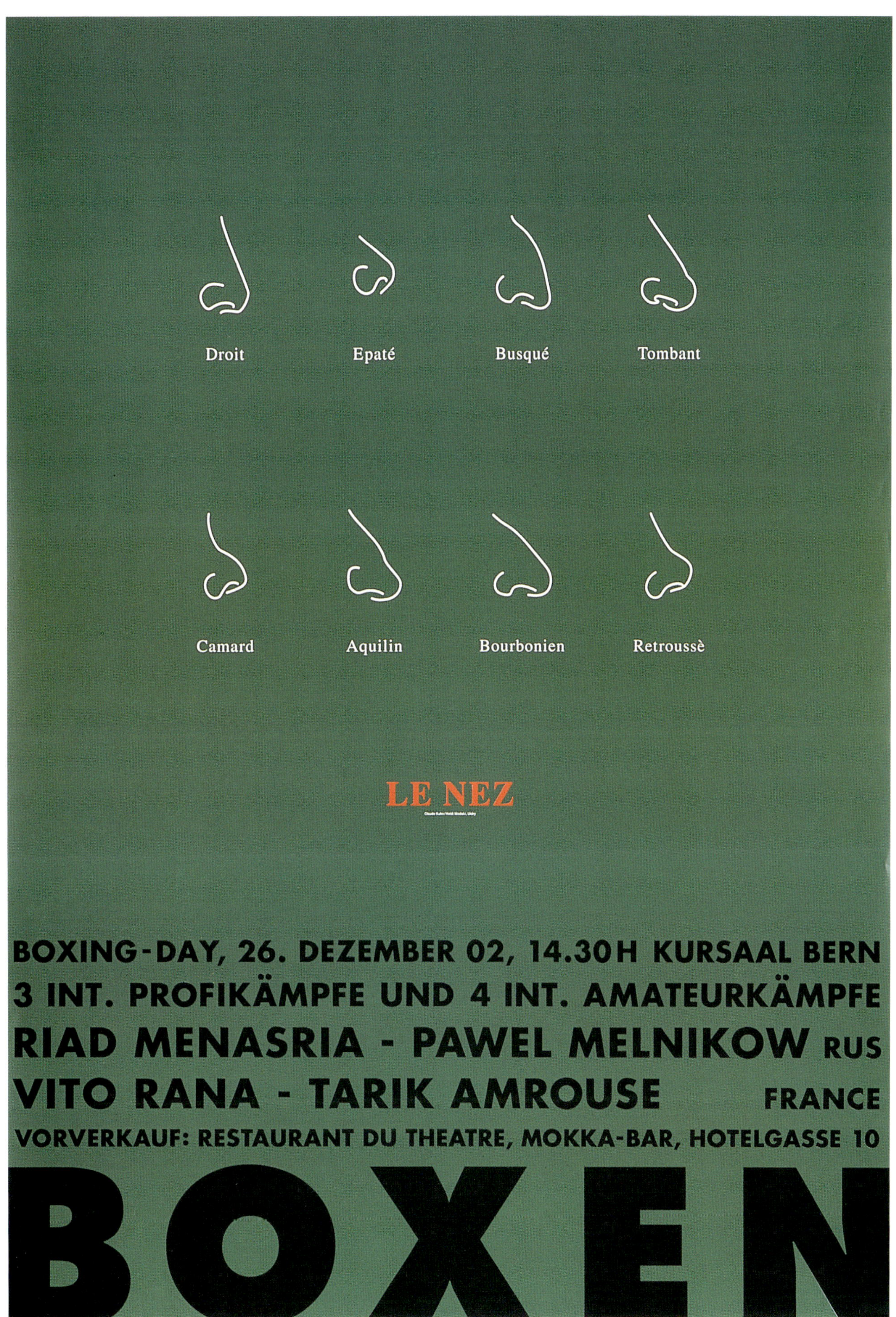

QN Graphic Design/Box Promotion Bern, Jan Eckmann

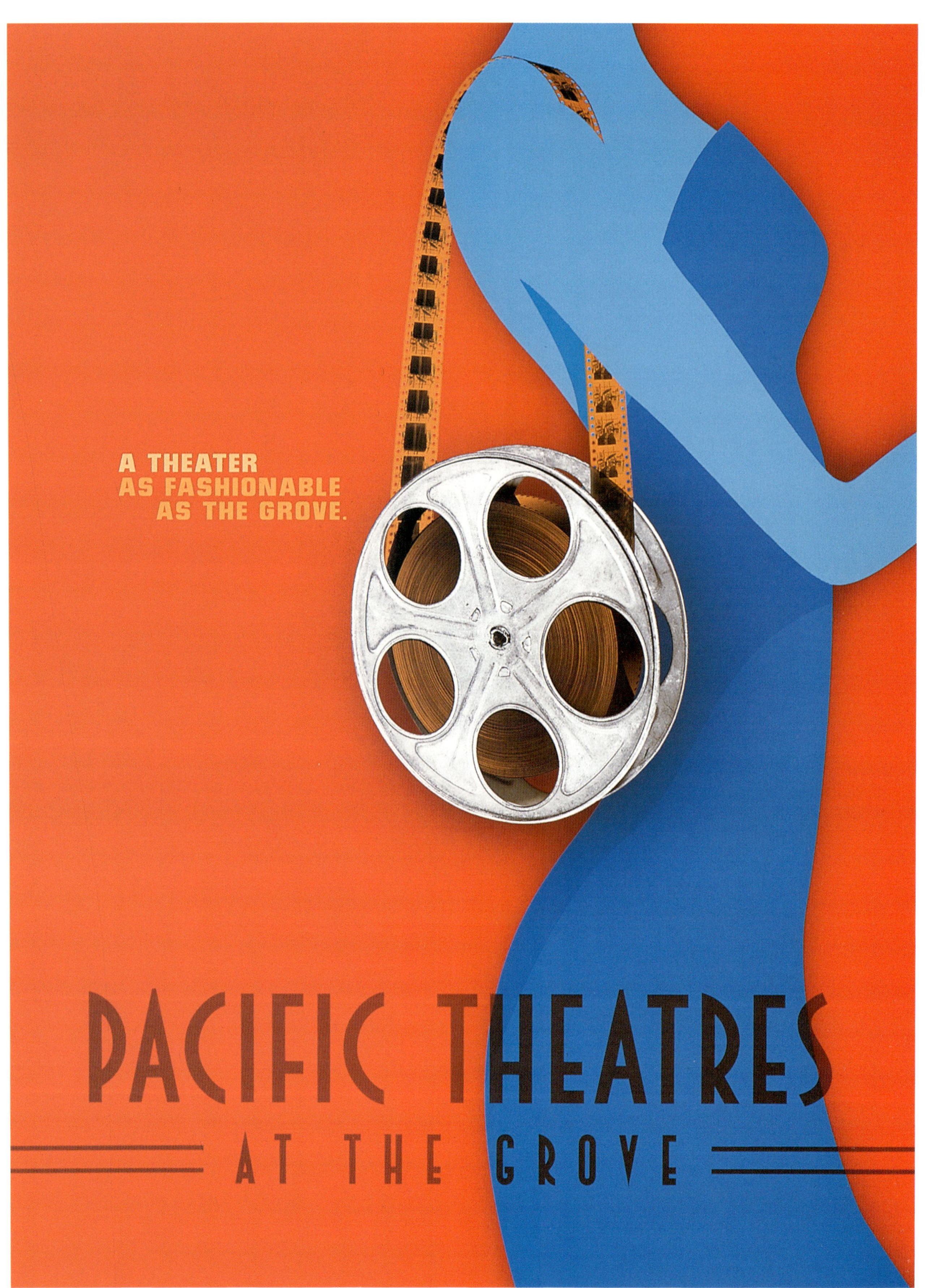

Wongdoody/Pacific Theaters

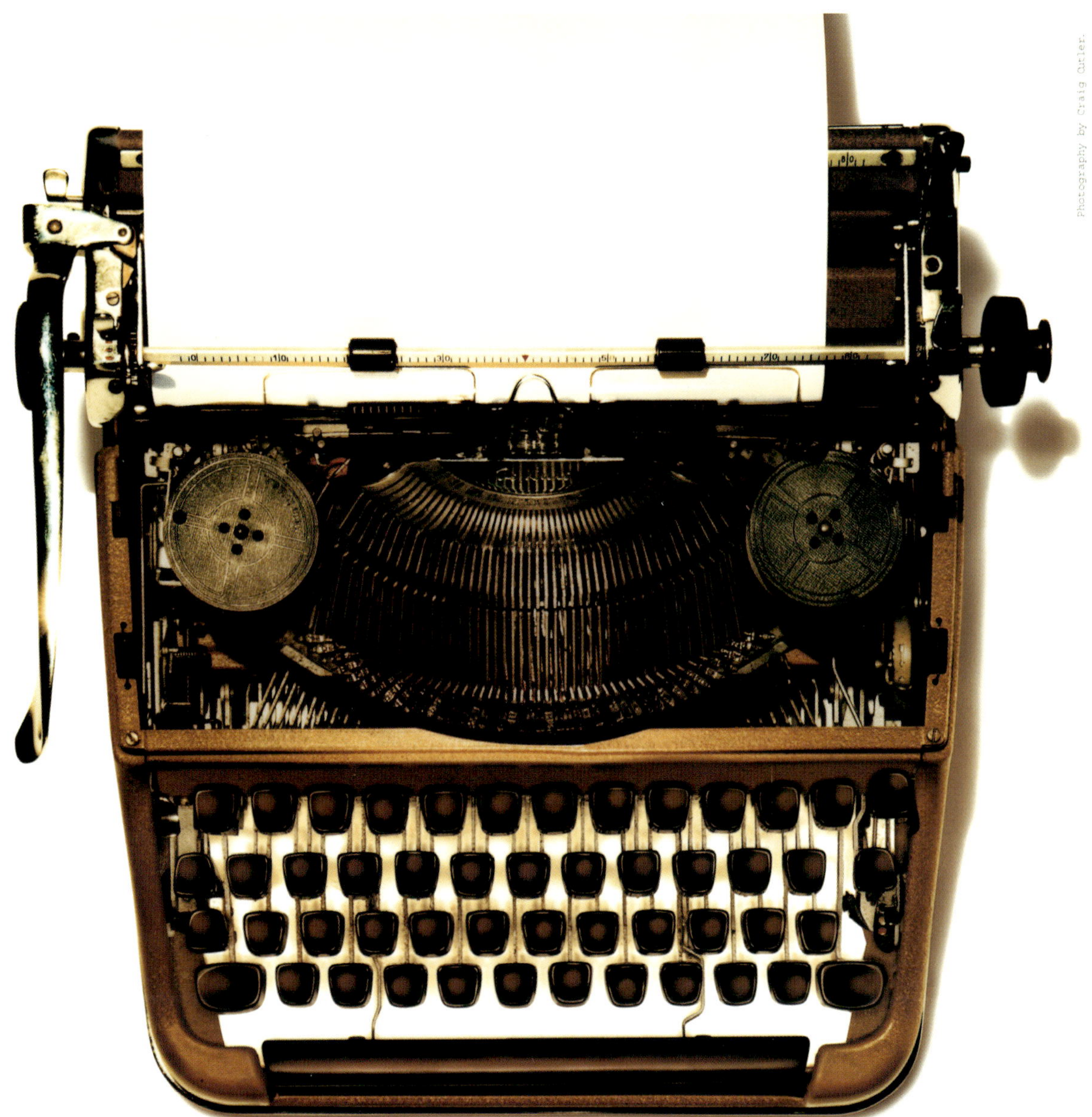

Photography by Craig Cutler.

Writer's Block

by Woody Allen

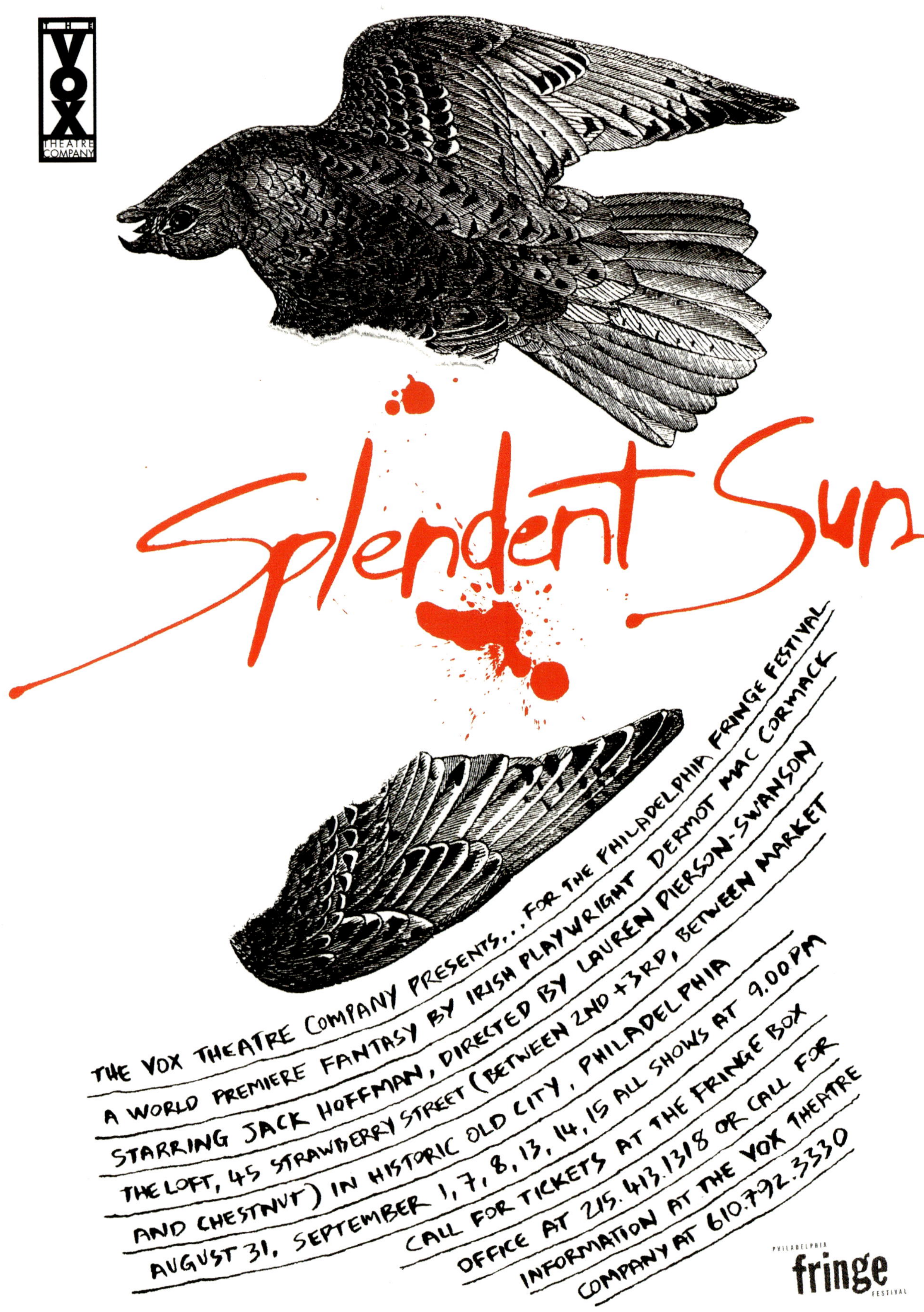
THE VOX THEATRE COMPANY
Splendent Sun
THE VOX THEATRE COMPANY PRESENTS... FOR THE PHILADELPHIA FRINGE FESTIVAL
A WORLD PREMIERE FANTASY BY IRISH PLAYWRIGHT DERMOT MAC CORMACK
STARRING JACK HOFFMAN, DIRECTED BY LAUREN PIERSON-SWANSON
THE LOFT, 45 STRAWBERRY STREET (BETWEEN 2ND + 3RD, BETWEEN MARKET
AND CHESTNUT) IN HISTORIC OLD CITY, PHILADELPHIA
AUGUST 31, SEPTEMBER 1, 7, 8, 13, 14, 15 ALL SHOWS AT 9.00PM
CALL FOR TICKETS AT THE FRINGE BOX
OFFICE AT 215.413.1318 OR CALL FOR
INFORMATION AT THE VOX THEATRE
COMPANY AT 610.792.3330
PHILADELPHIA fringe FESTIVAL

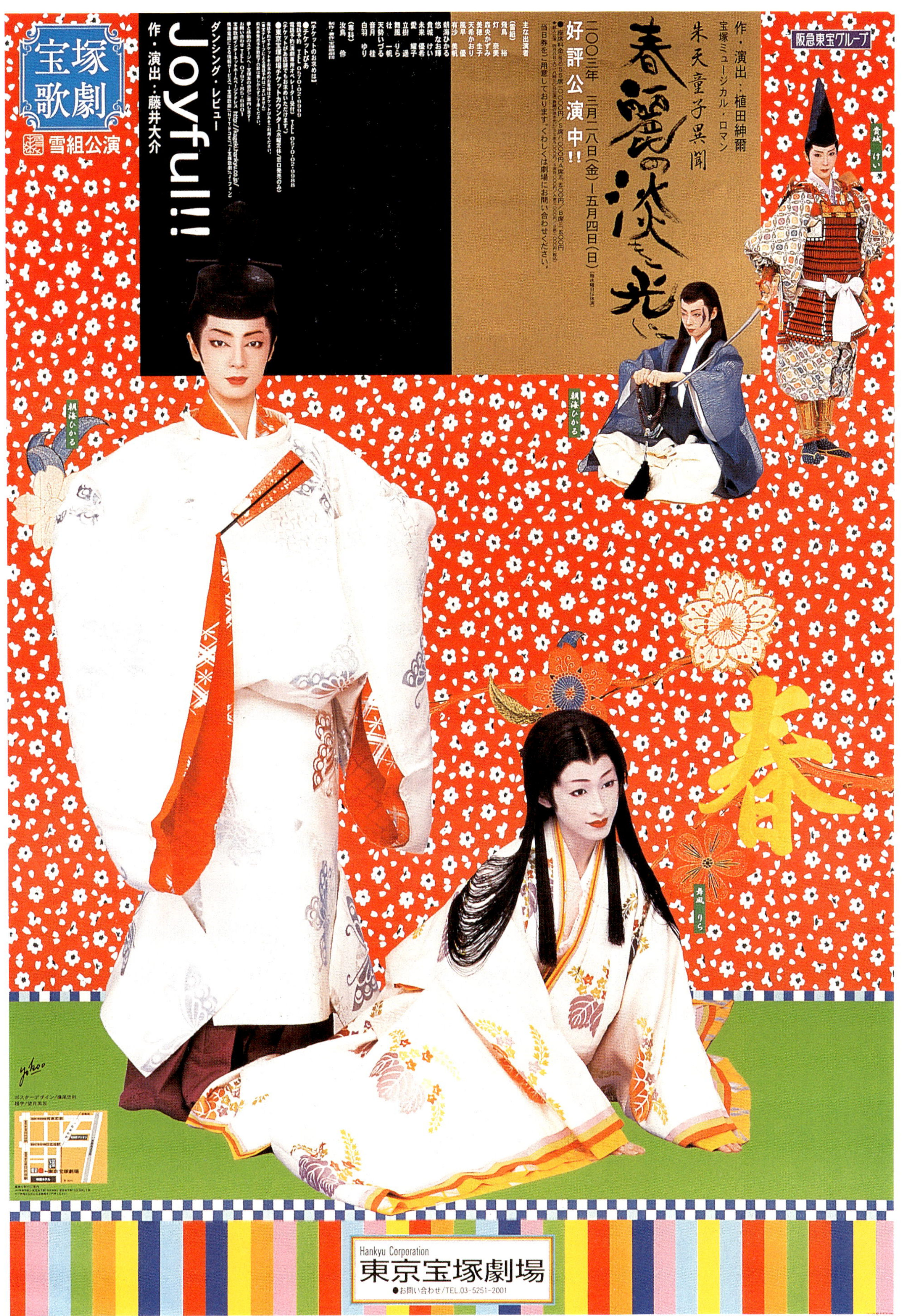

Yokoo's Circus Company, Ltd./Takarazuka Operetta Troupe

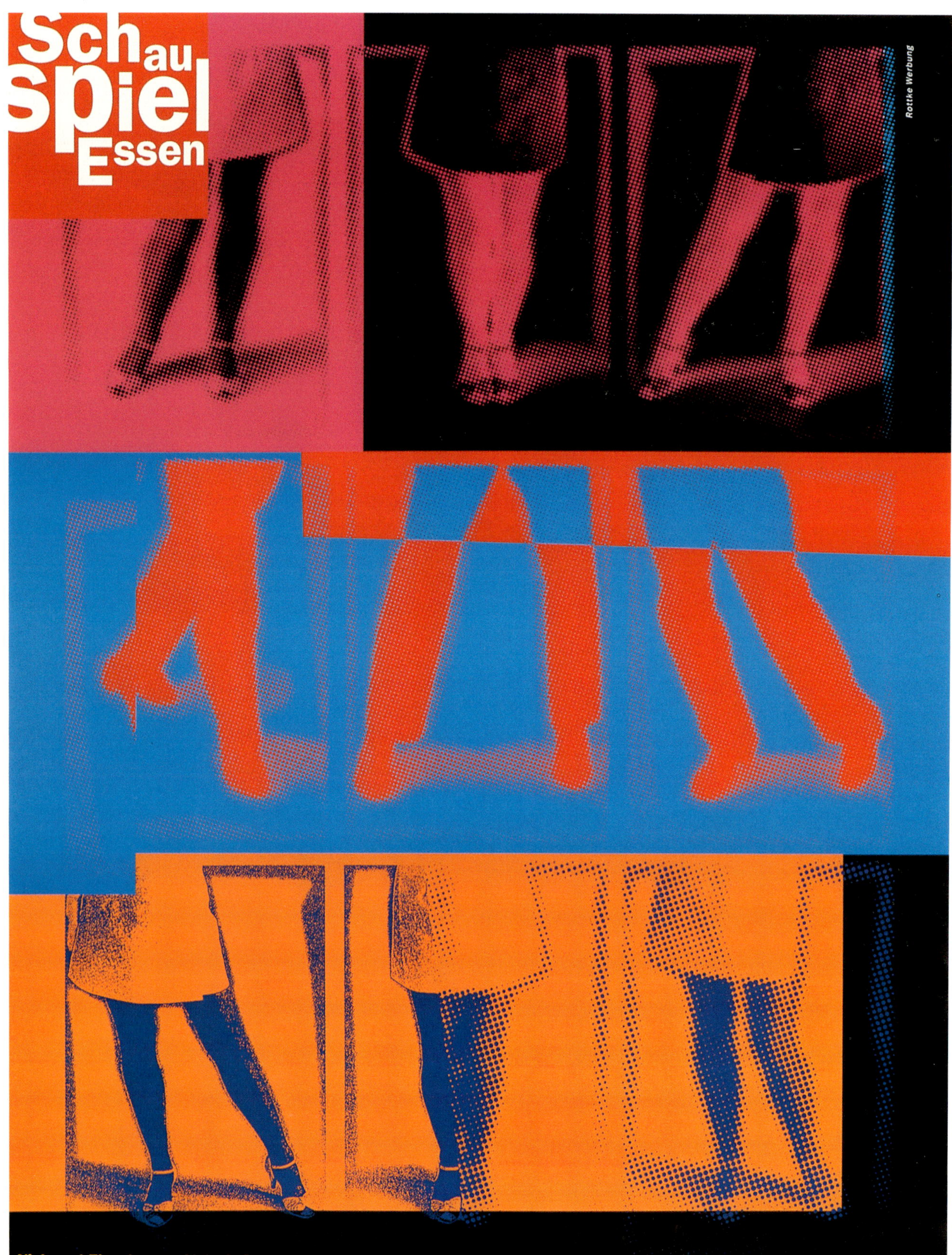

Rottke Werbung/Schauspiel Essen

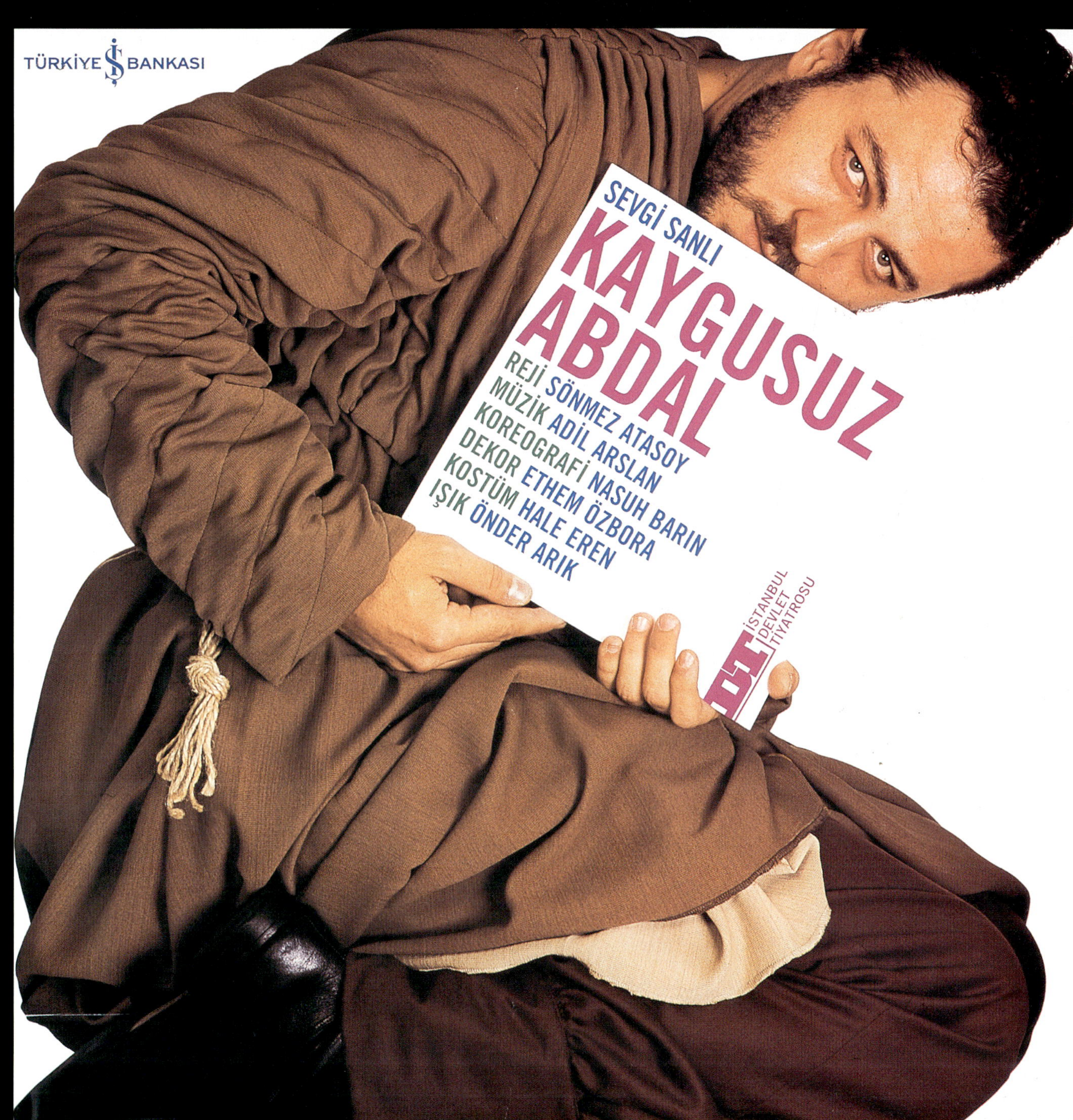
TÜRKİYE İŞ BANKASI
SEVGİ SANLI
KAYGUSUZ
ABDAL
REJİ SÖNMEZ ATASOY
MÜZİK ADİL ARSLAN
KOREOGRAFİ NASUH BARIN
DEKOR ETHEM ÖZBORA
KOSTÜM HALE EREN
IŞIK ÖNDER ARIK
İSTANBUL
DEVLET
TİYATROSU

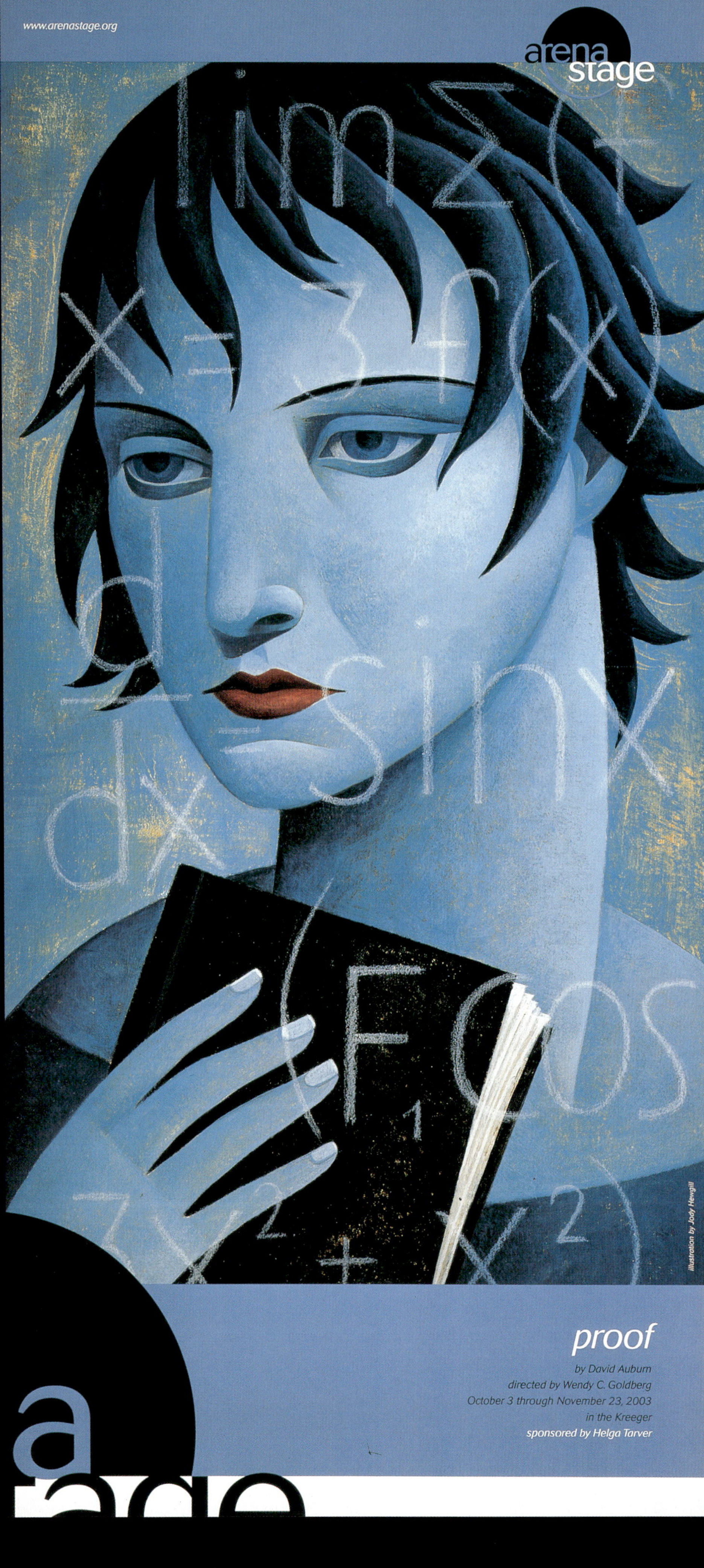

Mires>Design for Brands/Arena Stage

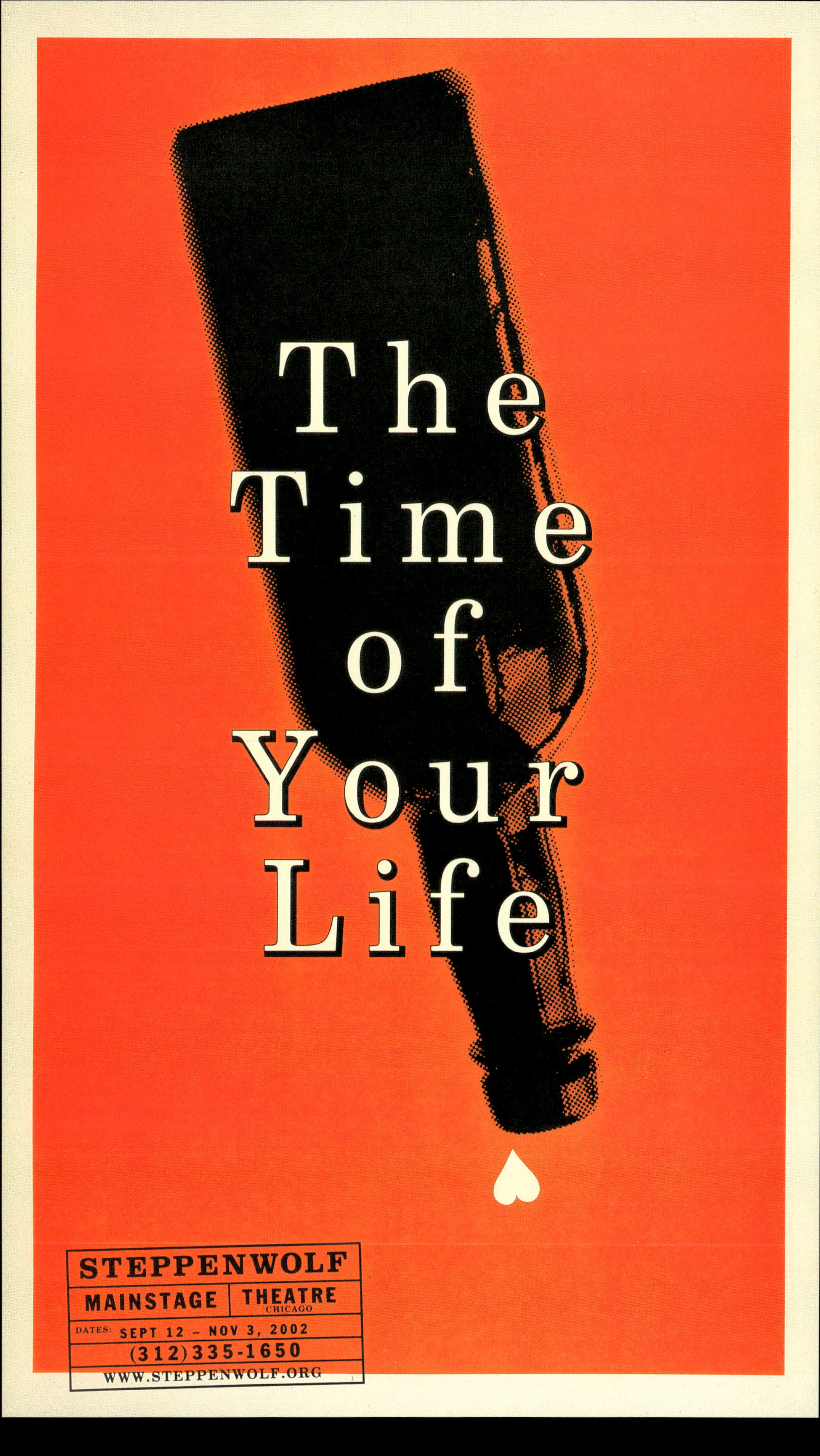

The Time of Your Life

STEPPENWOLF
MAINSTAGE THEATRE CHICAGO
DATES: SEPT 12 – NOV 3, 2002
(312) 335-1650
WWW.STEPPENWOLF.ORG

Sandstrom Design/Steppenwolf Theatre Chicago

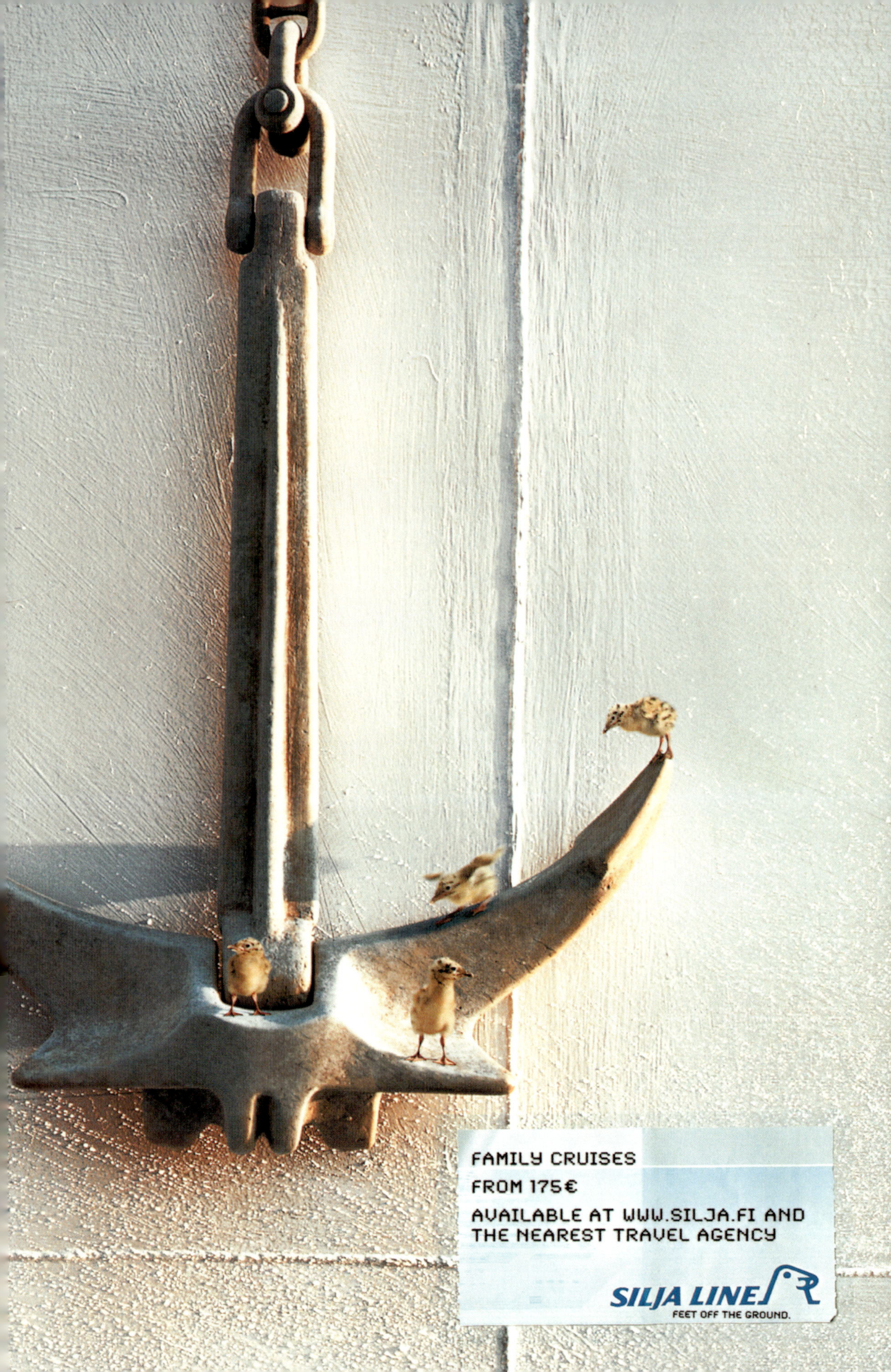
FAMILY CRUISES
FROM 175€
AVAILABLE AT WWW.SILJA.FI AND
THE NEAREST TRAVEL AGENCY
SILJA LINE
FEET OFF THE GROUND.

WILLAMETTE RIVER

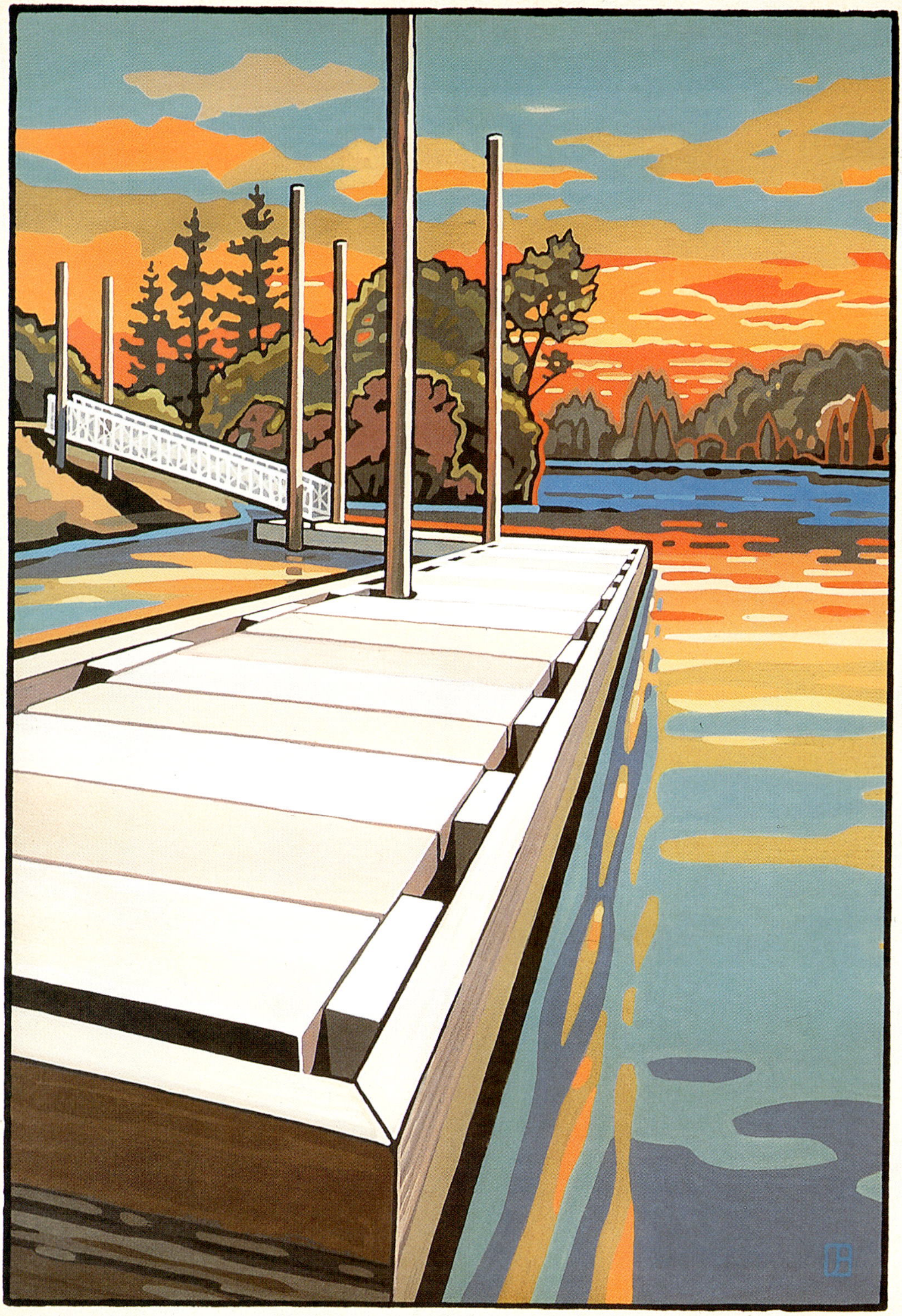

to **work** | to **play** | to **live**

See where it takes you.

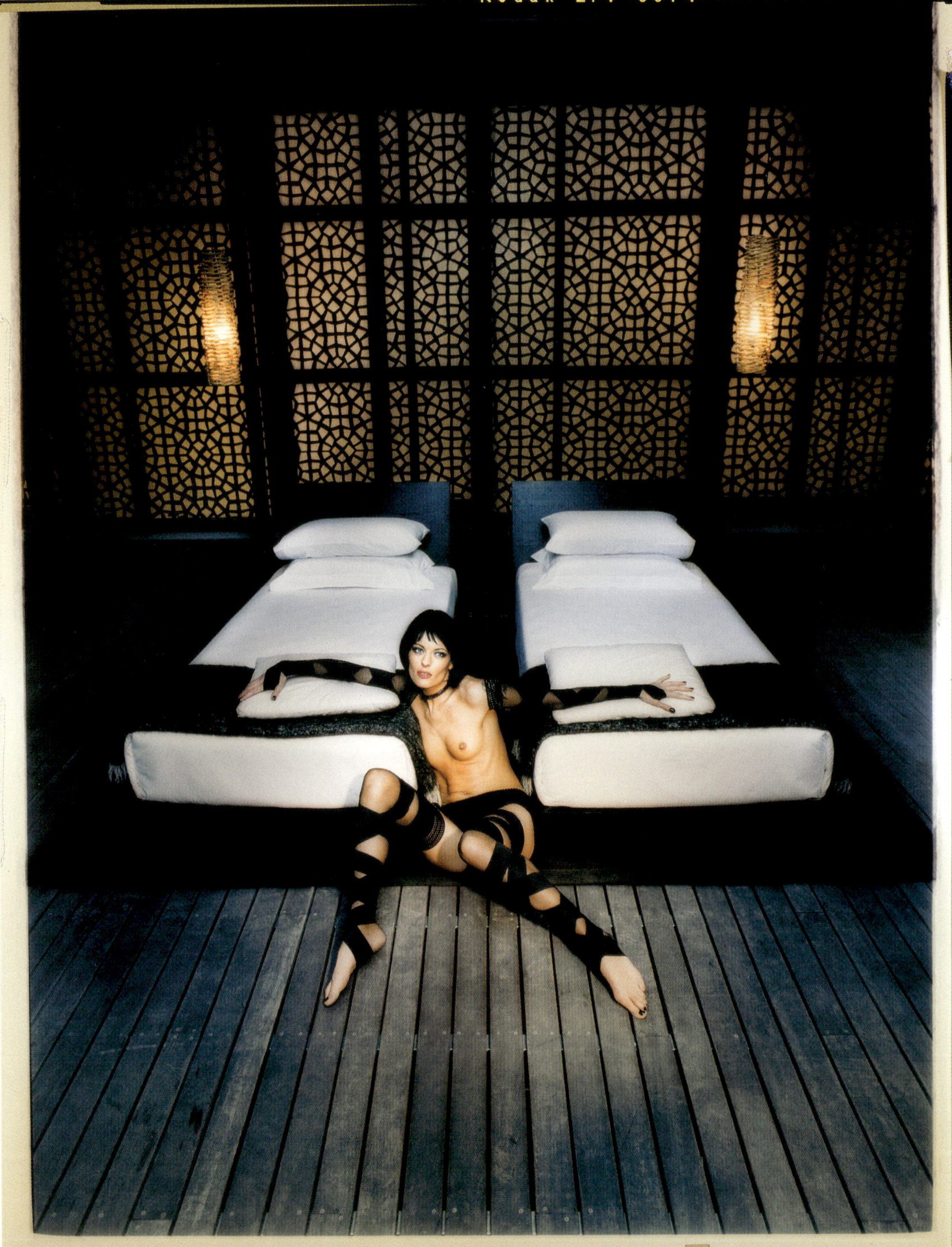

More than accommodating

THE PRINCE

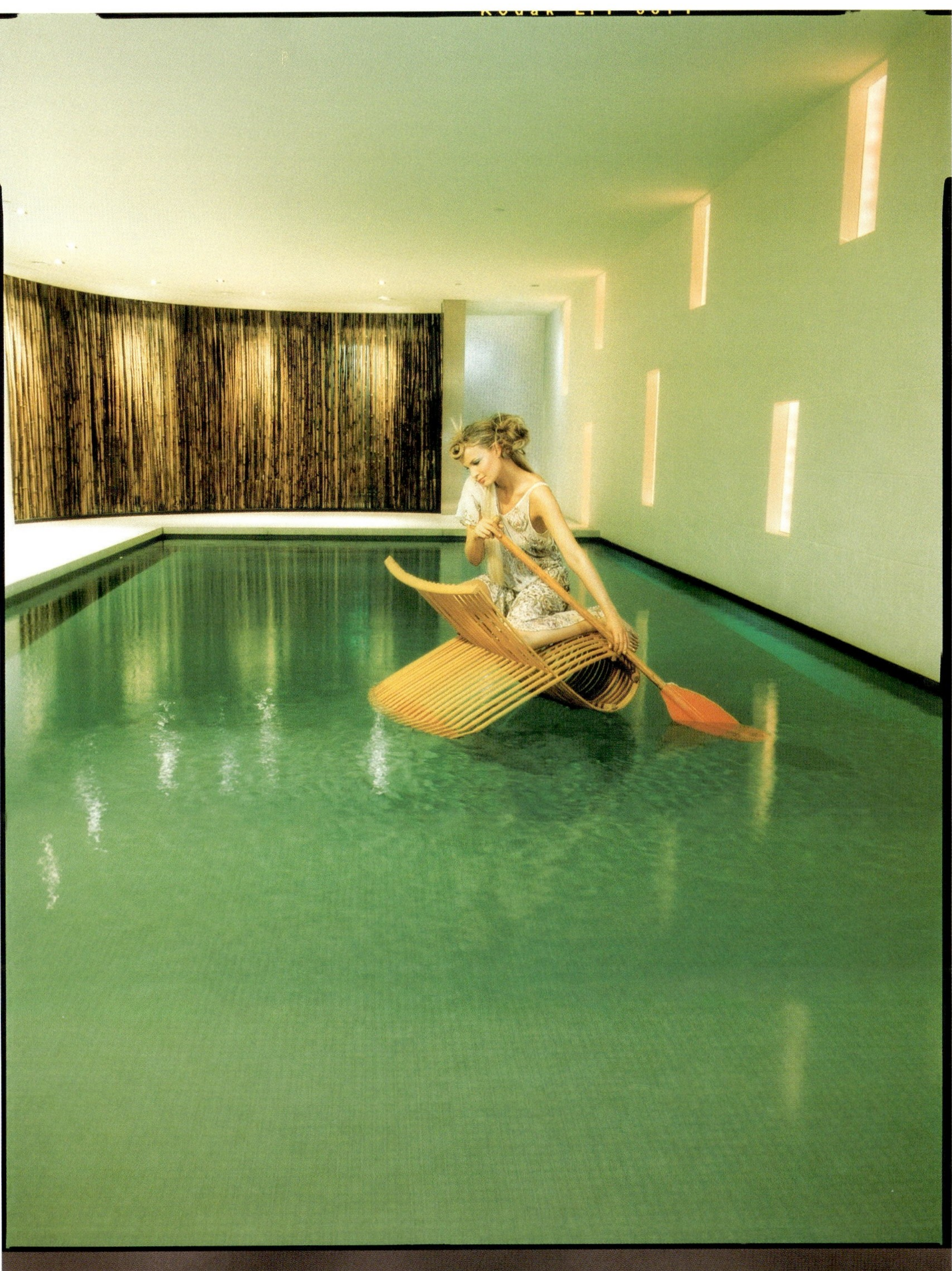

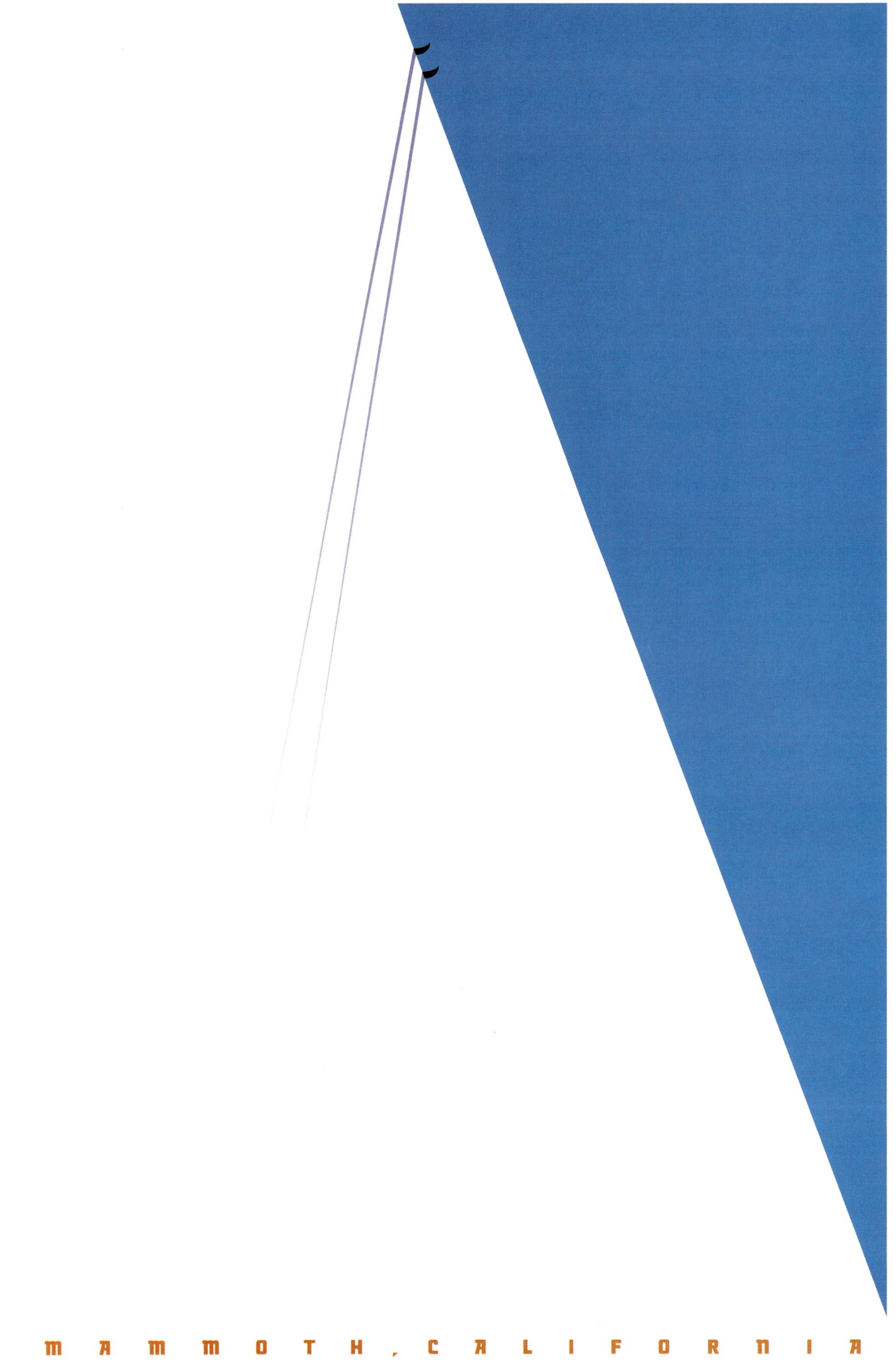

M A M M O T H , C A L I F O R N I A

SAN FRANCISCO® 0802-1	SAN FRANCISCO® 0802-2	SAN FRANCISCO® 0802-3	SAN FRANCISCO® 0802-4	SAN FRANCISCO® 0802-5	SAN FRANCISCO® 0802-6	SAN FRANCISCO® 0802-7	SAN FRANCISCO® 0802-8	SAN FRANCISCO® 0802-9	SAN FRANCISCO® 0802-10	SAN FRANCISCO® 0802-11	SAN FRANCISCO® 0802-12	SAN FRANCISCO® 0802-13
SAN FRANCISCO® 0802-14	SAN FRANCISCO® 0802-15	SAN FRANCISCO® 0802-16	SAN FRANCISCO® 0802-17	SAN FRANCISCO® 0802-18	SAN FRANCISCO® 0802-19	SAN FRANCISCO® 0802-20	SAN FRANCISCO® 0802-21	SAN FRANCISCO® 0802-22	SAN FRANCISCO® 0802-23	SAN FRANCISCO® 0802-24	SAN FRANCISCO® 0802-25	SAN FRANCISCO® 0802-26
SAN FRANCISCO® 0802-27	SAN FRANCISCO® 0802-28	SAN FRANCISCO® 0802-29	SAN FRANCISCO® 0802-30	SAN FRANCISCO® 0802-31	SAN FRANCISCO® 0802-32	SAN FRANCISCO® 0802-33	SAN FRANCISCO® 0802-34	SAN FRANCISCO® 0802-35	SAN FRANCISCO® 0802-36	SAN FRANCISCO® 0802-37	SAN FRANCISCO® 0802-38	SAN FRANCISCO® 0802-39
SAN FRANCISCO® 0802-40	SAN FRANCISCO® 0802-41	SAN FRANCISCO® 0802-42	SAN FRANCISCO® 0802-43	SAN FRANCISCO® 0802-44	SAN FRANCISCO® 0802-45	SAN FRANCISCO® 0802-46	SAN FRANCISCO® 0802-47	SAN FRANCISCO® 0802-48	SAN FRANCISCO® 0802-49	SAN FRANCISCO® 0801-50	SAN FRANCISCO® 0802-51	SAN FRANCISCO® 0802-52
SAN FRANCISCO® 0802-53	SAN FRANCISCO® 0802-54	SAN FRANCISCO® 0802-55	SAN FRANCISCO® 0802-56	SAN FRANCISCO® 0802-57	SAN FRANCISCO® 0802-58	SAN FRANCISCO® 0802-59	SAN FRANCISCO® 0802-60	SAN FRANCISCO® 0802-61	SAN FRANCISCO® 0802-62	SAN FRANCISCO® 0802-63	SAN FRANCISCO® 0802-64	SAN FRANCISCO® 0802-65
SAN FRANCISCO® 0802-66	SAN FRANCISCO® 0802-67	SAN FRANCISCO® 0802-68	SAN FRANCISCO® 0802-69	SAN FRANCISCO® 0802-70	SAN FRANCISCO® 0802-71	SAN FRANCISCO® 0802-72	SAN FRANCISCO® 1201-73	SAN FRANCISCO® 0802-74	SAN FRANCISCO® 0802-75	SAN FRANCISCO® 0802-76	SAN FRANCISCO® 0802-77	SAN FRANCISCO® 0802-78
SAN FRANCISCO® 0802-79	SAN FRANCISCO® 0802-80	SAN FRANCISCO® 0802-81	SAN FRANCISCO® 0802-82	SAN FRANCISCO® 0802-83	SAN FRANCISCO® 0802-84	SAN FRANCISCO® 0802-85	SAN FRANCISCO® 0802-86	SAN FRANCISCO® 0802-87	SAN FRANCISCO® 0802-88	SAN FRANCISCO® 0802-89	SAN FRANCISCO® 0802-90	SAN FRANCISCO® 0802-91
SAN FRANCISCO® 0802-92	SAN FRANCISCO® 0702-93	SAN FRANCISCO® 0802-94	SAN FRANCISCO® 0802-95	SAN FRANCISCO® 0802-96	SAN FRANCISCO® 0802-97	SAN FRANCISCO® 0802-98	SAN FRANCISCO® 0802-99	SAN FRANCISCO® 0802-100	SAN FRANCISCO® 0802-101	SAN FRANCISCO® 0802-102	SAN FRANCISCO® 0802-103	SAN FRANCISCO® 0802-104
SAN FRANCISCO® 0802-105	SAN FRANCISCO® 1001-106	SAN FRANCISCO® 0802-107	SAN FRANCISCO® 0802-108	SAN FRANCISCO® 0802-109	SAN FRANCISCO® 0402-110	SAN FRANCISCO® 0402-111	SAN FRANCISCO® 0802-112	SAN FRANCISCO® 0802-113	SAN FRANCISCO® 0802-114	SAN FRANCISCO® 0802-115	SAN FRANCISCO® 0802-116	SAN FRANCISCO® 0202-117
SAN FRANCISCO® 0802-118	SAN FRANCISCO® 0802-119	SAN FRANCISCO® 0802-120	SAN FRANCISCO® 0802-121	SAN FRANCISCO® 0802-122	SAN FRANCISCO® 0802-123	SAN FRANCISCO® 0802-124	SAN FRANCISCO® 0802-125	SAN FRANCISCO® 0802-126	SAN FRANCISCO® 0802-125	SAN FRANCISCO® 0802-129	SAN FRANCISCO® 0702-130	SAN FRANCISCO® 0802-131
SAN FRANCISCO® 0802-132	SAN FRANCISCO® 0802-133	SAN FRANCISCO® 0802-134	SAN FRANCISCO® 0802-135	SAN FRANCISCO® 0802-136	SAN FRANCISCO® 0802-137	SAN FRANCISCO® 0802-138	SAN FRANCISCO® 0802-139	SAN FRANCISCO® 0802-140	SAN FRANCISCO® 0802-141	SAN FRANCISCO® 0802-142	SAN FRANCISCO® 0802-143	SAN FRANCISCO® 0802-144
SAN FRANCISCO® 0802-145	SAN FRANCISCO® 0802-146	SAN FRANCISCO® 0802-147	SAN FRANCISCO® 0802-148	SAN FRANCISCO® 0802-149	SAN FRANCISCO® 0802-150	SAN FRANCISCO® 0802-151	SAN FRANCISCO® 0802-152	SAN FRANCISCO® 0802-153	SAN FRANCISCO® 0802-154	SAN FRANCISCO® 0802-155	SAN FRANCISCO® 0802-156	SAN FRANCISCO® 0802-157
SAN FRANCISCO® 0802-158	SAN FRANCISCO® 0802-159	SAN FRANCISCO® 0802-160	SAN FRANCISCO® 0802-161	SAN FRANCISCO® 0802-162	SAN FRANCISCO® 0802-163	SAN FRANCISCO® 0802-164	SAN FRANCISCO® 0802-165	SAN FRANCISCO® 0802-166	SAN FRANCISCO® 0802-167	SAN FRANCISCO® 0802-168	SAN FRANCISCO® 0802-169	SAN FRANCISCO® 0802-170
SAN FRANCISCO® 0802-171	SAN FRANCISCO® 0802-172	SAN FRANCISCO® 0802-173	SAN FRANCISCO® 0802-174	SAN FRANCISCO® 0802-175	SAN FRANCISCO® 0802-176	SAN FRANCISCO® 0802-177	SAN FRANCISCO® 0802-178	SAN FRANCISCO® 0802-179	SAN FRANCISCO® 0802-180	SAN FRANCISCO® 0802-181	SAN FRANCISCO® 0802-182	SAN FRANCISCO® 0802-183
SAN FRANCISCO® 0802-184	SAN FRANCISCO® 0802-185	SAN FRANCISCO® 0802-186	SAN FRANCISCO® 0802-187	SAN FRANCISCO® 0802-188	SAN FRANCISCO® 0802-190	SAN FRANCISCO® 0802-189	SAN FRANCISCO® 0802-191	SAN FRANCISCO® 0802-192	SAN FRANCISCO® 0802-193	SAN FRANCISCO® 0802-194	SAN FRANCISCO® 0802-195	SAN FRANCISCO® 0802-196

San Francisco Tones were collected over the span of a few days. We have tried to represent colors, names and places as accurately as possible. No bike messengers were harmed in the making of this poster. **Design** Character. **Printing** Graphic Arts Center / 415 703 8111. **Paper** Monadnock Paper Mills. Astrolite / Astrolite PC 100 / Caress / Dulcet.

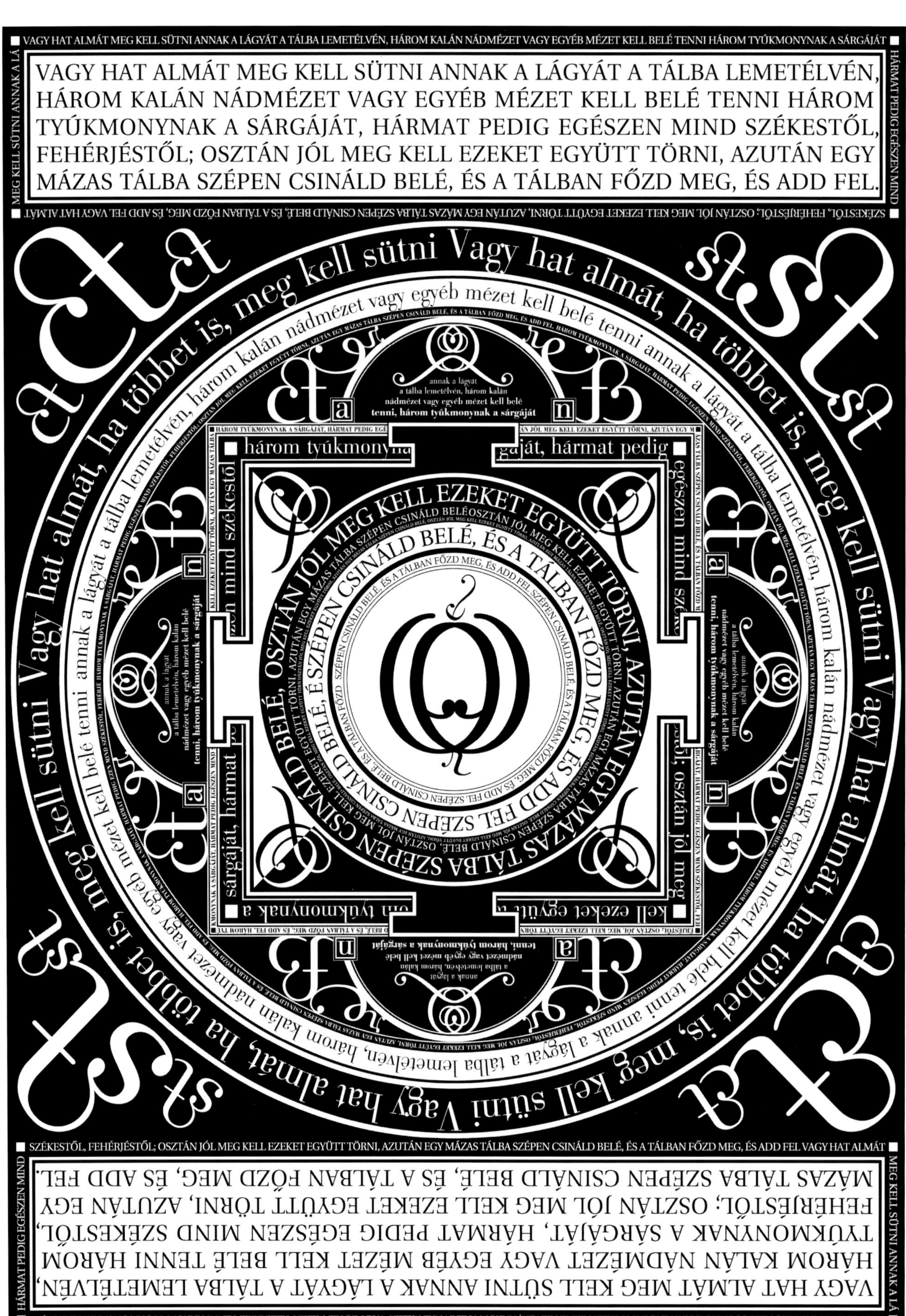

Art Force Design/Élofejek Csoport

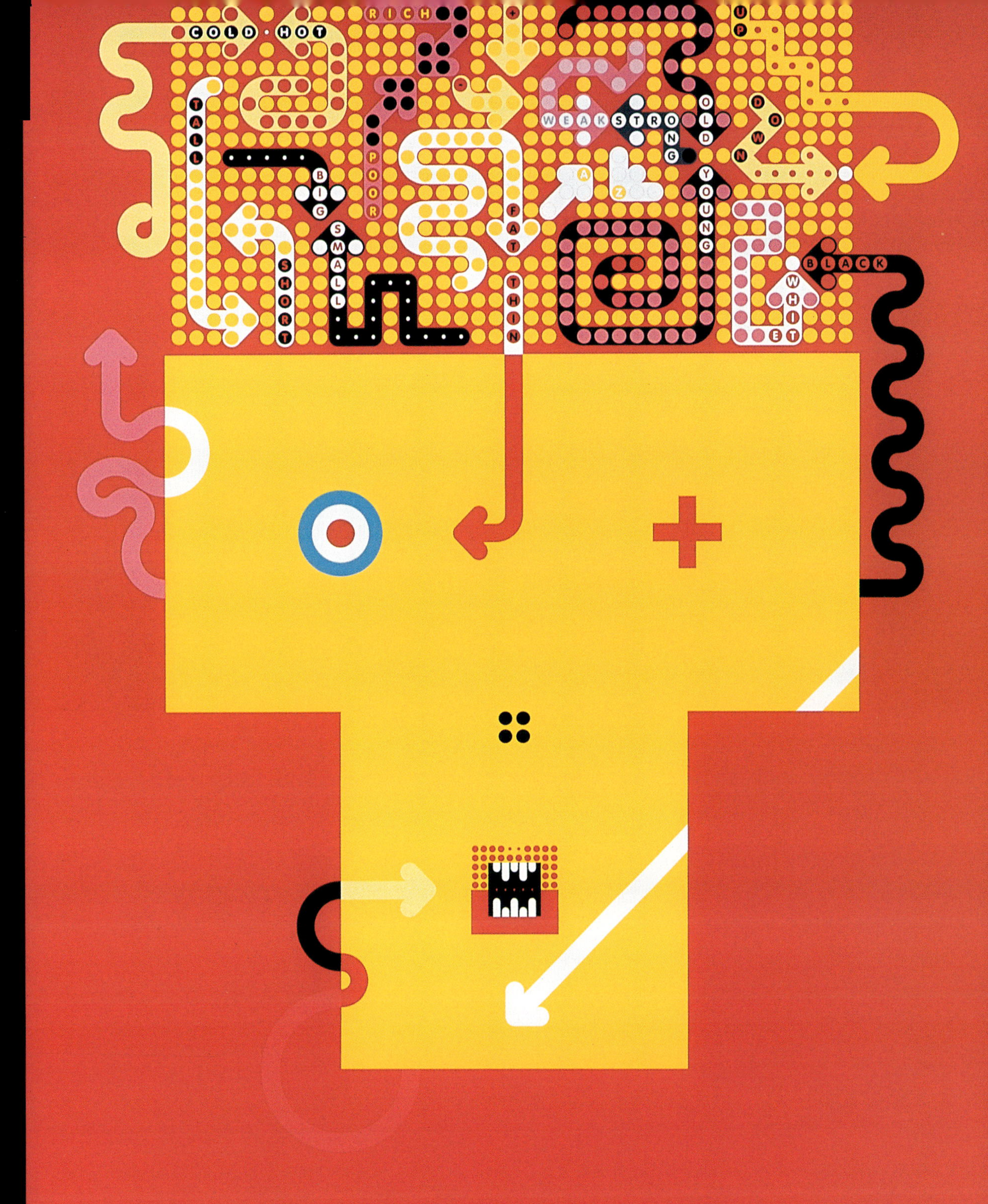

petergrundy

warhead

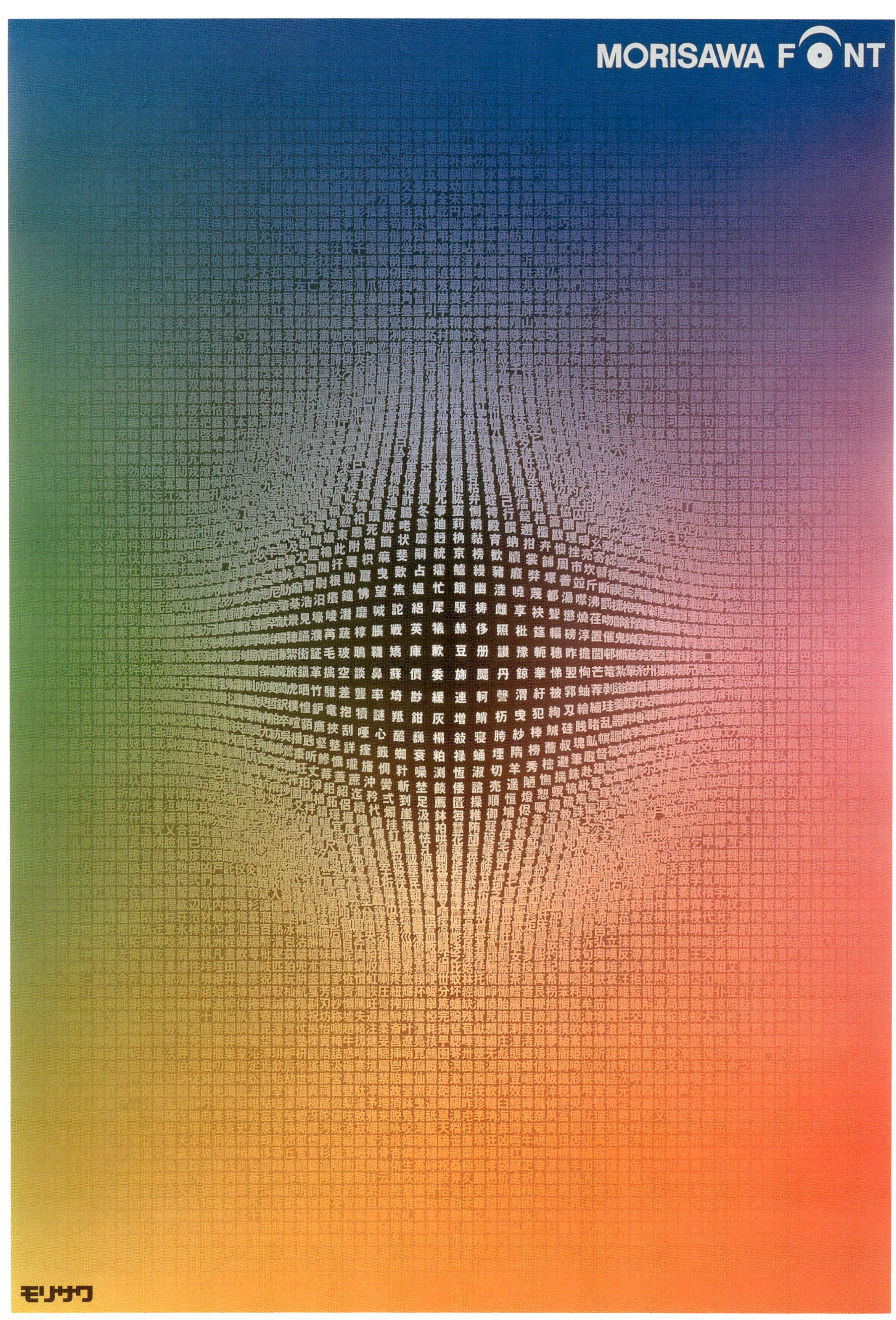

Shinnoske Inc./Morisawa & Company, Ltd.

Index

Credits

Page18
Lyceum 2003
Design Firm: Skolos/Wedell
Creative Directors: Nancy Skolos and Thomas Wedell
Designers: Nancy Skolos and Thomas Wedell
Photographer: Thomas Wedell
Size: 35.5 x 50 in.
Client: Lyceum Fellowship Committee
Paper: standard silkscreen
Printer: Uldry AG, Bern, Switzerland

Page19
Museum Exhibit Poster on Rem Koolhaas
Design Firm: Irene Yuan, for the Art Center College of Design
Designer: Irene Yuan
Size: 24 x 36 in.
Client: MOCA
Paper: Advantage Distribution, Azon semi-matte
Printer: Penpoint Graphics, Pasadena, CA

Page20
Leonard P. Zakim Bunker Hill Bridge
Design Firm: Francis Communications
Art Director: Keith M. Francis
Illustrator: Keith M. Francis
Size: 20 x 28 in.
Client: Millennium Graphics
Paper: Monadnock Astrolite 80# Smooth Cover, Premium Uncoated Brilliant White
Printer: Millennium Graphics, Norwood, MA

Page21
Genoa: Making the Space of the City
Design Firm: Nassar Design
Creative Director: Nelida Nassar
Art Director: Nelida Nassar
Designer: Margarita Encomienda
Photographer: Harvard Design School Students
Illustrator: Harvard Design School Students
Copywriter: Richard Marshall and the President and Fellows of Harvard College, Harvard Design School
Size: 27.5 x 40 in.
Client: Harvard Design School
Paper: Strobe Silk text 80#
Printer: Fit to Print, Abington, MA

Page22
Sticker
Design Firm: David and Goliath
Creative Director: Nigel Williams
Art Director: Will Chau
Photographer: Toby Pederson
Copywriter: Chuck Meehan
Size: 24 x 36 in.
Client: Kia Motors America
Paper: Vintage Clear, 100lb.
Printer: Applied Graphics, Los Angeles, CA

Page23
Solara Art Parts - Door
Design Firm: Saatchi & Saatchi Los Angeles
Creative Directors: Miles Turpin and Steve Landrum
Art Director: Dino Spadavecchia
Photographer: Kevin Necessary
Copywriter: Steve Austin
Size: 33 x 21 in.
Client: Toyota Motor Sales, Inc.
Paper: .020 C1S/Flexcon Busmark
Printer: Ultragraphics & Gangi Studios, Los Angeles, CA

Page24
Solara Art Parts - Fascia
Design Firm: Saatchi & Saatchi Los Angeles
Creative Directors: Miles Turpin and Steve Landrum
Art Director: Dino Spadavecchia
Photographer: Kevin Necessary
Copywriter: Steve Austin
Size: 33 x 21 in.
Client: Toyota Motor Sales, Inc.
Paper: .020 C1S/Flexcon Busmark
Printer: Ultragraphics & Gangi Studios, Los Angeles, CA

Page25
Elvis Rode
Design Firm: Shine Advertising
Creative Director: Mike Kriefski
Art Director: Mike Kriefski
Designer: Peter Bell
Copywriter: Bryan Judkins
Size: 12 x 24 in.
Client: Harley-Davidson Motor Company
Paper: 80# Finch Opaque Bright White Vellum Cover
Printer: The Printery, Milwaukee, WI

Page26
No Cages
Design Firm: Shine Advertising
Creative Director: Mike Kriefski
Art Director: Mike Kriefski
Designer: Peter Bell
Copywriter: Bryan Judkins
Size: 12 x 24 in.
Client: Harley-Davidson Motor Company
Paper: 80# Finch Opaque Bright White Vellum Cover
Printer: The Printery, Milwaukee, WI

Page27
Audi 2003 Racing Poster
Design Firm: McKinney + Silver
Creative Directors: David Baldwin, Dave Cook and Jonathan Cude
Art Director: Keith Greenstein
Illustrator: Dan Cosgrove
Copywriter: Jon Wagner
Production Manager: Lauren March
Size: 24 x 36 in.
Client: Audi of America
Paper: McCoy Silk 100# cover
Printer: Litho Inc., St. Paul, MN

Page28
100 Years of Alcoa in Flight
Design Firm: Arnold Saks Associates, Inc.
Creative Director: Arnold Saks
Art Director: Arnold Saks
Designer: Robert Yasharian
Copywriter: Alcoa Corporate Communications
Size: 22 x 32 in.
Client: Alcoa
Paper: 115lb. Scheufelen Job Parilux Silk Text White
Printer: Sandy Alexander Inc., Clifton, NJ

Page29
Red Hot
Design Firm: Brainstorm Advertising & Design
Creative Director: Joel Green
Art Director: Joel Green
Designer: Joel Green
Illustrator: Gary Overacre
Copywriter: Tara Green
Computer Graphics: Mike Ingram
Size: 12 x 16 in.
Client: Gallery of Love
Paper: 100 lb. uncoated Xerox brand
Printer: Impel Publishing, Atlanta, GA

Page30
Write with Might
Design Firm: Muller + Company
Creative Director: John Muller
Designer: Chris Kincaid
Copywriter: Justin Gardner
Size: 34.5 x 46 in.
Client: The Kansas City Screenwriters
Paper: 80# Productolith Dull
Printer: Limuli Printing, Kansas City, MO

Page31
Technology Trap
Design Firm: designbüro behr
Creative Director: Detlef Behr
Copywriter: Jochen Klein
Size: 60 x 80 cm
Client: Plakation Detlef Behr & Germar Wambach
Paper: 135 g/qm
Printer: Wery-Druck, Köln, Germany

Page32
DAS Call For Entry
Design Firm: Duffy Singapore Pte Ltd.
Creative Director: Christopher Lee
Art Director: Christopher Lee
Designer: Christopher Lee
Photographer: Geoff Ang
Size: 594 x 841 mm
Client: Designers Association of Singapore (DAS)
Paper: 120gsm Exel Bulky Satin (RJ Paper)
Printer: National Photo Engravers, Singapore

Page33
Art/Design/LA
Design Firm: Looking
Creative Director: John Clark
Art Director: John Clark
Designer: John Clark
Photographer: Donald Miller
Copywriter: Michael Dooley
Size: 21.5 x 30 in.
Client: AIGA Los Angeles, Harold's Gallery at Insync Media
Paper: Sappi Magno Dull 100# Cover and 100# Text
Printer: Insync Media, Los Angeles, CA

Page34
Say Your Prayers Call For Entries
Design Firm: Bohan Advertising/Marketing
Creative Director: Kerry Oliver
Art Directors: Kevin Hinson, Joe Weaver and Lisa Sarmento
Designer: Joe Weaver
Photographer: John Guider
Copywriters: Kerry Oliver and Darrell Soloman
Size: 16 x 22 in.
Client: Nashville Advertising Federation
Paper: French Parchtone
Printer: Lithographics Inc., Nashville, TN

Page35
No Software Support
Design Firm: ADK America
Creative Director: Daniel Yamada
Art Director: Daniel Yamada
Copywriter: Daniel Yamada
Size: 24 x 36 in.
Client: Fujifilm
Paper: 100# Gloss Book
Printer: Advanced Color Graphics, Claremont, CA

Page36
Media + HP
Design Firm: Seed Communications
Creative Director: Nancy Raff (Seed)
Art Director: Michael Mabry (Michael Mabry Designs)
Designer: Michael Mabry (Michael Mabry Designs)
Photographer: R.J. Muna
Copywriter: Stephen Emerson
Size: 36 x 24 in.
Client: Hewlett-Packard Company
Paper: Utopia 2 Matte
Printer: Anderson Lithograph, Los Angeles, CA

Page36
Recycling + HP
Design Firm: Seed Communications
Creative Director: Nancy Raff (Seed)
Art Director: Michael Mabry (Michael Mabry Designs)
Designer: Michael Mabry (Michael Mabry Designs)
Illustrator: Michael Mabry (Michael Mabry Designs)
Copywriter: Stephen Emerson
Size: 36 x 24 in.
Client: Hewlett-Packard Company
Paper: Utopia 2 Matte
Printer: Anderson Lithograph, Los Angeles, CA

Page36
Linux + HP
Design Firm: Seed Communications
Creative Director: Nancy Raff (Seed)
Designer: Michael Mabry (Michael Mabry Design)
Illustrator: Michael Mabry (Michael Mabry Design)
Copywriter: Stephen Emerson
Size: 36 x 24 in.
Client: Hewlett-Packard Company
Paper: Utopia 2 Matte
Printer: Anderson Lithograph, Los Angeles, CA

Page37
Explorers
Design Firm: Goodby Silverstein & Partners
Creative Directors: Steve Luker and Steve Silverstein
Art Directors: John Norman and Hunter Hindman
Photographer: Christopher Griffith, (Agent: MS Logan)
Size: Multiformat: Billboard to Adshell
Client: Hewlett-Packard

Page38
Dance Territory
Design Firm: Joseph Kaiser Art Direction
Creative Director: Joseph Kaiser
Art Director: Joseph Kaiser
Designer: Joseph Kaiser
Photographer: Michael Weschler
Size: 14 x 19 in.
Client: The Los Angeles Dance Invitational
Paper: 100 lb Camelot Matte Book
Printer: Design Printing, Beverly Hills, CA

Page39
3 Decades of Dance
Design Firm: Tom Bonauro
Creative Director: Tom Bonauro
Photographer: Christine Alicino
Size: 11 x 17 in.
Client: Margaret Jenkins Dance Company
Paper: Uncoated Evergreen text 70lb
Printer: Logos Graphics, San Francisco, CA

Page40
Mother of all Energy & Creativity
Design Firm: Michael Miller / Erich Chan & Associates
Creative Directors: Michael Miller Yu and Eric Chan
Art Directors: Michael Miller Yu and Eric Chan
Designers: Michael Miller Yu and Eric Chan
Photographer: Ivan Lee Hon Ching
Copywriter: Cat Tyrell
Size: 685 x 980 mm
Client: Hong Kong International Poster Triennial 2004
Paper: 157g Matte Art
Printer: Ching Yin Press, Hong Kong

Page41
Dayton... Cradle of Innovation Poster - Parking Meter Patent
Design Firm: Graphica, Inc.
Creative Directors: Nick Stamas and Mark Stockstill
Art Director: Greg Simmons
Designer: Greg Simmons
Illustrator: Greg Simmons
Copywriter: Graphica, Inc.
Size: 19 x 24 in.
Client: Graphica, Inc. and Progressive Printers
Paper: 80# Cover, Strobe Gloss
Printer: Progressive Printers, Dayton, OH

Page42
Dayton... Cradle of Innovation Poster - Ice Cube Tray Patent
Design Firm: Graphica, Inc.
Creative Directors: Nick Stamas and Mark Stockstill
Art Director: Greg Simmons
Designer: Greg Simmons
Illustrator: Greg Simmons
Copywriter: Graphica, Inc.
Size: 19 x 24 in.
Client: Graphica,Inc and Progressive Printers
Paper: 80# Cover, Strobe Gloss
Printer: Progressive Printers, Dayton, OH

Page43
Ass Kissing Machine
Design Firm: The Republik
Creative Director: Robert Shaw West
Designer: Brian Murray
Copywriter: Brian Murray
Size: 11 x 17 in.
Client: Serious Robots
Paper: Cougar Natural 80#
Printer: Future Graphics, Wendell, NC
The Ass-Kissing Machine was created for advertising agencies in search of new and exciting ways to make their clients happy through artificial means.

Page44
Season's Greetings
Design Firm: Images
Creative Director: Julius Friedman
Designer: Julius Friedman
Photographer: Geoffry Carr
Size: 24 x 36 in.
Client: Images and Hamilton Printing
Paper: Warren Lustro Gloss
Printer: Hamilton Printing, Louisville, KY

Page45
Fly on the Wall
Design Firm: Bozell & Jacobs
Creative Director: Robert Mucciaccio
Art Director: Erica Rowe
Designer: Wendy Biernbaum
Copywriter: Dan Walker
Size: 18 x 24 in.
Client: Bozell & Jacobs Internship Program
Paper: Utopia One, 100# Book, Dull
Printer: Barnhart Press, Omaha, NE

Page46
Constructivism
Design Firm: Amy Kalpakchyan
Creative Director: Amy Kalpakchyan
Art Director: Steve Madden
Designer: Amy Kalpakchyan
Photographer: Amy Kalpakchyan
Illustrator: Amy Kalpakchyan
Copywriter: Amy Kalpakchyan
Size: 2 x 3 ft.
Client: Art Center College of Design/Self-Promotion
Paper: Photo Matte Paper (7mil)
Printer: N2 Graphics, Pasadena, CA

Page47
ArtDesignStudio
Design Firm: ArtDesignStudio
Creative Directors: Vladimir Tsesler and Sergej Voichenko
Art Directors: Vladimir Tsesler and Sergej Voichenko
Designers: Vladimir Tsesler and Sergej Voichenko
Photographer: Andrej Shukin
Copywriter: ArtDesignStudio
Size: 70 x 100 cm
Client: Linea Grafic
Paper: 200g
Printer: Linea Graphic, Moscow

Page48
Resistance is Futile
Design Firm: Muller + Company
Creative Director: John Muller
Art Director: John Muller
Designer: John Muller
Photographer: Anna Velda
Size: 48 x 72 in.
Client: Muller + Company
Paper: Cougar Opaque
Printer: Limuli Printing, Kansas City, MO

Page49
Compostion of Drawing Series
Design Firm: Shin Matsunaga Design Inc.
Art Director: Shin Matsunaga
Designer: Shin Matsunaga
Illustrator: Shin Matusnaga
Size: 728 x 1030 cm
Client: Shin Matsunaga
Paper: Vent Nouveau VG
Printer: Kyodo Printing Co. Ltd, Tokyo, Japan

Page50
RISD Digital Media
Design Firm: Skolos/Wedell
Creative Directors: Thomas Wedell and Nancy Skolos
Designers: Nancy Skolos and Thomas Wedell
Photographer: Thomas Wedell
Size: 35.5 x 50 in.
Client: Rhode Island School of Design, Department of Digital Media
Paper: standard silkscreen
Printer: Uldry AG, Bern, Switzerland

Page51
AIGA Landor Associates Poster
Design Firm: Morla Design, Inc.
Creative Director: Jennifer Morla
Designers: Jennifer Morla and Brian Singer
Copywriter: Landor Associates
Size: 20 x 30 in.
Client: AIGA San Francisco Chapter
Paper: New Leaf Paper, Opaque Smooth 80# Text
Printer: Watermark Press, San Francisco, CA

Page52
RISD Faculty Biennial
Design Firm: Skolos/Wedell
Creative Directors: Nancy Skolos and Thomas Wedell
Designers: Nancy Skolos and Thomas Wedell
Photographer: Thomas Wedell
Size: 35.5 x 50 in
Client: Rhode Island School of Design Museum
Paper: Standard silkscreen
Printer: Uldry AG, Bern, Switzerland

Page53
Writing Studio
Design Firm: Malcolm Wadell Associates
Creative Director: Michael Maynard
Designer: Malcom Waddell
Photographer: Malcom Waddell
Size: 22 x 30 in.
Client: The Banff Centre
Paper: Weyerhaeuser, Cougar Opaque, 65lb Cougar Cover, Smooth Finish
Printer: The Banff Centre, Alberta, Canada

Page54
Blue Girl
Design Firm: Arnold Worldwide - St. Louis
Creative Director: Mark Ray
Art Director: Mark Halski
Photographer: Brad Wilson
Copywriter: Brad Fels
Print Production: David Christoff
Size: 18 x 24 in.
Client: Washington University Gallery of Art
Paper: 100# Text White Silk Finished Strobe
Printer: Kohler & Sons, St. Louis, MO

Page55
Green Boy
Design Firm: Arnold Worldwide - St. Louis
Creative Director: Mark Ray
Art Director: Mark Halski
Photographer: Brad Wilson
Copywriter: Brad Fels
Print Producer: David Christoff
Size: 18 x 24 in.
Client: Washington University Gallery of Art
Paper: 100# Text White Silk Finished Strobe
Printer: Kohler & Sons, St. Louis, MO

Credits

Page56
Oxbow Poster
Design Firm: Craig Frazier Studio
Creative Director: Craig Frazier
Art Director: Craig Frazier
Designer: Craig Frazier
Illustrator: Craig Frazier
Size: 14 1/8 x 21 1/2 in.
Client: The Oxbow School, Napa, CA
Paper: Carnival Smooth Cover: Pure White/ 80 lb., Stellar White/ 100 lb.
Printer: Watermark Graphics, San Francisco, CA

Page57
UC Berkely Real Estate Program, Haas School of Business
Design Firm: Saint Hieronymus Press
Creative Director: David Lance Goines
Art Director: David Lance Goines
Designer: David Lance Goines
Illustrator: David Lance Goines
Copywriter: Steve Chamberlin
Size: 17 3/8 x 24 in.
Client: Berkeley Real Estate Program, Haas School of Business, University of California, Berkeley
Printer: Saint Hieronymus Press, Berkeley, CA

Page58
The Crowden School
Design Firm: Saint Hieronymus Press
Creative Director: David Lance Goines
Art Director: David Lance Goines
Designer: David Lance Goines
Illustrator: David Lance Goines
Size: 17 3/8 x 24 in.
Client: The Crowden School
Paper: Monadnock Astrolite Brilliant White Smooth 80# Cover
Printer: Saint Hieronymus Press, Berkeley, CA

Page59
Chinese Character
Design Firm: Purdue University, Visual and Performing Arts
Creative Director: Li Zhang
Art Director: Li Zhang
Designer: Li Zhang
Photographer: Li Zhang
Illustrator: Li Zhang
Copywriter: Li Zhang
Size: 21 x 31.5 in.
Client: Taiwan Poster Design Association, Tung Fang Institute of Technology
Paper: #80lb White Mat
Printer: Purdue University, West Lafayette, IN

Page60
KQED & Entertainment
Design Firm: Pentagram San Francisco
Creative Director: Kit Hinrichs
Art Director: Kit Hinrichs
Designer: Leslie Stitzlein
Illustrator: Vivienne Flesher
Size: 16 x 20 in.
Client: KQED
Paper: Sappi McCoy 80# Cover Uncoated
Printer: Anderson Litho, San Francisco, CA

Page61
KQED & Children
Design Firm: Pentagram San Francisco
Creative Director: Kit Hinrichs
Art Director: Kit Hinrichs
Designer: Leslie Stitzlein
Illustrator: Gary Overacre
Size: 16 x 20 in.
Client: KQED
Paper: Sappi McCoy 80# Cover Uncoated
Printer: Anderson Litho, San Francisco, CA

Page62
KQED & Technology
Design Firm: Pentagram San Francisco
Creative Director: Kit Hinrichs
Art Director: Kit Hinrichs
Designer: Leslie Stitzlein
Illustrator: John Hersey
Size: 16 x 20 in.
Client: KQED
Paper: Sappi McCoy 80# Cover Uncoated
Printer: Anderson Litho, San Francisco, CA

Page63
UW School of Art Summer Programs 2003
Design Firm: John Rousseau Design
Creative Director: John Rousseau
Designer: John Rousseau
Photographer: John Rousseau
Size: 18 x 24 in.
Client: University of Washington School of Art
Paper: Lustro Dull 100lb Text
Printer: Olympus Press, Seattle, WA

Page64
Parallax View
Design Firm: Fred Drennan & Associates
Creative Director: Fred Drennan
Art Director: Fred Drennan
Designer: Fred Drennan
Copywriter: Ann Drennan (exegesis)
Typographer: David Bieloh
Size: 18 x 17 in.
Client: Fred Drennan & Associates
Paper: 100# Lustro Gloss Acid Free Coated Cover
Printer: Mix Printing Company, Inc., Carrollton, TX

Page65
Mind Meld
Design Firm: Fred Drennan & Associates
Creative Director: Fred Drennan
Art Director: Fred Drennan
Designer: Fred Drennan
Photographer: Tom Welch
Illustrator: Fred Drennan
Copywriter: Fred Drennan
Digital Artist: David Bieloh
Size: 18 x 17 in.
Client: Fred Drennan & Associates
Paper: 100# Lustro Gloss Acid Free Coated Cover
Printer: Mix Printing Company, Inc., Carrollton, TX

Page66
Propaganda 101
Design Firm: Insight Design Communications
Art Director: Tracy Holdeman
Designer: Lea Carmichael
Size: 24 x 36 in.
Client: Public Relations Society of America
Paper: French Paper, Packing Carton
Printer: Rand Graphics, Wichita, KS

Page67
Visiting Artists Program at FIT
Design Firm: Piscatello Design Centre
Designer: Rocco Piscatello
Size: 840 x 594 mm
Client: Fashion Institute of Technology
Paper: Neenah Paper, Classic Crest, Avalanche White, 80lb Text
Printer: Raad Graphic Arts, Saddlebrook, NJ

Page68
Icograda Congress Nagoya Japan 2003 "Visualoge"
Design Firm: Shin Matsunaga Design Inc.
Art Director: Shin Matsunaga
Designer: Shin Matsunaga
Illustrator: Shin Matsunaga
Size: 728 x 1030 cm
Client: Japan Graphic Designers Association, Inc.
Paper: Milt GA
Printer: Kyodo Printing Co., Ltd., Tokyo, Japan

Page69
Preserving the Past, Protecting the Future
Design Firm: Cummings & Good
Creative Director: Peter Good
Art Director: Peter Good
Designer: Peter Good
Photographer: Jim Coon (Jim Coon Photography)
Size: 24 x 36 in.
Client: Connecticut State Library
Paper: 80# Fox River Star White Sirius Smooth Cover
Printer: Creative Graphics Services, Inc., Newington, CT

Page70
Seven Deadly Environmental Sins (Global Warming)
Design Firm: Stephanie Knopp Designs
Creative Director: Stephanie Knopp
Art Director: Stephanie Knopp
Designer: Stephanie Knopp
Illustrator: Stephanie Knopp
Copywriter: Stephanie Knopp
Size: 18 x 22 in.
Client: Stephanie Knopp
Paper: Crown Vantage Graphika Cover, 80#
Printer: Color Comp, Inc., Pennsauken, NJ

Page71
(R)egrets?
Design Firm: Looking
Creative Director: John Clark
Art Director: John Clark
Designer: John Clark
Photographer: Rosalie Winard
Copywriter: John Clark
Size: 20 x 26 in.
Client: Wetland Action Committee
Paper: McCoy Silk 100# Cover
Printer: Gardner Lithograph, Buena Park, CA

Page72
Seven Deadly Envrionmental Sins (Greenhouse Gases)
Design Firm: Stephanie Knopp Designs
Creative Director: Stephanie Knopp
Art Director: Stephanie Knopp
Designer: Stephanie Knopp
Illustrator: Stephanie Knopp
Copywriter: Stephanie Knopp
Size: 18 x 22 in.
Client: Stephanie Knopp
Paper: Crown Vantage Graphika Cover, 80#
Printer: Color Comp, Inc., Pennsauken, NJ

Page73
First Crush
Design Firm: Riester~Robb
Creative Director: Dave Robb
Art Directors: Dave Robb and Ben Dveirin
Photographer: Michael Bisco
Size: 36 x 24 in.
Client: California Department of Conservation, Division of Recycling
Paper: 80 lb. Endeavour Gloss Cover
Printer: Eagle Press, Sacramento, CA

Page74
DSVC presents Frankfurt Balkind Partners Poster
Design Firm: Eisenberg and Associates
Creative Director: Marcus Dickerson
Art Director: Jeff Barfoot
Designer: Jeff Barfoot
Illustrator: Jeff Barfoot
Copywriters: Aubrey Balkind, Jeff Barfoot, Kent Hunter and Tom Lout
Size: 23 x 32 in.
Client: The Dallas Society of Visual Communications (DSVC)
Paper: Sappi McCoy Silk
Printer: Yaquinto Printing, Dallas, TX

Page75
Dinnerworks
Design Firm: Images
Creative Director: Julius Friedman
Designer: Julius Friedman
Photographer: Warren Lynch
Size: 24 x 36 in.
Client: Louisville Visual Art Association
Paper: Warren Lustro Gloss
Printer: Hamilton Printing, Louisville, KY

Page76
Victoria Polo Classic
Design Firm: Hangar 18 Creative Group
Creative Director: Nigel Yonge
Designer: Sean Carter
Illustrator: Sean Carter
Size: 22 x 30 in.
Client: Victoria Riding for the Disabled Association
Paper: Synergy Felt 100# Cover
Printer: Colortec Screen Printing, British Columbia

Page77
Elvis/Fashion Cares
Design Firm: GJP Design
Creative Director: Barry Quinn
Art Directors: Lisa Greenberg and Barry Quinn
Designers: Lisa Greenberg and Sebastien Howden
Photographer: Gabor Jurina
Illustrator: Karlock Levny
Size: 15.25 x 23 in.
Client: Fashion Cares/AIDS Committee of Toronto
Paper: curious iridescents - virtual pearl 80lb text from Arjo Wiggins
Printer: Bowne & Co., Inc., Toronto, Canada

Page78
2003 Picnic Poster
Design Firm: Herman Miller Inc.
Creative Director: Brian Edlefson
Designer: Brian Edlefson
Illustrator: Brian Edlefson
Size: 24 x 36 in.
Client: Herman Miller, Inc.
Paper: Centura Gloss 100# Cover
Printer: Continental ID, Sparta, MI

Page79
Ideo Event Poster
Design Firm: NDW Communications
Creative Director: Bill Healey
Designer: Bill Healey
Photographer: Hugh Kretschmer
Copywriter: Rob Linsalata
Size: 18 x 24 in.
Client: Art Directors Club of Philadelphia
Paper: Fox River Sundance Felt, 80# Text
Printer: Piccari Press, Warminster, PA

Page80, 81
Boat, Oar
Design Firm: Blattner Brunner
Creative Directors: Bill Drake and David Vissat
Art Director: David Vissat
Photographer: Tom Cwenar
Copywriter: Ray Pekich
Size: 40.5 x 10.25 in.
Client: Greater Pittsburgh Convention and Visitors Bureau
Paper: 7pt. Finch Fine Cover
Printer: Filmet, Pittsburgh, PA

Page82
Broken Word
Design Firm: Re:Public
Creative Director: Morten Windelev
Art Director: Marlene Hald
Designer: Marlene Hald
Size: 420 x 594 cm
Client: Gyldendal & Vega
Paper: Multiart silk, 170 g
Printer: Johnsen Offset, Grenaa, Denmark

Page83
2003 Ano Europeu da Pessoa com Deficiência
Design Firm: João Machado Design Lda
Creative Director: João Machado
Art Director: João Machado
Designer: João Machado
Copywriter: João Machado
Size: 70 x 100 cm
Client: CTT
Paper: Couché Mate 200grs.
Printer: Tecniforma Print, Portugal

Page84
DSVC Presents James Victore
Design Firm: Eisenberg and Associates
Art Director: Jeff Barfoot
Designer: Jeff Barfoot
Photographer: Phil Hollenbeck
Illustrator: Jeff Barfoot
Copywriter: Jeff Barfoot
Size: 16 x 25 in.
Client: The Dallas Society of Visual Communications (DSVC)
Paper: Unisource, Topkote Dull
Printer: Hill Printing, Dallas, TX

Page85
21st Annual Celtic Music Association
Design Firm: SullivanPerkins, Inc.
Creative Director: Ron Sullivan
Art Director: Brett Baridon
Designer: Brett Baridon
Illustrator: Brett Baridon
Size: 18 x 24 in.
Client: Southwest Celtic Music Association
Paper: Mohawk Superfine White Smooth 80# Cover
Printer: Blanks Color Imaging, Dallas, TX

Page86
Lewis Black
Design Firm: Aesthetic Apparatus
Designers: Michael Byzewski and Dan Ibarra
Size: 18 x 25 in.
Client: Stand Up! Records
Paper: French Paper - Whitewash
Printer: Screen Printed by Aesthetic Apparatus, Minneapolis, MN

Page87
Designing Across Borders
Design Firm: Purdue University
Creative Director: Li Zhang
Art Director: Li Zhang
Designer: Li Zhang
Photographer: Li Zhang
Illustrator: Li Zhang
Copywriter: Li Zhang
Size: 21 x 33 in
Client: Visual Communications Design, Purdue University
Paper: #80lb White Mat
Printer: Purdue University, West Lafayette, IN

Page88
Benny Au Talk To You
Design Firm: Amazing Angle Design Consultants Ltd.
Creative Director: Benny Au Tak-Shing
Art Director: Benny Au Tak-Shing
Designer: Benny Au Tak-Shing
Illustrator: Benny Au Tak-Shing
Size: 34 x 24 in.
Client: Polytrade Paper Corporation Limited
Paper: Phoenixmotion Xenon - Snow White 170gsm
Printer: Hoi Kwong Printing Co., Ltd., Hong Kong

Page89
Finish Line
Design Firm: Arnold Worldwide - St. Louis
Creative Director: Mark Ray
Art Director: Mark Halski
Illustrator: Mark Halski
Copywriter: Lori Jones
Print Producer: Dave Chrsitoff
Size: 17 x 22 in.
Client: St. Louis Marathon
Paper: 100lb Cougar Opaque Cover
Printer: Jerome Group, Judy Malpiedi, St. Louis, MO

Page90
Fight Night
Design Firm: Partners in Marketing, LLC
Creative Director: Michael Telesco
Art Directors: Amy Lucinski and Peter Ahl
Designer: Amy Lucinski
Illustrator: Warren Stanek
Copywriter: Crista Finn
Size: 22 x 28 in.
Client: Seneca Niagara Casino, Niagara Falls, NY
Paper: DigiPrint output Printer: Printing Prep, Buffalo, NY

Page91
Sierra Nevada 500
Design Firm: Alan Rellaford Graphic Design
Designer: Alan Rellaford
Illustrator: Alan Rellaford
Size: 16 x 20 in.
Client: Sierra Nevada 500
Paper: Entrada Fine Art Natural
Printer: Wolfe Printing, Chico, CA

Page92
2003 Monterey Design Conference Poster/Announcement
Design Firm: Volume Design, Inc.
Creative Directors: Adam Brodsley and Eric Heiman
Art Director: Eric Heiman
Designers: Eric Heiman and Elizabeth Fitzgibbons
Photographer: Marko Lavrisha
Illustrator: Eric Heiman
Size: 23 x 36.5 in.
Client: American Institute of Architects California Council
Paper: New Leaf Reincarnation Matte 80# text
Printer: California Lithographers, Concord, CA

Page93
Bare Bones - Creative Survival
Design Firm: Hill
Creative Directors: Chris Hill and Francois Robert
Art Director: Bobby Van Lenten
Designer: Bobby Van Lenten
Photographer: Francois Robert
Typographer: Bobby Van Lenten
Size: 14 x 24 7/8 in.
Client: Creative Summit
Paper: Cougar Opaque 80lb Cover
Printer: Wetmore Printing in Houston, TX

Page94
Art Director Confesses
Design Firm: Mike Salisbury LLC
Creative Director: Mike Salisbury
Art Director: Mike Salisbury
Designer: Jim Wojtowicz
Photographer: Tommy Lee
Copywriter: Mike Salisbury
Size: 26 x 28 in.
Client: Dallas Society of Communication Arts

Page95
Donate Your Legs
Design Firm: The Hiebing Group
Creative Directors: Barry Callen and Sean Mullen
Designer: Barry Kalpinski
Illustrator: Barry Kalpinski
Copywriter: Erik Zimmerman
Size: 11 x 17 in.
Client: Boys and Girls Club of Dane County
Paper: 80 # Cougar Opaque Cover
Printer: Sells Printing Inc., New Berlin, WI

Page96
Calories - Omaha Corporate Cup Run Poster
Design Firm: Bailey Lauerman
Creative Director: Carter Weitz
Art Director: Ron Sack
Designer: Ron Sack
Copywriter: Sarah Coker
Size: 15 x 20 in.
Client: Union Pacific Railroad
Paper: Carnival Vellum Cover and Tyvec
Printer: Eagle Printing, Lincoln, NE

Credits

Page 97
Black & White Ball Poster
Design Firm: SKM Group
Creative Director: Peter Campbell
Art Director: Dion Pender
Designer: Dion Pender
Photographer: K.C. Kratt Photography
Copywriter: Jim Bisco
Size: 15 x 23 in.
Client: Greater East Aurora Chamber of Commerce
Paper: International Via 80# Cover Natural White
Printer: Elma Press, Elma, NY

Page 98
Portraiture Between Narrative and Abstraction
Design Firm: Kolegram Design
Creative Director: Mike Teixeira
Designer: Jean-Francois Plante
Photographer: Jean-Francois Plante
Size: 17 x 22 in.
Client: Portrait Gallery of Canada
Paper: Domtar Solutions, Recycled White Vellum, 100 lbs. Cover
Printer: St-Joseph Corporation, Ontario, Canada

Page 99
Feed the Monster
Design Firm: HendersonBromsteadArt Co.
Designer: Hayes Henderson
Illustrator: Hayes Henderson
Size: 23.5 x 34 in.
Client: American Advertising Federation
Paper: French Butcher Block
Printer: Classic Graphics, Charlotte, NC

Page 100
25th Anniversary of Mana Screen "S"
Design Firm: Shin Matsunaga Design Inc.
Art Director: Shin Matsunaga
Designer: Shin Matsunaga
Size: 728 x 1030 cm
Client: Mana Screen Co., Ltd.
Paper: Vent Nouveau V
Printer: Mana Screen Co.,Ltd., Kumamoto, Japan

Page 101
Graphic Appetite Shin Matsunaga Poster Exhibition
Design Firm: Shin Matsunaga Design Inc
Art Director: Shin Matsunaga
Designer: Shin Matsunaga
Size: 728 x 1030 cm
Client: The Japan Foundation
Paper: Vent Nouveau VG
Printer: Kyodo Printing Co.,Ltd., Tokyo, Japan

Page 102
Graphic Appetite Shin Matsunaga Poster Exhibitions
Design Firm: Shin Matsunaga Design Inc.
Art Director: Shin Matsunaga
Designer: Shin Matsunaga
Size: 728 x 1030 cm
Client: The Japan Foundation
Paper: Vent Nouveau VG
Printer: Kyodo Printing Co.,Ltd., Tokyo, Japan

Page 103
25th Anniversary of Mana Screen "M"
Design Firm: Shin Matsunaga Design Inc.
Art Director: Shin Matsunaga
Designer: Shin Matsunaga
Size: 728 x 1030 cm
Client: Mana Screen Co., Ltd.
Paper: Vent Nouveau V
Printer: Mana Screen Co.,Ltd., Kumamoto, Japan

Page 104
Yokoo by Yokoos
Design Firm: Yokoo's Circus Co., Ltd.
Art Director: Tadanori Yokoo
Designer: Tadanori Yokoo
Painting: "Ukiyoe"
Size: 1030 x 728 mm
Client: The National Museum of Modern Art, Kyoto
Paper: Vent Nouveau V
Printer: Toppan Printing Co., Ltd., Tokyo, Japan

Page 105
Shinsengumi
Design Firm: Yokoo's Circus Co., Ltd.
Art Director: Tadanori Yokoo
Designer: Tadanori Yokoo
Size: 1030 x 728 mm
Client: Kyoto National Museum
Paper: Vent Nouveau V
Printer: Taihei Printing Co., Ltd., Japan

Page 106
Junction 3
Design Firm: Apre
Art Director: Koji Miwa
Designer: Koji Miwa
Size: 728 x 1030 mm
Client: Yoiko no Kai
Paper: Washi
Printer: Apre, Nagoya, Japan

Page 107
Graphic Design: Toyotsugu Itoh Series No. 2/2
Design Firm: Toyotsugu Itoh Design Office
Art Director: Toyotsugu Itoh
Designer: Toyotsugu Itoh
Photographer: Isao Takahashi
Illustrator: Toyotsugu Itoh
Size: 1030 x 728 mm
Client: "Graphic Design: Toyotsugu Itoh" Executive Committee
Paper: Mat coat (NIsshinbo Co.,Ltd. Vent Nouveau F white)
Printer: Process Center Co., Ltd., Nagoya City, Japan

Page 108
Lotenero Show Poster
Design Firm: Michael Lotenero Illustration + Design
Creative Director: Michael Lotenero
Art Director: Michael Lotenero
Designer: Michael Lotenero
Illustrator: Michael Lotenero
Copywriter: Michael Lotenero
Size: 18 x 24 in.
Client: Michale Lotenero/LaFon Gallery
Paper: Potlach Karma Bright White 80# Text
Printer: J.B. Kreider Company, Pittsburgh, PA

Page 109
Sagmeister in Japan
Design Firm: Sagmeister Inc.
Creative Director: Stefan Sagmeister
Designer: Matthias Ernstberger
Photographer: Tom Schierlitz
Size: 30 x 41 in.
Client: GGG Gallery, Tokyo
Paper: 200gsm, Matte Uncoated
Printer: Dai Nippon, Tokyo, Japan

Page 110
Ivan Mestrovic / the Croatian sculptor
Design Firm: Studio International
Creative Director: Boris Ljubicic
Art Director: Boris Ljubicic
Designer: Boris Ljubicic
Photographers: Damir Fabijanic, Zivko Bacic, Nenad Gattin, Ivo Pervan and phototecha Atelier Mestrovic
Illustrators: Boris Ljubicic and Igor Ljubicic
Copywriters: Ljilja Cerina and Boris Ljubicic
Size: 98 x 68 cm
Client: Fundacija Ivana Mestrovica / Ivan Mestrovic Foundation
Paper: Zanders kunsdruck 180 g
Printer: AKD - Agency for Commercial Works, Zagreb, Croatia

Page 111
TPLA Poster Exhibition in Warsaw by Tapani Aartomaa and Pekka Loiri
Design Firm: Original Loiri Inc.
Creative Director: Pekka Loiri
Art Director: Pekka Loiri
Designer: Pekka Loiri
Illustrator: Pekka Loiri
Size: 70 x 100 cm
Client: Galeria Krytykow Pokaz (Warsaw, Poland)
Paper: LumiArtSilk 200 gr
Printer: Seriprint Mainoskaari Oy, Lahti, Finland

Page 112
Dietrich, Forever Young
Design Firm: Garza Group Communications
Creative Director: Agustin Garza
Designers: Agustin Garza and Nadine Bosshard
Size: 18 x 27 in.
Client: Hollywood Entertainment Museum
Paper: 78# Topkote Cover
Printer: Dot Generator, Los Alamitos, CA

Page 113
Hollywood Salutes the Troops
Design Firm: Garza Group Communications
Creative Director: Agustin Garza
Art Director: Agustin Garza
Designers: Agustin Garza and Nadine Bosshard
Illustrator: Jon Conrad
Size: 18 x 27 in.
Client: Hollywood Entertainment Museum
Paper: 80# Smart White Cover Smooth
Printer: Dot Generator, Los Alamitos, CA

Page 114
Lanny Sommese Posters, Penn State Downtown Theatre
Design Firm: Sommese Design
Creative Director: Lanny Sommese
Art Director: Lanny Sommese
Designer: Lanny Sommese
Illustrator: Lanny Sommese
Size: 26 x 40 in.
Client: Penn State College of the Arts and Architecture
Paper: Epson Heavyweight Matte
Printer: Penn State Plotting Services, Pennsylvania State University

Page 115
Turn War into Warm
Design Firm: Amazing Angle Design Consultants Ltd.
Creative Director: Benny Au Tak-Shing
Art Director: Benny Au Tak-Shing
Designer: Benny Au Tak-Shing
Illustrator: Benny Au Tak-Shing
Size: 1000 x 700 mm
Client: Shenzhen Tai Tak Takeo Fine Paper Co., Ltd.
Paper: Take GA-100 - White 157gsm
Printer: Suncolor Printing Co., Ltd., Hong Kong

Page 116
Paper Living Exhibition Poster
Design Firm: Amazing Angle Design Consultants Ltd.
Creative Director: Benny Au Tak-Shing
Art Director: Benny Au Tak-Shing
Designer: Benny Au Tak-Shing
Illustrator: Benny Au Tak-Shing
Size: 36 x 24 in.
Client: Shenzhen Tai Tak Takeo Fine Paper Co., Ltd.
Paper: Mohawk Navajo - Brilliant White 148gsm
Printer: Suncolor Printing Co., Ltd., Hong Kong

Page 117
Paper Living Series
Design Firm: Amazing Angle Design Consultants, Ltd.
Creative Director: Benny Au Tak-shing
Art Director: Benny Au Tak-shing
Designer: Benny Au Tak-shing
Photographer: Benny Au Tak-shing
Illustrator: Benny Au Tak-shing
Size: 36 x 24 in.
Client: Shenzhen Tai Tak Takeo Fine Paper Co., Ltd.
Paper: Modera Tone - Ice 186gsm
Printer: Suncolor Printing Co., Ltd., Hong Kong

Page 118
Redhead
Design Firm: Arnold Worldwide - St. Louis
Creative Director: Mark Ray
Art Director: Mark Halski
Photographer: Brad Wilson
Copywriter: Brad Fels
Print Producer: Dave Christoff
Size: 18 x 24 in.
Client: Washington University Gallery of Art
Paper: 100# Text White Silk Finished Strobe
Printer: Kohler & Sons, St. Louis, MO

Page 119
Bald Guy
Design Firm: Arnold Worldwide - St. Louis
Creative Director: Mark Ray
Art Director: Mark Halski
Photographer: Brad Wilson
Copywriter: Brad Fels
Print Producer: Dave Christoff
Size: 18 x 24 in.
Client: Washington University Gallery of Art
Paper: 100# Text White Silk Finished Strobe
Printer: Kohler & Sons, St. Louis, MO

Page 120
Hozenji
Design Firm: Kokokumaru Inc.
Art Director: Yoshimaru Takahashi
Designer: Yoshimaru Takahashi
Photographer: Yoshimaru Takahashi
Size: 1030 x 728 mm
Client: Japan Graphic Desingers Association
Paper: Mr. B
Printer: Shinnihon Printing Co.Ltd., Osaka, Japan

Page 121
Color
Design Firm: Kokokumaru Inc
Art Director: Yoshimaru Takahashi
Designer: Yoshimaru Takahashi
Size: 1030 x 728 mm
Client: W-Clock
Paper: Mr. B
Printer: Shinnihon Printing Co.Ltd.

Page 122
Warhol Exhibit Poster
Design Firm: Jager Di Paola Kemp Design
Creative Director: Michael Jager
Art Director: Malcolm Buick
Designer: Denis Kegler
Photographer: Gerald Malanga
Size: 20 x 24 in.
Client: Robert Hull Fleming Museum
Paper: Hampden Paper Inc, 10pt, 2823-Brt. Silver Foil
Printer: Gary Blodgett at Color Shack, Huntington, VT

Page 123
Issey Miyake
Design Firm: Yokoo's Circus Co., Ltd.
Art Director: Tadanori Yokoo
Designer: Tadanori Yokoo
Painting: Tadanori Yokoo
Size: 728 x 1515 mm
Client: Issey Miyake Inc.
Paper: Vent Nouveau V
Printer: Akatsuki BP Co., Ltd., Tokyo, Japan

Page 124
21st Century Platinum
Design Firm: Exposed Design Consultants
Creative Director: David Clare
Art Director: David Clare
Designer: David Clare
Photographer: Peter Dazeley (Peter Dazeley Studios)
Size: 76 x 51 cm
Client: Peter Dazeley
Paper: Black Label gloss 130g
Printer: Maritime Printing, UK

Page 125
Zirkular
Design Firm: Air Design
Creative Directors: Vladimir Barinov and Vitali Stavitski
Art Director: Vitali Stavitski
Designer: Vitali Stavitski
Size: 600 x 900 mm
Client: Designteria
Paper: matte, 300 gr/sq.m weight paper
Printer: offset printing

Page 126
Body Language. Corporal Identity, 9th Triennial for Form and Content. USA and Germany
Design Firm: Uwe Loesch
Designer: Uwe Loesch
Size: 84 x 119 cm
Client: Museum of Arts & Crafts New York, Museum fur angewandte Kunst, Frankfurt am Main, Klingspor Museum, Offenbach
Paper: Offset Paper
Printer: ColorDruck Lemke, Essen, Germany

Page 127
Small Format Exhibit Promotion
Design Firm: 3dub Design
Designer: Michael Hellinger
Photographers: Andrew Baker and Michael Hellinger
Copywriters: Michael Hellinger and Zerbe Soderick
Printing Technologist: Donald Davis
Size: 95 x 19 in.
Client: Gallery R
Paper: Ivolaser uncoated 90lb text
Printer: Printing Applications Laboratory, Rochester, NY

Page 128
Seduction
Design Firm: Cole & Weber/Red Cell
Creative Director: Guy Seese
Art Director: Travis Britton
Designer: Travis Britton
Photographer: Mark Hooper
Copywriter: Jim Elliott
Digital Artist: Sean Onart
Size: 24.5 x 19 in.
Client: Seattle Erotic Art Festival
Paper: Graphika Linen, 80-lb Cover, Zinc-White
Printer: Security Press, Seattle, WA

Page 129
Jagda Members Poster Exhibition 2003
Design Firm: Shin Matsunaga Design Inc.
Art Director: Shin Matsunaga
Designer: Shin Matsunaga
Size: 728 x 1030 cm
Client: Japan Graphic Designers Association, Inc.
Paper: Vent Nouveau R
Printer: Kyodo Printing Co.,Ltd., Tokyo, Japan

Page 130
Jeux d'élégance (Games of Elegance)
Design Firm: Transphère SA
Creative Director: Didier Zanone
Art Directors: Irina Roffe and Frédéric Doms
Designer: Xavier Sprüngli
Copywriter: Didier Zanone
Size: 117.5 x 170 cm
Client: Bon Génie/Grieder
Paper: Poster Paper
Printer: Duo d'Art SA, Geneva, Switzerland

Page 131
Jeux d'élégance (Games of Elegance)
Design Firm: Transphère SA
Creative Director: Didier Zanone
Art Directors: Irina Roffe and Frédéric Doms
Designer: Xavier Sprüngli
Photographer: Nick Welsh
Copywriter: Didier Zanone
Size: 117.5 x 170 cm
Client: Bon Génie/Grieder
Paper: Poster Paper
Printer: Duo d'Art SA, Geneva, Switzerland

Page 132
Jeux d'élégance (Games of Elegance)
Design Firm: Transphère SA
Creative Director: Didier Zanone
Art Directors: Irina Roffe and Frédéric Doms
Designer: Xavier Sprüngli
Photographer: Christophe Lauffenburger
Copywriter: Didier Zanone
Size: 117.5 x 170 cm
Client: Bon Génie/Grieder
Paper: Poster Paper
Printer: Duo d'Art SA, Geneva, Switzerland

Page 133
Measuring Up
Design Firm: Dailey Interactive
Creative Director: Ron Taft
Art Director: Ron Taft
Designer: Ron Taft
Photographer: Ron Taft
Copywriter: Ron Taft
Typography: Jonathan Deiss
Size: 17 1/2 x 26 3/4 and 11 x 17 in.
Client: Big Headed Boxers
Paper: 120# McCoy Silk Cover
Printer: B & G House of Printing, Gardena, CA

Page 134
Edo Renaisance 2003 Food Festival
Design Firm: Shin Matsunaga Design Inc.
Art Director: Shin Matsunaga
Designer: Shin Matsunaga
Size: 728 x 1030 cm
Client: Chuo City
Paper: Mr. B
Printer: Sogo Printing Co.,Ltd, Tokyo, Japan

Page 135
Edo Renaissance 2003, Edo Tokyo Hana Parade
Design Firm: Shin Matsunaga Design Inc.
Art Director: Shin Matsunaga
Designer: Shin Matsunaga
Size: 728 x 1030 cm
Client: Chou City
Paper: Mr. B
Printer: Sogo Printing Co.,Ltd., Tokyo, Japan

Page 136
The Matrix Reloaded Niobe Teaser
Design Firm: Concept Arts
Creative Directors: Ron Michaelson, Lucinda Cowell and Mike Kaiser
Art Director: Adam Waldman
Photographer: Claudio Carpi
Size: 27 x 40 in.
Client: Joel Wayne/Warner Brothers
Paper: 100lb topcoat
Printer: Ivy Hill, Louisville, KY

Page 136
The Matrix Reloaded Agent Smith Teaser
Design Firm: Concept Arts
Creative Directors: Ron Michaelson, Lucinda Cowell and Mike Kaiser
Art Director: Adam Waldman
Photographer: Claudio Carpi
Size: 27 x 40 in
Client: Joel Wayne/Warner Brothers
Paper: 100lb topcoat
Printer: Ivy Hill, Louisville, KY

Page 136
The Matrix Reloaded Morpheus Teaser
Design Firm: Concept Arts
Creative Directors: Ron Michaelson, Lucinda Cowell and Mike Kaiser
Art Director: Adam Waldman
Photographer: Claudio Carpi
Size: 27 x 40 in
Client: Joel Wayne/Warner Brothers
Paper: 100lb topcoat
Printer: Ivy Hill, Louisville, KY

Credits

Page 136
The Matrix Reloaded Persephone Teaser
Design Firm: Concept Arts
Creative Directors: Ron Michaelson, Lucinda Cowell and Mike Kaiser
Art Director: Adam Waldman
Photographer: Claudio Carpi
Size: 27 x 40 in.
Client: Joel Wayne/Warner Brothers
Paper: 100lb topcoat
Printer: Ivy Hill, Louisville, KY

Page 137
Bangkok International Film Festival "Masters to Present"
Design Firm: Rod Dyer International
Creative Director: Rod Dyer
Art Director: Rod Dyer
Designer: Rod Dyer
Illustrator: Rod Dyer
Copywriter: Rod Dyer
Size: 18 x 27 in.
Client: Tourism Authority of Thailand
Printer: Amerin Printing, Bangkok, Thailand

Page 138
Cabaret
Design Firm: ArtDesignStudio
Creative Directors: Vladimir Tsesler and Sergej Voichenko
Art Directors: Vladimir Tsesler and Sergej Voichenko
Designers: Vladimir Tsesler and Sergej Voichenko
Photographer: Grigorij Liphshits (Minsk)
Copywriters: Vladimir Tsesler and Sergej Voichenko
Size: 70 x 100 cm
Client: The Central House of Cinema (Moscow)
Paper: 200 g
Printer: Linea Graphic, Moscow

Page 139
San Francisco International Film Festival No. 46
Design Firm: open
Creative Directors: Mark Frankel and Michael Manning
Art Director: Michael Manning
Designer: Michael Manning
Photographer: Michael Manning
Copywriter: Mark Frankel
Size: 27 x 34 in.
Client: San Francisco Film Society
Paper: Appleton Utopia Two
Printer: Vision Printing, San Francisco, CA

Page 140
Seattle International Film Festival Poster
Design Firm: Sedgwick Rd.
Creative Director: Steve Johnston
Art Director: Dave Sakamoto
Designer: Paul Rogers
Illustrator: Paul Rogers
Size: 12 x 18, 30 x 53, 47 x 68 in.
Client: Seattle International Film Festival
Printer: Valco Graphics, Seattle, WA

Page 141
Naqoyqatsi
Design Firm: Yokoo's Circus Company, Ltd.
Art Director: Tadanori Yokoo
Designer: Tadanori Yokoo
Size: 1030 x 728 mm
Client: Toshiba Entertainment Inc.
Paper: Vent Nouveau V
Printer: Dai Nippon Printing Co., Ltd., Tokyo, Japan

Page 142
Signal Ridge
Design Firm: Michael Schwab Studio
Art Director: Roger Scommegna
Designer: Michael Schwab
Illustrator: Michael Schwab
Size: 27 x 36 in.
Client: Signal Ridge Vineyard
Paper: French Construction
Printer: B & R Screen Graphics, Denver, CO

Page 143
Bonterra
Design Firm: Michael Schwab Studio
Creative Director: Owsley Brown III
Art Directors: Owsley Brown III and Leslie Bramwell-Smith
Designer: Michael Schwab
Illustrator: Michael Schwab
Size: 27 x 36 in.
Client: Brown-Forman Wine Estates
Paper: French Construction
Printer: B & R Screen Graphics, Denver, CO

Page 144
Anodyne Coffee Poster
Design Firm: CYD Design Ltd.
Creative Director: Cory DeWalt
Art Director: Cory DeWalt
Designer: Maureen Kane
Copywriter: John Schnieder
Size: 20 x 38 in.
Client: Anodyne Coffee Roasting Company
Paper: Hp Coated Heavyweight Matte
Printer: Kinkos Printing, Milwaukee, WI

Page 145
Motorcycle
Design Firm: DDB Seattle
Creative Director: Fred Hammerquist
Art Director: Randy Gerda
Designer: Nathan Zentz
Illustrator: Mitchell Markovitz (Rep: Munro Campaign)
Copywriter: Eric Gutierrez
Other: John Schupp
Size: 22 x 28 & 36 x 48 in.
Client: Domaine Ste. Michelle
Paper: 100# Cover, Potlatch McCoy Silk
Printer: Monarch Litho, Montebello, CA

Page 146
Steel Reserve Wallpaper
Design Firm: Turner Duckworth
Creative Directors: David Turner and Bruce Duckworth
Designer: Jonathan Warner
Illustrator: Jonathan Warner
Size: 24 in. x 9 ft.
Client: Steel Brewing Company
Paper: Silver Promavac Metallized Paper
Printer: Inland Printing Company, La Crosse, WI

Page 147
Olive
Design Firm: Gianfagna Jones
Designer: Tom Gianfagna
Illustrator: Tom Gianfagna
Size: 36 x 51 in.
Client: Tanqueray/Schieffelin & Somerset Co.
Paper: Conventry 100% Rag
Printer: Juan Rodriquez, S2 Atelier, New York

Page 148
Chez Panisse 32nd Anniversary
Design Firm: Saint Hieronymus Press
Creative Director: David Lance Goines
Art Director: David Lance Goines
Designer: David Lance Goines
Illustrator: David Lance Goines
Size: 17.5 x 24 in.
Client: Chez Panisse Cafe & Restaurant
Paper: Monadnock Astrolite Brilliant White Smooth 80# Cover
Printer: Saint Hieronymus Press, Berkeley, CA

Page 149
Absolut NYC
Design Firm: The Right Hand
Creative Director: Anatoliy Omelchenko
Art Director: Anatoliy Omelchenko
Designer: Anatoliy Omelchenko
Photographer: Anatoliy Omelchenko
Illustrator: Anatoliy Omelchenko
Copywriter: Anatoliy Omelchenko
Size: 13 x 19 in.
Client: Absolut Company (volunteer project)
Paper: Epson Photo Paper
Printer: Anatoliy Omelchenko, Epson Stylus Color 3000

Page 150
A City Seen Poster
Design Firm: Nesnadny + Schwartz
Creative Director: Mark Schwartz
Art Director: Mark Schwartz
Designer: Michelle Moehler
Photographer: Frank Gohlke
Size: 24 x 18 in.
Client: Cleveland Museum of Art and The George Gund Foundation
Paper: Sappi Lustro Dull 100#T
Printer: Fortran Printing, Cleveland, OH

Page 151
Confrontations 2003
Design Firm: Leonard Konopelski
Creative Director: Leonard Konopelski
Art Director: Leonard Konopelski
Designer: Leonard Konopelski
Photographer: Leonard Konopelski
Illustrator: Leonard Konopelski
Size: 37.5 x 25.5 in.
Client: Cosulate General of Republic of Poland in Los Angeles
Paper: HP photo glossy
Printer: New Image Graphics & Printing, Los Angeles, CA

Page 152
The 4085 and the CBOT
Design Firm: Sedlack Design Associates
Designer: Robert P. Sedlack, Jr.
Illustrator: Robert P. Sedlack, Jr.
Size: 20 x 36 in.
Client: New York Central Railroad Museum
Paper: Mohawk, Navajo, Brilliant White, 90# Cover
Printer: Rink Printing Company, South Bend, Indiana

Page 153
Welcome to the Museum
Design Firm: Studio International
Creative Director: Boris Ljubicic
Art Director: Boris Ljubicic
Photographers: Petar Dabac, Boris Ljubicic and Maja Moro
Copywriters: Toncika Cukrov and Boris Ljubicic
Size: 92 x 68 cm
Client: MDC Muzejski dokumentacijski centar/Museum Documentation Centre and Studio Intenational
Paper: Zanders kunsdruck 155 gr
Printer: AKD - Agency for Commercial Works, Zagreb, Croatia

Page 154
Dawn of the String Quartet
Design Firm: Cummings & Good
Creative Director: Peter Good
Art Director: Peter Good
Designer: Peter Good
Illustrator: Kirsten Desnoyers
Size: 22.5 x 37 in.
Client: Merck Paper: 80# Fox River Star White Sirius Smooth Cover
Printer: Wallace-Moore, Manchester, CT

Page 155
Cubanismo
Design Firm: Jager Di Paola Kemp Design
Creative Director: Michael Jager
Art Director: Steve Farrar
Designer: Fernando Munoz
Size: 22 x 26 in.
Client: Higher Ground
Printer: Gary Blodgett at Color Shack, Huntington, VT

Page 156
Das Rheingold
Design Firm: John Rieben Design
Designer: John Rieben
Illustrator: John Rieben
Size: 30 x 42 in.
Client: Obersimmental Opera
Paper: Rexam Glossy White
Printer: PG Exhibits, Denver, CO

Page 157
Turandot, Puccini
Design Firm: Olbinski Studio
Creative Director: Rafal Olbinski
Art Director: Rafal Olbinski
Designer: Rafal Olbinski
Illustrator: Rafal Olbinski
Size: 70 x 100 cm
Client: Allegro Corporation
Paper: Polaris 170g
Printer: Z.P. Bronishz

Page 158
Pilot Scott Tracy
Design Firm: Aesthetic Apparatus
Designers: Michael Byzewski and Dan Ibarra
Size: 19 x 25 in.
Client: Killdeer Records
Paper: French Paper, Recycled White
Printer: Screen Printed by Aesthetic Apparatus, Minneapolis, MN

Page 159
The Roots
Design Firm: Aesthetic Apparatus
Designers: Dan Ibarra and Michael Byzewski
Size: 19 x 25 in.
Client: First Avenue
Paper: French Paper - Smart White
Printer: Screen Printed by Aesthetic Apparatus, Minneapolis, MN

Page 160
Whoopee Cushion
Design Firm: Hoffman York Inc.
Art Director: Ken Butts
Photographer: Rich Bauer
Copywriter: Tom Jordan
Size: 24.25 x 31.5 in.
Client: What the Hale Music
Paper: 100# matte
Printer: ProGraphics, Waukesha, WI

Page 161
Hand Grenade
Design Firm: Hoffman York Inc.
Creative Director: Tom Jordan
Art Director: Ken Butts
Photographer: Rich Bauer
Copywriter: Tom Jordan
Size: 24.25 x 31.5 in.
Client: What the Hale Music
Paper: 100# matte
Printer: ProGraphics, Waukesha, WI

Page 162
Aero Blue
Design Firm: Rod Dyer International
Creative Director: Rod Dyer
Art Director: Rod Dyer
Designer: Rod Dyer
Illustrator: Rod Dyer
Copywriter: Brooks Branch
Size: 26 x 35 in.
Client: Brooks Branch
Printer: McGraw Publishing

Page 163
Mission of Burma
Design Firm: Methane Studios, Inc.
Creative Director: Robert Lee
Art Director: Mark McDevitt
Designer: Mark McDevitt
Size: 11 x 19 in.
Client: The Echo Lounge
Paper: French Paper (Smart White)
Printer: Ingram Screen Print, East Point, GA

Page 164
Symphony Poster
Design Firm: HendersonBromsteadArt Co.
Art Director: Hayes Henderson
Designer: Will Hackley
Illustrator: Will Hackley
Size: 19 x 37 in.
Client: Winston-Salem Symphony
Paper: Sundance Felt
Printer: Classic Graphics, Charlotte, NC

Page 165
Hurl It
Design Firm: Roman Brand Group
Creative Director: David Reyburn
Art Directors: Craig Moore and Gary Paultre
Photographer: Larry Ladig
Copywriter: Brian Harris
Print Production: Doyle Hoggatt
Size: 36 x 24 in.
Client: Indianapolis Opera
Paper: Satin Sheet with Lustre Laminate Overlay, 100# Cover
Printer: The Exhibit House, Indianapolis, IN

Page 166
Voante CD Release Poster
Design Firm: Aesthetic Apparatus
Designers: Dan Ibarra and Michael Byzewski
Size: 19 x 19 in.
Client: Volante
Paper: French Paper - Packing Brown Wrap
Printer: Screen Printed by Aesthetic Apparatus, Minneapolis, MN

Page 167
Pogorelich / piano concert
Design Firm: Studio International
Creative Director: Boris Ljubicic
Art Director: Boris Ljubicic
Designer: Boris Ljubicic
Photographer: Boris Ljubicic
Illustrator: Boris Ljubicic
Size: 68 x 98 cm
Client: Rotary Club Zagreb
Paper: Zanders kunsdruck 155g
Printer: AKD - Agency for Commercial Works, Zagreb, Croatia

Page 168
Hallelujah
Design Firm: Blattner Brunner
Creative Directors: Bill Garrison and David Hughes
Art Director: David Hughes
Photographer: Tom Gigliotti
Copywriter: Michael Guinta
Size: 12 x 17 in.
Client: Chapel of Blues
Paper: Mango/Porcelain Gloss
Printer: Filmet, Pittsburgh, PA

Page 169
Pearl Jam Chicago Show Poster
Design Firm: Ames Design
Designer: Barry Ament
Illustrator: Barry Ament
Size: 16.5 x 23.25 in.
Client: Pearl Jam
Paper: Finch Ultra-bright 80 lb cover stock
Printer: Clone Press, Seattle, WA

Page 170, 171
Slingshot
Design Firm: Taxi
Creative Director: Zak Mroueh
Art Director: Rose Sququillo
Copywriters: Jane Murray and Gaetan Namouric
Client: Mini - BMW Group Canada
3D billboard, where a fiberglass MINI (actual size) was attached to the board. The MINI is the 'ammunition' in a giant sling shot.

Page 172
Buntin Reid Rocks
Design Firm: Kolegram Design
Art Director: Mike Teixeira
Designer: Gontran Blais
Photographer: Headlight Innovative Imagery
Copywriters: Gontran Blais and Pat Newson
Size: 19.5 x 27 in.
Client: Buntin Reid
Paper: Luna Matte 100lb. Text
Printer: St-Jospeh Corporation, Ontario, Canada

Page 173
Different Feel
Design Firm: Log Cabin Studio
Creative Director: Brian Stauffer
Designer: Brian Stauffer
Illustrator: Brian Stauffer
Size: 24 x 36 in.
Client: Domtar Paper
Paper: Carrera White 80lb Cover Super Smooth
Printer: H+D Graphics, Miami FL

Page 174
Clampitt Paper Show
Design Firm: Savage Design Group, Inc.
Creative Director: Paula Savage
Art Director: Doug Hebert
Designer: Doug Hebert
Photographer: Scott Kohn
Illustrator: Doug Hebert
Size: 22 x 33 in.
Client: Clampitt Paper
Paper: Mohawk Ultrafelt, Cool White 80lb. Text
Printer: Page/International Communications, Houston, TX

Page 175
Faces of Ground Zero
Design Firm: Joe McNally Photography, Inc.
Creative Director: Joe McNally
Designer: Michael Iadanza
Photographer: Joe McNally
Size: 37 x 22 in.
Client: Joe McNally
Paper: 100T Strobe/McCoy Gloss
Printer: Bob Noto/RLN Graphics & Print Communications Group

Page 176
Disposable
Design Firm: GJP Design
Art Director: Lisa Greenberg
Designer: Lisa Greenberg
Photographer: Michael Myersfeld
Size: 50 x 50 cm
Client: Michael Myersfeld
Printer: Plasac, Toronto, Canada (bags); Colour Curve, Johannesburg, South Africa (posters)
For his promotion entitled "Disposable" Michael Meyersfeld photographed large sheets of plastic. The images were then sealed in plastic bags. All of the type was silkscreened onto the plastic. The result was a strange poster of an image of plastic that is viewed through plastic.

Page 177
Flying Male Nude
Design Firm: SamataMason
Creative Director: Greg Samata
Designer: Lynn Nagel
Photographer: Sandro
Size: 26 x 38 in.
Client: Center of International Photography Scavi Scaligeri Museum
Paper: Appleton Utopia 1 Dull
Printer: Kim Blanchette of Blanchette Press, Richmond, BC

Page 178
Make Life, No War
Design Firm: CreationHouse
Creative Director: Michael Miller Yu
Art Director: Michael Miller Yu
Designer: Michael Miller Yu
Photographer: Stephan Yu
Illustrator: Henry Yu
Copywriter: Cat Tyrell
Size: 685 x 980 mm
Client: Love & Peace Poster Show, Shanghai (China)
Paper: 157gsm Matte Art
Printer: Ching Yin Press, Hong Kong

Page 179
Colombia
Design Firm: Giotto
Art Director: Sandro & Silvio Giorgi
Designer: Sandro & Silvio Giorgi
Size: 70 x 100 cm
Client: Giotto
Paper: Couche Gala 150g
Printer: Imprenta Mariscal, Quito, Ecuador

Credits

Page180
War on Terror
Design Firm: Neutron LLC
Designers: Marty Neumeier and Josh Levine
Illustrator: Marty Neumeier
Size: 24 x 36 in.
Client: Another Poster for Peace
Paper: HP's LF Heavyweight Coated
The piece is meant to be printed from a PDF after being downloaded from the client's website (www.another-posterforpeace.com).

Page181
Fuel
Design Firm: Mirko Ilic Corporation
Art Director: Mirko Ilic
Designer: Mirko Ilic
Illustrator: Mirko Ilic
Size: 29.5 x 21 in.
Client: Anti-War Demonstration in Washington, DC 2003
Paper: Domtar, 90lb white, Stonehenge, 250 gr. warm white
Printer: NEBO Fine Arts Studio, Brooklyn, NY

Page182
Flag
Design Firm: Lowe
Creative Director: Dean Hacohen
Art Director: Dean Hacohen
Designer: Dean Hacohen
Illustrator: John Cheung
Copywriter: Dean Hacohen
Size: 23.5 x 19.5 in.
Client: USA Today (Tribute to 9/11)
Paper: Strobe 80lb cover stock
Printer: The CPS Group, New York, NY

Page183
Gun
Design Firm: Cima Communications
Creative Director: Fernando Rosario
Art Director: Jose M. Rivera
Designer: Jose M. Rivera
Photographer: Ernest Robles
Copywriter: Anibal Quiñones
Size: 17 x 22 in.
Client: Amnesty International Puerto Rico
Paper: photographic paper
Printer: Next Day Signs, San Juan, Puerto Rico

Page184
Williamson Printing Corporation Annual Report Promotion Poster
Design Firm: Eisenberg and Associates
Creative Director: Marcus Dickerson
Art Director: Frances Yllana
Designer: Frances Yllana
Illustrator: Frances Yllana
Copywriter: Frances Yllana
Size: 21 x 28 in.
Client: Williamson Printing Company
Paper: Utopia Dull
Printer: Williamson Printing Corporation, Dallas, TX

Page185
Primary Color Turbines Poster
Design Firm: Ph.D
Creative Director: Clive Piercy
Art Director: Clive Piercy
Designers: Clive Piercy and Heather Caughey
Photographers: Ron Slenzak and the Tennessee Valley Authority
Size: 24 x 36 in.
Client: Primary Color
Paper: Curious Metallic Anodized Cover
Printer: Primary Color, Irvine, CA

Page186
Primary Color Hands Poster
Design Firm: Ph.D
Creative Director: Clive Piercy
Art Director: Clive Piercy
Designers: Clive Piercy and Heather Caughey
Photographer: Ron Slenzak
Size: 24 x 36 in.
Client: Primary Color
Paper: Starbright Opaque Text Smooth
Printer: Primary Color, Irvine, CA

Page187
Santa Cruz Guitar
Design Firm: Craig Frazier Studio
Creative Director: Craig Frazier
Art Director: Craig Frazier
Designer: Craig Frazier
Illustrator: Craig Frazier
Size: 23 x 37 in.
Client: Santa Cruz Guitar Company
Paper: Beckett Expression, Super smooth text 100lb radiance
Printer: Watermark Graphics, San Francisco, CA

Page188
Kapka Series Posters for Keilhauer
Design Firm: Concrete Design Communications Inc.
Art Directors: Diti Katona and John Pylypczak
Designer: Claire Dawson
Photographer: Paul Weeks
Size: 37 x 24 in.
Client: Keilhauer
Paper: 17 lb Text UV Ultra
Printer: Transcontinental O'Keefe, Toronto, Canada

Page189
Kapka Series Posters for Keilhauer
Design Firm: Concrete Design Communications Inc.
Art Directors: Diti Katona and John Pylypczak
Designer: Claire Dawson
Photographer: Paul Weeks
Size: 37 x 24 in.
Client: Keilhauer
Paper: 67.5 lb Venetian Matte Text
Printer: Transcontinental O'Keefe, Toronto, Canada

Page190
See. Play. Live.
Design Firm: Muller + Company
Art Director: Jeff Miller
Designer: Jeff Miller
Photographer: Michael Regnier
Copywriter: Justin Gardner
Size: 27 x 38.5 in.
Client: Bolle Performance Eyewear
Paper: 100# Productolith Gloss, Dull Aqueous Coating
Printer: Limuli Printing, Kansas City, MO

Page191
Make Peace with the Sun
Design Firm: Muller + Company
Art Director: Jeff Miller
Designer: Jeff Miller
Copywriter: Justin Gardner
Size: 27 x 38.5 in.
Client: Bolle Performance Eyewear
Paper: 100# Productolith Gloss , Dull Aqueous Coating
Printer: Limuli Printing, Kansas City, MO

Page192
Bulthaup "Carrot/ Dough/Metal/Potato"
Design Firm: FCB Singapore
Creative Director: Robert Gaxiola
Art Director: Eric Yeo
Photographer: Teo Studio
Copywriter: Jay Phua
Size: 750 x 500 mm
Client: KHL Marketing
Paper: 190gsm art
Printer: National Photo Engravers, Singapore
This is a point-of sale campaign for a high-end kitchen brand. The idea here was to have each kitchen utensil roll, cut, or shred the actual poster it was printed on. Each poster was printed with a relevant background. The idea was to inspire people to get creative in the kitchen.

Page193
Bulthaup"Carrot/ Dough/Metal/Potato"
Design Firm: FCB Singapore
Creative Director: Robert Gaxiola
Art Director: Eric Yeo
Photographer: Teo Studio
Copywriter: Robert Gaxiola
Size: 450 x 900 mm
Client: KHL Marketing
Paper: 190gsm art
Printer: National Photo Engravers, Singapore
This is a point-of sale campaign for a high-end kitchen brand. The idea here was to have each kitchen utensil roll, cut, or shred the actual poster it was printed on. Each poster was printed with a relevant background. The idea was to inspire people to get creative in the kitchen.

Page194
Brunswick Billiard Poster Series (Cue)
Design Firm: IA Collaborative
Creative Director: Dan Kraemer
Designers: Jason Eplawy and Chris von Ende
Size: 26 x 40 in.
Client: Brunswick Billiards
Paper: 80# Solutions Super Smooth Carrara White
Printer: Active Graphics, Chicago, IL

Page195
Brunswick Billiard Poster Series (Chalk)
Design Firm: IA Collaborative
Creative Director: Dan Kraemer
Designers: Jason Eplawy and Chris von Ende
Size: 26 x 40 in
Client: Brunswick Billiards
Paper: 80# Solutioins Super Smooth Carrara White
Printer: Active Graphics, Chicago, IL

Page196
"Bowl/Candleholder/Kettle"
Design Firm: FCB Singapore
Creative Director: Robert Gaxiola
Art Director: Eric Yeo
Designer: Eric Yeo
Photographer: Shooting Gallery
Copywriter: Eddie Sep Han
Size: 594 x 420 mm
Client: Royal Selangor
Paper: 190gsm Art
Printer: A&P Co-ordinator Pte Ltd
Translation for Kettle: Sit. Take a seat. Please take the seat of honour. Tea. Make some tea. Make some good tea. (One should treat their friends/customers equally regardless of their status)
Translation for Candleholder: The wick of the candle will not glow if it is not lit. (Light, not only means physical brightness, but one's enlightenment when one receives good advice)

Page197
"Bowl/Candleholder/Kettle"
Design Firm: FCB Singapore
Creative Director: Robert Gaxiola
Art Director: Eric Yeo
Designer: Eric Yeo
Photographer: Shooting Gallery
Copywriter: Eddie Sep Han
Print Production: Eddie Han
Size: 594 x 420 mm
Client: Royal Selangor
Paper: 190gsm Art
Printer: A&P Co-ordinator Pte Ltd
Translation for Bowl: No fish can survive if the water is too clean. (No company can bear one whose requirements are too critical)

Page198
Mirra Promotional Poster
Design Firm: Herman Miller Inc.
Creative Directors: Andrew Dull and Steve Frykholm
Designer: Andrew Dull
Photographer: Nick Merrick (Hedrich-Blessing Photographers)
Copywriter: Dick Holm
Size: 25.5 x 33 in.
Client: Herman Miller Inc.
Paper: Monadnock Astrolite 80# Text
Printer: Steketee Van-Huis, Holland, MI

Page199
Introducing Filo Designed by Eoos for Keilhauer
Design Firm: Concrete Design Communications Inc.
Art Directors: Diti Katona and John Pyly
Designer: Claire Dawson
Photographer: Paul Weeks
Size: 37 x 24 in.
Client: Keilhauer
Paper: UV Ultra 17 lb Text Radiant White
Printer: Transcontinental O'Keefe, Toronto, Canada

Page200
Mona Lisa Smile
Design Firm: Kellam Montgomery Phillips Advertising
Creative Directors: J. Bernard Phillips and Steve Montgomery
Art Director: Steve Montgomery
Designer: Steve Montgomery
Copywriter: J. Bernard Phillips
Size: 20 x 15 in.
Client: Rowpar Pharmaceuticals
Paper: Productocith Text 100# Gloss
Printer: Composite Inc., Port Chester, NY

Page201
Berkeley Mills
Design Firm: Saint Hieronymus Press
Creative Director: David Lance Goines
Art Director: David Lance Goines
Designer: David Lance Goines
Illustrator: David Lance Goines
Copywriter: Steve Chamberlin
Size: 15 7/8″ x 24″
Client: Berkeley Mills
Paper: Monadnock Astrolite Brilliant White Smooth 80# Cover
Printer: Saint Hieronymus Press, Berkeley, CA

Page202
Rosie the Riviter
Design Firm: BBDO New York
Creative Director: Ted Sann
Art Directors: Frank Anselmo and Jayson Atienza
Designers: Frank Anselmo and Jayson Atienza
Copywriters: Jayson Atienza and Frank Anselmo
Retoucher: Joan Wood
Size: 24 x 36 in.
Client: The Ad Council
Paper: Super White High Gloss by Lindemaker
Printer: RC Communications, New York, NY

Page203
ServiceMaster "League of Heros"
Design Firm: Jeff Foster Illustration
Art Director: Lee Ann Christopherson (Design Take Out)
Designers: Jeff Foster and Lee Ann Christopherson
Illustrator: Jeff Foster
Client: Archer Malmo Adv. & Service Master

Page203
ServiceMaster "Flames of Fear"
Design Firm: Jeff Foster Illustration
Art Director: Lee Ann Christopherson (Design Take Out)
Designers: Jeff Foster and Lee Ann Christopherson
Illustrator: Jeff Foster
Client: Archer Malmo Adv. & Service Master

Page203
ServiceMaster "Drenched"
Design Firm: Jeff Foster Illustration
Art Director: Lee Ann Christopherson (Design Take Out)
Designers: Jeff Foster and Lee Ann Christopherson
Illustrator: Jeff Foster
Client: Archer Malmo Adv. & Service Master

Page204
YMCA
Design Firm: Saint Hieronymus Press
Creative Director: David Lance Goines
Art Director: David Lance Goines
Designer: David Lance Goines
Illustrator: David Lance Goines
Copywriter: Larry Bush
Size: 17 3/16 x 24 in.
Client: Berkeley-Albany YMCA
Paper: Monadnock Astrolite Brilliant White Smooth 80# Cover
Printer: Saint Hieronymus Press, Berkeley, CA

Credits

Page205
AIDS Proof
Design Firm: Vitamin Communications
Creative Director: Hyun Tai Kim
Art Director: Hyun Tai Kim
Photographer: Kyu Hwan Pyo
Copywriter: Jae Hak Kim
Size: 600 x 900 mm
Client: Visual Information Design Association of Korea
Paper: Matte, 300gr/sq. m
Printer: Offset Printing

Page206
Life Preserver, Arrow, Fishing Rod, Oar
Design Firm: Bailey Lauerman
Creative Director: Carter Weitz
Art Director: David Thornhill
Size: 18 x 24 in.
Client: YMCA
Paper: Epson Doubleweight Matte
Printer: The Photo Shoppe, Lincoln, NE

Page207
Put A Cross Over the Bottle
Design Firm: Pristop Communications
Creative Director: Mateja D. Zavrl
Art Director: Ivona Sutila
Designer: Ivona Sutila
Photographer: Medima D.O.O.
Copywriter: Saso Rajakovic
Size: 50 x 70 cm
Client: Red Cross Slovenia
Paper: Biomat
Printer: Cukgraf Tiskarna in Trgovina d.o.o., Slovenia

Page208
Quit Now
Design Firm: L.N. Kangas Design
Creative Director: Lauren Kangas
Designer: Lauren Kangas
Size: 19 x 24 in.
Client: Public Service Campaign
Paper: Potlatch Vintage Silk 100# Text
Printer: Matrix Inc., New York

Page209
Royal Caribbean Anti-Smoking Campaign Poster
Design Firm: Greteman Group
Creative Director: Sonia Greteman
Art Director: James Strange
Designer: James Strange
Client: Royal Carribean Cruise Lines

Page210
New York Post Posters
Design Firm: GSD&M
Creative Directors: Mark Ray and Ralph Yznaga
Art Director: Bryan Pudder
Photographer: Douglas Whyte
Copywriter: Trent Patterson
Size: 17 x 22 in.
Client: New York Post
Paper: Vintage Velvet 100# Cover
Printer: CSI, Austin, TX

Page211
New York Post Posters
Design Firm: GSD&M
Creative Directors: Mark Ray and Ralph Yznaga
Art Director: Bryan Pudder
Photographer: Douglas Whyte
Copywriter: Trent Patterson
Size: 17 x 22 in.
Client: New York Post
Paper: Vintage Velvet 100# Cover
Printer: CSI, Austin, TX

Page212
Lipsticks
Design Firm: Martin/Williams Advertising
Creative Director: Tom Kelly
Art Director: Jeff Jahn
Photographer: Davies Starr
Copywriter: Julie Kucinski
Size: 18 x 24 in.
Client: Target
Paper: 80 lb McCoy Silk Cover
Printer: Franklin Press, Inc., Plymouth, MN

Page213
Gumdrops
Design Firm: Martin/Williams Advertising
Creative Director: Tom Kelly
Art Director: Jeff Jahn
Photographer: Davies Starr
Copywriter: Julie Kucinski
Size: 18 x 24 in.
Client: Target
Paper: 80 lb McCoy Silk Cover
Printer: Franklin Press, Inc., Plymouth, MN

Page214
Kokomo
Design Firm: David Croy
Art Director: David Croy
Designer: David Croy
Typography: David Croy
Size: 28 x 36 in.
Client: Kokomo Cafe
Paper: French Frostone Polar White
Printer: Screenprinting by AAA Flag & Banner, Los Angeles

Page215
Tenkado Yohukuten Closing Sale
Design Firm: Nippon Design Center
Art Director: Yuji Koiso
Designer: Yuji Koiso
Photographer: Yuji Koiso
Copywriter: Yuji Koiso
Size: 1656 x 1230 mm
Client: Tenkado Yohukuten
Paper: Epson PX/MC Premium Matte Paper
Printer: Nippon Design Center, Epson digital ink-jet printer PX-9000

Page216
The Plays are Made with Rawlings
Design Firm: Muller + Company
Designer: Jeff Miller
Copywriter: Justin Gardner
Size: 45 x 60 in.
Client: Rawlings Sporting Goods
Paper: 100# Productolith Dull
Printer: Limuli Printing, Kansas City, MO

Page217
Back to the Game
Design Firm: PriceMcNabb
Creative Director: Alon Shoval
Designer: Patrick Short
Photographer: Brad Wilson
Illustrator: Patrick Short
Copywriter: Alon Shoval
Design Director: Patrick Short
Size: 31 x 21 in.
Client: PriceMcNabb
Paper: Artic Silk Dull 80# Cover
Printer: Classic Graphics, Charlotte, NC

Page218
Tiger Woods Foundation "Reach For Your Dreams"- Tiger Woods Junior Golf Clinic
Design Firm: Subzero Design
Creative Director: Bill Leissring
Art Director: Bill Leissring
Designer: Ted Wright
Illustrator: Ted Wright
Copywriter: Bill Leissrign
Size: 25" x 40"
Client: Tiger Woods/Coca Cola
Paper: 140lb Strathmore Cover 100% Rag
Printer: Color Associates, St. Louis, MO

Page219
Boxing-Day (International Boxmeeting)
Design Firm: QN Graphic Design
Art Director: Claude Kuhn
Designer: Claude Kuhn
Size: 70 x 100 cm
Client: Box Promotion Bern, Jan Eckmann
Paper: 120g Coated
Printer: Serigrafie Uldry, Bern

Page220
Purse
Design Firm: Wongdoody
Creative Director: Tracy Wong
Art Director: Pam Fujimoto
Designer: Pam Fujimoto
Illustrator: Patrick Jones
Copywriter: Tor Myhren
Size: 30 x 46 in.
Client: Pacific Theaters
Paper: 80# McCoy Silk Cover
Printer: Rainier Color, Seattle, WA

Page221
Writer's Block
Design Firm: Kirshenbaum Bond & Partners
Art Director: Karishma Mehta
Photographer: Craig Cutler (Craig Cutler Studios)
Client: Woody Allen/The Atlantic Theatre

Page222
Splendent Sun Poster
Design Firm: 21xdesign
Creative Director: Dermot Mac Cormack
Designers: Dermot Mac Cormack and Patricia McElroy
Illustrator: Dermot Mac Cormack
Copywriters: Dermot Mac Cormack and Lauren Peirson-Swanson
Size: 16 x 22 in.
Client: The Vox Theatre Company
Paper: 80# Karma Cover
Printer: Color Comp, Williamstown, NJ

Page223
In the Tender Light of a Fine Spring in Tokyo
Design Firm: Yokoo's Circus Company, Ltd.
Art Director: Tadanori Yokoo
Designer: Tadanori Yokoo
Photographer: Kensuke Okamoto
Client: Takarazuka Operetta Troupe
Paper: Vent Nouveau V
Printer: Toppan Printing Co., Ltd., Tokyo, Japan

Page224
Tanze/Dances
Design Firm: Rottke Werbung
Art Director: Helmut Rottke
Designer: Simon Strupath
Illustrator: Simon Strupath
Size: 84.1 x 118.9 cm
Client: Schauspiel Essen
Paper: Affichen-paper
Printer: Hermes-Druck, Dusseldorf, Germany

Page225
Kaygusuz Abdal (Abdal the Untroubled)
Design Firm: BEK
Creative Director: Bulent Erkmen
Art Director: Bulent Erkmen
Designer: Bulent Erkmen
Photographer: Sedar Tanyeli
Pre-Press: Kagan Gozen
Size: 68 x 68 cm
Client: Istanbul State Theatre
Paper: Sappi, 170gr mat coated
Printer: Offset Printing House, Istanbul, Turkey

Page226
Proof
Design Firm: Mires>Design for Brands
Creative Director: Scott Mires
Designer: Gale Spitzley
Illustrator: Jody Hewgill
Size: 12.75 x 26.5 in.
Client: Arena Stage
Paper: 80# Vintage Velvet Cover by Sappi
Printer: Smith Litho, Rockville, MD

Page227
The Time of Your Life
Design Firm: Sandstrom Design
Creative Directors: Joe Sciarrota (Ogilvy & Mather Chicago) and Steve Sandstrom (Sandstrom Design)
Art Director: Steve Sandstrom
Designers: Steve Sandstrom and Andrew Randall
Illustrators: Steve Sandstrom and John Bohls
Size: 24 x 36 in.
Client: Steppenwolf Theatre Chicago
Paper: Via Smooth Natural, 80# Cover
Printer: Seven Worldwide, Chicago, IL

Page228
Family Cruises
Design Firm: Hasan & Partners
Creative Director: Timo Everi
Art Director: Juha Larsson
Photographer: Markku Lähdesmäki
Illustrator: Jan Rudkiewicz
Copywriter: Niko Kokonmäki
Size: 80 x 120 cm
Client: Silja Line
Paper: Galerie Art Gloss 170g
Printer: JCDecaux Oy, Finland

Page229
Willamette River
Design Firm: Jeff Foster Illustration and ID, Inc.
Art Director: Shari Chapman
Illustrator: Jeff Foster
Size: 24 x 36 in.
Client: TriMet
Paper: Coronado 100 lb paper
Printer: GAC Printing, Portland, OR

Page230
More Than Accomodating Room
Design Firm: Hoyne Design
Creative Director: Andrew Hoyne
Art Director: Andrew Hoyne
Designer: Andrew Hoyne
Photographer: Eryk Fitkau
Copywriter: Andrew Anastasios
Typographers: Andrew Hoyne and Don Hatcher
Size: 840 x 594 mm
Client: The Prince of Wales Hotel
Paper: Edwards Dunlop, Sapphire Satin
Printer: Bambra Press, Port Melbourne, Australia

Page231
More Than Accomodating Pool
Design Firm: Hoyne Design
Creative Director: Andrew Hoyne
Art Director: Andrew Hoyne
Designer: Andrew Hoyne
Photographer: Eryk Fitkau
Copywriter: Andrew Anastasios
Typographers: Andrew Hoyne and Don Hatcher
Size: 840 x 594 mm
Client: The Prince of Wales Hotel
Paper: Edwards Dunlop, Sapphire Satin
Printer: Bambra Press, Port Melbourne, Australia

Page232
Ski Mammoth
Design Firm: David Croy
Art Director: David Croy
Designer: David Croy
Illustrator: David Croy
Size: 24 x 36 in.
Client: Mammoth, CA Chamber of Commerce
Printer: Digital Printing by Imagic, Hollywood, CA

Page233
San Francisco Tones
Design Firm: Character, San Francisco
Creative Director: Patricia Evangelista
Designers: Patricia Evangelista and Laura Vignale
Copywriters: Patricia Evangelista, Laura Vignale, Monika Shourie, Becky Hui, Rishi Shourie, and Benjamin Pham
Size: 24 x 18 in.
Client: Character, San Francisco
Paper: Astrolite, Monadnock Paper Mills
Printer: Graphic Arts Center, San Francisco, CA

Page234
Mandala
Design Firm: Art Force Design
Art Director: Zoltan Halasi
Designer: Zoltan Halasi
Size: 700 x 1000 mm
Client: Élofejek Csoport
Paper: Offset with Matte Folia
Printer: Mekkora Print, Budapest, Hungary

Page235
Warhead
Design Firm: Grundy & Northedge
Creative Director: Peter Grundy
Designer: Peter Grundy
Illustrator: Peter Grundy
Size: A1
Client: Peter Grundy
Paper: Parilux Silk 200g
Printer: Spin Offset Ltd., UK

Page236
Morisawa Font
Design Firm: Shinnoske Inc.
Art Director: Shinnoske Sugisaki
Designers: Shinsuke Suzuki and Jun Itadani
Size: 1030 x 728 mm
Client: Morisawa & Company, Ltd.
Paper: offset on Shin Shelurin, Heiwa Paper
Printer: Fuji Printing, Japan

CreativeDirectorsArtDirectorsDesigners

CreativeDirectorsArtDirectorsDesigners

Photographers Illustrators

Copywriters

DesignFirms

Clients

Clients

Printers

Printers

Directory of Design Firms

21xdesign
2713 South Kent Road
Broomall, PA USA 19008
Tel: 610.325.5422
Fax: 610.325.8227
www.21xdesign.com

3dub Design
455 Sunset Drive
Winston-Salem, NC USA 27103
Tel: 585.415.0669
www.3dubDesign.com

ADK America
5220 Pacific Concourse Drive,
Suite 130
Los Angeles, CA USA 90045
Tel: 310.725.9020
Fax: 310.725.9022
www.adkamerica.com

Aesthetic Apparatus
27 North 4th Street #301
Minneapolis, MN USA 55401
Tel: 612.339.3345
Fax: 612.339.6005
www.aestheticapparatus.com

Air Design
440, 3, Tverskaya Zastava Sq.
Moscow, Russia 125047
Tel: 7.095.504.7969
Fax: 7.095.250.3851
www.airdesign.ru

Alan Rellaford Graphic Design
1850 Humboldt Road #44
Chico, CA USA 95928
Tel: 530.892.8672

Amazing Angle
Design Consultants Ltd.
3/F, 510 Lockhart Road, Causeway Bay
Hong Kong, China
Tel: 852.2267.7213
Fax: 852.2267.6482
www.amazingangle.com

Ames Design
1735 Westlake Ave. N. 201
Seattle, WA USA 98109
Tel: 206.516.3020
Fax: 206.633.2057
www.amesbros.com

Amy Kalpakhcyan
1845 N. Altadena Drive
Altadena, CA USA 91001
Tel: 626.791.3486
Fax: 818.246.5020

Apre
Inukai Bldg. 1F, 2-18-2, Nagono, Nishi-ku
Nagoya, Japan 451-0042
Tel: 81.052.533.0971
Fax: 81.052.533.0971

Arnold Saks Associates, Inc.
350 East 81st Street
New York, NY USA 10028
Tel: 212.861.4300
Fax: 212.535.2590
www.saksdesign.com

Arnold Worldwide - St. Louis
701 Market St., Suite 200
St. Louis, MO USA 63101
Tel: 314.421.6610
Fax: 314.421.5627
www.arn.com

Art Force Design
Logodi u. 30
Budapest, Hungary 1012
Tel: 361.489.4730
Fax: 361.489.4731
www.artforce.hu

ArtDesignStudio
Pervomayskaja 2
Minsk, Belarus 220030
Tel: 375.17.227.3887
Fax: 375.17.227.3887
www.tsesler.com

Bailey Lauerman
900 Wells Fargo Center
Lincoln, NE USA 68508
Tel: 402 479 0276
Fax: 402 475 5115
www.baileylauerman.com

BBDO New York
1285 6th Avenue
New York, NY USA 10019
Tel: 516.413.3825
Fax: 212.459.5280
www.bbdo.com

BEK
Tesvikiye Bostan Sokak 13/4, Harbiye
Istanbul, Turkey 34367
Tel: 90.212.236.2705
Fax: 90.212.236.2708

Blattner Brunner
11 Stanwix Street, 5th Floor
Pittsburgh, PA USA 15222
Tel: 412.995.9500
Fax: 412.995.9550
www.blattnerbrunner.com

Bohan Advertising/Marketing
115 11th Avenue South
Nashville, TN USA 37203
Tel: 615.327.1189
Fax: 615.327.8123
www.bohanideas.com

Bozell & Jacobs
13801 FNB Parkway
Omaha, NE USA 68154
Tel: 402.965.4300
Fax: 402.965.4339

Brainstorm Advertising & Design
3802 Vinyard Court
Marietta, GA USA 30062
Tel: 770.973.0000
Fax: 770.973.0000

Character, San Francisco
487 Bryant Street, 3rd Floor
San Francisco, CA USA 94107
Tel: 415.227.2100
Fax: 415.227.2191
www.charactersf.com

Cima Communications
Urb. San Francisco,
1654 Tulipan St.
San Juan, Puerto Rico 00927
Tel: 787.622.7100
Fax: 787.622.7103
www.cimacomm.com

Cole & Weber/Red Cell
308 Occidental Ave. S.
Seattle, WA USA 98104
Tel: 206.447.9595
Fax: 206.340.1675
www.coleweber.com

Concept Arts
6422 Selma Ave
Hollywood, CA USA 90028
Tel: 323.461.3696
Fax: 323.461.6621
www.conceptarts.com

Concrete Design
Communications Inc.
2 Silver Avenue
Toronto, ON Canada M6R 3A2
Tel: 416.534.9960
Fax: 416.534.2184
www.concrete.ca

Craig Frazier Studio
90 Throckmorton Ave, Suite 28
Mill Valley, CA USA 94941
Tel: 415.389.1475
Fax: 415.389.1477
www.craigfrazier.com

Creation House
2/F 28 Sharp Street West, Wanchai
Hong Kong, China
Tel: 852.2572.9232
Fax: 852.2838.1375
www.creationhouse.com.hk

Cummings & Good
3 North Main Street, PO Box 570
Chester, CT USA 06412
Tel: 860.526.9597
Fax: 860.526.4454
www.cummings-good.com

CYD Design Ltd.
338 N. Milwaukee Street, Suite 401
Milwaukee, WI USA 53202
Tel: 414.277.9787
Fax: 414.277.8471
www.cyddesign.com

Dailey Interactive
8687 Melrose Avenue
West Hollywood, CA USA 90069
Tel: 310.360.3669
Fax: 310.360.1359
www.daileyads.com

David and Goliath
11755 Wilshire Blvd. Suite 2000
Los Angeles, CA USA 90025
Tel: 310.445.5200
Fax: 310.445.5201
www.dngla.com

David Croy
8306 Wilshire Blvd., Suite 886
Beverly Hills, CA USA 90211
Tel: 323.868.2298
davidcroy.com

DDB Seattle
1000 Second Ave, Suite 1000
Seattle, WA USA 98101
Tel: 206.464.0190
Fax: 206.447.1201

designbüro behr
Aachener Str. 7
Köln, Germany 50674
Tel: 49.221.258.4450
Fax: 49.221.258.4451
www.designbuerobehr.de

Duffy Singapore Pte Ltd.
25 Duxton Hill
Singapore 089608
Tel: 65.6324.2289
Fax: 65.6324.8265
www.duffy.com

Eisenberg and Associates
3311 Oak Lawn
Dallas, TXUSA 75219
Tel: 214.528.5990
Fax: 214.521.8536
www.eisenberg-inc.com

Exposed Design Consultants
PO Box 35575
London, UK NW4 4UH
Tel: 208.202.5964
Fax: 807.125.9115
www.peterdazeley.com

FCB Singapore
7 Temasek Blvd. #09-01 Suntec Tower 1
Singapore 038987
Tel: 65.6333.1300
Fax: 65.6333.4972
www.fcb.com

Francis Communications
137 Appleton Street
Boston, MA USA 02116
Tel: 617.529.2958
Fax: 617.859.8035
www.franciscomm.com

Fred Drennan & Associates
2208 Arbrook Blvd.
West Arlington, TX USA 76015
Tel: 817.465.6467
Fax: 817.465.8299
http://maxim.drennans.net

Garza Group Communications
35 East Union Street, Suite 2
Pasadena, CA USA 91103
Tel: 626.683.3395
Fax: 626.683.3398
www.garzagroup.com

Gianfagna Jones
174 West Street
Litchfield, CT USA 06759
Tel: 860.567.4470
Fax: 860.567.4469
www.gianfagnajones.com

Giotto
Juan Gonzalez N35-135 Of. 606
Quito, Ecuador
Tel: 593.2246.1075
Fax: 593.2246.1075
www.giottdg.com

GJP Design
154 Pearl Street
Toronto, Ontario, Canada M5H 1L3
Tel: 416.979.7999
Fax: 416.979.9750
www.gjpadvertising.com

Goodby Silverstein & Partners
720 California Street
San Francisco, CA USA 9108
Tel: 415.392.0669
Fax: 415.788.4303
www.goodbysilverstein.com

Graphica, Inc.
4501 Lyons Road
Miamisburg, OH USA 45342
Tel: 937.866.4013
Fax: 937.866.5581
www.graphicadesign.com

Greteman Group
1425 E. Douglas Ave, Suite 200
Wichita, KS USA 67211
Tel: 316.263.1004
Fax: 316.263.1060
www.gretemangroup.com

Grundy & Northedge
Power Road Studios
114 Power Road
London, UK W4 5PY
Tel: 208.995.2452
www.grundynorthedge.com

GSD&M
828 West 6th Street
Austin, TX USA 78703
Tel: 512.242.4736
Fax: 512.242.8800
www.gsdm.com

Hangar 18 Creative Group
#220-1737 W. 3rd Avenue
Vancouver, BC Canada V6J 1K7
Tel: 604.737.7111
Fax: 604.737.7166

Hasan & Partners
Pursimiehenkatu 29 - 31 B
Helsinki, Finland 00150
Tel: 358.424.6711
Fax: 358.917.7055

HendersonBromsteadArt Co.
105 West 4th Street, 6th Floor
Winston-Salem, NC USA 27101
Tel: 336.748.1364
Fax: 336.748.1268
www.hendersonbromsteadart.com

Herman Miller Inc.
855 East Main Street
Zeeland, MI USA 49464
Tel: 616.654.3000
Fax: 616.654.8210
www.hermanmiller.com

Hill
3512 Lake Street
Houston, TX USA 77098
Tel: 713.523.7363
Fax: 713.523.6624
www.hillonline.com

Hoffman York Inc.
1000 North Water Street
Milwaukee, WI USA 53202
Tel: 414.289.9700
Fax: 414.289.0417
www.hoffmanyork.com

Hoyne Design
Level One, 77a Acland Street
St Kilda, Victoria Australia 3182
Tel: 61.3.9537.1822
Fax: 61.3.9537.1833
www.hoyne.com.au

IA Collaborative
215 West Institute Place
Chicago, IL USA 60610
Tel: 312.337.2126
Fax: 312.337.2367
www.iacollaborative.com

Images
1835 Hampden Ct.
Louisville, KY USA 40205
Tel: 502.584.7954
Fax: 502.587.0926

Insight Design Communications
322 South Mosley
Wichita, KS USA 67202
Tel: 316.262.0085
Fax: 316.264.5420

Irene Yuan
1641 Orchard Drive
Santa Ana Heights, CA USA 92707
Tel: 818.571.0825

Jager Di Paola Kemp Design
47 Maple Street
Burlington, VT USA 05401
Tel: 802.864.5884
Fax: 802.864.8803
www.jdk.com

Jeff Foster Illustration
652 B Avenue
Lake Oswego, OR USA 97034
Tel: 503.636.4980
Fax: 503.636.0620
www.jefffoster.com

João Machado Design Lda
Rua Padre Xavier Coutinho, 125
Porto, Portugal 4150-751
Tel: 351.2261.03772
Fax: 351.2261.03773

Joe McNally Photography, Inc.
145 Palisade Street, Studio 389
Dobbs Ferry, NY USA 10522
Tel: 914.478.7728
Fax: 914.478.7719
www.joemcnally.com

John Rieben Design
W4550 Argue Road
New Glarus, WI USA 53574
Tel: 608.527.5550
Fax: 608.262.3607

John Rousseau Design
6702 Division Avenue NW
Seattle, WA USA 98117
Tel: 206.856.1070
Fax: 206.782.5397
www.rousseau.com

Joseph Kaiser Art Direction
607 N. Las Palmas Ave.
Los Angeles, CA USA 90004

Kellam Montgomery
Phillips Advertising
12 Great Oak Lane
Pleasantville, NY USA 10570
Tel: 914.741.0700
Fax: 914.747.684

Kirshenbaum Bond & Partners
15 East 32nd Street, 4th Floor
New York, NY USA 10016
Tel: 212.779.9755
Fax: 212.779.9780
www.craigculter.com

Kokokumaru Inc.
507 Unihigashiumeda 7-2,
Minamiogimachi Kita-ku
Osaka, Japan 530-0052
Tel: 81.6.6314.0881
Fax: 81.6.6314.0806
www.kokokumaru.com

Kolegram Design
37, boulevard St.-Joseph
Gatineau (Hull),
Quebec Canada J8Y 3V8
Tel: 819.777.5538
Fax: 819.777.8525
www.kolegram.com

Directory of Design Firms

L.N. Kangas Design
129 West 88th Street, #4B
New York, NY USA 10024
Tel: 212.877.3336
Fax: 212.877.9559
www.lnkangas.com

Leonard Konopelski
1101 South Holt Avenue, Suite 3
Los Angeles, CA USA 90035
Tel: 310.657.2262
www.leonardkonopelski.edu

Log Cabin Studio
641 Zamora Avenue
Coral Gables, FL USA 33134
Tel: 866.220.3142
Fax: 305.445.3279
www.brianstauffer.com

Looking
333 Main Street
El Segundo, CA USA 90245
Tel: 310.322.6330
Fax: 310.322.3096
www.lookinglax.com

Lowe
One Dag Hammarskjold Plaza
New York, NY USA 10017
Tel: 212.605.8000
Fax: 212.605.4712
www.loweworldwide.com

Malcolm Wadell Associates
6 Yule Avenue
Toronto, Canada M6S 1E8
Tel: 416.761.1737
Fax: 416.761.9684

Martin/Williams Advertising
60 S. 6th Street, Suite 2800
Minneapolis, MN USA 55402
Tel: 612.340.0800
Fax: 612.342.9700
www.martinwilliams.com

McKinney + Silver
333 Corporate Plaza
Raleigh, NC USA 27601
Tel: 919.828.0691
Fax: 919.821.5122
www.mckinney-silver.com

Methane Studios, Inc.
175 Paula Drive
Tyrone, GA USA 30290
Tel: 404.226.6744
www.methanestudios.com

Michael Lotenero Illustration + Design
33 Linshaw Avenue
Pittsburgh, PA USA 15205
Tel: 412.922.2989
Fax: 412.922.0999
www.lotenero.com

Michael Miller/Erich Chan & Associates
2/F 28 Sharp Street, West, Wanchai
Hong Kong, China
Tel: 852.2572.9232
Fax: 852.2838.1375
www.creationhouse.com.hk

Michael Schwab Studio
108 Tamalpais Avenue
San Anselmo, CA USA 94960
Tel: 415.257.5792
Fax: 415.257.5793
www.michaelschwab.com

Mike Salisbury LLC
25 18th Ave.
Venice, CA USA 90291
Tel: 310.392.8779
Fax: 310.392.9488
www.mikesalisbury.com

Mires>Design for Brands
2345 Kettner Boulevard
San Diego, CA USA 92101
Tel: 619.234.6631
Fax: 619.234.1807
www.miresbrands.com

Mirko Ilic Corporation
207 East 32nd Street
New York, NY USA 10016
Tel: 212.481.9737
Fax: 212.481.7088
www.mirkoilic.com

Morla Design, Inc.
463 Bryant Street
San Francisco, CA USA 94107
Tel: 415.543.6548
Fax: 415.543.7214
www.morladesign.com

Muller + Company
4739 Belleview
Kansas City, MO USA 64108
Tel: 816.531.1992
Fax: 816.531.6692
www.mullerco.com

Nassar Design
11 Park Street
Brookline, MA USA 02446
Tel: 617.264.2862
Fax: 617.264.2861

NDW Communications
100 Tournament Drive, Suite 230
Horsham, PA USA 19044
Tel: 215.957.9871
Fax: 215.957.9872
www.ndwc.com

Nesnadny + Schwartz
10803 Magnolia Drive
Cleveland, OH USA 44106
Tel: 216.791.7721
Fax: 216.791.9560
http://www.NSideas.com

Neutron LLC
444 De Haro Street, Suite 212
San Francisco, CA USA 94107
Tel: 415.626.9700
Fax: 415.626.9711
www.neutronllc.com

Nippon Design Center
1-13-13 Ginza, Chuo-ku
Tokyo, Japan 104-0061
Tel: 81.3.3567.3524
Fax: 81.3.3564.9445

Olbinski Studio
142 E. 35th Street
New York, NY USA 10016
Tel: 212.532.4328
Fax: 212.532.4348

open
39 Midway Avenue
Mill Valley, CA USA 94941
Tel: 415.378.8271
Fax: 415.743.3999

Original Loiri Inc.
Selkamerenkatu 7 C 43
Helsinki, Finland 00180
Tel: 358.9.685.2854
Fax: 358.9.685.2072
www.originalloiri.fi

Partners in Marketing, LLC
4476 Main Street, Suite 206
Amherst, NY USA 14226
Tel: 716.839.4141
Fax: 716.839.4144
www.pimllc.com

Pentagram San Francisco
387 Tehama Street
San Francisco, CA USA 94103
Tel: 415.896.0499
Fax: 415.896.0555
www.pentagram.com

Ph.D
1524a Cloverfield Blvd.
Santa Monica, CA USA 90404
Tel: 310.829.0900
Fax: 310.829.1859
www.phdla.com

Piscatello Design Centre
355 Seventh Avenue, Suite 304
New York, NY USA 10001
Tel: 212.502.4734
Fax: 212.502.4735
www.piscatello.com

PriceMcNabb
1001 Morehead Square, 5th Floor
Charlotte, NC USA 28203
Tel: 704.375.0123
Fax: 704.335.5804
www.pricemcnabb.com

Pristop Communications
Trubarjeva cesta 79
Ljubljana, Slovenia 1000
Tel: 386.1.23.91.200
Fax: 386.1.23.91.210
www.pristop.si

Purdue University
552 Westwood Street
West Lafayette, IN USA
Tel: 765.494.3072
Fax: 765.496.1198
http://web.ics.purdue.edu/~lzhang3

QN Graphic Design
c/o Naturhistorisches Museum,
Bernastrasse 15
Bern, Switzerland 3005
Tel: 41.31.350.72.30
Fax: 41.31.350.74.99

Re:Public
Laplandsgade 4
Copenhagen, Denmark 2300
Tel: 45.7020.9890
Fax: 45.7020.9690
www.re-public.com

Riester~Robb
1410 Abbot Kinney Blvd., Suite 100
Venice, CA USA 90291
Tel: 310.392.4244
Fax: 310.392.2595
www.riester.com

Rod Dyer International
151 S. Camden Drive
Beverly Hills, CA USA 90212
Tel: 310.860.9923
Fax: 310.859.9538
www.roddyerinternational.com

Roman Brand Group
117 East Washington Street
Indianapolis, IN USA 46204
Tel: 317.686.7800
Fax: 317.686.7880
www.romanbrandgroup.com

Rottke Werbung
Dominikanerstrasse 19
Dusseldorf, Germany 40545
Tel: 49.211.588712
Fax: 49.211.588338
www.rottke-werbung.de

Saatchi & Saatchi Los Angeles
3501 Sepulveda Blvd.
Torrance, CA USA 90505
Tel: 310.214.6000
Fax: 310.214.6160
www.saatchila.com

Sagmeister Inc.
222 West 14th Street
New York, NY USA 10011
Tel: 212.647.1789
Fax: 212.647.1788
www.sagmeister.com

Saint Hieronymus Press
1703 Martin Luther King Way
Berkeley, CA USA 94709
Tel: 510.549.1405
www.goines.net

SamataMason
101 South First Street
Dundee, IL USA 60118
Tel: 847.902.8601
www.samatamason.com

Sandstrom Design
808 SW 3rd Ave., Suite 610
Portland, OR USA 97204
Tel: 503.248.9466
Fax: 503.227.5035
www.sandstromdesign.com

Savage Design Group, Inc.
4203 Yoakum Blvd., 4th Floor
Houston, TX USA 77006
Tel: 713.522.1555
Fax: 713.522.1582
www.savagedesign.com

Sedgwick Rd.
1741 1st Ave. South
Seattle, WA USA 98134
Tel: 206.971.4200
Fax: 206.971.4299
www.sedgwickrd.com

Sedlack Design Associates
817 Forest Avenue
South Bend, IN USA 46616
Tel: 574.246.9817
Fax: 574.631.6312
www.sedlackdesign.com

Seed Communications
1372 Ocean Avenue
Emeryville, CA USA 94608
Tel: 510.595.1888
Fax: 510.594.8976
www.seedcom.com

Shin Matsunaga Design Inc.
98-4, Yarai-cho, Shinjuku-ku
Tokyo, Japan 162-0805
Tel: 81.3.5225.0777
Fax: 81.3.3266.5600

Shine Advertising
612 W. Main Street
Madison, WI USA 53703
Tel: 608.442.7373
Fax: 608.442.7374
www.shinenorth.com

Shinnoske Inc.
6th floor, 2-1-8 Tsuriganecho Chuoku
Osaka, Japan 540-0035
Tel: 81.6.6943.9077
Fax: 81.6.6943.9078
www.shinn.co.jp

SKM Group
5166 Main Street
Williamsville, NY USA 14221
Tel: 716.630.4000
Fax: 716.630.4020
www.skmgroup.com

Skolos/Wedell
125 Green Street
Canton, MA USA 02021
Tel: 781.828.0280
Fax: 781.828.0435
www.skolos-wedell.com

Sommese Design
100 Rose Drive
Port Matilda, PA USA 16870
Tel: 814.353.1951
Fax: 814.865.1158

Stephanie Knopp Designs
334 West Allens Lane
Philadelphia, PA USA 19119
Tel: 215.242.2932
Fax: 215.242.9231

Studio International
Buconjiceva 43
Zagreb, Croatia HR-10000
Tel: 385.1.3760171
Fax: 385.1.3760172
www.studio-international.com

Subzero Design
301 N. Water Street, Suite 360
Milwaukee, WI USA 53202
Tel: 414 347 1500

SullivanPerkins, Inc.
2811 McKinney Ave., Suite 320,
LB111
Dallas, TX USA 75204
Tel: 214.922.9080
Fax: 214.922.0044

Taxi
495 Wellington Street, Suite 102
Toronto, ON Canada M5V 1E9
Tel: 416.979.7001
Fax: 416.979.7626
www.taxi.ca

The Hiebing Group
315 Wisconsin Avenue
Madison, WI USA 53703
Tel: 608.256.6357
Fax: 608.256.0693
www.hiebing.com

The Republik
313 West Main Street
Durham, NC USA 27701
Tel: 919-824-6487

The Right Hand
335 93rd Street
Brooklyn, NY USA 11209
Tel: 718.748.940
Fax: 718.748.9406

Tom Bonauro
34 Portola Street
San Francisco, CA USA 94137
Tel: 415.641.1184
www.tombonauro.com

Toyotsugu Itoh Design Office
402 Royal Villa Tsurumai,
4-17-8 Tsurumai, Showa-ku
Nagoya, Japan 466-0064
Tel: 81.52.731.9747
Fax: 81.52.731.9747

Transphère SA
36, rue des Maraîchers
Geneva, Switzerland 1205
Tel: 22.807.27.00
Fax: 22.807.27.10

Turner Duckworth
164 Townsend St. #8
San Francisco, CA USA 94107
Tel: 415.495.8691
Fax: 415.495.8692
www.turnerduckworth.com

Uwe Loesch
Mettmanner Str. 25
Dusseldorf-Erkrath, Germany D-40699
Tel: 49.211.55.848
Fax: 49.211.55 84.610

Vitamin Communications
#210 K.P.C.C. 506
Shinsa-dong, Kangnam-gu
Seoul, Korea 135-120
Tel: 82.2.3018.0031
Fax: 82.2.3018.0032

Volume Design, Inc.
2130-B Harrison Street
San Francisco, CA USA 94110
Tel: 415.503.0800
Fax: 415.503.0818
www.volumesf.com

Wongdoody
83 South King Street, Suite 814
Seattle, WA USA 98104
Tel: 206.624.5325
Fax: 206.624.2369
www.wongdoody.com

Yokoo's Circus Co., Ltd.
5-22-2 Seijo Setagaya-ku
Tokyo, Japan 157-0066
Tel: 81.3.3482.2826
Fax: 81.3.3482.2451

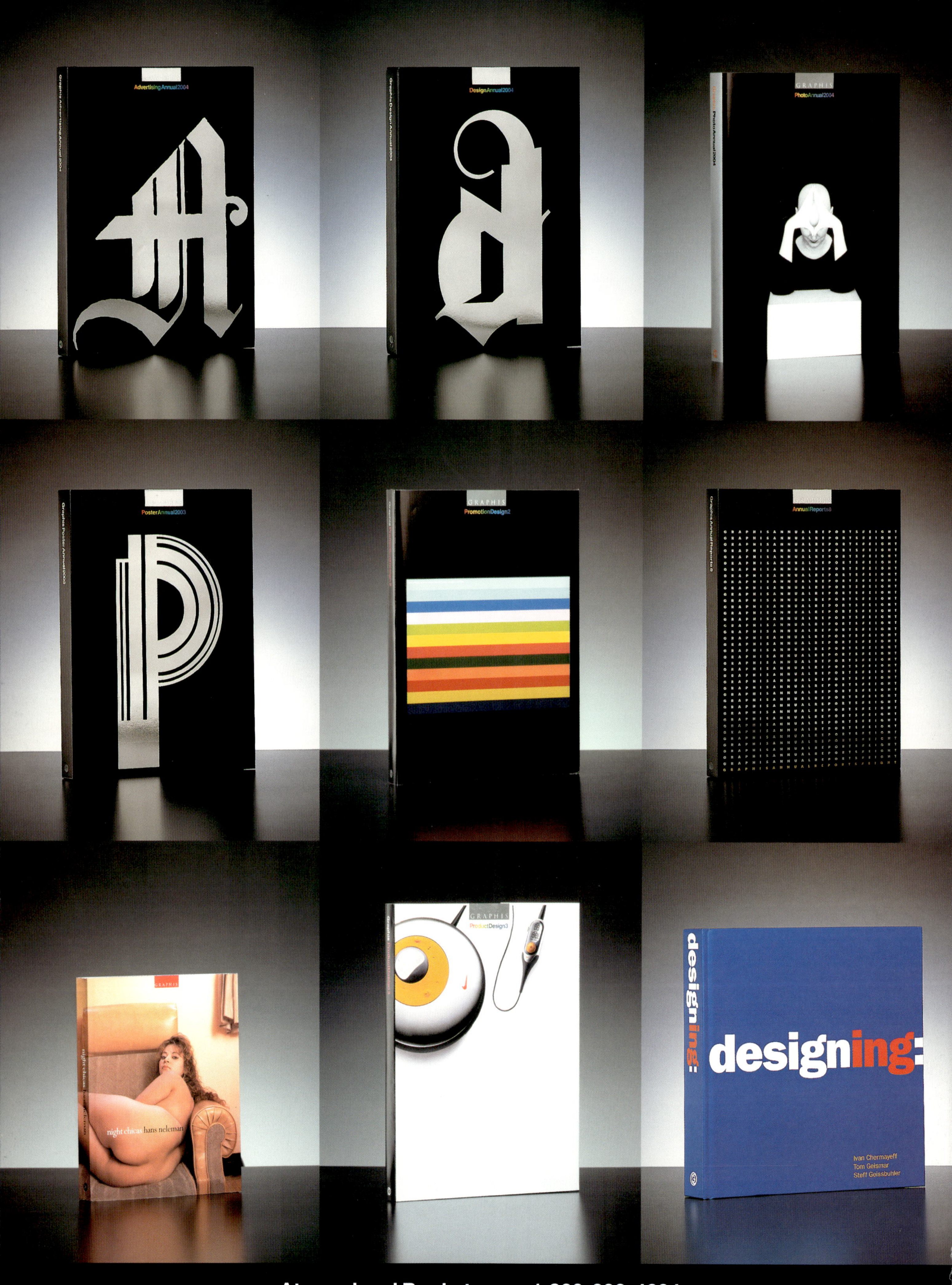
AdvertisingAnnual2004
DesignAnnual2004
GRAPHIS
PhotoAnnual2004
PosterAnnual2003
GRAPHIS
PromotionDesign2
GRAPHIS
AnnualReports8
GRAPHIS
night chicas hans neleman
GRAPHIS
ProductDesign3
designing:
designing:
Ivan Chermayeff
Tom Geismar
Steff Geissbuhler

ORDER FROM ANYWHERE IN THE WORLD.

Yes, even from Christmas Island.

DESIGN›› JON CANNELL DESIGN & BALANCE PROGRAMMING›› SYSTEMS CATALYST FLASH DESIGN›› GARN CREATIVE

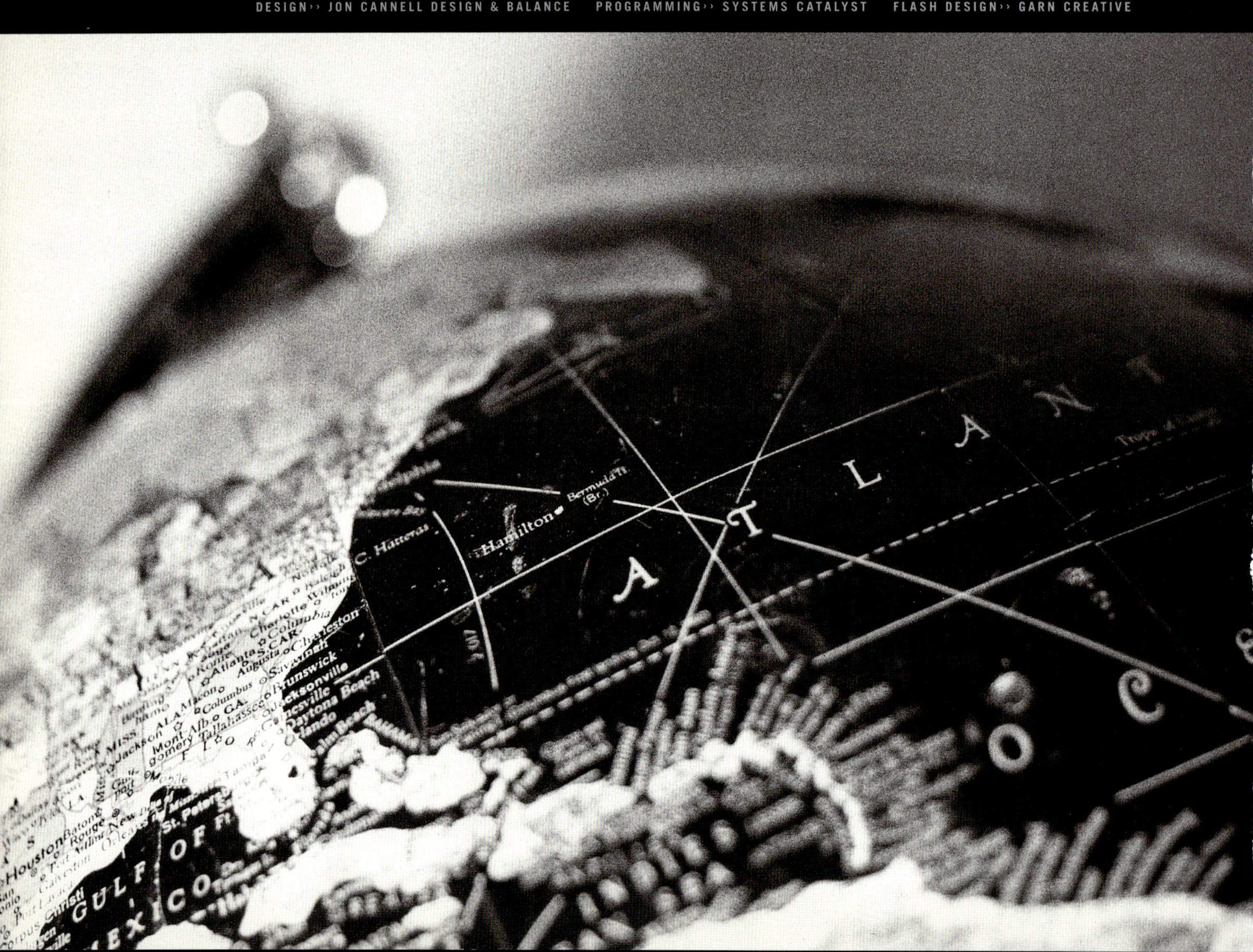